ESPRIT DE CORPS

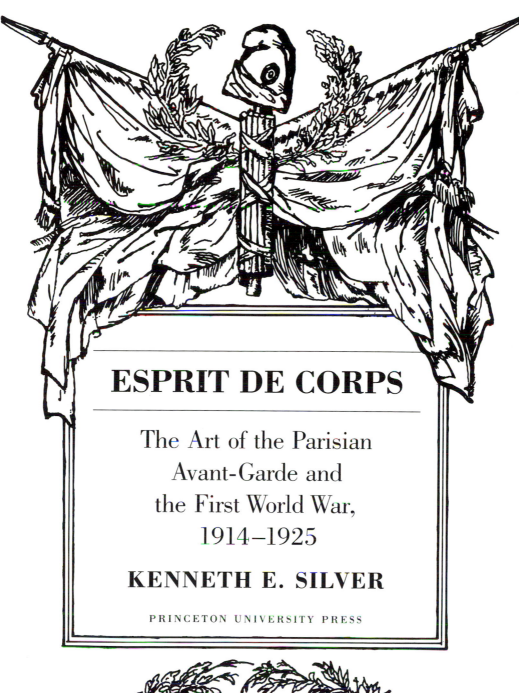

ESPRIT DE CORPS

The Art of the Parisian
Avant-Garde and
the First World War,
1914–1925

KENNETH E. SILVER

PRINCETON UNIVERSITY PRESS

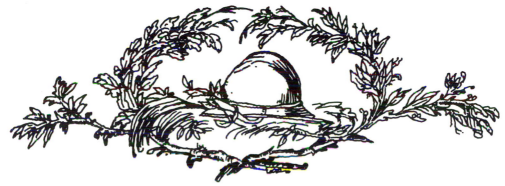

Published by Princeton University Press, 41 William Street,
Princeton, New Jersey 08540

Library of Congress Cataloging-in-Publication Data

Silver, Kenneth E.
Esprit de corps : the art of the Parisian avant-garde and the First World War,
1914–1925 / Kenneth E. Silver.
p. cm.   Bibliography: p.   Includes index.
ISBN 0-691-04052-4 (alk. paper)
1. Avant-garde (Aesthetics)—France—Paris—History—20th century.
2. Nationalism and art—France—Paris. 3. Painting, French—France—Paris.
4. Painting, Modern—20th century—France—Paris. 5. Art and society—
France—Paris. I. Title.
N6850.S56 1989   709′.44′361—dc19   89-3735

This book has been composed in Linotron Bodoni

Printed in the United States of America by Princeton University Press,
Princeton, New Jersey

The title page is an adaptation of Bernard Naudin's cover for the *Bulletin des
Armées*, 1915.

Designed by Laury A. Egan

For my parents, Raymond A. and Sylvia K. Silver

and for my teachers, Carol H. Krinsky, New York
University, and Robert L. Herbert, Yale University

"La culture nationale pure? Cela s'appelle l'onanisme."

ELIE FAURE

La Danse sur le feu et l'eau, 1920

Contents

List of Illustrations

NOTE: Titles have been translated into English except where the original French forms part of the work (as in fig. 2 below) or where the French title is well known in the English-speaking world.

7. J. Nam, "The Cubists!" ("Les Cubistes"). Back cover of *La Baïon-nette* (23 November 1916).

8. L. Métivet, "Marianne and Germania." Cover of *La Baïonnette* special issue (18 April 1918).

9. L. Métivet, "Marianne and Germania," pp. 242–43.

10. L. Métivet, "Marianne and Germania," pp. 244–45.

11. L. Métivet, "Marianne and Germania," p. 248.

12. L. Métivet, "Marianne and Germania," p. 252.

13. H. Léka, *Intellectual and Soldier* (*Intellectuel et militaire*), 1915. Musée d'Histoire Contemporaine—BDIC, Hôtel National des Invalides, Paris.

14. L. Métivet, "Marianne and Germania," p. 253.

15. G. Arnoux, *Maurice Barrès, Patriot/Writer* (*Maurice Barrès, L'Ecrivain Patriote*), c. 1914–18. Private Collection.

16. H. Matisse, *The Red Studio*, 1911. Museum of Modern Art, New York.

17. P. Picasso, *Still-Life with Cards, Glasses, and Bottle of Rum* ("*Vive la France*"), 1914–15. Private Collection.

18. P. Picasso, *Guillaume Apollinaire, Artilleryman* (*Guillaume de Kostrowitzky, Artilleur*), 1914. Private Collection, Paris.

19. R. Bonfils, *Joffre*, 1916. Private Collection.

20. R. Dufy, *The Four Aymon Sons* (*Les 4 Fils Aymon*), 1914. Musée d'Histoire Contemporaine — BDIC, Hôtel National des Invalides, Paris.

21. R. Dufy, *The Allies* (*Les Alliés*) (detail), c. 1916. Musée d'Histoire Contemporaine—BDIC, Hôtel National des Invalides, Paris.

22. A. Bourdelle, *To the Deputies Slain for the Fatherland* (*Aux Deputés, morts pour la patrie*), c. 1918. Musée Bourdelle, Paris.

23. L. Marcoussis, Plan for artillery emplacement, 1915. Musée d'Histoire Contemporaine — BDIC, Hôtel National des Invalides, Paris.

24. R. Duchamp-Villon, *Rooster* (*Gallic Cock*), 1916 (cast 1919). Hirshhorn Museum and Sculpture Garden, Smithsonian Institution, Washington, D.C.

25. J. Dunand, Helmet design for French army, 1918. Private Collection, Paris.

26. A. Gleizes, *Return* (*Le Retour*), 1915. Reproduced in *Le Mot* no. 20 (July 1915).

27. R. de la Fresnaye, *Conquest of the Air*, 1913. Museum of Modern Art, New York.

130. Delegation of French *Mutilés de Guerre*, Congress of the Versailles Treaty, 28 June 1919. Postcard.

131. L. Lévy-Dhurmer, *Motherhood* (*Maternité*), c. 1914–18. Musée d'Histoire Contemporaine—BDIC, Hôtel National des Invalides, Paris.

132. C. Le Vieil, *For the War Loan, the Sacred Union* (*Pour l'emprunt, Union Sacrée*), 1917. Musée d'Histoire Contemporaine—BDIC, Hôtel National des Invalides, Paris.

133. E. Benito, *The Farewells*, c. 1914–18. Musée d'Histoire Contemporaine—BDIC, Hôtel National des Invalides, Paris.

134. C. Léandre, *The Soil of France* (*La Terre de France*), 1917. Musée d'Histoire Contemporaine—BDIC, Hôtel National des Invalides, Paris.

135. G. Arnoux, "The Good Frenchman contributes to the War Loan" (Le Bon Français souscrit à l'Emprunt) from *Le Bon Français*, c. 1914–18. Private Collection.

136. H.M.R., Images from *French Women at Work for the Nation*, c. 1914–18. Musée d'Histoire Contemporaine—BDIC, Hôtel National des Invalides, Paris.

137. Gerda-Wegener, "La Mode Nationale." Cover of *La Baïonnette* (27 December 1917).

138. Anonymous, Patriotic *faïence*, c. 1914–19. Musée d'Histoire Contemporaine—BDIC, Hôtel National des Invalides, Paris.

139. H. Matisse, *The Music Lesson*, 1917. Barnes Foundation, Merion, Pennsylvania.

140. C. Huard, *Holy France / The Knitter* (*Sainte France / La Tricoteuse*), c. 1914–18. Musée d'Histoire Contemporaine—BDIC, Hôtel National des Invalides, Paris.

141. J. Marchand, *The Guardian of the Home* (*La Gardienne de Foyer*), c. 1915. Reproduced in *L'Elan* no. 3 (March 1915).

142. J. Metzinger, *The Knitter*, 1919. Musée National d'Art Moderne, Centre Georges Pompidou, Paris.

143. Anonymous, Seal of the City of Paris, n.d. Private Collection.

144. O. Friesz, *The Entry of the French into Strasbourg*, 1918. Musée d'Histoire Contemporaine — BDIC, Hôtel National des Invalides, Paris.

145. E. Aubry, Medallion (*La Somme*) for the Peace Festivities, Paris, 14 July 1919. Musée d'Histoire Contemporaine—BDIC, Hôtel National des Invalides, Paris.

146. The Etoile—Arc de Triomphe during the Peace Festivities, Paris, 14 July 1919.

147. J. Galtier-Boissière, *Procession of the Mutilés de Guerre, 14 July*

169. R. de la Fresnaye, *Portrait of Jean-Louis Gampert*, 1920. Musée National d'Art Moderne, Centre Georges Pompidou, Paris.

170. A. Gleizes, *Self-Portrait*, 1919. Musée d'Art Moderne de la Ville de Paris.

171. H. Matisse, *The Plumed Hat*, 1919. Museum of Modern Art, New York.

172. H. Matisse, *Odalisque with Red Trousers*, 1921–22. Musée National d'Art Moderne, Centre Georges Pompidou, Paris.

173. A. Renoir, *Odalisque (Algerian Woman)*, 1870. National Gallery of Art, Washington, D.C.

174. H. Matisse, *Odalisque with Green Sash*, 1926–27. Baltimore Museum of Art: The Cone Collection.

175. J.A.D. Ingres, *Odalisque and Slave*, 1842. Walters Art Gallery, Baltimore.

176. Capiello, Poster for Exposition Coloniale (Marseille, 1922).

177. Jean Droit, Poster for Olympic Games (Paris, 1924).

178. J. Metzinger, *Harlequinade*, 1925. Present collection unknown.

179. A. Derain, *Harlequin and Pierrot*, 1924. Collection Jean Walter and Paul Guillaume, Musée de l'Orangerie, Paris.

180. J. Magrou, *Monument to the Genius of the Latin People*, 1921. Garden of the Palais Royal, Paris.

181. P. Picasso, *Bathers*, 1918. Fogg Art Museum, Cambridge, Mass.

182. P. Picasso, *Bathers*, 1921. Present collection unknown.

183. P. Picasso, *La Source*, 1921. Museum of Modern Art, New York.

184. P. Picasso, *Three Women at the Spring*, 1921. Museum of Modern Art, New York.

185. P. Picasso, *La Liseuse*, 1920. Musée National d'Art Moderne, Centre Georges Pompidou, Paris.

186. N. Poussin, *The Arcadian Shepherds (Et in Arcadia Ego)*, 1638. Musée du Louvre, Paris.

187. P. Puvis de Chavannes, *The Shepherd's Song*, 1891. Metropolitan Museum of Art, New York.

188. P. Puvis de Chavannes, *La Source*, 1869. Musée de Reims.

189. P. Picasso, *The Pipes of Pan*, 1923. Musée Picasso, Paris.

190. P. Picasso, *Mother and Child*, 1921. Art Institute of Chicago.

191. H. Lebasque, Poster for Peace Loan, 1920. Private Collection.

192. G. Severini, Study for *Family of the Commedia dell'Arte*, c. 1922. Severini Collection, Rome.

193. A. Gleizes, *Mother and Child*, 1920. Pochoir, published in *Der Sturm*, 1921.

194. R. de la Fresnaye, *Mother and Child*, 1923. Present collection unknown.

195. P. Picasso, *Dancing Couple*, 1921–22. Musée Picasso, Paris.

196. P. Puvis de Chavannes, *Hope*, 1871. Musée du Louvre, Paris.

197. P. Picasso, Drawing on fragment of *L'Excelsior* (23 July 1923), 1923. Musée Picasso, Paris.

198. G. Braque, *Canéphore*, 1922–23. Musée National d'Art Moderne, Centre Georges Pompidou, Paris.

199. G. Braque, *Canéphore*, 1922–23. Musée National d'Art Moderne, Centre Georges Pompidou, Paris.

200. A. Bourdelle, Study for *Noble Burdens*, 1910–11. Musée d'Orleans.

201. R. de la Fresnaye, *Les Palefreniers*, 1922. Kunstmuseum, Berne.

202. R. de la Fresnaye, *Portrait of Guynemer*, 1922. Musée National d'Art Moderne, Centre Georges Pompidou, Paris.

203. R. de la Fresnaye, *The Sick Man in Bed*, 1922. Collection Françoise Mare-Vène, Paris.

204. R. de la Fresnaye, *Self-Portrait*, 1925. Present collection unknown.

205. P. Picasso, Curtain for *Le Tricorne*, 1919. Seagram Building, New York.

206. G. Braque, Curtain for *Les Fâcheux*, 1924. Sumner Collection, Wadsworth Atheneum, Hartford, Connecticut.

207. J. Gris, Costume design for *Les Tentations de la bergère*, 1924. Sumner Collection, Gift of Mr. and Mrs. John Lee Bruce in Memory of A. Everett Austin, Jr., Wadsworth Atheneum, Hartford, Connecticut.

208. F. Léger, Set design for *La Création du Monde*, 1923. Dansmuseet, Stockholm.

209. F. Picabia, *Monument to Latin Stupidity* (*Monument à la Bêtise Latine*), 1921. Reproduced in *391* no. 16 (10 July 1921).

210. J. Hugo, Costume design for *Les Mariés de la tour Eiffel*, 1921. Dansmuseet, Stockholm.

211. P. Picasso, Drawing of costume worn at the Beaumont *Bal des Jeux*, 1922. Collection H. de Beaumont, Paris.

212. F. Picabia, *Portrait of Max Goth*, 1917. Reproduced in *391* no. 1 (1 February 1917).

213. P. Picasso, *Three Musicians*, 1921. Museum of Modern Art, New York.

214. P. Picasso, *Studies*, 1920. Musée Picasso, Paris.

Acknowledgments

I AM INDEBTED to many people and numerous institutions for the realization of this book, which has been a long time in the making. I want to thank, first of all, the National Endowment for the Humanities, which provided me with funds for travel, research, and writing. In Paris, I am indebted to the staff of the Musée d'Histoire Contemporain (formerly the Musée des Deux Guerres), at the Hôtel National des Invalides, particularly to the curator, Cécile Coutin, and to Laure Barbizet, my good friend. I want to also thank Hélène Seckel and Marie-Laure Bernadac of the Musée Picasso. Jacques Thuillier of the Collège de France helped me over a number of administrative hurdles, for which I am grateful. Monique Manoury-Schneider provided access to the materials in the Robert Delaunay estate and introduced me to Sonia Delaunay. Françoise Mare-Vène was always generous with the materials of her father, André Mare, and she has been a warm friend as well. I am only sorry that my dear friend, the late Jean Guéry, whose love for France and knowledge of his country were of inestimable value to me, will not read this book.

In the United States I want to thank numerous friends and colleagues as well. Susan Ball, Romy Golan, Billy Klüver, and Julie Martin, and Pamela Sharpless Richter, the Fine Arts Librarian at Washington Square College, all provided me with valuable information. I am especially grateful to Yona Zeldis McDonough, my former student, who has helped with the arduous task of collecting illustrations and has been a loyal friend and a supporter of this book for so long. Paul Tucker and Sarah Brett-Smith, who were there at the start of this project, provided the intellectual challenge and moral support so necessary for any extended research. Michael Marrinan and Mary McLeod both read early versions of this manuscript and their suggestions and criticisms have, I hope, enormously improved it. Zack Karantonis encouraged and assisted me in more ways than I can enumerate, and I thank him for having helped to make this book a reality.

This project began when I was a graduate student at Yale and

I want to thank there both Anne Coffin Hanson and Vincent Scully for their advice and guidance. Most of all I am indebted to Robert L. Herbert, who showed me a history of art that looks as new and vital to me now as it did in New Haven thirteen years ago.

New York
April 1986

ESPRIT DE CORPS

"In the nightmare through which we are passing"

I

O**N** 2 A**UGUST** 1914, the day France declared war on Germany, Pablo Picasso, who was vacationing in Avignon, escorted his friends Georges Braque and André Derain to the railroad station for the journey to Paris, where the two Frenchmen would soon join the army. "We never saw each other again," Picasso said—*Nous ne nous sommes jamais revus*—whereas, in reality, the trio saw a good deal of each other, for many years, over the course of their long lives.[1] What Picasso meant was that although the three emerged from the Great War—*la Grande Guerre*, as the French called it for so long—ostensibly unchanged, nothing was ever quite the same after 2 August. A sentiment akin to this, a feeling that a way of life came to an end as France went to war in the summer of 1914, was elaborated by Rémy de Gourmont, literary critic and editor-in-chief of the *Mercure de France*. "There is a great sense of melancholy," he wrote in 1915,

> in thumbing through the publications and little magazines of all kinds which appeared at the same time as the outbreak of the war. . . . How happy seem the times when we seriously discussed the future of Cubism, or the respective merits of free and regular verse! There was a moment in the month of August when I firmly believed that all that was finished forever, that we would never again care about art, or poetry, or literature, or even science . . .[2]

Needless to say, as the critic himself soon realized, "all that" was by no means finished—art not only would flourish again in France, but would continue to be made in the midst of war, both at the front and in Paris. Yet, as we shall see, Gourmont was right to feel that a certain kind of delight, whereby Cubism and poetic experimentation were the most important things in the world, vanished in August 1914, to be replaced by a far more austere, moralistic, and circumspect cultural climate.

In contrast to Picasso's and Gourmont's retrospective evocations of the summer of 1914, Juan Gris's state of mind at the moment of the war's outbreak was without any kind of poetical self-consciousness. As a non-Allied foreigner (a Spaniard, like Picasso) who had left his homeland to escape conscription, Gris was plunged into a desperate frenzy: "I have no idea where you are," Gris wrote from Collioure on 1 August to Daniel-Henry Kahnweiler, his Paris dealer who, as a German, was fortunate to have been in Italy when war was declared,

> or whether amidst all these troubles of war you will receive this letter. At all events, the fact is that panic is increasing from hour to hour. . . . The reservists have been called up; the foreigners, summoned to the town hall to reveal their most intimate secrets, have been involved in a mass of fines and proceedings for not having their papers in order, and some have been threatened with expulsion. . . .[3]

On 3 August Gris again wrote to Kahnweiler, "I have been advised to go, and when I said that I didn't want to unless formally ordered to do so, I was told to be prepared even for that. But where shall I go?"[4] And again, on 16 August:

> what will happen to all of us? . . . All those of us who had sketched out our way through life must now change everything temporarily and get along as best we can. For, my dear friend, I can see that in the nightmare through which we are passing, previous engagements are no longer valid and each of us must make his own way. How? I don't know.[5]

Over and above the immediate fear of expulsion, Gris had already sensed that even the daily lives of himself and his friends were being radically altered; the free-wheeling, bohemian world of Montmartre and Montparnasse was, at least for the moment, a vanished way of life. More ominous, though (and it may in part be a warning to his dealer), is the remark that "previous engagements are no longer valid and each of us must make his own way." The friendships, financial arrangements, alliances, and even animosities among companions of disparate national origins were suddenly suspended. To a greater or lesser degree it was to be *sauve qui peut*.

For many Parisian artists, French and foreign, the prospect

was simpler than for Gris—they became soldiers. By the first winter of war, Braque, Derain, Charles Camoin, Raymond Duchamp-Villon, Roger de la Fresnaye, Albert Gleizes, Moise Kisling, František Kupka, Fernand Léger, Jean Metzinger, Henri Dunoyer de Segonzac, Jacques Villon, Maurice de Vlaminck, and Ossip Zadkine, among many others, were all at the front; even Matisse, already forty-five years old, tried to enlist. Not that all Parisians, let alone all Frenchmen, went to war or attempted to do so. Robert Delaunay was in Spain with his wife Sonia in August and chose to remain on the Iberian peninsula for the duration of the war. Marcel Duchamp was exempt from the draft and, like Delaunay, decided that it would be best not to be in Paris as a noncombatant—he left for New York in 1915, while the United States was still neutral in the conflict.

Few of the most important members of the pre-war avant-garde remained in Paris, and those that did, with the exception of Matisse, were foreigners: Picasso, Gris, and Gino Severini, the Italian Futurist, were among them. Although they were fortunate to remain in France and yet to avoid the bullets and poison gas of the trenches, being a civilian in Paris during wartime, especially for healthy young men, brought hazards of its own. With the front so close—less than seventy-five miles from the capital—Paris was like a vast army encampment, which made it all the more difficult for a noncombatant to pass unnoticed or avoid accusations of cowardice and disloyalty. Louis Sabattier's glamorized depiction of the Café de la Paix in 1917 (fig. 1) testifies to the overwhelming presence of uniformed soldiers. It is no wonder that Picasso went out in public much less, preferring to remain at home working during the first, clamorously patriotic year of war; that Gris did his best to avoid the cafes and the newly established canteens for artists; or that the poet and *bon vivant* Jean Cocteau, who despite his best efforts to enlist was rejected for military service, should have outfitted himself with a wardrobe of unofficial uniforms.[6] Things had become so bad for civilian men in Paris that in a letter of 1 April 1915, to Kahnweiler, who was now in Switzerland, Gris repeated a request that he had made to his dealer the previous winter—in order to avoid discovery that he was in communication with an "enemy" German, mightn't he (Gris asked) correspond by way of his sister in Madrid? With a sort of apologetic desperation, he wrote:

> You who are absent cannot imagine how every foreigner here is suspect, no matter what his nationality . . .

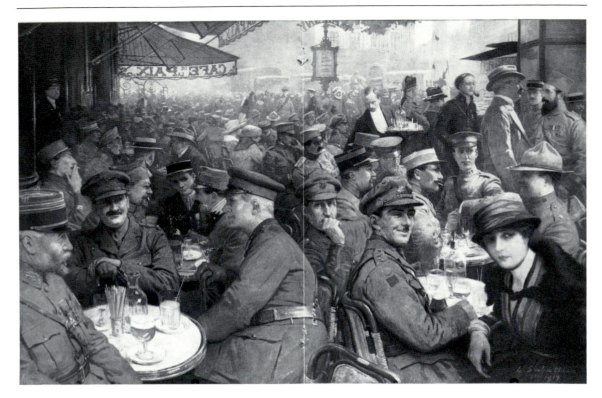

1. L. Sabattier, *The Café de la Paix in Wartime*, 1917. Reproduced in *L'Illustration* (26 January 1918).

What I am telling you is an absolute fact, so I think it is much better for us to carry on our correspondence via Madrid, in order not to arouse my concierge's suspicions. I can see you laughing at my suggestion. . . . but don't forget that at the present nothing is more important than the opinion of a concierge. Every day one is aware of the petty malice of one's neighbors. . . . An anonymous letter is the most favored method.

. . . Take it from me, *mon cher ami*, that it is not enough to have a clear conscience: one also has to give the appearance . . . they say appalling things in the canteens of Montmartre and Montparnasse and make terrible accusations against myself and against anyone who had dealings with you.[7]

Of course, the most popular and the least sophisticated French accusation against the Germans during wartime was of barbarism: Baron Kervyn de Lettenhove, a Belgian, referring to the German march through his country in August (the destruction of the town hall of Louvain and the decimation of the medieval Flemish Cloth Hall at Ypres were the most notable artistic casualties) wrote of the "Huns" and "Vandals" who, "after

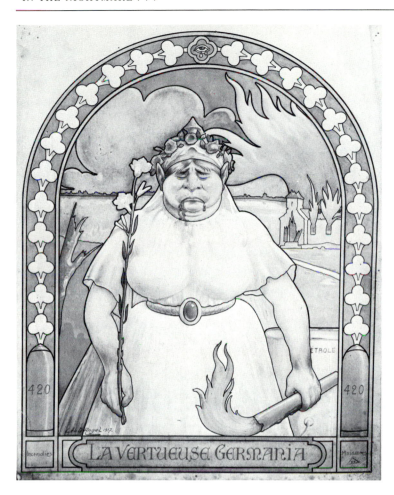

2. L. d'Angel, *Virtuous Germania* (*La Vertueuse Germania*), 1917.

the cruelest massacres, burned the most beautiful monuments, destroyed all that science venerated and art glorified,"[8] while artists such as Léo d'Angel created *Virtuous Germania* (fig. 2), of 1917, in which the enemy is personified as a gross peasant woman bearing a torch. The greatest outcry against the German destruction of culture arose from an event which helped to galvanize world opinion against the invader: the bombing, in September, of Reims Cathedral (fig. 3). This atrocity became a symbol of France aflame—invoked, for instance, in a commemorative seal (fig. 4) in which a classically draped allegorical figure stands before the *tricolore* and points to the burning cathedral in the distance, as she exhorts her countrymen: "Frenchmen! Don't Buy German/Remember 1914!" Even Romain Rolland, France's most famous wartime pacifist, who was in Swiss exile, found a place to mourn the destruction of Reims in his celebrated 1915 tract *Au dessus de la mêlée*: "Our France

3. Reims Cathedral (photo taken 19 September 1914, during bombardment by Germans). Postcard.

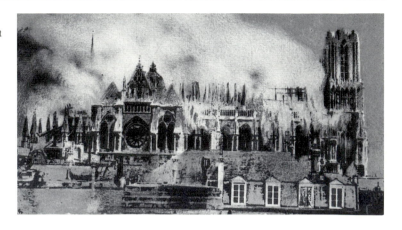

which bleeds with so many other wounds," he wrote, "has suffered nothing more cruel than the attack against her Parthenon, the Cathedral of Reims, 'Our Lady of France.' . . . A piece of architecture like Reims is more than one life; it is a people—whose centuries vibrate like a symphony in this organ of stone."[9]

Of specific concern to Gris and Kahnweiler were anti-German accusations which depicted a subtler assault on French civilization, a cultural subversion that was supposedly of long standing. One Tony Tollet gave a lecture in Lyon, in 1915, titled "On the Influence of the Judeo-German Cartel of Parisian Painting Dealers on French Art," and it was surely that kind of thing that Gris was hearing in Montmartre and Montparnasse. "I want to speak to you," Tollet began,

> of the crushing and pestilent influence that the cartel of painting dealers has had on French art for the last twenty years. I want to show you by what maneuvers they came to falsify French taste; what influence they exerted to force the specimens with which they had first furnished their offices on our great public collections, and how they had imposed works stamped with German culture—Pointillist, Cubist, and Futurist, etc.—on the taste of our snobs. . . . Everything—music, literature, painting, sculpture, architecture, decorative arts, fashion, everything—suffered the noxious effects of the asphyxiating gases of our enemies.[10]

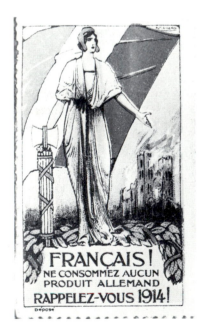

4. Anonymous (artist's name illegible), *Remember 1914!* (*Rappelez-vous 1914!*), c. 1914–18. Commemorative stamp.

Even if Tollet could offer no evidence to substantiate this supposed conspiracy of modern art dealers to corrupt French taste—and he refrained from giving names—some of his audience must have been aware of the preponderance of German-

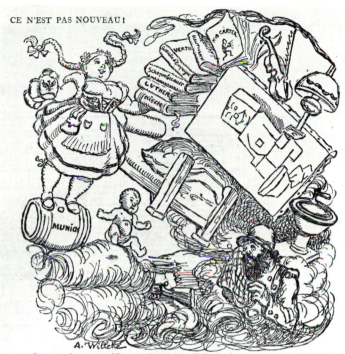

CE N'EST PAS NOUVEAU!

— *Des gaz asphyxiants ! à c't'heure !... Oh ! là là !... Voilà plus de quarante ans qu'ils nous en ont empestés Made in Germany !.* (Dessin de WILLETTE.)

5. A. Willette. "It's Not New!" ("Ce n'est pas nouveau!"), c. 1914–18. Photograph.

Jewish names, of both Frenchman and foreigners, among the Parisian dealers—Wildenstein, Bernheim, Berthe Weill, Adolphe Basler, and of course Kahnweiler—a fact which, while proving nothing in particular about treason, nonetheless bestowed a semblance of credibility on an otherwise incredible theory. Moreover, essentially the same notion of the Germanic invasion of French culture was available in a shorthand version in a satirical illustration by the well-known cartoonist Willette. Called "It's Not New!" (fig. 5), the cartoon draws an analogy between the German assault on French troops during the war and the German assault on French culture before the war. At the lower right we see the French foot-soldier, the *poilu* (so called because, at least early in the war, he was usually unshaven), wiping away the tears caused by poison gases loosed by the Germans, "Asphyxiating gas, at this point . . . Oh! la la! . . . For more than forty years they've plagued us with everything marked *Made in Germany*!" And, by way of showing us this, Willette draws, rising from the gaseous smoke, a German beer-hall waitress standing on a keg marked *Munich*; books with authors' names like Nietzsche, Luther, Schopenhauer,

Goethe; a violin (meant to symbolize German music); a toilet
bowl (symbolic of German industrial manufacturing, and placed
here because Willette could not resist the scatological reference, a phenomenon we shall see elsewhere); and, most important for us, at the middle right, a large "Cubist" painting in
which a baby and a bowl are rendered in a cubic manner that
the audience knew was supposed to signify modern art. These
kinds of images obviously helped turn public opinion against
the purveyors of Cubism, who, if they were foreigners, and Germans as well, were already in trouble enough: both Kahnweiler
and Wilhelm Uhde, one of the most important early collectors
of Cubism, had their collections confiscated as enemy goods by
the French government.[11]

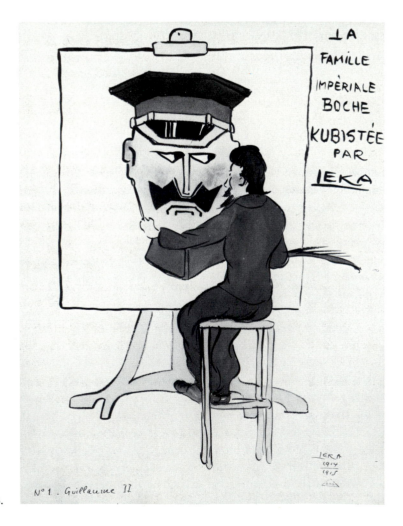

6. H. Léka, "The Boche Imperial
Family Kubified" ("La Famille
impériale boche kubistée"), 1914–15.

But it was not just Germans and art dealers that were now under attack—nothing less than modern culture itself was besieged, as the war gave the conservative forces in France the ammunition they needed to go on the offensive. Cubism in particular, one of the most obvious expressions of the modern spirit, was seen as the advance guard of the enemy. For instance one artist, an illustrator named Léka, created a series of Cubistic portraits of the Germans during 1914-15, his *La Famille impériale boche kubistée* (fig. 6). Without having to make the patently untrue assertion that Cubism was a German art form, the artist nonetheless associated the modern style with the enemy by rendering the royal family in a supposedly Cubist mode. Furthermore, by spelling the word "Cubist" with a "K" he makes it ostentatiously Germanic (the "K" is almost nonexistent in French) and also makes a subtle reference to Kubbrand bouillon cubes, a French household product, then of German manufacture, that was banned in France during the war.[12] Less subtle was Jacques Nam's cartoon "Les Cubistes," published in full color on the back cover of the leading wartime humor magazine *La Baïonnette* of 23 November 1916 (fig. 7). Drawn in what was the standard French caricature of the German—fat, red-headed, and bespectacled—and standing before his latest work (which includes a number of prominently displayed K's, two of which are placed right next to each other so that one is encouraged to pronounce them in quick succession, enunciating "kaka," the French infants' word for feces), this Cubist proclaims, with what is meant to be Germanic vanity, "Fortunately we're here to renew art!" Whether this is supposed to mean that the Germans invented Cubism, or simply that they are attracted to Cubism, is not made clear, and it hardly matters—the point was to indict modern art as being somehow, in some way, Germanic.

Some commentators, of course, were well aware that Cubism was a Parisian, and specifically a French and Spanish, phenomenon, but that made little difference. A popular critic of the period, Madame Aurel, referred to Cubism, Futurism, and Orphism collectively as "this convulsed art, for which Gleizes, Metzinger, Apollinaire, and Boccioni, and not long ago Severini, established the rules with the most erudite malice, this art which, although born in this country, is no more French for that . . ."[13] What she looked forward to in the future, she wrote in her pamphlet *The Commandment of Love in Post-War Art*, was an end to the divisive and chaotic aesthetics of the pre-war period. Similarly, the critic Camille Mauclair admitted that "It is

7. J. Nam, "The Cubists!" ("Les Cubistes"). Back cover of *La Baïon-nette* (23 November 1916).

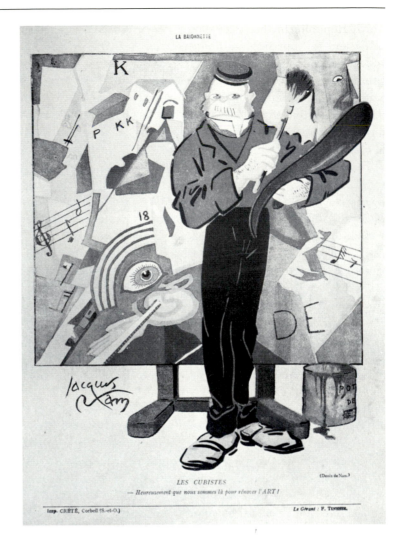

incorrect to say that this bizarre conception . . . is of German origin. It is Spanish and French, as Futurism is Italian," yet this did not, he wrote in 1918, alter the fact that Cubism was unhealthy for France and must be considered "the last and insurmountable consequence of this total abandonment of the natural paths of color and drawing."[14]

In fact the assault on modern art, and on Cubism in particular, that flared up so quickly upon the declaration of war was only the tip of an iceberg; although it was an extremely important and highly visible sign of conflicts that had long been raging within French culture, the wartime attack on the Parisian avant-garde was but one aspect of a larger struggle—at that point nearly a half-century old—to define French culture of the

Third Republic in the wake of the defeat by the Prussians in 1870 and the uprising of the Commune the following spring. Indeed, so important was this struggle for self-definition to the course of Parisian art during and after World War I that it is worth pausing briefly to review the period between the French defeat in 1870 at the hands of the Germans and the chance for *revanche* that, for so many Frenchmen, was represented by war in 1914.[15]

Fortunately, we can find out just what we need to know—not a textbook history, but rather a record of what many French themselves believed to have happened to the nation between 1870 and 1914—in the form of a comic book, a fairy-tale for adults, that appeared as a special issue of *La Baïonnette*, on 18 April 1918. In its sixteen pages, Lucien Métivet's "Marianne and Germania, the Story of a Bonnet and a Helmet" provided the French wartime public with a grossly distorted but eminently recognizable cultural history and moralizing tale after La Fontaine's fable, with France in the role of the self-indulgent grasshopper and Germany the part of the hard-working ant. The cover already tells us a great deal (fig. 8). France, at left, is represented by Marianne, the female incarnation of the French nation that dates back to the Revolution; she is pretty, svelte, and insouciant, wearing her Phrygian cap (the bonnet of the title, and another Revolutionary symbol) with all the stylishness of the classic *gamine*. Germania, at the right, is just as true to type: again she is fat, thick-lipped, and bespectacled, with a glum expression to match the austere Wagnerian helmet that sits upon her ponderous—and obviously evil—brow. All of the details have been prejudicially chosen: Marianne's portrait is set in a frame that includes the French cock at the top flanked by roses and, below, a bow and a quiver of arrows associating her with Diana, the virgin huntress of Antiquity; the entire image is set upon the slenderizing stripes of the *tricolore*. Unfortunate Germania! Her portrait is seen as through a glass darkly—not only is the background shaded, but her frame is composed of a leather whip forming the oval, sabers falling vertically at left and right, and a small rifle crossing the whip's handle below, all topped by a vulturous-looking German eagle. Not surprisingly, this dour and dumpy portrait is set against the unflattering horizontal stripes of the German flag.

The story begins with the birth of the two infant nations. A smiling Marianne/France is born *en plein air* (fig. 9) as the sun rises behind her cradle and the *coq gaulois*—Chanteclaire—announces the blessed event. In the clouds above this secular

8. L. Métivet, "Marianne and Germania." Cover of *La Baïonnette* special issue (18 April 1918).

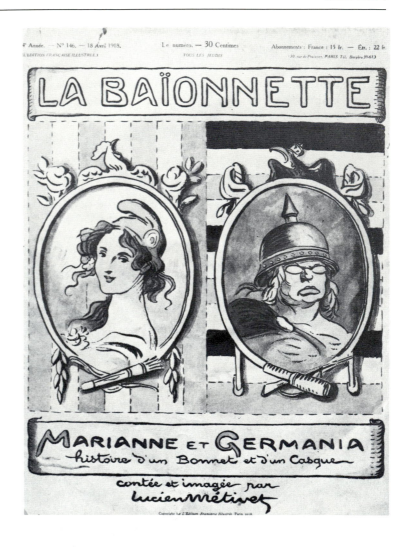

nativity, the bouncing babe is attended by France's great men; reading clockwise from upper left are Charlemagne, Henri IV, Louis XIV, Napoleon, Louis Philippe, and Francis I. The narration tells us that "in the most beautiful country in the world . . . Marianne was born on a stormy day. Guns and cannons were firing and, from the East, the winds of an unjust defeat blew on the capital. But, while the wind was blowing, the child . . . had the singular good fortune to become sovereign of a magnificent domain . . ."[16] In reassuringly picturesque language, we have been told of the origin of the Third Republic: the "unjust defeat" is the Franco-Prussian War of 1870 and Napoleon III's surrender to the Germans at Sedan, followed immediately by the first proclamation of the Republic; the siege of

Paris by the Germans, with the Parisians holding out through the terribly cold and pestilential winter until January 1871; Wilhelm II's crowning as German Emperor at Versailles on 18 January and the Prussian parade down the Champs-Elysées on 1 March; and, finally, the two bloody months of the Commune in 1871, followed by the eventual triumph of the new Republic under Adolphe Thiers. Every Frenchman was intimately familiar with the agonizing facts of the birth of the Third Republic—the so-called *l'année terrible*—so that Métivet can draw and narrate in a kind of idealized shorthand and still be certain of getting his point across. Meanwhile, over to the right is pictured Germania's infancy as the new German empire unified under Count von Bismarck. Baby Germany, her mouth opened in what appears to be a colic scream, is wrapped in swaddling clothes. Already wearing her pointed helmet, she sits upon a gruesomely carved throne in the dark recesses of a Teutonic *Schloss*, and is watched over by Bismarck himself, dressed up as a barbarian warlord. Taken together, the two images of national birth make an unequivocal point: France is born in the clear light of freedom and Germany in the shadow of medievalistic authority.

9. L. Métivet, "Marianne and Germania," pp. 242–43.

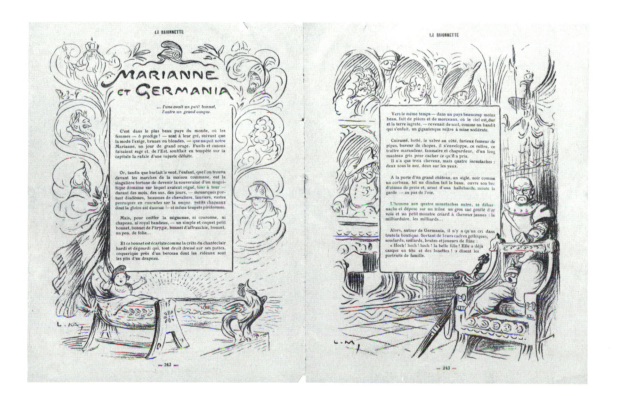

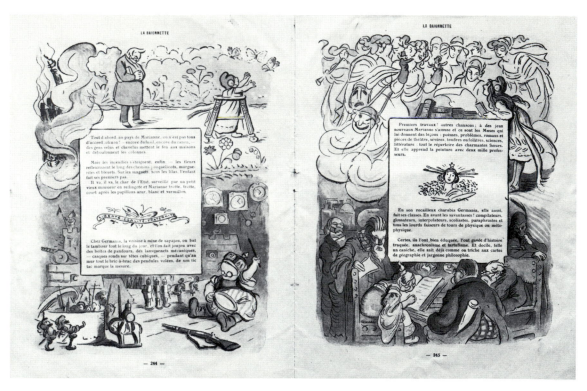

10. L. Métivet, "Marianne and
Germania," pp. 244–45.

As the story continues (fig. 10), Marianne leads the most
charmed of childhoods—at the upper left we watch as she takes
her first steps within the confines of a stroller, chasing butter-
flies, under the watchful gaze of her tutor (who is none other
than Adolphe Thiers), and at the upper right she pursues her
studies surrounded by a bevy of benevolent and talented muses:
"poems, problems, novels, and plays," reads the narration, "severe, tender, or frolicsome; science, literature: the entire repertory of the charming Sisters. And she learns painting with two
thousand professors,"[17] presumably all the great artists that
France has ever produced. Germania's childhood could not, of
course, be more different: we watch her beat her drum and play
with toy soldiers at the lower left (all to the insistent tick-tock-
ing of the Germanic cuckoo-clocks on the wall behind) and at
the lower right she is already slouched over her books, reading
monstrously large tomes undoubtedly written by the miserable-
looking *Herren Professoren* who surround her. A little heavy-
handedly, even for this heavy-handed piece of propaganda, Métivet depicts Mephistophiles standing watch over Germania's
early education. Here as throughout "Marianne and Germania"—with an exception we will come to shortly—the

French scenes are depicted in pale, pastel shades of blue, green, pink, and yellow, and the German scenes in browns, blacks, creams, oranges, and reds.

But all does not continue to go well for Marianne and the Third Republic. Although she is the epitome of grace and wholesome sexiness, by the 1890s (fig. 11), Marianne has become too casual in her statesmanship, too indulgent of the increasing havoc around her. She fans her brow coquettishly as the *Guignol parlementaire*, as Métivet puts it, is enacted. The reference here is, of course, to the Dreyfus Affair, the *cause célèbre* that divided the country into opposing ideological camps of the Left (the defenders of Dreyfus) and the Right (his accusers), though not always strictly along party lines.[18] We ought to have the facts of the case in our minds, for the Affair in many ways is the history of the Third Republic in microcosm. In 1894 Captain Alfred Dreyfus, a wealthy Alsatian, and the only Jewish officer on the general staff, was convicted in a court-martial of selling state secrets to the Germans and sentenced to solitary confinement on Devil's Island. Although Dreyfus protested his innocence, the French army, a fervently anti-Semitic Catholic stronghold as well as one of the last bastions of the monarchists in the Republic, turned a deaf ear. At this point public opinion was strongly behind the army and against the supposedly treacherous Jew. In 1896 a Colonel Georges Picquart, chief of intelligence, uncovered evidence identifying one Major Ferdinand Esterhazy as the real author of the *bordereau* (the list of secrets for sale) that Dreyfus was thought to have written. But Picquart was silenced by the authorities, and Esterhazy was immediately tried and acquitted by the army. Now Emile Zola stepped into the case, urged on by Dreyfus's brother Mathieu: in an open letter to President Félix Faure, the famous *J'Accuse*, Zola claimed the judges were in collusion with the war office. Zola was in turn himself tried and convicted of libel, whereupon he exiled himself to England. By now, though, the Affair was out in the open, and both public opinion and the political and cultural establishment were sharply divided: the most famous Dreyfusards, aside from Zola, included Georges Clemenceau, Jean Jaurès, Charles Péguy, and Anatole France; the best-known anti-Dreyfusards were Edouard Drumont, Paul Déroulède, Maurice Barrès, and Charles Maurras. The two sides now replayed most of the major political dramas that had been enacted in France since 1789. The single most important question was the matter of authority—the state versus the individual—and it was from this, in a manner of speaking, that all other questions flowed: monarchy vs. republic, church vs. state, army vs. civil authority, France vs. her enemies (real or imagined, domestic or foreign), old aristocratic France vs. new bourgeois France, and Christian vs. Jew (really a mythic re-enactment, with biblical precedent, of almost all of the other antagonisms). That is not to say that the lines were always clearly drawn or that there was not a certain amount of waffling on both sides—Clemenceau's famous remark that, had another Jew stood accused, the extremely conservative Dreyfus himself would have been an anti-Dreyfusard, is very much to this point. A crucial element was the army's sense of its prerogatives: not only was it loath to admit error, but it believed, on principle, that it should not be held accountable for its actions. Indeed, even after it was admitted that Dreyfus had been unfairly accused, his enemies nonetheless considered that, even in retrospect, his demand for justice under the law was treasonous, an outsider's disrespect for what ought to be sacrosanct authority. Yet, despite the calumnies and difficulties that Dreyfus endured, he was finally pardoned by President Emile Loubet and in 1906 was exonerated by the supreme court of appeals, reinstated in the army, and decorated with the Legion of Honor (but not until after the union of Church and State had been broken, in 1905, in large part as a result of the Affair). As we shall see throughout this book, the Dreyfus Affair, in both form and content, would continue to influence French society for decades.

But let us return to our story of "a Bonnet and a Helmet." Although the Dreyfus Affair, according to Métivet, should have brought Marianne to her senses, it has not. She continues to amuse herself grandly, holds great expositions (like that of 1900), and welcomes the world, with open arms, to the City of Light.

> She receives friends—emperors and kings from southern and northern climes, who have come from far and near in golden clothes, in pointed and square caps, some even with pagodas on their heads. With her accustomed grace, she knows how to entertain them: parades and cavalcades, and regattas, great fountains here and there, in tra-la-la festivities, and galas at the opera: Faust—Romeo—Samson and Delilah![19]

This image of France as fun-loving, unserious, and self-indulgent at the *fin de siècle* was a widely held stereotype and was often used by the forces of reaction to chastise the nation for its anti-authoritarian waywardness. In one of the best-known books of the war, *Les Traits éternelles de la France* of 1916 (translated into English as *The Undying Spirit of France*), Barrès, one of the famous anti-Dreyfusards, put it this way:

> We were mistrusted. They said of us: "They are no longer what they were. . . . France is a nation grown old, an ancient nation." . . . Among those who spoke there were many who looked upon us without animosity, sometimes even with sympathy. According to them, France had in the past laid up a vast store of virtues, noble deeds, and glorious achievements beyond compare, but today is seated in the midst of these like an old man in the evening of the most successful of lives, or still more, like certain worthy aristocrats of illustrious lineage, who have charming manners, superb portraits, royal tapestries, books adorned with coats of arms, all denoting sumptuous but trivial luxury.
>
> It was in this, as we well understood, that we came to be regarded as jaded triflers, far too affluent and light-hearted, with pleasure as our only concern; the French people were supposed to allow impulse and passion to determine the course of their lives, pleasure being the supreme good sought . . . and to Paris came representatives of every nation in the world to share in this pleasure.[20]

While such a reputation—deserved or not—might even be acceptable in peacetime, in the midst of war it was demoralizing and therefore dangerous. As one source saw fit to express it, "France of the pre-war period . . . saw herself as a woman . . . in her nervousness, her depressions, her fits of anger, her periods of weakness, and the injustice of her verdicts."[21] Germania, on the other hand, demonstrated all the "manly" strengths, if not the virtues. "In her gothic, ostrogothic palace," Métivet recounts, "she received not friends but vassals . . . She never offers her hand, but rather a fist, sometimes in a glove which is not a velvet one."[22] The accompanying illustration shows Germania upon a throne, gloved in chain mail, with various exotic-looking monarchs (presumably France's enemies) kissing her booted feet.

As the tale nears its conclusion, we find ourselves in the period immediately preceding the war (fig. 12), c. 1900–14. The narrator cries, "Pretty Marianne! Be careful!—your bonnet with its cockade is beginning to look like a dunce's cap!" What has happened to that nice little girl in rompers? Having gone beyond mere youthful exuberance, the French Third Republic,

11. (*left*) L. Métivet, "Marianne and Germania," p. 248.

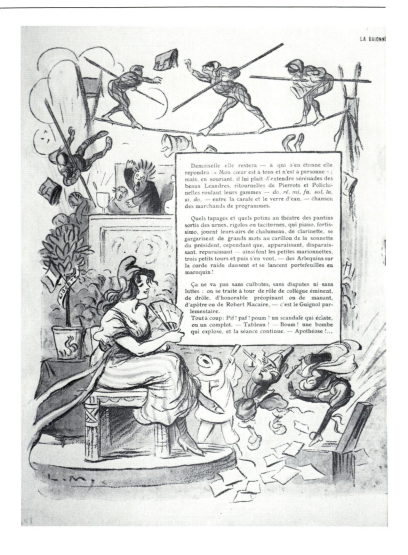

12. (*facing page*) L. Métivet, "Marianne and Germania," p. 252.

according to Métivet, is on the verge of real, mature decadence; Marianne is a bit delirious. Her Phrygian bonnet, as we see in the upper right, is not really a dunce's cap, but Métivet's idea of its equivalent in the world of style: it has become a high-fashion chapeau with its little cockade now exaggerated into a great, arching plume. At the upper left, we see Marianne in a swooning surrender, as she dances with a sinister-looking character: "Look how she is swept off her feet in a fantastic vertigo, frenetic dances, crazy dresses, odalisque culottes, sultan's turbans—her head turned round, with green hair—enough to make you think she's lost her rudder."[23] With her bizarre clothes and her indecent dances—surely a reference to *fin-de-siècle* dances like the *chahut*, the *chaloupe*, and the tango, all

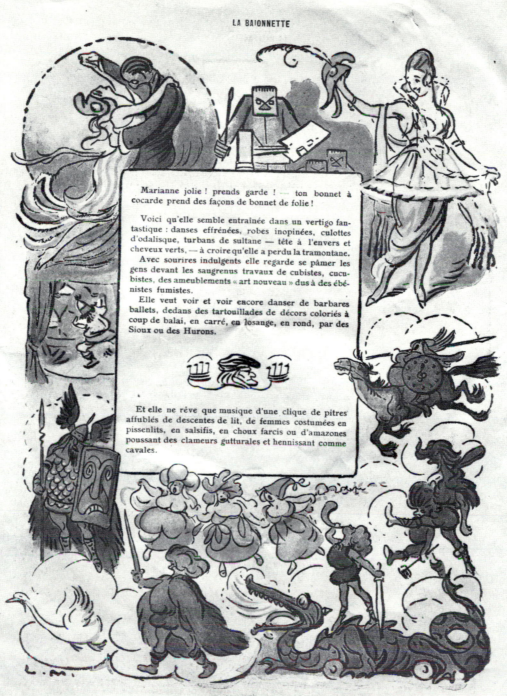

LA BAIONNETTE

Marianne jolie ! prends garde ! — ton bonnet à cocarde prend des façons de bonnet de folie !

Voici qu'elle semble entraînée dans un vertigo fantastique : danses effrénées, robes inopinées, culottes d'odalisque, turbans de sultane — tête à l'envers et cheveux verts, — à croire qu'elle a perdu la tramontane.

Avec sourires indulgents elle regarde se pâmer les gens devant les saugrenus travaux de cubistes, cucubistes, des ameublements « art nouveau » dus à des ébénistes fumistes.

Elle veut voir et voir encore danser de barbares ballets, dedans des tartouillades de décors coloriés à coup de balai, en carré, en losange, en rond, par des Sioux ou des Hurons.

Et elle ne rêve que musique d'une clique de pitres affublés de descentes de lit, de femmes costumées en pissenlits, en salsifis, en choux farcis ou d'amazones poussant des clameurs gutturales et hennissant comme cavales.

— 252 —

of which were read as signs of moral degeneracy—Marianne is a grown-up *mondaine*, and only the worse for it. We may particularly notice the green-tinted robot-like creature at the top center, wielding a paintbrush in one hand and a square palette in the other, who is meant to be a Cubist painter (and therefore is depicted as a cube), and the dancing American Indian at the left, just beneath the image of Marianne herself dancing.

> With indulgent smiles she watches as people are tricked by the ridiculous work of the cubists, cu-cubists, "art nouveau" furniture made by insane cabinetmakers. She wants to see, again and again, the barbarian ballets danced, with conglomerations of decor painted with broom-sized brushstrokes, square, lozenge-shaped, round, by Sioux and Huron.[24]

Not only does Marianne dress strangely and dance immodestly, but she also tolerates the making of crazy paintings and the presentation of "barbarian ballets," which, despite the mention of Sioux and Huron, is actually a reference to the Ballets Russes' 1913 production of *The Rite of Spring*, with its primitivistic sets and costumes by Nicholas Roerich.[25] But whether it was native American or native Russian was of little difference to Métivet and those who shared his cultural predispositions— it was all part of the deranged and un-French recent history of Parisian aesthetics (and, as a composite image, it is quite close to Willette's cartoon "It's not new!"). And that is only the top half of this page, which is meant to depict France's moral and cultural degeneracy in one vast tableau. On the bottom of the page we find an orgy of Wagnerism (with a sketch of the composer himself in the midst of the block of type): Valkyries and Rhine Maidens, Siegfrieds and dragons. Metivet tells us that Marianne "dreams only of music made by a clique of buffoons . . . with amazons screaming a guttural clamor and neighing like mares."[26]

Indeed, the art of Richard Wagner as well as the French cult of Wagner symbolized for many nationalists the total domination of France by Germany since the time of the Franco-Prussian war. Wagner is a major focus of *Hors du joug allemand* (Out from Under the German Yoke): *Mesures d'après-guerre*, of 1915, by Léon Daudet (son of Alphonse, the famous author of *Lettres de mon moulin*), second-in-command to Charles Maurras at *Action Française*, the extreme-Right, Royalist newspaper. *Hors du joug allemand* is but a long diatribe on the idea that French culture had been continuously infiltrated by German ideas since 1870 (i.e. the German "yoke"), and that decades of "Kantism" had led to a "sickening of the French soul." The *joug allemand* is a reference not only to philosophy (the nineteenth-century German métier par excellence), but also to the Bismarckian "blood and iron" that supports a larger *Kulturkampf*[27] which manifests itself in every aspect of German society. This is what Léka meant when he drew *Intellectual and Soldier* (fig. 13) carousing together arm-in-arm, and it is why Daudet singled out Wagner especially: ". . . With Wagner the issue is a methodical and systematic glorification of Germanic legends . . . [Wagnerism] forms, whether we like it or not, an integral part of the conquering and absorbing intentions of German imperialism . . ." For this reason, "the devotion to Wagner is costly," he explained, "because he denationalizes the French in the manner of a Kant or a Hegel or a Schopenhauer." When Daudet declares that "these 'motifs' of Wagner's are military commands in the German language," which like a high-pitched dog whistle can be heard only by Germans, it is because of his belief that where the enemy is concerned—and this includes anyone with whom Daudet does not agree—the supposedly purely formal elements of art are inevitably colored by political ideology. It is not an accident that Daudet says: ". . . the dramas of Wagner are an avant-garde and do not readily relinquish any high ground they have taken," because much as Léka does when he spells the word Cubist with a "K," Daudet means his reader to associate all forms of avant-garde art with the anti-French aims of the enemy.[28]

Daudet's reading of French culture after 1870 was but a variation on the established right-wing plaint which was just as often concerned with economics as with ideas. Edouard Driault, in his book of 1918, *Plus rien d'allemand* (Nothing Else German), claimed that "France before the war was invaded by German products; she sent herself to a German school. The future of her industry, of her beautiful qualities of national genius were threatened, already compromised,"[29] and this is just what Métivet depicts (fig. 14) on the page facing Marianne's pre-war degeneracy: Germania is bent over her accounts as her factories produce at peak capacity, while German trains roar past and ships set out from German harbors exporting German goods throughout the world. Of course, the story does not end here: the point of Métivet's fable was not simply to reprimand the French for their excesses and insufficiencies in the past, but to convince them that despite their waywardness they still had the stuff of which victories were made. Published during the last German offensive in the spring of 1918, when it was not at all clear that the Allies would prevail, this story of a bonnet and a

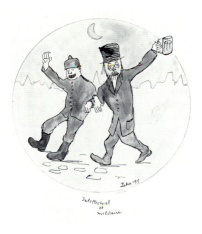

13. H. Léka, *Intellectual and Soldier* (*Intellectuel et militaire*), 1915.

14. L. Métivet, "Marianne and
Germania," p. 253.

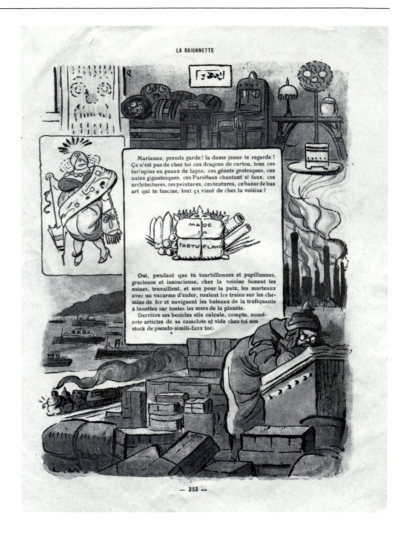

helmet has a miraculous finale: Marianne comes to her senses
at the last moment, transforms herself from a *mondaine* into a
Medusa-like avenging deity, and finally grabs Germania's helmet which she "brandishes like a trophy" of victory. Happily
for France this fairy-tale ending, which still seemed dubious in
April, blossomed into reality by the following November.

Having made our way, in abbreviated form, through this popular wartime history of the Third Republic, we ought to catch
up with the real events of the war's outbreak that mythologies
like "Marianne et Germania" were meant to explain, celebrate,
or rectify. Indeed, the French nation, as in Métivet's story, experienced a sobering sense of collective *déjà-vu* as the Germans
marched through Belgium in August 1914—this had happened
to them before. Was it possible that Paris was to be invaded yet

again by the Germans, for the second time in less than fifty years? Were they about to be again humiliated as the enemy marched down the Champs-Elysées? The government could not afford to chance it: on 1 September all administration was moved from Paris to Bordeaux, followed by the exodus of a large number of civilians from the capital. But although von Kluck's army, following Count von Schlieffen's much-vaunted plan of attack, came within twenty-five miles of the capital, they were to get no closer this time. The first Battle of the Marne began on 6 September, and by the 12th the French had successfully repelled the Germans, who retreated to a point north of the Aisne, where they would remain for the duration.

The French told themselves—and for all we know it may have been the truth—that the reason for their victory at the Marne and the Germans' failure to invade Paris was precisely the French people's resolve not to see a repeat of 1870. The American writer Edith Wharton, a French resident, described the mobilization in just this way:

> After the first rush of conscripts hurrying to their military bases, it might have been imagined that the reign of peace had set in. . . . Paris scorned all show of war, and fed the patriotism of her children on the mere sight of her beauty. . . . It seemed as though it had been unanimously, instinctively decided that the Paris of 1914 should in no way resemble the Paris of 1870, and as though this resolution had passed into the blood of millions born since that fatal date, ignorant of its bitter lesson.[30]

In fact, France's sudden unanimity in the face of the enemy was neither instinctive nor congenital, but was the result of a political coalition formed at the moment of mobilization. On 4 August, in a speech to the National Assembly, President Poincaré coined a term which was to be used over and over again during the course of the war: *union sacrée*. In the war which they were about to embark upon, he said, the nation "will be heroically defended by all her sons, for whom nothing will break the sacred union against the enemy," which was a rhetorical way of saying—as everyone well understood—that all forms of party politics must yield in the name of France's defense.[31] Commenting upon the President's use of the term, one writer explained that it meant, in plain language, that the myriad individual identities that had for so long fought for supremacy— "Socialists, radicals, progressivists, conservatives, republicans, monarchists, Freemasons, clericalists, blockists, nationalists"—must cease and desist.[32]

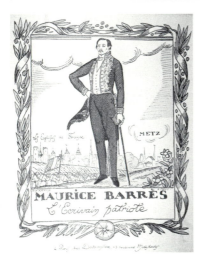

15. G. Arnoux, *Maurice Barrès,
Patriot/Writer* (*Maurice Barrès,
L'Ecrivain Patriote*), c. 1914–18.

In practice, though, the non-partisan Sacred Union meant a virtual capitulation of the Left to the Right, signaled, before a single life had been lost to enemy fire, by the assassination in Paris on 31 July (literally on the eve of mobilization) of Jean Jaurès, the Socialist leader. Indeed, though the killing was the act of a fanatic, it had a specific political objective—the French Left had long called for reconciliation with the Germans, and Jaurès in particular not only blamed capitalism for the war crisis but assured the French working class that the German working class would never take up arms against their brethren to the west, a mistaken notion that cost him his life as the Germans prepared to march on Belgium.[33] The Left in general was forced into a position of having to prove its patriotism—Anatole France, Zola's famous defender in the Dreyfus Affair, at seventy years of age, beseeched the Minister of War, "Make me a soldier"[34]—while the Right, which had long militated to keep the defeat at Sedan alive by calling for *revanche* (revenge and retrieval of the lost provinces of Alsace-Lorraine), appeared vindicated by the German invasion. The reputation of Barrès, for instance, nationalist poet, advocate of *revanche*, self-appointed protector and bard of Lorraine, was never higher (fig. 15). The circulation of *Action Française* skyrocketed: Marcel Proust, André Gide, Auguste Rodin, and Guillaume Apollinaire (who had enlisted in the French army as an artilleryman) were all wartime subscribers to the ultra-Right nationalist magazine.[35]

It therefore comes as no surprise that it was the Right's cultural interpretation and paradigm—of a cosmopolitan, decadent, and demented France suddenly come to her senses as a result of the war—that soon came to prevail, especially after the first Battle of the Marne: "Germany thought she faced a dissociated, a frivolous nation," the Premier, René Viviani, said, but "ignorant of the French soul" she was now being punished for her errors.[36] Of course, it was important that the French rely on their illustrious distant past for moral sustenance, so that among the most popular motifs for expressing France's wartime power was the image of a return to sources and especially of a "reawakening." Charles Saroléa called his patriotic book of 1916 precisely that, *Le Réveil de la France*. He wrote:

> Since the beginning of the war, in all her acts, in her reverses as well as her successes, France has refuted the claims of her enemies. She has proved that those who loved and believed in her were right. She has disconcerted her critics and filled them with astonishment . . . It is the

ancient heroism, the ancient vitality that is affirming itself. The well-informed foreign journalists, whose entire horizon is limited to the cafes along the boulevards, are surprised by this sudden revelation of order and reserve, of devotion and sacrifice.[37]

Barrès, in turn, who had made much of France's reputation for frivolity, now said that it was no wonder that the "undiscerning foreigner" had failed to see the real France, for it remained remote from the crowd, revealed only at "every French fireside";[38] and yet another commentator, André Beaunier, said that the decadent aspect of France before the war was finished: "The new France will be conscious of her power, not to abuse it, but to be no longer timid."[39]

Most important for our interests is that this notion was also applied to culture. If the supposedly frivolous French had proven that they could overcome the pre-war malaise and fight off the barbarian invaders, so Daudet reasoned, the arts in France could finally stem the tide of unhealthy foreign influences. "It was high time," he wrote, "that the warlike and liberating date of 1914 put up a barrier to this inundation. One of the most beautiful privileges of arms is the restoration of values of all kinds, and especially intellectual [ones], that were previously neglected or renounced."[40] According to this logic, the onset of war was not only a phenomenon that destroys but one that also produces a new, or a renewed, mode of thought. This is what another critic, Clément Janin, meant when he referred to "this war which is not only a destroyer but is fecund," in an article of 1917 on print-making during the war.[41] Of course, when Daudet said that "a huge field, which German culture was monopolizing, thus opens to our intellectual, artistic, and scientific activity,"[42] he included avant-garde tendencies under the rubric of "German culture," as part of the congestion that had to be cleared away for the new "field" of restored values.

Perhaps Mauclair best expressed the sense of 1914 as a turning point for French culture, a place of departures not unlike Picasso's place of epiphany, the train station at Avignon: "The war," he wrote, "has figuratively but powerfully dug a trench between yesterday's ideas and those of today. . . . We have all been thrown outside ourselves by a tremendous shock."[43]

II   The Rewards of War

Pierre Albert-Birot, editor of *Sic*—the new "little magazine" of the Parisian avant-garde—asked his "newly enlisted readers," in the inaugural issue of January 1916, to respond to the question: What will the war mean to art? From one of those readers, who was allowed by army censorship to be identified simply as "Victor R. . . . of the corps of A. Sector," a reply was published in the March issue, summing up the positions of Daudet and Mauclair in the tersest way possible: "It won't take even five lines to say that the war will mark the point of departure for a new era." Infantryman "Louis B.," in a slightly more brutal fashion, made reference to the nation's supposed pre-war malaise: "The war is horse medicine," he said, "that cures when it doesn't kill." While saying nothing precise about this transformed new era, both soldiers imply that whatever is in store for the French arts will be for the better.[1] So thought another of *Sic*'s readers, Gabriel Boissy of "Sector 139" (who must have been stationed in Paris, since we know his name), who in mufti was editor-in-chief of the Parisian cultural magazine *Commedia*. Boissy gave a more extended account of the "re-awakening" motif:

> This war, drenched in blood, gives soil for our sensations, our feelings, our ideas to take root: these will all be based on realities, and no longer on dreams or memories. The sense of limits and of the relative, father of the arts, comes back, and separates us from the chimeras of the superhuman absolute, of which Germany is dying.
>
> We will date ourselves from this war, pivot of history, instead of from a too-distant past. *It measures men against each other and from it surges a new nobility.* The war's violent necessities re-establish the sapped hierarchy. . . . Freed from their vanquished soul, the French will have— they have already—a soul of masters, a creative spirit: they finally believe in themselves, without waiting for approbation from the past or from afar. Henceforth they will flower with the impetuous ease of a people rejuvenated or, rather, purified by sacrifice.[2]

Like many others, Boissy sees the outbreak of war as a positive, liberating force; his prediction that the struggle will give the French a renewed sense of self-worth is an indirect allusion to the widespread conviction that victory in the Great War would avenge the defeat of 1870. Not unlike Mauclair, who had written that "danger alone makes us measure the full beauty of what we possess,"[3] *Sic*'s reader uses the imagery of measurement, which he relates to a wider picture of pre-war versus wartime reality: the period before 1914 is seen as a limitless nightmare without scale or proportion, and the period after the start of war as its antithesis—a reawakening to a healthily rooted world of limits and fixed landmarks. By now we recognize those poisonous vapors that had filled the vacuum of the pre-war nightmare: these "dreams and memories," these "chimeras of the superhuman absolute," are another version of Daudet's "sickening Kantism," of Tollet and Willette's "asphyxiating gases" of Germanic *Kultur*. Just as Métivet's Marianne was shaken out of her pre-war delirium, so here France is rejuvenated and purified by the catastrophe. French culture before 1914 had been rootless, dreamy, amorphous, cosmopolitan, exotic, defeated, and chimerical; henceforth—*en revanche*—it would be victorious, masterful, hierarchical, rooted, measured, fully conscious, and limited—all this conveyed not in a right-wing political tract, but in a magazine of the artistic avant-garde.

Most extraordinary in this soldier's analysis is its most basic assumption that life is better during the war than it was in the preceding peaceful period. Where in August 1914 Gris had called the war a nightmare through which he and his friends would have to pass, and looked back upon the halcyon days before the war as a reality which had to be forfeited, Boissy blithely and even exultantly reverses the terms: peace was a bad dream, the war is a comforting reality. In fact, this conception of the war as essentially good for France was the accompaniment of a more generalized patriotism that increased as war progressed. Gris himself, who at the outbreak had spoken of "a war which does not concern me by virtue of either my nationality, my character, or my ideas,"[4] struck a very different chord in a letter that he wrote to his friend at the front, the art critic Maurice Raynal, in October 1916:

> I'm terribly sorry to hear that you are in the thick of it once again. But don't get downhearted . . . When it is all over, you'll be able to rest peacefully without the pangs of egoism and remorse which those of us who haven't taken part in the campaign will feel. For my own part, I assure you

that I am continually ashamed of that peacefulness which
you envy.[5]

To be sure, Gris's change in tone must be due at least in part
to a change in correspondent: it was to his exiled German dealer
that he was writing in 1914, but to a French friend and soldier
two years later. Nonetheless, the artist's willingness to express
himself in this way indicates the degree to which Boissy's view-
point had come to predominate. Royalist literary critics and
avant-garde painters alike had come to share a basic belief in
the morality of the French war effort, as well as a newborn faith
in the salutary effects of war.

For instance, in a letter from the trenches to Vlaminck, Derain wrote that he was "always thinking about this good god of
painting," and like Boissy and Daudet he saw the war as a purifying influence on French culture: "Everything is going to
change," he wrote, "and we will have simpler ideas."[6] Derain's
feelings seem in turn to have influenced those of Henri Matisse,
who in a letter of June 1916 recounted how

> Derain, who came back yesterday, displayed a state of
> mind so marvelous, so grand, that in spite of the risks, I
> shall always regret that I could not see all the upheavals.
> How irrelevant the mentality of the home front must appear
> to those who are at the front.

Like Gris, Matisse was obviously experiencing a good deal of
noncombatant's guilt, so that he contrasts Derain's marvelous
and grand spirit with his own petty civilian preoccupations. At
this moment he considered even his art to be of a second order
of importance: after writing in the same letter, in reference to
his latest creative exertions, "I can't say that it is not a struggle," he caught himself and continued:

> —but it is not the real one, I know so well, and it is with
> special respect that I think of the *poilu.* . . . This war will
> have its rewards—what a gravity it will have given even
> the lives of those who did not participate in it if they can
> share the feelings of the simple soldier who gives his life
> without exactly knowing why, but who has an inkling that
> the gift is necessary.[7]

For Matisse, relative value here depends not upon the difference between pre-war and wartime, but upon the distinction
between front and home front. Thus, although Matisse gives no
indication of sharing in the Right's condemnation of pre-war

Parisian art, he arrived at an almost identical notion of the potential benefits of the war. Just as Boissy had written that it "gives root" to feelings which had previously been amorphous, so Matisse saw a healthy coming down to earth, saw a profundity in the *poilu*'s combat experience that would bestow a new emotional ballast on each and every Frenchman.

If Matisse experienced the crisis of identity to which all noncombatants were subject, he had even more reason than most to scrutinize his modus vivendi. Because while his wife and children were safely installed at Clamart (Issy), the rest of his family, in Bohain-en-Vermandois, near Saint-Quentin, found themselves behind enemy lines. To make matters worse, his brother was being held in Heidelberg as a civilian hostage by the Germans. No wonder he wrote to his friend Marcel Sembat, the *député* and wartime Minister of Public Works: "Derain, Braque, Camoin, Puy are at the front risking their lives . . . we've had enough of staying behind . . . how might we serve the country?" to which Sembat replied, *tout court*, "By continuing, as you do, to paint well."[8] This may have been a less than satisfactory answer for Matisse, who did not credit his art with the kind of reality that seemed important in the midst of the national struggle. But Sembat's response was more than merely a polite brush-off offered to a middle-aged civilian. The Minister was only too aware that it was not at all obvious that the arts would flourish, or even survive, in wartime. Not only were certain styles and modes, as we have seen, now considered to be tainted with Germanic affiliation, but many would be prepared to dismiss all artistic endeavor as a frivolous luxury at a time of national emergency. Sembat, along with other commentators, took the question seriously—considered it a national concern—and (as his letter to Matisse shows) set about offering a patriotic rationale for independent artistic pursuit.

It was at France's darkest moment, during the German offensive at Verdun in the spring of 1916, that the first major salon since the start of war opened in Paris: the Triennale, in which Matisse agreed to exhibit, was held in the Jeu de Paume from 2 March to 15 April. Needless to say, the terrible events at France's eastern frontier could not be ignored by the Triennale's organizers; in fact, they now had the perfect opportunity to make an equation between France's military and her artistic efforts. In the introduction to the show's catalogue, after first making the requisite reference to "the Hun, the stupid Hun, with dirty and rank-smelling skin," the critic Clément Janin went on to expostulate:

. . . the longer the war is prolonged, the longer the energy of the nation affirms itself. . . . Look at this astounding nation, ordinarily so changeable, today so calm in its hope. . . . Life is beginning again everywhere, everyone contributes an evident good will, under pressure from officialdom, to establish, paralleling our offensive force, a moral force whose first source is the normal use of our faculties. . . . And so, let the arts and letters also be taken up again![9]

For the critic, as for the politician and the propagandist, the distinguishing characteristic of the war is not death but renascent life. For Janin, art is no less a part of the war effort than is the military; it is an element of the moral force that complements the force at the front. Essential here is the critic's statement that the origin of this moral power is "the normal use of our faculties," which is really an extension of the now-familiar dreaming-and-waking metaphorical inversion. If the French can behave normally (in effect, "by continuing to paint well") then they must, perforce, be awake; they can feel certain of their ability to act rationally, never to be lost in some inchoate imagination of disaster. Normal life, which includes the normal functioning of the arts, here becomes an important reassurance for the nation. In fact, it is also, as Janin points out, a recompense *avant la lettre.*

Ah! what revenge if the historian who will write about the gigantic struggle and the epic courage of our people finds here and there the masterpiece born in the tempest and acclaimed by the future! What triumph if he can cry: "While the barbarians destroyed the cathedrals of Reims, of Louvain, of Soissons, the 'Halles' of Ypres, the Belfry at Arras, France, feeling her genius aroused, repaired these disasters. She gave back to Humanity what it had lost!" That is why the renewal of artistic preoccupations when the horde of Attila is ninety kilometers from the City of Light—when that city must extinguish her lights each night, to attenuate the severity of the attacks—has something very noble about it. There is also something very touching.[10]

Most important, though, for artists like Matisse who did not see combat, Janin painted a heroic tableau in which they were prominently featured:

Our army has put up such a strong barrier to the enemy, saying to him "You will go no further," that the painter, with confidence, has seized his brushes, the sculptor his rough sketches, the engraver his burin, and the ceramist his wheel and his glaze. All have set to work, and without dissociating themselves from the tragedies played out communally in the trenches, hearts beating in agreement with the hearts of the heroes, who are often their sons and brothers, all have wanted to participate, according to their means, in the sacred defense and the Victory.[11]

In even more forceful language, the poet and critic Charles Morice expounded on "The Necessity of Intellectual Work" on the front page of Georges Clemenceau's newspaper, *L'Homme Libre*, in December 1917. (A recent recruit to the Parisian avant-garde—Charles-Edouard Jeanneret, soon to rechristen himself Le Corbusier—thought Morice's article important enough to clip it from the newspaper and insert it in his files, with relevant passages underlined in red pencil.) Morice begins by adopting the voice of the narrow-minded, chauvinistic philistine:

"The resumption of our intellectual life at this moment? Impossible! Too much blood, too many death rattles. . . . Let us make war!"

To which, in his own voice, he replies:

Make war? . . . How? Each according to his métier. I ask you, since the war began, has the doctor—not only he who treats our wounded, but also the old civilian doctor— ceased to cure, or the judge ceased to judge, or the master to teach, or the industrialist and merchant to produce and sell? Why, then, are the writer and artist alone constrained to remain unemployed? By what exclusive privilege should they be forbidden to work and live, when their effort, more than any other, can unite with patriotic thought, can inspire and propagate it, when they too are healers, judges, awakeners of souls, and good fighters in their fashion?[12]

Just as first Daudet and then Janin had seen the clear interrelationship of culture and politics, so Morice gives the writer and the artist a crucial role to play in the war effort, as the propagandists and shapers of thought. Whereas, according to Mauclair, "in the stupor and disarray of the first weeks of war, writers and artists painfully felt their uselessness,"[13] as the war progressed artistic endeavor was converted by commentators like Janin and Morice into a patriotic obligation. With a heightened sense of reality, seriousness, and mission, the artist's role as warrior for the moral defense of France was being defined.

Of course, the most superb rationalizations always fall somewhat short of the mark, failing to assuage each man's personal sense of inadequacy. During the last year of war, in a letter to his friend Camoin (who was in uniform), Matisse expressed the persistent feelings of uselessness that Sembat's reply had evidently not alleviated. Maybe it was because his younger son Pierre had just followed the older son, Jean, into the army that Matisse felt especially uneasy:

> I work enormously all day long, and with ardor; I know that there is only that, good and sure. I can't engage in politics [*Je ne puis faire de politique*] as, alas, almost everyone does, so to compensate I have to make strong and sensitive paintings. Ours is a career of forced labor, without the certainties that allow one to sleep tranquilly. Every day I have to have worked all day long to accept the irresponsibility which puts the conscience to rest. . . . What do you have to say about events?[14]

Although Matisse had not been reassured by arguments (like Morice's or Janin's) to the effect that every working French artist was perforce a part of the rampart against the enemy, he nonetheless had come to accept the notion that art and politics were inevitably linked. So, as Sembat had urged him to, he continued to paint. His reference to "forced labor" is indicative of a developing wartime definition of art as duty and obligation (even if done only for oneself), as opposed to an unfettered play of the imagination, or a self-generated, even entrepreneurial inventiveness. If the patriotic defenders of art during wartime could not convince the artistic community of its inherent morality, they nonetheless managed to cleanse art of some of its more frivolous and self-serving associations.

Indeed, how differently is the creative process depicted in a pre-war work like Matisse's *The Red Studio* (fig. 16) of 1911 and in his wartime *Piano Lesson* (pl. I) of 1916.[15] Gone, at least for the moment, in 1916 is the lush red atmosphere that engulfed the artist's creative life before the war; gone is the vegetation spilling forth in natural arabesques from a vase in the foreground, as if in friendly challenge to the artistic simulacra which surround it; gone, in the *Piano Lesson*, is the joyous her-

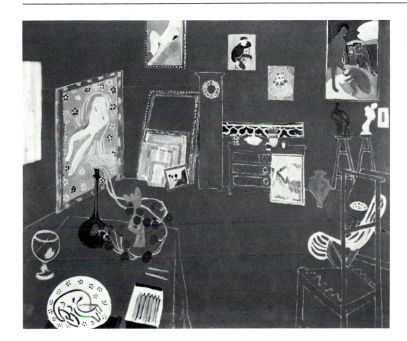

16. H. Matisse, *The Red Studio*, 1911.

meticism of the artist's life in the warm, red space of his imagination. Instead, a young and only half-attentive boy-artist (the
model was Matisse's son Pierre, but portrayed much younger
than he was in fact) sits at the Pleyel, watched over by his taskmistress and regimented by the metronome, dwarfed by the
enormity of his project. The atmosphere is no longer thick with
the slightly vertiginous "scarlet" fever of art, but gray and
squared-off, with only an exasperatingly open window at the
left, its slash of green reminding Pierre of his freedom denied,
of his friends on the street, of the natural life. The ecstatic joy
and lyricism of making art are now reduced to the narrow horizontal band of arabesques formed by the continuous frieze of
the music stand and the balustrade and, at his right, to a tiny
Matisse bronze of a lounging nude, who tauntingly suggests the
sensual fulfillment (and aesthetic flights) which he has little
chance of experiencing. If *The Red Studio* is a pre-war image of
art at its most private and secure, the *Piano Lesson* is an image
of art as it was in the process of being defined during the war:
as discipline, as obligation, as a life of "forced labor," but a life
which, if it held little promise of sensual reward, implied something grander, more heroic, more sublimely moral. The imagery, format, and color of the *Piano Lesson* of 1916 embody
the new rooted "sense of limits and of the relative"; its alert,
upright, gray verticality could not be in stronger contrast to the

recumbent, red format of the earlier painting, with its pre-war dreaminess and exoticism. In fact, the *Piano Lesson* was painted within months of Matisse's statement that one of the rewards of war would be a sense of "gravity" bestowed on even the civilians, if they could share "the feelings of the simple soldier who gives his life without exactly knowing why, but who has an inkling that the gift is necessary." If only unconsciously, Matisse has endowed little Pierre with precisely this sense of confused, innocent, but not undignified obligation; he is at once *petit garçon, artiste, poilu.*

If the *Piano Lesson* is indelibly marked by the Great War, it was by no means intended by the artist as a patriotic statement. Aside from a vague notion of making "strong and sensitive" paintings, Matisse himself was probably unaware of how thoroughly his pictorial thinking was being shaped by wartime attitudes. In fact, he seems to have been equally impervious to the contemporary attacks on Cubism—the *Piano Lesson*, along with other paintings of 1915–16, is if anything more and not less Cubist than his pre-war work (the most immediate source for Matisse's interest in Cubism was Gris, with whom he became friendly during this period).[16] The evolution of Picasso's wartime art, on the other hand, displays a very different aesthetic response to social exigencies. In fact, he was among the very first members of the Parisian avant-garde to create, after 1 August, a work with explicit patriotic reference. During the fall/winter of 1914–15 he painted a still-life (fig. 17), in what has been called his "rococo" Cubist style, wherein decorative patterning, an arch recycling of Seurat's neo-Impressionist dotting, and a jumble of compositional devices combine to form a rather playful if sophisticated Cubist image. What distinguishes this picture from similar ones of the period, and marks it as an immediate response to the declaration of war, is the insertion of a little piece of patriotic faience at the lower left: a white cup that bears the words "Vive la" followed by a pair of crossed *tricolores*. The game, of course, is to fill in the word "France," and the painting is now, appropriately, referred to as the *Vive la France* still-life.

To discuss the "influence" of the Great War on Picasso's art by making reference to *Vive la France* would be fatuous. Aside from the inclusion of a patriotic slogan, which is no more than a detail, the painting is essentially no different in form and content from the works that Picasso produced during the previous spring and early summer. We can find no major thematic shift that would be equivalent to the ideas embodied, if only uncon-

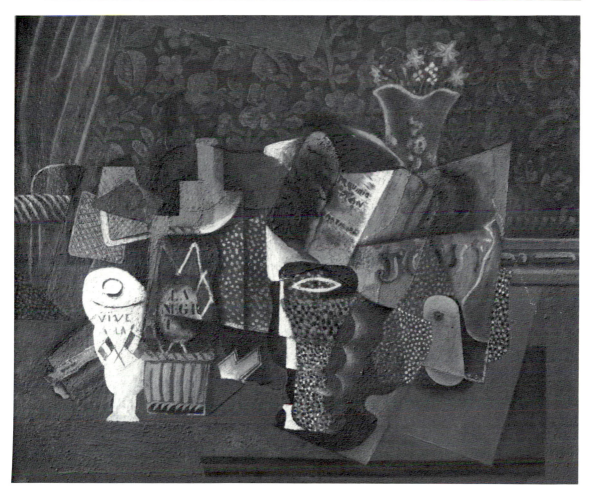

17. P. Picasso, *Still-Life with Cards, Glasses, and Bottle of Rum* ("*Vive la France*"), 1914–15.

sciously, in Matisse's picture of 1916. Indeed, the nationalist slogan within the context of this avant-garde table-scape seems ironic, the patriotic emblem perhaps a bit trivialized by the unexpected juxtaposition. This is not to say that Picasso intended ridicule, only that he appears not to have thought very deeply about the mixture of nationalism and "Kubisme." Yet even at the very start it must have been obvious to Picasso, as a foreigner and noncombatant, that there were to be difficult times ahead for such as he, and we are told that by the first winter he was already suffering from accusations of cowardice and bad faith.[17] Perhaps that is why he quickly realized his mistake: the combination of explicit patriotic reference and Cubism in *Vive la France* was not to be repeated in his painted oeuvre. And when, as we shall see, he again attempted to combine patriot-

ism and Cubism in a single work—the ballet *Parade*, of 1917—
the public would inform him in no uncertain terms of his *faux-
pas*.

Two other explicitly patriotic references in Picasso's art were
essentially private and comradely, and neither made use of any
form of Cubist referent. One was a little sketch, again with the
words "Vive la France," that he sent to his friend André
Salmon.[18] The other was a rapidly executed "doodle" that he
created for Guillaume Apollinaire (fig. 18) and sent to him in
December of 1914. Although of Polish and Italian descent and
of Russian nationality, Apollinaire enlisted in the French army
as early as 5 August 1914 and joined the artillery corps; he rose
to be a *Maréchal des logies*, and sustained a serious head wound
only eight days after he was naturalized a French citizen on 9
March 1916.[19] Picasso's little drawing was made in the first
flush of patriotic ardor and is a playful tribute to the heroism of
his closest friend. Instead of trying to wedge a bit of nationalist
sentiment into his pre-war Cubism, Picasso here adopts the
simple format and crude drawing of the *images d'Epinal*, the
folkloric, brightly colored broadsides (first woodcut, then after
1850 lithographic) produced since the sixteenth century in
Epinal in eastern France. With anachronistic saber in hand,
with cannon behind, map of the territory alongside, and
heaven-sent rays of victorious sunlight breaking through the
storm clouds above, "Guillaume de Kostrowitzky / Artilleur /
1914" (the legend is inscribed upon a *tricolore* rendered in
gouache) is a sweet spoof of the prototype.

While the drawing of Apollinaire hardly qualifies as a work
of art in the public sense—it was no more than a billet-doux—
it nonetheless demonstrates how accurately Picasso gauged the
direction that popular artistic taste was taking. As Janin was to
point out retrospectively in 1917: "And yet another effect of the
war: the renaissance of the *image d'Epinal!*"—a revival which
began almost immediately on the heels of the outbreak, when
the artist E. G. Benito published the first new wartime *image
d'Epinal*, an "Entry of the French into Mulhouse (9 August
1914)."[20] This was followed over the next four years by countless other examples, including Arnoux's image of Maurice
Barrès (fig. 15), by Robert Bonfils's heroic portrait of Maréchal
Joffre (fig. 19) and by a charming series of six images called
"L'Alphabet de l'Armée" (pl. II) by the talented but forgotten
artist Pierre Abadie.

The reasons for the renewed interest in the *image d'Epinal*,
with its simple format and equally simple delineation, are clear:

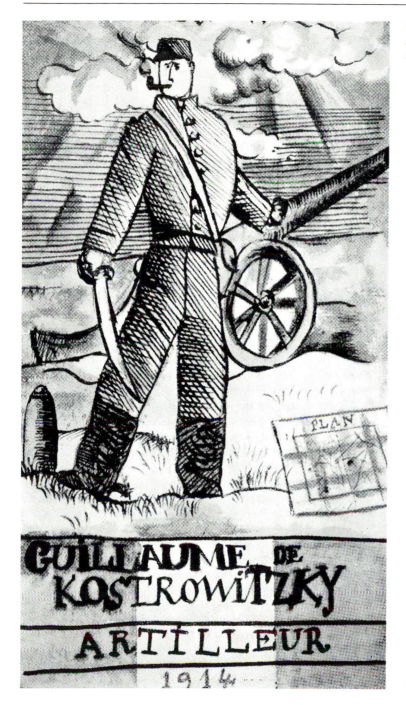

18. P. Picasso, *Guillaume Apollinaire,
Artilleryman (Guillaume de
Kostrowitzky, Artilleur)*, 1914.

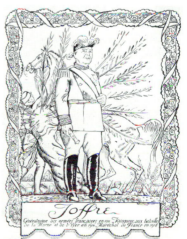

19. R. Bonfils, *Joffre*, 1916.

20. R. Dufy, *The Four Aymon Sons*
(*Les 4 Fils Aymon*), 1914.

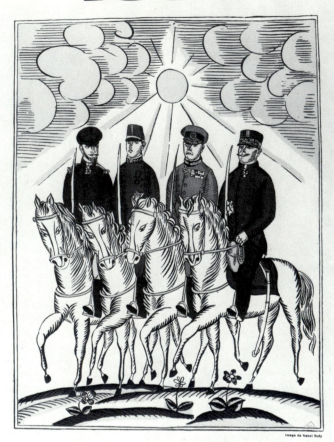

it was easy to imitate and produce, and, just as in the past, it
was an art form designed to appeal to a large audience—a truly
popular art. Moreover, it was indisputably French, and effective
at rousing public sentiment in a war that was intended as a
revanche for the humiliation of 1870 (the town of Epinal is,
moreover, in Lorraine, near the captured regions which France
hoped to retrieve). Especially for the avant-garde or marginally
"advanced" painter, the *image d'Epinal* offered yet one further
advantage: not only was it untainted with Beaux-Arts associa-

tions, while remaining figurative, but in its naiveté it partook of a kind of primitivism which was congenial and even familiar to late-nineteenth- and early-twentieth-century artists.

Raoul Dufy is perhaps the artist who became best known for his wartime *images d'Epinal*. After first driving a van for the military postal service, Dufy went to work for the government propaganda bureau, creating posters and pamphlets for the war effort (he seems also to have worked at the then-new Musée de la Guerre, under Camille Bloch). Most of his graphic work for the government was in the *image d'Epinal* style, as for example his *Les 4 Fils Aymon* poster (fig. 20), based on eighteenth-century models;[21] the four medieval brothers of French legend are here transformed into the military commanders of the four Allied nations in 1914 (l. to r.: Russia, Belgium, Britain, and France). In a letter of 1916, Dufy spoke of a series to be specifically aimed at the colonial forces fighting for France: "Allow me to describe this idea to you: it is to recount in colored pictures (like the *images d'Epinal*) the events of the war involving our native soldiers in the colonies, so that on the walls of the barracks and homes of the Blacks in Africa and the Yellow races in Asia there would be a record of their participation in the Great War, just as our own peasants once had pictures of the Napoleonic Wars in their cottages. My idea has already been very well received in various departments of the Minister of the Colonies, and I thought it would be worth putting it to the propaganda office."[22] Indeed, the idea was approved, and the result is *The Allies*, subtitled "Petit Panorama des Uniformes" (fig. 21).

The propagandistic *image d'Epinal* was but one very limited artistic response to war. There were any number of other ways in which artists could put their talent to work for the common cause. Traditionalists like the sculptor Antoine Bourdelle, whose art had always been at the service of more public forms of expression, proceeded to produce numerous war memorials, as for example his project for the Palais Bourbon, *To the Deputies Slain for the Fatherland* (fig. 22). Louis Marcoussis, Polish émigré and Cubist follower, made studies for artillery and camouflage emplacement (fig. 23), just as many other artists, such as André Dunoyer de Segonzac, worked for the army camouflage unit.[23] La Fresnaye, when he was not actually fighting on the front lines, would dash off occasional pieces for regimental activities,[24] as would Raymond Duchamp-Villon (fig. 24).[25] Jean Dunand, who with his sybaritic lacquer-work would become one of the leading lights in French decorative arts in the

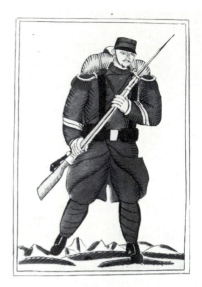

CHASSEUR A PIED.

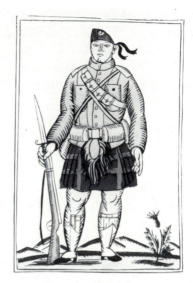

SOLDAT ÉCOSSAIS.

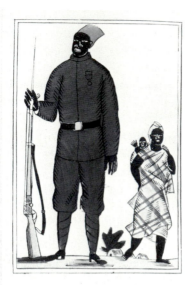

TIRAILLEUR SÉNÉGALAIS

21. R. Dufy, *The Allies* (*Les Alliés*)
(detail), c. 1916.

1920s, designed a new helmet for the army (fig. 25). Although the Armistice was signed before the helmet could go into production, its creator nonetheless received the Cross of the Legion of Honor for his exertions (the helmet's novelty was a movable mesh visor meant to reduce the incidence of blinding).[26]

Yet none of these works—Picasso's little sketch of Apollinaire, Dufy's official propaganda *à l'Epinal*, Dunand's helmet— provided a viable model for serious artistic work during the war. It was one thing to break off one's normal work momentarily to dash off a sketch or poster, or to take on practical wartime tasks such as camouflage; it was another matter altogether to remain committed to an artistic style which, as in Picasso's case, had been declared subversive and treasonous. With the new wartime requirement that art contribute to the national cause, and with the added assumption that a new seriousness, a "gravity," would be forthcoming in French culture, it was not at all clear that the pre-war avant-garde artist could produce anything that would be deemed appropriate to the times. Given that an artist of serious intent could not go on turning out folkloric prints ad infinitum, and that, on the other hand, too radical a style—even with a patriotic reference, such as Picasso's *Vive la France* still-life—could hardly satisfy the new conservative tastes, what were the alternatives?

Indeed, the treacherous waters of national ideology during *la*

Grande Guerre were all the harder to navigate because few of the avant-garde's pre-war leaders were in any position to take the helm after August 1914. Guillaume Apollinaire, Albert Gleizes,[27] and Maurice Raynal, each of whom had been an important spokesman for advanced French art, were in uniform; many of the other artists were themselves at the front; and one of the primary sources of financial support for avant-garde painting, Daniel-Henry Kahnweiler, was in exile in Switzerland. Juan Gris, for instance, had nowhere to turn for the sale of his work, although the French dealer Léonce Rosenberg, despite having been called up, managed to take up some of the slack created by Kahnweiler's absence.[28] True enough, the two leading painters of the avant-garde, Picasso and Matisse, were both around Paris and highly productive during the war—offering at least a model of unimpeded creativity. But even here there was a problem, since one of the two was a noncombatant foreigner—thus doubly to be mistrusted. In fact, almost by default Matisse found himself assuming a good deal of responsibility for protecting various members of the Parisian avant-garde after August 1914.[29]

Among the first to attempt to assume direction of the rudderless avant-garde after war was declared were Jean Cocteau and Amédée Ozenfant, neither of whom had been in the forefront of the Parisian scene until war broke out.

Cocteau, hardly waiting a moment, was the first to throw his hat into the ring. The war was but three and a half months old when, under the direction of the designer Paul Iribe, he helped

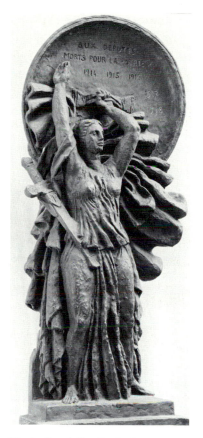

22. A. Bourdelle, *To the Deputies Slain for the Fatherland* (*Aux Deputés, morts pour la patrie*), c. 1918.

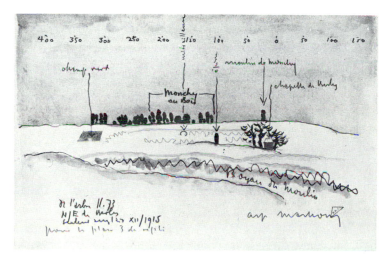

23. L. Marcoussis, Plan for artillery emplacement, 1915.

24. R. Duchamp-Villon, *Rooster*
(*Gallic Cock*), 1916 (cast 1919).

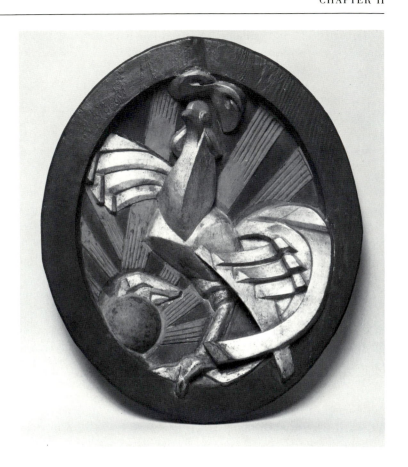

25. J. Dunand, Helmet design for
French army, 1918.

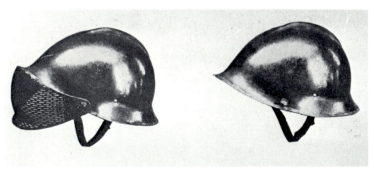

publish the first issue of the new magazine *Le Mot* on 28 November 1914. The title, with its biblical evocation, was sol-
emnly appropriate to France's new-found militarism and to its
editors' objective of laying down the cultural law during the national crisis. Its position vis-à-vis both the avant-garde and the
anti-modernist reaction was equivocal at best, as we shall
shortly see. Nonetheless, *Le Mot* saw as one of its primary tasks

the rescue of modernism and imaginative creative endeavor from the accusations of Germanic affiliation. "Ah!" they sighed,

> let us safeguard the treasure of France. Don't let what has been slowly constructed be damaged through haste and error; let us be careful not to throw away the good grain with the bad. Confusion is already arising. Shoddy goods from Munich and the masterpieces of the pure French tradition are put into the same sack, and the young painters are reproached for Berlin influence.[30]

If the editors seem far from unprejudiced—jingoistic, and anything but cosmopolitan (it is the "pure French tradition" they are defending, not internationalism)—this is hardly surprising at the very start of war. Considering the kinds of attacks that Aurel, Mauclair, Daudet, Tollet, and Léka would shortly be launching against art in Paris, the avant-garde was sorely in need of even this admittedly timid form of defense.

In an article of March 1915 (the entire life-span of *Le Mot* was only eight months) called "Let's be reasonable," the editors attempted a slightly more judicious separating of the grain and chaff. The article began,

> Wagner is indigestible but brilliant. Munich is atrocious, but it must not be confused with a pure French return to sublime simplicity. I will no longer brush my teeth with Odol, but I will not deprive myself of Schubert, Bach, or Beethoven.[31]

Wise-cracking and *"au courant,"* *Le Mot* considered itself a voice of reason in the midst of an unreasonable, even hysterical, chauvinism. There was no need to go too far, Cocteau and Iribe insist—we can still listen to classic German music, even if we boycott their products or find Wagner now beyond the pale—and Cocteau returns to the same ideas in an ode, "Le Grande Pitié des Victimes de France," dedicated to Maurice Barrès, in issue no. 8.[32]

In some fundamental ways, *Le Mot*'s reading of culture was not very different from that of the more reactionary critics. Its cultural stance, for example, was predicated on the now-familiar pre-war/wartime dichotomy: the position that the years preceding 1914 were more hazardous than the war in progress. The notion of pre-war decadence and internal disunity is central to the magazine's philosophy:

> Before the war, nothing but mines! nothing but trenches!

Nothing but malaises, hunger strikes, alliances, invaded provinces, atrocities, unstable borders.[33]

This succinctly described and took to its logical conclusion the right-wing doctrine that, since France was already in a state of war—an ideological civil war—in August 1914, she had merely to direct her efforts eastward against the true enemy. Indeed, in accordance with that position, the editors provided the standard wartime interpretation of 1914 as the date of France's liberation, for the war rescued France from her confusion, her dreaminess, and allowed her people to gain a renewed sense of value, proportion, and reality:

The war breaks out; immediately a roaring cannon and a cathedral in flames reveal to each his ear and his eye. He hears! He sees! He is undeceived! His amorphousness is metamorphosed in passion . . . the concrete evidence of the drama revealing to him the relative worth of living . . .[34]

In fact, according to Iribe and Cocteau—who here echo the now-familiar refrain of the cleansing, curative powers of the war—it was as a celebration of the "liberating date" of mobilization that *Le Mot* was conceived. Explaining that their magazine would be uncontaminated by commercialism, they provided an editorial formula for this wartime journal:

Our program is to make a journal born of the war and nourished by the war; a journal that always shows the same face, but animated each week by a different expression . . .[35]

Then, in a voice that is clearly that of Cocteau alone, the editors offer their credo:

Between TASTE and VULGARITY, both unpleasant, there remains an *élan* and a sense of proportion: THE TACT OF UNDERSTANDING JUST HOW FAR YOU CAN GO TOO FAR. *Le Mot* hopes you will follow it on this path of France.[36]

In describing as supremely French a path of judicious experimentation—a middle road that sounds like the very definition of *chic*—Cocteau is of course addressing himself specifically to the Parisian artists of modernist tendencies, in effect warning them that extreme forms of aesthetic endeavor will have to be moderated. Even less cheerful was the editorial statement of two months later: "*Le Mot* asks its devoted readers to follow it, believe in it, and have confidence in it. It hopes to become, little by little, the organ of common sense, equilibrium, and intellectual order."[37]

Despite the powerfully conservatizing mission that *Le Mot* assigned to itself, it was nonetheless far less fervent in its cultural chauvinism than the editors' credo might seem to promise. In response to Cubism, for instance, there was at least a hesitation and a reluctant acceptance of the movement's role in pre-war aesthetics. In an article of June 1915, "Ism," probably written by Cocteau, artistic vanguards are declared to be narrow-minded, but not evil: "Let's hope that the post-war era will bring about the death of the 'ism,' " it said. "Cubism was appropriate for a large public, . . . Cubism was appropriate, and a little simple, as Impressionism was, in its time." It then went on to say that "isms" were nonetheless antithetical to individual expression, and should be abandoned, concluding with the statement "Let's be on guard against GermanIsm."[38] Still, this was a far more moderate view of the avant-garde than tended to prevail.

The magazine's artistic tastes were also less parochial than we might have expected. Wondering (as Albert-Birot would the next year) about the war's possible influence on art, the editors asked:

> . . . What will it mean for musicians like Igor Stravinsky and Maurice Ravel, for painters like Albert Gleizes and Bonnard, for poets like the Comtesse de Noailles and Paul Claudel, for writers like André Gide and Valéry-Larbaud?[39]

"Eclectic" is the best description of such a disparate group; aside from the obvious point that all but Stravinsky are French, the artists would appear to have little in common. Probably the strangest coupling here is that of Bonnard and Gleizes, strange less for its mix of generations and aesthetics than of relative stature—Bonnard was already a major older figure, with a public identity; Gleizes was relatively unknown outside the avant-garde. Yet, it was *Le Mot*'s nationalism that forced this peculiar configuration, since the most appropriate name here was that of Picasso—the younger Parisian star who, as a noncombatant and a neutral, could not be mentioned. "The *métèque* cannot love our journal,"[40] wrote the editors in issue no. 7 (Stravinsky was exonerated for the time being, as Russia was the third great ally until 1917).

Gleizes—the patriotic artist-soldier, serving at the front until his demobilization in 1915—had the great virtue at this moment

26. A. Gleizes, *Return* (*Le Retour*), 1915. Reproduced in *Le Mot* no. 20 (July 1915).

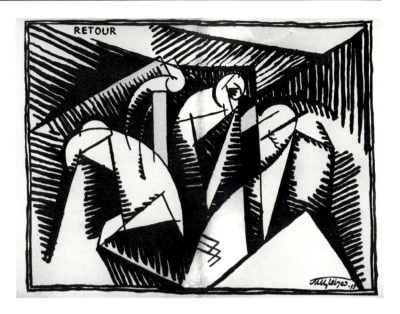

of being French. It was with evident pride that the editors re-produced his drawing *Return* (fig. 26), a Cubistic rendition of the aftermath of battle, as a full-color two-page spread in July 1915. But Gleizes's artistic and cultural opinions, as published in *Le Mot*, were surprisingly inconsistent with the editorial slant. Despite the fact that he gave voice to the kind of hortatory patriotism that Iribe and Cocteau liked, his views on pre-war versus wartime—as expressed in an article entitled "It is in los-ing itself in the sea that the river remains faithful to its source"—were another matter:

> The present conflict throws into anarchy all the intellectual paths of the pre-war period, and the reasons are simple: the leaders are in the army and the generation of thirty-year-olds is sparse. . . . From this moment on, *Le Mot* wants to prepare for the post-war period. . . . *Le Mot* watches over the audaciously creative French spirit. The writers and artists with whom you will some day claim the honor of belonging to the same race are almost all in the line of fire. Nonetheless, nothing blinds their conscience and their love. The past is finished. It was great. Let us have the wisdom not to make it seem odious as we leave it behind. We remain faithful to it in going, with courage, as far as we can.[41]

Gleizes certainly strikes the right note, telling us that *Le Mot* is anticipating the victory by protecting the "esprit de France"; he fortifies Gallic pride with words like "honor" and "race." But he directly contradicts Cocteau when he encourages the French artistic community to go "as far as we can"—not for him the compromise of "understanding just how far you can go too far." This, of course, is consistent with his positive view of the pre-war period, a view which again contradicts Cocteau's notion of that period as an amorphous era of "malaise." Gleizes, who had good reason to feel proud of the years before 1914 and of the avant-garde culture in which he had played such a major role, says simply "It was great." The Cubist painter and theorist envisions no new start for France, no epochal break with the past, but the opposite: he swears fidelity to it, a loyalty which can be demonstrated only by continuing to be audacious. Yet Gleizes too rewrote the past as he wanted to see it: when he says that the reason artistic direction is presently in disarray is that "the leaders are in the army," he conveniently chooses to ignore the presence, hard at work in Paris, of the *foremost* Parisian modernist—Picasso. This tendency to write Picasso out of the history of art will become a recurring motif in the wartime and post-war years.

Another Cubist painter championed by *Le Mot* was Roger de la Fresnaye, who was also in uniform. Even more to the editors' taste than the middle-class Gleizes, La Fresnaye was from an old aristocratic family, with a name to prove it. Unfortunately, he was also the victim of a rather formidable gaffe on the part of the editors. Lamenting the wartime loss of many French geniuses on the *champ de bataille*, the editors cried in January 1915:

> Charles Péguy, you would have avenged Reims! La Fresnaye, in one of your fresh canvases you would have concentrated the inventive heroism of our tri-colored youth of earth and sky![42]

In fact, although he would be seriously wounded later on, La Fresnaye was alive and healthy, and the magazine had to apologize for having jumped the gun on his martyrdom. But the reason for so lamenting his putative death (along with the authentic demise of Péguy) is clear enough. In his pre-war work La Fresnaye had demonstrated that the new Cubist language could be used to patriotic, distinctly nationalistic effect. Where Picasso's iconoclasm visually undermined such obviously bourgeois ideologies as nationalism, from the very start La Fresnaye had managed to separate Cubism's pictorial subversions from its thematic and ideological ones. Whether it was the straightfor-

27. R. de la Fresnaye, *Conquest of the Air*, 1913.

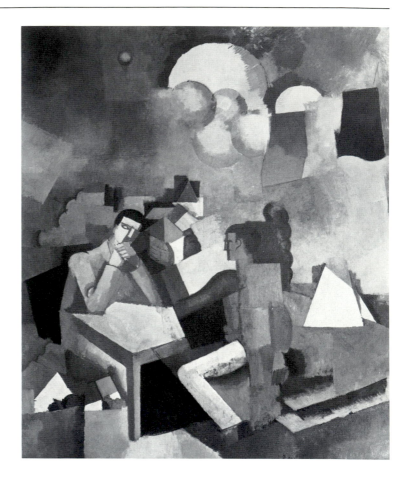

ward heroizing of the French military, as in the 1911 *Artillery*, or the eulogizing of a more general French spirit of invention, as in his *Conquest of the Air* of 1913 (fig. 27), La Fresnaye's orientation had always been emphatically "tri-colored."[43]

Dufy was another favorite of *Le Mot*'s editors. They reproduced several of his wartime prints, including *Tirez les premiers, messieurs les français*, which depicted a British officer quaintly inviting his French allies to enjoy the first shot of the battle,[44] and his *The End of the Great War* (fig. 28), where the *coq gaulois*, Chanteclaire, sings a hymn to victory to the tune of "The Wandering Jew." With the German eagle crushed beneath the cock's claws and Joan of Arc's spirit rising from the ashes of the Cathedral of Reims, Dufy had made precisely the kind of unabashedly French image that Cocteau and Iribe liked. Their comment on the print: "*Voilà*, a bit of the excellent tradition of the *Epinal tricolore*."[45]

In short, *Le Mot* presented, at this early moment in the war,

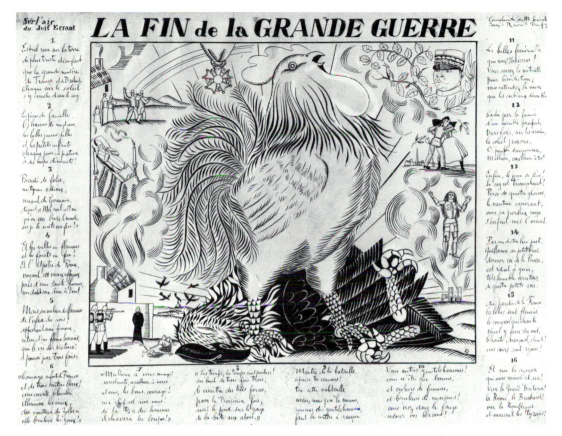

28. R. Dufy, *The End of the Great War* (*La Fin de la Grande Guerre*), 1915. Reproduced in *Le Mot* no. 13 (6 March 1915).

a mixed aesthetic. Its editorial position espoused a rather conservative reading of culture, yet one of its contributors dissented. There was no strong visual style to speak of, since *Le Mot* carried relatively few illustrations other than ironic line-drawings by Cocteau, signed with the name "Jim" (Gleizes's *Return* was one of the rare works of art reproduced). Indeed, in terms of a visual aesthetic *Le Mot* represents Cocteau's pre-history; by the next year he would begin to actually ally himself with avant-garde painting. But his collaboration with Iribe in 1914–15 already shows Cocteau establishing his working method: his hestitation between self-consciously modernist culture and anti-modernist reaction will be transformed into an aesthetic of ambiguity; what had been equivocation will become pluralism, and will put Cocteau in the ideal position to influence the course of events in the Parisian art world.

Le Mot was surely the model for the second avant-garde magazine to appear during the first year of war, *L'Elan*. Amédée Ozenfant, its founder-editor and the principal contributor, had, like Cocteau, been on the periphery of the pre-war avant-garde.[46] Exempt from military service, he made his first contribution to the war effort in editorial work for the propaganda bureau on the rue Vivienne, alongside Dufy. Perhaps sensing a lack of direction on the part of the avant-garde after August, Ozenfant decided to strike out on his own with a wartime journal of advanced tastes. The first issue of *L'Elan* appeared on 15 April 1915, just ten weeks before the demise of Cocteau's journal. In fact, we have already noticed "*élan*" as one of the key words on Cocteau's "path" of French finesse, and Ozenfant's choice of title left no doubt as to his magazine's orientation: *élan* was among the most patriotic and optimistic words that could be spoken in wartime France.[47] This short, accented vocable, expressive of jumping, flying, ardor, and enthusiasm, was popularized through Henri Bergson's concept of *élan vital*, but it took on a more specifically belligerent connotation in the vernacular of the French army. If Bergson had functioned, in the pre-war years, as a kind of Gallic response to nineteenth-century German philosophy (especially to the pernicious doctrines of Kant, Hegel, and Nietzsche), *élan* was the Ecole Supérieure de la Guerre's answer to France's defeat in 1870 at the hands of the Prussians. In tactical terms, *élan* meant that France would take the offensive in matters military, just as the Germans subscribed to the aggressive gospel of war according to their famous theorist, Count von Schlieffen. With her smaller population and army, France had far less reason than Germany to believe that she could succeed in an *offensive à outrance*. But this was precisely the essence of *élan*, an almost mystical term meant to express France's "will to succeed," her military *je ne sais quoi*, an ancient Gallic spirit which, despite her limited means, would spell the difference between the humiliation at Sedan and victory in the war to come. All French vitality and *panache* were concentrated in Ozenfant's title.

The cover of the magazine's first issue (fig. 29), drawn by Ozenfant, exemplifies the magazine's title and betrays its early date in the war. Superimposing a bejeweled Dame Victory on a map of the Allied lines in France and Belgium, Ozenfant created a witty image of the "brow [and] necklace of Victory" by punning on the French word *front*, which means both "brow" (or "forehead") and, as in English, a military front. Of course, the cleverness, *chic*, and optimism of *L'Elan*'s first cover would not have been possible by the fall of the following year. After the battles of Verdun and the Somme, after the year-long bloodletting of 1916, when the front would budge neither for the Ger-

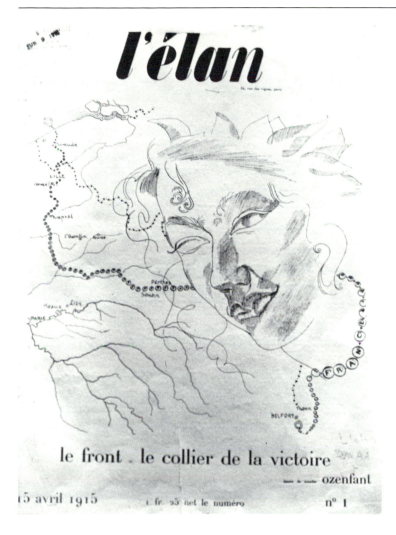

29. A. Ozenfant, "Brow and Necklace of Victory" ("Front et collier de la Victoire"). Cover of *L'Elan* (15 April 1915).

man offensive nor for French *élan*, when the war of attrition became an undeniable reality, the same picture would have seemed a bad joke.

But the "front et collier de la Victoire" was, nonetheless, a perfect symbol of *L'Elan*'s double-flanked militancy: its whole-hearted patriotic contribution to the war effort and its strong defense of the Parisian avant-garde. Not that Ozenfant himself was making difficult or advanced pictures, or that even the majority of artists whose work he reproduced were working in extremely radical styles. André Dunoyer de Segonzac, one of the editor's favorite artists, sent back from the front rather traditional, if slightly "improvisational," sketches; Sonia Lewitzka, a Polish émigrée, created folkloric images based on styles of

30. J. Metzinger, *Nurse*, c. 1914–16.
Reproduced in *L'Elan* (1 February
1916).

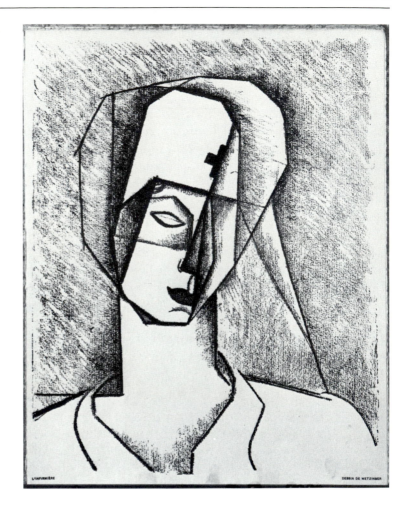

her native country; and Lucien Mainssieux drew patriotic cartoons. But there was more than a faint Cubist reference in Jean
Metzinger's image of a Red Cross nurse (fig. 30), which appeared in issue no. 9, of February 1916. Moreover, Ozenfant
was completely forthright about his magazine's modernist orientation, even if the imagery was unequivocally nationalist.
"*L'Elan* . . . affirms that it is the journal of avant-garde thought
about art and the spirit," he wrote in the eighth issue. "It gath-
ers all free efforts and testifies that the war has not diminished
the *élan* of thought in France."[48] And recognizing that it was not
enough simply to proclaim support of advanced Parisian culture, Ozenfant went further, by launching a counterattack
against the avant-garde's critics. Léon Daudet was savaged by
way of a footnote: in a mock *enquête* conducted at the zoo, a

monkey (!) was asked "What do you think of the war?" and his pompous, reactionary views were footnoted thus: "By the way, it seems to us that M. Léon Daudet made the same remark in his remarkable work *L'Avant-guerre*. . . ." (a reference to Daudet's 1913 book *L'Avant-guerre, études et documents sur l'espionnage juif-allemand en France depuis l'affaire Dreyfus*).[49] Mauclair and another critic, Emile Bayard, were ridiculed for their reactionary defamation of Cubism in a piece penned by Granié, a well-placed magistrate sympathetic to the Cubists;[50] and in another issue, a right-wing critic was invented named "Geoffrey Wenceslas de Viel-Buze" (Old Nit-Wit), who said things like, "Since Claude Lorrain French art has been sullied with Germanism."[51]

Ozenfant's defense of the avant-garde took the effective approach of refusing to take the reactionary critics seriously. Which is not to say that *L'Elan* appeared frivolous or unserious in regard to the war effort; to the contrary, the magazine proclaimed its devotion to the cause on almost every page, and its high quality of production—its fine stock, tipped-in plates, and superb printing—was meant as a kind of affirmation of French aesthetics and culture. Indeed, its first statement of purpose read:

> The foreigner may think that art in France belongs only to peace. Those who are fighting, our friends, write to us how much more strongly the war has attached them to their art: they would like some pages in which to show it. This journal will be those pages. The foreigner can but admire this elegant insouciance, this fidelity to art. This French journal is also the journal of our allies and our friends. . . . It will fight against the Enemy, wherever he is, even in France. Entirely disinterested, it will be expensive, its only goal being to propagandize on behalf of French art, of French Independence, in sum, of the true French spirit.[52]

Although Ozenfant was far more cosmopolitan in his tastes than Cocteau and Iribe had been in *Le Mot* (significantly, his "French" journal is also the magazine of "allies and friends," which left room for even noncombatant, neutral friends like Picasso), *L'Elan* was no less patriotic for all its liberality. In fact, although toward the end of its run *L'Elan* would reproduce work by foreigners and noncombatants like Severini and Picasso, the magazine's contributors were overwhelmingly French (or at least were, like Apollinaire, foreigners who were fighting for France).

Moreover, the terms in which the avant-garde was defended were nationalist, as for example when Ozenfant wrote ironically:

> It is in the midst of war, during leisure time in the trenches, that Braque, Derain, La Fresnaye, Léger, L.-A. Moreau, A.-D. de Segonzac, Allard, Apollinaire, and so many others persevere—O, paradox!—in perpetrating and advocating . . . BOCHE PAINTING.[53]

Yet by offering a nationalist defense of the artists in question, Ozenfant was unwittingly fighting the reactionaries on their own terms. His effort to create in *L'Elan* a united front against wartime reaction, while it was not unsuccessful, nonetheless was carried on at a certain cost to his magazine's claims to disinterestedness. Despite Ozenfant's valiant efforts, his reasoning entailed a tacit acceptance of the values of conservative wartime art criticism. For instance, those artists at the front who "write to us how much *more* the war has attached them to their art" echo a now-familiar theme: the war restoring a sense of values and gravity to the artistic enterprise. More important, Ozenfant's foreigner observing "this elegant insouciance, this fidelity to art" recalls Janin's theme when he introduced the Triennale show:[54] that art was essential to national morale as a demonstration of the French ability to function normally, even under stress. This idea must have been important to Ozenfant, because he used it again in another article. In issue no. 5, on the page facing a drawing by Segonzac, appeared "A propos d'un dessin," where *L'Elan*'s editor wrote:

> . . . The beautiful drawing . . . by our collaborator and friend A.-D. de Segonzac is further evidence adding to the certainty that the French, even outside of their accustomed surroundings and despite the constant diversity of such a new existence, can preserve with a truly PEACEFUL unselfconsciousness the perfect possession of all their faculties . . . Faced with the lucidity of these lines, how can one imagine that the artist is himself a soldier, that he fights, and that the same hand has in successive moments commanded an attack and drawn this contour? . . . Let's admire this force which is French force.[55]

The editor's conception of art as a normalizing activity (presented as the antithesis of combat) was, in turn, closely related to another of his positions: the duty to be discreet about the unpleasant realities at the front.[56] On the first page of the seventh issue, of 15 December 1915, Ozenfant reprimanded the

French press for their gory reportage. "Why these bloody images?" he asked,

> these corpses, these sufferers, on every page of the most
> timid newspapers . . . ? Poor, heroic soldiers, hard task
> of fighting! but when you fall, lamented ones, wouldn't it
> be better to turn our backs? Faced with agony, the civi-
> lized pull the curtain. One must love life; O yes! let us
> admire our poor soldiers who sacrifice their lives, but let
> us cover their corpses as well as those of our enemies.[57]

Although he could hardly have realized it, the amalgamation of
these two ideas—on the one hand that art is normative, and on
the other that images are potentially dangerous (and therefore
must be controlled)—by the end of the war would radically alter
the ideological complexion of the Parisian avant-garde. This
was only the beginning of an important cultural transformation,
whereby the avant-garde's function as critic, disrupter, and ad-
versary of the establishment would be gradually but effectively
discredited.

If Gleizes's article was the exception that proved the editorial
rule of *Le Mot*'s denigration of the pre-war Parisian avant-garde,
then André Lhote's article, "Totalisme," published in issue no.
9, is the exception that demonstrates *L'Elan*'s editorial embrace
of pre-war audacity. Not that Lhote, a young painter who could
only benefit by pronouncing a negative judgment on the pre-war
scene, comes right out and says so; on the contrary, he first
lauds Cubism as "the most ardent expression" of the "rational"
technique inaugurated by Cézanne. But the point is that the
Cubists' success in rationalizing visual expression has been
achieved, in his view,

> despite a certain unhealthiness—the disease of one-up-
> manship that arises from the obsession with "personality
> at all costs" and that ends up turning unsoundly based and
> overly experimental techniques into a formal system.

Having linked Cubism with illness, obsession, individualism,
and exaggeration, Lhote goes on to say that now, during the war,
the suspension of the often petty studio quarrels of the pre-war
period "arouses today, in every thoughtful artist who is freed
from the aggressive exaggerations of yesterday, a just evaluation
of pictorial processes . . ."—the now-familiar idea of the war's
calming restoration of a sense of values in contrast to pre-war
extremism. Not surprisingly, Lhote urges his readers (i.e., the
other artists of the Parisian avant-garde) toward moderation:

"Recognizing the insufficiency of a single method," he writes,
"let us not confine ourselves to any exclusive *parti-pris*."
Rather, "let us take advantage of this tragic vacation . . . to
attempt an expressive totalization of pictorial values."[58] This,
for all its obfuscation, was nothing other than the safe middle
road that Cocteau recommended for France, "the tact of understanding just how far you can go too far." Indeed, Ozenfant was
aware that Lhote's article might be viewed rather unfavorably
by members of the Parisian art world, and he actually went so
far as to add a signed disclaimer at the end of "Totalisme":
"*L'Elan*, being completely independent, is interested in all experiment. . . . The opinions expressed are only those of their
author." Ironically—or perhaps it is a question of Ozenfant's
protesting too much—he himself would express very similar
opinions by 1918.[59]

But, whatever *Le Mot* and *L'Elan* did or did not do for the
Parisian avant-garde, neither Cocteau nor Ozenfant could answer the most vexing dilemmas; neither had any proposals to
make regarding *praxis*. It was one thing to say that a "French
path" could be found between stifling "good taste" and vulgarity, but it was something else to specify what that art might look
like. Ozenfant could claim that his journal would propagandize
for a spirited and independent French art, but what form, after
August 1914, would that art take? How could the various forms
of pre-war art that had been deliberately provocative, often
ironic, and usually iconoclastic become serious, measured, and
simplified? How could an art be nationalist if it was produced
by a heterogeneous group of cosmopolitans? How could art that
had been born and flourished in the supposedly frivolous years
before 1914 declare itself to be part of France's post-mobiliza-
tion reawakening?

And there remained yet another dilemma. Even if the pre-
war artist was willing to capitulate by introducing explicitly patriotic subjects into his art, and even if he agreed thereby to
draw back from some of the more abstruse formal issues, he
would still not be fulfilling the "normal" and "insouciant" role
for wartime art that both Janin and Ozenfant had so generously
assigned it. Explicitly patriotic art was no normal use of the
faculties; nor was it insouciant or peaceful. Even if veiled in an
unaltered Cubist pictorial structure, the use of demonstrably
nationalist themes—themes quite alien to most of the pre-war
avant-garde—was both an abnormal turning of one's faculties to
the task of moral defense and a proof not of insouciance but, to
the contrary, of concern and even fear. Of course, the artist

would have ignored the anti-Cubist, anti-internationalist, anti-avant-garde wartime doctrines very much at his peril. Although they offered no formula for how it was to be realized, what France's spokesmen (both those allied with and those ranged against the avant-garde) demanded was that art be patriotic without being obvious about it—that it be, in some sense, un-worried, yet conscious of the national mission. Explicitly patriotic art might be a suitable stop-gap measure, but it could be no more than that, while the critics waited for a deeper, more profound demonstration of French spirit.

Indeed, we have already heard the first part of what was to be a solution to the avant-garde's predicament, although no one could have known it at the time. When Sembat told Matisse that he would be serving France by "continuing to paint well," the Minister of Public Works was subtly altering the terms of the debate. According to Sembat, it was not a question of what patriotic efforts Matisse made or what subjects he chose to paint (for instance, Matisse might have joined the war effort by making a loan poster or designing a cenotaph—probably the kind of thing that the painter had had in mind). Rather, Sembat says, Matisse's patriotism would be ratified by the *quality* of his art. Of course, though Sembat might be confident that Matisse's "continuing to paint well" would in itself be a contribution to French culture, less sympathetic critics would probably not agree. Nonetheless, the Minister's instructions to his favorite artist offered at least a partial solution to the dilemma of the avant-garde in wartime. Whatever it might mean for a patriotic artist to "paint well"—and it was not yet clear what that did mean—it was plainly *not* going to be found in ostentatiously nationalistic subject matter or patriotic iconography.

Coincidentally, it is again in relation to Matisse's art that we find what was to become the most popular, if rarely explicitly stated, formula for making an art that was simultaneously disinterested and patriotic, and it was once again Janin who enunciated it in his discussion of wartime printmaking. Matisse's brother was being held hostage by the Germans, and the artist was therefore especially anxious to contribute to the war effort in some way. So although Matisse did not divert his art into propagandistic channels, he decided to donate some of the proceeds of his art to the cause by way of a series of prints to be sold, as a group, for the benefit of the "civilian prisoners of Bohain-en Vermandois." Made during the first winter of war, the suite consists of eleven images: nine portrait "heads," one half-length double portrait (fig. 31), and one full-length figure.[60]

31. H. Matisse, *Double Portrait*
(*Mme. Juan Gris*) (from the "Bohain
Suite"), 1914–15.

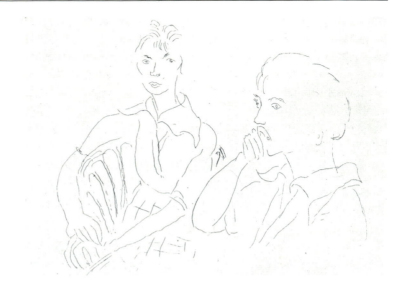

As in Matisse's pre-war prints, these are distinguished by
quick, light lines that describe the subject without excessive
modeling or cross-hatching and have the look of spontaneous,
off-the-cuff depictions. The Bohain series is a handsome group
of portraits, but unexceptional and even somewhat bland in
terms of style and expression. Yet Janin saw much more in the
suite than a present-day observer is likely to:

> We have here certain works made at the moment of war for
> the *ouevres de guerre*, but representing no war subjects. By
> their inspiration, their destination, and their process, they
> are incontestably within our domain. Figures of such sim-
> plicity, drawn with an etching stroke, with a purity of con-
> tour that makes us think alternately of Ingres and of M.
> Rodin, that Matisse has pulled in fifteen examples for the
> benefit of the prisoners of Bohain-en-Vermandois. M.
> Henri Matisse, whose formula of pictorial abbreviation is
> often difficult to accept, is, on the contrary, in these etch-
> ings and in his lithographic sketches, entirely deserving of
> approbation, and even, I might say, of admiration.[61]

In implying that Matisse's pre-war work was too "abbreviated"
for his taste, Janin is undoubtedly thinking of Matisse as leader
of the Fauves. Although Fauvism had been too exclusively a
French movement and, by 1917, was too far in the past to incite
the kind of invective that befell Cubism during the war, it nonetheless did come in for a good deal of criticism after 1914. Mauclair, for one, grouped it with Symbolism, Cubism, and Futur-

ism as part of the "arbitrary" wave of painting that followed
Impressionism.[62] This new series of prints, though, was different. Though his language at times seems to confuse moral judgment and artistic evaluation, Janin finds these prints "incon-
testably within our domain" by virtue of their *style*, and only
incidentally because they are for the benefit of prisoners of war.
In their purity and simplicity (which we cannot fail to recognize
as part of the post-1914 "rewards of war"), these prints elo-
quently proclaim their French character—in every respect, that
is, except in their subject matter. This is not to say that there
was anything unpatriotic about portraiture;[63] only that the in-
contestably French qualities of a work were revealed by implication—by style—rather than proclaimed by subject. According to Janin, whether Matisse had intended it or not, his Bohain
prints were precisely the kind of "normal" artistic endeavor that
testified to French vitality. They deserve approbation by virtue
of their simplicity and purity, "inspired" by the great French
tradition, "destined" for a worthy cause, and executed in a traditional medium or process. This was the answer to the avant-
garde's dilemma: it could demonstrate its patriotism best by
finding a style and making artistic references that were implicitly, but strikingly, French.

Janin was but one of many critics who, by the middle of the
war, were making a necessary equation between quality in art
and national self-assertion. Aurel, who had labeled Cubism as
"cosmpolitan" and "foreign and flashy in its over-combined
quality," declared that "true art is always territorial, even *nationalist*, carrying the mark of each land, even the ties of each
nation";[64] while the poet, novelist, and critic Francis Carco, in
the catalogue to an exhibition of 1917, wrote, "We have all
learned since the war began—and we should never forget—how
much everything that is the manifestation of a nation's art is
equally the testimony of its moral force."[65] In much the same
way, the young art historian Henri Focillon said that art must
now "enter the battle" because it represented nothing less than
"the program of a race and the embodiment of our instincts."[66]
And in another essay, written in May 1918 during the last German offensive, Focillon exhorted the French to reclaim their
national identity, "Let us come back to ourselves," he wrote,

> to our past, to our remotest origins, to all the monuments
> of our effort, to all that we have given of intelligence and
> virtue. History is not an arid meditation, a retreat in time.
> It is the memory of a people. It does not turn one away,
> but exhorts and encourages to action.[67]

32. Anonymous, Cover of *La Race*
(1 February 1916).

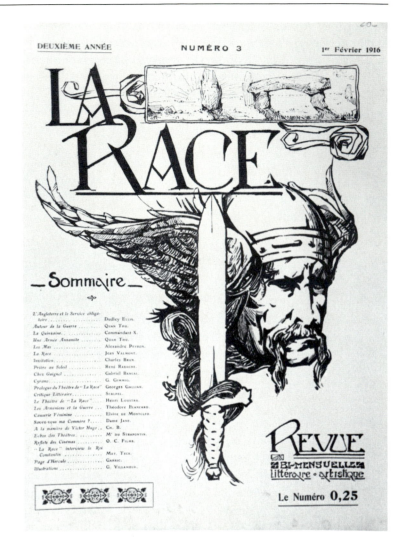

This was published in 1919, in a collection called *Les Pierres de France*, which in its combination of the telluric and the autochthonous conveys a national message closely allied to that proffered by a wartime magazine, *La Race*, founded in Marseille in 1915. Its cover (fig. 32) featured a bellicose Gaulois and a vignette depicting dolmens and menhirs—literally "the stones of France"—at the "dawn" of Gallic creation.

For us, what is most significant in all of this is the idea that nationalism is less a matter of content than of form; less a subject for art than a style. As Lucien Roure (a political writer otherwise unconcerned with aesthetics) put it,

Each country . . . has its own character. It represents a
distinct combination of intellectual and moral qualities is-
suing from the soil, from the climate, from the race, above
all from culture and history . . . The fatherland is, with all
that, a certain form of feeling, of thinking, of wanting; it is
a certain manner of understanding and expressing the
truth . . .[68]

Ironically, it was not in the art of Matisse or in that of any
other French painter that the new "manner of understanding"—
the specifically "French" form of feeling—was most quickly
and strikingly manifested in wartime Paris. For if Picasso was
the first to attempt to insert an inappropriate bit of patriotic sentiment into his Cubist art after the start of war, so Picasso was
also the first to see the error of his ways and to make amends.
If there was any reference to either Ingres or Rodin in Matisse's
Bohain series, of the sort that Janin saw, it is not at all easy for
us to perceive. But when in the summer of 1914 Picasso began
an oil painting, *The Painter and His Model* (fig. 33), which he
seems not to have shown to anyone,[69] and when thereafter he
drew two portraits which will be discussed shortly—one of his
good friend the poet Max Jacob (fig. 39), in January 1915
(which was published in the final issue of *L'Elan* the next year),
and another in August of the art dealer Ambroise Vollard (fig.
40)—a stylistic transformation in the direction of *la tradition*
was strikingly apparent.

As a volte-face from Cubism, *The Painter and His Model* is
unequivocal: illusionism had come back full-force if, owing to
the picture's unfinished state, inconclusively. Although only the
model, part of the landscape on the easel, and a portion of the
rear wall—on which hangs a palette—have been painted (in
various flesh and earth tones), the entire composition has been
delineated in pencil. Apart from the protagonists, this includes
a table at the right on which sits a still-life; the top edge of a
chimney mantel just behind; a small rug on which the nude
stands; a chair for the painter; and the indication of a doorway
at the left.

But despite the fact that the picture is barely begun as a
painting, it bears the imprint of long deliberation: there is, for
instance, hardly a line that has not been carefully set down,
and this is because Picasso made numerous studies for the figure of the painter and at least three studies for the figure of the
model. Moreover, although there is no known study for the composition as a whole, the image was not an entirely new one for

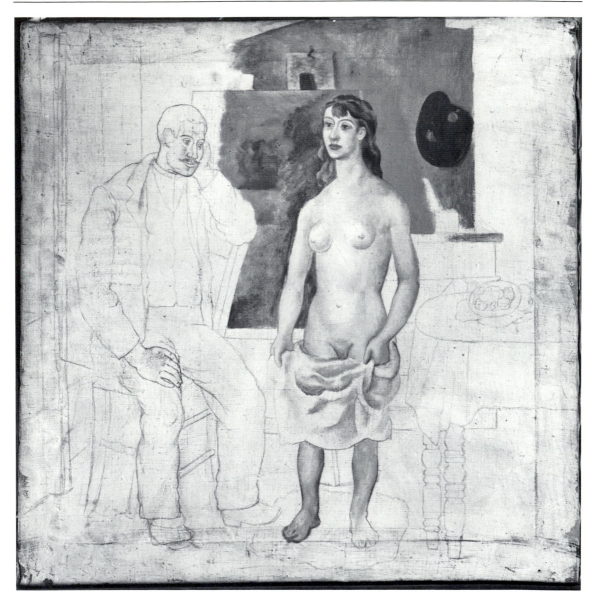

33. P. Picasso, *The Painter and His Model*, 1914.

Picasso. It reiterates one of his key compositional types of the Blue Period: the two figures facing off (if not looking at each other) at the center, physically proximate yet irremediably separated by a vertical caesura, revive the compositional sign for psychic alienation that Picasso had used to such effect in *Poor People on the Seashore (The Tragedy)* (fig. 34) and *La Vie* (in the Cleveland Museum), both of 1903 (there is even a study for the latter which includes an intervening easel positioned simi-

larly to that in *The Painter and His Model*).[70] The image of the
wistful and ungainly male gazing at, or musing upon, female
beauty is also recognizable from paintings like *The Acrobat and
Young Equilibrist* of 1905 (now in the Pushkin Museum).

The obvious question is: why in the summer of 1914 does
Picasso recollect so powerfully his pre-Cubist themes and compositions? And the answer is to be found in part, I think, in
looking beyond Picasso's own work to the artistic sources for
The Painter and His Model, a picture whose proclaimed subject
is, after all, self-consciously artistic. To begin, the melancholic
artist is an important early-nineteenth-century theme, the most
famous example of which may be Géricault's *Portrait of a
Young Man in an Artist's Studio* (fig. 35) (then known as *Por-*

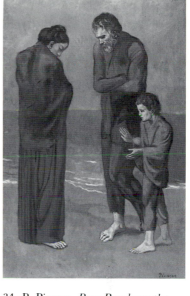

34. P. Picasso, *Poor People on the
Seashore* (*The Tragedy*), 1903.

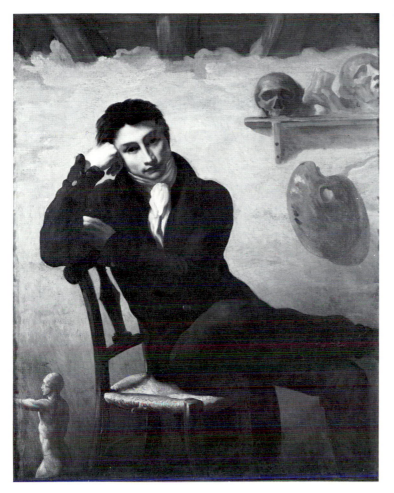

35. T. Géricault, *Portrait of a Young
Man in an Artist's Studio*, c. 1819–20.

36. P. Cézanne, *Seated Man*
(*The Smoker*), c. 1895–1900.

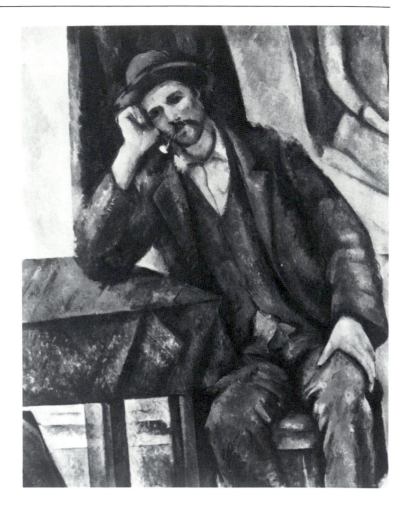

trait of an Artist in His Studio), which Picasso, like every other
Parisian artist, knew first-hand at the Louvre. Of course the
head resting on the hand is a *topos* of melancholy dating back
to medieval physiology, but the combination of melancholic
pose and palette as signs of the artistic temperament is Romantic. Even more important for Picasso, this melancholic pose was
one which Cézanne gave to numerous portraits of peasants,
such as the *Seated Man* (fig. 36), more or less immediately the
precedent for the figure of the painter.[71]

But, as is typical of Picasso's most ambitious pictures prior
to 1908—*La Vie*, *Family of Saltimbanques*, *Demoiselles d'Avignon*—*The Painter and His Model* is referentially impacted: if
we may rightly think of it as generally Cézannean, we must also
recognize the picture's indebtedness to Courbet, since the con-

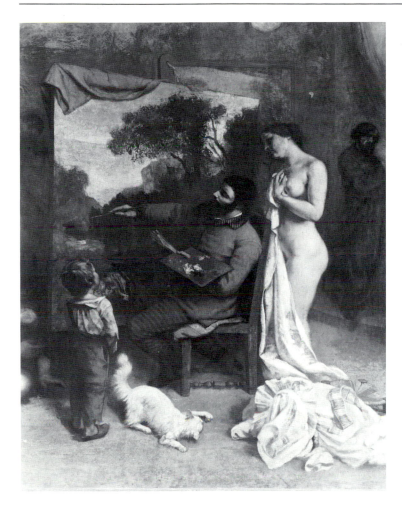

37. G. Courbet, *The Studio of the Painter* (detail), 1854–55.

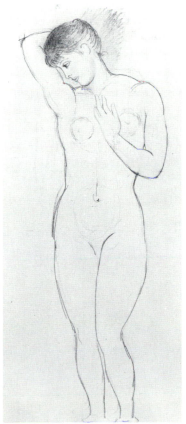

38. P. Picasso, *Bather*, 1914.

stellation of painter, model, and landscape-in-progress upon the easel (which turns the model into a muse, as she is serving no literal function vis-à-vis the work at hand) is taken from the central group of the *Studio* (fig. 37). One of Picasso's studies for the model (fig. 38) points us specifically toward Courbet's great *machine*: turned to the left with her hand modestly raised to her bosom (and hair demurely pulled back behind her head), she would, like Courbet's muse, have stared down protectively at the artist. But Picasso has changed the scale—the painter is now gargantuan, as tall seated as the model is standing—so that the no-longer-modest nude (whose drape, unlike that of Courbet's muse, is lowered so as to expose the pudendum) now looks across toward, but not really at, the artist.

To be sure, there is nothing especially surprising in Picasso's

interest in Courbet (even though the latter had not previously
figured importantly in Picasso's work): the first Realist was generally taken as a grandfather figure for the Parisian avant-garde,
significant perhaps even more for his independence from artistic authority than for the specifics of his aesthetic program.
Only two years earlier, in 1912, Gleizes and Metzinger had
written in their famous essay *Du Cubisme*: "To evaluate the importance of Cubism, we must go back to Gustave Courbet. . . .
it is to him that we owe our present joys, so subtle and so powerful."[72] Yet it is not in the emulation of Courbet's picture that
the meaning of Picasso's unfinished work will be found, but in
the distance that Picasso puts between his picture and the *Studio*. In a nearly square compartment, the painter and model are
set in isolation, not snug at the center of a complex social configuration which, in Courbet's image, unfolds to the left and
right. They are without context—alone—a kind of modern,
post-Edenic couple, cursed with knowledge of their state of
less-than-grace. Unlike Courbet's self-representation, Picasso's
melancholic artist does not paint (or even look as if he might be
amorous); his palette hangs on the wall, now a nagging reminder
of defeat rather than an attribute of vocation. And as melancholy here is specifically presented as psychic alienation, we
understand how a composition that originates in Courbet is metamorphosed into an image whose mood and figural style, in its
awkwardness and earthbound corporeality, is so closely akin to
Cézanne's.

How appropriate that in this summer of 1914, when he was
staying in Avignon, so near Aix-en-Provence—Cézanne country—Picasso should turn toward him who had been his most
important artistic source for nearly a decade, especially when,
in August, Picasso himself was suddenly transformed from a
Courbet-like godhead for the Parisian avant-garde into a Cézannean *grand isolé* in the Midi. Although it has been argued that
The Painter and His Model was begun in the early summer,
before the outbreak of war, and was left incomplete as a result
of the turmoil caused by mobilization,[73] I think, to the contrary,
that the picture as we know it was conceived after the mobilization—that is to say, after 3 August—as a kind of *retour de la
gare*, an expression of Picasso's intense sense of abandonment
after the departure of Braque and Derain, when his situation as
a displaced foreigner ineluctably brought him back to those difficult early years in Paris. Perhaps the picture was left unfinished as a calculated effect—at once an homage to Cézanne's

unfinished pictures and a sign of the abandoned artist's impuissance.

But anything we might say about *The Painter and His Model*
is important only as it pertains to Picasso's personal development; although it is doubtful that it was conceived as a private
work of art it became one, which the artist kept from the public.[74] However, the important naturalistic works that followed
this one, the drawings of Jacob (fig. 39) and Vollard (fig. 40),
quickly became known throughout the Parisian art scene and
were taken as a sign of changing times. It is clear to us that the
two famous seated portraits evolved from the figure of the

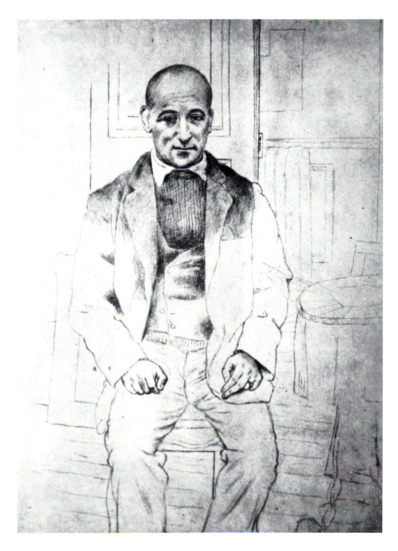

39. P. Picasso, *Portrait of Max
Jacob*, 1915.

40. P. Picasso, *Portrait of Ambroise Vollard*, 1915.

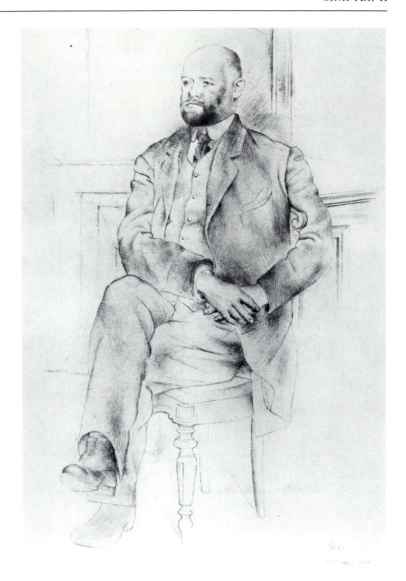

painter in *The Painter and His Model*. But by the first winter and second summer of war, the mood of Picasso's illusionistic representations, which are now portraits rather than narrative types, has changed: Jacob looks pensive but not unhappy; Vollard (drawn a few months later) is elegantly but impressively reserved. Within the year, Picasso has simultaneously lowered his sights and worked up his technique. Both the figure of Jacob and that of Vollard are meticulously, if selectively, detailed; the chiaroscuro is subtly nuanced (created by feathery cross-hatching). In comparison with the figure of the fully rendered model in the oil painting, there is in these presentation-style drawings a lighter touch, a more delicate rendering of tonal value.

As has always been noted, there is another artistic reference in the drawings of Jacob and Vollard, one that is unmistakable and unmistakably different from the reference in *The Painter and His Model*. Now it is not to the rebellious Courbet or the reclusive Cézanne that Picasso pays homage, but rather to the most public, confident, conservative, and quintessentially French of artists, Jean-Auguste-Dominique Ingres. It is to Ingres specifically (as for instance in his studies for the portrait of M. Louis Bertin) and to Beaux-Arts practice generally that Picasso refers in these two great drawings: from the use of the hard pencil on high-quality paper to the method of working up only parts of the figure (in a kind of Neoplatonic coming-into-being), Picasso recollects an artistic tradition that he himself had seemed to kill off, once and for all, in 1907. There is more than a touch of irony here, for Picasso was well aware of being the foremost iconoclast of Parisian art. But this did not preclude the recognition by his close friends that there was something else too in his new style. André Level, in a letter of 14 January 1915, to Apollinaire at the front, wrote:

> . . . as for him whom we cherish more than all others and who fortunately is in no danger, he is expanding every day, while becoming more precise and, by way of drawings that make you think of Ingres, surpasses him [i.e. Ingres] while amusing himself.[75]

"Expanding," becoming more "precise," surpassing the great exemplar of French art—all this Level saw alongside the fun of Picasso's iconoclastic regression. If style and artistic reference were the wartime proof of patriotism—if, as Gris said, it was not enough to have a clear conscience, but one had also to give the appearance—then Picasso was, if with amusement, going to be certain that his style and reference were unimpeachable (although, as we shall see later, there were many who resented what they considered Picasso's far too obvious atavism). In fact, these drawings require no further explication at this point, because their enormous cultural significance as well as their direct impact on the wartime Parisian avant-garde will become clear in the succeeding chapters. Suffice it to say that Picasso's momentous decision to make meticulously delineated parodies of Ingres was but the first step in his progress toward a new artistic persona.

Instead, let us conclude here with the words of the critic Jacques Vernay, who in a review of the Triennale of 1916, published in the *Gazette des Beaux-Arts*, provided an early prediction of the enormous changes that would take place in French art over the next decade. Musing on the last war (i.e., the Franco-Prussian defeat of 1870) and its artistic repercussions (i.e., the birth of Impressionism), Vernay commented on the possible artistic consequences of the present war. Reasoning on the basis of "action/reaction," from social event to artistic phenomenon, Vernay explained to his readers that, since a "revolutionary" artistic milieu was the result of the last war (in reaction to the conservative Second Empire that preceded it), what they could expect to see after *this* war, which was preceded by a revolutionary aesthetic in the arts, would be a conservative shift:

> With the formidable shock of a quasi-universal war, it is certain that unexpected forms, ideas, and aspirations will be born out of new efforts and out of tests lived through. Such is the march of time. Without comparing the past to the present as rigorously as some *retardataire* types do, one can recall that after 1870 a new set of tendencies succeeded the too-fixed forms of the Second Empire. But where one would risk being fooled is in counting on a movement precisely patterned upon that one, to imagine that art will go "still further," so to speak, on the pre-war roads where it saw itself advancing.
>
> In reality, if things should proceed in an absolute action/reaction, flux/reflux fashion . . . after the kinds of shocks we have felt . . . , then what would be produced after the war of 1914 would be diametrically opposed to what happened after 1870. This would be a reaction or a renaissance, if you will, of classical tendencies against those of liberty in excess. There would again be a search for form and line as passionate as the search for deformation between 1900 and 1913; and there would be a rejection of the "arabesques" and the overworked *rapprochements* of flat tones as extreme as the [*sc.* pre-war] claim that these simplified, not to say simplistic, developments were "the ultimate."[76]

Faulty as Vernay's theories of culture might be (and there is really no valid basis for his flux/reflux theory), his forecast was absolutely correct. His description of a reactionary wave—first

foreshadowed by Picasso's new naturalism so early in the war—
accurately anticipated much that was to happen in Paris in the
succeeding years.

III *Comme il faut*

DESPITE the nationalistic tone of *Le Mot* and *L'Elan*, and the reference to Ingres in Picasso's two portrait drawings of 1915, there was scant evidence to support Jacques Vernay's prediction of a classical reaction when he wrote his review of the Triennale in April 1916. To the contrary, had he been at all conversant with the activities of the Parisian avant-garde (and it is doubtful that he was), he might have predicted an acceleration of pre-war extremism, rather than a withdrawing from it. If Vernay had read Albert-Birot's declaration "Tradition/Death, France/Life," which appeared the same month in *Sic*, he might well have imagined that the anti-Cubist campaign had been completely ineffective and that French art would indeed go "still further" on its pre-war road. Albert-Birot wrote:

> The French Tradition: is to break the shackles
> The French Tradition: is to see and understand everything
> The French Tradition: is to search, discover, create . . .
> Therefore the French Tradition IS TO NEGATE TRADITION
> Let's follow the tradition[1]

This was not, to say the least, a manifesto of "classical tendencies against those of liberty in excess."

Even more emblematic of the avant-garde's continued vitality at the beginning of 1916 was the work that Gino Severini exhibited in his "First Futurist Exhibition of the Plastic Art of War" at the Galerie Boutet de Monvel from 15 January to 1 February. Picasso, Gris, and Ozenfant were among the visitors to the Italian's show, which must have been an exciting event for a Parisian avant-garde that was generally lacking in aesthetic stimulation. It must also have been reassuring to find that, in the face of the anti-modernist campaign, Severini was presenting himself to the wartime public as (to use Christopher Green's terms) "a painter whose approach still carried the Bergsonian emphasis on the many-layered dynamism of experience, whose work was still aggressively anti-rational and poetically impure."[2] In paintings like *La Guerre* (fig. 41) (probably one of the two studies exhibited for the painting *Synthèse plastique de l'idée:*

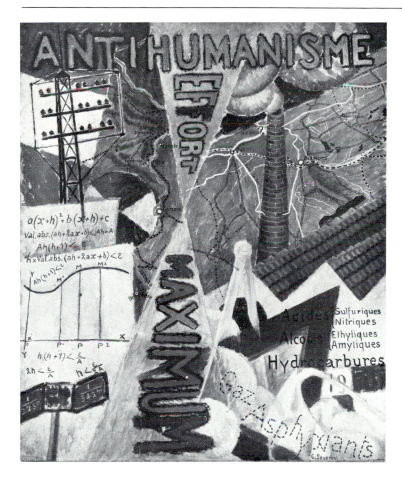

41. G. Severini, *War* (*La Guerre*), 1915.

"*Guerre*"), the artist ignores the signposts that might direct him toward *Le Mot*'s tactful "middle-road of France."

Rejoicing in the pre-war Futurist's dream of a virilizing European conflagration, this painted collage proclaims "ANTI HUMANISME" as the war's highest value. Contrary to all notions of moderation, the words "EFFORT MAXIMUM" are broadcast (unfortunately from a pictorially uninteresting locus) across maps of Belgium and Northeastern Italy; over the rooftop of a munitions factory (notice the chemical notation for acids and alcohols); and alongside algebraic equations, a mathematical curve, and a high-tension pylon. *La Guerre* is a visual explosion in High Futurist style that assaults the viewer's senses, as well as his sense of humanistic values. Severini's war is waged by the combined forces of technological theory and destructive practice.

Which is not to say that the Futurist painter was uninterested in the war's more down-to-earth aspects. Although he remained

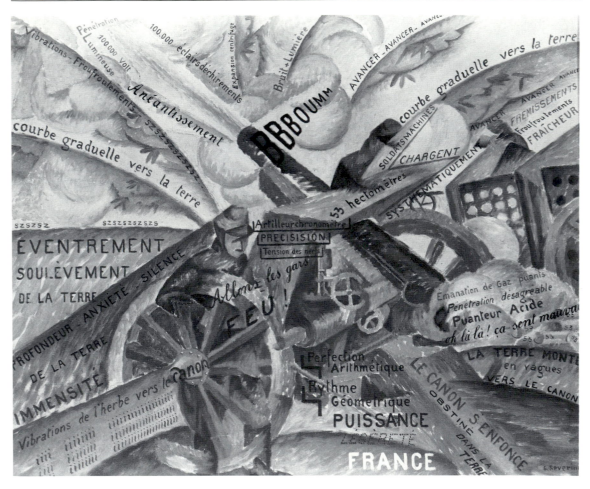

42. G. Severini, *Cannon in Action*,
1915.

in Paris as a civilian, he must have been enthralled by the stories that he heard of the new trench warfare, for he paid homage
to it in his *Cannon in Action* (fig. 42) of 1915.

Severini here recognizes the human element of war in the
person of an artilleryman (had he heard stories from Apollinaire?), but it is a presence so dwarfed by the immense modern
weapon that mere humanity is reduced to the role of servant to
the mechanical hero. Aside from the sensory descriptions which
the artist inscribes on his canvas ("noise and light," "advance,
advance, advance," "annihilation," "fire"), by means of radiat-
ing lines of force he attempts to convey the emotive life of the
cannon and surrounding territory: "disembowelment, raising of
the ground"; "the earth mounts in waves toward the cannon";
"the cannon embeds itself obstinately in the earth"; and even
"vibration of the grass toward the cannon"! But if *Cannon in*

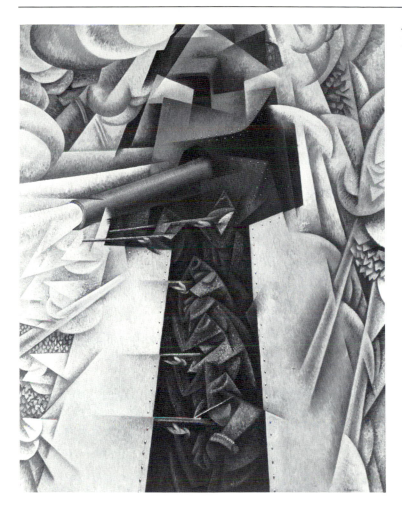

43. G. Severini, *The Armored Train*, 1915.

Action, with its Cubist-Futurist fragmentation, defies the idea of a "middle-of-the-road" aesthetic, Severini is nonetheless careful to include a patriotic reference that would not have been uncongenial to the editors of *Le Mot* or *L'Elan*. In a series of visual steps that descend from the weapon, he writes: "arithmetical perfection / geometrical rhythm/POWER/LIGHTNESS/FRANCE."

Even more striking, but of a very different order, is Severini's most famous wartime painting, his *Armored Train* (fig. 43) also of 1915. Forgoing the spatial ambiguity and the verbal coefficient of collage, the painter here gives us a breathtaking, almost silent malevolence (in contrast to the sensory cacophony of *La Guerre* and *Cannon in Action*). Making use of a low-flying-bird's-eye-view, rapidly receding orthogonals, and an icy palette of blue, green, and white, Severini creates a ruthless picture of an immaculately modern war. No clanking, obstinate machinery or bedraggled soldiers—the hooded sharpshooters are like a perfectly synchronized chorus line as, to the accompaniment of the crackling artillery at the front of the train, they fire into the countryside from their effortlessly speeding vehicle. It is worth noting that there appears to be no chance here for bodily damage; bloodless and efficient, the diabolical marksmen fire on a landscape that reveals not a single enemy soldier. But perhaps this image of a war without human cost is not as contradictory as it seems, because for Severini—a civilian and a prominent modernist—in early 1916 the new German enemy may have seemed personally less threatening than the incorporeal enemy that he and his Futurist confreres had been fighting ever since 1910: the past—inherited civilization, tradition, and everything homey, rustic, academic, or pre-technological.

Severini's was certainly the most thoroughgoing wartime attempt to make an oeuvre that would embody the catastrophe at hand, and to do so in an appropriately modern language. But if he was the best-known civilian avant-garde painter of the war, there were many soldier-artists who created modern images of the front from first-hand experience. Albert Gleizes, for instance, who was conscripted in 1914, painted the gouache *Return*, which was reproduced in *Le Mot* (fig. 26). In a cross-hatched Cubist style, with a somber and restricted palette of brown, ochre, and white, Gleizes depicts the age-old pathos of war through the descending curves of the fatigued backs of the *poilus*, and at the same time he renders the modernity of this particular war in the nexus of opposing diagonals.[3] Contrary to the message communicated by Severini's works, to the effect that the Great War is totally unlike any in the past, Gleizes's *Return* represents a contemporary reversion to older themes, something like Géricault's 1818 image of a return from battle, the *Cart with Wounded Soldiers* (now in the Fitzwilliam Museum).

Among the most popular subjects depicted by artists at the front are what we may call genre scenes, the everyday life of the *poilu*, typified by Fernand Léger's *Card Party* of 1917 (fig. 44) and Jacques Villon's *At Ease (The Officers' Bridge Game)* of 1915 (fig. 45), which are identical in theme although drastically different in ambiance and style (Léger's is a Cubist card party of enlisted men, while Villon's represents a game of bridge among officers, depicted in an elegant, fin-de-siècle mode).

Which is not to say that the most felicitous marriage of modern form and wartime subject—the representation of destruction

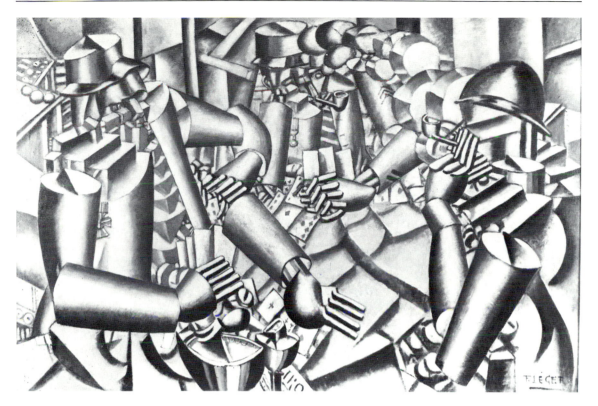

44. F. Léger, *The Card Party*, 1917.

by means of Cubism's analytic language—went unconsum-
mated. For if Léger found Cubism appropriate for life in the
trenches (trench warfare itself being an essentially new form of
battle), it was equally appropriate for his view of Verdun (fig.
46), which was almost completely destroyed during the famous
battle. Indeed, despite the increasingly anti-modernist tone of
much Parisian art writing, Cubism flourished at the front.
While, back in the capital, Dufy was casting the Allied generals
in the roles of the Aymon brothers, Picasso was beginning to
draw like Monsieur Ingres, and Matisse was pulling a conservative suite of engraved portraits for the war effort, a number of
artistes combattants who had been only marginally avant-garde
before the war were actually being converted to Cubism while
in uniform. André Mare, for example, although he had collaborated with Raymond Duchamp-Villon on the *Maison Cubiste* of
1912, was still a rather traditional painter and draftsman at the
outset of war. In the artist's wartime sketchbooks we can trace,
almost month by month, his development from a talented and
traditional portrayer of his comrades (fig. 47) to a proficient
practitioner of Cubism (fig. 48)—here used to depict the great

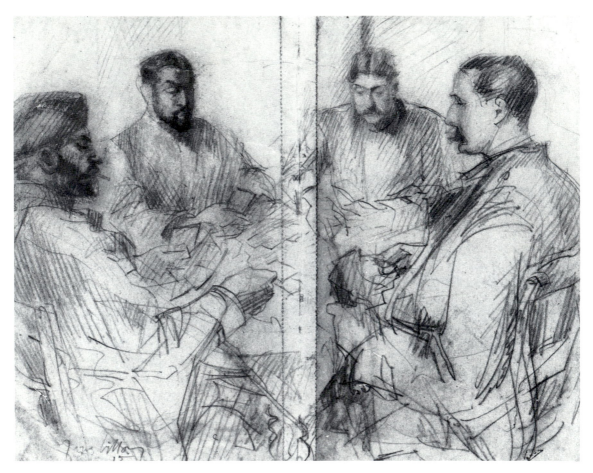

45. J. Villon, *At Ease (The Officers'*
Bridge Game) (Au repos: Le bridge
des Officiers). 1915.

moment when, as a newspaper headline reads: "*l'Ennemi de-*
mande l'armistice." Even more striking is the artistic evolution
of the soldier-artist André Fraye from a "non-controversial
member of the Salon d'Automne" before the war, "who had
never painted anything remotely Cubist,"[4] to a forthright modernist by 1918, as can be seen in a battle scene rendered in
transparent planes and ambiguously disposed forms (fig. 49).

How can we account for this seeming contradiction of a nas-
cent aesthetic conservatism at home and a thriving pictorial
radicalization at the front? How is it that while Cubism had become an enemy style in Paris, artists who had been only nominally connected to avant-garde circles in the pre-war years
actually moved toward that so-called "Boche" style as
combatants? The first and most obvious point to consider is
that, although Paris and the front were less than seventy-five

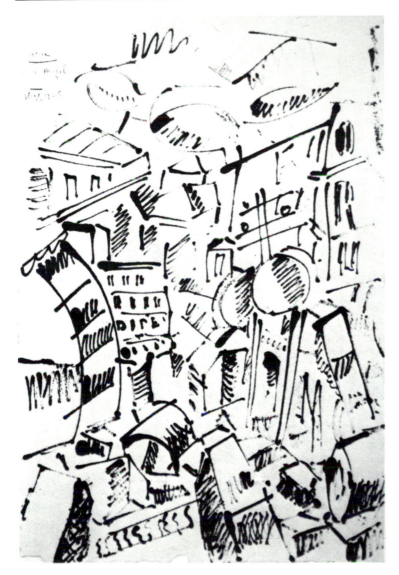

46. F. Léger, *Verdun, la rue Mazel,*
1916.

miles apart, they were absolutely separate worlds. A soldier
who traveled, without difficulty, back to the capital for an after-
noon's leave would be traversing an incalculable distance ideologically. Paris during the war was so congested with myth,
fiction, propaganda, prohibitions, and proscriptions that the
most basic realities of wartime life were, at best, only dimly
perceived. Compared to the home front, the front itself was
rather free of ideology, aside from the most basic tenet that the
Germans were to be killed. This is not surprising: the army, by
its very nature as an organization of absolute or near-absolute

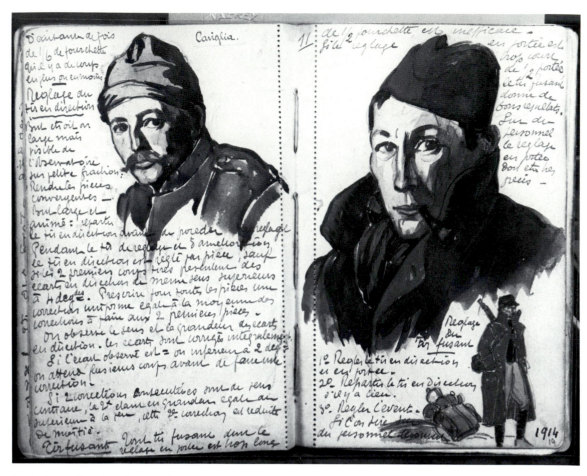

47. A. Mare, Drawing, from notebook,
1914.

control, eliminates ideological positions. Here is how Raymond Duchamp-Villon, whose address at this point was simply "With the armies," put it in a letter from the front to the American collector John Quinn, on 8 April 1916:

> I have to apologize for not having answered you since so long a time. You know how little we are ourselves for the present, and you cannot imagine the effort necessary to evade by the mind, even for a moment, the world of the war. In fact, it is a world, really, which is complete in itself, in its ways and in its ends.
>
> For what counts the thought of one man in this whirlwind, and above all, what is that thought able to do? We are as far away from Paris, where some friends are working now, as from New York. Any connection between intellectual life and us is broken, and for an undetermined time.[5]

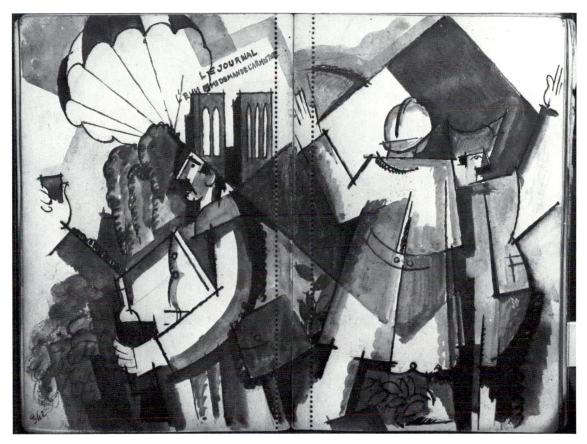

48. A. Mare, Drawing, from notebook, 1918.

And he goes on to credit the war with those benefits that others thought they perceived: "Perhaps this rest forced upon our artistic faculties will be a benefit. I know already, now, I have a clearer and surer vision of the road passed over and the road to go over."

But if the rigidly defined hierarchy of military structure obviates, except under the most adverse conditions, the need for ideological persuasion, the home front is its mirror image. For the civilian population of relatively free individuals whose social hierarchy is (compared to the military's) tenuous and almost ineffectual, ideology and propaganda are the necessary means by which all collective action is affected. While the feelings or attitudes of the individual soldier are negligible to the structure of the army, those of the civilian are essential to his deportment and are therefore carefully scrutinized and controlled on the home front. In effect, while the soldier is subject to the total regulation of his actions by the army, the subtleties of his

49. A. Fraye, *Scene of Battle*, 1918.

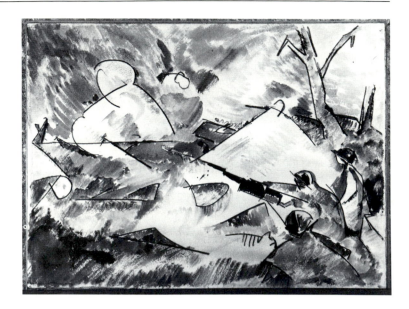

thought process, having been rendered powerless to affect his life, are relatively ignored, while the mind of the civilian, still capable of instigating deviant and even subversive behavior, is given no such latitude. In artistic issues, this meant that while a civilian artist like Gris lived under the constant scrutiny of both his concierge and the art critics, a soldier-artist like Fraye answered only to his commanding officer, for whom the supposedly subversive elements of Cubism mattered little in relation to the omnipresent enemy artillery across a few yards of barbed wire.

The existence of, in a very real way, two distinct cultures—that of the front and that of the home front—helps to explain Cubism's vitality in the trenches of the Great War. Its dissonant, visually explosive style was an especially appropriate language in which to describe the destructive powers of modern warfare. Cubism offered both a system for the breaking down of forms and a method for organizing pictorial decomposition. For a war that—with its trench fighting, new incendiary devices, modern artillery, and poison gas—was unprecedented in almost every way, Cubism's lack of association with the past was the analogue of the *poilu*'s general sense of dissociation. As a new visual language with a radically altered perspective, Cubism was an excellent means for portraying a war that broke all the rules of traditional combat. For those who had actually been in the trenches, the image of a wounded cuirassier could not possibly translate or epitomize lived experience: Cubism, on the other hand, for rendering one's comrades whether at leisure or in the midst of battle, seemed to have the ring of truth. Not surprisingly, the new Cubist careers of the "converts"—of Mare and Fraye, as well as others—did not outlast their tours of duty; all resumed working in far more traditional, naturalistic styles after their return from the front.[6]

But on the artistic home front of 1916, Gino Severini's exhibition was the most famous and most public demonstration of putting pre-war style (whether we call it Futurist or Cubist) to wartime use. Aside from his newfound, if momentary, celebrity the most striking effect of Severini's show was the lack of impact that it made on his bank account: he did not sell a single work from his exhibition of war pictures.[7] Artists' preferences notwithstanding, war subjects in modernist style were extremely unpopular; the Parisian public preferred to see the war handled in the traditional manner, by artists like Charles Fouqueray (fig. 50), who confirmed its home-front mythologies of battle. The civilian French had little taste for war imagery by 1916, because the morbid realities were in apparent contradiction of the "progressivist" implications of modernism, the facts in the process of giving the lie to the celebratory quality of Severini's plastic art. The Battle of Verdun, the great mid-war German offensive, began in February 1916 while Severini's pictures were still on the wall and would continue until July. The total ground gained by the Germans, at the cost of two-thirds of a million German and Allied lives, was a pitiful 130 square miles (in other words, an area one-eighth the size of Rhode Island)! And no sooner had the German offensive come to an end than the Allies' equally ineffective offensive began at the Somme. This time, at the cost of over a million lives, the gain for the Allies was 120 square miles. No one in his right mind could expect Severini's "Anti-humanism" to seize the public imagination.

On a more personal level, the year following Severini's show was also a period of new, or at any rate newly confirmed, artistic alliances. He was starting to become friendly with Jean Cocteau,[8] and if their friendship appears to have had no tangible repercussions in the art or life of the Italian painter, we can hardly doubt that Severini was privy to the poet's tactful advice on making art during wartime. Of more immediate consequence, though, was Severini's other new friendship of the period, with Amédée Ozenfant. Indeed, we know from Severini's autobiography that although he was not terribly interested in the

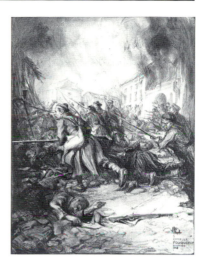

50. C. Fouqueray, *Dixmude*, 1915.

art made by *L'Elan*'s editor, he listened carefully to his words.
It is from Severini that we discover that Ozenfant was more explicitly anti-Cubist in private than he appeared in print, that he
chastised the Cubists for having "a tendency to adopt an abstruse attitude, scorning the public and judging it imbecilic,"
and that "even though he spared Picasso and Braque," Ozenfant, "without being precise, launched anathemas right and left
against any and all Cubists."[9] Furthermore, Severini's position
within the Cubist-Futurist camp (he was one of the original
signers of the First Futurist Manifesto) was being altered on
other fronts too. Now, for instance, he was seeing a good deal
of Henri Matisse, French elder statesman of the Parisian avant-
garde and temporarily, at least, one of its formidable protectors.
Severini tells us that it was at this moment that he was gaining
a new appreciation of Matisse's "value as a painter and as a
man," at his time of "full artistic maturity and maturity of
thought."[10] The Italian, it should be added, had good reason to
feel kindly toward Matisse, because the French painter gave
him tangible support during the war: he sent collectors to Severini's studio and also asked him to assemble, for appropriate
financial remuneration, a collection of late-nineteenth-century
and early-twentieth-century French art for a Swiss collector.[11]
Finally—and it is not the least important aspect of Severini's
life as a civilian in wartime Paris—it must be remembered that
he had married into a French family and a rather patriotic one
at that. His wife, Jeanne, was the daughter of the poet Paul
Fort, editor of the review *Vers et Prose* and, more recently, author of the patriotic poetry cycle *Les Poèmes de France*, which
he issued in broadside form. When Severini made a collage portrait of his *beau-père* in 1915 (Musée National d'Art Moderne,
Centre Georges Pompidou), which he showed in his exhibition
the next year, he made sure to include a copy of the issue of
the *Poèmes* that featured his recent work "La Cathédrale de
Reims" (an ode to the famous monument assaulted by the barbarians) and various examples of the poet's pre-war writings,
along with a fake moustache and Fort's eyeglasses and cummer-
bund.

Within months of the "First Futurist Exhibition of the Plastic
Art of War," Severini had painted both the *Portrait of Jeanne*
(fig. 51) and a *Motherhood* (fig. 52), which, as avatars of a classical renaissance, make Picasso's two Ingres drawings look
rather tame in comparison.[12] The themes of Severini's two new
paintings are neither Futurist nor warlike, but are intimate,
wholly personal glimpses of the artist's family life. Not that Severini is simply renouncing more public, socially relevant ma-

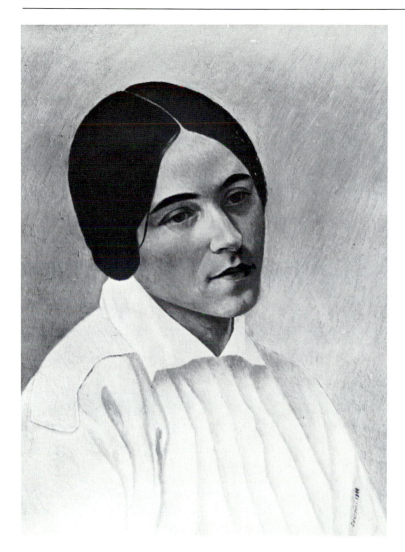

51. G. Severini, *Portrait of Jeanne*, 1916.

terial for strictly private iconography; he must have realized that his *Motherhood* was, if only by inference, part of a long, venerable tradition in the West. In the light of his pre-war art, the Mother and Child image as well as the portrait of his wife—with her pleated, demurely buttoned shirt and pulled-back hair—seem pointedly unprovocative. In fact, we have little to say here about style *per se*: there is no specific recollection of past masters (as in Picasso's invocation of Ingres) and certainly no irony of any kind. If anything, it is their very lack of irony or art-historical reference that make these two works remarkable. Severini has forsaken his "Plastic Art of War" not for an esoteric allusion but for the blandest kind of representation, adequate drawing, unexceptional modeling, and rather dry paint technique.

52. G. Severini, *Motherhood*, 1916.

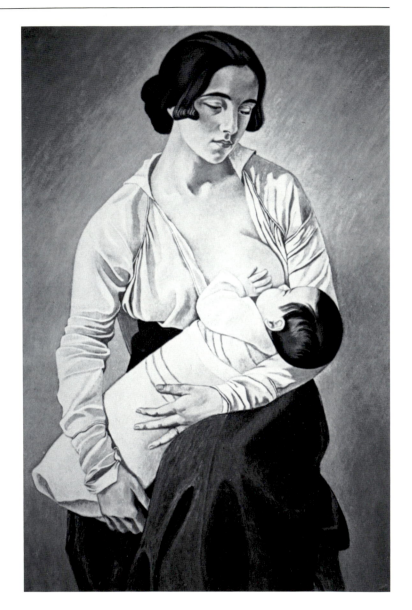

Yet at least one observer, Amédée Ozenfant, saw a kinship between Picasso's Ingres-style drawings and Severini's new traditionalism. He published reproductions of a study for Severini's *Motherhood* and of Picasso's *Portrait of Max Jacob* in the long-delayed final issue of *L'Elan* (no. 10) in December 1916, together with Ozenfant's own first truly anti-Cubist statement, "Notes sur le Cubisme."[13] He also asked Severini to exhibit the portrait of Jeanne at a show he had organized at the premises of the dressmaker Mme. Bongard, sister of the couturier Paul

Poiret, and André Salmon asked him to exhibit the *Motherhood*
at another show at the Galerie Barbazangue. Thus Severini's
new style did not go unheralded, although there were some artists, like Jean Metzinger, who found the new conservative trend
highly objectionable.[14]

If Vernay's prediction of a "renaissance of classical tendencies" was becoming ever more accurate, it was still not until the
spring of 1917 that the new classicism was actually declared to
be a valid course for the avant-garde by a member of the avant-
garde. That was on 15 March, when the poet Paul Dermée published "Quand le Symbolisme fut mort," in another new wartime
magazine, *Nord-Sud* (founded by Pierre Reverdy). Dermée ratified the new trends that were beginning to make themselves
apparent:

> . . . the life of literature continues, and a very sure in-
> stinct guides it in its evolution. . . . After a period of ex-
> uberance and force must follow a period of organization, of
> arrangement, of science—that is to say, a classic age.[15]

This idea of the dawning of a new classic age is a far more
precise reward of war than those of which we have already
heard so much—such as gravity, order, and a sense of measure.
It is interesting to find a member of the avant-garde using the
same word, "classic," chosen by so conservative a critic as Vernay. And Dermée, like Vernay before him, also establishes a
historical paradigm: from "exuberance" to "organization." In
essence we are hearing again the familiar pre-war/wartime distinction between "decadence" and "health," except that Dermée has eliminated all value judgment from the motif. Instead
of proclaiming a classic age as a conscious political or artistic
reaction against pre-war frivolity or subversion, he writes as if
the change were a law of nature. Freed, as it were, from all
partis pris, the new classicism is merely part of history's ineluctable progress, larger than any individual artistic personality
and not even temporally rooted in the present war. This meant,
in effect, that the pre-war artist of avant-garde tendencies could
respond to a new sense of "organization" not because France
demanded patriotism, but because history demanded classicism. No guilt need attach to the abandonment of certain artistic attitudes: pre-war exuberance was not bad, it was merely a
thing of the past, and no advanced artist in Paris wanted to be
retardataire. The new classic age that was dawning was the
next, and inevitable, direction for the modern sensibility.

But if the avant-garde began to see a new classicism as one

53. G. Quesnel, "In Front of the
Ruins of the Colosseum" ("Devant les
ruines du colisée"). Cover of
Le Pêle-Mêle (14 November 1915).

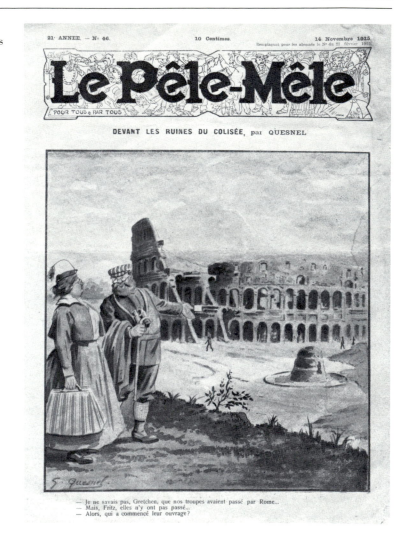

of the rewards of war only in 1917, the equation of France and
Classical Antiquity had long been a commonplace of national
propaganda. That equation was in fact the other side of the coin
that bore the imprint of Germania the Barbarian. The cover of
the popular magazine *Le Pêle-Mêle*, for 14 November 1915 provided precisely the kind of essential link that was made between the French notion of Germans and the French view of
themselves. The cartoon, drawn by Quesnel (fig. 53) is titled
"Devant les ruines du Colisée" (Before the Ruins of the Colosseum). A German couple, Fritz and Gretchen, stand gazing
upon the most famous ruin of Imperial Rome. The reader would
know, of course, that they were Germans even without their
names, for they are the spitting images of Métivet's Germania

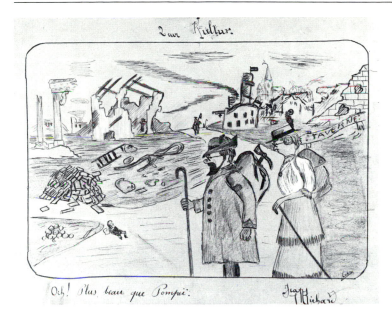

54. J. Richard, "Their Culture" ("Leur Kultur"), c. 1914–18.

and of every other caricature of Germans during the war. But it is the couple's relationship to the heritage of Antiquity that is most important here. With arm extended toward the Colosseum, Fritz says to his mate:

—I didn't know, Gretchen, that our troops had passed through Rome . . .
—But Fritz, they haven't passed through here.
—Well, then, who began their work?[16]

These blinkered, bourgeois Germans, ignorant enough to see in the Colosseum's ruins only the brutal handiwork of their compatriots, and coarse enough to take pride in it, show an even deeper depravity in their inability to feel the melancholy that is every cultured Occidental's obligatory response to the decline and fall of classical civilization. Of course, to the French the ruined Colosseum stood for the ruins of France and Belgium; and this cartoon is a satirical echo of, for instance, the commemorative seal with the image of the burning cathedral of Reims that was mentioned in chapter I (fig. 4). In fact, the identification of Antique with contemporary ruins is manifest in the work of another artist, probably an amateur, who seems to have been inspired by Quesnel's image in *Le Pêle-Mêle*. In Jean Richard's "Leur Kultur" (fig. 54) a German couple again contemplates ruins, this time in Belgium (as we can tell by the signpost "Taverne"). This German, who knows his history somewhat better than Fritz, declares: "Ach! more beautiful than Pompeii!" Faced once again with the destruction of civilization, it is not the neo-classical sigh of melancholy that escapes from the German's lips, but the guttural ecstasy of the true barbarian.

With increasing frequency as the war progressed, the accusation of German barbarism was coupled with the affirmation of French "civilization" and "humanity." The Goth was the antagonist in a propaganda drama whose hero of course was France, the inheritor, preserver, and defender of classical culture. Ernest Lavisse, in his wartime tract *France = Humanity*, stated unequivocally, "We do not pretend to be sufficient unto ourselves. We are the disciples of Antiquity, from which our language comes directly. The best of ancient 'humanity' has passed into us,"[17] clearly implying that the Germans were somewhat less than human. In *Les Grandes Pensées de la France à travers ses grands hommes* of 1916, Augustin Rey wrote of "this French language so sublime in its clarity, its limpidity, its loyalty, proclaiming the race's invincible faith in its destinies," and more specifically of President Viviani's words as "vivid, vital, incisive, the classical beauty of expression closely united with a marvelous adaptation to the demands of the present hour."[18] France's classical heritage, proclaimed in the light and clarity of its Romance tongue, could still provide sustenance. France's connection with ancient culture, called decadent by her detractors, was called venerable by her spokesmen. In a lecture on 17 March 1915, André Beaunier discussed the *esprit nouveau* of French strength in this way:

> The Renaissance has been defined as "a newness which is not new"; it resuscitated a magnificent past, Antiquity. The novelty proclaimed in the two words "New France" is not new either. . . . An ancient tradition is renewed . . . we are again on the beautiful and good path, broad and well lit by the sun of France.[19]

The ever-fervent Barrès, patriot of the *Revanche*, saw the German assault on France as evidence of the barbarians' desire for those pleasures of southern civilization of which the French were so proud. In the postwar discussion of the need for fortifications in the east (which would in time result in the ill-fated Maginot Line), Barrès said:

> . . . for centuries [we have seen] a perpetual march of populations from beyond the Rhine toward the milder regions.

. . . We should protect ourselves by bastions in the east of France. These bastions consist of fortifications, and if possible they should even more consist of peoples who are organized to filter Germanic elements through their French and Latin sentiments.[20]

Within nine months of the start of war, the cultural significance of the Antique, Mediterranean, and specifically Latin world took on added meaning. The French sense of a mission to defend the best and oldest in Occidental culture was reinforced when Italy, which had remained neutral during the fall and winter of 1914–15, joined the Allied cause in April 1915. It was a major triumph for partisans like the poet Gabriele d'Annunzio, who, as early as the first fall of the war, had published an "Ode to the Latin Resurrection" in *Le Figaro*.[21] The land of the Roman Empire, the Renaissance, and the Catholic Church had at last entered into the struggle against the barbarians. It was a sure sign that God was on the side of the Latins in their current travail, and it gave new weight to the idea of the *Grande Guerre* as a sacred war against the infidels and the forces of darkness. Jean Cocteau greeted Italy's entrance into the war on the cover of the 15 June 1915 issue of *Le Mot* with a composite image called *Dante avec nous* (Dante on Our Side) (fig. 55). Here, Dante sports a Phrygian cap with the ancient laurel wrapped around it. Inside the issue could be found the editors' dedication to their new southern allies:

> Let us salute with love a people who might have chosen to sleep on palm leaves under the olive trees of Latium, and who, with a tuft of feather from our cock over their ear, marries us . . . —Let us salute, at the threshold of a sacred Inferno, the meeting of Dante and Marianne.[22]

Despite her wayward behavior in the pre-war years, Marianne had finally married within the Latin family. In fact, in many ways the cultural and moral significance of Italy's decision to join the cause was far more important than the military alliance. It ratified a war of classicists and Latins against the barbarians in a way that France by herself could not do. The influential philosopher Emile Boutroux, in *The Idea of Liberty in France and Germany*, constructed a long and complicated argument to prove that the French were the inheritors of Antique reason while the Germans, both malevolent and pitiable, were descended in spirit from a confused, autocratic, medieval mysticism. He united both the Antique and the Christian into a workable legacy for the French (and, by implication, for the Italians

55. J. Cocteau, *Dante on Our Side*
(*Dante avec nous*). Cover of *Le Mot*
(15 June 1915).

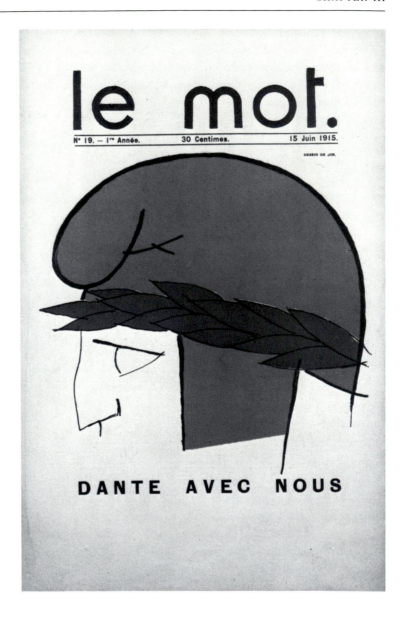

as well): he wrote, "If French thought proceeds from the tradition called classical, she is equally the inheritor of the Christian tradition. The latter in no way contradicts the classical tradition," and elsewhere, "the French idea of liberty is not a modern invention, but is the fruit of the twofold Greco-Roman and Christian tradition."[23] Of course the French had to tread carefully where matters of Catholicism were concerned; the clerical issue was still a very live one, as likely to divide as to inspire. In general, the wartime usages of the term "Latin" partook of a

hierarchical tradition that could be of timely use, while leaving
aside most issues of dogma or worship. It was a call to order
and an appeal to family, in the larger, national sense. By 1917,
the year when the new classic age was being heralded in the
Parisian avant-garde, the propagandistic literature showed a
marked preference for Antique, classical, and Latin evocations,
which by extension led to the increasing use of the terms "civilization," "Occident," and "humanity." In that one year appeared Ferrière's *L'Esprit latin et l'esprit germanique*, Anatole
France's reissued *Le Génie latin*, Gaillard's *Le Germanisme et
les cultures antiques*, Mithouard's *La Terre d'Occident*, Athen-
ius's mystical *Notes sur l'harmonie: Le crime allemand et sa
faute d'harmonie*, Mathieu's *Le Rôle de la France dans la civilisation*, and Rey's *La Guerre Européene et les enseignements de
l'histoire; L'Union des nations latines: France et Italie.*[24]

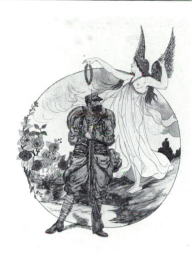

56. G. Domergue, *1916* (*New Year's
Greeting*), 1915.

This essential tenet—that the French were not "sufficient
unto" themselves but were descended from and protected by the
best of ancient humanity—achieved concrete realization in the
visual campaign. Antique goddesses representing Victory,
Glory, Humanity, and Civilization, and often an unspecified
combination of all these personae, flew above the skies of
France. An incarnation of "la Victoire" holds a laurel wreath
above the head of a scruffy *poilu* in a New Year's greeting for
1916 (fig. 56); her great wings protect the gravely wounded soldiers in Lambert's image of 1915 (fig. 57); and stylishly coiffed,
with olive branch raised high, she carries a dead soldier to his
resurrection in Boutet's painting of 1917 (fig. 58). Louise Abbéma, eschewing all narrative, created a tiny oil portrait of the
same goddess as a devotional image for 1916 (fig. 59). Two of
the Antique personages who presided over France's destiny
have an intimate *tête-à-tête* of a quite didactic nature in Gerbault's small gouache (fig. 60): Cupid, in the garb of a Roman
warrior with a cockade on his helmet, tells his mother, Venus,
that "Love of country is the greatest love," undoubtedly to remind a nation of self-professed sensualists that patriotism must
take precedence over other more immediate forms of gratifica-
tion. On an anonymous postcard (fig. 61), Victory distributes
olive branches, each with a streamer marked with a battle (Mulhouse, Marne, Liège, et al.), to Allied soldiers—"Glory to you,
noble combatants for Right and Justice."

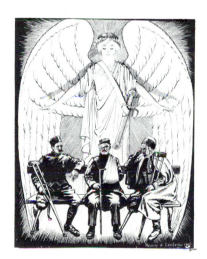

57. M. de Lambert, *Guardian of the
Valiantly Wounded*, 1915.

These Antique deities were often merged with France's own
Marianne, known by her Phrygian bonnet or her cockade. Like
that benevolent Parisienne St. Geneviève, Marianne succors
her people in a charcoal sketch by Steinlen (fig. 62); she com-

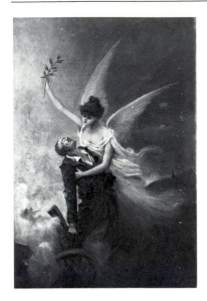

58. H. Boutet, *Untitled*, 1917.

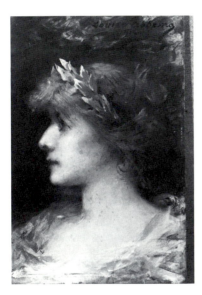

59. L. Abbéma, *Victory*, 1916.

forts a ravaged Verdun in Nam's pen-and-ink drawing of 1916 (fig. 63); and she kneels by the hearth alongside Marshal Joffre on Christmas Eve 1915 (fig. 64), when, much to her astonishment, a tiny "Victoire" appears from the chimney, brandishing sword and *tricolore*, in a gouache by Cocteau's friend Paul Iribe that was used as the cover for *La Baïonnette*. Naturally, Marianne could be found spreading her seed "à tous vents," here in a drawing by Othon Friesz, the former Fauve (fig. 65); rather more practically, helping the French citizenry to pile sacks of money onto the ramparts (fig. 66)—"le meilleur rempart"—in Tournelle's 1917 image; and, with utmost dignity, accompanying the martyred French soldier on high in an etching by another of Cocteau's friends, Benito, his apotheosis of the *poilu* (fig. 67). Not surprisingly, "la pucelle," Joan of Arc herself, made a return engagement during the Great War: in Gennaro's design for a commemorative plaque of 1915 (fig. 68), and summoned forth by the Savior—"Go forth . . . daughter of France, the time has come!"—in a postcard of the same year (fig. 69). And in yet another variation, France's daughter is merged with Marianne imagery to become a symbol of the lost provinces: "La Lorraine est française!" another image proclaims, above three lines from Victor Hugo and a depiction of a pretty Lorraine peasant girl whose bonnet sports a cockade.

The various French deities also came to the rescue of France in the form of the great monuments of the French artistic past. The figure of "la Marseillaise" from Rude's *Chant du Départ* on the Arc de Triomphe flies in all her righteous wrath above the streets of Paris, to the cheers of the Parisians, in Steinlen's charcoal drawing of 1915 (fig. 70); the entire group haunts the reveries of a French prisoner of war (fig. 71) in Tavernier's image of the same year; and in Sem's National Loan poster, la Marseillaise presides over the transformation of ancient Gallic warriors into contemporary *poilus*, without ever leaving her post on the Arc de Triomphe (fig. 72). Other heroic works from French art history also made their way into wartime imagery. Carpeaux's 1860 *Ugolino* is transformed into a French prisoner of war tormented by his exile in an image of 1916 by Dupont (fig. 73). In a drawing by the well-known illustrator Léandre, the Poor Fisherman "à la manière de . . . Puvis de Chavannes" (fig. 74) becomes a symbol for a frail, vulnerable France, while "the britannic Amphitrite, who laughs at the Kaiser's mines and Zeppelins, takes the *pauvre pêcheur* under her protection."[25]

Although not of French origin, the Nike of Samothrace had been a resident of France, at the Louvre, for so long that she could not escape her patriotic duty: in Reb's 1915 cartoon "Those who have seen" (fig. 75), she testifies to triumph in adversity. A bandaged French Zouave with cane and his wounded, much-decorated commanding officer come upon the statue during a stroll through the Louvre: the Zouave turns to his companion and, gesturing to the Antique ruin before them, asks what this other ancient Victory had done to assure Greek fortune.[26] Although she provided solace and acted as an *exemplum virtutis* for these Frenchmen, the Victory of Samothrace appears as a rebuke to the neutral Greeks on the cover of Ozenfant's *L'Elan* (fig. 76): "un bel élan," Ozenfant writes over the figure, "mais ni tête ni bras" (she has spirit, but no brains and no brawn). In their refusal to join the Allied cause, the present-day Athenians are unworthy of their exalted heritage.

A large and varied cast of allegorical figures, traditional symbols, and patriotic monuments was, then, called back into national service after August 1914. Although these were mostly neglected images that had long ceased to fire the imaginative life of the public, such was the nature of the national emergency—such was the apparent need for moral reassurance—that these stock characters of older brands of nationalism and nationalist revival looked plausible again. Perhaps not surprisingly, along with this renewed dawning of the gods came the re-emergence of classical values as they were defined and propagated by the French Right. Edouard Driault wrote that since the outbreak of war the French had "finally understood that Germany waged war against all Latin civilization," and that

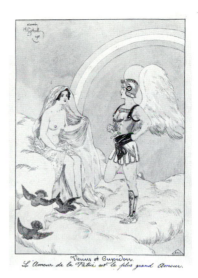

60. H. Gerbault, *Venus and Cupid*, c. 1914–18.

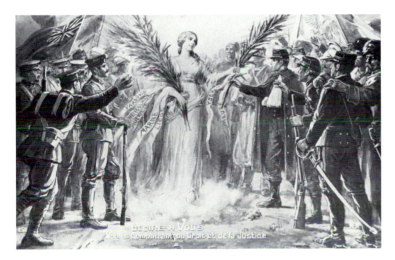

61. Anonymous, *Glory to You* (*Gloire à Vous*), c. 1914–18. Postcard.

62. T. Steinlen, Illustration for
Journée française du secours national,
1915. Postcard.

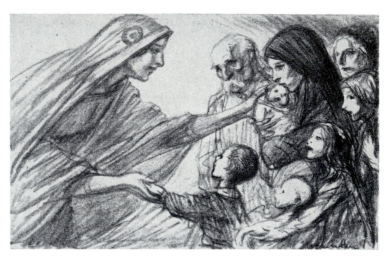

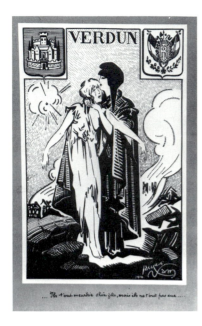

63. J. Nam, *Verdun*, 1916.

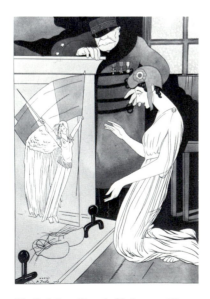

64. P. Iribe, *French Christmas: Victory*
(*Le Noël de la France: la Victoire*),
1915.

"French art, so pure, so sober, so classical,"[27] could now reassert itself as it could not since 1870. Similarly, Mauclair, who had labeled Cubism as one of the results of the Germanic invasion of culture, saw the war as the ideal moment for the return to lost values:

All our artistic activity should be a return of passion for our mother. By this love, intensified by suffering, we will again become classicists, fervent devotees of the cathedral, of the village, of the sense of place, of the sky, cherishing them the more for having defended them, for having measured the price, not confusing them with anything else, only dreaming of venerating them better. The epochs when a classical tradition has flourished are made of nothing other than this simple and healthy feeling.[28]

Mauclair's conception of the classical tradition seems rather provincial to say the least; to equate "classicism" with a love of mother, hearth, and homeland is to play very freely with cultural terms (although his intention is obvious: he means this as an indictment of the pre-war cosmopolitans). But both during and after the war the terms *classique* and *classicisme* came to represent all manner of values, depending on the user. Of course, the flexible use of the concept was not new with the Great War. In French artistic parlance, "classical" is used to describe not only Antiquity and the Italian Renaissance, but also the court art of Francis I at Fontainebleau; the art of Poussin and his contemporaries during the *grand siècle*; the painting of David and his followers at the end of the eighteenth century;

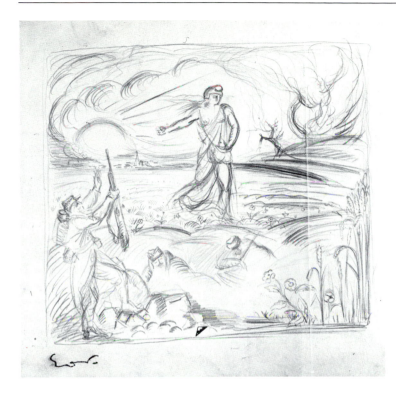

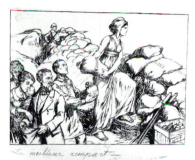

65. O. Friesz, *The Sower* (*Elle sême à tous vents*), c. 1914–18.

66. J. Tournelle, *The Best Defense* (*Le Meilleur Rempart*), 1917.

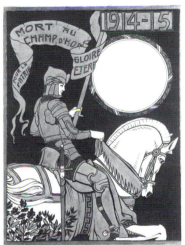

and the art of Ingres, the great representative of *le style classique* in the nineteenth century (not to mention still later "classicists" like Puvis de Chavannes, Aristide Maillol, and André Derain). It is, after all, part of the usefulness of this loose conception of classicism that it can be stripped of its historical

68. G. de Gennaro, *Slain for the Fatherland* (*Mort pour La Patrie*), 1915.

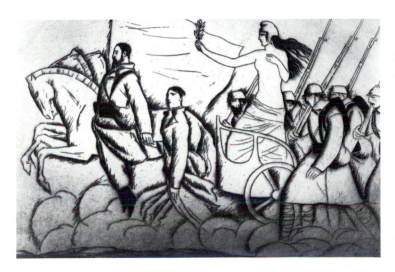

67. E. Benito, *Immortality*, c. 1914–18.

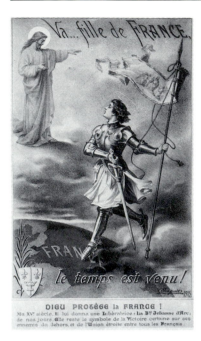

69. Anonymous (artist's name
illegible), "Go forth . . . Daughter of
France, the time has come!" ("Va . . .
fille de France, le temps est venu!"),
1915. Postcard.

70. T. Steinlen, *La Marseillaise
Rallying the Parisians*, 1915.

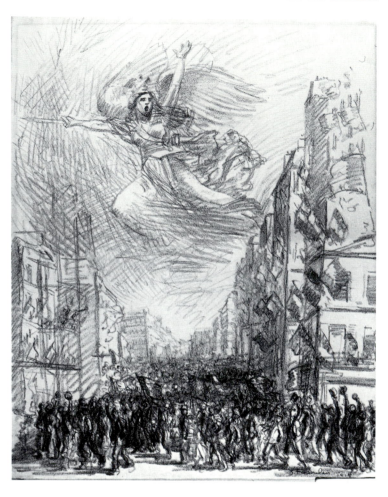

specificity and used to bind together disparate events with a
label that may signify no more than approval. Nonetheless, for
all that "classicism" is, and was, subject to manipulation, after
the start of war in 1914 it always referred to a new national
sense of self-identity.

Auguste Rodin, for instance, when asked in 1917 about his
thoughts on the German invasion of French culture, replied
with a fervor typical of his countrymen:

> Here's what I think: we will do well to abandon all the
> chimeras coming from a sick mind and return to the true
> ancient tradition, old as the centuries, instead of making
> things without value. For a while now, the cities of Europe
> have been ravaged by these barbarians. We don't need

German influence, but rather that of our most beautiful
classic traditions.[29]

Rodin is presumably offering his own "classic" art as the answer to German barbarism. Yet, however he conceived of the
barbarian/classic polarity, its invocation by one of the greatest
living masters of French art is testimony to the power of images
by artists like Quesnel and the words of critics like Daudet. A
more subtle interpretation of the differences between French
and German culture, appropriate to the role of the historian,
came from Focillon. After first admitting to his own *parti pris*—
"In what tone can we speak of the magnificent and beautiful
things with which genius has endowed our enemy?"—he nonetheless concludes, while perusing a volume of German art, that

> even through these images an obsessive Germany appears.
> The Greco-Roman mind, the French classical mind, is ad-
> dressed to the universal reason of man, everywhere, for all
> time. . . . Modern German art rests on German man, Ger-
> man reason, and German nature. . . . Never have we been
> further from the spirit of the Renaissance, from classical
> thoughts, from the Greco-Latin method—invented not for
> the tribe but for all humanity.[30]

In some ways this is a far more affecting argument than the
flat-footedly chauvinistic one that saw the enemy as no better
than animals. It not only gave the Germans a certain dignity
and made them therefore worth opposing, but it enlarged the
French cause to include all civilized peoples. In fact it was precisely this line of reasoning that Apollinaire followed in an essay in *Nord-Sud* in October 1917: "The duty of the French is
superior to all other patriotisms, because at all times in her
history France has never been uninterested in the destinies of
humanity . . . the duty of the French is melded in the great
human tradition."[31] In other words, to be a German patriot was
to be narrowly nationalistic; but to be a French patriot was to
be something larger and better, not only a Latin and an "homme
classique," but a humanitarian.

Although he had declared the end of the "period of exuberance" and signaled the commencement of the "period of organization, of arrangement, of science . . . a classical age," Paul
Dermée was fearful that amidst all this cultural chauvinism his
fellow artists (and particularly poets) might interpret his call to
order as a ratification of academicism and become mere copiers
of the past. "To be sure," he told his readers, "it is necessary

71. P. Tavernier, *Prisoner!*, 1915.

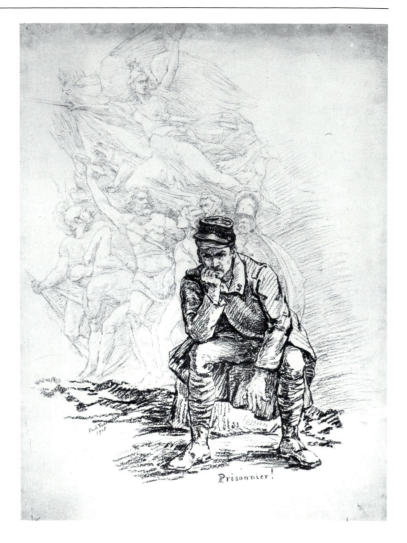

to see through the error of the neo-classicists who, in giving us the seventeenth century as a model, want an impoverishment of our lyricism and our language."[32] He was not only worried that his announcement of a new classical age might lead to pastiche (which in time, as we shall see, it did) but was also well aware that he was coming dangerously close to sounding like the avant-garde's arch-enemy, the extreme Right. "They claim," Dermée went on to say of these right-wing critics from whom he wanted to be distinguished, "that classical verse is necessary for classicism. Certain of them even believe that classicism is an ideal that we cannot obtain without a king."[33]

The reference here is unmistakable: those who believed that France could not regain her classical tradition without the res-

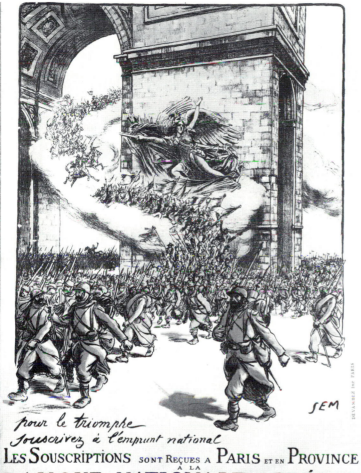

pour le triomphe
souscrivez à l'emprunt national
LES SOUSCRIPTIONS SONT REÇUES A PARIS ET EN PROVINCE
À LA
BANQUE NATIONALE DE CRÉDIT

toration of the king were the Royalist party, the *Action Française,* and, in particular, their outspoken leader, Charles Maurras. It was the extreme Right that had been propagandizing for
a French return to classicism for nearly twenty years, just as it
was the extreme Right that had warned since 1870 that the Germans would again be marching on France. Originally a literary
critic and part of the circle around the poet Jean Moréas and
his neo-classical "Ecole romane," Maurras extended Moréas's
ideas into the realm of politics in the late 1890s.[34] Maurras's
political/cultural theory, formulated as part of the campaign
against Captain Dreyfus, would be echoed in the campaign
against Germany during the Great War: the Germans were barbarians; French culture was based on a "twofold tradition" of

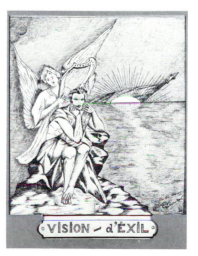

73. C. Dupont, *Vision of Exile* (*Vision
d'Exil*), 1916.

74. C. Léandre, *In the Manner of Puvis de Chavannes* (*A la manière de Puvis de Chavannes*), c. 1915.

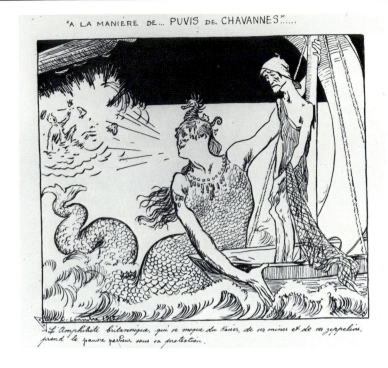

classicism and Catholicism; the barbarian culture had weakened the great French traditions since 1870; the task of all good Frenchmen was to rid France of non-indigenous elements. Maurras's collaborator, Léon Daudet (from whom we have already heard a good deal), predicted after war began that "young Frenchmen will return to the humanities, notably to this irreplaceable Latin training."[35] Although most Parisian artists and critics chose, at least in public, to ignore the fact, the source of the new classicism during the war was indisputably the French Right, and Dermée—rather more perspicacious than most of the promulgators of the new period of "organization"— was aware that to invoke a new classic age was to risk finding oneself in the company of the French Right.

Nonetheless, Dermée's statement was but a reformulation of the new sobriety that Derain, Matisse, and countless critics had already perceived as one of the rewards of war. In a later article in *Nord-Sud*, "Un Prochain Age classique," Dermée invoked an old metaphor for the passage from "exuberance" to "organization": "The crazy stallion of our passions is firmly bridled. The reins are pulled up short . . . the mastery of self is the moral and aesthetic ideal of the classic epochs."[36] Although he does not refer to the pre-war Parisian avant-garde as sick, decadent,

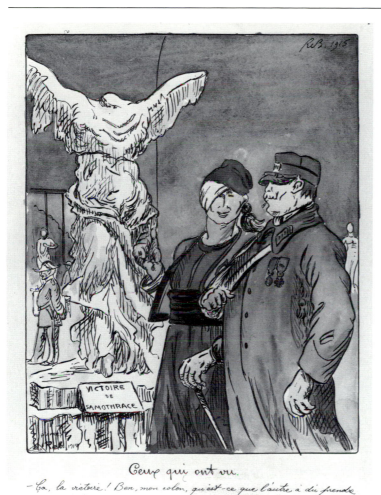

75. Reb, "Those who have seen,"
1915.

Ceux qui ont vu.

— Ça, la victoire ! Ben, mon colon, qu'est-ce que l'autre a dû prendre
pour son rhume ?

or frivolous, his image of the "crazy stallion" is only a more
exalted version of the same idea. In the "coming classical age,"
of course, the rearing steed is tamed, and, as Boissy had
watched the "sense of limits and of the relative, father of the
arts" return to France as a result of the war, so Dermée posits
self-control as the artistic and moral ambition of all classical
epochs.

In the December 1917 issue of *Nord-Sud*, Georges Braque,
now discharged from the army and convalescent after being
wounded, also saw self-imposed limitations as the essence of
the artistic enterprise. His article "Pensées et réflexions sur la
peinture" presents twenty aphorisms, from "1. In art, progress
consists not in extension but in the knowledge of its limits" to

76. A. Ozenfant, "Un bel élan," Cover
of *L'Élan* (1 June 1915).

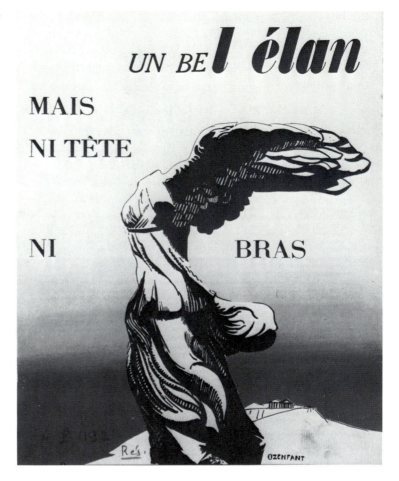

"20. I love the rule which corrects emotion." Along the way,
Braque also decreed that "14. The senses deform, the mind
[*l'esprit*] forms. Work to perfect the mind. There is no certainty
except in what the mind conceives."[37] To be sure, the supremacy of the mind's conception over the senses' perception had
been an essential tenet of Cubism from the very start. But the
aphoristic style of Braque's condensed, gemlike "thoughts and
reflections on painting" is in marked contrast to the far less
rigorous, more contemplative style of his famous statement of
1908–9:

> I couldn't portray a woman in all her natural loveliness
> . . . I haven't the skill. No one has. I must therefore create
> a new sort of beauty, the beauty that appears to me in
> terms of volume, of line, of mass, of weight, and through

the beauty interpret my subjective impression. Nature is a mere pretext for a decorative composition, plus sentiment. It suggests emotion, and I translate that emotion into art. I want to expose the Absolute, and not merely the factitious woman.[38]

Braque's basic ideas have not changed, but his emphasis has. Where emotion is "translated" and transmuted in the earlier statement, it is "corrected" and "contained" by 1917; where he created a "new sort of beauty" in the pre-war years, it is knowledge of the *limits* rather than the expansion of artistic language that now accounts for progress. And, if Braque made no reference whatsoever to classicism in his article in *Nord-Sud* but merely echoed Dermée's sanctioning of self-control, he was in fact beginning to think in terms of a new classical age (which would not really appear in his own art until after the war). In his notebook, while convalescing, he made the observation that "the pre-classical style is a style of rupture; the classical style is a style of development,"[39] invoking once again the before-and-after leitmotif of wartime discussion. We shall see later that it is the linking of "pre-classical" and "rupture" that will give birth to the term "analytic" as a description of pre-war—and hence outdated—Cubism.

There is no question, though, that the most powerful and direct influence on the avant-garde's new classicism was the result of a rendezvous that took place late in 1915, when the composer Edgar Varèse introduced Cocteau and Picasso. Perhaps if times had been better for Picasso the meeting would not have proved so fateful for both Spaniard and Frenchman. It was truly the winter of Picasso's discontent: his lover, Eva (Marcelle Humbert), was at that moment very ill (she died on 14 December); his closest friend and collaborator, Braque, had sustained a serious head wound earlier in the year; and, as we know from Juan Gris, it was a period when a civilian artist, and especially a non-Allied alien, could not even show his face in Montparnasse without risking verbal abuse.[40] Picasso, who remained in Paris, may have been handed more than a few white feathers (symbol of cowardice), especially after the New Year when the German assault at Verdun began. It comes as no great surprise that when summer came he moved out of Montparnasse (and the Parisian spotlight) to the quiet suburb of Montrouge.

Nor is it surprising that after April 1916, when his most important pre-war defender, Guillaume Apollinaire, was gravely wounded at the front, the Spaniard was happy to have a new friend. To Picasso, with his world collapsing around him—his lover recently deceased, his dealer exiled, his other friends ailing or dying, his ego and self-esteem under persistent attack—Cocteau must have appeared as a godsend. Born into the *haute bourgeoisie*, with a cousin in the diplomatic corps, well connected to the now-fashionable patriots like Maurice Barrès and Léon Daudet, Cocteau had another virtue: he very badly wanted to please Picasso. A propagandist and popularizer as if by instinct, Cocteau knew how valuable his entrepreneurial skills could be to the Spaniard in distress. Although *Le Mot* had given him a certain measure of notoriety in wartime Parisian art circles, his association with artists like La Fresnaye and Gleizes was simply not enough to win him a place at the center of the Parisian avant-garde: only a liaison with Picasso could do that. Now, it is true that Cocteau's aesthetics, as expressed in his magazine, seem rather old-fashioned compared to Picasso's, and that he was even opposed to the extremism manifested by the pre-war avant-garde. But it does not appear that this discrepancy bothered Cocteau; perhaps he understood that his tastes were not yet fully mature. Having conquered, at least in some respects, the world of Parisian high society, he now wanted to explore bohemia. As Cocteau himself was to write:

> There were two fronts: the war front and then in Paris there was what might be called the Montparnasse front . . . which is where I met all the men who helped me emerge from the famous Right in which I had been living . . . I was on the way to what seemed to me the intense life— toward Picasso, toward Modigliani, toward Satie. . . . All those men who had given proof of their Leftism, and I had to do the same. I was . . . suspect on the Right, which I was leaving, and suspect on the Left, where I was arriving. . . . The man who made it possible for me to stick at the controls was Picasso. Picasso at once considered me a friend and took me around to all the groups. He introduced me to the painters and poets. . . . There were no politics at the time, no political Left or Right, there was only a Left and Right in art, and what we were full of was the patriotism of art . . .[41]

Cocteau's analysis of his situation during the early months of 1916 hinges on the kinds of wartime dualities that we have come to recognize. In this case it is a pair of dualities: the war front versus the home front, and the "famous Right" versus the

"Left." His language is thoroughly permeated with wartime motifs—the idea of men giving proof of their credentials and being suspect in opposing camps; his use of the phrase "stick at the controls" (probably acquired from his friend, the heroic flying ace Rolland Garros). It is interesting to note too that artistic issues *per se* seem beside the point here; it was toward a more intense life that Cocteau was drawn. Nor can we fail to notice how effortlessly he raises his situation (and himself) to heroic stature by evoking images of battlefront and crisis.

Most crucial, though, is the way in which Cocteau uses the terms "Left" and "Right." In French usage these can signify not only the two sides of the political spectrum but also the *rives gauche et droite* of Parisian geography. The problem is that the two usages may or may not be congruent: the Right Bank, as a symbol of established culture, can signify the political Right, but not necessarily; the Left Bank, often associated with bohemianism, has been used as a symbol of Leftist politics, but not always. It is characteristic of Cocteau's pronouncements that we cannot be certain of how he intends "Left" and "Right" to be understood here, and he compounds the ambiguity by giving us a second set of dualities, that of the war front and the "Montparnasse" front. When he refers to those artists who had "given proof of their Leftism" (and we sense a touch of condescension here), he seems at first to be using the word mainly in a political sense, yet he goes on to deny that these artists were partisan in any but an artistic sense. We do know that the Sacred Union of wartime France was not wholly false in its celebration of national unity in the face of the enemy. "Since the mobilization," André Beaunier wrote, "we have witnessed a splendid national somersault. In an instant, parties forgot their quarrel. . . . No more politics; instead of politicking, this unanimous wish: save France."[42]

But of course Cocteau's claims for the non-partisan nature of French political life during the war rested upon the tacit acceptance of a lie (albeit one that was formulated from the top), because what characterized French society after August 1914, was far less a true non-partisanship than the triumph of the Right and the capitulation of the Left effected under the aegis of non-partisanship. Cocteau himself was keenly aware of the *modus operandi* of the Sacred Union: it was in *Le Mot* that he first proposed the de-polarization of French culture, whereby artists were asked to give up their pre-war extremism and follow the safe middle road of sanctioned, French moderation. Paul

77. P. Picasso, *Portrait of Jean
Cocteau in Uniform*, 1916.

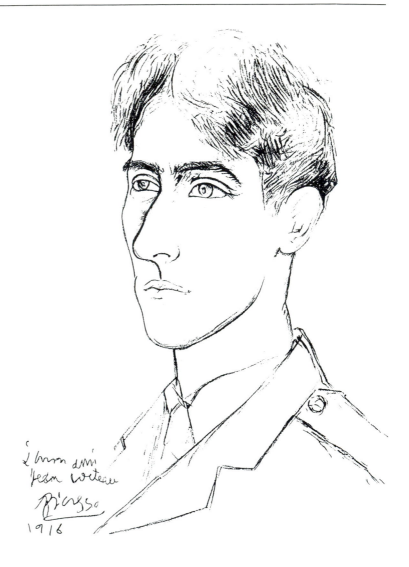

Dermée, by proclaiming classicism as a historical, artistic evolution rather than as a political shift, allowed the avant-garde
to "pull up on the reins" without the guilt of having compromised; Cocteau goes one step further. By exploiting the myth of
the Sacred Union and the virtual disappearance of politics, he
cleared the way for his own and Picasso's lateral movements
through French culture.

The ease with which Cocteau could move from the "famous
Right" to the Left, as if he were doing no more than crossing
the Pont Neuf, is an indication not only of his own protean sen-

sibilities, but of a more general shift in wartime attitudes. The pre-war distinctions between the establishment and the opposition, between the Faubourg St.-Honoré and Montparnasse, were becoming blurred. If the war effort required loyal, non-partisan Frenchmen, Cocteau decided, he was going to be that loyal, non-partisan Frenchman for the Parisian avant-garde. Picasso, as we shall see, would play the liaison officer for Cocteau's move to that now vague region called the Left, just as the French poet would function in the same capacity for the Spanish painter's shift in the opposite direction.

To celebrate the new friendship, Picasso drew Cocteau's portrait (fig. 77) which, in the wartime style "d'après Ingres," is a kind of double masquerade. Not only has Picasso here disguised himself as the exemplar of nineteenth-century French classicism, but Cocteau is also disguised: he appears in one of the pseudo-military uniforms that he had made for him, and that he wore habitually during the war years. He was in fact in the army, but despite his best efforts and to his great disappointment, he was only a member of the auxiliary, and passed most of his service in Paris (first as a member of the medical corps on the rue François Ier and later as a clerk for the *état majeur*). Although he was thus safe from the accusations of cowardice that civilians had to endure, Cocteau's unglamorous service was a far cry from the heroism of which he dreamed and of which, by all accounts, he would have been capable. His situation was clearly the inspiration for *Thomas l'Imposteur*, his wartime novel about an underage French boy who lies his way into the army (posing as the son of a famous general) and who finally dies a hero's death at the front.[43] Picasso's little portrait, with the sitter's intense gaze and firmly set jaw, seems to have met the requirements of the poet's imaginative life to perfection. He wrote to his friend Valentine Hugo, on 1 May 1916: "This morning posed for Picasso in his studio. . . . He is beginning an 'Ingres' head of me—very suitable for portrait of young author to accompany posthumous works after premature death."[44]

Picasso was giving Cocteau at least the illusion of heroism and seriousness that he so desired, and he must have been gratified to join the gallery of Picasso's military portraits in the Ingres style. By the end of the war these would include—aside from the famous series of drawings of the bandaged and decorated Apollinaire (fig. 78)—pictures of Léonce Rosenberg, soon to be one of Picasso's new dealers, portrayed in elegant military greatcoat and leggings (fig. 79), and the author Riccioto Ca-

78. P. Picasso, *Portrait of Guillaume Apollinaire in Uniform, Bandaged,* 1916.

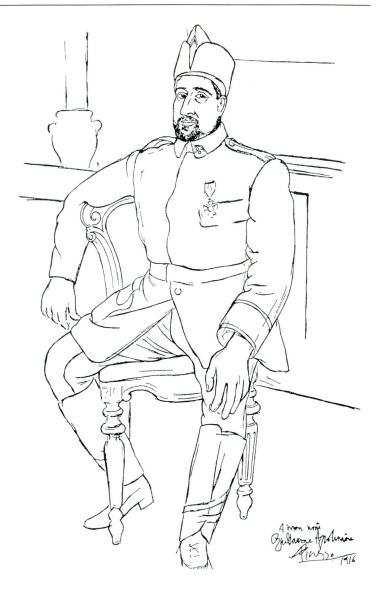

nudo, editor of the pre-war avant-garde journal *Montjoie,* shown holding a dignified cane and wearing the exotic uniform of the Zouave (fig. 80).

If it was Picasso who introduced Cocteau to the "Left" of Montparnasse and allowed him to "stick at the controls," it was the young Frenchman who facilitated Picasso's wartime entry into the *beau monde* of the Right Bank, and who thus almost single-handed transformed Picasso's wartime existence from one of defensive isolation to one of contentment and even luxury. There were, of course, others who would have been happy to help if they could. But neither Apollinaire nor Braque, both

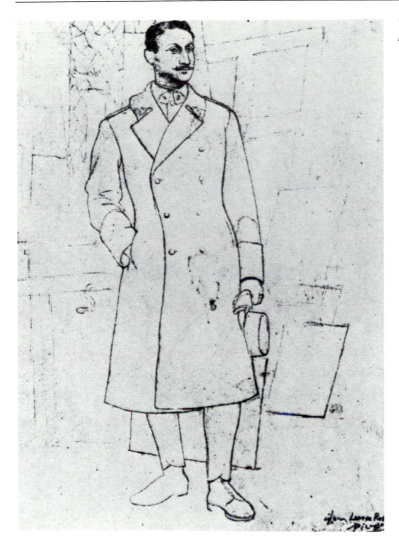

79. P. Picasso, *Portrait of Léonce Rosenberg in Uniform*, 1916.

wounded and home from the front, had the strength; Ozenfant hadn't the right connections; and critics like Maurice Raynal were still combatants. Only Cocteau had the combination of energy, connections, and force of will that could assure Picasso of a place on the Right. And it was only a few weeks after the portrait session that Cocteau began his efforts on Picasso's behalf (and therefore on his own too) by arranging a meeting between the Spaniard and Serge Diaghilev, artistic director of the Ballets Russes.

Diaghilev's Ballets Russes occupied a special place in prewar Parisian culture—at once stylish and scandalous, very much a Right Bank phenomenon but highly controversial in that

80. P. Picasso, *Portrait of Riccioto Canudo in Uniform*, 1918.

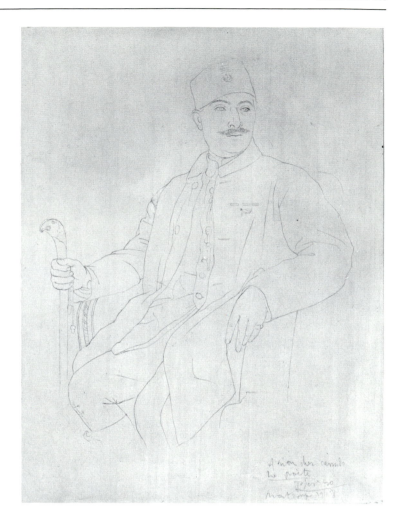

context. Diaghilev himself was both the darling and the gadfly of Parisian high society. Acceptable in all the right drawing rooms, but unpredictable; a soother of egos and a betrayer of convention; a friend and a fiend at the same time, Diaghilev (with Bakst, Fokine, Stravinsky, and Nijinsky in tow) was perhaps the premier purveyor of artistic newness to an excited Parisian audience. At the same moment that the Cubists were shocking a very small public with their pictorial inventions, Diaghilev was shocking a much larger and more bourgeois group of spectators with his Oriental and primitivistic extravagance and sensuality. The Cubists and the Ballets Russes represented two different faces of the pre-war avant-garde, with the opulence of Diaghilev's aesthetic and the mundane iconoclasm of the Cubists existing in distinct and separate realms.[45] Cocteau had been part of the "Famous Right" form of aesthetic provocation: he was an intimate of the Diaghilev circle, one of the Ballets Russes' most fervent supporters, and even one of their collaborators in 1912 (he wrote the scenario for Michel Fokine and Reynaldo Hahn's *Le Dieu bleu*, in which Nijinsky starred); and when, that same year, *The Rite of Spring* caused such an uproar at its premiére, Cocteau accompanied the ballet's composer, Igor Stravinsky, to Switzerland. But by 1916 Cocteau seemed to be shifting away from that Right Bank brand of artistic radicalism.

In fact, he was not exactly saying goodbye to his pre-war past: rather, by means of the rendezvous that he arranged between Diaghilev and Picasso in the late spring, he was about to bring the Right and Left together on a new middle ground, precisely as he had advised in *Le Mot*. Cocteau's matchmaking was not, to be sure, entirely disinterested. The "sacred union" which he was bringing about between the two most famous *agents provocateurs* of the pre-war period was meant to benefit all parties concerned. What Cocteau had in mind was the collaboration of the great Spaniard and the great Russian on a ballet of his own invention, for which Erik Satie was already writing the music. For Diaghilev, who had recently broken off with his famous protégé, Nijinsky, it would be a chance to work with another genius, Picasso. For Picasso, in turn, the collaboration must have promised at least a certain amount of assured income; a certain degree of anticipated legitimacy for his "Kubist" efforts, as a result of participating in a Right Bank theatrical event; and most important, one suspects, it was an opportunity to escape both from his sense of isolation, by collaborating with other artists, and from Paris (the troupe was based in Rome), with its painful memories of Eva's death. Finally, for Cocteau, it would not only be his first chance to collaborate with Picasso but would assure him stage center (snug between the "famous Right" and the Left) on the Parisian scene, announcing his cultural ascendancy. By August all parties were in agreement. Picasso would create the sets and costumes; Satie would finish his score; Léonide Massine would choreograph Cocteau's story; and all (except Satie) would convene in Rome the next winter to work under the watchful eye of Diaghilev, in preparation for the opening in Paris.

Parade, as the new ballet was called, created a sensation at its première at the Théâtre de Châtelet on 18 May 1917.[46] Organized as a benefit for the *mutilés de guerre* of the eastern Ardennes region (several sections were reserved for the actual vic-

tims), with the cream of Parisian high society as its sponsors—
including the Comtesse de Chabrillon, the Comtesse de Che-
vigné, and the Comtesse de Beaumont—*Parade* was intended
to be a dazzling and memorable event. Yet, although it is among
the most celebrated manifestations of modernism, *Parade* did
not dazzle as its organizers had hoped: it fizzled and, according
to some accounts, threatened to break into chaos. When they
heard Satie's dance-hall melodies, saw Picasso's Cubist set and
costumes, and watched Cocteau's strange little story unfold,
many in the audience were not at all amused. In a vein that was
typical of wartime Paris, they booed the production, shouting
"métèques," "boches," "trahison," "art munichois," "em-
busqués," and every other epithet that signified unpatriotic behavior. Some witnesses even claim—no doubt apocryphally—
that the audience was on the verge of assaulting the performers
until Apollinaire—uniformed, bandaged, decorated—mounted
the stage and intervened on behalf of the cast.

What was the *Parade* scandal all about? First, it has been
plausibly argued that the audience's response that May evening
is anticipated in Cocteau's libretto. It is the story of a *théâtre
forain*, an itinerant theatre group, that establishes makeshift
quarters on a Parisian street (fig. 81). In an effort to induce the
passersby to attend the show, the troupe presents a *parade*, the
come-on or sideshow that was part of the street-theatre tradition. The performers in this preview include a Chinese Magician, a Little American Girl, and a pair of acrobats, as well as
three "managers": one in fancy dress (fig. 82), one "from New
York" (fig. 83), and a third in the form of a horse. The action is
best understood in Cocteau's own words:

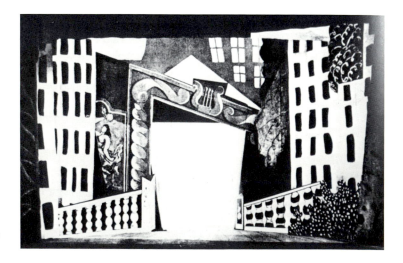

81. P. Picasso, Set for *Parade*, 1917.
Photograph.

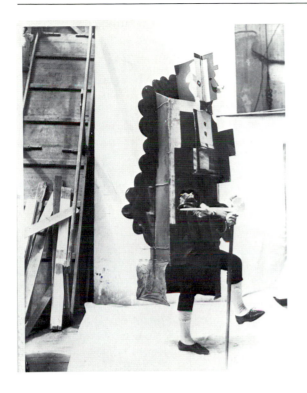

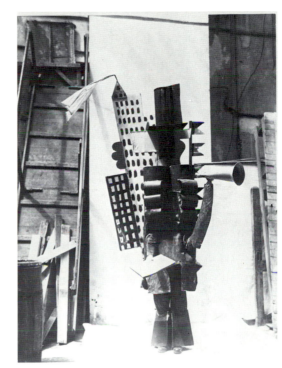

82. (*left*) P. Picasso, Costume for *Parade*: "Manager in Fancy Dress," 1917. Photograph.

83. (*right*) P. Picasso, Costume for *Parade*: "Manager from New York," 1917. Photograph.

Parade. Realist ballet.

The scene represents the houses of Paris on a Sunday.

Théâtre forain. Three music hall numbers serve as the Parade.

    Chinese prestidigitator.

    Acrobats.

    Little American girl.

Three managers organize the publicity. They communicate in their extraordinary language that the crowd should join the parade to see the show inside and coarsely try to make the crowd understand this.

No one enters.

After the last act of the parade, the exhausted managers collapse on each other.

The Chinese, the acrobats, and the little girl leave the empty theatre. Seeing the supreme effort and the failure of the managers, they in turn try to explain that the show takes place inside.[47]

The point here is clear enough: it is a parable of the travails of the avant-garde, whereby the public is not interested in making the kind of effort necessary to appreciate new (and true) art. Instead, despite the exertions of the propagandists and artists themselves, the audience remains oblivious to the spirit of a profound work, satisfied to ignore or condemn it on the basis of a superficial encounter.

It is probable, though, that the audience at the Théâtre de Châtelet—with an appropriate irony—failed even to understand Cocteau's elliptical story line and was simply reacting to Satie's strange music and Picasso's Cubist set and costumes, specifically the costumes of the "managers." This should have surprised no one, considering the fact that Cubism had been labeled *boche* and all advanced art treasonous since the start of war. In the light of the patriotic argument that the artist's duty was to defend the cultural patrimony, *Parade*'s avant-garde qualities must have seemed intolerably glib to many in attendance. Furthermore, as everyone in the audience was perfectly aware, the production's designer was a Spaniard, a noncombatant, and the most notorious pre-war artistic iconoclast; and the Ballets Russes was the same group of Russians who had created so many scandals before 1914. Even more damaging was the fact that revolutionary activity had begun in Russia. The French feared that a revolutionary proletarian government would pull Russia out of the war (as in fact it did less than a year later). Diaghilev, in his initial enthusiasm for the revolutionary cause, had even unfurled the red flag at a performance of *Firebird* just two weeks before the première of *Parade*. Foreigners, revolutionaries, avant-garde artists, and startling production values all combined to form a volatile mixture that exploded in the faces of its authors. The critic Guy Noël wrote the next day that *Parade*'s makers should "reserve these revolutionary arts for Red Russia—if even Russia will accept them!"[48] There was simply no room in wartime Paris for such deviant behavior.

The obvious anomaly in all this is how Cocteau, so sensitive to public opinion—he who had admonished the Parisian avant-garde to be discreet in its modernism, to know "just how far you can go too far"—could have committed such an obvious faux pas. How could he, of all people, have imagined that a Cubist ballet would be cheered by a French public, especially when he had been one of the formulators of the new "path of France"? Did he really think that the audience would enjoy his show? Perhaps the excitement that Cocteau felt in working for the first time with Picasso, the greatest Parisian *enfant terrible*, accounts for a good deal. He may have experienced such a sense of euphoria with his new collaborator as to make them both believe that anything was possible, even in the midst of wartime.

The standard interpretation of the scandalous outcome of the ballet's première in May 1917 equates effect and intention: *Parade* is almost always seen as one of the great *épates* of the bourgeoisie and as a successful attempt to scandalize. But I think that the quality of the intended provocation has been misunderstood, for we find on closer inspection that *Parade* was only in part a Cubist manifestation, and that its authors' intention had been to *pique*, to surprise, but finally to charm the audience and not to antagonize it. Cocteau, Picasso, Satie, and Diaghilev had been neither oblivious to the audience's reaction nor disdainful of it: they had merely miscalculated it.

In fact, when the curtain went up to the opening bars of Satie's overture, it looked like Cocteau's *Parade* might be just what the public wanted. They saw not a Cubist display but the first great public and monumental example of the new avant-garde neo-classicism—an overture curtain of sublimely Latin sentiment painted by Pablo Picasso, a Latin artist (pl. III). In the manner of the most convincing patriotic art, Picasso's curtain was Latin—and French—not by way of any direct reference to the war at hand, but by allusion. Around the table at the right are gathered not a group of Cubist inventions, but two Harlequins from the *commedia dell'arte*; two lovely young women in rustic, quasi-rococo *bergère* costume; an Italian sailor at the right; a Spanish guitarist at the left; a smiling, benevolent blackamoor behind; and, at their feet, a faithful canine.[49] Several of the characters are obviously identical in type to those of Picasso's Rose period, except that here there is no angst, no brutal poverty, no malaise of any sort. To the contrary, this happy Latin party is being entertained by the sweet play-within-a-play at the left: a circus group that includes a winged bare-back rider (accompanied by a monkey ascending a ladder) poised above a tender, familial scene of a mare (got up as Pegasus) and a suckling foal.

And it is not by chance that the scene looks so Latin, even Italian, because we can now positively date Picasso's commencement of work on the curtain to the moment of his trip to Italy with the Ballets Russes, and even more specifically to a moment just after his brief journey to Naples. For it was there, in his wanderings around the old city and port with Stravinsky, that Picasso acquired a postcard reproduction of a pen-and-ink drawing by the early-nineteenth-century Neapolitan genre

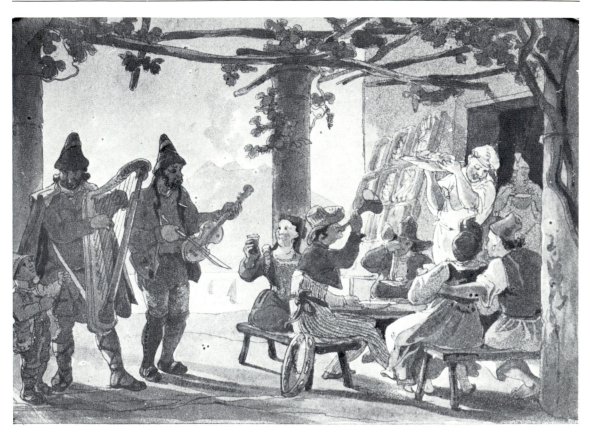

84. A. Vianelli, *Taverna*, early 19th
century. Postcard.

painter Achille Vianelli, titled simply *Taverna*, on which he
based the overture curtain for *Parade* (fig. 84).[50] Here is the
festive party scene at the right, and at the left the performance
which the revelers observe, and which Picasso has transformed
from a small group of itinerant musicians into his charming object lesson in familial piety (enacted by friendly fauna and a
make-believe angel). The setting too is but a transposition of
elements in Vianelli's picture: the closed-off region to the right;
the column located at the center; the mountain landscape, specifically Vesuvian in the Neapolitan original, more generally Italianate in the *Parade* curtain. Picasso's major changes are the
transfer of the scene to a backstage setting and the addition of
curtains, a ruined Roman arch in the background (surely the
remains of a viaduct), and foliage, which replaces the view of
the Bay of Naples in the original. Perhaps owing to a generalized reference to Watteau's art—specifically to pictures like
The Delights of Life (fig. 85)—the total effect is both more artificial and more eclectic than the Vianelli scene; Picasso's image

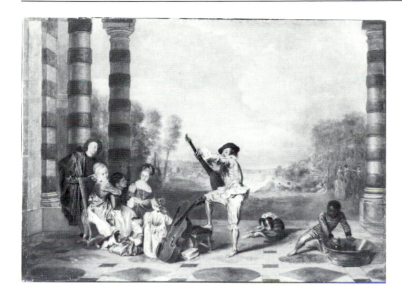

85. A. Watteau, *The Delights of Life*, c. 1715.

is no longer local, but a summation of the sources and mythic sterotypes of the Latin tradition.

In other words, before the audience had any notion of Cocteau's tale of frustrated creativity or Picasso's Cubist managers or the more radical aspects of Satie's score, they were presented with a composite of all that was best, most carefree, and most comforting under the clear skies of the Mediterranean world, where could observe an image of perfect artistic complicity—that between the diners at the right and circus performers at the left. Most important, all of this was rendered in Picasso's new illusionistic style, which seems to have produced the desired effect: the audience, which anticipated a modernist assault, was delighted with what it saw and with what it heard. It was certainly no accident that Picasso's first major public appearance of the war should be so unabashedly Latin and traditional in form. Nor is it accidental that the color scheme of the overture curtain evokes both the red, white, and blue of the French flag and the red, white, and green of the Italian flag.[51] Needless to say, for all the reassurance that the curtain offered in its style, content, and general look, it was far from sufficient to defend what followed from the audience's wrath—which may even have been more intense when, faced with the Cubist aspects of the main body of *Parade*, the audience realized how deceptive first appearances could be.

Yet *Parade*'s collaborators really had thought that, with the help of Picasso's overture curtain, with a star-studded list of the performance's sponsors, and with the good will generated by a benefit for a patriotic cause, they could insinuate themselves into the heart of conservative French culture.[52] In the evening's program notes, in which he coined the term "sur-réalisme," Guillaume Apollinaire wrote that *Parade* was "the point of departure of a series of manifestations of the *Esprit nouveau*, which will not fail to seduce the elite and which promises to transform arts and manners in universal exhilaration."[53] Obviously, this was neither a revolutionary credo nor an *épate* of the bourgeoisie; it was an invitation to and, as Apollinaire admits, a seduction of the elite. That elite included (aside from the *grandes dames* who sponsored the event) people like Gabriele d'Annunzio, to whom Apollinaire wrote an ode, "Aux Grandes Hommes, la Patrie reconnaissante," published the following month in *Nord-Sud*;[54] Léon Daudet, with whom Apollinaire was now communicating and to whom he wrote from his hospital bed, "It is really necessary that those who are of your opinion help you," and in a postscript, "You can always correspond with me through your newspaper by using the term *trépané*";[55] and Cocteau's friend Maurice Barrès, who had given Cocteau the ancient coin with an image of Alexander the Great that *Parade*'s author wore to the première.[56]

Furthermore, when Apollinaire said that *Parade* marked the beginning of a "new spirit," he was not talking about a renewed burst of revolutionary activity—as is almost always presumed—but practically its opposite. Not only did he write in those same program notes that Satie's score was "so clear and simple that one will recognize the marvelously lucid spirit of France herself," but several months later in a lecture entitled "The New Spirit and the Poets," he went on to say:

> The new spirit which we can already discern claims above all to have inherited from the classics solid good sense, a confident spirit of criticism, a wide view of the world and the human mind, and that sense of duty which limits or rather controls displays of emotion.[57]

Moreover, this conception of *l'esprit nouveau* as a classicizing, controlling sensibility was, yet again, linked quite specifically to France: "the new spirit [is] a particular and lyric expression of the French nation, just as the classical spirit is a sublime expression, *par excellence*, of that nation."[58] In fact, the term "esprit nouveau" was not coined by Apollinaire, as is again generally assumed, but was chosen by the poet from that extraordinarily rich harvest of patriotic wartime bywords. It meant

the same thing as France's "reawakening" after August 1914—
her new sense of strength, control, and equilibrium. Indeed,
the phrase appeared in the historian Charles Saroléa's book *The
Reawakening of France* (*Le Réveil de la France*), more than a
year before it showed up in the notes to *Parade*: "One speaks
today of a 'new spirit' [*d'un 'esprit nouveau'*], of a dramatic
transformation of the French character . . ."[59] For Apollinaire,
then, *Parade* was the start of a new era in the arts; a classical
and patriotic era of lucid, restrained modernity that would find
the French elite among its adherents.

It may in part have been Cocteau's belief that "exhilaration"
[*l'allégresse*] would be acceptable during wartime that accounts
for the fiasco of *Parade*. In an article that appeared on the day
of the première, Cocteau explained:

> Our wish is that the public may consider *Parade* as a work
> which conceals poetry beneath the coarse outer skin of
> slapstick. Laughter is natural to Frenchmen: it is impor-
> tant to keep this in mind and not be afraid to laugh even
> at this most difficult time. Laughter is too Latin a weapon
> to be neglected.[60]

Cocteau hoped that in blending slapstick and poetry, Latinism
and laughter—in juxtaposing the patriotic overture curtain with
the Cubist mise-en-scène—he would find his "path of France."
In a letter to the editor of the *Mercure de France*, published five
months after the première of *Parade*, Apollinaire insisted on the
Latin aspect of Cubism as a movement:

> All of the merit of this "creation"—such merit as there
> is—is entirely and incontestably due to Pablo Picasso and
> Georges Braque. They are the true "creators" of a school
> which could consequently be described as Franco-Spanish
> or, more simply, Latin.
>
> It is true that since the start of war it has so expanded
> that . . . one might call it cosmopolitan, if its Latinity were
> not confirmed yet again by its crucial inclusion of Italian
> Futurism. It is therefore correct to call "Latin" a school
> whose principal adepts are French, Spanish, and Italian.
> In any case, it was born on French soil and the artists who
> constitute it work in Paris, which means that the term "Pa-
> risian" might not be at all a bad description.[61]

Indeed, the Parisian dimension of *Parade* has, except in the
most general way, been ignored, probably because it is in the
production's Cubist aspect that this dimension resides. And

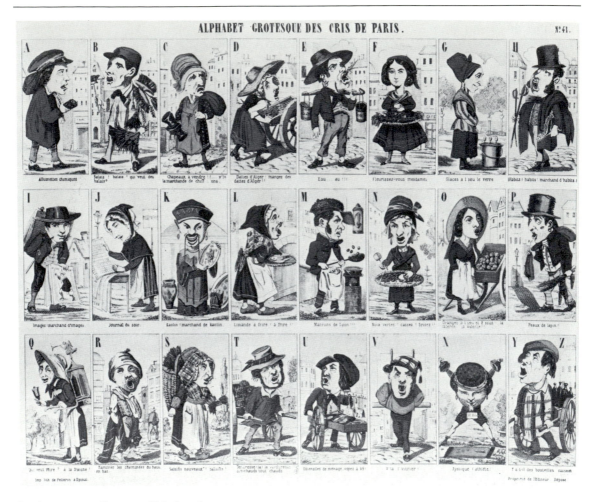

86. Anonymous, *Grotesque Alphabet of the "Cris de Paris,"* 1858.

once again it is to the *image d'Epinal* (as we already know, a particular interest of Cocteau's) that we must refer—specifically, to the genre of images called the *Cris de Paris*, the centuries-old visual lexicon of the street vendors whose "cries" were usually arranged in alphabets, as in the *Alphabet grotesque* (fig. 86). This sequence, much favored for children's reading lessons, displayed a Parisian street cry for each letter of the alphabet—for example, *Allumettes chimiques!* for "A," *Balais, Balais!* for "B," *Chapeaux à vendre!* for "C," and so forth. *Parade* is but a magically transformed page of the *Cris de Paris* wherein the Parisian vendors have become artists, critics, and dealers trying desperately to catch the public's attention. In Cocteau's notes for *Parade* it is the word "crier"—not *houer, hurler,* or *pousser*—that recurs, as in "Cris des trois managers,"

and "Parade/Cris/crier/cris."[62] Luckily, owing to Picasso's early
sketches for the managers (fig. 87) we can trace the evolution
of the idea of using the *Cris de Paris* as it must have first been
suggested to the artist by Cocteau. We can see how closely the
early, partly Cubist idea for the managers is modeled on the
Parisian street vendors of the *Cris*, many of whom were famous
for carrying their wares on their backs—note especially the letter "I" in fig. 86, who is the *marchand d'images* (in fact, he is
the vendor of *images d'Epinal!*), a bit of self-advertising that
the Pellerin printers included in this and other similar alphabets; note also the drink vendor at the letter "Q," the salsify
peddler at "S," and especially the *Vitrier*, who always carried
his panes of glass on his back like so many free-floating Cubist
planes. If we look at the real thing, or as close as we can get to
it—photographs of the *petits métiers* under the Second Empire
(figs. 88 and 89)—we find a confirmation of Picasso's source
material: in images of a man with a sandwich-board and a cocoa
vendor. Once we know the sources in the *Cris de Paris* and the
Parisian street, Picasso's Cubist managers look a bit less
strange.

The great surprise, though, is the discovery that even that
most enigmatic character of *Parade*, the Chinese Magician (fig.
90), was drawn from the *images d'Epinal* and the *Cris de Paris*.
For if we look at the figure under "K," the figure who cries *Kaolin!*, we find a Chinese porcelain merchant (fig. 91). Although
he is unquestionably an anomalous character in this chart of
Parisian types, he turns out to have been, in fact, a standard
figure in the *alphabets grotesques* of the *Cris de Paris*.[63] His costume and headgear may vary, but he always looks more or less
like Picasso's Chinese Magician in *Parade*.

It is easy, with hindsight, to see that Cocteau was wrong in
expecting the audience—mostly Parisians who had grown up
picturing the world through the same visual conventions as
he—to recognize these *images d'Epinal* brought to life; Picasso
had so subsumed this aspect in his Cubist designs that all trace
of popular visual tradition vanished. Yet, despite the failure to
unite classicism and Cubism, the Latin arts with the Parisian,
Parade was Cocteau's first important attempt to unite the Parisian "Left" and "Right" (he was later quite specific on this
point):

> I understood that there existed in Paris an artistic Right
> and an artistic Left, which were ignorant or disdainful of
> each other for no valid reasons and which it was perfectly

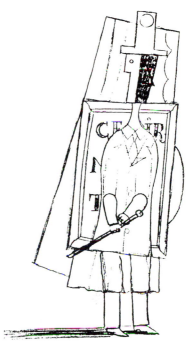

87. P. Picasso, Study for Manager in
Parade, 1917.

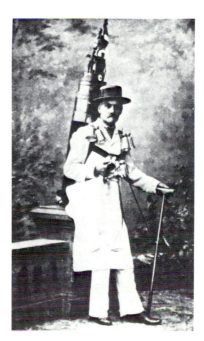

88. Anonymous, Photograph of cocoa
vendor, Paris, Second Empire.

possible to bring together. It was a question of converting Diaghilev to modern painting, and . . . the modern paint-ers, especially Picasso, to the sumptuous, decorative es-thetic of the ballet; of coaxing the Cubists out of their isolation, persuading them to abandon their hermetic Montmartre folklore of pipes, packages of tobacco, guitars, and old newspapers . . . the discovery of a middle-of-the-road solution attuned to the taste for luxury and pleasure, of the revived cult of French "clarity" that was springing up in Paris even before the war . . . such was the history of *Parade*.[64]

Only someone for whom the artistic Right and Left had "no valid reasons" for mutual disdain could have conceived of the radicalization of Diaghilev and the *embourgeoisement* of Pablo Picasso. Cocteau was quite right to think that the artists could find their way to a middle-of-the-road solution, that Diaghilev could shift his focus from Orientalism and lush decor to Mont-martrean avant-garde aesthetics, and that Picasso was ready for a little Right Bank fraternization. Cocteau's mistake vis-à-vis *Parade* was his estimation of the audience's ability, in 1917, to make similar accommodations. By 1921 the public was in fact so disposed, and when *Parade* was again performed it met with great success.[65] But at the wartime première it was too early for the Parisian public to accept classicism and Cubism as equal partners in an advanced aesthetic. For the time being, *Parade* would have to remain not the marvelous *succès de scandale* that it would become in legend but Cocteau's grossest miscalcula-tion of the prevailing cultural mood. He was to make no such mistakes in the future.

If *Parade* failed to seduce the elite as its creators had hoped, Picasso's Latinate overture curtain was nonetheless an an-nouncement of themes and styles just emerging. In fact it was not the painter's first wartime use of *commedia dell'arte* subject matter. In December 1915, during that terrible month of per-sonal disasters, Picasso created a dark, slightly chilling, and highly abstracted *Harlequin* (fig. 92). The picture, composed of several large, overlapping planes (of which the foremost repre-sents Harlequin's costume), pleased the artist enormously. He wrote to Gertrude Stein, "I have done a painting of a Harlequin which in the opinion of myself and several others is the best thing I have done."[66] It has been conjectured, correctly I think, that this macabre image owes its sinister palette and deathly face to Picasso's mood when, as Eva lay dying in the hospital,

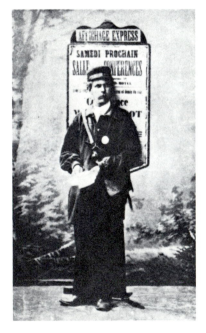

89. Anonymous, Photograph of *homme-affiche*, Paris, Second Empire.

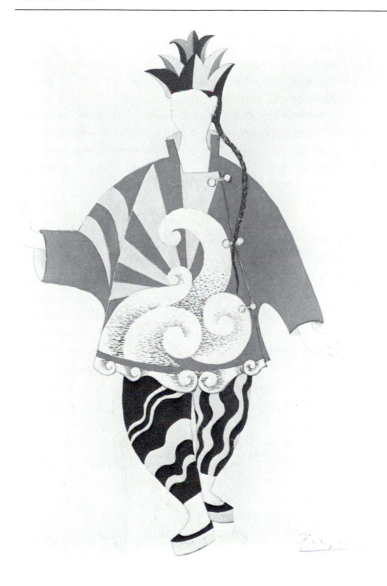

90. P. Picasso, Costume for *Parade*: "Chinese Magician," 1917.

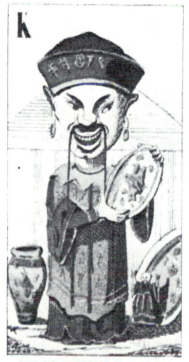

Kaolin ! marchand de kaolin.

he roamed through Montparnasse lonely and besieged.[67] The artist's reversion to a *commedia dell'arte* subject here represents a hermetic withdrawal toward private symbols at a moment of personal crisis.

But if that first appearance of Harlequin after 1914 was the result of a strictly internal need, it is clear that by the time he designed the curtain for *Parade* the meanings of that same iconography were at least as social and public as they were personal and idiosyncratic. The style and meaning of another *Harlequin*, painted in 1917 (fig. 93), have been adjusted to the

91. Anonymous, *Grotesque Alphabet of the "Cris de Paris,"* 1858 (detail of fig. 86).

92. P. Picasso, *Harlequin*, 1915.

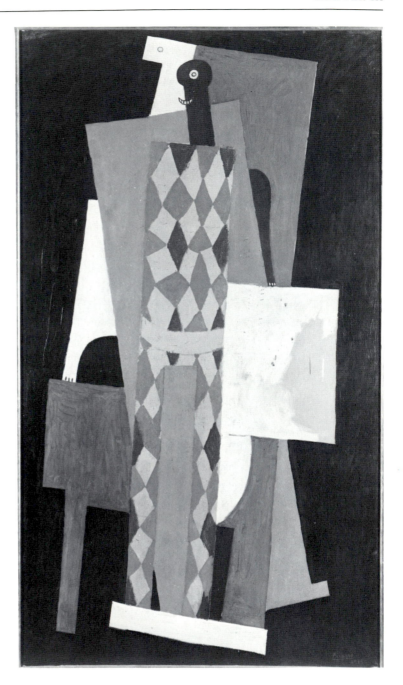

new, distinctly Latin, and far more traditional conception of the *commedia*. Rendered in the new realist mode proclaimed by the drawing of Jacob, the Barcelona *Harlequin* is a full-blown revival of *belle peinture*. Melancholic in mood, this immaculately shorn and shaved figure, dressed in what appears to be a silken

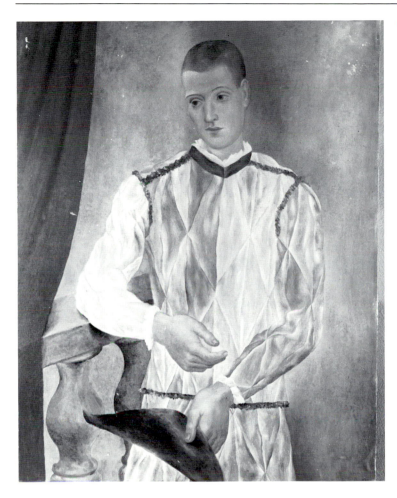

93. P. Picasso, *Harlequin*, 1917.

costume of pale pinks, blues, and greens, is as far from his
Cubist counterpart of 1915 as he is from the pitiable, under-
nourished Harlequins of the Blue and Rose periods. Leaning
against a balustrade (over which is draped the same kind of lush
red curtain that envelops the *Parade* scene), he is neither
Saltimbanque nor circus clown, but a carefully turned out *jeune
homme bourgeois*. He might be a ballet dancer from the Russian
troupe, an actor in the midst of a soliloquy, or simply a *distrait*
party-goer in fancy dress who watches the other revelers from a
discreet spot on the terrace. Whichever he is—and Picasso,
typically, gives no indication of the precise degree of reality or
illusion with which he is endowed—we sense in him a sadness
that is internal rather than social in nature. The Harlequin of
1917 is not an impoverished bohemian; he is a sensitive, artis-

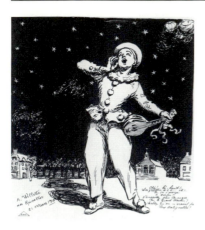

94. A. Willette, "La Chanson de Pierrot," 1915.

tic youth whose emotional perturbations produce *ennui*, not *angst*.

Such was the beginning of Picasso's new involvement with the Latin family of the Italian *commedia*. The next year he made a number of studies of Pierrot, partly based on old engravings that he had acquired in Italy, as well as a major painting (Museum of Modern Art) derived from these figures. While Picasso's recent involvement with the ballet was certainly the most direct influence on this renewed interest in theatrical types, the conventional illusionistic mode of these works, along with their lack of implied social protest, brought them extremely close to an acceptable affirmation of French wartime values. Whether or not he knew of a 1915 cartoon by Willette[68] called "La Chanson de Pierrot" (fig. 94), in which the serenading figure, as a symbol of France, sings defiantly in the face of the Kaiser's Zeppelins, he could hardly have been unaware of the symbolic nature of the line drawings (figs. 95 and 96) which he himself produced for Jean Cocteau's book *Le Coq et l'Arlequin* in 1918. Symbols of French and Latin culture respectively, the *coq Gaulois* and Harlequin, along with the Ingres-style head of Cocteau that the poet had speculated would be appropriate as accompaniment to a posthumous volume of poetry, were the illustrations for this highly nationalist tract.[69]

Cocteau's *Le Coq et l'Arlequin*, which was written just after the debacle of *Parade* and included an apologia for it, was subtitled "Notes autour de la musique." It was dedicated to the young composer Georges Auric and was intended, at least in part, as a justification of the music of Erik Satie. More generally, it was a call to order for French music, advocating a return to the virtues of classical aesthetics and protesting against the foreign influences that French music had welcomed. The book began with a variation of Cocteau's well-known slogan for *finesse*—"Tact in audacity, that's knowing just how far you can go too far"[70]—which, since the failure of *Parade*, was more on his mind than ever before, just as the issue of French versus German culture, which had been an *idée fixe* since *Le Mot*, continued to obsess him. "We should be quite clear," he wrote,

> on the misunderstanding of "German influence." France, whose pockets were full of seeds of grain, carelessly let them fall about her; Germany gathered the seeds, brought them to Germany, planted them in a chemical soil from which grew a monstrous scentless flower.[71]

Nothing new in this: it is the old argument (made by Aurel and others), that the worst aspects of French culture were the result of her prodigality—Cocteau's image here is that of Marianne "la semeuse," sowing her grain "à tous vents." Of course in terms of music this was simply fallacious; France had never had a musical tradition comparable to that of the dreaded barbarian enemy. But this was unimportant. *Le Coq et l'Arlequin* was not a book of music theory, but a nationalist polemic intended to reaffirm Cocteau's patriotism. Having been caught red-handed, as it were, consorting with the now non-Allied Russians, and hampered by a reputation as a frivolous cosmopolitan, Cocteau wanted to be absolutely clear on where his sympathies lay, even if it meant a bit of disloyalty to his intimates. Most notably, the music of his good friend Igor Stravinsky was henceforth to be considered unhealthy as an inspiration for French endeavors:

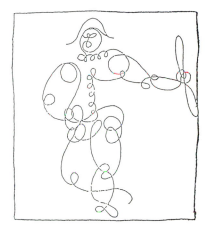

95. P. Picasso, Figure of Harlequin for Jean Cocteau's *Le Coq et l'Arlequin* (1918).

> Debussy deviated; because of the German ambush he fell into the Russian trap . . . when I say "Russian trap," "Russian influence," I do not mean to say that I disdain Russian music. Russian music is admirable because it is Russian music. French Russian music or French German music is perforce a bastardization, even if it is inspired by a Mussorgsky, a Stravinsky, a Wagner, or a Schoenberg.[72]

What he wanted instead was, not surprisingly, a "French music for France," one that would be simple and lucid, as opposed to the vagaries of Impressionism: "Impressionism is a side-effect of Wagner," he said, "the last rumblings of a dying storm. The school of Impressionism substitutes sun for light and sonority for rhythm." In place of the sonorities and fluctuations of the late-nineteenth-century aesthetic, Cocteau proposed the classical formula: "Our music must be constructed to the measure of man." And after claiming, with his usual wit, that "you can't get lost in the Debussy mist as you can in the Wagner fog; but you can catch cold there," he went on to tell the reader: "The Latin style is to play without using the pedals; Romanticism pedaled all-out. Pedal Wagner, pedal Debussy."[73]

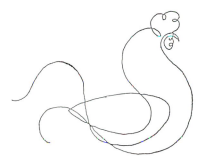

96. P. Picasso, Figure of the Cock for Jean Cocteau's *Le Coq et l'Arlequin* (1918).

All of this, from anti-Wagnerism to anti-Impressionism, from the association of Germany with Romanticism to the equation of French tradition with Latin formation, is extremely close to the ideas in Daudet's *Hors du joug allemand* of 1915. Simplicity, clarity, proportion—these were authentically Latin and were the only path to truly French art. As Cocteau demonstrated so

well, the turgid, narrow, and boring cultural theories of the extreme Right could, with a bit of wit and ironic distance, seem
fresh again.

As much as anyone else, it was Picasso who was showing
Cocteau the virtues of the light touch. In the notebooks which
he compiled while working on *Parade*, Cocteau jotted down,
apparently verbatim, something that Picasso had said to him:
"Work with three colors; too many colors makes Impressionism."[74] And if the poet already had a classicizing and Latinate
bias by the time of their collaboration, he must have been
pleased to see, in addition to Picasso's interest in the *commedia
dell'arte*, such other efforts as his series of Italian peasant girls
(fig. 97). Straightforwardly posed, dressed in embroidered pin-

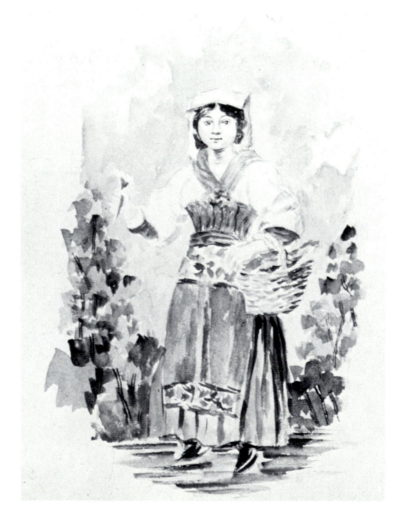

97. P. Picasso, *Italian Flower Girl*,
1917.

afores, with traditional peasant coifs, and usually carrying a rustic basket, these peasants are cribbed from popular imagery, from prints and postcards of the kinds that the artist found on his Italian journey (fig. 98).[75] Of course, there is another important source, a high art source, for this series, and that is in the work of Corot. In one of his rare line-for-line copies from past art, Picasso made a small sketch, clearly no more than an *aide-mémoire*, of one of Corot's sweet young women (fig. 99). Zervos dates the drawing to 1920, by which time, as we shall see, Corot's name was often being invoked as one of the exemplars of the great French tradition and therefore worthy of emulation. There is again at least a touch of irony in these Italianate studies, and the irony is still more pronounced in a variation on this theme: a group of fishmongers, rendered in the purified Ingres line, whose gargantuan proportions and free way with the slimy fish must have been intended as sexual jokes.[76] The Italian peninsula, with its regional types and unchanging way of life, captivated the Spaniard, who, after all, was from a quite similar Mediterranean culture. But how much more appealing must his Latin origins have seemed in the midst of a war in which—or so the French and Italians told themselves—this ancient way of life might be crushed under the barbarian's heel. If back in Paris his *Kubisme* was considered pro-German, Picasso's voyage to Italy proved him once again to be made of the right stuff.

Perhaps more remarkable than the frankly *retardataire* "peasant girl" gouaches, and certainly (because it is an oil painting) more nearly a major work in his oeuvre, is his 1917 Cubist adaptation of the Latin theme, *L'Italienne* (fig. 100). In much the same way that *Parade* juxtaposed a traditionally rendered image of the *commedia dell'arte* with Cubism, *L'Italienne* combines the traditionally coiffed Mediterranean peasant (again, with embroidered dress and straw basket) with Cubist style. Indeed, the juxtaposition of the drawings and gouaches with the painting epitomizes Picasso's way of dealing with the modernist/classicist dichotomy until at least 1925. Unlike a number of other artists (Severini and La Fresnaye, for instance) who by the 1920s had renounced Cubism altogether, Picasso would continue to work in a Cubist mode of one kind or another. As we shall see, he neither spoke out against Cubism nor abandoned it in practice. Rather (and we have already begun to observe the process), Picasso simply increased the number of styles in which he worked, establishing an entire spectrum of

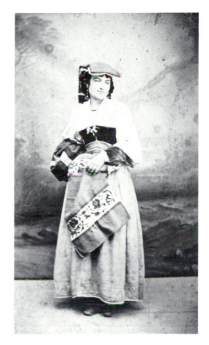

98. Anonymous, *Italian Peasant Girl*, late nineteenth or early twentieth century. Photograph.

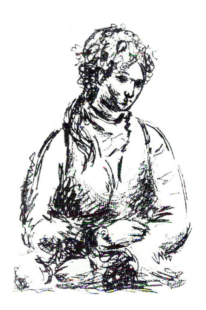

99. P. Picasso, Drawing after Corot's *Mlle. de Foudras*, 1920.

100. P. Picasso, *L'Italienne*, 1917.

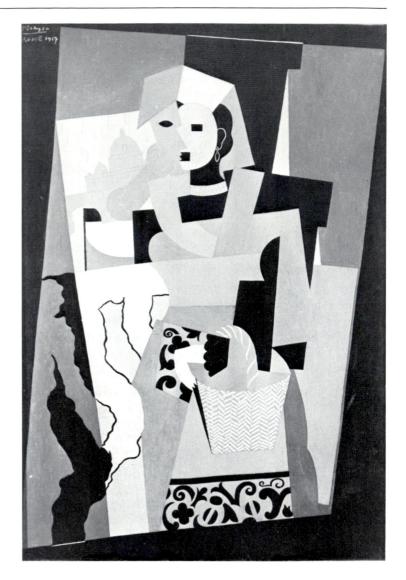

traditional modes as a counterpoise to his various Cubist procedures. We have already seen three different academic inflections—an "Ingres" drawing style, a pseudo-academic painting style (as in the Barcelona *Harlequin*), and the picturesque gouaches. Picasso employed a considerable number of other non-Cubist, illusionistic styles as the post-war period approached. Correspondingly, his quotations of and glosses on the past history of painting steadily increased in the 1920s at the same time that he continued to make Cubist art.

Unlike other periods in his career, where we can sense a dominating impulse that shapes all the work of a given moment,

Picasso is truly an eclectic during and after the Great War. The brilliance of his eclecticism is of course unmistakable: perhaps at no other moment does he seem to be so many different and consummate artists at once. But—and this will become clearer as we move into the post-war years—there is a striking lack of focus too. Such was the power of the political and social regimes of war and Reconstruction, and so in conflict were their ideologies with those of pre-war Parisian society, that for an artist like Picasso who was committed to both his earlier aesthetic discoveries and to his own well-being, the only solution was to hedge his bets and play all ends against the middle. Picasso's artistic eclecticism during these years demonstrates, perhaps better than any written evidence, the ideological turbulence of the period. Nonetheless, Picasso was a skilled and graceful navigator. He painted his way through the cross-currents and unpredictable winds of French culture as no one else could.

To describe the 1917 *L'Italienne* as Cubist in technique and Latin in subject is to imply that there is a Cubist form that can exist independently of a Cubist subject—in this case the Latin subject being, somehow, at odds with the Cubist technique. While these distinctions may seem more semantic than substantive, whether to call this a Cubist painting is very much to the point, considering what we know of Cubism's wartime reputation. From an art-historical perspective, *L'Italienne* would be called Cubist for obvious reasons, owing to its geometry, abstracting of forms, overlapping planes, and ambiguous spatial conformation; and, in order for us to recognize that it does not look like Cubist painting of c. 1909–12, it would be further designated as a Synthetic rather than Analytic Cubist work. (We shall have more to say about these terms later.) For most intents and purposes, it is accurate to see *L'Italienne*, with its shifting planes and multivalent readings, as Cubist in its assertion of a relativistic world view, of which indeterminacy and contingency are the most striking physical embodiments. But to so describe the painting and affirm its place in the continuum of Picasso's, and Cubism's, development is to give little or no place to subject matter in our definition of Cubism. Yet we cannot help noticing that an Italian peasant girl (perhaps being kissed by a vinelike Harlequin) standing in front of St. Peter's (or at any rate a Baroque church, in the upper left) is, by pre-war standards, as unlikely a subject as we can imagine. The five short years that separate this picture from *Ma Jolie* (fig. 101) of 1912, with its quasi-Impressionist facture, its allusions to popular cul-

101. P. Picasso, *Ma Jolie*, 1912.

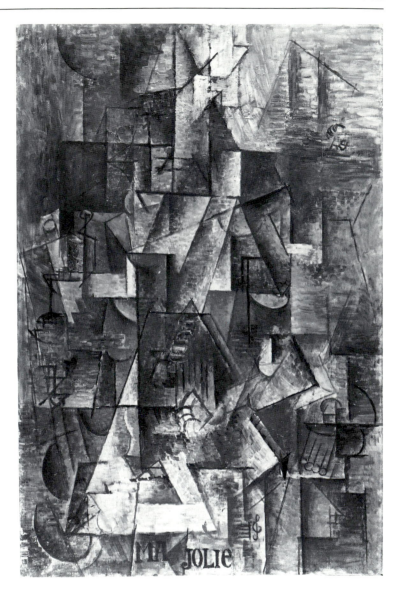

ture, its high degree of abstraction, and its ironic declaration of a wholly personal conception of the meaning of beauty, seem far longer in terms of the transformation of values that the two pictures represent. As a result of the wartime "Latinizing" campaign and Picasso's journey to Italy at the beginning of the classical revival, we have moved from the strictly personal, contemporary, and dissenting frame of mind that the 1912 portrait represents, to that in which a picture of a woman as the symbol of an old and durable culture can be rendered, incongruously, in the most up-to-date formal language.

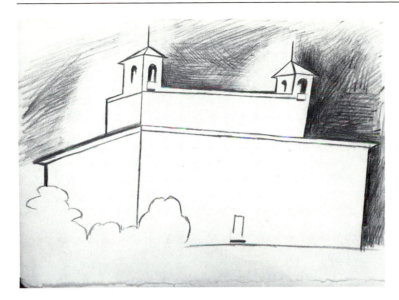

102. P. Picasso, *Villa Medici, Rome*, 1917.

While, after all is said and done, there may be some intended irony in the adaptation of Cubist techniques to a subject
that could not be less Cubist (by a pre-war conception of that
term), it was a singularly appropriate subject for an artist like
Picasso, who seems always to have evaluated his art in the light
of the past masters. Like Corot in the early nineteenth century
and Poussin in the seventeenth, Picasso, when he went to Rome
in 1917 to work with the Ballets Russes, must have been delighted that it was his turn to embark on the Italian journey. In
this context, his drawings of the Villa Medici (fig. 102) assume
added significance. Now that the values of pre-war bohemia
were no longer operative, he could indulge his artistic atavism
to whatever extremes he chose. Besides, he was with Cocteau,
whose self-designated mission was that of coaxing the Cubists,
"and especially Picasso," out of their isolation and of "persuading them to abandon their hermetic Montmartre folklore" to
convert them to the luxurious pleasures and "French clarity" of
his middle-of-the-road solution. Cocteau was in no doubt that
the pre-war Cubist iconography, which seems rather neutral to
us, was not that at all but was "hermetic"—anarchic and unsavory. It will become increasingly clear, as we look beyond
Picasso at other Parisian painters, that this transformation from
bohemianism to a more traditional aesthetic was a change that
encompassed more than just Picasso and Cocteau. It was because of paintings like *L'Italienne* that, when Cocteau published a little book on Picasso in 1923, he could say, with evi-

dence to support him, that "here, then, is a Spaniard, provided with the oldest French recipes (Chardin, Poussin, Lenain, Corot) . . ." and add in a footnote: "I don't emphasize Spain. Picasso is from here. He has devoted all his powers, all the ruses of his race, to learning from the school and being of service to France."[77] We shall see later how many other French ingredients Picasso added to his Cubist *pot-au-feu*.

Nor was it only in his art that Picasso was beginning to forsake bohemia. He had now fallen in love with a very proper, even stuffy, young woman: a ballerina from Diaghilev's troupe, the daughter of a Russian colonel—Olga Koklova. When the Ballets Russes traveled to Spain in 1917, Picasso made a portrait of his new girlfriend *bien élevée* (fig. 103). The picture is

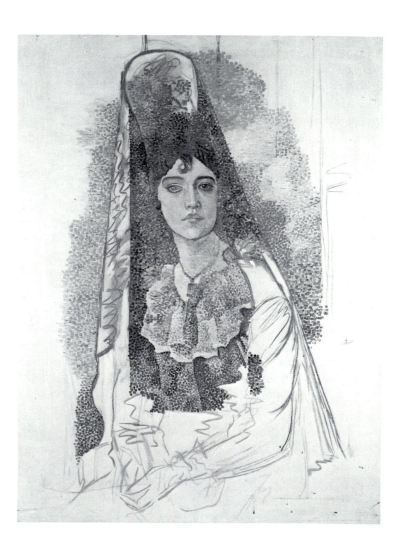

103. P. Picasso, *Portrait of Olga*, 1917.

closely related to the Italian peasant girl series, except that here
the artist uses a real, living woman to embody the Mediterranean ideal. Although Russian, Olga is portrayed *à l'espagnol* in
this pointillist portrait. Covered in a mantilla of old lace, wearing what appears to be an heirloom pendant around her neck,
her hands decorously folded in her lap, Olga looks none too
trustfully out at the viewer. Again, there is no hint of bohemia
or the Parisian Left Bank—no popular song titles, no frank
sexuality, and not even the ghost of Cubism. This is a portrait
of the kind of old-fashioned, haughty girl that Picasso could
bring home to his family, and it is rendered in the kind of academic style that his own father had practiced and taught at the
academy.

Olga Koklova was also the kind of woman that a man could
bring into society, and in the summer of 1918 (on July 12) Pablo and Olga were married. In keeping with the artist's new
Right Bank legitimacy, it was to Biarritz, Europe's most fashionable resort, that the newlyweds went for their honeymoon.
They stayed there as the guests of the Chilean socialite Eugenia
Errazuriz, who was now a close friend of the Picassos.[78] To
amuse himself, and perhaps as a way of thanking his hostess
for her hospitality, Picasso decorated one of the rooms in her
villa, *La Mimoseraie*, with neo-Renaissance line drawings (figs.
104 and 105), in the midst of which was inscribed the first
stanza of Apollinaire's poem "Les Saisons":

> Those were the happy days we strolled along the beach
> Go early in the morning hatless and barefoot
> And as swiftly as a toad's tongue darts
> Love wounded crazy hearts as well as wise[79]

The poet was touched by his friend's homage and on 11 September wrote to Picasso, "I am also very happy that you have decorated the villa at Biarritz and proud that my verses are there."
Aware of Picasso's new artistic directions, Apollinaire continued, in reference to his own work: "What I am doing now will
accord better with your present preoccupations. I am trying to
renovate the poetic tone, but in the classic rhyme."[80]

But if his traditionalizing preoccupations were being manifested in an ever-expanding repertory of subjects and styles, the
figure who presided over Picasso's neo-classicism was still
Jean-Auguste-Dominique Ingres. As one of the most recent exemplars of French classicism, on whose shoulders the mantle of
le style français was draped, Ingres was not only the symbol of
sanctioned French art but was also seen as an antidote to every-

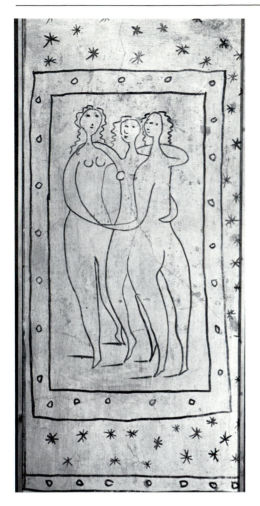

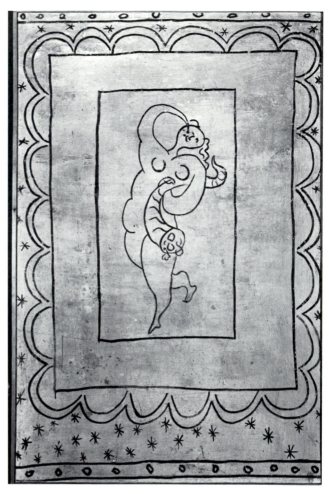

104. (*left*) P. Picasso, Wall decorations for Errazuriz villa, *La Mimoseraie*, Biarritz, 1918.

105. (*right*) P. Picasso, Wall decorations for Errazuriz villa, *La Mimoseraie*, Biarritz, 1918.

106. (*facing page*) P. Picasso, *Portrait of Olga*, 1917.

thing that deviated from the "path of France." When Jean Cocteau in *Le Coq et l'Arlequin* said that "Debussy translates Claude Monet into Russian" (associating Impressionism with foreignness), whereas "Satie remains intact . . . he speaks of Ingres,"[81] he was probably also thinking of Picasso's art. He may even have been thinking specifically of the artist's *Portrait of Olga* (fig. 106) of late 1917, one of the most beautiful portraits of Picasso's long career. Indeed, it is his most direct (and his largest) Ingres-style work, very similar (as Phoebe Pool pointed out) to Ingres's *Madame Devaucey*.[82] As in the case of his *L'Italienne*, where we had concrete evidence of Picasso's study of Corot, we also have in 1917 a direct line-for-line copy from Ingres (fig. 107), a drawing of the figure of Livia from Ingres's *Tu Marcellus Eris* (fig. 108). Although the drawing

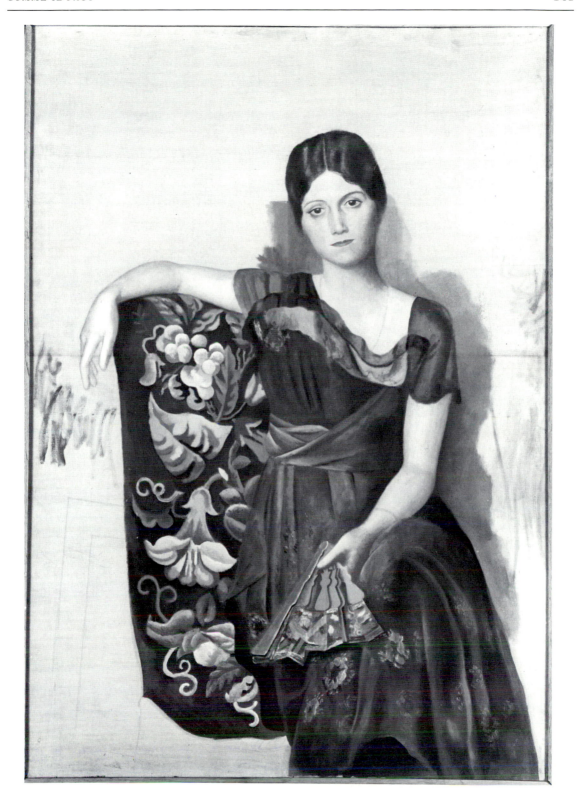

bears no resemblance to the *Portrait of Olga*, it clearly provided him with a model for the dignified, classic demeanor that he bestowed on the woman who would soon be his wife. Olga appears a little softer and more wistful here than in the Spanish picture, although her carefully parted hair (in the style that ballerinas favor to this day), her tightly pursed lips, and the tensed muscles of her neck all convey an air of utter propriety. Depicted in a palette of grays, flesh tones, and greens, combined with the buff of the unpainted ground and red highlights, with a fan held in her lap (a symbol of reserve and Old World manners), attired in a printed silk dress, and with her arm so elegantly draped over the back of an embroidered, flower-

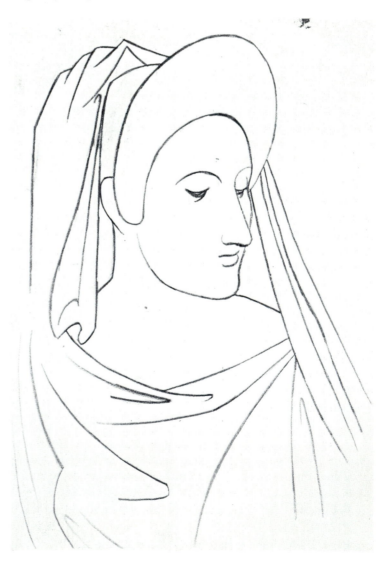

107. P. Picasso, Drawing of the figure of Livia from J.A.D. Ingres's *Tu Marcellus Eris*, 1917.

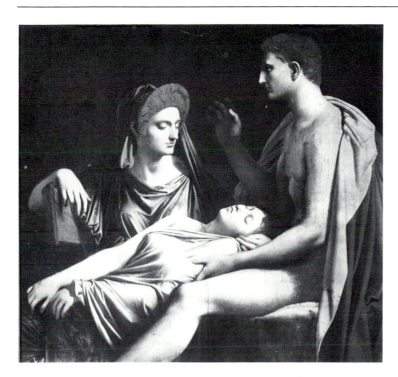

108. J.A.D. Ingres, *Tu Marcellus Eris*, 1813.

patterned chair, the portrait of Olga Koklova could not be further from Picasso's pre-war portraits of Fernande Olivier and Marcelle Humbert. Neither a primitive icon nor a Cubist construction, it is a portrait of the first woman whose relationship with Picasso was legitimized by marriage. Olga appears here as the symbol of all that was most comfortable and *chic* on the Right Bank, where in fact the Picassos now resided (upon their return from Biarritz, *chez* Errazuriz, the couple moved to an apartment on the fashionable rue la Boétie, just down the street from Pablo's new dealer, Paul Rosenberg, brother of Léonce). To be sure, the *Portrait of Olga* could never be mistaken for one of the immaculately finished works of Ingres. The brilliant incorporation of the unpainted ground which, with the pencil lines and slashes of gray-green paint on both sides, brackets the figure (literally making a quotation of the central form), establishes Picasso's distance from Ingres by way of Cézanne's unfinished canvases. Yet, ironically, the painting becomes all the more elegant in a specifically twentieth-century way. Just like the marriage of Pablo and Olga—the avant-garde artist and the White Russian ballerina—the portrait stylistically weds the improvised and the premeditated. Cocteau's aesthetic of the

Left and the Right joined together in French clarity is stunningly realized in this portrait *comme il faut*.

By this time, late in the war, Picasso was already becoming a bit distant from his old crowd: Juan Gris noted, just after the war, that Picasso "produces some fine things still," when he had a moment between "a Russian ballet and a society portrait"—obviously a bitter reference as much to a style of living as to an aesthetic. Max Jacob was not often asked to the new apartment, and even Georges Braque was much less intimate with his former collaborator.[83] There is a revealing anecdote related by Ernest Ansermet, in which the conductor arrived at the painter's hotel room in Barcelona one night during Diaghilev's tour there. Picasso was getting ready for a night at the ballet and was dressed in formal attire. As Ansermet tells the story, Picasso placed his top hat on his head, looked at himself in the mirror, and murmured: "Monsieur Ingres."[84] The irony of course is unmistakable; more than anyone, Picasso was aware of how radically his life had changed in just a few short years. Nonetheless, it is interesting to note Picasso's acute sense of the relationship between an artist's life and his oeuvre. To draw and to paint like Ingres meant more than a shift in the aesthetic of art; it also signaled a shift in the art of living.

The dealer and collector Wilhelm Uhde, whose stock of paintings, as we know, was confiscated by the French government at the outbreak of war, wrote a book about Picasso in 1928. *Picasso et la tradition française* is not, as its title seems to imply, a study of the French qualities of the Spaniard's art but rather an exposition of what Uhde considered to be Picasso's debt to *German* culture (the book's title is but another example of the kind of rhetorical disguise that the moment demanded). With the insight and even sympathy of a fellow foreigner, the German wrote:

> At Paul Rosenberg's gallery, Pablo Picasso came running down the stairs, pulling me excitedly into the room where his pictures were. I found myself in front of a large portrait in what is called the "Ingres" style. The stiffness of posture, a forced sobriety, seemed to hide a pathetic secret . . . what did these paintings mean? Was it an intermediate phase, a game, handsome but without significance? . . . or, rather, at a moment when hate ruled men, when Roman circumspection fought a pitched battle against cloudy German metaphysics, did Picasso feel that he was being pointed at by countless people who reproached him

for his profound feelings of affinity with Germany and accused him of being secretly in league with the enemy? Was
he trying to align himself with the specifically "French"
side, and do these paintings attest to the torment of his
soul?[85]

Uhde goes on to say: "It is difficult to find an answer to these
questions" and, less tactfully, "As for obtaining one from him,
one could hardly imagine such a thing." Although one art historian has called this passage from Uhde's book "a fundamental
misunderstanding of the character of Picasso, whose intellectual courage was without fault his whole life long,"[86] I think that
the acuity of the German's conjecture speaks for itself. As Gris
had said to Kahnweiler only two weeks after war began, previous engagements were no longer valid—each Parisian artist
had to make his own way.

IV Internecine Warfare

As early as April 1916, the young painter and critic Bissière had written in the magazine *L'Opinion*:

> I apologize for using the word "cubist"; it describes a school which was perhaps necessary at its moment, but whose usefulness has ceased to make itself felt, and whose disappearance seems almost a *fait accompli*.[1]

Bissière was overstating his case. Far from having disappeared, Cubist art of one kind or another was still being made (in Paris and elsewhere) by almost all of its pre-war practitioners. But his statement of Cubism's obsolescence and demise is important not only because it announces a new generation's challenge to its predecessors—signifying, in effect, that Cubism was no longer new—but also because it acknowledges that something had changed even within the Cubist enclave. If the major figure of the movement could draw like Ingres, paint the Latin family *en tricolore*, and turn to Corot and Baroque Rome for subject matter, then a perceptive observer might well question Cubism's *raison d'être*. Carco, who said "art is for a country . . . the testimony of its moral force," also spoke with confidence, in December 1917, of Cubism's passing.

> Do you remember—before the war—the diversity of views, opinions, tendencies, directions, theories in French pictorial art? The grossest extravagances became a daily spectacle—and amid this chaos we had to fight in order to declare that Cubism was no more than an error—and that experiment for experiment's sake was an idle preoccupation.[2]

Apparently, he and his friends no longer had to fight for their anti-Cubist opinions, because the pre-war multiplicity of directions was now a thing of the past. We may recall that André Lhote, another young painter, had previously (in the February 1916 issue of *L'Elan*) referred to Cubism as a "disease . . . that arises from the obsession with 'personality at all costs,'" had charged it with "unsoundly based and overly experimental tech-

niques," and had called for an "expressive totalization of pictorial values," which was but another way of declaring the end of the pre-war "diversity of views."

Far more extraordinary, though, were the kinds of things being said not by outsiders and ambitious newcomers but by the very leaders of the pre-war Parisian avant-garde. As we know, Robert Delaunay was in self-imposed exile on the Iberian peninsula for the duration of the war. Considering his alleged pacifism, and remembering that before the war he had been the single most important link between French and German artists (particularly through Franz Marc, Auguste Macke, and Wassily Kandinsky), we might expect to hear Delaunay bemoaning the war and the concomitant eradication of internationalist culture. He was in fact greatly disturbed by the kinds of things that were being said about him and his friends back in Paris, especially by the conservative critics. "The old-timers," he wrote to Albert Gleizes during the winter of 1915–16, "have made use of the situation: called us deserters, A.W.O.L., calumnies, slander . . ." and complained that even the young "have had a disgusting role in all this . . . they said modern painting was German . . . stabbed us in the back."[3] Yet, as it happens, Delaunay himself was becoming as virulently jingoistic, anti-Cubist, and calumnious as the old-timers and the young. In a letter of 12 December 1916, Delaunay wrote to a friend that the "newest art" was "in reaction or rather in opposition to all the painting or artistic tendencies called Cubist-Futurist" and that "among the young there is a great reaction against this amorphous art, and these profiteers are no longer *à la mode*—it's finished." And in a chilling postscript, he wrote:

> I am delighted with what you say . . . this stupid painting which was made by certain mystifiers who, for the most part, were foreigners to France, but who fooled the world by saying "made in Paris" . . . I am happy to see that there are men . . . who have not allowed themselves to be invaded by this rot: as I said, which is not French, but of which we are now obliged to cleanse Paris—great Paris, which forever renews itself.[4]

He repeated the latter motif in another letter to Gleizes ("the sweeping-up begins"[5]) and again, in a letter of 1917, to his friend Felin Elias ("the young French painters have begun the cleaning-up"[6]). And Delaunay did not confine his ideas to personal correspondence. While in Barcelona, in 1917, he wrote a letter in the newspaper *Vell i Nou* in which he referred to the

period of the pre-war Parisian avant-garde as an "epoch of poor painting, hysterical, convulsive, destructive, . . . these Futurist [and] Cubist hoaxes . . . neither painting nor art."[7]

It becomes clear, very early in his wartime correspondence, that in adopting (although from a considerable distance) the new anti-Cubist attitude Delaunay had a particular target in mind. After telling Gleizes that owing to the war "the foreigners and the old-timers have profited too much from the current lack of cohesion," he goes on to say that certain parties "want to make the French painters out to be followers of the famous genius,"[8] by whom he meant, of course, Picasso. Delaunay's vexation at Picasso's fame must have begun long before the war, and perhaps because Guillaume Apollinaire had labeled Delaunay an Orphist the French artist felt able to denounce Cubism and Futurism. The strong nationalism of wartime allowed Delaunay to vent his pent-up hostilities, and so, just like the conservative critics whom he elsewhere attacks, he took the opportunity to berate Picasso for his exploitation of French culture. In another letter to Gleizes Delaunay made his anger plain. First, in reference to the Ballets Russes, which he had just seen in Barcelona in November 1917, he wrote, "*Parade* is a completely crazy story—no success here, or even curiosity, when confronted with this hysterical thing—that's the only correct word . . . hysteria—painting of a sick mind—tortured . . ." Then he went on to speak of Picasso's recent "return to tradition," a topic which he must already have touched on in the correspondence with Gleizes, for he writes:

> What you say à propos Picasso . . . now, having left behind Cubist incomprehensibility, he accommodates himself marvelously with his so-called classic period of these drawings which have neither father nor mother."[9]

Later, c. 1920–21, Delaunay elaborated on this idea:

> Comparison of the Cubists, who equivocate by going back to old means . . . like Picasso, who imitates Bouguereau, being unable to obtain the purity of Ingres (Ingres already being a "neo," there is no serious or possible development).[10]

Indeed, Delaunay's attacks on Picasso's neo-traditionalism might well be considered as the groundwork for a valid indictment of the Spaniard's accommodations to the conservative wartime regime. That is, we might see them as such if Delaunay were an artist who, having chosen exile from chauvinistic Paris,

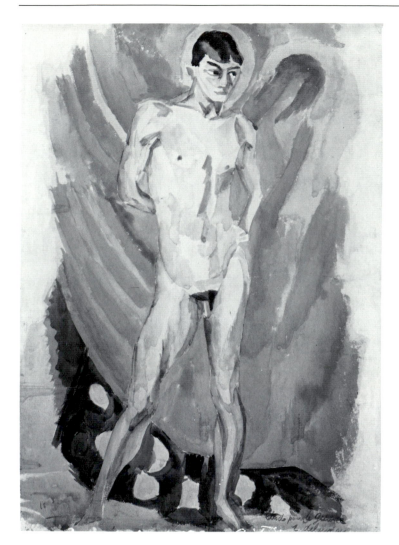

109. R. Delaunay, Study for *Le Gitan*, 1915.

was defending internationalism and attempting to preserve his own pre-war stance. We have already heard, of course, that De-launay could be less than generous in regard to foreigners after the war began; moreover, despite his accusations against Pi-casso, he himself was moving in the direction of the new tradi-tionalism he was condemning. His *Le Gitan* (fig. 109) of 1915 is among the first works to indicate a softening of Delaunay's sharp-angled, fragmented pre-war aesthetic. Even in compari-son to the figures of the Three Graces in his 1912 *The City of Paris* (fig. 110)—itself still a traditional work in a number of ways—the image of the Spanish gypsy boy is remarkably aca-demic. There is none of the fragmentation or prismatic pattern-

110. R. Delaunay, *The City of Paris*, 1912.

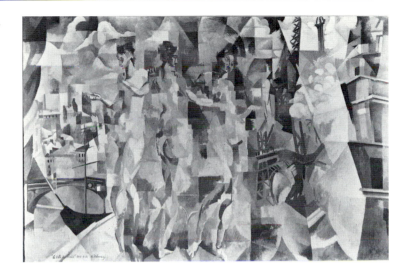

ing of the 1912 figures: the gypsy's body is conventionally rendered, although the schematization of planar transitions (particularly apparent in the lower part of the legs) hardly follows the rules of correct drawing. What gives the figure a "modern" look is the abstract geometric ground against which the boy poses (it may be one of Sonia Terk Delaunay's "simultaneous" fabrics). But the figure is clearly posed against the abstract pattern, so that there is not the slightest confusion between figure and ground. We are left with but a reminiscence of Delaunay's pre-war fragmentation, presented merely as the background to a rather banal figure study.

Even more striking than the *Gitan* of 1915 is a 1918 watercolor portrait (fig. 111) of Léonide Massine. As the identity of the sitter indicates, Delaunay himself was by now in the company of the Ballets Russes, having been asked by Diaghilev to create the settings for his ballet *Cléopâtre* (with costumes by Sonia Delaunay). Again, we see that it was not Delaunay's resistance to the new trends that accounts for his denigration of Picasso, for he was following more closely than anyone in the footsteps of the "famous genius." Not only was he working for Diaghilev—the first Parisian artist to do so after Picasso—but he was also clearly aware of Picasso's new illusionistic portrait style. The portrait of Massine, painted in Sitges, is altogether conventional in conception. Although the portrait is only an *étude*, the planes of the face have been carefully modeled, and the sitter's distant gaze and superbly erect posture remind us of the heroizing qualities of Picasso's drawing of Cocteau. The

Spaniard might be a "foreign mystifier," and his drawings might seem inauthentic to the Frenchman, but his influence was powerful enough to divert the course of Delaunay's art even as he railed against it.

Back in Paris, the changes within the avant-garde camp were becoming increasingly apparent. The two almost shockingly conventional works that Gino Severini produced within months of his first (and last) "Futurist Exhibition of the Plastic Art of War," the *Motherhood* and *Portrait of Jeanne*, are not typical of Severini's wartime art (although, as we shall see, he was to revive this kind of illusionism in the early 1920s). Instead, what we observe is a more gradual softening of the Italian's pre-war

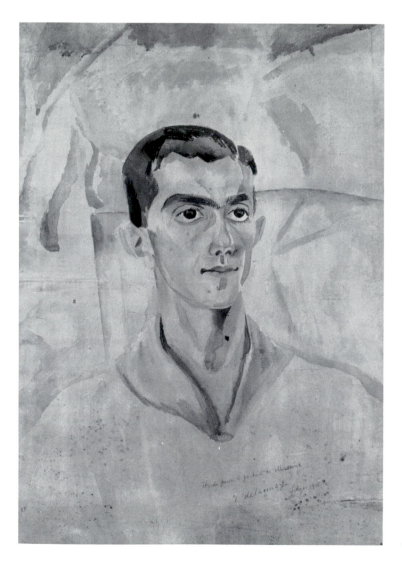

111. R. Delaunay, Study for *Portrait of Léonide Massine*, 1918.

112. G. Severini, *Mother and Child*, c. 1916.

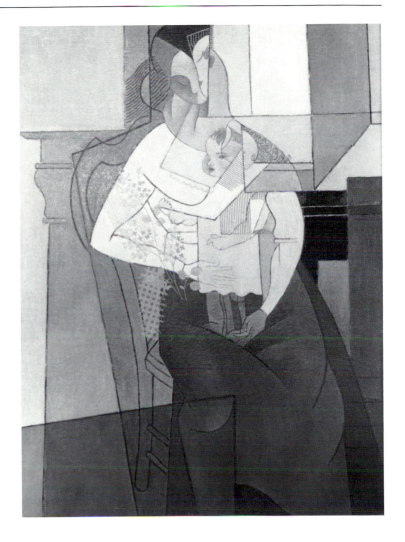

modern aesthetic, the first stage of which, after the momentary venture into illusionism, is a move away from Futurism toward the comparatively stable Cubism of another portrait of his wife and newborn child (fig. 112). In other words, Severini presented himself with three pictorial options: to continue with his pre-war Futurist art (such as he exhibited at the Galerie Boutet de Monvel); to make an about-face, as in his illusionistic *Motherhood* (fig. 52); or, as in *Mother and Child*, to pursue a Cubist direction. Perhaps not surprisingly, it was this third possibility that he chose, because, in effect, a kind of subdued Cubism was the compromise aesthetic between his revolutionary Futurism and a reactionary neo-traditionalism. In both a personal and a public sense, it was probably more comfortable, in the

midst of the wartime conservatism, to modify his pre-war aesthetic radicalism than to attempt to deny it. Severini must have
been artistically dissatisfied with the conventional nature of his
illusionistic works, a dissatisfaction increased by the knowledge
that any reputation he had gained before the war had been as a
modern and progressive artist. To abjure that pre-war reputation
all at once would have been inconceivable. In time Severini
would become central to the post-war attack on pre-war aesthetics, but not until he had thoroughly exhausted his avant-
garde investments.

Perhaps the most striking example of Severini's artistic dilemma is his *Appearance of the Angel to Punchinello* of 1917[11]
(fig. 113). The subject, as far as I am aware, is unique in the
history of art: Gabriel, the annunciating angel, enters (airborne)
from the left, carrying a message to the guitar-strumming Punchinello and his clarinet-playing companion Arlecchino. Severini's narrative is baffling, to say the least. We might even

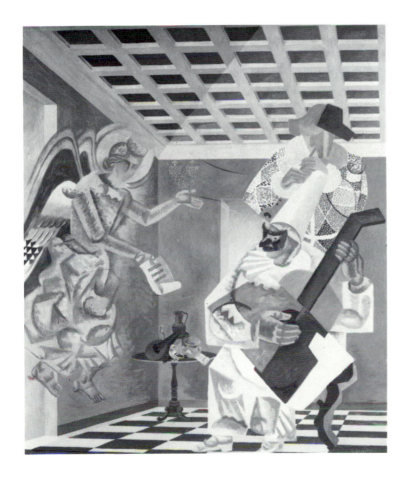

113. G. Severini, *Appearance of the
Angel to Punchinello*, 1917.

conclude that the artist himself was not altogether certain of the meaning of his iconography, considering the equally bewildering mélange of styles: a perfectly traditional neo-Renaissance depiction of the room, replete with checkerboard tiling and coffered ceiling; an Analytic Cubist or pre-war Futurist rendering of the angel (with his/her shifting planes and volumetric modeling); and the depiction of the two musicians, to the right, in the newer, more geometric, largely unmodeled Cubism of paintings like Picasso's *L'Italienne*, of the same year. The subject matter is also of the new Latin kind that Picasso was exploring in 1917, except that Severini has doubled the Spaniard's recipe. Not only does he make use of the *commedia dell'arte* at the right (and it is likely that the *Appearance of the Angel to Punchinello* was painted after the première of *Parade*), but he adds an equal quantity of Christian iconography. This is hardly surprising, however, since Severini and Picasso had almost identical handicaps and virtues in wartime Paris: both were civilians, foreigners, and Latins. Whether Severini's situation as an Allied civilian (in contrast to Picasso's as a neutral noncombatant) was more or less congenial is difficult to say; that he exploited his Latin roots in 1917 is obvious. In fact, he said as much in the preface to the catalogue of his New York exhibition in that year:

> In the works that I am exhibiting, works belonging to different periods, one may discern a search for a balance between reason and sensitivity. Also, while obeying the tendency toward composition which I have inherited from the Old Italians, I have wanted to attain a new classicism, through the construction of the "picture."[12]

Severini speaks in the wartime artistic language that we have heard so often and with such frequency after 1916: balance (between mind and emotions, the same balancing act that Dermée and Braque spoke of); the Latin inheritance (the reference to "the Old Italians" is meant quite specifically; he appears to have based the *Appearance of the Angel* on a School of Bellini *Annunciation* (fig. 114); and, most strikingly, his invocation of the key phrase of 1917, "new classicism."

Yet for all that this kind of talk was becoming commonplace within the Parisian avant-garde, it is nonetheless an extraordinary shift in sensibility for Severini. Despite his words to the New York viewers, it is difficult to see a work like his *Cannon in Action* (fig. 42) as exemplifying a search for balance, reason, or sensitivity. We should not forget that Severini had been one

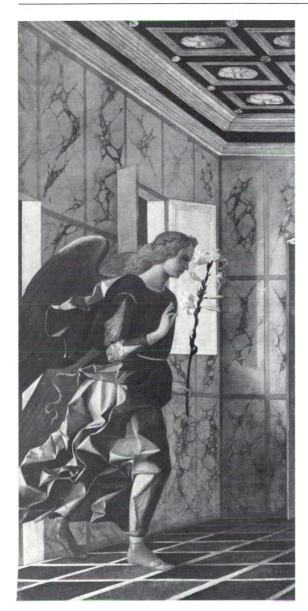
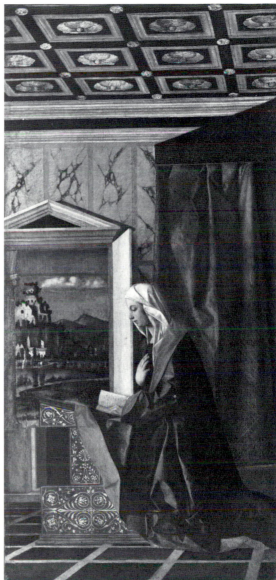

114. School of G. Bellini,
Annunciation, c. 1500.

of the signers of the Manifesto of Futurist Painters in 1910,
which declared:

> We will: 1. Destroy the cult of the past, the obsession with
> the ancients, pedantry and academic formalism. 2. Totally
> invalidate all kinds of imitation. . . . 7. Sweep the whole
> field of art clean of all themes and subjects which have
> been used in the past.[13]

That he could so blithely now refer to "Old Italians" and "new classicism" bespeaks a sensibility that must have been at war with itself. There can be no more blatant, and even saddening, demonstration of the impact of conflicting wartime demands than Severini's *Appearance of the Angel to Punchinello*, in which Cubism, Latinism, and Christianity are invited to cohabit in a Renaissance villa. Picasso might artistically bob and weave (with a soupçon of irony) through the wartime strictures, but other artists who attempted to balance the same contradictory elements simply could not carry it off. So great are the visual inconsistencies and so outlandish are the narrative elements in Severini's painting that the result is, at best, a forgettable effort at accommodation.

Although our earliest evidence of the war's impact on a Parisian artist came from another resident alien, Juan Gris, we have not yet looked at the effect which the wartime atmosphere had on his painting. It was clear, in his letters to Kahnweiler, that he felt lonely, confused, and frightened. Like Picasso, Gris was a Spaniard in wartime Paris, with the same equivocal status vis-à-vis French public policy. We should not forget that as early as 3 August 1914 he had written to his German friend that "all of us who had sketched our way through life must now change everything and get along as best we can," which turned out to be an accurate forecast of his wartime experience.

Like Severini, Gris too was befriended by Matisse, who included a portrait of Juan's wife, Josette, in his Bohain-en-Vermandois series of 1915 (fig. 31). But Gris seems not to have had as wide a circle of bright young Frenchmen surrounding him as had the former Futurist Severini, and he did not have the aid of Cocteau, who was busily introducing Picasso to the right people. The entire period of the war seems to have been an unhappy time for him,[14] although he did not remain completely resistant to the new patriotism. We have already seen the signs of his accommodation to wartime circumstances, as for instance when he wrote to Raynal in October 1916 that he was "continually ashamed of that peacefulness which you envy." Even more interesting is a letter to Kahnweiler of September 1915 where Gris reveals the extent to which his aesthetic conceptions were also accommodating themselves, if unconsciously, to prevailing attitudes:

> Nowadays when I have finished working I don't read serial novels but do portraits from life. They are very good likenesses and I shall soon have as much skill as a Prix de

Rome winner. It is a perpetual thrill for me to discover how it is done. I can't get over it because I thought it was much more difficult.[15]

Gris's portraits were probably inspired by Picasso's Ingres-style works, begun in January 1915, and when he says that he will soon be as proficient as a Prix de Rome winner, he is as well aware as Picasso was of the irony of an avant-garde painter aspiring to the highest honor of the Ecole. And indeed it is extraordinary to hear one of the pioneers of Cubism claim with evident pride that his portraits are "very good likenesses." Yet there is no reason to doubt that he is being straightforward here. Gris makes us aware of the limits that pre-war Cubism had imposed on its practitioners—i.e., portrait drawing from life was simply not part of the modernist program. Seen in this light, the anti-Cubist campaign did provide at least a momentary sensation of engaging in illicit activity, as Gris indulged in the old-fashioned pleasures of mimesis.

A drawing that he made the next year of Josette (fig. 115) must be close to the likenesses of which he wrote to Raynal. While there is a certain degree of fracturing here (near the neck and ear, and in the squared-off bangs), it is essentially a rather traditional piece of draftsmanship. As in Picasso's portraits of Jacob and Vollard (figs. 39 and 40), Gris chooses to work in the medium of hard pencil, eschewing the charcoal and softer pencils that he had favored in his pre-war drawings. It is evident in this portrait of Josette that he takes particular delight in the contrast between the sharp, clean lines of contour and the larger planes modeled in chiaroscuro. Although the image, unlike those of his fellow Spaniard, is not intended as a specific quotation from Ingres or from any other past master, it does have the precise and pristine look of an academic drawing.

But if the portrait of Josette was no more than vaguely academic in appearance, Gris made specific reference to the French artistic past in a major painting of 1916, *Woman with Mandolin* (fig. 116). If, as it appears, the painting is correctly dated, then we have one striking instance of an artist other than Picasso taking the lead in the wartime neo-traditionalism, for Gris's painting is a direct quotation of Corot's *Girl with a Mandolin* (fig. 117). As such it is a precedent for, rather than a derivation from, *L'Italienne* of 1917. Both in its subject—that of the beautiful, mythic Italian peasant—and its style—Cubism adapted to Corot's rendering of the woman's sensuous curves—it anticipates the new "Latin Cubism" of Picasso's picture of the

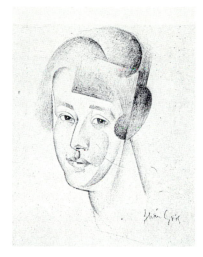

115. J. Gris, *Portrait of Josette*, 1916.

116. J. Gris, *Woman with Mandolin
(after Corot)*, 1916.

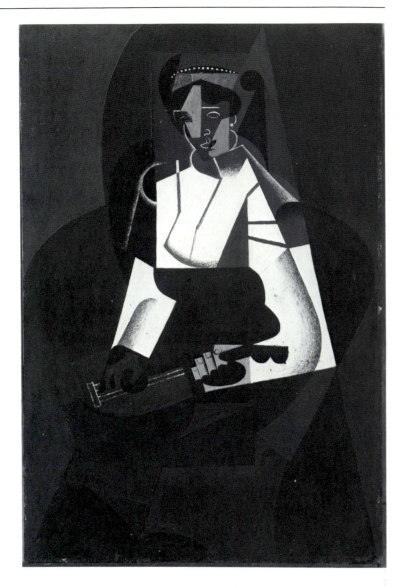

next year. Since Gris did not travel to Italy, wartime Paris must
have been sufficiently Latinized in its outlook to encourage such
non-allusive references to the current struggle. *Woman with
Mandolin* was just the kind of work which by its "origin and
destination" was unquestionably of the French domain.

Moreover, Gris's new-found Latin tastes were not confined to
his painting *d'après* Corot. Just as Picasso and Severini were
demonstrating in 1917, so Gris found that new inspiration could
be derived from the venerable *commedia dell'arte*: in December
he painted two portraits of Harlequin, one of them a seated fig-

ure with guitar (fig. 118). Obviously, Gris has not gone to the
traditionalizing lengths of Picasso's Barcelona *Harlequin* (fig.
93), nor has he attempted (as Severini so infelicitously did) to
introduce a neo-Renaissance context for his figures. Instead, in
place of the still-life objects and collaged elements of his pre-
war Cubism, Gris has simply brought his prismatic style to bear
on the popular Latin character. Of course, his Cubist style has
changed: the angles are less acute, the paint application is
smooth rather than stippled, and the face is left relatively intact, except where a shadow can justify an abrupt fracture. This
is the same rather orderly Cubism as that of the *Woman with
Mandolin.*

As it was for Picasso and Severini, the *commedia dell'arte*
continued to serve as an important theme in Gris's art until the
mid-1920s. In 1925 the French scholar Pierre Duchartre, in his

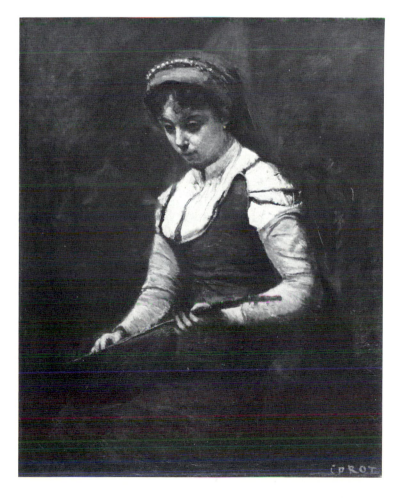

117. C. Corot, *Girl with a Mandolin,*
c. 1860.

118. J. Gris, *Harlequin with Guitar*,
1917.

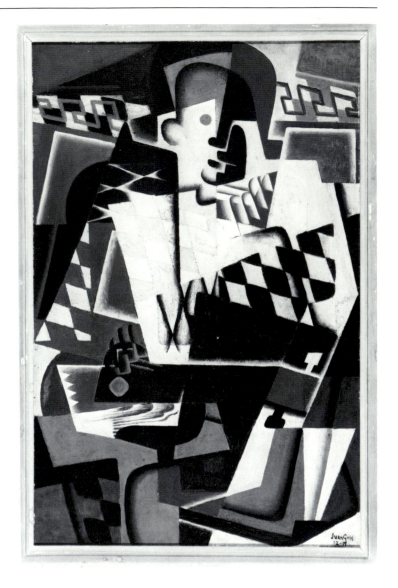

La Comédie italienne, recognized that the three Latin avant-garde painters had, through their Harlequins and Punchinellos, their Pierrots and Columbines, joined a venerable tradition:

> The Italian Comedy is forever being reborn . . . the Fra-tellini, Grock, . . . the Ballets Russes, . . . Molière, . . . Marivaux, Verlaine, Debureau, . . . Callot, . . . Gillot, Watteau, Lancret, Giovanni Battista Tiepolo, . . . Guérin, Picasso, Severini, Gris, Lombard, [Umberto] Brunelleschi, Claude-Lévy and so many others . . . small and great have saluted each other across the centuries; they are all

in part members of the illustrious, joyous, and forever flourishing family which could carry on its banner as a motto: "All genres except the tedious."

Duchartre also alluded to that aspect of the *commedia dell'arte* which was so valuable to the French and Italian wartime regimes, but which was seldom explicitly talked about, namely the *commedia* as a paradigm of normal collective behavior: "No Othello, no Hamlet, no Phèdre or Chimera, no one who agitates his mind with overpowering emotions . . . the *commedia dell'arte* is a complete world where each can find his nourishment." He advocates the popular and healthy tradition as an antidote to the eccentric, libidinous, murderous, incestuous, and abnormal heroes of the theatre. And not only was the Italian comedy a nourishing world from which exceptional, or deviant, behavior was eliminated, but it was equally an artistic genre in which all artists could share: "Poets, musicians, writers, painters of talent or genius, [otherwise] the most strongly opposed to each other, meet in their common love for the *commedia dell'arte*."[16]

But far more important than Corot or the *commedia dell'arte* for the wartime development of Juan Gris was the art of Paul Cézanne. Perhaps in much the same way that Picasso, in *The Painter and His Model* (fig. 33), turned to Cézanne for reassurance during the summer of 1914, Gris—clearly in search of something too—returned to the art of Cézanne in an almost obsessive fashion after 1916. Now, this would seem to mark no deviation at all from Gris's pre-war interests and might even, to the contrary, be seen as a way of confirming that the aesthetic concerns of the Cubists were, in the deepest sense, unchanged by the war. Cézanne, after all, had been the great ancestor-figure in the development of Cubism from its earliest origins. Indeed, if an artist's style were something static and immutable, open only to a single interpretation, there would be nothing remarkable in Gris's continued interest in Cézanne's work. But of course the art of Cézanne was subject to multiple interpretations, dependent on the interpreter's prejudices as well as on the moment when he looked at the work. For instance, while Picasso, Matisse, and Derain all turned to Cézanne for guidance during the period 1905–7, the work of each is unique, the result of having drawn different, and even antithetical, conclusions from Cézanne. Likewise, the Cézanne that Juan Gris was looking at between 1910 and 1914 was a very different artist from the one he saw between 1916 and 1918.

In 1916, Gris made numerous drawings after paintings by

119. J. Gris, Drawing after
P. Cézanne's *Self-Portrait* (1886?),
1916.

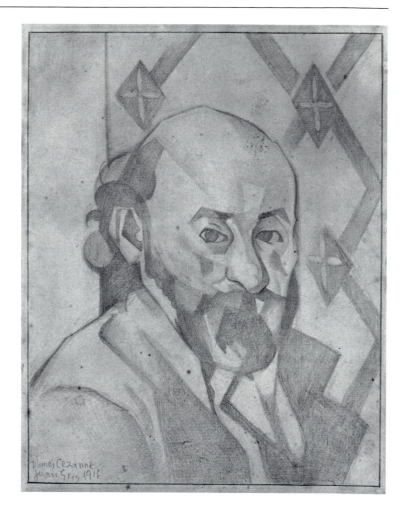

Cézanne, including a self-portrait (fig. 119) and a small *Three Bathers* (fig. 120) the original of which belonged to Matisse and which Gris undoubtedly saw at his home. We can speak of Cézanne's influence on Gris during this period far more precisely than we can of the pre-war years, simply because the Spanish artist was *copying* Cézanne's paintings between 1916 and 1918, whereas (as far as I am aware) we have not a single copy *per se* before the war. Similarly, while the influence of Cézanne on the pre-war Cubism of Picasso and Braque was apparent in almost every picture they painted (especially between 1908 and 1910), that influence never took the form of drawing or painting *d'après* Cézanne. Indeed, for the Parisian avant-garde before 1914 the very notion of "influence" was one which precluded the academic apprenticeship that had been practiced since the Renaissance and earlier. The pre-war Cubists, including Gris, did not aspire to Cézanne's aesthetic but rather enlarged upon it; they exaggerated, reworked, extended what they saw as the central ideas, impulses, suggestions, or values in Cézanne's vision, and each argued, at least pictorially, for his own interpretation of the work. It is hardly incidental to this highly sophisticated pre-war conception of influence that it was after Cézanne's death in 1906 that he became, so quickly and prodigiously, the mentor of Picasso and Braque. Since the intention of the self-proclaimed avant-garde before the war was to explore and create the new, the unseen, and the untested, it would have been old-fashioned and self-contradictory to paint at the side of the revered figure.[17]

In effect, by making literal copies after Cézanne during the war, Gris legitimized his relationship to the French painter. From a position which, before the war, might best have been described as one of inspiration or suggestion, Gris now established himself vis-à-vis Cézanne in the more regular and more easily discernible relationship of apprentice to master. Where Gris and his fellow Cubists had seen Cézanne as a reclusive and undervalued talent (all the more esteemed for having been "au dessus de la mêlée" for so long), who with his proto-Berg-

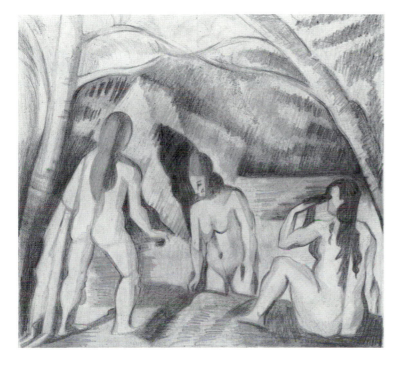

120. J. Gris, Drawing after P. Cézanne's *Bathers* (c. 1875), 1916.

sonian vision of shimmering planes and relativistic perspectives seemed to reach across the perturbations of the *fin de siècle* toward a modern aesthetic, Gris now makes Cézanne into the Master from Aix, as copyable and secure of his place in the tradition as Corot.

The style of the copies also attests to this new view. Instead of Cézanne's stunning pictorial fabric of conflicting planes and *passages*, which had been so inspirational to Gris's own pre-war refracted style, the Spaniard, in part by his reduction of the Impressionist palette to black and white, imparts a solid, stony quality to the forms which they do not possess in the original. To be sure, the faceting to which Gris subjects Cézanne's forms, apparent in the bathers and self-portrait, is in part Gris's effort to assimilate the pictures to his own Cubist experience, not unlike Delaunay's rather planar treatment of parts of his *Gitan*. And like Delaunay's these slight exaggerations in geometry tend to increase, rather than deny, the sense of volume: precisely the opposite of Gris's earlier use of Cézanne as a source for the organized analysis and decomposition of the visual field. Even more important, though, is what has not been done to Cézanne's pictures; they have been left intact. Gris here presents Cézanne not as the obsessive rebel who often left his paintings unfinished, but rather, in an almost textbook fashion, as a maker of key iconic monuments, reference points of unimpeachable style.

In significant segments of the avant-garde, we have already begun to see a subtle but quite definite shift in the modern artist's relationship to past art: in Picasso's blatant allusions to Cézanne, Ingres, and Corot; in Severini's talk—and use—of the "Old Italians"; in Gris's reworking of Corot and his copies of Cézanne; and in all three artists' new interest in the *commedia dell'arte*. And in Georges Braque's "Pensées et réflexions sur la peinture" of 1917 we find again the more traditional notion of the past as something to be embraced (rather than negated or neglected) that was beginning to emerge in the midst of war. Although he was quite emphatically opposed to copying,[18] Braque's first statement of principle—"1. In art, progress consists not in extension but in the knowledge of its limits"—was the verbal equivalent of Gris's more respectful attitude toward Cézanne. In fact, while Gris would remain a Cubist painter until the end of his short life in 1927, he would henceforth make art with a new sense of tradition and of the weight of history. Kahnweiler tells us that Gris (probably in 1919) said, referring to his recent work, somewhat pitifully, "My work may be bad 'great painting' but at least it's 'great painting.' "[19] As Sembat had told Matisse that he could best serve France by continuing to "paint well," so Juan Gris, like almost every Parisian artist, was no longer painting only for himself or his colleagues. Now all were making art with at least an eye out for such abstract glories as France, civilization, and eternity. The burden of such a new set of ambitions must have been enormous.

The war, with its complex network of alliances, loyalties, requisites, and prohibitions, was putting a terrible strain on personal relationships among Parisian artists, critics, and friends. Toward the end of 1916, Gris wrote to Raynal: "Ever since the war broke out, all the civilians I come into contact with have their minds warped by events. There's not one of them intact; all have broken down under the pressure."[20] Although he did not explain precisely what he meant by this, we can surmise that at least some of the tension was caused by the clash between pre-war and wartime values. There was, for instance, a further unpleasant development of the *Parade* fiasco. The music critic Jean Poueigh, having written a derogatory review of the ballet in the *Carnet de la Semaine*, received a postcard from Erik Satie that contained nothing but the following line:

> Monsieur et cher amie,
> Vous êtes un cul, mais un cul sans musique.
> (You are an asshole, and an unmusical asshole at that.)
> Erik Satie.

The critic sued Satie for defamation of character (the suit hinged on the fact that Satie's note was not in a sealed letter, but was readable by Poueigh's concierge). The composer was arraigned on 15 July 1917 in the Fifth Chamber of the Civil Court where, typically in wartime Paris, the matter soon escalated to an issue of patriotism—Poueigh's lawyer, José Théry, referred to the avant-garde as *boche*. Dunoyer de Segonzac, La Fresnaye, Derain, Braque, Léger, and Apollinaire were all asked to testify—which they did in uniforms and decorations— in Satie's defense. He lost nonetheless, was fined a total of 1100 francs (no more than a token sum), and was condemned to eight days in prison, a sentence which he served.[21]

Even earlier, before *Parade*, things had started to heat up. As Gris told Raynal, at a banquet given in honor of Apollinaire (now the gravely wounded patriot) on New Year's Eve, to celebrate the publication of *Le Poète assassiné*, the participants fell to arguing among themselves. Mme. Aurel, an anti-Cubist but a good friend of Apollinaire, was booed and prevented from delivering her tribute to the poet; the party broke up in chaos.[22] Then there was another incident which again we know of by way of Gris's correspondence with Raynal:

> Haven't you heard about the Reverdy-Rivera incident? During a discussion about painting at Lhote's, Rivera slapped Reverdy's face, so that the latter went for him. I hear that lots of china was broken, and one pane of glass. Metzinger tried to intervene and get them to fight it out in a duel, but that didn't work. I don't know whether we shall see more of such incidents.[23]

Max Jacob gave a slightly fuller version of the story in a letter to the couturier and art collector Jacques Doucet, explaining that a small crowd had gone to Lhote's after a dinner organized at the restaurant Lapérouse by Léonce Rosenberg for the artists in his gallery, with the addition of the poet Pierre Reverdy, "While we became livelier and livelier in the studio," Jacob elaborated,

> Pierre arrogantly raised himself up on the Cubist pedestal: he treated his friends there with such little respect that Monsieur Ribera [sic] felt insulted and slapped him . . . Reverdy yanked Ribera's hair while screaming: the crowd of people there threw themselves on the combatants.[24]

Indeed, by 1918 the incident was already somewhat legendary and had acquired the term "l'affaire Rivera" when André Salmon wrote about it in *L'Europe Nouvelle*.[25] And the fight at Lhote's was not an isolated event, but was symptomatic of the kinds of internecine conflicts that were disrupting the Parisian avant-garde. Just three months after the Reverdy-Rivera squabble, there was another "such incident," dubbed by one critic "the Cubist quarrel,"[26] which began with another theatrical production, this time the première of Apollinaire's play *Les Mamelles de Tirésias*, on 24 June. Presented under the auspices of Birot's *Sic*, with sets and costumes by Serge Férat, it was a farce with a serious and timely theme: the distressingly low French birthrate, and the need to make more children *pour la patrie*. As Apollinaire says in the prologue:

> Ecoutez ô Français la leçon de la guerre
> Et faites des enfants, vous qui n'en faisiez guère.
> (Listen, O Frenchmen, to the lesson of the war
> And make children, you who have hardly made them at all).

This time, though, it was not the bourgeois public which was
up in arms, but members of the Parisian avant-garde. Shortly
after the première, the following letter appeared in the newspaper *Le Pays*:

> [As] Cubist painters and sculptors, we protest against the
> mistaken connection that has tended to be drawn between
> our work and certain literary and theatrical fantasies that
> it is not for us to judge. Those among us who have taken
> part in the events of "Art et Liberté" and *Sic* formally de-
> clare that they [ed. "the events"] have nothing in common
> with their [ed. "our own"] plastic innovations.
>   signed: Metzinger, Juan Gris, Diego Rivera, Lhote,
> Lipchiz, H. Hayden, Severini, Kisling[27]

This curious letter both says very little and says a great deal.
What it does not tell us, or the readers of *Le Pays*, is just what
it is that the authors want to repudiate in "literary and theatrical
fantasies" (such as *Les Mamelles*, one of *Sic*'s events). Yet it is
perfectly clear, despite the fact that the writers consider themselves "Cubists," that there is something unsavory from which
they want to dissociate themselves. Moreover, they have taken
the trouble of making this declaration in the pages of a major
newspaper in language that can best be described as legalis-
tic—"nous protestons," "il ne nous appartient de juger," "déclarent formellement"—all in order to establish a distinction
between terms that do not seem to us as especially freighted
with meaning: "fantasies" and "plastic innovations." However,
the connotations of the word "fantasy" will shortly become apparent, along with the reasons why a group of artists who were
all foreigners (with the exception of Metzinger) might want to
distance themselves from it. One immediate result of the letter
was that Apollinaire was understandably infuriated by it. Writing to Reverdy on 28 June he referred to the group (four of
whom had been at Lhote's studio in March) as "a band of fat-
heads who invaded Cubism,"[28] and chalked their hostility up to
jealousy and the hope of financial gain.

But all of these quarrels and disagreements were fairly minor
in comparison with what I shall refer to as the Poiret Affair,
after *Parade* the greatest *cause célèbre*—with perhaps even
wider-ranging implications—of the wartime avant-garde. Although almost completely forgotten now, the wartime tribula-
tions of Paul Poiret, the most famous couturier of the period,
form the essential background against which many of the avant-
garde's difficulties must be viewed. The Affair began almost ex-

actly one year after the start of war, on 7 August 1915, with the appearance of a short piece in the moderate Left magazine *La Renaissance politique, littéraire, et artistique* entitled "Juste Sévérité." Although unsigned, it was probably penned by the magazine's editor, Henri Lapauze (well known to art historians for his work on Ingres). The entire piece went as follows:

> We have all cried out loudly against the *boche, munichois, berlinois* fashions that were imposed on the French. The Germans have in their newspapers taken it upon themselves to give us stronger reasons for our pre-war indignation toward them, as M. Léon Daudet says.
>
> A cartoon in *Simplicissimus* shows a German cavalryman consoling his wife. "Na," he says to her, "don't cry, Else, I myself shall order you your new dress from Poiret!" From Poiret, you've really read it! What does M. Poiret think of that? Is it perhaps that, despite himself, he had *boche* taste, by which the Germans recognized him even then as one of theirs? After the war, M. Poiret will have to seek pardon from Frenchwomen; he will most certainly need it.[29]

On the basis of a cartoon in Germany's most famous humor magazine, France's *enfant terrible* of the fashion world was found guilty of *boche* sympathies. Not surprisingly, the article's author was quite familiar with Daudet's arguments—he had probably just read *Hors du joug allemand*—for the Royalist critic is credited with the inspiration for the indictment. We recognize, of course, this line of so-called reasoning from the accusations against Cubism, whereby the German attraction to a French work of art testifies not to the work's power to extend French influence abroad, but rather to its weakness and even its subversive quality—i.e. its susceptibility to enemy tastes. Where the German cartoonist intended to mock the German worship, even in the midst of war, of things French, *La Renaissance* chose to see instead the basis for an indictment of a famous but unorthodox French cultural figure.

Unfortunately for the couturier, the story did not end there. Several months later *La Renaissance* renewed the attack with increased vigor, again through the medium of an unsigned article. "La Mode Changera" (Fashion Will Change), published on 16 October 1915, began as follows:

> It [fashion] will no longer allow itself to be influenced by a certain *goût munichois*; everyone tells us so, and even M.

Poiret unceasingly proclaims the necessity of returning to
national traditions. Why not believe in M. Poiret's good
will? He has been subjected to such cruelties that he
would have to lack all feeling to persevere. And M. Poiret
is far from lacking in feeling. He is an intelligent and
suave man. So suave that he went to extremes, certain that
he would be followed by the snobbism of foreigners and by
the emotionally disturbed persons who were made so by
the overheated life of the pre-war period.[30]

Here the author seems to get more to the point: Poiret has been
one of the central figures in Marianne's pre-war delirium of foreign snobs and indigenous neurotics. And this was only the first
half of the article. After summing up the attack on the couturier
with the statement, "As for fashion, then, I think we are all in
agreement, or nearly so," the writer then extended his indictment to other venues:

But . . . for furniture? Shall we still consent to be the vassals of the disgusting taste of Mlle. Martine, of the Ecole
Martine, of the Maison Martine? Shall we still tolerate the
blacks, greens, reds, yellows, and the *b...ochonneries* that
have been imposed on our tables, our consoles, our seats,
etc.? Shall we not burn all this German garbage, influenced by Munich, Dresden, Stuttgart, and promoted by
our art magazines—all or almost all our art magazines?
Burn it, I say, burn all of it—and let's hope that we never
hear of it again.[31]

In fact, this assault on the "disgusting taste" of Mlle. Martine
turns out to be a further attack on Poiret, because the Ecole
Martine and the Maison Martine (named after one of the couturier's daughters) were the decorative-arts subsidiaries of the
House of Poiret.[32] Moreover, the attack on the Parisian arts has
widened to the extent that the French art magazines are also
implicated in the foisting of German-influenced "blacks,
greens, reds, and yellows" on French furniture. The author,
perhaps not surprisingly, rises to the fever pitch characteristic
of all witch-hunts as he exhorts his readers to "burn all of it."
Paul Poiret could hardly allow such attacks to continue without attempting to defend himself. Accordingly, on 6 November
1915 his lawyer filed suit against *La Renaissance* for defamation
of character, asking for 20,000 francs damages. This was the
moment that Henri Lapauze and his cohorts were waiting for. In
the next issue of *La Renaissance*, after publishing the complete

text of the summons, the editors replied (under the title "The Trial of German Influence on French Decorative Arts and French Fashion"):

> M. Poiret's lawsuit delights *La Renaissance*. No more propitious occasion has ever been offered to us to explain what we mean by *boche* art, or, if you prefer, by German influence on the French decorative arts and fashion.
>
> It's time that certain things were said. *La Renaissance* will say them. She will bring before the French magistrates of the Ninth Chamber precise facts and texts. The eloquent and eminently well-qualified voice of M. Léon Bérard will, that day, express the feelings of everyone, and since it has pleased M. Poiret to bring this action he will very quickly realize that, to judge a national cause that concerns all of us, there are judges in Paris.[33]

The magazine's reply to Poiret's suit is chilling, not least because of its expression of delight in receiving the summons. This trial was meant as a warning that any kind of deviant behavior could be mercilessly pursued by the furies of French right thinking.

But before going further we must ask whether there was any basis at all for the accusations against Poiret—was he somehow in connivance with the enemy, on either a political or a cultural level? The answer seems to be No; no evidence was ever produced, and we have none, to show that Poiret was disloyal in any way. In his 1930 autobiography, Poiret makes no direct mention of his trial in the pages of *La Renaissance* (he was probably glad that it was by that time in the distant past), but he does provide at least part of the reason why he was attacked as pro-German. For one thing, he was an outspoken admirer of the German decorative arts before the war, which he considered much more forward-looking than anything then being produced in France. He frankly admitted his close friendship with the Freudenberg brothers of Berlin, directors of the decorative-arts exhibitions in Berlin and Vienna before the war; and he knew all the important figures in Germany and Austria, notably Josef Hoffmann, Bruno Paul, and Hermann Muthesius. After August 1914, of course, these associations were liabilities. And, as if his pre-war ideas were not enough, he happened to have been in Germany on business until the beginning of July 1914, a fact which a month later became the basis for his arrest by the French military authorities (he was eventually cleared of all charges and taken into the army).[34]

But these circumstances only partially explain why Poiret was singled out for abuse. Equally important is the context in which the decorative arts in France, even more crucially than painting or sculpture, had been debated before the war, and it is the phrase *goût munichois*— "Munich taste"—that provides the focus. Specifically, it referred to a major cultural event of the pre-war years: the exhibition of Munich decorators at the 1910 Salon d'Automne. Having impressed a number of important French *décorateurs* at an exhibit in Munich in 1908, the Germans, as a symbol of good will (and out of a very real interest on the part of their French counterparts), were invited to come to Paris two years later. They were given the entire decorative-arts section at the Grand Palais that fall, and what they exhibited was, by French standards, extraordinary. Instead of an eclectic grouping of furniture and *bibelots* mounted helter-skelter, the Munich decorators presented "ensembles"—entire decorated rooms in which every element, from furniture to lighting, wallpaper and window treatment, was created under the supervision of a single designer. Today, of course, this kind of room has become a commonplace of interior-design publicity. But such was not the case before 1910, when, at least in France, the manufacture and diffusion of the decorative arts was rather *ad hoc*.[35]

The impact of the show was enormous, and it was greeted with a mixture of awe at the German accomplishment and criticism of the Bavarian aesthetic. Naturally, the exhibition and the reaction took on a political cast from the very start, with the competition between German and French arts, as well as between German and French cultures in general, at stake. Writing in 1910, Vauxcelles explicitly saw the competition as one between the Latin and Germanic peoples; although he admitted that the Germans were better organized, more attentive to fine craftsmanship, and better trained, he found the ensembles ponderous and unoriginal. He was not without praise, though, for some of what he saw, and he felt that the French decorative-arts schools could take a lesson or two from German pedagogy.[36] Indeed, the critic could hardly have dismissed the show altogether: he himself was on the board of the Salon d'Automne, along with such other notables as André Gide, Gustave Kahn, Charles Morice, Auguste Rodin, and, most interestingly, none other than Henri Lapauze, later to be editor of *La Renaissance* when it was the scourge of every sign of Munich taste in French culture.[37]

By 1915, however, the Germans were no longer just competitors: they were enemies, and the tone of all discussions about French versus German arts was correspondingly escalated. "Do you recall . . . the Salon d'Automne, when we invited the Munich decorators?" asked Vauxcelles in an article in 1915, going on to say of the rooms he had seen at the exhibit:

> How gloomy and funereal were those pavilions and "music rooms"! . . . the orange and light-green vestibule of Herr Karl Jaeger, with Pompeian mosaics; the colossal boudoir of Herr Theodore Veil; the library of Professor Paul-Ludwig Troost (boredom oozed from the walls); the violet bedroom of Herr Adalbert Niemeyer, where the bed was made of lead and the armoire of granite; and the morose barracks, the *salon de "restauration"* designed for you to stuff yourself with Protestant sausages while listening to a little symphony of Mahler—all this horrible German architecture, where armies of "Professoren" in gold-rimmed glasses slug away, makes us appreciate by contrast the exquisite and nuanced taste of our French furniture-makers, great-grand-cousins of the Crescents and the Rieseners. The sense of measure, the harmony, the winged tact are things of ours. One could die of mildew in a *boche* interior.[38]

Another critic, Frédéric Masson, in his wartime article "Munich Arts and Its Apostles," said that the art of Munich represented

> a style in which everything is violent, shocking, burning, in which the tones explode one against another, the crudest and most intense that one could imagine. That's the Munich style. And one sees greens whose acidity turns the stomach, crossed with lilac stripes that accompany a blood-red line; and what yellows! and what pinks! The goal pursued—and attained—is to knock you flat, to hit the retina with a thoroughly Germanic blow of brutality: the *boche* blow![39]

Yet if we look for ourselves at those German ensembles of 1910, such as Karl Jaeger's vestibule (fig. 121) or Emmanuel von Seidel's music room (fig. 122), we may be somewhat surprised that these rooms could ever have provoked such intense dislike. It is true that the rooms were rather heavy in their neoclassical architectonics; there *is* something a bit funereal here. But the critics had led us to expect interiors totally lacking in grace or proportion, fit only, perhaps, for the barbarians that

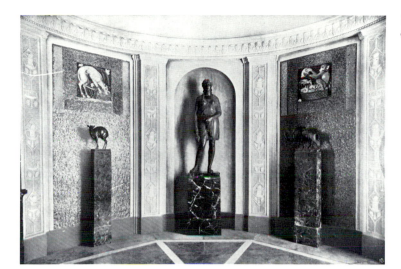

121. K. Jaeger, *Vestibule*, Exhibition of Munich Decorators, Paris, 1910.

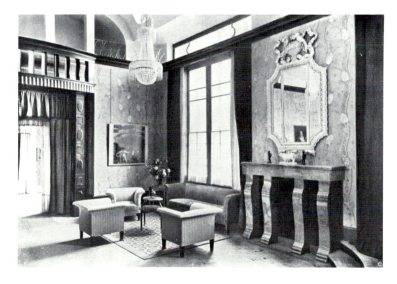

122. E. von Seidel, *Music Room*, Exhibition of Munich Decorators, Paris, 1910.

the French were so fond of depicting in their propaganda; and this is obviously not what we find. Indeed, apart from the few sincere aesthetic criticisms, we should probably conclude that the biggest problem with the Munich interiors of 1910 was that they were—quite simply—too good, that they were successful in a way that the French would have liked to be themselves. Here was a kind of modern classicism, or neo-classicism, that was very convincing.[40]

But beyond issues of taste, of French versus German style, the story of *art munichois* presented larger, more crucial ques-

tions. Although these were only implied before the war, Vauxcelles states them quite explicitly in 1915:

> The problem—a problem that embraces economic, social,
> and national issues—is to know if French taste, French
> style, and French furnishings are going to abase them-
> selves before the products of Munich and Berlin. And that
> alone matters.[41]

The question of French and German economic competition in
the exportation of decorative arts had been central to the *art
munichois* controversy from the very start. As early as the 1900
Exposition Universelle in Paris the French were becoming extremely concerned over foreign, and especially German, invasion of what had hitherto been an exclusively French market. If
the figures are to be believed, the Germans were already overwhelmingly the leading exporters of decorative arts in the world
by 1913.[42] They were dealing a serious blow to the French
economy, which relied heavily on world demand for *le goût
français*. The stature of French taste could be measured in
francs, and it may be for precisely this reason that the issue of
French versus German style could ever have been so hotly debated in the first place. Vauxcelles, preparing the way for the
post-war period, concluded by saying:

> After the war of cannon fire, another war, on the terrain of
> the industries of art, will have to be vigorously pursued.
> And there again we must win.[43]

We can now understand the ideological reverberations of calling
Poiret's art "Germanic" in the wake of the *art munichois* debate.
Of course, the clothes that Poiret designed were not in any visual sense "*munichois*," nor for that matter especially German
in any other way that we can discern. It was really a question
of attitude; what earned Poiret such abuse was his cosmopolitanism, and Lapauze's use of a provocative vocabulary. This is
not to say that the term *munichois* was wholly without a visual
coefficient—albeit unjustified—when used to describe Poiret's
pre-war creations. The decorative arts in Paris before the war
display a further aspect of the contemporary conception of *art
munichois*, one that specifically referred to Poiret but that had,
ironically, nothing whatever to do with Germany, and that was
the term *Orientalisme*.

In fact, the craze for things "Oriental" (i.e. Near Eastern) in
pre-war Paris was not even of Paul Poiret's invention. It was the
Ballets Russes that started all the excitement with *Shéhérazade*

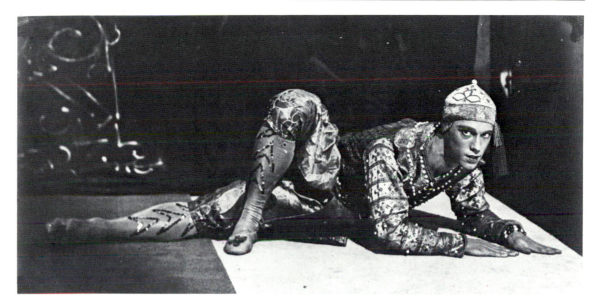

123. Anonymous, Photograph of
Nijinsky as the Golden Slave in
Shéhérazade, 1910.

in 1910. Nijinsky danced the famous role of the Golden Slave
(fig. 123) in this story, in which the ladies of the harem, while
the Sultan is away, participate in an orgy with the court slaves,
only to be massacred upon the potentate's return. *Shéhérazade*
was a great success of the 1910 season at the Paris Opéra (a
season that also featured *The Orientals* and *Firebird*). When
Paul Poiret threw a party on 24 June 1911, he decided to call
it "La 1002ième Nuit"—in honor of Shéhérazade—and asked
all his guests to appear in Oriental costume, with himself and
his wife as the sultan and consort (fig. 124). Soon Poiret was
popularizing the Oriental "look" in women's fashions, featuring
a long tunic that flared at the hem, worn over a straight and
narrower skirt to the ground, as for example in a 1913 creation
called *Sorbet* (fig. 125). These Poiret dresses were the last word
in pre-war Parisian high fashion.

We see how easy it was, then, with just a little bit of distance, to confuse the "Oriental" and the *munichois*: both had
burst onto the Parisian scene at exactly that same moment in
1910—two great aesthetic invasions from beyond French borders. It is no wonder that the architect Adolphe Dervaux, writing in *La Grande Revue* in 1916, could implore his colleagues:

We must turn toward the French tradition! the only one
that, by the intelligent use of our material resources in our
climate, can satisfy the conditions of our temperament. Let

124. Anonymous, Photograph of Paul
and Denise Poiret in costume for
"1002nd Night" party, Paris, 24 June
1911.

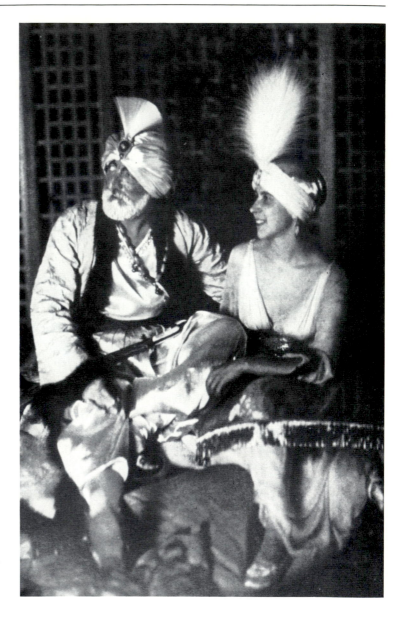

us forget all foreign efforts if they are opposed to these
conditions. Let us follow neither Munich "art," which, as
such, is not wanted, nor any decadent or exotic art.[44]

Later, the critic Jean-Louis Vaudoyer, in his review of the first
Salon d'Automne after the Armistice, warned young decorators
to be on guard against the various manifestations of pre-war
decadence, including the "harem of Shéhérazade, as M. Bakst

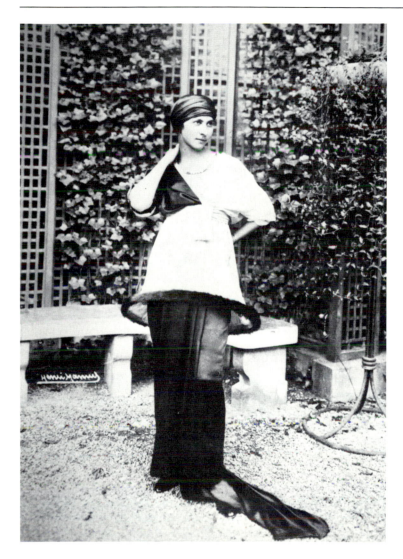

125. P. Poiret, *Sorbet*, 1913.

represented it," and the *goût munichois* as it was exemplified in furniture design.[45]

Furthermore, the facts of the war provided irrefutable evidence—so the patriots said—that the Orient was totally unreliable and even dangerous. Despite her traditional allegiance to England and France, Turkey came into the war on the German side in September 1914 (primarily because of her distrust of Russia). As a result, Orientalism was now not only foreign but pernicious: the well-known fashion illustrator Georges Barbier created an image of "Vieille Turquie" (fig. 126) in 1915, in which a swarthy, turbaned sultan stands in a perfumed garden

126. G. Barbier, "Old Turkey"
("Vieille Turquie"), 1915.

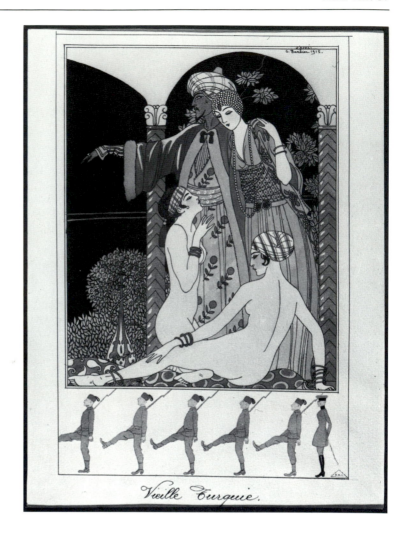

adored by his wife and two naked slave-girls, while below five
Turks march in goose-step precision to the command of a
German officer. Another popular illustrator, Gerda-Wegener
(French, despite a German name),[46] drew a parody of Turkey's
involvement in the war (fig. 127) in which a buffoonish potentate puts his hands to his ears, as sweat drips from his brow and
his concubines collapse together in a heap, as a result of the
fighting in the Dardanelles: "They can hear the cannon in Constantinople," reads the caption. Is it only an accident that the
cowardly sultan, hiding under the pile of silk pillows and
pouffes, bears a striking resemblance to Paul Poiret (compare
the figure with the photograph of the designer, fig. 124)? In fact,
this full-page cartoon appeared in *La Baïonnette* on 15 July

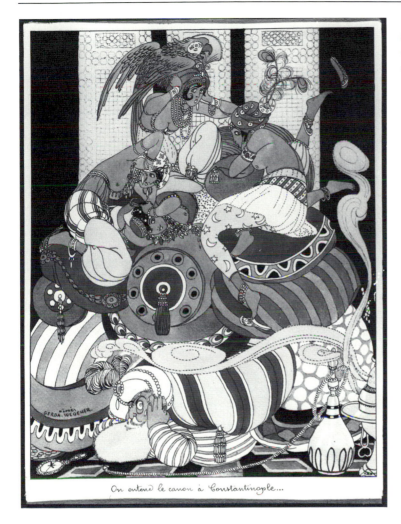

On entend le canon à Constantinople...

127. Gerda-Wegener, "They can hear the cannon in Constantinople" ("On entend le canon à Constantinople . . .") c. 1914–18.

1915, only weeks before Lapauze's first attack on Poiret in *La Renaissance*.

For Royalists and racists like Léon Daudet, the realities of the war's political alliances confirmed what they had thought all along about the German cultural invasion:

> This architecture, painting, engraving, furniture . . . invaded the Parisian scene. After German Hellenism we had German Orientalism, this screeching modernism of the aesthetic, of which the unhappy are so proud. . . . Nonetheless, in these discordant monsters could be discerned the aspirations of German imperialism, her sights trained on Baghdad and elsewhere. The stamp that is put on these theatrical Turkeries retained a political significance.[47]

Not only that: for many Frenchmen, the alliance of Turkey—
i.e. the "Orient"—with the enemy was preordained; France, as
the embodiment of all that was finest in the Occident, had a
sacred mission to preserve the classical West against any Eastern incursions. The nation's cultural spokesmen were quick to
explain how the association of Germany with the East had come
about. The philosopher Emile Boutroux wrote, early in the war,
that the French concept of freedom descended from the Greeks,
while the Germans had inherited an Oriental notion "that
placed man and the world under the absolute control of tran-
scendent powers and ineluctable fates."[48] In 1916 the Abbé
Delfour, a right-wing cleric, wrote in his *La Culture latine* that
the Germans did indeed have a Mediterranean inheritance, but
that it was of the "Greco-Oriental" rather than the Hellenic
strain, and that "Greco-Oriental civilization is, without any possible question, of an inferior quality."[49]

Finally, despite the apparent logic of the wartime conceptualizations (that of Occident vs. Orient, civilization vs. barbarism) and the concrete fact of Turkey's alliance with the enemy,
I think we can ascribe much of the French desire to repudiate
the "Oriental" as an attempt to distance herself from her own
worst fears. The qualities which the French found so appalling
in the so-called Orientals and in Oriental culture in general—
indolence, frivolousness, and an overindulgence in the sensual
and sexual—were, as we are well aware, the same qualities that
the French feared in themselves. Calling those now-threatening
character traits "Oriental" and then proclaiming oneself to be,
in contrast, of the Occident was ideologically efficient: the
French at once disposed of their self-contempt and reinforced
hatred of the enemy. Of course, loyal Frenchmen and resident
foreigners of a perfect patriotism might sometimes be innocent
casualties of the propaganda offensive. If we look again at Lucien Métivet's portrayal of Marianne's pre-war cultural dementia (fig. 12), we notice how freely the satirist mixes foreign and
indigenous elements. We have already noted Cubism's place
atop the delirium, and of course Wagner's place below. Now,
though, we recognize that the high-fashion Marianne at the upper right—dressed, as Métivet says, in "unexpected dresses,
odalisque culottes, sultan's turbans"—is a specific reference to
the "Oriental," *munichois* styles of Paul Poiret (compare Marianne's dress to fig. 125) and that the "Indian" dancing in front
of the teepees at the middle left is not in fact a *peau rouge*, but
a reference to Diaghilev's Ballets Russes (not, in this case, to
one of his orientalizing productions, but specifically to the set,

costumes, and dancing of the 1913 *Rite of Spring*). Cubism, Poiret, Ballets Russes, Wagner, and *art munichois* are now inextricably bound together in an anarchic pre-war cultural maelstrom.

We probably now have more than a clue as to the meanings implicit, though never stated, in the letter which Metzinger, Gris, et al. wrote to the newspaper *Le Pays* after the première of Apollinaire's *Les Mamelles de Tirésias* in June 1917. Remember that they wanted to dissociate themselves from "certain literary and theatrical fantasies," and to distinguish these from their own "plastic innovations." It may well be that our artists were thinking long and hard about the woes that had befallen Paul Poiret, for the word "fantasy" appears a number of times in discussions of Poiret, and the meaning of the word is almost always negative after the start of war. Vauxcelles denigrated pre-war fashions as "sartorial fantasies, pheasant-like, Batignolle-Persian,"[50] and the fashion critic Jeanne Ramon Fernandez, in the *Gazette des Beaux-Arts*, linked fantasy with anarchy in her overview of French styles. "It would have been difficult, the year before the war," she wrote,

> to undertake a serious critique of fashion, because the absence of a governing principle in the creations of the couturiers foredoomed all analysis to failure. The most radical anarchy reigned then; it was all individual and momentary fantasy, fantasy guided by the concern for realizing original and surprising fashions, and encouraged by women's surrender of their will into the hands of the couturier.[51]

As it was for Vauxcelles and Fernandez, the word "fantasy" was almost surely a negative one for the signers of the letter to *Le Pays*, conveying far more than fairy-tales or light-heartedness, something closer to dementia and anarchy. Especially in the immediate wake of the *Parade* scandal, it was probably best to make sure that the public did not confuse the seriousness of "plastic innovation" with the ill-conceived fantasies presented to the French public under the auspices of *Sic* and the "Art et Liberté" group. Indeed, the invocation of the latter organization brings us to the conclusion of the Poiret Affair.

Needless to say, by the time that Poiret served the magazine with a summons for slander, the damage to his reputation was already immense; little could be worse than a public accusation of treason in the midst of war. Yet he did achieve a victory over Lapauze and *La Renaissance*, pyrrhic though it may have been. The magazine agreed to drop the matter and apologize in print if Poiret would agree not to sue. As part of the settlement reached, *La Renaissance*, on 15 September 1917, published all the letters that both parties had received in support of their respective positions.[52]

Interestingly, few supporters of the magazine's campaign against Germanic taste actually mentioned Poiret by name, although one respondent did say that "The Martine style comes directly from Munich in its stiffness of forms, and from Polynesia in its barbarian violence of color."[53] Most of the support for *La Renaissance* took the form of a general attack on things German. Eugène Delard, curator of the Musée Galliéra, wrote: "German influence. . . . alas! dear friend, it was undeniable, detestable . . .";[54] M. R. Falcou, Director of Fine Arts and Museums of the City of Paris, seconded the opinion: "The German influence on architecture and decorative art was incontestable in the ten years that preceded the war."[55] Georges Cain, curator at the Musée Carnavalet, said to Lapauze, "My answer is simple and can be summed up in four words, 'You are absolutely right' ";[56] Arsène Alexandre, critic and Inspector General of the Museums, wrote that it was obvious that "the Germans and their agents or dupes" wanted to destroy all that was best in French art—"this alliance of simplicity, clarity, and the sense of proportion"—and that "the wound was deep";[57] and Léonce Bénédite, curator at the Musée du Luxembourg, said, "I can only associate myself with those who band together to combat all that remains of influence from beyond the Rhine on our arts," and expressed the hope that after the war French artists would again adhere to "our venerable traditions of taste, that is to say of proportion and tact."[58]

Not surprisingly, the letters of support for Poiret written during the two years since the accusations had first started to appear in *La Renaissance* were mostly from artists, rather than from functionaries in the Parisian art establishment. André Derain wrote, evidently with a great deal of feeling: "I know that you have been mistreated lately, and while in principle I think that one must endure such things with complete indifference, I understand that it is bitter at this moment to be insulted in such a fashion."[59] Raoul Dufy, a close friend and collaborator of Poiret, wrote an indignant note: "I understand that you are accused of defending *boche* art! . . . You, whose character is so French, so Parisian, who rightly had such a success in France and in the entire world, to be the object of M. Lapauze's accusation! It's stupefying!"[60] And from Max Jacob came: "My dear friend, I was more indignant than surprised by the attacks

of which you have been the object since the outbreak of the war
and before it. Not surprised, because men of your value have
always been victims; but indignant, because the injustice is
much too shocking."[61]

The painter Fauconnet did not mention the decorative arts in
his letter in support of the couturier, but instead made reference
to the accusations against Cubism:

> One can be a good patriot and know nothing about chem-
> istry. Everyone agrees on that. But some good patriots
> will, relying on their emotions, declare out of ignorance
> that Cubism is German. It has already happened. The
> truth is that they know nothing about painting. Cubism was
> founded, if one may so speak, by Picasso and Braque, one
> a Spaniard and the other a Frenchman. It's in France that
> it developed, and it's a Latin product.[62]

Two letters were especially enlightened, and enlightening.
One was from Jacques-Emile Blanche, the conservative society
portraitist, who was an intimate of Poiret and the Ballets Russes
circle. He decided to set matters straight on the Poiret Affair:

> Since this is a question of fashion, and since the name of
> M. Poiret has been pronounced, it remains to say that it
> seems to me that, with his audacity and the Oriental taste
> of his productions, M. Poiret has exerted a potent and most
> beneficial influence on fashion. I see nothing German at
> all in that . . . The furniture, the knick-knacks, the toys
> called *munichois* date from the Ballets Russes. The only
> authentic novelty, in the combination of lines and decora-
> tive colors, came to us from the Russian spirit. The name
> of Léon Bakst . . . can be read, if one will take the trou-
> ble, on many labels from which people have wanted to
> erase it.[63]

Of course by the following winter, when the Russians signed
their peace treaty with the Germans, even this simple truth
could not have been enunciated safely. But André Dunoyer de
Segonzac, the author of the other informative and perceptive
letter of support for Poiret, went beyond the particulars of the
attacks. He said of Lapauze and his slander:

> So that's the "Sacred Union." It is the revenge of the
> "Critic" and the "Functionaries of Art" against all those
> who had had the courage to affirm themselves in creating
> something. . . . To call you *boche*, it's truly too stupid!

You, who had all the independence of spirit, fantasy, and
candor of the child of Paris that you are! . . . If one does
not dare to speculate on the French mentality after the
war, one can at least formulate some hopes. All those who
love the country and understand her real interests will
hope to see her abandon her spirit of routine which frustrated living forces and paralyzed any initiative. In many
ways, Revolutionary France has become more conservative
than Medieval Germany. The examples are unfortunately
too numerous.[64]

The painter could not have read more accurately the cultural
program of the *Union Sacrée*, based as it was on a combination
of *revanche* and *ressentiment*.

Of course, what many artists understood was that the Poiret
Affair was only the tip of the iceberg—what was said of fashion
and the decorative arts was also being said of painting and
sculpture; what had happened to Poiret might happen to them
as well. One of the positive results of the scandal, in fact, was
a reinvigorated sense of group solidarity, which took concrete
form in the establishment of "Art et Liberté," an association of
artists for the defense of artistic freedom, as well as an exhibiting and organizing society that was quite active during 1917–
18.[65] Its manifesto was published as part of the pro-Poiret dossier in *La Renaissance*:

the undersigned protest publicly against the discord that
some are attempting to sow in the midst of war, in hostility
to artists of value, who are perfectly French and are participating in the essential glorification of the nation.

They [the signatories] have found that when these criticisms, insinuations, and attacks do not verge on impudent
accusations of immorality, they manifest themselves under
the form that is currently more injurious than all others,
that of stigmatizing all new effort as "*boche* work."[66]

Among those who signed were Igor Stravinsky, Henri Lebasque, Jean Poueigh (the critic who had sued Satie after *Parade!*), Henri Matisse, Gino Severini, Pierre-Albert Birot, Kees
Van Dongen, Jean Metzinger, Moise Kisling, Georges Rouault,
Albert Marquet, Constantin Brancusi, Luc-Albert Moreau,
André Lhote, and Auguste Herbin, among others. Mme. Aurel,
although she was willing to support Poiret against accusations
of Germanism, had this to say: "I sign this for all artistic renewal, except for cubes, not liking geometry, and I forbid my

name to be used without this disclaimer preceding."[67] Even Louis Vauxcelles agreed that Poiret was not *boche*, although he reserved the right to dislike his decorative forays.[68] Jean Cocteau, on the other hand, said that he could not sign with "Art et Liberté" owing to certain (unnamed) nuances in their protest with which he was not in accord.[69]

But, in spite of "Art et Liberté" and whatever other benefits one might attribute to Lapauze's attack on Poiret, the cost had been high. Hereafter, no matter how much an individual or group might believe itself to be above the battle, it was not so; a kind of bohemia, thinking (correctly or not) that it was essentially free from scrutiny, ceased to exist. Segonzac knew this when he forebodingly remarked that "one does not dare speculate on the French mentality after the war." It was one thing to defend a fellow artist and to express righteous indignation at an unjustified slander; it was something else to attempt to return to cosmopolitan values in the face of the wartime campaigns. Whether one liked it or not, the cultural biases of the Sacred Union were now and for the foreseeable future a fact of French life. We might even say that the resolutely optimistic tone—the call to order, proportion, organization, and moral purity—of the *Union Sacrée* became a national style. A rather unhysterical assessment of French painting, which without really attacking pre-war art affirmed the new values, was offered by Bissière in the same article, "Le Revéil des Cubistes," with which we began this chapter. After his statement of Cubism's demise as a *fait accompli*, he said:

> . . . it is realizations that we need now. The French school during the last ten years has amassed all sorts of material, attempted experiments of all sorts and often hazardous ones. It is about time to bring order out of this chaos and to build. We are sorry that among these audacious and often admirably talented experimenters we have yet to meet the constructors whom our generation is calling for with such yearning and who, not being content merely to collect beautiful stones, will know how to put them together to raise up a vast and solid house.[70]

Bissière's central image of building provides a key to many of the themes and styles of post-war French art. For architecture, both in terms of the physical reconstruction of France and as a more widely applied "constructive" metaphor, was in the process of becoming, along with *la France classique*, a crucial aspect of all Parisian artistic discourse.

V   *Fluctuat nec mergitur*

IF THE IDEOLOGICAL PROGRAM of French wartime propaganda was fashioned mostly from half-truths, misconceptions, stereotypes, and, when necessary, outright lies, the destruction of the homeland at the hands of the invader was a visible fact. It was convenient and even amusing to invent a "Fritz" and "Gretchen" who blithely took a ruin of Antiquity for a recent German accomplishment. But this was no more than a trope for the total devastation of towns like Arras (fig. 128), a way of salvaging something from the smoldering ruins. To be sure, this was one of the central roles of wartime cultural propaganda: the transformation of harsh and potentially demoralizing reality into usable, belligerent, moral indignation. When Ozenfant exhorted his countrymen, in *L'Elan*, to "draw the curtain" on their wounded and dying brothers, he was prescribing a method of survival. The course of war is too fast and inexorable for reflection or protracted grief. Like all invaded peoples, the French had to come to terms with the realities of their situation and to respond instantaneously.

By the time the war came to an end in 1918, the extent of

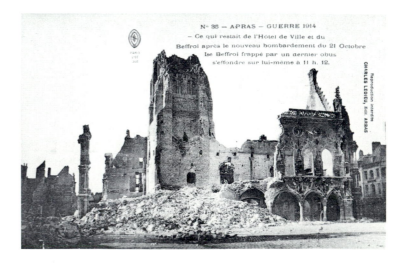

128. Arras, 1914. Postcard.

the devastation was enormous: of the 3,524 cities, towns, and villages that had been occupied by the enemy and the 805 localities unoccupied but evacuated by the French, 1,039 were completely destroyed, 1,235 were more than 50 percent damaged, and most of the others were more or less damaged. Some 293,039 homes were destroyed and another 435,961 nearly destroyed; 6,147 public buildings, including churches, schools, and town halls, were destroyed, and over 10,000 others were seriously damaged. France had to remake 52,734 kilometers of roads and nearly 5,000 kilometers of railway track, and 3,220 bridges, culverts, and other structures had to be restored; 1,036 kilometers of canals and navigable streams had to be either dredged or cleared of obstruction. Not only was Arras reduced to rubble, but so were Senlis, much of Reims, Verdun, Ypres, Lens, and Soissons, to name only the most famous of the "wounded" cities.[1]

This was apart from the greatest loss, that of life itself: approximately 1,356,000 Frenchmen were dead, and a horrifying four and a quarter million were wounded. While many artists took up the theme of the bravely impaired, as in Maurice Rétif's contemporary updating of Brueghel's *Blind Leading the Blind*, his *Gassed Men* (fig. 129) of 1918, the average Frenchman had no choice but to see it with his own eyes. The committee of the *Mutilés de Guerre* came to Versailles on 28 June 1919 for the peace conference, as lobbyists for the cause of the wounded. Their presence (fig. 130) had such an impact on the gathered statesmen—an impact which could not have been produced by any collection of statistics—that orders were given for the war wounded to receive the seating priority—even before pregnant women—which they still enjoy on all French public transport.

Faced with unprecedented physical destruction, France devised a program of reconstruction that was equally without precedent, and did so with extraordinary speed. As William Mac-Donald, an American observer sent to France after the war, put it: "The beginning of reconstruction is almost identical with the beginning of war. . . . within a few weeks the first steps had been taken looking to the relief of the departments which had been invaded . . . There is no 'period of reconstruction' separate and distinct from the period of war, but war and reconstruction went on together so long as the war continued."[2] The nation did not have the luxury of waiting until some imagined peace was regained in order to rebuild roads, railways, homes, and churches—life had to be rehabilitated even while it was still being destroyed. Nowhere was this need for immediate recon-

129. M. Rétif, *Gassed Men* (*Les Gazés*), 1918.

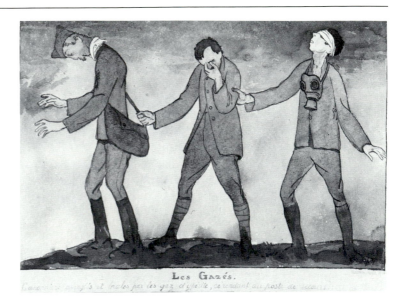

Les Gazés.

struction more pressing than in regard to human life: the tragic
reality of the war-mutilated led, for instance, to important ad-
vances in the technology of plastic surgery. In an article of
1917, "The Art of Restoring Faces," the writer observed that
"the war, with all its mutilations and deformations, has favored
the development of what one might call aesthetic surgery . . .
Nothing has become more common than a glass eye neatly
placed or . . . a hideous scar cleverly masked."[3] In other
words, if the reconstruction program as such did not begin until
after November 1918, the rebuilding and repairing of the seri-

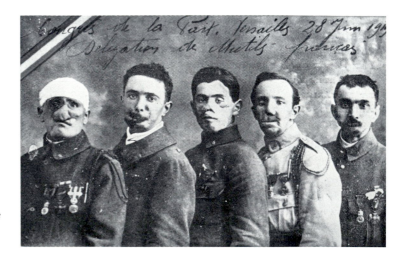

130. Delegation of French *Mutilés de
Guerre*, Congress of the Versailles
Treaty, 28 June 1919. Postcard.

ously wounded nation was in progress for well over a decade, from August 1914 until Armistice Day 1927, when André Tardieu, Minister of Public Works, officially declared that reconstruction was completed.

In his article "The Beautiful, the True, and the Reorganization of the City," published in *La Grande Revue* in April 1916 (in the midst of the Battle of Verdun), the architect Adolphe Dervaux reminded his fellow Frenchmen that they could not push architectural issues aside as irrelevant to the task at hand. His argument was almost identical to the one Charles Morice used to justify wartime intellectual pursuits. "There is the war!" Dervaux said,

> All efforts, all thoughts are shaped by the terrible concern of the moment: THE WAR! Nonetheless, and because of this catastrophe, it is of the utmost urgency that we be concerned with architecture—at the same time as cannon, munitions, and the resumption of business. The question posed since August 1914 is how cities and villages damaged or destroyed by the bombs and fires will be re-established.[4]

By the second year of war, "La Renaissance des Cités" was founded, an unpaid advisory society of architects, artists, engineers, bankers, lawyers, and others, who helped compile reports on reconstruction issues. In 1916, the Association Générale des Hygiénistes et Téchniciens Municipaux, an umbrella group of urbanists, organized a major exhibition that opened just a month after Dervaux's article appeared. The "Exposition de la Cité Reconstituée," which was on view from 25 May to 15 August at the Jeu de Paume in the Tuileries Garden, was perhaps the most important public event for French architecture during the war. Raymond Poincaré, President of the Republic, cut the ribbon on opening day, a commemorative medal was struck, and the fraternity of French architects and city planners was given a prominent place in which to demonstrate their importance to the war effort.

New construction, of course, all but came to a standstill during the war except, as the exhibition's title indicated, when it was a matter of "reconstituting" essential venues. But although architectural commissions were, for all intents and purposes, nonexistent after August 1914, the war did nonetheless help to reaffirm the profession's prestige by providing an expanded conception of its social mission. Dervaux, for one, claimed a vast territory for architecture:

Now, to recreate or reconstruct a city is assuredly a question of national economy, but it's also one of architecture.
To provide sanitation for a densely populated region, to
join the banks of a river by a bridge, that's architecture.
To plan effectively for the needs of a whole community, to
study the social customs and the needs of the inhabitants
to facilitate their work, their education, their leisure—that
is, to practice individual or collective psychology—is still
architecture.[5]

Obviously, this is special pleading—the image of the architect
as analyst and social psychologist seems rather far-fetched. Yet
such was the metaphorical power of the imagery of architecture
and construction that one author, Béard d'Aunet, chose for a
book that had nothing whatever to do with architecture the title
Pour remettre de l'ordre dans la maison (To Restore Order in the
House), intended as a shorthand for social reconstruction.
André Beaunier, in his *Les Idées et les hommes* of 1915, described the "new spirit" engendered by the war in the vocabulary of reconstruction: "the French soul remade and France re-
built: these two phenomena united in a single epiphany."[6]

The social relevance of architecture and construction for wartime and post-war France is evident. But there was yet another
reason why discussions of architecture and construction moved
to the forefront of much of artistic debate after August 1914—
because of all the visual arts, in terms of both creation and
reception, architecture was the most collective endeavor. Despite the fact that neither during the war nor afterward would
architecture become the most widely *practiced* of the arts—in
any real sense of quantitative activity, painting and sculpture
would continue to far outpace architecture—the collective art
of designing and building gradually became the rhetorical
touchstone to which the more individualistic arts had now, at
least in the critical debate, to pay homage.

The issue of collectivity was not a minor concern for the
French who, with their highly touted love of independence, had
nonetheless to exert a collective national effort. Just like their
real or imagined pre-war decadence, the patriotic spokesmen
had to come to terms with a real or imagined French sense of
individualism. "Malevolent critics could say that France oscil-
lated between despotism and anarchy," wrote Boutroux,

And it is fashionable, especially beyond the Rhine, to say
that the French are committed to an ungovernable individualism. The individual in France, according to this opin-

ion, considers himself literally sovereign. He would find the only rule governing his conduct in the satisfying of his own wishes, his desires, his whims.

But this stereotype, he goes on to say, is unfounded:

> If the present war has particularly reminded the French of the duty to subordinate the individual will to a higher law, it has, by this call, simply stimulated the harmonious development of all their natural predilections. . . . It is in keeping with the Frenchman's innermost nature to reconcile individual value with submission to the law of duty.[7]

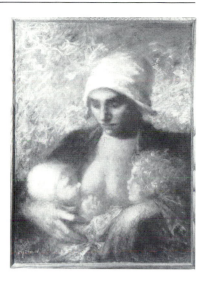

131. L. Lévy-Dhurmer, *Motherhood (Maternité)*, c. 1914–18.

Of course, as with every assertion regarding the French character during the Great War, self-definition was modified not only by how the French had previously thought of themselves but also by how they had defined the enemy. Where the issue was the reconciliation of the individual and the group, the French were hampered to a certain extent by the fact that they had repeatedly described the Germans as a race of mindless vassals, a culture in which devotion to the Emperor and the nation was the *sine qua non*. If France was going to proclaim that she too possessed the social cohesion necessary to wage and win a war, then a distinction had to be drawn between German and French ideas of collectivity. One writer, for instance, said that "without desiring to see the Latin race transformed into disciplined automatons" like the Germans, he nonetheless hoped that the French would put strict controls on their behavior and work as an efficient collective unit. As a model for this kind of duty to the community, he proposed a "Latin" paradigm for self-control and abnegation—the monastery.[8]

Needless to say, the cloistered orders were hardly a suitable model of collective behavior for the nation at large. For one thing, the production of children was essential to the future of France: the already very low French birthrate could only suffer as a result of the absence of men at home.[9] Consequently, we find a vast wartime iconography of family and fecundity. The former Symbolist Lévy-Dhurmer produced several patriotic mother-and-child images during the war, including a pastel (fig. 131) in which two children cling to the full breasts of a nurturing Marianne-like mother. In Le Vieil's maquette for a War Loan poster published in the *Bulletin des Armées de la République* on 21 November 1917 (fig. 132), human reproduction is shown as one sphere in the four-part collective endeavor of the *Union Sacrée*: "Fight, Give Birth, Farm, Contribute." But to ex-

132. C. Le Vieil, *For the War Loan,*
the Sacred Union (*Pour l'emprunt,*
Union Sacrée), 1917.

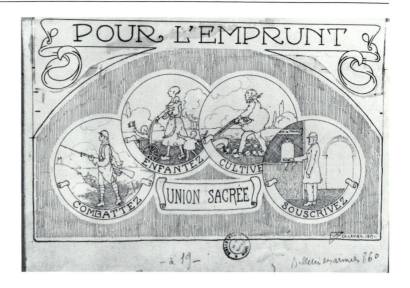

toll the family also meant that the familial tragedies which
would befall so many had to be justified in terms of the national
cause. Cocteau's friend Benito, borrowing a motif from the late
eighteenth century, executed a "call to arms," a kind of secular
Holy Family (fig. 133) in which a noble French soldier bids his
wife and infant child a fond *adieu*. The well-known illustrator
Léandre drew another family scene, entitled *The Soil of France*
(fig. 134), in which a soldier-farmer is leaving for the front: his
wife takes the reins of their workhorse; he embraces his baby
daughter one last time; and his son, filled with the same patriotic ardor as Rude's volunteers on the Arc de Triomphe, steps
forward to assume the man's role during his father's impending
absence. According to the fervent nationalist Maurice Barrès,
it was only the "easy and cosmopolitan pleasures of Paris" that
blinded foreigners to this true France, the France of hearth and
home—now the world was becoming aware of "the underlying
force present at every French fireside."[10]

But along with building up the social unit of the family—
which was both essential in and of itself and crucial as a model
for a unified nation—the collective endeavor had to be reinforced on many other fronts. Apart from making children, Le
Vieil depicted fighting, farming, and subscribing to war loans
as social obligations. Arnoux, in his portfolio of five wartime
images rendered in *image d'Epinal* style, *The Good Frenchman*,
included not only him who "cultivates the soil," him who "fights
for his country," and him who "contributes to the War Loan,"
but even him who "assures the resumption of business"—the

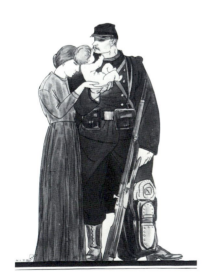

133. E. Benito, *The Farewells*, c.
1914–18.

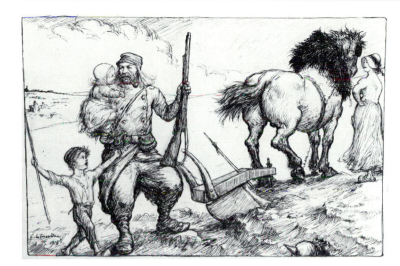

134. C. Léandre, *The Soil of France*
(*La Terre de France*), 1917.

businessman (fig. 135). In a felicitous reworking of Marx (who had himself reworked Louis Blanc), Boutroux spoke of France's wartime need for collective action in this way:

> All devote themselves to the common task, each according to the place that he occupies or to which he is assigned . . . it is essential that the French persuade themselves thoroughly of the role of organization in the accomplishment of human tasks . . . to take one's place in the world is to practice, on the largest possible scale, the most advanced methods of organization.[11]

But again, as we are well aware, it was not enough in wartime France to merely instruct the population in its obligations—it was also expedient to raise even mundane tasks to the level of mythic labors. An anonymous artist whom we know only by the initials H.M.R. portrayed the female French munitions worker (fig. 136) with classical proportions and Olympian calm. However it was to be accomplished, France had to act as a unit, and this is what Gabriel Boissy meant when he wrote to *Sic*, in 1916, that "the war's violent necessities re-establish the sapped hierarchy"—to wit, that the urgency of the war necessitated a return to older class relations, where prerogatives and obligations were fixed and "reliable."

So well organized did the French attempt to become in their collective endeavor that even *la cuisine française* was not exempt from the wartime attentions of efficiency experts and other authorities. Baudry de Saugnier published a *Nutritional Re-*

135. G. Arnoux, "The Good
Frenchman contributes to the War
Loan" (Le Bon Français souscrit à
l'Emprunt) from *Le Bon Français*, c.
1914–18.

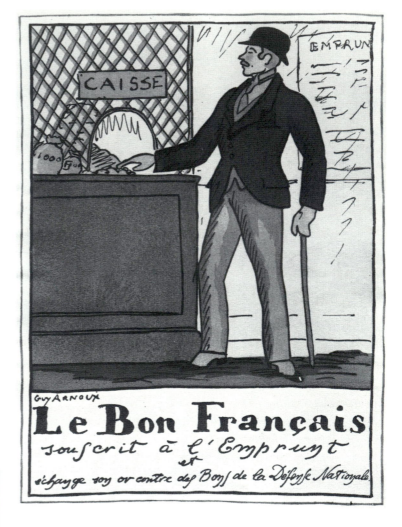

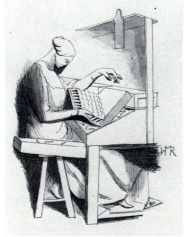

136. H.M.R., Images from *French
Women at Work for the Nation*,
c. 1914–18.

minder, with a chart of the principal leftovers and their caloric
value; and, in order to make his point more clearly, he renamed
the kitchen the "alimentary laboratory." Two researchers, La-
pique and Richet, created a "Scientific Society for Nutritional
Science and the Rational Nourishment of Man." On 24 June
1916 the newspaper *Le Matin* arranged a "lunch of delicious
garbage" (*déjeuner de la poubelle délicieuse*), to which celebri-
ties from all walks of French life were invited, in order to demonstrate to the already very frugal French how they could become even more creative in their use of leftovers. Victory
Gardens also sprang up all over Paris—string beans and carrots
were cultivated in the Luxembourg Garden; the Bibliothèque
Nationale was said to grow the best cabbage in town. Perhaps

even more surprising than the wartime bureaucratization of food was the attempt at a French national regime of fashion. On 5 August 1917 a "National Shoe" was introduced in the hope that the ever-stylish French might forsake their sartorial preoccupations for the national cause and all agree to purchase the same dowdy brown oxford. A wartime Frenchwoman in a pair of "National Shoes" was featured on the cover of the 27 December 1917 issue of *La Baïonnette* (fig. 137): wearing a dull gray shift, she stands encircled by centuries of her forebears, all in extravagantly fashionable outfits, and the realization of her debasement brings tears to her eyes. Not surprisingly, the national shoe was unsuccessful, and thus the "National Fabric," then in the planning stages, was never to see the light of day.[12]

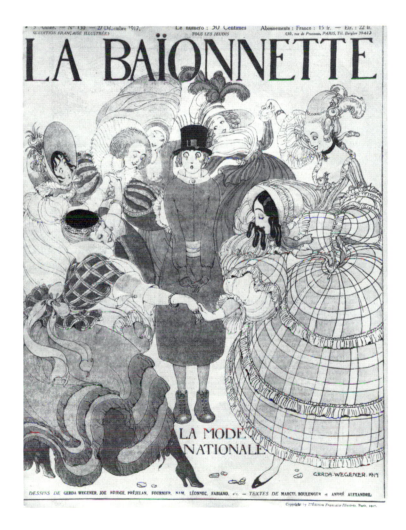

137. Gerda-Wegener, "La Mode Nationale." Cover of *La Baïonnette* (27 December 1917).

Of course, the greatest fear—should the nation fail in its collective endeavor—was of revolution, a possibility that loomed ominously in the light of 1870–71; in the minds of most Frenchmen, for better or worse, the Franco-Prussian humiliation and the Commune were inextricably linked. As has already been noted, still more timely was the example of France's erstwhile Russian ally, which underwent not only the most radical revolution in history in the very midst of *la Grande Guerre*, but which then signed an independent peace treaty with the enemy at Brest-Litovsk. Thus, for the French, by 1917, the waging of war and the staving-off of revolution went hand in hand. Yet this presented a special problem for France, which was emotionally and ideologically bound to its own Revolution of 1789 and its principles of freedom—indeed, the nation constantly stressed the difference between the clear light of modern French liberty and the darkness of Germany's medievalistic obedience to its rulers. How could France reconcile the current need for hierarchy and social control with the values of 1789? Or, conversely, how could the nation decry revolution without seeming to repudiate its own revolutionary past?

In fact, the task seems to have defeated even France's best theoreticians, for we find little discussion of the Revolution in wartime literature—the Left, as we have said, maintained an extremely low profile during the war, and the Right would not have cared to invoke 1789 in any case except, as we shall shortly see, to bemoan its outcome. But the Revolution nonetheless could not be ignored, because the nationalist energies which could be elicited by the single greatest moment in modern French history were too valuable to the current effort to go unexploited. What was needed was the stimulation of collective solidarity without the unleashing of collectivism. The most that the French could do was, as we have already seen, to suggest by way of revolutionary and popular symbols—Marianne, the Phrygian bonnet, the *image d'Epinal*—that the old feelings could come to the aid of the new effort. Typically, the revolutionary *faïence populaire* of the 1790s was revived during the Great War, but in place of slogans like "Death to Tyrants" and "Long Live Liberty without License" these ceramics now carried, as on the little cup in Picasso's *Vive la France* still-life of 1914, simple expressions of patriotism (fig. 138).

On the other hand, any number of spokesmen from the Right were now presented with an ideal opportunity to launch a repudiation of the Revolution and its values—the Enlightenment and Jean-Jacques Rousseau were usually blamed for having

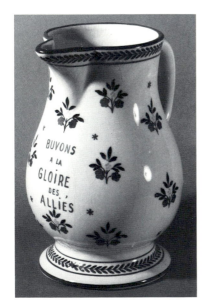

138. Anonymous, Patriotic *faïence*, c. 1914–19.

started all the trouble, especially as it pertained to the issue of
the individual and the collectivity. "Kant, of course, did not
point the cannons that have ruined the Cathedral of Reims, any
more than Jean-Jacques Rousseau set the guillotine in motion,"
wrote the Theosophist Sar Péladan, "but they molded the minds
of the bombardiers and the *sans-culottes.*"[13] Boutroux believed
it was important to distinguish between a healthy freedom and
too much freedom: "French thought does not ratify the exaggerated assertion of Rousseau," he wrote, "which attributes an 'absolute and naturally independent existence' to the individual."[14]
The Royalist Daudet went even further: "Rousseau himself is a
direct derivation from Martin Luther and . . . his impassioned
introspection is the unquestionably legitimate offspring of the
'libre examen' . . . One knows where this path has led and will
always lead: to *individualism.*"[15]

As we have seen before, artists and critics of almost every
persuasion in wartime Paris were soon in the embrace of prevailing social doctrines, not the least of which was the denigration of "individualistic" pursuits in favor of collective action.
Mme. Aurel, as part of her wide-ranging attack on avant-garde
painting, accused Derain, Picasso, and Braque of having
caused "a divorce between themselves and the wider public,"
by which she meant that the avant-garde, and especially the
Cubists, were guilty of elitism—a particular subspecies of individualism—and of a disdain for the public at large which
could not comprehend the avant-garde artist's abstruse artistic
methods;[16] and Mauclair stated flatly that individualism had
proved inadequate, that what was needed now was a real doctrine of the French school.[17] In the preface to a book on post-
war architecture and decorative arts, published in 1915, Maurice Denis asked: "What are we waiting for, in order that a great
epoch may be possible in France?" And he answered his own
question thus:

> Oh, above all, [for] victory! And then [for] a return to good
> sense. Revolutionary prejudices, the excesses of individ-
> ualism, the love of paradox, the fetishism of the unex-
> pected and the original—all the blemishes on our art are
> also the blemishes on French society.[18]

Denis, though, was not a wartime convert to the new enthusiasm
for collectivity and aversion to revolutionary aesthetics. A devout Catholic, the painter had been a firmly entrenched member
of the right-wing intelligentsia before the war. In fact, by 1912
he was a member of the editorial board of the virulently pa-

triotic (and anti-Semitic) magazine *L'Indépendance*, a board that included also Georges Sorel, Vincent d'Indy, Maurice Barrès, and Paul Bourget.[19]

Far more sweeping in his indictment of the avant-garde and in his remedies for an ailing French culture was André Michel, art historian and curator at the Louvre. In a major article that appeared in the *Revue Hebdomadaire* of 1917, entitled "L'Art français après la Guerre," Michel was especially concerned about this issue of individual and collective roles in the artistic process. In answer to those artists and critics who were forever extolling the virtues of individual genius and originality, he wrote:

> With a light heart I brave the disdain of these great men by recalling as a truth the evidence that in the greatest creative epochs the artist was at once the servant and the spokesman of the community; he had the responsibility to express not his sacrosanct personality, his ineffable independence, his esoteric originality, but the communal beliefs on which the *cité* was founded and around which its life was organized. And he found that instead of separating himself from this dependence, the visual power of the artist found there, if I may put it this way, a support, a reinforcement, and a surer and more effective inspiration.

Michel chose to see in the past a Golden Age when the individual and the community were harmoniously bound together, a time when everything that the artist said was meaningful to all of his compatriots. And lest we think that Michel is talking only about the past, or alluding to the present only indirectly, he brings his discussion right to contemporary issues:

> One could go further and, by uniting the excesses of individualism and the abuse of reason, sketch out a theory of Cubism. True, there is nothing that is completely absurd, as the indulgent Renan said; but we have reached a time when it is well to realize that not all sophisms are equally inoffensive. And it is here that, for the health, the future, the flowering of French art, I permit myself to appeal to all those responsible for our art, before the eyes of France and of the world. . . . The need, one might say the fervent need for a return to style, to composition, which makes itself felt even at the very headquarters of today's anarchy, is not, I have reason to believe, a new mystification; it is one of our firmest reasons to count on tomorrow. It is here,

in this need, that artists, even those that are most individualistic in the dangerous sense of the word, will understand the necessity of laws, the benefit of subordination; it
is here that the truly strong individualists will steel themselves and will triumph.[20]

If avant-garde art in general, and Cubism in particular, was
now also subject to the accusation of being too individualistic—
and, in this sense, unpatriotic in its failure of collectivity—it
was from within the avant-garde as well that the accusations
came. After seeing an exhibition of recent art at Mme. Bongard's gallery in 1916, which included works by Marie Laurencin, Raoul Dufy, Othon Friesz, Luc-Albert Moreau, Henri Matisse, and Roger de la Fresnaye, Bissière said that he found the
show regrettable from a number of points of view, not least because artists of this group, "seeming to consider singularity as
an end and not a means, linger over their experiments with a
slightly unhealthy relish and an excessive complacency. Each
one . . . delights in the contemplation of his little find."[21]
André Lhote, we may recall, in the article "Totalisme" which
he published in *L'Elan* in 1916, had said that the pre-war Parisian artists were infected with "the disease of one-upman-
ship," a product of "the obsession with 'personality at all
costs' "—i.e. the malady of individualism. Most important,
though, major artists were thinking in these terms as well.
Léger's most famous statement as to the influence of the war on
his art—"I was dazzled by the breech of a 75mm gun, open and
with the sun shining on it, a magic spell of light on white metal
. . ."—is, in fact, the culmination of a reminiscence in which
he discussed the transformation which the war wrought in his
social milieu:

> I left Paris completely immersed in an abstract method, a
> period of pictorial liberation. Without any transition I
> found myself on a level with the whole of the French peo-
> ple; once I was in the Engineers, my new friends were
> miners, navvies, workers in wood and metal. There I dis-
> covered the French nation.[22]

Léger here confirms the accusation of a divorce between artist
and public which Aurel, Mauclair, Michel, and others had lev-
eled at the Parisian avant-garde, although we do not sense that
he regrets his period of immersion in abstraction or condemns
its effects. The war, though, changed all this for him—it is
nothing less than "the whole of the French people"—the French

nation—that he discovered in the army corps of Engineers, a milieu antithetical to the insular avant-garde that he had known before the war. "Once I had bitten into this reality," he goes on to say, "the object was, and remained, essential to me."[23] The period of his abstract *contraste des formes* had come to an end; now he would create an art that spoke directly to the collective life of the modern Frenchman in a language of recognizable "things." His *Card Party* of 1917 (fig. 44) was among the first statements of this new, more accessible, non-individualistic approach in Léger's art.

There were other signs too that some form of collectively oriented behavior, and a concomitant relinquishing of individualism (apart from patriotic activities *per se*), was expected of Parisian artists, especially during the latter part of the war. The submission rules for a Salon in the spring of 1918 "for the benefit of the war effort" were as follows: "This exhibition, having been planned for a dreadfully restricted space, demands of each artist, whoever he may be, a small sacrifice of his personality. Whoever he may be, he will have the right to only one work."[24] Even the two Parisian titans from whom we would least expect a sacrifice of personality for one another's sake—Pablo Picasso and Henri Matisse—gave an unprecedented sign, one never to be repeated, that they were not intransigent individualists. From 23 January to 15 February 1918, Picasso and Matisse exhibited together, in a two-man show, at the Galerie Paul Guillaume. Interestingly, the catalogue, written by Apollinaire, makes no mention of this truly remarkable collaboration; in fact, the two artists are not even discussed in the same essay. The poet and critic simply wrote two one-page pieces, one on each artist, that appeared side by side. It is probably a good guess that Picasso and Matisse asked Apollinaire to preserve this measure of their artistic selfhood.

Apart from the changes it wrought in the behavior of artists, the ideological demand for collectivity affected artistic production in important ways. Knowing as we do the wartime accusations against the avant-garde—of individualism, elitism, unpatriotic liaisons—we are now in a position to comprehend what has hitherto been among the least explicable occurrences in modern art: Matisse's decision to make a second version of his great *Piano Lesson* (pl. I) of 1916. So brilliantly does the painting articulate its theme, so economically, so gravely, and with such elegance does it enunciate a world-view, that it is difficult to imagine in what sense Matisse thought he could improve upon it. Yet by the next year he had completed *The Music Lesson* (fig. 139), which is astonishing not only because it is so

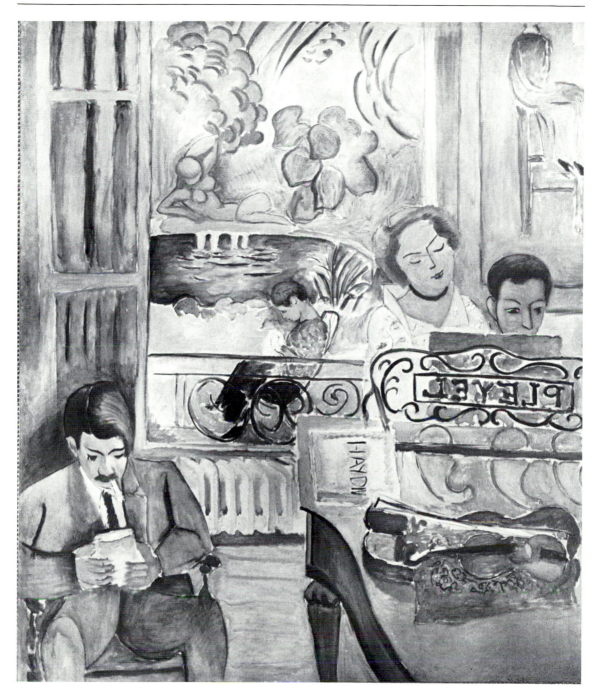

139. H. Matisse, *The Music Lesson*, 1917.

obviously an attempt to redo the earlier picture (the two paintings are almost exactly the same size, 8 × 7 feet, and have a quite similar if not identical palette), but also because of its all too apparent lack of inspiration. Almost programmatically, Matisse turns his back on everything that was abstract, difficult, and poignant in the work of the previous year. First, with the scaling-up of the figures (increasing their size in relation to the space) and the elimination of the important vertical thrust created in the *Piano Lesson* by the paired light-blue strip of window molding and ochre edge of wall, the image loses monumentality: the *Music Lesson* looks square and stable in comparison to the austere verticality of its predecessor. Furthermore, in 1917 a *horror vacui* has overtaken Matisse, so that in place of the balustraded open window with a large swath of bright green—symbolic of the natural world outdoors—there is now a veritable riot of foliage and garden accoutrements, including a lily pond, a waterfall, and an enormous piece of sculpture (the artist's own *Reclining Nude I*, of 1907). Everywhere we look, what was empty is now full, what was suggested is now literally declared and elaborated. If the severe rectilinear structure on which Matisse built his story in the *Piano Lesson* communicates constraint, then the predominance of rococo-like curves in the *Music Lesson* conveys ease. The painting of 1916 is a product of that extraordinary moment in Matisse's art when he turned to Cubism both for its formal rigor and for its potential for symbolic abstraction, while the painting of the next year recapitulates the strategies of traditional picture-making.

But of course the formal transformations that have taken place are corollary to the change in iconography and theme. If, as we saw earlier, the *Piano Lesson* of 1916 represented a dramatically altered conception of the artistic endeavor from that demonstrated in the *Red Studio* of 1911, a change that we might schematically characterize as from self-indulgence to self-denial, equally drastic is the transformation between 1916 and 1917. Now, though, the terms of the problem have been altered: the lone creator and his enterprise are no longer the subject— the individual's pursuit of the sublime has become the collectivity's shared endeavor, in this case that of familial complicity. Pierre's distracted glare in 1916 has become bland concentration; instead of the disciplinarian taskmistress impersonated by the artist's own *Woman on a High Stool* (whose contours have been bent into gentle curves and whose head has been lopped off), Pierre's teacher is now his lovingly firm sister Marguérite. The elder Matisse son, Jean, reads as he puffs on a cigarette in the lower left (replacing the provocative nude perched there in the *Piano Lesson*—she is now in the garden, recumbent and petrified, her sexuality chastened). Madame Matisse sits in the garden too—knitting or sewing—just beyond the balustrade, rounding out this vision of the happy French family, the kind we know, and Matisse knew, so well from patriotic imagery. Indeed, *la tricoteuse* was a much-replicated nationalist French image of family values, as in Huard's line-drawing *Holy France (The Knitter)* (fig. 140) or Jean Marchand's wood-block print, reproduced in issue no. 3 of *L'Elan* (15 March 1915) (fig. 141), entitled *The Guardian of the Home*. It was apparently such an evocative image that even after the war, in 1919, we find Metzinger making a Cubist knitter (fig. 142). And, although the mother is placed centrally in the scene, the *paterfamilias* is appropriately absent—presumably, according to the wartime conceit, at the front. Pierre Schneider points out, in a strictly biographical interpretation, that Matisse painted this picture of his united family expressly as a consolation for what was soon to be an empty hearthside: Pierre, who had enlisted in the armored cavalry, was now to be joined by Jean, who had been called up into the Air Force ground staff.[25] We might then extend this argument a bit further and say that Matisse offers a picture of *la bonne famille française* at precisely the moment when he himself, as a French parent, was being asked to make the sacrifice that was expected of all patriotic parents.

But it is neither the iconography—which, obviously, is patriotic without declaring itself as such—nor the style alone that has changed between 1916 and 1917, nor simply the two of them combined. Rather, the sum total of the imagery conclusively alters a third key aspect, that of the relationship between Matisse and his audience. The spectator is no longer asked to make the imaginative exertions that were required by the *Piano Lesson*—no longer asked to accept metaphoric readings of color or symbolic interpretations of shape, such as noting that the triangular slice in Pierre's face relates the young boy at once to the pyramidal metronome and to the slice of green in the window, so that he is placed at the fulcrum of the opposing forces of art and of life. For that matter, the spectator need no longer "hear" the persistent beat of the metronome; we know by the sheet music now placed on the edge of the piano that what is being rehearsed is something classically sanctioned like Haydn. Everything is spelled out in *The Music Lesson*, comprehensible to even the most obtuse viewer. Matisse could hardly now be accused by Aurel or others of "elitist" artistic practice,

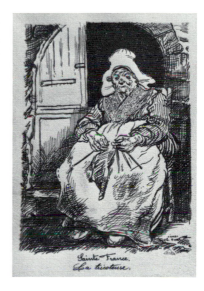

140. C. Huard, *Holy France / The Knitter (Sainte France/La Tricoteuse)*, c. 1914–18.

141. J. Marchand, *The Guardian of the Home* (*La Gardienne de Foyer*), c. 1915. Reproduced in *L'Elan* no. 3 (March 1915).

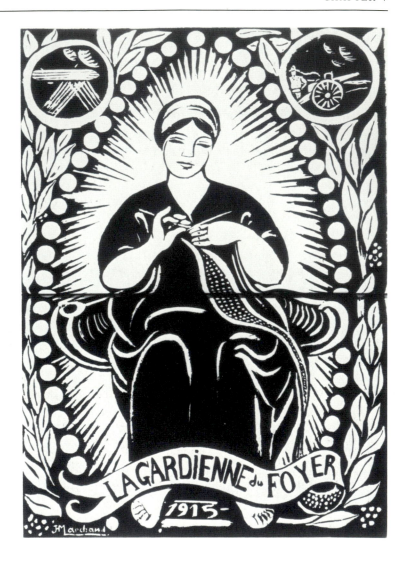

of putting a distance between himself and his public in 1917, for the painting sets itself apart from the various brands of modernism that the conservative press found objectionable.[26] Although Daudet's description of *art munichois* as "this brutal lighting, in these flat, harsh colors, in this symbolism of sharp angles which appear necessary to the excitation of weighty nervous systems," could have been applied without difficulty to the *Piano Lesson*, the soft tonalities and gentle curves of the *Music Lesson* would thwart any attempt to label it "Germanic." Most significantly, every major duality which the *Piano Lesson* invokes—between inside and out, discipline and indulgence, mind and body, art and life—has been banished from beneath

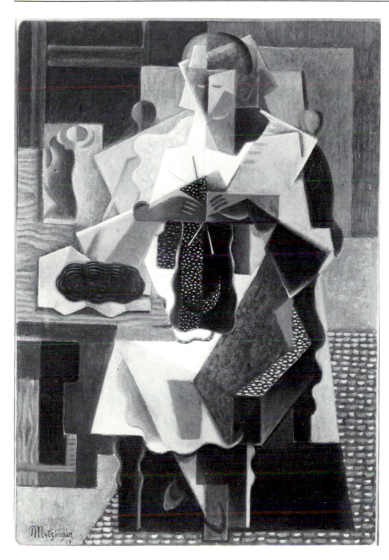

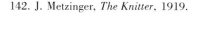

this patriarchal roof; no such metaphysical dilemmas intrude upon the Matisse family, and no such conflicts can disturb the spectator. In the *Music Lesson* Matisse takes a decisive step back from the modernist precipice onto the safer ground of traditional formulae.

But let us return to that aspect of the collective wartime regime which we touched on earlier, the new significance given to architecture and metaphors of construction in the visual arts. We have already heard Bissière's exhortation to "bring order to this chaos and to build," and his appeal to his own generation to raise a "vast and solid house" of the arts. In 1917, Lhote also

found his way to the architectural metaphor, when he wrote that
the "taste for architecture" to be discerned in the art of Poussin,
Claude, David, and Ingres (the French classicists) would make
an excellent example for contemporary artists,[27] while the next
year, in *Le Coq et l'Arlequin*, Cocteau explained that innovations
in art were acceptable if the classical bases of the work were
sound, and he too turned to the new constructive metaphor:
"One may criticize the color of the bedrooms," he wrote; "it
hardly matters, as long as the house is solidly built, lacking
nothing from top to bottom."[28] The constructive conceit was especially reassuring to a nation that was experiencing the most
destructive war in memory.

And there was yet one further reason why architecture was
becoming the metaphor of choice in so many artistic discussions: namely, that the pre-eminence of architecture in the visual arts—its position as the highest and purest art to which the
other arts aspired—was a basic tenet of academic theory. It had
been Charles Blanc, in his famous *Grammar of the Arts of Design* of 1870, who said:

> In a word, the art of statuary and that of painting, if they
> are in their emancipation more animated, more lively, and
> freer, are never grander or prouder than in their austere
> obedience to the laws of architecture.[29]

At a moment when all manner of old formulations, especially of
a classicistic bent, were beginning to sound good again to artists
and critics, Blanc's statement of architecture's supremacy in
the arts must have looked better than it had for many years.
Indeed, we find it in one version or another in critical writing
throughout the war. Dervaux wrote that it is architecture which
has always indicated the "degree of civilization" of an epoch,
and that after the Great War France too would be judged by "the
standard of that art which is called the art of peace: Architecture."[30] Even closer to Blanc, in fact really nothing more than
a paraphrase, were the words of André Michel, who having already decried individualism in the arts (and exalted the ancient
role of the artist as *porte-parole* for the community) now said of
architecture: "In all great creative epochs, it is she who was the
central art and the matrix of all the other arts, who were subordinated to her instructions and benefitted from her inspiration."[31] But Michel did not stop there. He went on to provide
his readers with the conceptual framework for understanding
the primacy of architecture specifically as a symbol of social
control and hierarchy:

It would take too long to recall here how sculpture and
painting were for such a long time no more than her collaborators, and what grandeur, what force they drew from
the apparent restraints she imposed on them. As well as a
higher plastic value, a prouder, more monumental allure,
they gained thereby a fuller awareness of their social purpose. Today, of course, we see all about us the independence, the sovereignty, and I would even say the tyranny
of the fantasy of the artist, who despises above all the philistine incapable of fathoming the sublimity of his genius or
of his intentions.[32]

The past versus the present; a Golden Age and a base contemporaneity; the cognizance of social obligation and the contempt
of the public that characterizes modern elitism—these are the
associated contrasts which Michel derives from his primary
duality: the control imposed by architecture on the one hand,
and the modern-day anarchy of the "sovereign" artist on the
other.

Michel's use of architecture as a symbol of social order and
control did not mean that he had special insight into the political implications of academic theory, for once again it had been
the French Right and Charles Maurras in particular who had
made the artistic and political liaisons clear to whoever was interested between the time of the Dreyfus Affair and the Great
War. The interrelated spheres of social order, structure, and
classicism were the ideological foundation on which the Royalist built his world-view. "If our France remains strong," he
wrote in a well-known essay of 1896, "it is because she was put
together by classical architects. One recognizes the marks of
their fine and energetic hand; I consider them, among others,
to be the Catholic Church and Roman administration, ancient
counselors of the Kings of France."[33] And it was not just the
union of Church and State that was essential to this classically
constructed nation, according to Maurras. It was equally the
recognition that the general good must always come before the
needs of the individual—*Salus populi suprema lex esto*, in Cicero's formulation—even if, as Maurras pointed out repeatedly
during the years of the Dreyfus Affair, the individual had to be
denied justice for the good of the state. Concomitantly, to promulgate a wartime re-evaluation of the significance of architecture, and to propose it as the touchstone of the arts, was to
withdraw from almost all that had been called modern in
France; to denigrate painting and sculpture as tyrannically in-

dividualistic and hopelessly beyond the control of the mother art was, if unwittingly, to accept the Right's cultural critique. For it was nothing less than the democratization of culture that was in question here. When the Right accused the Parisian avant-garde of elitism, it was not because of an objection to elites *per se*; on the contrary, it was the Right, and especially the Royalists, who considered France's salvation to lie first in the restoration of that "natural" elite, the Royal house. In effect, everything that had happened since 1789 was considered to have been for the worst. In one form or another it was a general indictment of bourgeois, "parliamentary" France, of *The Stupid Nineteenth Century*, as the Royalist Léon Daudet unashamedly referred to it in a well-known book of 1922.[34]

According to this interpretation, among the earliest and most dangerous forms of individualism and "revolutionary prejudice" had been Romanticism. We already know that Wagnerian aesthetics were considered anathema to the French precisely because, in the wake of 1870, their impact had been so great. Wagner's French popularity was the proof of the power of those noxious later-Romantic vapors. Both Cocteau and Daudet, as we have seen, were among those who shared these anti-Wagnerian sentiments and helped propagate them (anti-Wagnerism was, in fact, a central motif of Daudet's *Hors du joug allemand*). But blaming Wagner for the corruption of French culture was unsatisfactory for obvious reasons. If it was merely a question of expunging Wagnerism from the arts in France, then the cleansing process was a fairly minor affair. But to indict Romanticism itself was to launch a campaign whose historical justifications could be pushed as far back (with some maneuvering) as the Enlightenment and which could be as thoroughly damning of the French subversives as of the German infiltrators. Moreover, such an indictment was so vague and general that almost any artist or thinker or movement could be called Romantic (and hence un-classical). Maurras, with a far more brilliant mind than his sidekick Daudet, had recognized this before the turn of the century. In fact, he accounted for his own intellectual development from cultural critic to political theorist in terms of his discovery of the dangers of Romanticism: "We had seen the ruins in the realm of thought and taste before noticing the social, military, economic, and diplomatic damage that generally results from democracy," and it had been "by analyzing the literary errors of romanticism that we were led, indeed dragged, to study the moral and political error of a State involved in revolution."[35] To be sure, Maurras was not uninformed about his subject and hence was well aware that Romanticism nonetheless had also been an important influence on the growth of French nationalism, of which he wholly approved. He found especially laudable the Romantic interest in indigenous French themes. The problem, as he saw it, was that the French had come to accept and propagate a "Gothic" or cosmopolitan style, even a Germanic style, and that nothing could be worse for the nation, or further from her classical roots, than this. He established an updated version of the older Classic/Romantic antithesis, with Dante, Racine, and Poussin representing the pure, classical, Latin impulse, and Musset, Baudelaire, Rimbaud, and their spiritual predecessor Jean-Jacques Rousseau symbolizing the unhealthy, un-French, Romantic subversion of the Great Tradition.[36]

As one of the spearheads of the New Classic Age for the French arts, and as an essential promoter of the new classicism for the avant-garde, the magazine *Nord-Sud* translated many of Maurras' ideas into the modernist idiom even while the magazine claimed in print that it opposed Royalist politics.

Paul Dermée's statement that "the mastery of self is the moral and aesthetic ideal of the classic epochs," which appeared in *Nord-Sud* in his article "Un Prochain Age classique," was accompanied, we recall, by the Romantic image of the rearing horse: "The crazy stallion of our passions is firmly bridled." But in that same article he went even further to make clear that the "coming classical age" would be in marked contrast to the entire Romantic strain in French culture:

> Rousseau, the adoration of nature, unbridled lyricism, the insurrection of slaves, the rights of peoples, the "vivre sa vie," [the philosopher Henri] Bernstein, and finally Bergson and his metaphysics of the *élan vital* are all but one and the same attitude before the world: Romanticism. The classic arts exist only where intelligence reigns supreme.[37]

As extraordinary as it may seem for a self-proclaimed member of the avant-garde to lump together Rousseau, lyricism, revolution, "the rights of peoples," and Bergson in order to dismiss it all as Romantic, as opposed to the intellectual remoteness of classical art, Dermée was not, as we are by now aware, exceptional in his attitudes. For him as for Maurras, Michel, Daudet, and many others, artistic and social issues were self-evidently linked; the term "Romantic" was as good as any to describe the qualities that bound men and ideas, nature and attitudes, together over time. There is hardly an element in Dermée's Romantic repertory that we have not heard already, or that we will not find developed after the war.

In terms of the history of painting, the wartime use of "Romanticism" was less important as a description of Delacroix or Géricault's art (although it was, of course, always understood in that way too) than for its extension into the late nineteenth century. The art of the Napoleonic period and the Bourbon Restoration, although Romantic, was far enough away to pose no immediate threat to current practices; Courbet's Realism, although undesirable still to many conservative critics, had been so diluted by academic practice that it too seemed unthreatening. (Besides, the term "Realism" gave added protection in the midst of a war in which so high a value was placed on being in touch with reality, as opposed to an amorphous dream-state.) Impressionism, on the other hand, was so recent, so powerful, and so closely associated with the period following the national humiliation of 1870 that it gradually became the artistic *bête noire* not only of the Right, but of the nominally progressive avant-garde as well. Besides, in the midst of the national emergency, its rebelliousness—its rejection of academic practice and validation of the *refusés*—made Impressionism seem even less desirable. Lhote, in 1916, said that although it could not be denied that contemporary artists might still benefit from the "lively teachings of Impressionism," the movement was nonetheless highly problematical as a precedent. "Since Giotto," he wrote,

> from whom he derived his greatness, David was the most considerable of the masters whose clear and logical teaching galvanized a generation. The Romantic wave, of which Impressionism was the outcome, renewed the poorly harnessed deliquescences of the eighteenth century, provoked the disfavor of all precise teaching . . . and led to a pictorial empiricism based on feeling alone.[38]

If the linking of Romanticism, Rousseau (i.e. eighteenth-century deliquescences), feeling (i.e. individual feelings), and Impressionism is only summarily indicated here, by 1920 Lhote would refer to Impressionism as the "religion of instinct, of pure talent . . . negation of all principles, total innovation, anarchy,"[39] and Mauclair (although an admirer of Monet!), after damning Impressionism for its interest in the mere "caprices of light" and its excessive concern with "the notation of modern life," also saw the movement as a dangerous negation of authority, in particular the authority of the Ecole.[40]

Most important for the development of art in Paris, the major figures almost all evinced an ever-increasing distaste for Impressionism. Léger, who considered his art to be descended from Impressionism, nonetheless noted that by 1918 he and his friends were in "violent reaction" against Impressionism, and that a "return to local color, broader areas of unbroken color and larger forms was the character this revolt took" in his painting.[41] Picasso's famous statement, "Work with three colors, too many colors makes Impressionism"—which we know from Cocteau's *Parade* notebooks—was enunciated in 1917, in Rome, where the capriciousness of Northern light may have looked less appealing than ever beneath the constant Mediterranean sun. Interestingly, although it was in Rome that Picasso's Latinity, classicism, and anti-Impressionism were being confirmed, the Paris-based Spaniard saw nothing of ancient greatness in contemporary Italian endeavor: "The Futurists," Picasso said, "are the Impressionists of ideas,"[42] meaning that the anarchic qualities of Futurism were a legacy of Impressionist revolt. In part, Picasso was advancing the cause of Cubism during the war by pushing Futurism, as it were, to the left, thereby creating a more moderate anti-Impressionist place for Cubism at the center. It is noteworthy that Severini himself was in complete agreement—not perhaps surprisingly considering the rather drastically neo-traditional aspects of his artistic production during 1916–17. In a letter to Walter Pach, written in October 1916 in anticipation of his New York exhibition the following March, the Italian said of his recent *Woman Seated in a Square*:

> In the painting is evidenced the effort to reconcile the spirit of Futurist experimentation (continuation of Impressionism) with the spirit of Cubist experimentation (reaction to Impressionism). And at this moment all the painters are [moving] there [i.e. in that direction].[43]

That is to say, this kind of Cubist work by Severini, which we have earlier described as occupying a middle ground between revolutionary Futurism and reactionary renunciation of all modernist tendencies, was regarded by the artist as having been, at the same time, a work that was attempting to take a compromise position vis-à-vis Impressionism.

Indeed, ascribing the legacy of Impressionism to various other modernist movements (as we have just seen in the case of Futurism) or, alternatively, calling other movements Romantic (Cocteau wrote: "Make no mistake here, Cubism was a classicism after the Romanticism of the Fauves"),[44] allowed a wartime notion of Cubism to be forged which extricated it from the "stupid" nineteenth century and its societal ills. This meant in effect that while Cubism's newness had been a liability at the beginning of the war, it now could also be an asset. Cocteau was an important propagator of anti-Impressionist attitudes—he wrote to Gleizes in 1919, "More and more I'm against Impressionist decadence . . . Yes, of course, Renoir [is good], but I say down with Renoir the way I say down with Wagner"[45] (interestingly, as we shall see later, Renoir would soon be revived for the Parisian avant-garde, but as an Old Master and not as an Impressionist). In *Dans le ciel de la patrie*, his 1918 patriotic ode to French wartime aviation, Cocteau also wrote:

> The Impressionist painter looked at nature through eyes squinting at the sun; Cubism today rediscovers the austere discipline of the great epochs, renounces pretty games, and becomes the pretext for a new architecture of the sensibility.[46]

Armed with the particulars of wartime cultural debate, we understand just how much Cocteau has said in these few lines: as a symbol of the nineteenth century, and especially of the period after the Prussian defeat and the Commune, Impressionism was flat-footedly empirical and even ape-like in its artistic ambitions, whereas Cubism—according to the poet—is the antithesis: it retrieves a glorious past by abandoning frivolity and self-indulgence in order to construct a firm basis for a French aesthetic.

The wartime preference for the austere over the frivolous, for the classical over the Romantic, and for almost any artistic manifestation over Impressionism partook, moreover, of a set of cultural referents that were deeply ingrained in French, and especially Parisian, consciousness. We may recall that Saroléa, in *Le Réveil de la France*, had written of an *esprit nouveau*, the catchphrase for a morally reconstructed France—borrowed by Apollinaire in his program notes for *Parade*—that had been coined in the 1890s by the forces of the *ralliement*, the new Republican realignment with the old clerical and aristocratic elites, effected in order to defuse the Socialist threat. Saroléa used another term as well, this time a Latin one, to depict the nation at war in 1916. "We are convinced in our hearts," he intoned,

> that thou shalt emerge from thy tragic ordeal as radiant as ever. The motto of thy capital—*Fluctuat nec mergitur*—is

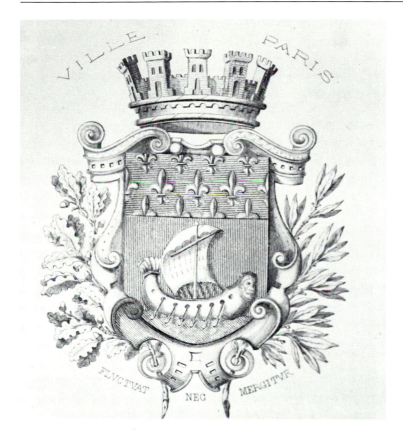

143. Anonymous, Seal of the City of Paris, n.d.

engraved on every page of thy chequered annals. The bark which carried the fortunes of France, like the bark of Lutetia, has been "ever tossed on the waves, but it has never submerged." How often in thy past history did everything seem lost! Yet thou didst keep thy stout heart and still thou didst challenge thine enemies.[47]

As the reader may be aware, the motto *Fluctuat nec mergitur*, along with the image of a sailing ship on the waves (fig. 143), is the insignia of the City of Paris; "to be tossed on the waves, but never to sink" is a verbal and visual symbol of the firm and dependable ship of state, which can withstand the onslaught of enemies both internal and external to the nation (and its capital city). Like so many other symbols, *Fluctuat* and the bark of Lutetia had a renewed significance for France under seige during the Great War. Henri Lavedan, the great historian of Paris, found himself drawn to the imagery when in the spring of 1918 the Germans mounted their last offensive against the capital. In the 15 June 1918 issue of *L'Illustration*, he wrote:

Paris, personifying the France which, in these breathless hours, rushes forward and baffles fate, Paris for two weeks has absorbed the thoughts of the entire world. . . . Thus Paris . . . at this moment again takes her coat of arms, her traditional and sacred effigy. On the ocean of her ancient history, raised up for the last four years, again and again one sees the Vessel lurch, descend, and regain her place. On the streaming colors of tears, of blood reappears in golden letters the unshakable motto: *Fluctuat nec mergitur*.[48]

The imagery of standing firm amidst the swelling sea and stormy skies, of remaining constant and unchanging in the face of adversity's flux, had a kind of daily, if essentially unconscious, reality for the Parisians. And it signified something else as well: for just as Saroléa's term *espirt nouveau* was intimately linked (as Debora Silverman has shown) to late-nineteenth-century politics, so *Fluctuat nec mergitur* was another product of that same conservative Republican *ralliement*. Incised in a number of public buildings after 1889, the banderole and motto became symbols of the Third Republic and its ability to withstand the attacks of the regime's enemies, especially its socialist enemies, and, as imagery that dated even further back to Louis XIV and Napoleon III, it was a kind of shorthand for a traditional, enduring notion of the state.[49] Surely André Mare was thinking neither of the symbol of Paris nor (consciously) of the anti-Impressionism of the wartime Parisian critics when he arrived in Venice, as a soldier, in 1916. Yet it was while gazing into the canals of that quintessentially Romantic city (Charles Maurras considered it a symbol of Romantic decadence)[50] that Mare saw the failures of Impressionism. "The modern painters lacked the sense of structure," he wrote:

> they made pink palaces, reflections in water, and gondolas, but they did not understand that moving water is only the antithesis of a severe and rigid architecture lined up in shadows and in plans where the color is not a covering and is never an end.[51]

Once again, it is construction and architecture that function as the antidote for the flux of moving water and reflected light. Although the history of Impressionism would later be written as essentially the triumph of formal values over subject matter, it is clear that, at least during World War I, the visual flux of Impressionism was often understood as being the objective correlative of the fluctuating society from which it issued.

When Braque made his famous declarations—"the senses deform, the spirit forms," "emotion should not be translated by a nervous tremor," and "I love the rule that corrects emotion"— he was probably not consciously aware that his anti-emotional, anti-sensual, anti-Impressionist attitudes were part of a larger system of meaning that ideologically connected such diverse elements as the rebuilding of French cities, Jean-Jacques Rousseau, and the Parisian coat-of-arms; any more than Jacques Vernay understood how accurate and how resonant was his prediction that after the war "there would again be a search for form and line as passionate as the search for deformation between 1900 and 1913." Gino Severini could hardly have known that he was laying down the guidelines for the post-war history of French art when he spoke of "deformation and reconstruction," and when (in his article in the *Mercure de France*, "La Peinture d'avant-garde," in 1917) he referred to the "architecture of painting" and declared, further on, "I think that the collective and anti-individualist aesthetic to which I have just alluded prepares an artistic epoch which will finally realize the universality of style."[52] Indeed, each one of these statements was personal; each one expressed an individual response to phenomena, even though, as we have seen, each individual response was indelibly marked by the exigencies of the moment. Could Ozenfant have predicted, when in issue no. 9 of *L'Elan* he published an excerpt from Plato's *Philebus*, that he was inaugurating a new Neoplatonism in the Parisian avant-garde,[53] or that in 1919 Erik Satie would compose his classicizing oratorio *Socrate*, based on the Victor Cousin translation of the Dialogues? Certainly the critic René Chalupt knew, at least in artistic terms, what he was saying when he referred to Satie's oratorio as "ce dessin":

> This drawing of such strict and precise line, where trickery has no place, this just and temperate light, without zone of chiaroscuro (so propitious for hiding shortcomings), which never flits off with Impressionist butterfly-wings, this subtle and wise equilibrium of the score engraved on these pages . . . it's a little as if M. Ingres, at the request of Victor Cousin, had illustrated these passages from the Dialogues of Plato.[54]

Chalupt had obviously read Cocteau's anti-Romantic tract; he probably knew Picasso's Ingres-style drawings; and he surely was aware that the term "Impressionist" was at that moment among the least complimentary epithets that one could attach to a work of art. But it is doubtful that anyone was aware of the reasons *why* Plato was enjoying a revival, aside from the most obvious fact of his Antique origins, or why change and fluctuation in general seemed so unattractive to almost all Frenchmen. For the same reasons that André Mare could not have understood, as he gazed into the Venetian waters, that his preference for the rigid architecture of lines and clear shadows was part of a larger search for stability in the face of war, so transformations in philosophical taste and bias were never considered in their timely aspect, but were discussed in a kind of absolute, purist realm of thought.

It seems not to have occurred to Saroléa that the reason he devoted an entire chapter to Henri Bergson's philosophy in *Le Réveil de la France* was precisely that, as the most important French philosopher of the pre-war period, Bergson with theories of change, relativism, and flux was now, in 1916, out of step with wartime ideology. We have already heard Dermée refer to "Bergson and his *élan vital*" as Romantic, and although Saroléa was an admirer of the philosopher he did want to know whether Bergson's system could now provide the constants and absolutes that it had hitherto seemed to deny. "So far, then," he wrote,

> the philosophy of Bergson has proved an inspiration to the student of Ethics and of Theology, but it is not necessary to travel a long way before he realizes that even to the liberal student of Christian Theology the new philosophy raises as many problems as it solves and that it bristles with contradictions. For Bergsonism is pre-eminently the philosophy of Change, of a ceaseless Becoming. Theology is concerned with the Immutable and the Everlasting. In Bergson's conception Time and Duration are the very web and woof of life. Theology is merged in Eternity. Bergsonism is the philosophy of Chance, of accidental variations. Creative evolution proceeds by eruptive, explosive, vital outbursts. All Christian theology is Teleology.
>
> Bergsonism emphasizes nothing more constantly than diversity. Creative evolution has again and again been deflected on divergent lines. The World of Instinct follows one line of development. The World of Intellect follows another. On the contrary, religion is based on unity and continuity. Revealed religion, supernatural religion, is the deposit of a revelation vouchsafed to mankind once and for all.

This being so, Saroléa goes on to say, what does Bergson intend to do about his philosophical position: will he continue to be the advocate of chance, change, and fluctuation, or will he discover a new certainty in his work?

> It is an interesting subject for speculation whether . . . he
> will address himself to these questions, or whether, as he
> has done in the past, he will stop short of the answer and
> the ultimate reality? Will he refrain from putting the cop-
> ing-stone to his philosophical structure?[55]

Bergson was, of course, an extremely important source for pre-war Parisian aesthetics, and when Saroléa says that Bergsonism is "the philosophy of Change, of a ceaseless Becoming," he might as well have been talking about Picasso's *Ma Jolie* (fig. 101) or Delaunay's *City of Paris* (fig. 110), in which nothing is "vouchsafed" once and for all, but rather in which the world seems to dissolve in its own complexity.

Despite the interpretation of Cubism as a "classical" reaction of form and line against Impressionist color and divisionism, there is no denying that far more basic to Analytic Cubism was its quantum leap toward an art of change, becoming, and process. In Saroléa's evocation of Bergson's creative evolution proceeding by eruptive, explosive, vital outbursts (in contrast to the revelatory, teleological form of Christian thought), we hear echoes of all the statements that were made after 1914 about the pre-war period: Cocteau's description of those years as "nothing but mines, nothing but trenches," years of "atrocities, unstable borders"; Tollet's "asphyxiating gases of our enemies"; Métivet's image of Marianne fanning herself as French society literally explodes around her. And when he offers in contrast Theology, concerned with the "Immutable," the "Everlasting," we remember that it was not only the devout but the whole French people that clung to the immutable and everlasting during the hard years of war, both as a means of reassurance that they would survive the crisis and as a reminder that they were fighting for the everlasting, enduring principles of Occidental culture.

Obviously, to ask Henri Bergson to renounce the concepts of duration and the *élan vital* was tantamount to the total abandonment of Bergsonism, just as asking the Cubists and Futurists to forfeit those same qualities of fluctuation meant nothing less than the abandonment of nearly everything they had invented. Yet this is precisely what was being asked of the Parisian avant-garde, even by its own members and most fervent supporters. So powerful was the wartime need for absolutes—even patently fallacious ones—and so self-evident seemed the rightness of these values in the midst of the national emergency that such attitudes appeared to be beyond question. When Léonce Rosenberg, the Cubist dealer and critic, published his article "Pourquoi choyez-vous?" (Why Kid Yourself?) in October 1918, just days before the Armistice, he provided a schema for the evolution of Cubism and avant-garde art in general. He wrote:

> The evolution of the true artist consists of the following three successive phases:
>
> Imitation—Interpretation—Creation
>
> First Phase: He reproduces *directly* the appearance of nature. He renders an image.
>
> Second Phase: He expresses the visible face of nature through his *humanity*; he exteriorizes an *impression*.
>
> Third Phase: Retaining from nature only the constant and the absolute, free in his choice of the necessary elements for the *structure* of his work, he realizes the *Spirit*. His work becomes *Reality*.[56]

By the end of the war the Parisian avant-garde had, quite self-consciously, passed from the second to the third of Rosenberg's phases: from Bergsonian dynamics, Impressionism, and Analytic Cubism to Platonic statics, structure, and Synthetic Cubism.

Blue Horizons

VI

O̲ₙ 11 N̲ₒᵥₑₘᵦₑᵣ 1918 the German peace delegates surrendered to France in Marshal Foch's railway car at Rethondes, close to Compiègne. Beginning that night and for almost two days afterward there were Armistice celebrations in every city, town, and hamlet in France. After more than four years of war fought almost entirely on French soil, the peace had been regained, and the *revanche* of which the French had long dreamed was accomplished. The French army marched into Strasbourg to reclaim the "lost provinces" of Alsace and Lorraine and were greeted by the local peasantry, dressed in provincial costume—a scene that the former Fauve Othon Friesz captured for posterity (fig. 144)—and proudly holding aloft images from the town of Epinal, in Lorraine.[1] Back in Paris, the allegorical figure of *Strasbourg* in the Place de la Concorde, draped in black crepe since August 1914, was unveiled. It was an extraordinary moment for France.

But the real celebration of the Armistice, for which no one had been prepared in November, was deferred until Bastille Day of 1919, after the signing of the Treaty of Versailles on 28 June. Together, the city of Paris and the national government allocated close to six million francs for the victory festivities and employed more than two hundred artists to decorate the *voie triomphale*, which stretched the entire length of the Champs Elysées.[2] The Place de la Concorde was encircled with tall flagpoles, each of which flew a *tricolore* along with the other Allied flags, as well as an ornamented escutcheon; a series of paired pylons lined the Champs-Elysées; mid-way to the Arc de Triomphe, at the Rond-Point, were altars to France's "martyred cities" (Soissons, Verduns, Reims, Arras, et al.), composed of a flaming brazier complemented by *trophées*, great piles of captured German armaments, each surmounted by a *coq Gaulois*, the whole encircled by medallions (fig. 145) commemorating the victorious Allied battles of *la Grande Guerre*. The Etoile (fig. 146) was decorated in much the same manner as the Place de la Concorde.

The grand *défilé* of the army began at eight thirty on the

144. O. Friesz, *The Entry of the
French into Strasbourg*, 1918.

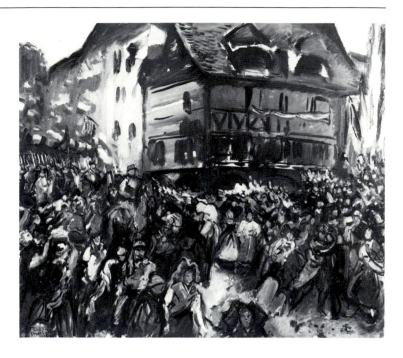

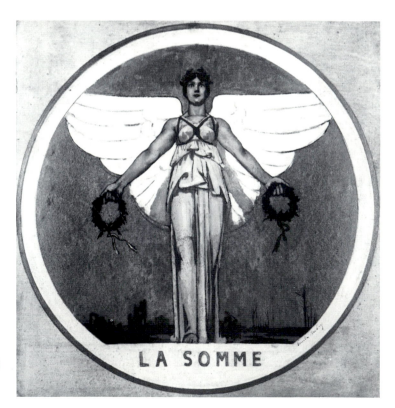

145. E. Aubry, Medallion (*La Somme*)
for the Peace Festivities, Paris, 14
July 1919.

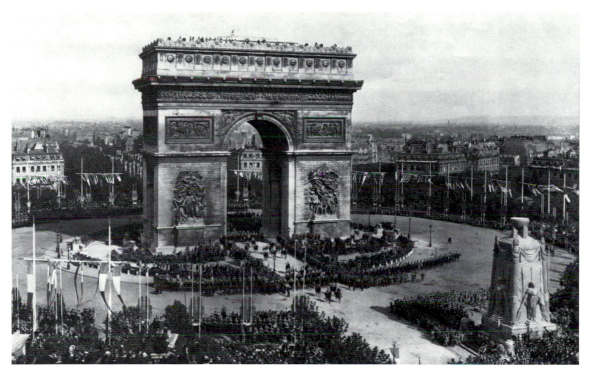

146. The Etoile—Arc de Triomphe during the Peace Festivities, Paris, 14 July 1919.

morning of 14 July when the first troops marched toward the Arc de Triomphe to the tune of the *Marseillaise*. As living testimony to France's heroic suffering, it was the *mutilés de guerre* that led the way—facially disfigured, some blinded, bandaged, many with limbs missing, many others on crutches, all decorated—these were the solemn advance guard of the great procession as depicted by the painter Galtier-Boissière (fig. 147). The progress of these broken Frenchmen through the heart of Paris must have been a tremendously moving and pathetic sight; the bystanders threw flowers and called out benedictions all along their halting march. The day of the Armistice the previous November had been too exhilarating an occasion for sadness and mourning. But 14 July was something very different, a consecrated day when the war, in all its misery and final triumph, was honored. After a mandated minute of silence that followed the arrival of the mutilated soldiers at the Arc de Triomphe came the more splendid military display: "Then in the great portal, through which shone the most beautiful sun of Austerlitz," intoned Maurice Barrès in the *Echo de Paris*, "silhouettes surged forth. The *poilus* came through the Arc de Triomphe."[3] At their head were the two designated triumphant

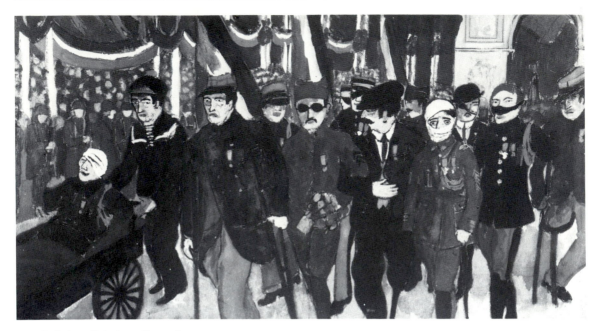

147. J. Galtier-Boissière, *Procession of the Mutilés de Guerre, 14 July 1919.*

maréchaux, Joffre and Foch (fig. 148), on horseback; and just behind them was Pétain, followed by first the French and then the Allied troops. All, of course, were greeted by the thunderous applause of what seemed like the entire French nation lining the streets. It was a day that France would long remember.

Only one contretemps, seemingly, struck a sour note in the festivities, and that, ironically, was an artistic matter. Before Bastille Day even got under way, during the weeks of hasty preparation for decorating the monumental *allée*, someone decided that the enormous Cenotaph for the War Dead (fig. 149), designed by André Mare with his friends Gustave Jaulmes and Louis Süe, was *munichois*! Of gilded staff, equipped with wheels so that it could be removed from its place under the central portal of the Arc de Triomphe when the parade began, the monument displayed four Victories, each with a pair of wings that had been removed from actual French army aircraft.[4] Fasces bound the corners; trophied swags draped the base; and a giant brazier formed the pinnacle of an ensemble which one could agree was not extremely attractive, but which nevertheless had been designed and executed in a matter of weeks by loyal French soldiers. Yet its colossal size, its severity, and perhaps the fact that it was designed by artists who had been, if only marginally, part of the "advanced" Parisian art scene all

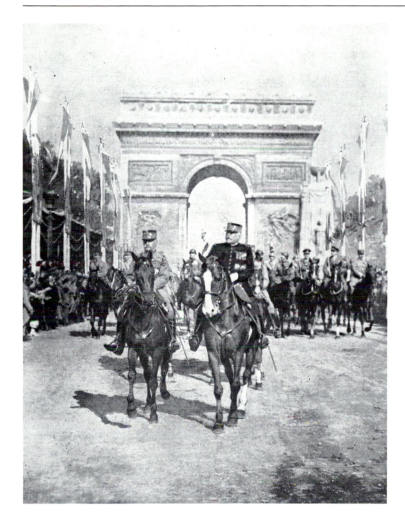

148. Marshals Foch and Joffre riding at head of parade for Peace Festivities, Paris, 14 July 1919.

ended up working against it when on 13 July the critic for *L'Eclair* wrote, "Under the Arc de Triomphe, the monument to the dead is in the process of being completed. It nastily bottles up the triumphal portal; it seems crushing and heavy and slightly *munichois* in style, despite its high artistic merit and grave emotion."[5] Jean Cocteau, who had himself suffered from this kind of accusation at the première of *Parade*, went even further and wrote in *Paris-Midi* that "the Cenotaph could have come straight from Munich."[6] More damaging still, the politicians soon threw themselves into the fray. *Le Pays* reported that no less a figure than Georges Clemenceau, Prime Minister and seventy-six-year-old heroic victor of the Great War—The Tiger—had passed judgment on the cenotaph:

149. G. Jaulmes, A. Mare, and L. Süe, *Cenotaph for the War Dead,* Peace Festivities, Paris, 14 July 1919.

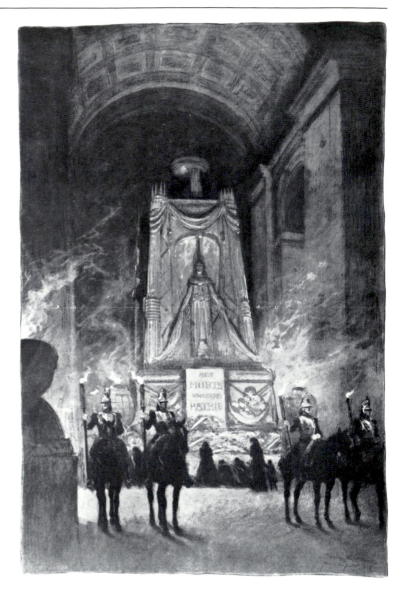

M. Clemenceau saw the cenotaph and he said, "It's imposing." . . . M. Clemenceau saw the cenotaph again on 14 July and he said, "It's ignoble," in his haughty, laconic way that is the enemy of circumlocution. Then he took the trouble, quite unnecessarily, to bolster up his new opinion. And he spoke of "Boche art" of "Munich inspiration." Finally—since everything in France just now ends up by being demolished—he gave the order to demolish it.[7]

Far from having been put to rest with the Armistice, the issue
of German influence on French culture was still lively in 1919.
Fortunately, though, Mare and his colleagues were not without
their defenders: Roger Allard offered his support in the pages
of the *Nouveau Spectateur*,[8] and on 10 August the critic for the
Carnet de la Semaine, after praising the "pure and simple lines"
of the Cenotaph, reminded his readers that these artists were
"among the most ardent reformers of the French decorative arts,
taking up the battle against Munich"; and besides, they were
veterans.[9]

To be sure, most artistic demonstrations of patriotism were
received with the good faith in which they had been offered.
Mare himself created, for example, a wallpaper for the Armistice, "The Allies" (fig. 150), based in part on a gouache in his

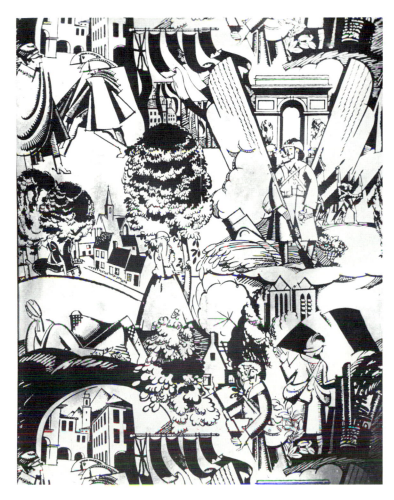

150. A. Mare, Wallpaper design,
"The Allies," 1919.

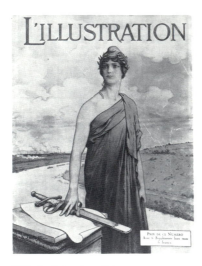

151. L. Sabattier, "France
Victorious." Cover of *L'Illustration*
(5 July 1919).

wartime notebooks (fig. 48).[10] Henri Matisse painted a victory
bouquet that he titled simply *Flowers, 14 July*;[11] and the academic artist Louis Sabattier, whose view of the Café de la Paix
in wartime we saw at the outset of our study (fig. 1), fashioned
an allegorical figure of "France Victorious" for the cover of *L'Illustration* (fig. 151). Paul Poiret, doing his best to put the *Renaissance* affair behind him, gave parties: one on the night of the
Armistice and a second on the night of 14 July 1919, to which
"le tout Paris" came in droves.[12]

But in ways more significant than victory parties or patriotic
wallpaper, the war continued to influence, and even shape,
French life after November 1918. For if reconstruction efforts
had begun in France even in the midst of war, it was now the
moment for the French nation to devote itself wholeheartedly to
that effort; if France's political, economic, and social way of life
had been altered and transformed to meet the challenge of the
enemy, it was now time for France to rebuild a normal peacetime society. In 1920 two political analysts, Henri Bornecque
and Germain Drouilly, wrote in rather glowing terms of the
"fight for moral unity" that had been carried out against the
"divisive and revolutionary forces" unleashed by the demobilization. "There were suspicions and accusations, conflicts and
strikes, even attempts at revolution," they wrote, the work not
of loyal Frenchmen but of "the internal enemies of France, *métèques*, profiteers, and united troublemakers."[13] There, of
course, was the rub—now that the Germans were no longer "at
Noyon" (in Clemenceau's habitual phrase), the Sacred Union
was no longer sacred. The government's greatest fear, as intense
as ever, was of revolution after four arduous years of regimen-
tation for army and civilians alike. The French Left was once
again active: when Raoul Villain, Jaurès's assassin, was acquitted of the crime in April 1919, it provoked bloody clashes
on May Day; major strikes—something the French had not seen
for a long time—were called in 1919 and 1920. Indeed, during
the spring of 1919 labor won several important concessions
from a frightened government, including the legalization of collective bargaining and the eight-hour work day. Especially in
the light of the successful revolution in Russia and the November Revolution in Germany (even though the latter was abor-
tive), "the most important single issue of the elections of 16th
November 1919 was bolshevism."[14]

As it turned out, the Left did not even win a victory at the
polls in November 1919, for it was the coalition of conservative
parties, the *Bloc National*, that came to power—the first time

that a right-wing chamber had been elected since the founding
of the Third Republic in 1871. Because the majority of the new
deputies were ex-soldiers, it was called the *Chambre Bleu Horizon*, after the "Horizon Blue" color of the serviceman's uniform. It should be pointed out, nonetheless, that the *Bloc National* was equipped with no real doctrine, apart from a general
disposition toward patriotism and the status quo—but for the
time being, that was enough to keep the Right in office. Bornecque and Drouilly succinctly outlined the Blue Horizon regime of post-war French recovery:

> They preached to the rich and the managerial class of nec-
> essary sacrifices, to everyone of productivity and the strict-
> est economy, of the reconciliation of the classes on the
> altar of work, of the return of all the uprooted to the nour-
> ishing land, of the elementary hygiene indispensable to
> the betterment of health, and of the love of family [as] the
> only socially powerful force, the creator of a new genera-
> tion.[15]

Nothing really new here; this was but an updated version of the
program of national discipline and moral rearmament that had
brought France through her darkest hours.

For the Parisian avant-garde, the post-war period was heralded by a series of major events that were almost simultaneous
with the Armistice. On 7 October the French lost their foremost
sculptor of the pre-war avant-garde, Raymond Duchamp-Villon, who died at the Cannes military hospital of blood poison-
ing, in the wake of a long battle with typhoid. Then on 9
November only two days before the cessation of fighting,
Guillaume Apollinaire (né Kostrowitzky), weakened by the in-
fluenza that swept through Europe in 1918, finally succumbed
to the head wound of which the poet himself had said, "a beautiful Minerva is the child of my head."[16] The funeral service was
held at the Church of Saint Thomas Aquinas, near his apartment, just off the Boulevard Saint-Germain. And within a week
of the death of the author of *The Cubist Painters* (published just
five years before) appeared the first post-war manifesto written
for the avant-garde, in the form of a tract that declared the
death of Apollinaire's beloved pre-war cause in its very title:
Après le Cubisme. Written by Amédée Ozenfant (who had been
out of the public eye since the demise of *L'Elan*), in partnership
with the young painter-architect-critic Charles-Edouard Jeanneret, *Après le Cubisme* is exemplary for both its critique and its
prescriptions.

For instance, the authors' attitude toward the pre-war period was the standard post-1914 opinion:

> Art before the Great Test [*la Grande Epreuve*] was not alive enough to invigorate the idle, nor to interest the vigorous; society then was restless, because the direction of life was too uncertain, because there was no great collective current to force to work those who had to work nor to tempt to work those who did not have to. Era of strikes, of lawsuits, of protests where art itself was but an art of protest. Gone are those times at once too heavy and too light.[17]

There is little here that is unfamiliar to us: the pre-war period viewed as somehow less alive than the period of war; pre-war society as restless and uncertain, a divided culture fraught with protest, in which individualism vitiated any sense of community; an era "at once too heavy and too light," lacking any sense of value or proportion. The restoration of value is brought about by the war, which the authors significantly call the "Great Test," and of which they also say in the essay, "The Great Competition [*la Grande Concurrence*] has tested everyone, it has gotten rid of obsolete methods and in their place imposed those that the struggle proved to be the best"[18]—in other words, the Sacred Union was a kind of filter that separated the men from the boys and the moribund from the healthy. Furthermore, there was at the moment of the Armistice a new timeliness and significance to what must have been a fairly stale interpretation by 1918; when Jeanneret and Ozenfant evoked an era "of strikes, of lawsuits, of protests," they could hardly have been unaware that they were speaking of matters that were once again near at hand.

As the title indicates, Cubism was the reference point for their discussion; it was the very symbol of an art that was "itself an art of protest." "The last of the schools," they wrote, "was Cubism. It was truly of its epoch, this troubled art of a troubled epoch."[19] This was precisely what the Green Kubist presiding over Marianne's delirium in Métivet's cartoon-strip had been meant to indicate. "The art of today," they went on, "which was [once] avant-garde art, is no more than a rear-guard, pre-war art, that of a self-indulgent society,"[20] an assertion that summarily deprived Cubism of any claim to progress. Not that Cubism was the only target of Jeanneret and Ozenfant's critique. They liked neither Fauvism, which they clearly found sloppy—

> The Fauves deny; their paintings are, in effect, feeble in technique, their conception no less so; the fashion for it has passed.[21]

—nor anything smacking of Romanticism, which they considered to be very overly individualistic and elitist—

> Up to the age of Romanticism, artists lived in their own time; the Romantics broke that connection, considering themselves as beings apart, outside of their epoch. Such an attitude, perhaps understandable in that regressive period, would not be justified today.[22]

If the authors of *Après le Cubisme* took a firm stand vis-à-vis the recent and distant past, they were equally unequivocal (though unspecific) in their hopes for the future of art: "Enough games," they scolded; "We aspire to a serious rigor."[23] Statements like this earned for Ozenfant and Jeanneret Gris's mocking description as "the high-minded assembly."[24] Individualism and frivolity were to be replaced by art's union with a governing body of law because, as they saw it, "Science and great Art have the common ideal of generalizing, that which is the highest goal of the spirit . . . Art must generalize to attain beauty."[25] This idea was closely linked to other standard anti-Romantic notions: in philosophical terms, the superiority of the intellect over the senses; in visual terms, of line over color ("the idea of form precedes that of color,"[26] they wrote); and in cultural terms—with wearisome predictability—of the civilized over the barbarian:

> If the Greeks triumphed over the barbarians, if Europe, inheritor of Greek thought, dominates the world, it is because the savages liked loud colors and the noisy sound of tambourines which engage only the senses, while the Greeks loved intellectual beauty which hides beneath sensory beauty.[27]

Here again there is nothing surprising in their new Platonism; hadn't Braque already said, by 1917, "the spirit [the mind] forms; the senses deform"? There is, however, something a bit surprising here, not in the conceptualizations but in their phraseology: where they invoke the classic/barbarian dichotomy, it is not France that is the "inheritor of Greek thought," as it had been for every other spokesman, but Europe that dominates the world. Indeed, as we watch Jeanneret and Ozenfant's artistic and polemical development in the 1920s, we shall find that although they embraced nearly every one of the wartime attitudes with which we are so well acquainted, and in time made an art and inaugurated a movement that was the direct result of the wartime French atmosphere of prejudices and propaganda, exigencies and ideology, they almost never stated their ideas in specifically nationalist terms. Although their paintings and their theories during the 1920s were the fullest realization of post-1914 French national attitudes, they dedicated themselves to and reached out toward an international audience.

Central to the ideas developed in *Après le Cubisme* is the authors' conception of purity and purification. "The war ends," they proclaimed, "everything is organized, everything clarified and purified; factories rise, and already nothing is as it was before the war"[28]—but another way of stating the beneficial aspects of *la Grande Epreuve*, which filters and restores (and it is very close in theme to Paul Dermée's "coming classical age" of organization, arrangement, and science). Jeanneret and Ozenfant continue:

> Here, order and purity illuminate and orient life; this orientation will make the life of tomorrow a profoundly different life from that of yesterday. To the extent that the latter was troubled, uncertain of its path, to the same extent that which is beginning . . . is lucid and clear.[29]

The exaltation of the idea of "purity" had, as we know, been linked to the war from quite early on. Gabriel Boissy had said that the French people would "flower with the impetuous ease of a rejuvenated people or, rather, a people purified by sacrifice," and André Beaunier wrote of France after August 1914 as a place where "everything is changed. The sky opens up; it is purified and grows lighter . . . We were ill; and we recover our health. In our souls, in our spirits, and in our hearts, all is put in order."[30] In a slightly different vein, we may recall, Delaunay said in 1917 that "the young French painters have begun the cleaning-up." In fact, Jeanneret and Ozenfant had very big things in mind for the word "purity," for this was the name by which they had decided to call their post-Cubist art—*le Purisme*. Endowing the word with an almost anthropomorphic quality, and even with an emotive life, they wrote:

> Purism fears the bizarre and the "original." It seeks the pure element with which to reconstruct organized paintings which seem to be made by nature itself.[31]

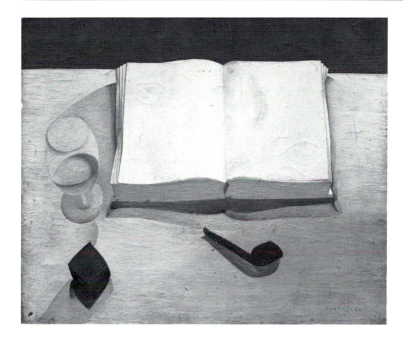

152. C.-E. Jeanneret (Le Corbusier), *Still-Life with Book, Glass, and Pipe*, 1918.

Did the authors realize how thoroughly their Purism was imbued with the impurities of French wartime and post-war prejudices? Did they know that what Purism feared was identical with the nation's fears; that the bizarre and original were otherwise known as revolution, anarchy, and individualism, which were also considered anathema to the organized reconstruction of the French nation, of the *patrie* restored to its proper role? Whether they did or not, they certainly hoped that their chosen name and their stated positions would be more congenial to post-war Frenchmen than the movement they were hoping to supplant. "Purism," they wrote, again imputing to their movement a human consciousness, "thinks that Cubism has remained, no matter what anyone says of it, a decorative, ornamental, and Romantic art."[32] Such an assessment put Cubism in a class with such despised internationalist movements as *Art Nouveau*, Orientalism, *art munichois*, and the entire range of pre-war cosmopolitan frivolities.

But as is often the case in the history of art, the new Purists' theory ran far ahead of their practice, even though their first exhibition of paintings followed the publication of *Après le Cubisme* by no more than a month. Among the works shown at the Galerie Thomas from 22 December 1918 to 11 January 1919 was Jeanneret's *Still-Life with Book, Glass, and Pipe* (fig. 152), which hardly seems to justify the polemic that was its apologia. Or perhaps it does to the extent that, if this is Purism, it does indeed appear to fear the bizarre and original (only to replace it with something bland) and is by all means pure and organized (but this is not difficult, considering how reduced the means have become). When the Purists spoke of "paintings which seem to be made by nature itself," they were merely talking at this point about naturalistic painting. Although *Après le Cubisme* presented an argument that was meant to go "beyond" Cubism and espouse "Science," Jeanneret's painting looks strikingly like the kind of work that many Parisian artists made ca. 1908–9 on their way *into* Cubism. So conventional-looking is it that a viewer in the winter of 1918 would not see it as a rejection of anything in particular, unless he was equipped with both the publication of 15 November and a Cubist work alongside as comparative material. For the Purist, verbal polemic and critique were substituted for an artistic past, so that only text and painting together (i.e. polemic and illustration) could convey the sense of artistic renovation.

In fact, when *Still-Life with Book, Glass, and Pipe* is examined in the context of *Après le Cubisme*, its programmatic reworking of Cubism becomes obvious. If we compare it to Pablo Picasso's *The Bottle of Pernod* (fig. 153) of six years earlier, we can see how thoroughly Jeanneret has rejected Picasso's free-floating space, his simultaneity, his Bergsonian sense of flux, and the general proliferation of signs and symbols that make up this Cubist café still-life. In place of visual complexity, the Purist gives us the stark image of an open book with clean white pages, a kind of Neoplatonic *tabula rasa* on which a new historical chapter is beginning. Although we could not know it without Jeanneret and Ozenfant's statement that Cubism was a "decorative, ornamental, and Romantic art," we see to what extent the Purist still-life does, in a sense, accuse Picasso's picture of these shortcomings. But however organized, clear, and pure Jeanneret's picture looks there is nothing scientific here; and the vigor which the Purists claimed for post-war art seems to live rather in Picasso's pre-war picture.

But on the issue of the preference for the intellectual over the sensual, and in view of their coining of the phrases "the Great Test" and "the Great Competition," the *Still-Life with Book, Glass, and Pipe* does seem to confirm the authors' verbal statements. After all, Jeanneret's painting is about the life of the mind; it is the view from the perspective of the reader, as he looks down upon his immaculate book, alongside which are

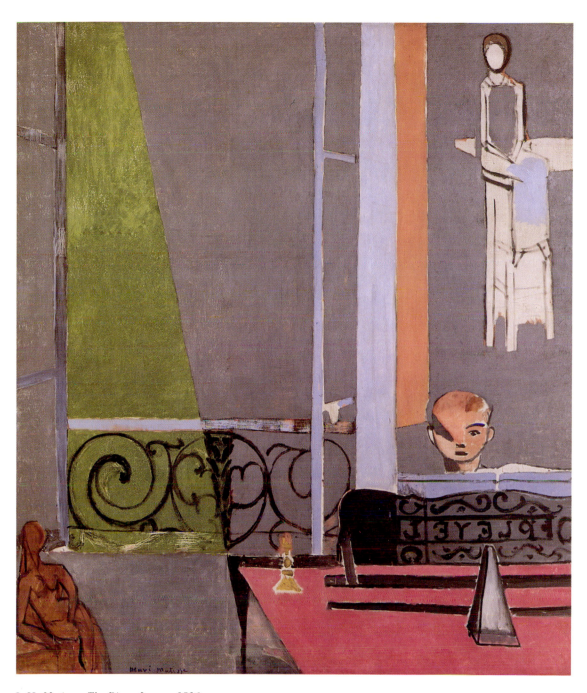

I. H. Matisse, *The Piano Lesson*, 1916.

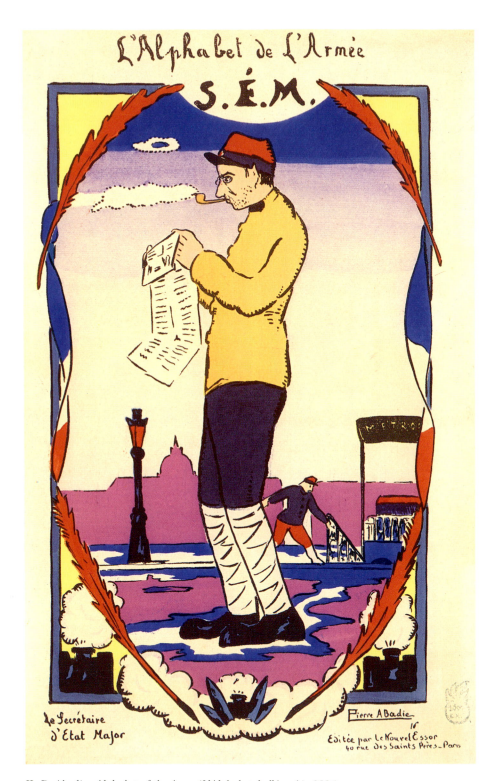

II. P. Abadie, *Alphabet of the Army* (*L'Alphabet de l'Armée*), 1916.

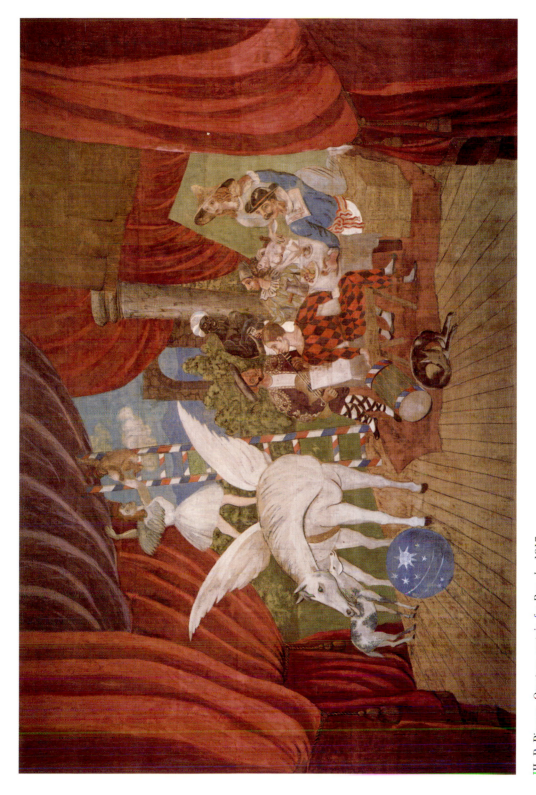

III. P. Picasso. Overture curtain for *Parade*, 1917.

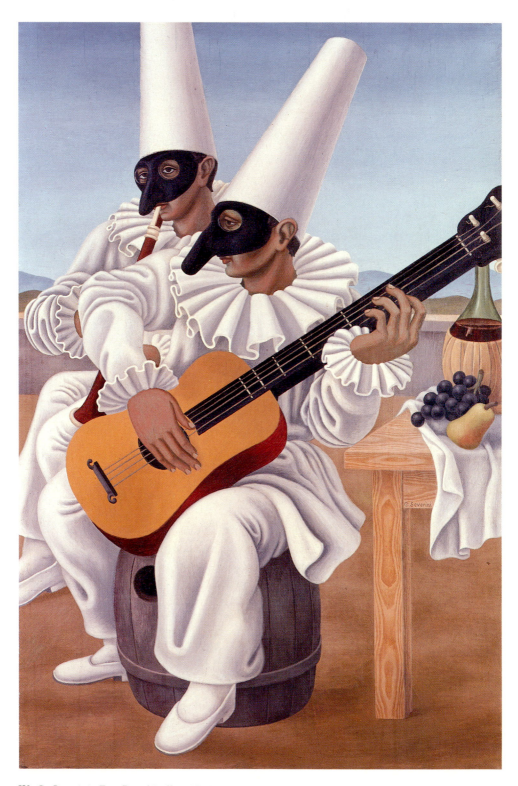

IV. G. Severini, *Two Punchinellos*, 1922.

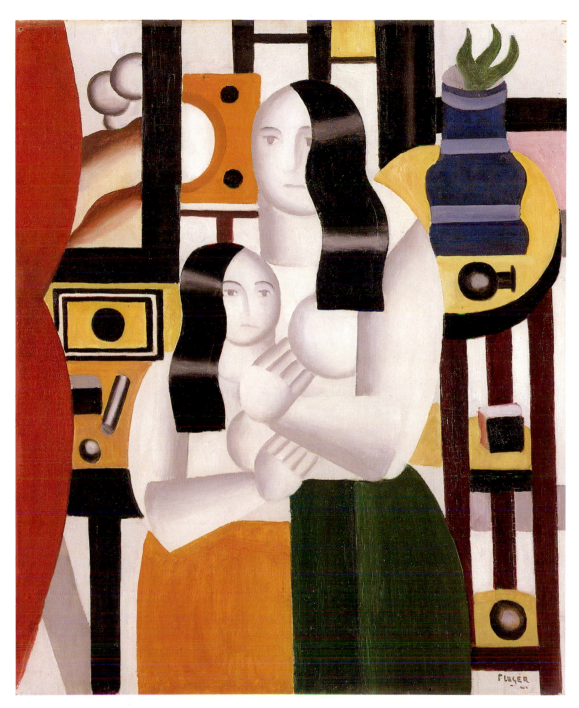

V. F. Léger, *Mother and Child*, 1922.

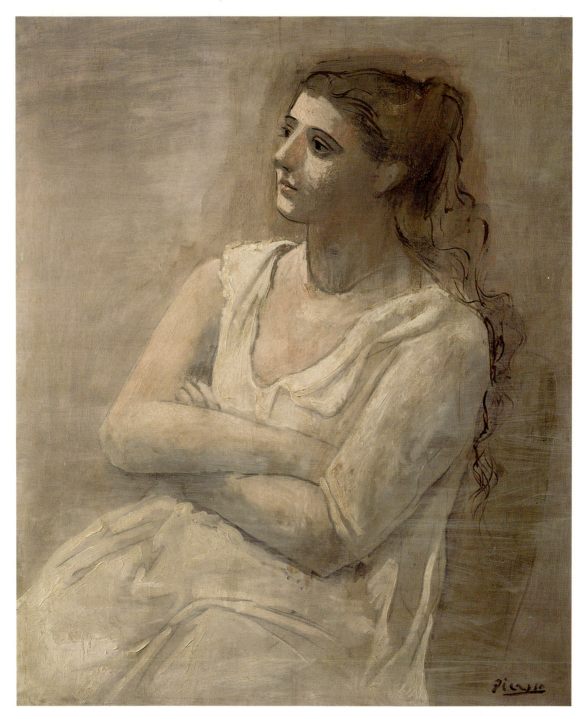

VI. P. Picasso, *Woman in White*, 1923.

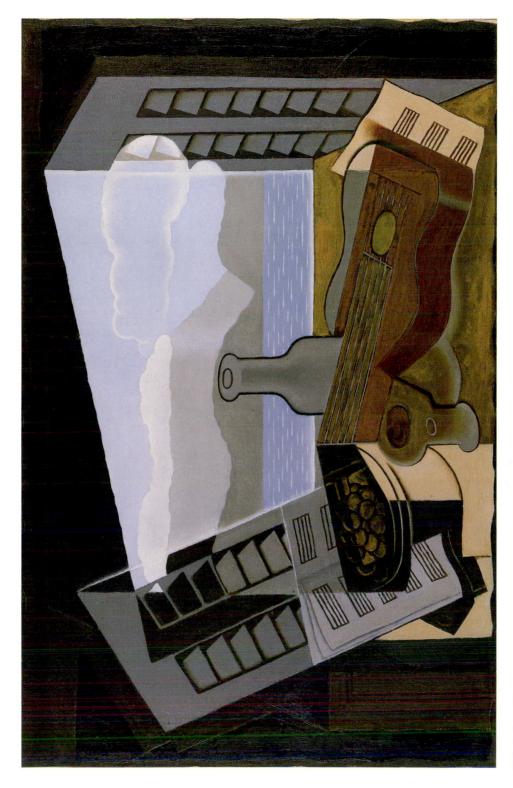

VII. J. Gris, *The Open Window*, 1921.

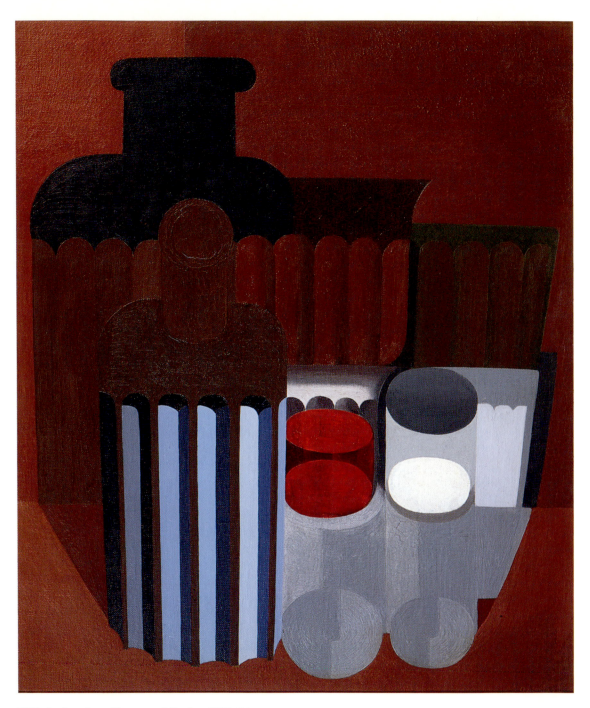

VIII. A. Ozenfant, *Glasses and Bottles*, 1922–26.

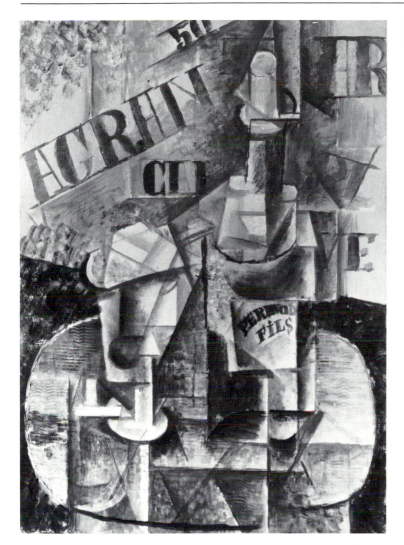

153. P. Picasso, *The Bottle of Pernod*, 1912.

ranged his glass of wine or cognac (only a third full), his pipe, and his matches. Indeed, this is clearly a mature-man's-eye-view of study, while Picasso's picture contains only images of amusement and sociability. In *The Bottle of Pernod* we are located in a café where the only semblance of a text is the visual cacophony caused by advertisements, newspapers, perhaps snippets of conversation. Of course the central image is of that bottle and the accompanying glass, a vessel that can be filled and refilled, toward the goal not of self-improvement but of inebriation, of the loss of self-control and clarity. If Picasso's rather sober palette and harsh, modern geometry are usually considered to be the antithesis of a Romantic art, we now understand that in terms of subject matter and even, to a certain extent, of metaphor the Purists could see in Cubist art a visual counterpart of Symbolist (i.e. late Romantic) poetry, the realization of Rimbaud's "drunken boat." We might even go so far as to invent a kind of "Marianne and Germania" moralizing fable in the comparison (and one, we can imagine, that would not have displeased Jeanneret): while the inebriated Cubist fritters away his time at the café, the Purist remains at home, diligently studying his texts, puffing on his pipe, and taking only an occasional sip from his glass. Although this style of conventional painting did not long satisfy Jeanneret and Ozenfant, it was nonetheless their first attempt at forging a new aesthetic for the post-war years.

The Purists were by no means alone in declaring that a new, more rigorous age had dawned for France, though they were the first to say it after the Armistice. For André Salmon in 1920, for instance, it was as simple as the statement "The era of the virtuosos is closed,"[33] by which he meant that individualistic manifestations were no longer the order of the day. Roger Allard went on at greater length in *Le Nouveau Spectateur* to describe the same phenomenon, specifically referring to the Salon d'Automne of 1919:

> Sale before inventory. Tomorrow we begin again with new stock. The Salon of 1919 resembles too closely that of 1913 not to be a liquidation of stock. We didn't hope for a miracle, a fireworks of blinding revelations, and we envisioned the "benefits of war" with appropriate skepticism. But lacking a benefit there is a fact . . . the means no longer correspond to new values. *All prices have gone up* . . . That which formerly conferred a manner of originality and permitted an adroit practitioner to make a name for himself in a salon of painting today excites, by his air of indigence or by his usurped opulence, only commiseration mixed with annoyance.
>
> Certain words have acquired a clear meaning. They are sonorous gongs that one dare no longer strike without a motive. People will no longer say so generously that a work is "audacious"; they will no longer pretend to believe that a clown who does the same trick every night is "audacious."[34]

Although he had been a pre-war supporter of the Parisian avant-garde (and would generally remain one in the post-war years), Allard, like Salmon and the Purists, has no patience left for the "audacity" or individualism of adroit artist-clowns. Like many others before him, Allard builds his critique of the contemporary scene on the metaphor of evaluation, in this case assuming the persona of the shopkeeper coming to terms with the economics of inflation (eminently appropriate in the hyperinflationary post-war French economy). While far too perspicacious to believe that the war's benefits would be immediately forthcoming—and proclaiming his wholly justified skepticism with such talk—he nonetheless believes in the new values. As a critic, he is sensitive to language. He duly notes the abuse of terms like *les bienfaits de la guerre*, and points out that the post-war period is a time of words, catch-words, slogans, and abbreviations—indeed, that "certain words have acquired a clear meaning," with the example that "audacity" now signifies something negative where once it seemed to be a term of praise. To a certain extent he may have been referring (if unconsciously) to the manifestations of Parisian Dada around 1919—and on this subject there will be more to say at a later point. For now, it is sufficient that we recognize the bias in the Parisian avant-garde against anything too audacious both in painting and, not surprisingly, in the decorative arts. In the spring of 1919, for instance, the critic Jean Laran wrote in *Art et Décoration*: "The war has taught us a hard lesson which must not be lost"—i.e., that the French decorative arts need to "prune the tree of dead branches and cease producing bizarre oddities," to put an end to the supposed virtue of "novelty at all costs"; no more "backward houses," no more "chairs with five legs."[35]

But if, as the critic Jean-Louis Vaudoyer wrote in 1919, "innovation at all costs is no longer in style; we are calming ourselves and organizing,"[36] then artistic inspiration had to come from sources other than that which had been provided by the metaphors of modernity; if the artist could not look toward the future, then there was only one other direction in which he could look—backward—and for Vaudoyer this was as it should be. "We will see," he wrote,

> that the past is no longer an enemy to be demolished or disdained but, on the contrary, it is an auxiliary, an ally, a discreet inspiration, with proven and living virtues.[37]

This had been one of the lessons of the Great War: that France's past (or her supposed past) was her closest ally; that, as Focillon said, "history is not an arid meditation . . . it does not turn away but exhorts, encourages to action."[38] And even if Picasso had not been responding to a conscious change in attitude when he first turned back to Ingres in 1915, or Gris when he began to draw *d'après* Cézanne just slightly later; even if Matisse had never intended a reference to Rodin or to Ingres in his Bohain series; and even though Severini may have been unaware of how crucial was his decision in late 1916 to try his hand at a bit of academic painting, by 1918 the re-emergence of historical reference was a given for the avant-garde. In fact, the moment had never been more propitious for such a backward glance, not only because the French nation in general was now busy counting its dead and quantifying its losses, but also because the artistic necrology was formidable by 1919, especially in regard to the recent past. Three of the great surviving figures of the nineteenth century had just died—Rodin and Degas in 1917, and Renoir in 1919—and if the reputation of Impressionism had declined rapidly of late, the reputations of these individual artists were probably as high as they had ever been. Of the Impressionists, only Claude Monet was still alive, and with the installation of the *Water Lilies* in the Orangerie, at Clemenceau's invitation,[39] his legend, if not his artistic influence, was secure.

Another, more tangible encouragement to think about the past was provided by the post-war reopening of the Louvre, the nation's treasure house of sanctioned art history. Starting in January 1919, the Egyptian and Assyrian galleries were reopened, and by the next year the Salon Carré, the Grande Galerie, and the French galleries were open to the public.[40] "After a long period of being closed, the Louvre reappears," wrote Bissière, who continued, "many of today's painters have entered it with a new heart . . . with a desire to meet some of the great works there and with the secret hope of finding in them a lesson and a justification."[41] But it was not *any* works of the past that the young artists wanted to see, not even especially the masterpieces of the Italian Renaissance, according to the painter and critic:

> To the splendors of the Italians they have preferred the little lost galleries where sleeps the art of the men of their race, testimony to the clear and lucid French spirit, spirit of earthly realities. . . . They found themselves in the presence of their true origins, and they have understood that it was not necessary to search elsewhere for guides and supports.[42]

As we know, the turn toward the French masters of the past (and, for artists less parochial than Bissière, toward other elements of the Latin heritage) had been apparent for a number of years, although the "rappel à l'ordre," as André Lhote called it,[43] certainly became more insistent in the post-war period. Lhote himself, who had said in 1917 that it was in "Poussin, Claude Lorrain, David, and Ingres" that one finds a "taste for architecture," and "often perfect equilibriums," now wrote in 1920 that Fouquet was "our highest national reference,"[44] and the same year, in his article "First Visit to the Louvre," it was "Jean Fouquet, Le Nain, Ingres with his drawings of such prodigious acuity and style"[45] that were his favorites. Allard, in 1919, after stating that "three apples on a plate can suffice to give the idea of a highly gifted painter"—clearly a reference to Cézanne—nonetheless went on to say that "a landscape by Claude or the *Shepherds of Arcadia* give a prouder idea of art and humanity."[46] And Gris, whose studio in the 1920s was "decorated entirely with reproductions of the work of the French painters: Fouquet, the brothers Le Nain, Boucher, and Ingres,"[47] wrote to Daniel-Henry Kahnweiler in 1919:

> I would like to continue the tradition of painting with plastic means while bringing it to a new aesthetic based on the intellect. I think one can quite well take over Chardin's means without taking over either the appearance of his pictures or his conception of reality.[48]

But this formidable task, as we shall see later, was beyond Gris's abilities. More typical of the avant-garde's new interest in the French masters was a modest attempt at homage like Braque's *Memory of Corot—Woman with Mandolin* (fig. 154) of 1922–23, which was (as far as I am aware) only the second illusionistic work that Braque had made since the advent of Cubism. Bissière said of Braque, just after the war, "I recognize in this artist the essential gifts of our race: this sense of proportion and this severe grace which are born only in France, likewise this disdain for ephemeral appearances and this need for profundity."[49]

Far more deeply involved in a thorough perusal of *la grande tradition*, French and Italian, was Roger de la Fresnaye, whose actual uses of the artistic past seem to have begun in earnest in Tours, when he was hospitalized there at the very end of the war in October 1918, after having been gassed in the trenches. Albeit an eclectic sampling of the Latin sensibility, La Fresnaye's post-war studies firmly place him in the historicist mode, the first example of which is a watercolor made at Tours (fig. 155) and based on Le Sueur's (or Vouet's) *Saint Sebastian succored by Saint Irene* in the collection of the local museum. Still

154. G. Braque, *Memory of Corot:*
Woman with Mandolin, 1922–23.

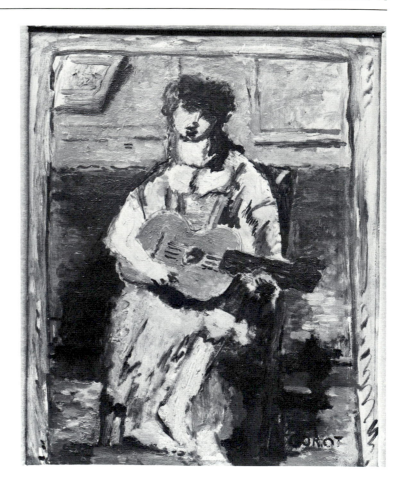

somewhat in the quasi-Cubist mode of his pre-war art, it was
followed in the next year by quite close copies of Goya tapestry
cartoons. Then came a more folkloric-looking *Sacred Heart Ap-*
pearing to Saint Margaret Maria dated 1919–20; drawings of
Eve after Raphael's figure on the ceiling of the Stanza della
Segnatura; and other drawings after Michelangelo and Fra
Lippo Lippi, Botticelli and Pollaiuolo.[50] Although we shall look
more closely at La Fresnaye's post-war painting later, it can be
noted here that he was thinking a good deal about traditional
techniques, as exemplified by his statement to a friend in 1922
that he had found the solution to the "execution of the ancients
and particularly Poussin," which consisted in using "oil to flu-
idify the color."[51]

We already know that by the end of the war Apollinaire felt
that his poetry was moving in a "classic" direction much akin
to his friend Picasso's artistic development. In August 1918,

just a few months before his death, Apollinaire encouraged Picasso in another related direction, toward the specifically French: "I would like to see you make large paintings like Poussin," he wrote at the end of the summer, "something lyrical like your copy of Le Nain,"[52] referring to the Spaniard's recent "neo-Impressionist" copy (fig. 156) of *The Peasants' Repast* in the Louvre. Although clearly part of Picasso's post-1914 study of the French past and, in its form *d'après* Le Nain, exemplary of the new apprenticeship to old masters being served by so many members of the Parisian avant-garde, the painting would hardly qualify as an example of the "clear and lucid French spirit" or even, for that matter, as respectful. Having changed the format from Le Nain's horizontal to vertical; neglecting to include a child in the doorway at the far right and also a baby

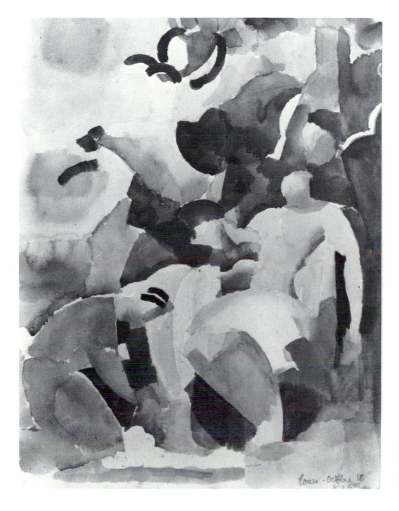

155. R. de la Fresnaye, Study after Le Sueur's (or Vouet's) *Saint Sebastian Succored by Saint Irene*, 1918.

156. P. Picasso, *The Peasants' Repast
(after Le Nain)*, 1917–18.

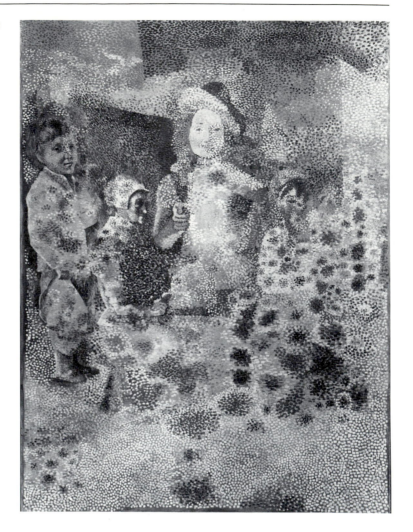

(perhaps a just-baptized infant) on the woman's knee at the right, as well as a cat in the lower left; altering the relative scale of the figures to the point of nonsense; and, most obviously, exploding Le Nain's image of familial piety with the brightly colored confetti of a mock-Seurat pointillism, Picasso has totally subverted the form and content of the French master. Although there is some evidence, in the form of a highly worked-up drawing (a figure study [Zervos, xxx, no. 147] of the boy at the left), that Picasso may have also taken a more serious interest in Le Nain's aesthetic, the painting nonetheless typifies his extremely ambivalent relationship to the past, especially during the last year of the war and following the Armistice.

Another work of 1918, the tiny *Bathers* (fig. 157) which he made in Biarritz during the summer, exhibits a similarly ironic and distorted remembrance of things past, in a crazy-quilt of French art history. Picasso's first source for the *Bathers* is none other than Puvis de Chavannes, specifically the famous *Young Girls by the Seashore* of 1880 (fig. 158).[53] The Three Graces motif; the poses (standing woman, now turned forward, with hair in hand; the reclining "Odalisque" with raised arm, now disposed from left to right; the third figure, at the lower right, with hair falling forward to reveal the nape of her neck); the seashore setting; and even the particulars of the compositional devices (the tripartite division of shoreline, sea, and sky echoing the three figures; the precise intervals at which the bathers are cut by the simplified lines of the landscape; the outcropping of land at the left which has been transformed into volcanic rock and, at the same time, moved to the right, to form a natural pillow for the reclining woman) are all direct quotations from Puvis's famous picture. Indeed, Puvis was an ideal source of inspiration at a moment when classicism and French values were being consistently invoked. André Michel, for instance, lumped together "landscape, plein-airism, Impressionism, division[ism], optical mixing" as "indefensible eccentricities" and "aberrations," but saw Puvis as a Christ-like figure who had cleansed the temple: "At the moment when, on so many fronts, mediocrity seemed about to triumph, didn't a Puvis de Chavannes appear, in the nick of time, to restore all her dignity to French art?"[54]

Of course, the changes that Picasso makes are numerous and funny: these are not eternalized neo-classical goddesses draped *à l'antique* but modern girls wearing the latest *maillots de bain*; it is not the unspecified and eternalized sea of Puvis at which these women luxuriate, but a modern resort, with a picturesque lighthouse and a breeze-tossed skiff in the background; and at least one figure, the standing brunette in the striped suit, is the opposite of languidly ethereal—she is a modern bacchante, a Biarritz "jazz-baby" who seems lost not in reverie but in the throes of a latter-day Dionysian ritual (although perhaps she is no more than a member of the new breed of sun-worshiper). Furthermore, Picasso has also produced an artistic amalgam without precedent, because if the highly respectable Puvis is one component of the source and reference for the 1918 *Bathers*, the other major source here is the Sunday painter and customs-inspector Henri Rousseau, *dit le Douanier*. In the high-keyed color scheme of gray, green, and blue setting, juxtaposed

157. P. Picasso, *Bathers*, 1918.

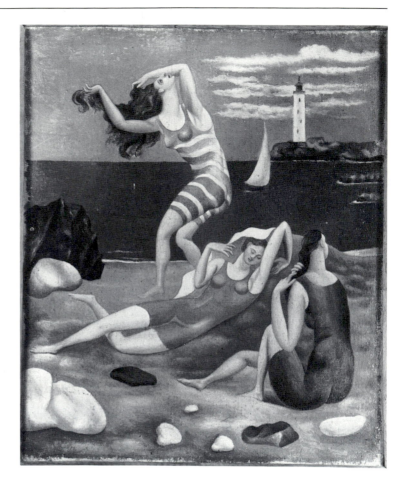

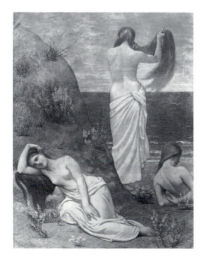

158. P. Puvis de Chavannes, *Young Girls by the Seashore*, 1880.

with the hot pink, orange, and light blue of the bathers' outfits, as well as in the stripe motif, we can see that it is to a work like Rousseau's *Soccer Players* (fig. 159) that Picasso has turned for his leavening. Nor is it only the color scheme that Picasso takes from France's most famous folk artist; he has also borrowed the rather primitively rendered poses, awkward distortions, frozen gestures, and childlike arrangement, as well as the polished appearance of the modeling (partaking of intense white highlights, the Douanier's idea of volume). Indeed, Picasso has made of the combination of Puvis and the Douanier Rousseau a tour de force, a demonstration of his artistic power, not only in blending such stylistically contradictory artists but in making a mixture that in cultural terms was unthinkable. Like oil and water, Puvis the *Chevalier* of the Legion of Honor, he of the sanctioned national and religious iconography, and Rousseau the Sunday painter were irreconcilable quantities—or so one would have thought.

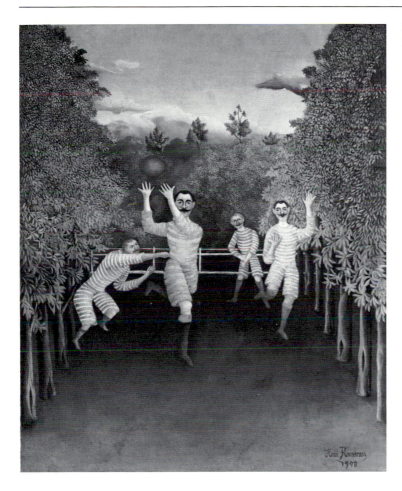

159. H. Rousseau, *The Soccer Players*, 1908.

Picasso's two historical graftings of 1918, that of Le Nain on Seurat and of Puvis on Rousseau, were but a continuation of the artist's new concern with art history that had begun in 1914. With homage and irony in various proportions, he continued to make reference to the French repertory in the years following the Armistice. Appropriately, in 1919 it was to Renoir that Picasso devoted a good deal of thought, both in a drawing of the recently deceased master (fig. 160), based on a popular photograph,[55] and in a series of pencil studies after Renoir's painting *Le Ménage Sisley* (fig. 161). Nineteenth-century peasant painting, and probably Millet specifically, also captured Picasso's fancy that year; the result was a series of sleeping farm workers, executed in charcoal and pencil, and a famous gouache (fig. 162). Not surprisingly, we also find in 1919 a large series of ballet images—some were executed on the spot as the artist watched Olga's colleagues dance, others were drawn from photographs of the Diaghilev troupe, and still others are pure in-

160. P. Picasso, *Portrait of Renoir*, 1919.

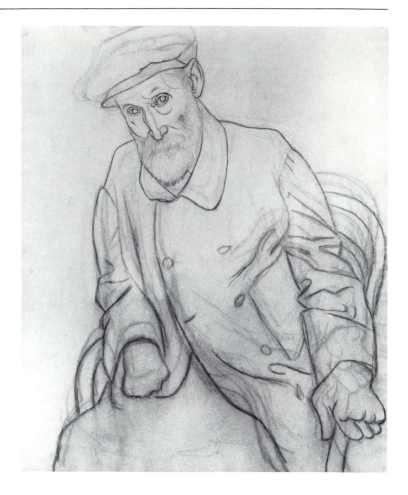

ventions (fig. 163)—that both rejoice in and make fun of that most famous balletic oeuvre, Degas's pictures of the ballet at the Paris Opéra.[56] The next year Picasso also copied Corot's *Mlle. de Foudras* (fig. 99) and made several other drawings that are very reminiscent of Puvis.[57] But of all the Spaniard's various tributes to the French tradition, it was still the classicist Ingres who was the greatest inspiration for Picasso's post-war draftsmanship. Drawing had by now become a major aspect of Picasso's art. Of the three exhibitions of his work held in Paris between 1919 and 1925—all at Paul Rosenberg's gallery—two, those of 1919 and 1924, were of drawings (the 1919 show, which included watercolors, was criticized by Allard for its preponderance of historical pastiche: "everything, including Leonardo, Dürer, Le Nain, Ingres, Van Gogh, Cézanne, yes, everything . . . except Picasso";[58] the 1924 exhibition was titled simply "Cent dessins."). Only in 1921 did Picasso show

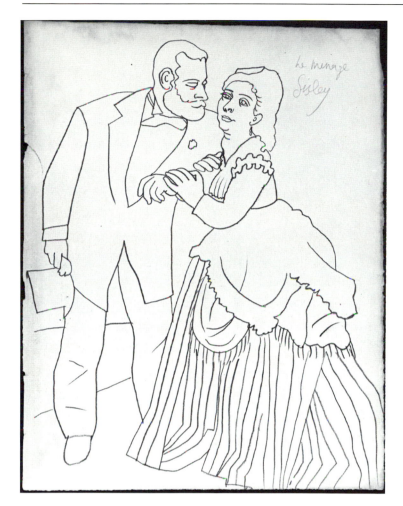

161. P. Picasso, Study after Renoir's *Le Ménage Sisley*, 1919.

paintings, and then not again in Paris until 1926. A large proportion of the drawings were Ingres-inspired not only in their
purified line, but also in their subject—portraiture—which included drawings of Erik Satie, Léon Bakst, and André Derain
(fig. 164), in the last of which Picasso has enlarged the painter's
hands to gargantuan proportions. And it was not just in the art
of Picasso that Ingres was experiencing a post-war revival: his
name was being invoked and his art scrutinized widely. A major
exhibition of the nineteenth-century master's work, installed at
the "Hôtel des commissaires-priseurs," from 7 June to 12 June
1921, opened to great acclaim, including an article by Léonce
Bénédite, curator of the Luxembourg Museum, who noted that
the show was very timely: "While Delacroix has been somewhat
relegated to the shadows, Ingres, for a number of years now,

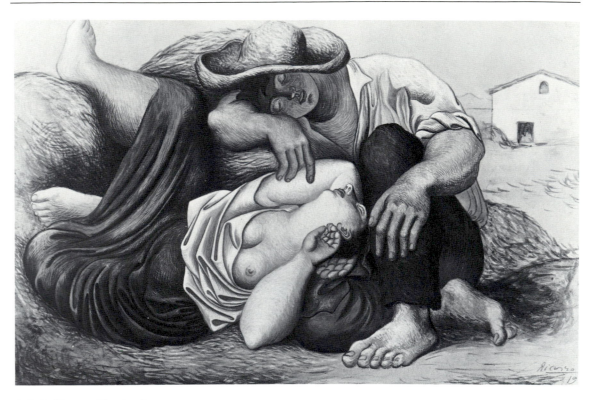

162. P. Picasso, *Sleeping Peasants*,
1919.

has been attracting the attention of artists and of the public."[59]
Organized for the benefit of disfigured war veterans, the exhibition of Ingres's mostly idealized humanity was accompanied
by a special issue of *La Renaissance de l'Art Français et des
Industries de Luxe*, the new post-war magazine of the arts, published by none other than Henri Lapauze and conceived as an
adjunct to his *La Renaissance (politique, economique, littéraire
et artistique)*. With ten articles by the leading authorities and
would-be authorities on Ingres's oeuvre, and with numerous illustrations of the master's work, it was a major effort at trying
to create taste, by the journalist who had recently persecuted
Paul Poiret for his supposed German affiliations.

No friend of advanced Parisian art, Lapauze nevertheless was
aware of the new importance of Ingres in the work of Picasso,
and he wasted no time in mentioning this, rather disdainfully,
in his article "Une Nouvelle Leçon de Ingres." "M. Picasso and
my young compatriots André Lhote and Bissière, so sympathetic to the Ingrist sensibility—from which they are much further removed than they think—will be followed in their turn by
the ardent young, as they followed their elders," wrote Lapauze;
the reason for this, he went on to explain, was that every artist,

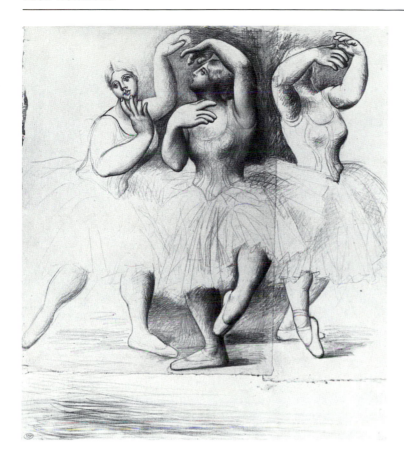

163. P. Picasso, *Ballet Dancers*, 1919.

whether he deserves to or not, "wants to be able to claim Ingres for himself."[60] After all, says the critic parenthetically, the Cubists were preceded in their admiration for Ingres by those revolutionaries of yesteryear, Cézanne, Degas, Denis, and Signac.[61] Indeed, Ingres's new lesson, according to Lapauze, is that of proportion and good sense, an antidote for contemporary malaise:

> this exhibition, for the benefit of the facially wounded, valiant ones who sacrificed themselves for their country, arrived at the right time. Our young artists are going crazy, alas!, not knowing where to turn. I can see that they really are trying to find their way in entirely good faith, but no one is there to point it out to them. People speak glibly today of reconstruction, of order, and of discipline. And they think they are hearing M. Ingres himself talking.[62]

Arsène Alexandre's article in the same issue of *La Renaissance*, entitled "To understand Ingres is to understand Greece and France," puts forth the by now unsurprising if fatuous the-

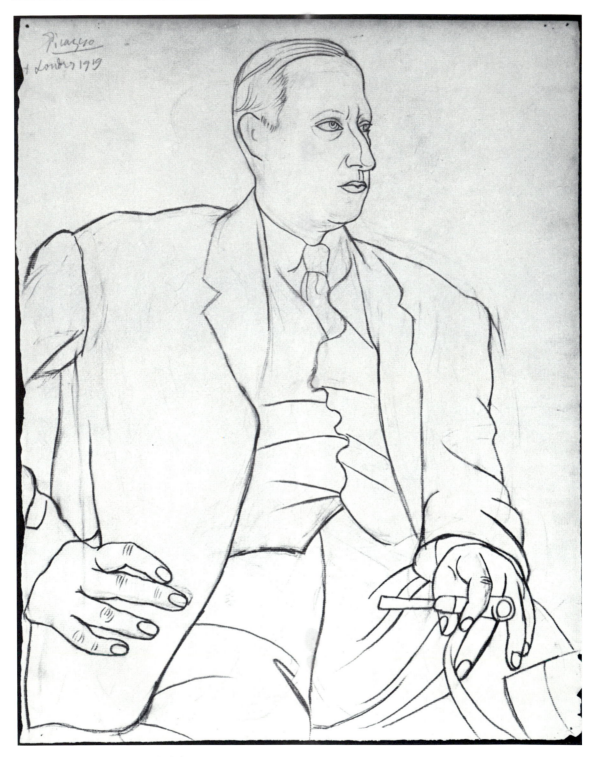

164. P. Picasso, *Portrait of André Derain*, 1919.

sis that of all the Allied nations France is the most Hellenic, the "Greece of Euripides, Socrates, Plato, Praxiteles, Phidias." In turn, he goes on to say, it is in Ingres's work that "the tendencies of a race are revealed," and these, like France herself, are a product of the artist's "supreme Hellenism." In reference to Ingres's *Birth of the Muses* ("this little . . . sober picture") Alexandre says, "Such a work will always bestow on men of Greco-Latin race and culture a light and calm intoxication that can help them to bear the doubts and burdens of life"; and this Mediterranean opiate could not have arrived at a more propitious moment, "when we have hardly awoken from the Germanic ascendancy that assaulted our minds in the form of asphyxiating systems much more dangerous than poison gases . . ." Yet again, as ever since the very beginning of the now historic war, it is "lucidity, clarity, luminous enthusiasm, and intelligent goodness" that will dispel the alien vapors and restore the nation to full health, courtesy of J.A.D. Ingres.[63]

But perhaps the most important lesson that the current revival of Ingres has to teach, according to Alexandre, is that history will heal all wounds and reconcile all differences. Could Ingres and Delacroix, sworn rivals, have imagined that they would both now bask in the beneficent glow of history, the critic asks, now that the classicist and the Romantic had both become exemplars of the great French tradition? "We rejoice that France," he exclaims, "by a marvelous equilibrium that is hers alone, could give birth at the same time and in the same country to two geniuses so representative of opposing tendencies."[64] But the test of a powerful culture lies in its ability to assimilate contrary but indigenous tendencies, according to Alexandre, and it is the passage of time that is the nation's greatest ally:

> A century of distance effects many rapprochements and metamorphoses. Leveling the sheerest summits as well as creating an elevated observation point for our eyes, it transforms a revolutionary into a classicist and a classicist into a revolutionary, which is a way of bringing them into harmony.[65]

The transformation of revolutionaries into classicists, by way of the art of Ingres, was in fact taking place in ateliers all over Paris. Gris, for example, who had begun to draw "like a Prix de Rome winner" during the war, took his neo-Ingres draftsmanship even further after the Armistice. As Picasso had first done in 1915, Gris made a pencil portrait of Max Jacob in 1919 (fig. 165), and a portrait of Daniel-Henry Kahnweiler in 1921

165. J. Gris, *Portrait of Max Jacob*,
1919.

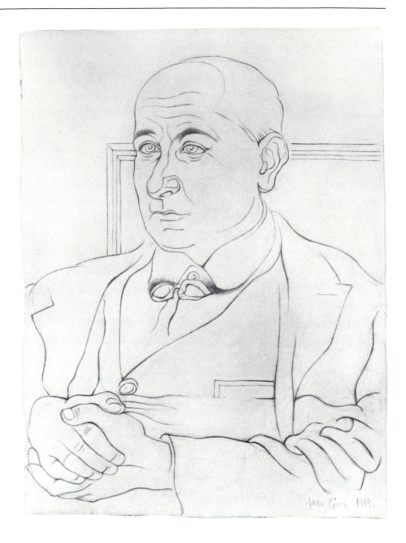

(fig. 166): in both portraits nearly every trace of Cubism has
been expunged and in its place is a pristine line with only the
most discreet areas of modeling. Kahnweiler, who had returned
to Paris from exile in February 1920, is posed before a stack of
canvases, a perhaps slightly bitter reference to his sequestered
property (stored in a damp ground-floor apartment in the rue de
Rome) which at that moment was being auctioned off by the
French government.[66] Gris also created a suite of portrait prints
in 1921, of which he pulled fifty examples.[67] We have already
heard the artist say that he hoped to be able to take over "Chardin's means" without making pictures that would look like his.
In a letter to Kahnweiler in November 1921, implying that he
had at one time felt differently, Gris wrote:

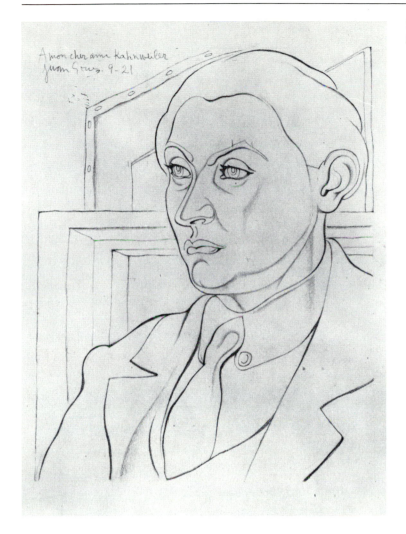

166. J. Gris, *Portrait of D.-H. Kahnweiler*, 1921.

I have been thinking about what is meant by "quality" in an artist. . . . Well, now I believe that the "quality" of an artist derives from the quantity of the past that he carries in him—from his artistic atavism. The more of this heritage he has, the more "quality" he has.[68]

While perhaps unsurprising in this retrospective era of French art, this is nevertheless an astonishing statement to hear from one of the leading members of the pre-war Parisian avant-garde.

Needless to say, it was Picasso whom Gris was thinking of when he spoke of artistic atavism, and it is Picasso's name that we hear over and over again in relation to the post-war traditionalism, and especially in all matters involving the art of

Ingres. Delaunay, who with his wife Sonia had returned to Paris from their Iberian exile, was annoyed by the direction of Picasso's art as well as by the Spaniard's ever-flourishing career. In the winter of 1923–24 he wrote of Picasso's "superficiality" and "habitual snobbery" and referred to his myriad art-historical references as "this continuity in pillage that individualists dare to call 'tradition.' "[69] Abbreviating Picasso's name to a simple "P"—as if he could not bear to write out the name in full—Delaunay disdainfully described Picasso's career this way:

> P with his periods: Steinlen, Lautrec, Van Gogh, Daumier, Corot, negroes, Braque, Derain, Cézanne, Renoir, Ingres, etc. etc. etc. Puvis de Chavannes, neo-Italian . . . these influences prove the lack of seriousness, in terms of construction and sureness.[70]

Yet once again, even while he was damning the "famous genius," Delaunay was still mimicking Picasso—he too made a gallery of traditionally rendered portraits, in about 1922–23, including those of Boris Kochno, the dance critic and secretary to Diaghilev (fig. 167), the poets Ilizaid Zdanevich, Ivan Goll, and his wife Claire, as well as Philippe Soupault, Louis Aragon, Tristan Tzara, and Bella Chagall.

Meanwhile, Delaunay's compatriot Roger de la Fresnaye, busily surveying the history of art for guidance, also found what he was looking for in Ingres. Whereas in the midst of war much of his work was still at least marginally Cubist, as exemplified by a watercolor of a café scene with soldiers and waitress (fig. 168), by the post-war period we find not only a large group of Ingres-style drawings, but full-scale neo-traditional oil portraits, like that of the man who appears to have been his lover, Jean-Louis Gampert (fig. 169).[71] In reference to a portrait he was painting in 1921, La Fresnaye told André Mare that he wanted to "make it like M. Ingres."[72]

But, as Delaunay's coments on Picasso's eclecticism prove, the Spaniard was resented even though he was the instigator of the Ingres revival that held the avant-garde in thrall. For one thing, the artist was financially more successful than ever, in part because he had begun to appeal to an expanded audience—not just the group of advanced collectors who had bought his work in the pre-war years, but now also a more conservative clientele that frequented the gallery of Paul Rosenberg, brother of Léonce (Paul's taste, in contrast to that of his brother, was quite traditional). More important, though, Picasso's aesthetic brew at this point was a combination of revolution and reaction,

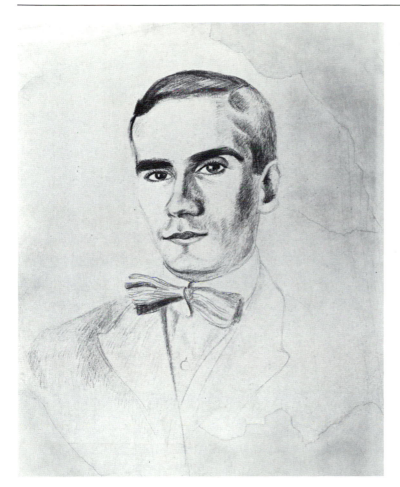

heavily seasoned with irony, and it was this last quality which was so difficult for his peers to tolerate: Picasso was able to eat his cake and have it too. Even when the works seem ironic in their invocation of the new traditionalism, they managed to please the collectors nonetheless. Indeed, just as André Level had said of the 1915 portrait of Jacob that Picasso was "surpassing" Ingres, purifying, enlarging, and clarifying his art while amusing himself, so in the post-war Ingres-style drawings he demonstrates by means of caricature (as, for example, the enlarged hands in the portrait of Derain) an unshakable confidence in his own "artistic atavism." In comparison to Albert Gleizes's self-portrait of 1919 (fig. 170), where the artist not only attempts to convince us of his commanding presence by means of a pipe but also wears a cape, forcing us to make a comparison with Ingres's own famous self-portrait as a young

168. R. de la Fresnaye, *La Madelon*, 1917.

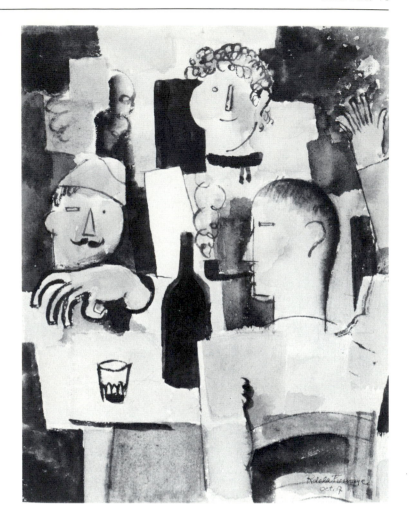

man, Picasso's drawings seem ineffably light and self-assured.[73]

As we have noticed, the Ingres influence (or the Picasso-cum-Ingres influence) tended to take the form of drawing rather than painting, usually resulting in schematized, nearly unmodeled linear drawing. This preference for *le dessin*, for form over color, for precise line over anything too atmospheric or painterly, was of course Ingres's own preference. It was an essential tenet of academic art, part and parcel of the descending order of priority among the visual arts, i.e. from architecture to sculpture to painting. We are already well acquainted, furthermore, with the French wartime discussions of construction and architecture, whereby social order and socially sanctioned behavior were intimately associated with these academic principles (and we have heard the Purists, for instance, say that "the idea of form precedes that of color"). For the Parisian avant-garde after 1918, as for the more conservative artists and critics, the painterly was associated with Romantic and Impressionist art, with all that was fragmentary, socially divisive, and individualistic. The rhetoric of the "asphyxiating gases" of the despised enemy could be turned on anything that was too "gaseous" or ill-defined.

But academic precedent was not, I think, the only reason for the enormous popularity of drawing after the war. If each portrait drawing was an isolated demonstration of the "quantity of the past" (to use Gris's phrase) that each artist carried in him,

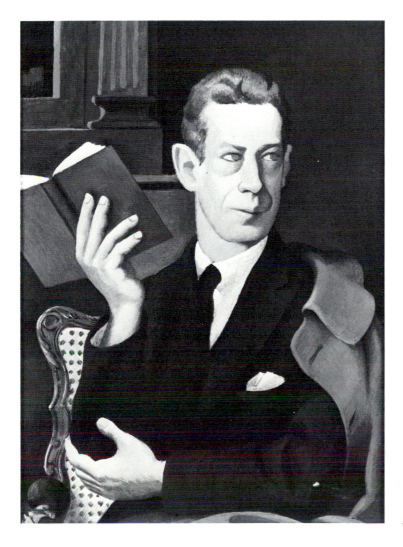

169. R. de la Fresnaye, *Portrait of Jean-Louis Gampert*, 1920.

170. A. Gleizes, *Self-Portrait*, 1919.

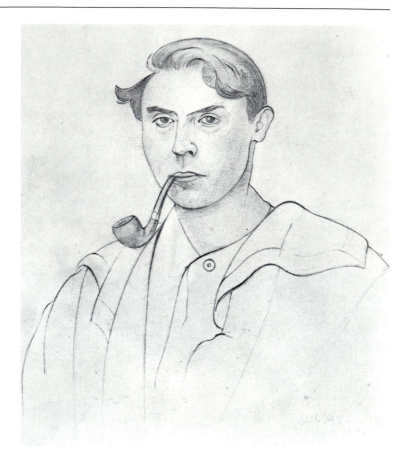

each artist's "gallery of Ingres" was nevertheless a genre quite distinct from that artist's paintings, which often, as we shall see, continued to be in some sense Cubist. In this way an artist's traditionalism and his modernism could continue to coexist. Of course, the precedent for this division—the avant-garde oeuvre broken down into the constituent elements of atavism and modernity—had been established by Picasso in the distinction between *Parade*'s classicizing overture curtain and its Cubist set, costumes, and story. Although the proportion of traditionalism to modernism might vary from artist to artist, the bifurcated mode of production, with one foot in each camp, was widely practiced in the post-war years. It was, after all, much easier for an artist like Gris, who had a large investment in his pre-war accomplishments (and who was also experiencing a crisis of confidence about his talent), to put the most blatant manifestations of his atavism into the minor genre of drawing: only because he could tell himself that the "Prix de Rome"-style

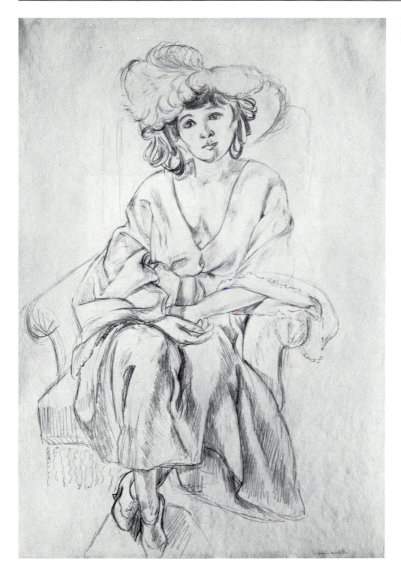

171. H. Matisse, *The Plumed Hat*, 1919.

drawings which he began during the war were a form of diver-
sion (instead of reading serial novels) had he been able to commence his artistic retrogression. To be sure, there were other
ways of distancing oneself from the evidently reactionary quality of the new illusionism. It could even be a form of challenge,
as it was for Picasso, to see if one could be both modern and
traditional in a single work. In his 1917 *Portrait of Olga* (fig.
106), for instance, we saw how Picasso diluted Ingres with Cézanne, how the game became one in which the more conservative, fully illusionistic style of one master could be undermined

by the sketchiness of the more recent artist. But since most of
the Parisian artists had neither Picasso's deep commitment to
the past (and his academic skills) nor his self-consciousness (or
sense of irony), it was in the Ingres-style work that they located
and demonstrated their sense of tradition.

Although his homage would take a very different form, Henri
Matisse was by no means immune to the Ingres revival or the
new interest in academic draftsmanship that flourished in the
post-war period. During 1919, in Nice, he made a large group
of drawings and a painting depicting his model Antoinette under the wide brim of a feathered hat (fig. 171). If neither the
delineation of the drawings nor the handling of the paint is especially redolent of Ingres—the technique being too loose and
free to evoke his style—these images are nonetheless rather traditional-looking, elegant, and, in the relationship of studies to
finished paintings, exemplary of the academic practices that
were generally lacking in the work of the younger artists imitat-
ing Ingres.

But, in fact, it was neither in draftsmanship nor portraiture
that Matisse found his way back to Ingres after the war. Instead,
the living French master—himself now past the half-century
mark—paid tribute to Ingres, and to the French tradition generally, by painting odalisques in orientalized settings, as for example his *Odalisque with Red Trousers* of 1921–22 (fig. 172).[74]
Not only is the Ingres of the *Turkish Bath* a referent for Matisse,
but so are Delacroix and, most pointedly, Renoir, in particular
his *Odalisque* (fig. 173) of 1870—the open-legged pose, the
slightly cocked head, the headdress, and of course the loose-
fitting harem pants, gathered beneath the knee, all reveal Matisse's debt to the recently deceased Impressionist (although the
bare-breasted provocativeness of the twentieth-century odalisque is Matisse's own doing). Indeed, Renoir's art was much
on Matisse's mind at this moment: he had visited the old painter
during the winter of 1917–18 at Cagnes, and in the next year,
when Renoir died, Matisse expostulated to an interviewer, "Oh,
Renoir was a marvel! . . .I've always thought that no other epoch offered a nobler, more heroic story, a more magnificent accomplishment than that of Renoir."[75]

The direct influence of Ingres's harem pictures on Matisse
becomes obvious somewhat later in the decade, especially apparent in a group of odalisques of about 1926–28, such as the
Odalisque with Green Sash (fig. 174) of 1926, which are deri-
vations of Ingres's two famous *Odalisque and Slave* pictures of
1839 and 1842 (fig. 175). Matisse has transformed his prede-

cessor's imaginative re-creation of harem life—wherein the highly erotic nude lies in an opium-induced trance, as she is serenaded by one of the sultan's slaves—into a much tamer, thoroughly aestheticized studio scene. Retaining Ingres's red and green palette, Matisse has defused the scene's sexuality and alien excitations by first eliminating the hookah and then substituting a large brazier for the musician (although he has been careful to retain the figure's pyramidal shape in the form of the inanimate object); Matisse has also made the important addition here of a small Louis XV table, which helps to westernize the setting.

Still, given the unsavory associations of "Orientalism" during the war, it is surprising that in the 1920s Matisse presented himself more than ever as an *orientaliste* (albeit one with an impressive artistic pedigree). It was not as if Matisse had been spared the invective heaped on other members of the Parisian avant-garde. Michel repeatedly attacked the Fauves (although not Matisse by name) in his article in the *Revue Hebdomadaire* in 1917; and Jacques Vernay, who (we recall) first predicted a "renaissance of classical tendencies" after the war (in reaction to pre-war "liberty in excess" symbolized by "the 'arabesques' and . . . *rapprochements* of flat tones"—probably a reference to the pre-war exoticism of the Ballets Russes and Matisse), mentioned the artist by name in 1916, saying that Matisse's art was "too far outside the realm of painting" to merit discussion.[76] At least in part, then, Matisse's decision to re-engage with the Orientalist motif must have been a conscious self-affirmation in the face of anti-Orientalist critics. As the most prominent Orientalist painter of the pre-war avant-garde—for whom North Africa and Islamic art had been of enormous importance—he may well have felt that he wanted all the more to remain true to his own earlier convictions or even to return nostalgically to more youthful enthusiasms.

But that must remain a matter of conjecture; what is certain is the concrete reality of the post-war French colonial adventure. Indeed, the colonial movement was at its height and France's empire at its greatest extent just after the war, and the war itself had been partly responsible for this. The French territories, especially those of North Africa—Algeria, Tunisia, Morocco—had supplied soldiers, as well as raw goods, for the Sacred Union; France proudly referred to herself as a nation of "100 million" (a figure that, because it included all the inhabitants of the colonies, effectively made France more populous than Germany). Furthermore, the victory of the Great War was

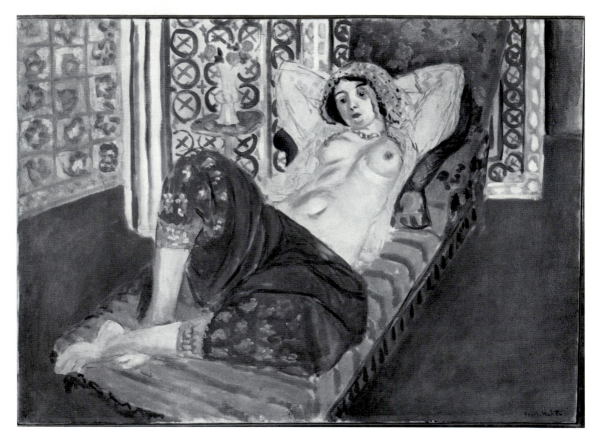

172. H. Matisse, *Odalisque with Red Trousers*, 1921–22.

seen as a vindication of French civilization and as such provided the mandate for France's civilizing mission abroad. Finally, in the light of French fiscal losses as a result of the war, the exploitation of the colonies was put forth as a get-rich-quick scheme that might function as a kind of non-negotiable reparations. Needless to say, Millerand's conservative *Bloc National* and the "Blue Horizon" Chamber of Deputies tended to be highly sympathetic to the colonial cause. By April 1920, the journal *L'Afrique Française* waxed lyrical over the current state of affairs: "We are witnessing a veritable crusade in favor of colonial development, in parliament, in the press . . . and among the public at large."[77] In 1923 Albert Sarraut, Minister of the Colonies for most of the early 1920s, published his famous *La Mise en valeur des colonies françaises* (The Development of the French Colonies), a tract that became "the bible of post-war imperialism."[78]

In keeping with France's venerable tradition of aestheticizing

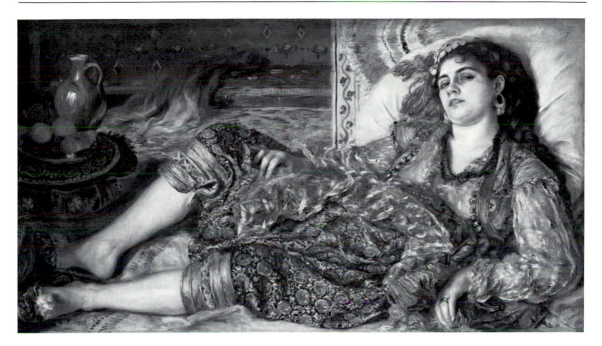

173. A. Renoir, *Odalisque (Algerian Woman)*, 1870.

colonial expansion, a major exhibition of Moroccan art was installed at the Pavillon de Marsan in the middle of the war, from March to October 1917. Organized under the auspices of one of France's greatest colonial leaders, General Lyautey, Resident of Morocco—who was a vigorous and effective defender of indigenous Moroccan culture, insofar as it could survive in the imperial context—the exhibition was a timely tribute to one of the colonies that were contributing to the war effort.[79] It was also a forecast of things to come: on a far vaster scale was the Exposition Coloniale held in Marseille—France's traditional gateway to the Orient—from April to November 1922.[80] The show was a great success, the most important post-war manifestation of the nation's continued commitment to empire, as demonstrated by Cappiello's poster (fig. 176) in which *La France*, gowned *en tricolore* and sporting the laurel wreath of her still recent victory, calls forth with a beckoning gesture the bounty (including here wheat, fruit, cotton, and silks) of her colonies, allegorized below. Of course, there is another implication here as well, that France's relationship to her colonies is reciprocal—the gesture of calling forth is also a gesture of elevation, for *La France* promises to raise these noble and generous savages to enlightenment.

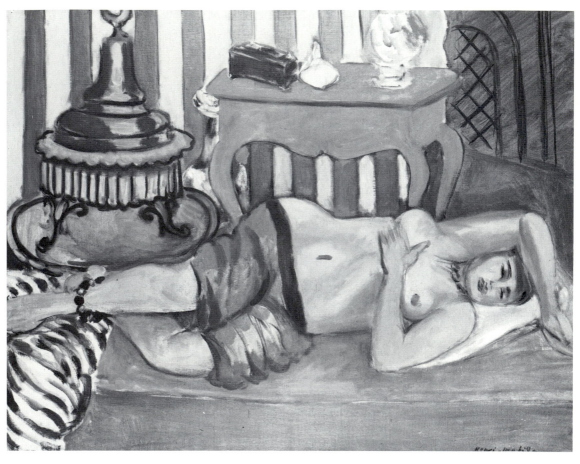

174. H. Matisse, *Odalisque with
Green Sash*, 1926–27.

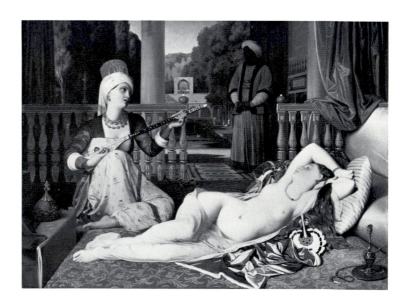

175. J.A.D. Ingres, *Odalisque and
Slave*, 1842.

And just as Lapauze's *La Renaissance de l'Art Français et des Industries de Luxe* had devoted a special issue to Ingres in April 1921, so precisely one year later an elaborate special number was devoted to "Richesses d'Art de la France Coloniale." With over 100 pages and 150 illustrations, the issue was an impressive ensemble of articles, all by major authorities, dealing with the art of France's imposing roster of colonies, protectorates, and mandated territories in Africa (Algeria, Morocco, Tunisia, Sudan; Guinea, Ivory Coast, Dahomey, Cameroon, Gabon, French Congo, Ogowe, Chad; Somalia, La Réunion, Madagascar), the Middle East (Syria, Lebanon), Indochina (Cambodia, Laos, Viet Nam), India (Pondicherry), Oceania (New Caledonia, the New Hebrides, the Marquesas, Tahiti), and the Americas (Gaudeloupe, Martinique, Guiana, Saint-Pierre, Miquelon). It was again Arsène Alexandre (who had offered the intriguing notion that to "understand" Ingres was to "understand" Greece and France, and who was apparently considered an expert on cross-cultural theories) who wrote the foreword to the issue, dedicated to Minister Sarraut and illustrated with Puvis's *Marseille: Gate to the Orient*. Filled with the kind of racist colonial attitudes that went mostly unquestioned for so long (i.e., the Orient is mysterious, sensual, aromatic, dreamy, intoxicating, etc., whereas France is "civilized and regulated"), Alexandre's article concluded by bringing the discussion home. Of the effect that exposure to all this art of the colonies might have on France, he wrote, "European artists, without *Africanizing*, *Asianizing*, or *Oceanianizing* themselves, can nonetheless always try to refresh the imagination and sharpen the eye."[81] The specific wording of this can help us to better understand the character of Matisse's Orientalism in the 1920s, for the critic's use of the reflexive—"sans s'*africaniser*," etc.—expresses something difficult to render in English, namely that the influence which the colonies can exert on Western art must not be internalized: rather than recast himself or his art in the African, Asiatic, or Oceanian mold, the artist should use the art of the colonies to renew and refresh, but not to remake or revolutionize, his art.

Indeed, this distinction—between a passive and an aggressive relationship to the culture of the colonies—is the same one that obtains between Matisse's own Orientalism even as late as 1916, when he painted *The Moroccans* (Museum of Modern Art), and that of the 1920s, as in the *Odalisque with Red Trousers*. In the first case, the Islamic culture of Morocco and elsewhere was a vehicle for and perhaps an instigator of Matisse's

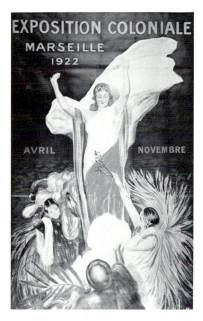

176. Cappiello, Poster for Exposition Coloniale (Marseille, 1922).

pictorial radicalism (which does not mean, to be sure, that there is necessarily anything politically radical in this aesthetic);[82] in the second case, the same culture is completely subordinated to Western pictorial rules and traditions—delectation replaces involvement. In 1922 the Orient nourishes a long-standing relationship between East and West, just as the colonies were expected to nourish the metropolis. Of course, a recumbent and available female nude is a far cry from the fully dressed, prayerful males of *The Moroccans*.

Now we understand that it was not altogether by chance that the *Odalisque with Red Trousers* (painted in Nice in 1921) became the first painting by Matisse bought by the French state for a Parisian museum. It was bought for the Luxembourg by none other than Léonce Bénédite, who in his article on Ingres in the *Gazette des Beaux-Arts* the previous June (at the time of the large exhibition) had reproduced the 1842 *Odalisque and Slave* (fig. 175). Matisse's painting had been on exhibit in his Bernheim-Jeune show of February–March (1922), and it was there that Bénédite saw the picture and asked to buy it, just three weeks before the Colonial Exhibition opened in Marseille.[83] Matisse the pre-war Orientalist innovator might not create the art of which state museum collections were made; but Matisse the inheritor of Delacroix, Ingres, and Renoir—the appreciator of colonial "refreshment"—had earned his place in the pantheon.

Writing during the war, the critic Jean Paulhan accounted for the ever-increasing rush toward tradition on the part of the Parisian avant-garde by means of a boomerang theory: "An anarchist," he wrote, "from the day when he recognizes the existence of an authority, threatens thereafter to become more authoritarian, and more *purely* authoritarian, than anyone in the world."[84] He might well have been thinking of Gino Severini, except that the full force of the former Futurist's retrenchment was not really apparent until 1921. That year he published a book whose title could serve as the motto for the Parisian postwar avant-garde, *From Cubism to Classicism: Aesthetic of the Compass and Number*. Not content with having found the path of virtue for himself, Severini wanted to show his colleagues the error of their ways as well, and his book is a description of his own journey from revolutionary aesthetics before 1914 to the classical point of view after the Armistice. Interestingly, Severini completely ignores his own specifically Italian and Futurist beginnings, in favor of French, i.e. Cubist, origins. But this historical sleight of hand is minor indeed, considering how close the painter has come to the ideas of Aurel, Daudet, and Mauclair by 1921. "At the start of the century," he begins,

> artistic anarchy was at its peak despite the very laudable efforts of some. That is due to causes in the moral and social order, no doubt, but it is not my intention to examine this aspect of the problem. Perhaps from time to time I shall be forced to allude to these, but if I decide to publish these notes, it is above all to show and to emphasize to artists of my generation the aesthetic and technical causes of this disorder, and to indicate the path by which they can escape them.[85]

As it was for so many others, the root of the contemporary problem—the disorder to which Severini repeatedly alludes—was "individualism," the lack of social cohesion and resultant concern with self which doomed the artist to marginality: "There was a fierce search for *originality*," he wrote, "but, with only fantasy and caprice as a basis, little was achieved, in general, but *singularity*." During the course of the nineteenth century, he explained, artistic matters got increasingly out of hand, especially when "After Ingres, whose benign influence has been a great support, more and more brazen efforts, often divergent and contradictory," came to prevail.[86] Yes, it is Severini, the pre-war Futurist, who sounds like a disappointed old schoolteacher here, and he was evidently enjoying fantasies of becoming a member of the academy, for he proposed the formation of a new art school—"not, obviously, an old Ecole replastered and repainted in fresh Impressionist colors, like the Ecole des Beaux-Arts, but an *Edifice*, a brand-new monument, having from the foundation to the roof, as generating principles, the eternal laws of construction that we find at the foundation of the art of all times. . . ."[87]

Clearly, certain ideas were so closely associated that the invocation of one inevitably led to the enunciation of the others; in this case, Severini is ineluctably led from anarchy, over-individualism, and caprice to Ingres, the Ecole, and "laws of construction." These last are very important for him:

> The best painters, the most talented, sincerely believed (and many still believe) that they can lead painting to construction and style by *deformation*. . . . The most intelligent of the artists are beginning to realize nonetheless that

it is not possible to build anything solid on caprice, fantasy, or good taste, and that, in sum, nothing good is possible without the Ecole.[88]

For Severini, the essential struggle is between the empirical and the "spiritual," and he is on the side of the latter—all great art derives from general laws and from sound practices, based on numbers: "The artists of our epoch do not know how to use a compass, a protractor, or numbers. Since the Italian Renaissance," he says, "the laws of construction have gradually been forgotten."[89] In fact, Severini traces the error of empiricism all the way back to the ancients, with the Ionians as the empiricists and the Dorians as the standard-bearers of the "spiritual conception." Unfortunately, according to Severini, even the Renaissance chose poorly and found itself in the naturalist camp *avant la lettre*—"Instead of exalting Homer, Virgil, Cicero, et al., it would have been better to follow closely Orpheus, Pythagoras, Aristotle, and Plato . . ."[90] Finally, the former Futurist and now classicist brings the issues up to date, and finds a timely lesson in the past:

> We find ourselves today, after an interval of several centuries, in an identical situation. Today, one speaks a great deal about the great Greek civilization, we claim it as our own, and we declare ourselves Hellenists, but it is not recognized that it is generally of an Ionian Hellenism, of paganism and of Epicurianism, that we are speaking. . . . Will we have a new Pythagoras capable of reuniting and ordering all the good forces that we feel around us and which truly tend toward a new renaissance?[91]

Severini's last rhetorical question, whether there is a "Pythagoras" on the horizon—one who could reunite and order all the "good forces" and bring about a renaissance—was the kind of part-social, part-aesthetic question that was being asked by many of his contemporaries. André Mare, for instance, less hopeful in the midst of "the immense destruction in which we live," wrote in about 1921–22 that what society lacked was "a man who is at once poet, soldier, and legislator, capable of regrouping all that is valuable in France and of giving a soul to the indifferent nation."[92] Added impetus was given to this post-Armistice search for a powerful, poetic, Romantic hero in 1921 by the centennial of Napoleon's death—a slew of publications appeared and ceremonies in Napoleon's honor were held all over Paris, at the Trocadéro, Notre Dame, the Sorbonne, and the Invalides.[93] Abel Gance's epic film *Napoléon* premièred in 1926 and represented the climax of the centennial craze. Of course, for those who were willing to replace aesthetics with politics, and who deeply believed that society had reached a point of anarchic disunion which only law, order, discipline, and "constructive" policies could counteract, there was some-one—a Latin and an Italian—who was at that very moment promising to be that "new Pythagoras," the "poet, soldier, and legislator" who would regroup all the "good forces" to bring about a renaissance: and that was Benito Mussolini.

Indeed, fascism, the movement of reaction *par excellence*, was the inevitable next step for many thinkers of the Right—for instance, Léon Daudet, who in August 1922 said that it was a positive national reaction against the "evils of communism."[94] Furthermore, fascism was one of the most obvious destinations for those who had traveled the route from anarchism to social order, as Il Duce had himself: formerly a Socialist, Mussolini had by 1922 turned viciously against his former comrades, was quelling all political agitation on the Left, and was declared Premier at the King's invitation. That is not to say that all or even most of those who hoped for a powerful leader to bring post-war Europe out of her bereavement became fascists; only that such a desire, with its associated ideas, was abroad in the early 1920s. We have only to look at the official French poster, by Jean Droit, for the Olympic Games of 1924 (fig. 177), the eighth modern Olympiad, held in Paris, to recognize how prev-alent and even acceptable an ideal of orderly, quasi-militarized youth was in the post-war years.[95] Or consider the immensely popular and influential author Gabriele d'Annunzio, who held the formerly Austrian but Italian-speaking city of Fiume under military siege in 1921—crossing the line from a certain kind of aesthetics to a certain kind of politics was becoming *de rigueur*. Even the young André Malraux, later to be an important spokesman of the anti-colonial Left, before becoming a Gaullist after World War II, could write in 1923, in the introduction to a book of Charles Maurras's writings, that "to go from intellec-tual anarchy to the Action Française is not to contradict oneself, but to construct"—in other words, to go from extreme Left to Right might be seen as a positive development. He also said of the Royalist's writing: "His work is a suite of constructions des-tined to create or maintain a harmony. Above all, he prizes and admires order, because all order represents beauty and force."[96] Construction, Action Française, order, Mussolini, discipline, classicism, Maurras—these were all elements of a post-war at-

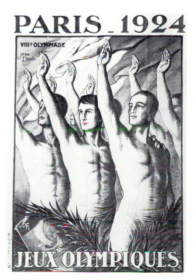

177. Jean Droit, Poster for Olympic Games (Paris, 1924).

titude shared by the Latinate victors of the Great War. For the
Italians, it was to determine the next quarter-century of their
political life; for the French, it was a major element in a much
more varied landscape of ideologies, which would find its most
devastating expression in Pétain's Vichy.

But we have moved ahead of the Severini of 1921. Can we
fail to be disappointed when we find, after his discussion of the
need for "the compass and number," for construction, and for a
new Pythagoras, that Severini's idea of a post-war artistic renaissance is manifested in his 1922 painting of two Punchinellos (pl. IV)? Even more emphatically than Jeanneret's still-life
of 1918, Severini's picture looks like the work of an artist who
had never ventured beyond the most banal forms of representation. And unlike his traditionalist forays in 1916, this was not
an isolated demonstration of atavism but typified a major component of his work after the Armistice, which included a vast
array of *commedia dell'arte* pictures, among them a series of
murals that he executed in 1922 for the Sitwells at their villa in
Montegufoni, outside Florence.[97] Obviously, there is not the
slightest reference here either to Futurism or to Cubism, except
for the extent to which the *commedia* had already been established as a genre dear to Picasso. It may be significant that so
many of Severini's Punchinellos and Harlequins peer out, with
plaintive eyes, from behind masks—these actors of the Italian
Comedy often look trapped by the artifice of their métier. Severini himself must have been perfectly aware of how far his art
had changed in only a few years: it was as if his "Plastic Art of
War" had been made by another artist in another life.

Not that Severini was alone in his preference for *commedia
dell'arte* subject matter after the war; it was a genre that, as we
have observed, first came back into popularity in the wartime
art of Gris and Picasso. In 1925 Metzinger created a *Harlequinade* (fig. 178) in a style as conventional as Severini's; and Derain made a number of pictures on the theme, of which the most
important was his 1924 *Harlequin and Pierrot* (fig. 179), a big,
square canvas that depicts two very melancholy troubadours
who step forward towards the viewer. The picture borders on the
tragic, not only by way of the implied lyric to lost love that the
iconography conveys, but also in the startlingly low quality of
Derain's draftsmanship. For that matter, post-war expressions
of Latinity were often aesthetically maladroit: in 1921, for instance, the "League of the Latin Intellectual Fraternity," an organization composed of representatives from the Allied or
nearly Allied "Latin" nations, with the goal of fostering culture,

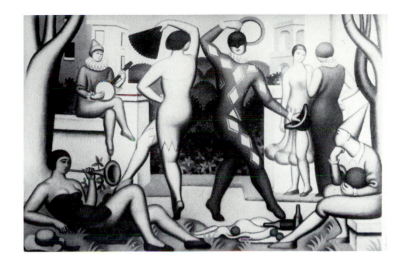

178. J. Metzinger, *Harlequinade*, 1925.

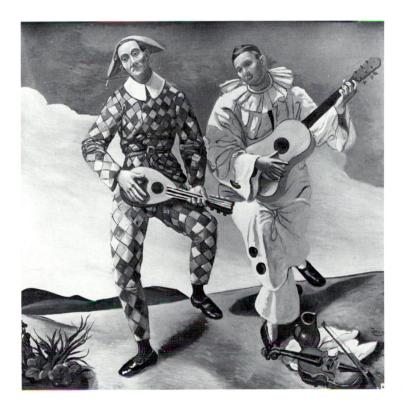

179. A. Derain, *Harlequin and Pierrot*, 1924.

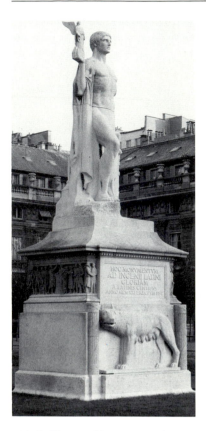

180. J. Magrou, *Monument to the Genius of the Latin People*, 1921. Garden of the Palais Royal, Paris.

placed in the garden of the Palais Royale a statue that remains in place to this day (fig. 180). Sculpted by Jean Magrou, it is dedicated and titled *To the Genius of the Latin People* (Au génie latin) and represents a young man (the Latin Genius in question) who holds in his hand a victory—the Allied victory, of course—and stands upon a pedestal whose bas-relief evokes the Roman she-wolf and the Declaration of the Rights of Man. The statue is, as most will attest, rather unattractive—classical in the *munichois* or even crypto-fascist manner. Ironically, it was André Malraux—who sang the praises of Charles Maurras in 1923—who, as Minister of Fine Arts under De Gaulle many years later, would try to have the Latinate monstrosity removed from the garden, to no avail.[98]

But it should be emphasized that the specifically Latin strain was only a sub-category of the much larger phenomenon of classicism, which after four long wartime years of gradual re-emergence, had come back with full force after the Armistice. In high culture it was represented by Paul Valéry, André Gide, Raymond Radiguet, and Julien Benda in the literary sphere, as was duly noted by the critic Jacques Rivière in the first post-1914 issue of the *Nouvelle Revue Française*, of 1 June 1919: "We think we can perceive a direction to which the creative instinct of our race, as new and hardy as ever, is in the process of committing itself . . . we will speak about everything that seems to forecast a classical renaissance."[99] Satie's cantata *Socrate*, which he said he would like to be "white and pure, like the Antique,"[100] and Stravinsky's ballet *Pulcinella* (combining *commedia dell'arte* themes and neo-classical harmonies) were only two of the many manifestations of the new post-war classicism in music, which was occurring simultaneously with what Christopher Green has called the "popular" manifestations of the new classicism that included both the Eurythmics of Jacques Dalcroze and the *méthode naturelle* of physical education taught by Georges Hébert at Deauville (one magazine in August 1919 reproduced a picture of Lieutenant Hébert's pupils, dressed in Greek tunics, as they exercised on a lawn at the fashionable resort; it was captioned "Une fresque de Puvis de Chavannes animée.").[101] We might say of post-war France, as Hans Baron said of fifteenth-century Florence, that an "almost dithyrambic worship of all things ancient pervaded the cultural atmosphere."[102]

The gradual and steady "classicizing" of the Parisian avantgarde art world was also described by André Salmon in his book of 1920, *L'Art vivant*. For him, the French were in the "first days of an indisputable renaissance," for the simple reason that it was only after the war that the twentieth century got under way: "It seems that the twentieth century begins with the Armistice and that there were twenty years of 'between-centuries' [*entre-siècles*] since the Exposition Universelle." According to the critic, this chance to finally begin the new century was signaled by the satisfying "classical order," although he warned against the emptiness of the "neo-classics" pure and simple, preferring a profound sense of collective feeling (among writers and painters) that would "alone favor the classical order." While at one of the Salons of 1919 he announced the demise of that recent artistic past:

> . . . all that makes Impressionism what it is belongs henceforth to a phase that is finished. The first free Salon of the post-war period, the "Armistice Salon" of 1919, "this mortal triumph of clearly ranked values" . . . proves it.[103]

In the same way, the distinction between the "realist" genres of the nineteenth century and the "mortal triumph of clearly ranked values" (i.e. classicism) was a given for Edmond Viollier. In his 1924 article "Toward the Classical Order—Classical Technique," he wrote that artists had to cease making use of the *plein-air* prejudice for "direct" painting, and once again take up classical technique, the studio methods that signified freedom from gross contingency:

> This conception, which tends with all its young energies toward a liberation from the transitory and the exceptional—that is, from all individualism—necessarily implies a universality of number and duration. . . . This technique we define as "classical," as opposed to the direct technique.[104]

Yet it is entirely possible that had it not been for Pablo Picasso the new classicism in the post-war avant-garde would have been of far less consequence than it was. For if he was the first, strongest, and most prolific practitioner of the wartime revival of traditional draftsmanship, he was equally the best and most unabashed neo-classicist after the war. Although his various reworkings of the French tradition around 1918–21 broadened his approach to the past, the first real indication that Picasso's art would take on a specifically classical—i.e. Antique—complexion was his justly famous drawing of *Bathers* (fig. 181) of 1918. Reminiscent of Ingres's *Turkish Bath* both in

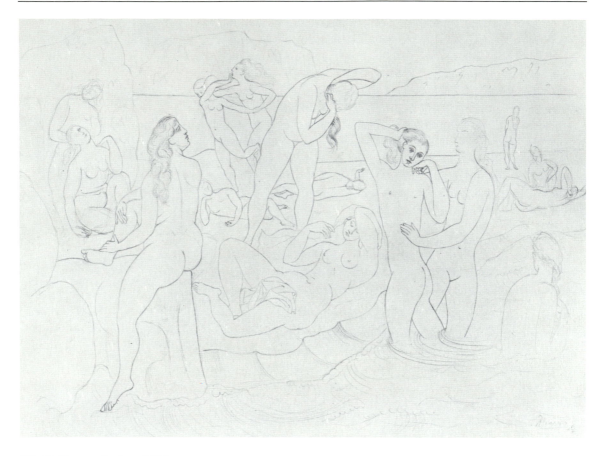

181. P. Picasso, *Bathers*, 1918.

specific poses and in its general homo-erotic orgiastic abandon, the drawing also is indebted to the bathers of Renoir, as well as to more distant Renaissance and Baroque motifs (note especially the twin "Apollo and Daphne" couples, at the near right and in the rear). The setting, though, is obviously Mediterranean; the arrangement is flattened and frieze-like; and the entire image has been emptied of chiaroscuro and blanched "white and pure, like the Antique." By 1921, Picasso went still further toward a high, serious classical *mise-en-scène* (fig. 182): now the figures are heavier, the composition has been purged of all extraneous elements (there is only a horizon line now to indicate depth). The facial expressions are also serious, as befits the action, in which a central character—a dancer or exerciser—performs for her fellow Olympians (in one of the drawings, dated 29 April, there is even an instructor, with staff in hand);[105] they gaze at her with what seems to be analytic scrutiny. These scenes may be Picasso's classicizing transformation

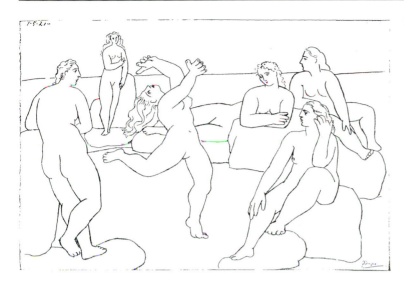

182. P. Picasso, *Bathers*, 1921.

of the Ballets Russes classes and rehearsals to which he sometimes accompanied Olga.

By the summer of 1921, which he spent at Fontainebleau,
Picasso was turning once again to "la Tradition" for guidance
in his classical endeavor, this time to the court painting of Francis I. Inspired by the image of a river goddess based on an
engraving by Rosso, in the king's gallery in the chateau,[106] Picasso made a series of drawings in which he attempted several
different groupings of nymph, dog, and tipped water jug, set on
a sculptural base of rock. These were studies for a painting executed that summer (fig. 183) in which the lapping canine has
been eliminated, a riverbank setting has been sketched in, and
the river-goddess figure has been more modestly draped in classical garb and turned, as it were, to stone. The result is that we
are uncertain whether this is a "real" mythological goddess or a
piece of sculpture; whether her static pose, indifferent gaze,
and enclosed bodily profile are meant to symbolize an eternal
incarnation of woman or an ossified yet living symbol of art—
precisely the kind of epistemological uncertainty that Picasso
so delights in creating.

All of these endeavors at depicting the classicized nude, in
which we see a fairly steady progression from slender and
highly sexualized types to heavier, more monumental, sculptural, and asexual classical figures, were a prelude to his first
major "classical" painting, the famous *Three Women at the
Spring* (fig. 184).[107] In this large picture (80 ¼ × 68 ½ inches)
of 1921, nearly square, dark-toned, and monumental in every
sense, we are struck first by this most traditional of female fig-

183. P. Picasso, *La Source*, 1921.

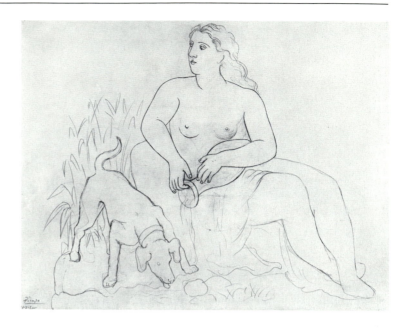

ure-groupings, the triad or threesome, which has so often appeared as images of the Graces and Fates: Picasso himself had
exploited the grouping before, for instance in his *Three Women*
of 1908. The body types are obviously very close to the sub-
stantial nudes of the exercise squadrons we have just seen—
they are massive and earthbound, fashioned after the Greek
style of depicting goddesses and muses in the image of a robust
humankind. Here, so enormous and dense are the figures that
they seem weighed down by their own amplitude; their gestures—whose rhetorical meaning eludes us—seem the result of
great effort. The square composition, in turn, is but an extension of the figures' proportions. This grouping looks as if it
could have been designed for a metope of the Parthenon, and
this is not surprising since the forms all derive from sculpted
prototypes.[108] As in the Fontainebleau painting, the figures are
draped in the Antique style, the falling pleats of their white
chitons like so many flutings in a Doric column. The colors too
are "Greek": flesh tones and terra-cotta; brown, black, and
white, and a residual gray. In fact, although the general types
for these highly modeled Graces are based on work in three
dimensions, they are also descended from fresco painting. Picasso's 1920 charcoal sketch of a woman's head, with a finger
pressed against her brow in a pose of contemplation, is based
on the figure of Arcadia from the Hercules and Telephus fresco

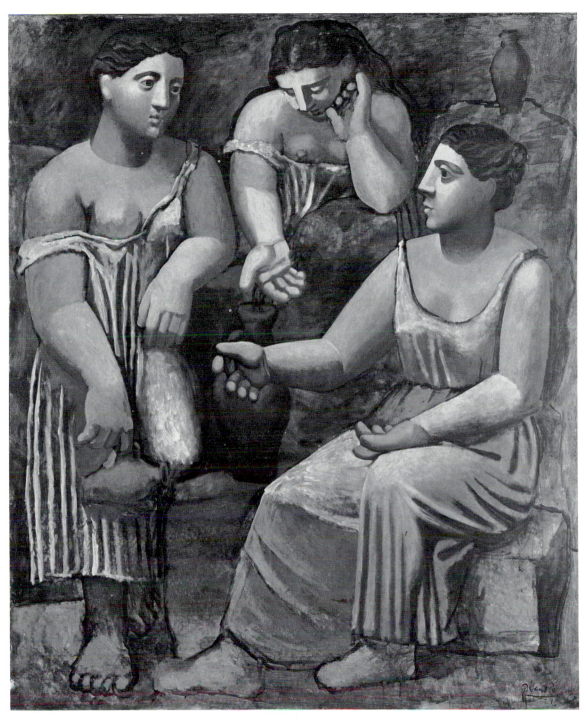

184. P. Picasso, *Three Women at the Spring*, 1921.

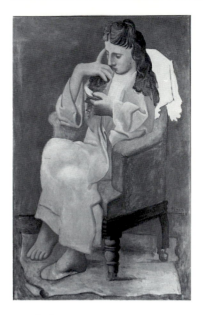

185. P. Picasso, *La Liseuse*, 1920.

from Herculaneum, which Picasso knew and which earlier had been the model for the pose of Ingres's *Madame Moitessier*. That same year, he used the head-and-hand pose for the picture called *La Liseuse* (fig. 185), which is the immediate forebear of the gigantic figures of *Three Women at the Spring*.[109]

Aside from the more or less direct influence of Antique sources, Picasso also looked to French sources for *Three Women at the Spring*—especially to the art of Nicolas Poussin, for whom a monumental and intentionally awkward and unbending figure style was the Baroque embodiment of classicism. The seventeenth-century French master is invoked both formally and iconographically: the frieze-like style and the theme—women who have gone to the spring, or fountain, to fill their *hydriae*—are reminiscent of famous works that Picasso must have known from the Louvre, like the *Eliezar and Rebecca at the Well*, while the placement of rustic figures in an arcadian setting, grouped about a central point, strongly suggests that Picasso was thinking about pictures like *The Arcadian Shepherds* (*Et in Arcadia Ego*) (fig. 186), an image whose meaning may have been all the more poignant for the artist since it was Apollinaire, only months before his death, who had expressed the wish to see Picasso make "large paintings like Poussin."

But at least as important is yet again, the influence of Puvis de Chavannes. The group of three Greek maidens (one of whom carries a water jug) in *The Shepherd's Song* (fig. 187) of 1891 is an obvious precedent for Picasso's picture. Freed, as it were,

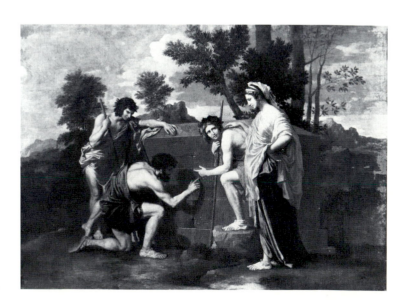

186. N. Poussin, *The Arcadian Shepherds* (*Et in Arcadia Ego*), 1638.

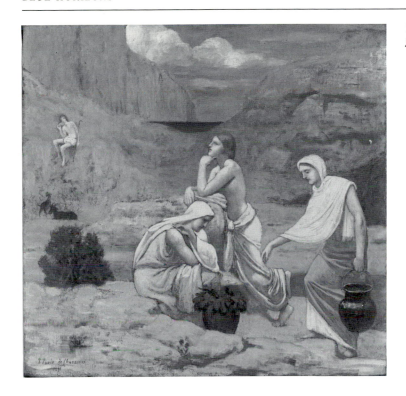

187. P. Puvis de Chavannes, *The Shepherd's Song*, 1891.

from the specific allegorical meanings of Poussin, the Antique vision of Puvis may have looked especially congenial to Picasso, who for his *Three Women at the Spring* was clearly more interested in the iconic power of gesture and placement than in narrative. But that is not to say that the theme is unimportant. So close is Picasso's picture to Puvis's *At the Fountain* of 1869, now in Boston, for which the *La Source* now in Reims (fig. 188) is a study, that the picture's subject is worth taking seriously. For whether we call it *Three Women at the Spring* or *At the Fountain*, the theme is in fact *la Source*, that old pun in art that means at once a spring or stream (at the point at which it wells up from the earth; also a fountain); the "source" of artistic inspiration—the "stream" of civilized humanity at which one is nourished and replenished; and, of course, in its strictly allegorical incarnation, the female form which embodies *la Source*, both as a muse and as the origin of biological life. Ingres, Courbet, and Renoir had all painted *la Source*, but always as a highly eroticized lone nude female in a watery glade. Picasso, like Puvis de Chavannes before him, takes the high road; he chastens, accessorizes, and Hellenizes the scene, and in the process makes us aware of how rich the subject is. What more appropriate theme for Picasso at this moment, when he was im-

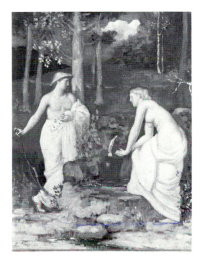

188. P. Puvis de Chavannes, *La Source*, 1869.

mersed in a thorough investigation of artistic sources, searching for inspiration and rejuvenation in the art of the past? Just as the French nation during the war turned to *l'histoire*—in its dual aspect of history and "story" or myth—for moral support, so Picasso creates a mythic Antique world that nonetheless has the weight and reassuring gravity of truth.

Picasso's classicism was an important artistic vein that he continued to mine until the mid 1920s. For instance, in 1923 he again went back to Puvis as a source—specifically, to *The Shepherd's Song*—to create a male complement to his image of mythic feminity, *The Pipes of Pan* (fig. 189), the dimensions of which are almost identical to those of the two earlier pictures. Again, the artistic sources here are a combination of the French (the motif of the shepherd's pipe comes directly from Puvis's picture) and the Antique (the standing boy at the left is modeled on the *kouros* type that had long interested Picasso). The palette in *The Pipes of Pan* is, on the other hand, much brighter than in *Three Women at the Spring*: the stagelike setting opens up in back to reveal two different but equally saturated shades of blue—a darker one for the sea, a slightly more yellowed one for the sky—and these are exquisite partners for the pinks, flesh tones, ochres, whites, blacks, and grays of the foreground. To a certain extent the change in tonality and palette from the work of 1921 to this painting may be due to the locales in which they were executed: the earlier one in the Ile-de-France, at Fontainebleau, the later one at the Mediterranean resort of Antibes. While the three women are unquestionably Antique, the two boys in *The Pipes of Pan* are temporally more equivocal in appearance: they could be either the real-life ancient models for the Greek *kouroi* or present-day peasant boys on the beach. In fact, as has recently been suggested, they are probably Sicilian peasant boys in Taormina—Picasso may have based *The Pipes of Pan* on a quasi-pornographic photograph of such boys, c. 1900, by Wilhelm von Gloeden.[110] But Picasso does not really want us to be certain of the context, but prefers to create eternal Mediterranean types.

There is certainly nothing accidental in the change in subject from *Three Women at the Spring* to *The Pipes of Pan*, a change that is part and parcel of the change in gender. For while the Antique women are eternally relegated to collecting water from "the source," these two boys are ephebes, on the threshold of adult responsibility—in this case, the responsibility of making art: one of the boys plays the shepherd's pipe—the pipes of Pan—while the other listens, perhaps in preparation for song. This is Picasso's picture of the young "classic" artist. There

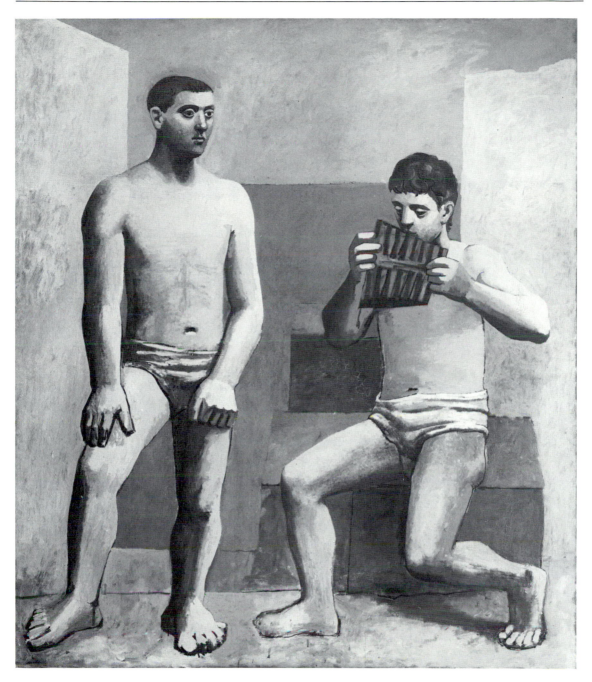

189. P. Picasso, *The Pipes of Pan*, 1923.

may even be an autobiographical element here. Based on the artist's Cubist painting *Three Musicians* of 1921 (which will be discussed in the next chapter),[111] *The Pipes of Pan*, in its pairing of the two boys, is perhaps a recollection of Picasso's intense artistic partnership with Braque (who in fact played the concertina) and/or his friendship with Apollinaire, a pipe-smoker, for whom the shepherd's pipe was a significant symbol.[112] At any rate, it is enough that we recognize how thoroughly "male" this painting is in comparison to *Three Women at the Spring*: how both the setting and figures are here composed of straight lines and sharp angles, while it is curves and softened edges that distinguish the "female" picture of 1921.

Between 1921 and 1924, Picasso created a vast oeuvre in the classical style that included Antique heads, single figures, and other groupings in the "classic" and traditional manner. All, in various combinations, are derived from Greek and Roman art and academic models, as well as from the art of Poussin, Ingres, Renoir, and Puvis de Chavannes. Picasso sketched in the classic style, drew in pastel, painted in gouache and oil, made prints, and generally indulged in the neo-traditional conceit. Among his favorite themes—and one that would have been congenial to Poussin, Renoir, and Puvis—was that of *maternité*, which, as has often been pointed out, was the direct result of the birth of his first child, Paul, in February 1921. That year he painted the large *Mother and Child* (fig. 190). With its stable horizontal format, made all the more insistent by the repeating horizontals of shoreline and horizon; with its reduced and earth-bound color scheme of blues and pink/brown/white; and with its completely enclosed, bounded, static forms, this *maternité* becomes a kind of emblem of the mythic endurance of the human species. The schematization of form and gesture bestows a quality of the archetypal, as if this were Everymother and Everychild. The obvious contrast between the mother's calm (in which the line of the horizon is also the line of her brow) and the child's innocent movements—his complicated and twisting baby-form that breaks through his mother's enclosed outline as he reaches up toward her face and the sky—symbolizes the difference betwen maturity and new life. The baby's squirming energy is contained and sheltered in the mother's steadfast and watchful care.

If such a description seems to suggest larger social issues—for instance, that of Marianne's steadfast care for her *enfants* during the four long years of war—it is not by chance, any more

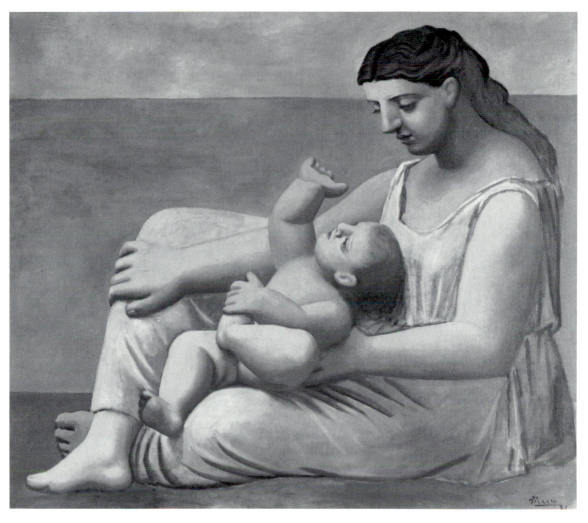

190. P. Picasso, *Mother and Child*,
1921.

than the fact that Picasso's family images (the overture curtain
for *Parade* and the reworking of Le Nain) preceded the birth of
his own child. It was not just during wartime but also, and with
increased determination, after the war that the French preached
the virtues of *fécondité*. It was, in fact, during 1921, the same
year in which that Picasso first painted his large *maternités* and
the same year in which his son was born, that the "Exposition
Nationale de la Maternité et de l'Enfance" took place in the
Bois de Boulogne, during June and July. On the honorary committee for the show, organized for the benefit of the "oeuvres
départementales de Natalité," were all the familiar French
names: Maurice Barrès, René Viviani, Emile Boutroux, Henri

Poincaré, and even Henri Bergson. As the spokesman wrote in
the exhibition's catalogue:

> On the day after the war in which, despite her numerical
> inferiority, France of the Marne and of Verdun triumphed
> by her heroism and her genius over the savage onslaught
> of an empire of sixty million inhabitants, it became indis-
> pensable to compress into a powerful visual synthesis the
> disastrous effects of the decline in the birthrate and the
> remedies that must at all costs be put in hand to alleviate
> it. . . . The future of the race itself is in the balance, and
> nothing would be more cruelly ironic than to see its flame
> extinguished at the moment when it burns with its bright-
> est light. If France is the light of the world, it is important
> not only for our country but even for the human species
> that this lighthouse never cease to cast its luminous beam
> on to the uncertain road. What do we need to accomplish
> this? That the wonderful torchbearers who are our children
> may come into the world in great enough numbers! For
> every extinguished lamp, at least one lamp must be lit.[113]

It is probably true that had it not been for the birth of Paul,
Picasso would not have created his numerous "mother and
child" pictures of the early 1920s; but had it not been for the
officially sanctioned significance of the theme, making the *maternités* specially meaningful for his French audience at that
moment, Picasso might well have been satisfied with a strictly
private artistic record of his newborn child and not gone on to
create these images of "the human species," classicized testi-
monials to the fecundity of the race. Even if he had wanted to,
he could not have ignored the reproductive propaganda that was
everywhere in evidence—for example, a Peace Loan poster by
Henri Lebasque (fig. 191) of 1920, in which industrial production is equated with human reproduction: a mother and suckling
babe, with an older child seated alongside reading, are before
a hedge in the foreground; behind, a building is under construction, and in the far distance the post-war French factories produce at peak capacity. Certainly, official policy provided an impetus for the creation of the mother-and-child themes that
proliferate in the art of the Parisian avant-garde. Severini had
already turned to the maternity theme at the time of his son's
birth in 1916 (fig. 52), and now, in about 1922, he painted a
Family of the Commedia (fig. 192) that includes a *maternità*.
Albert Gleizes painted a nearly abstract *Mother and Child* (fig.
193) in 1920. Léger made numerous mother-and-child pictures
in the early 1920s (pl. V). And it was at this point, in 1923,

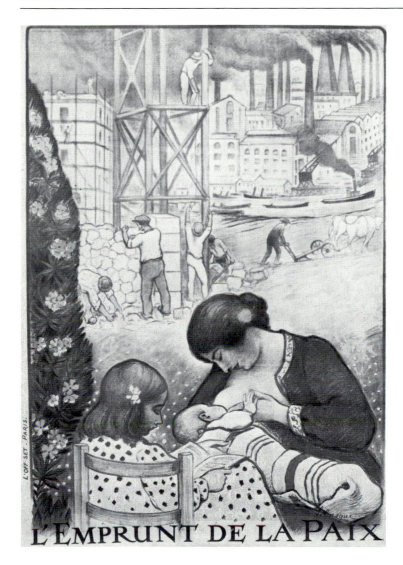

191. H. Lebasque, Poster for Peace Loan, 1920.

that La Fresnaye made the only *maternité* in his oeuvre (fig. 194).

In our discussion of Picasso's neo-classical works of 1919–24 we should not lose track of the first, most immediate, and most influential "source" for the imagery and the artistic conceit—that is, the repertory company of Victories, Glories, and *Patries*, all those winged creatures or earthbound deities who represented at once *La France*, Marianne, and the Nation. These mythical women had watched over France in her darkest hours and were also symbolic of her triumph in 1918—for example, as depicted in Louis Sabattier's cover of *L'Illustration* for Bastille Day 1919 (fig. 151). To understand a painting like

192. G. Severini, Study for *Family of
the Commedia dell'Arte*, c. 1922.

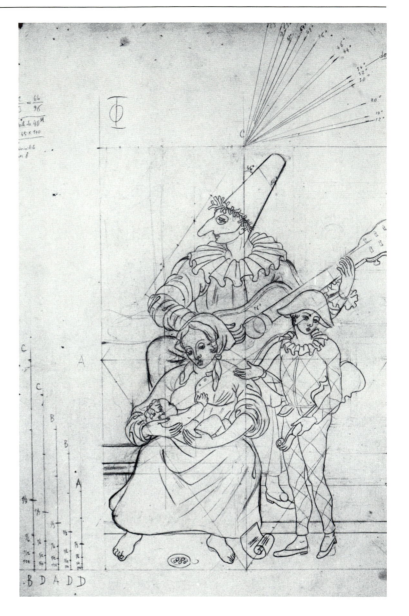

Picasso's *Woman in White* (pl. VI) of 1923, it is essential that
it be viewed within the context of that well-established touring
company of nationalist guardian figures. Of course, Picasso has
painted no allegory: the seated figure is far too generalized to
function as a specific symbol. The woman herself could be modern or ancient; her hairstyle and her dress—really her drapery—are vague enough to be timeless, although the classical
allusion is obvious. She could easily be, though, an actress or
dancer at rest, which may well have been the inspiration for the
picture. Unlike Sabattier's cover for *L'Illustration*, there is no

Phrygian cap here, no sword laid to rest, no peace treaty or
even a background (Sabattier's allegorical figure stands above a
French river on which ships pass, carrying the post-war produce of the farmland on the right and the manufactured goods
made in the factories at the far left). Yet I think that Picasso's
ability in this painting "to breathe new life and charm into so
exhausted a style as the neo-classic"—as Alfred Barr said of
the *Woman in White*[114]—nonetheless depends on the significance and poignancy of France's wartime and post-war allego-
ries.

Especially when the *Woman in White* is seen alongside other
images like Louise Abbéma's little oil painting *Victory* (fig. 59),
we begin to realize that the attitude evoked in Picasso's painting—so essentially a study in mood—is extremely close to the
noble and protective character of the patriotic figures. Like

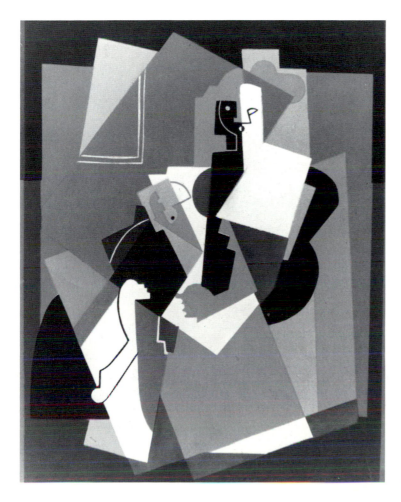

193. A. Gleizes, *Mother and Child*,
1920. Pochoir, published in *Der
Sturm*, 1921.

194. R. de la Fresnaye, *Mother and Child*, 1923.

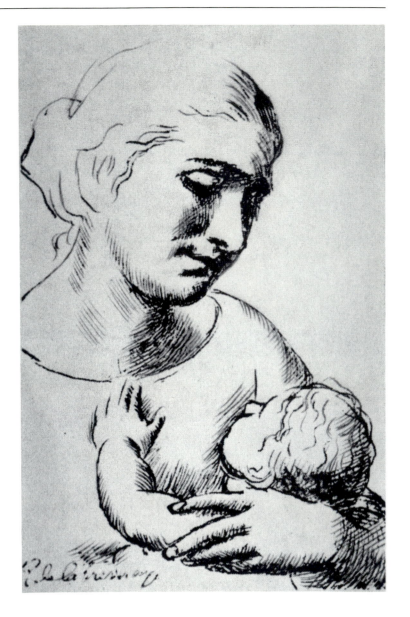

those in Abbéma's and Sabattier's pictures, Picasso's woman looks to the left; her gaze is elevated and her chin is held high; she establishes a relationship with something beyond the confines of the picture's space but significantly does not engage with the viewer. She is also charming: her figure is ample; her long neck, her well-defined brow, and especially her eyes are beautiful. Most important, though, is the very subtle tension in her face, betrayed by the slightly stiff neck, the closed mouth, and especially the deep-set eyes completely surrounded by shadow. In fact, it is precisely this same combination of tensed

neck, mouth, and eyes that raises Abbéma's and Sabattier's figures, too, above the mundane concerns of ordinary mortals.
These women's task, after all, was nothing less than the guard-
ianship of the French nation and—as indicated by their laurel
wreaths and classical garb—the protection and defense of a far
more ancient culture. They are at once the symbols for and the
protectors of Western civilization in perpetuity.

Besides, we have good reason to see patriotic, allegorical
precedents lurking behind Picasso's *Woman in White* because
we know that the artist had only the year before attempted to
create a non-allusive patriotic allegory in his *Dancing Couple*
(fig. 195), a large oil-and-pastel image of 1921–22. As Linda
Nochlin has pointed out, what at first appears to be an ordinary
if strangely "melancholy, lumpish pair" is a rather more complex image:

> on second glance, the patriotic motif asserts itself: the man
> wears bright blue; his head is haloed with a chalky powder
> blue. He clasps his partner around the waist. . . . She
> wears a white dress, reminiscent of classical drapery in its
> simplicity and fluted pleats. On her head is a wonderful,
> squashy, acid-red-orange hat—a contemporary Phrygian
> bonnet. She turns her profile to the left. Presto! It is La
> République, Marianne, La France—with a profile
> strangely reminiscent of Picasso's own—embraced by a sol-
> emn representative of *le peuple*. Whether or not it was De-
> lacroix's Liberty that Picasso had in mind, or one of the
> innumerable variants on the popular allegorical figures of
> French nationhood, there is no doubt about the specifically
> French implications of the tricolor scheme here.[115]

Moreover, once again Picasso could have found in the art of
Puvis de Chavannes the ideal model for creating the non-allusive, or secret, allegory pictures in which, as Robert Goldwater
said of Puvis, it was the "joining of allegory with mood, of conventional description with reflection and description" that "al-
lows the spectator the luxury of personal reverie and association."[116] We have already seen Léandre's invocation of Puvis's
Poor Fisherman of c. 1915 (fig. 74), in which the Christ-like
fisherman so easily became a symbol of France's fragile condi-
tion during wartime. Even more appropriate as a model for Picasso's post-war neo-classicism was Puvis's *Hope* (fig. 196) of
1871, a picture as famous as his *Poor Fisherman*. Like Picasso's own dancing couple of 1920, Puvis's allegory contains a
double-edged signification: what at first appears to be a simple
painting of Hope as a lovely young girl, extending a laurel

195. P. Picasso, *Dancing Couple*,
1921–22.

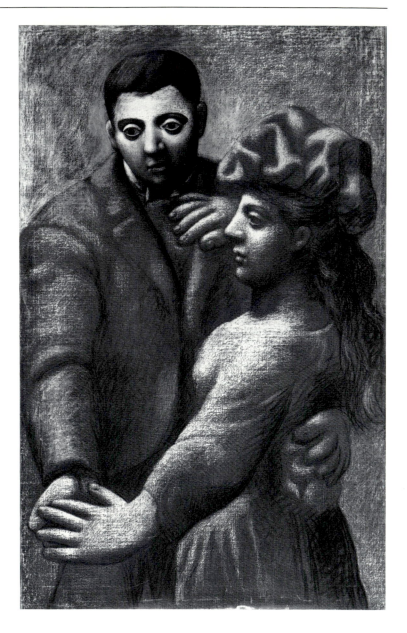

wreath, turns out, on closer inspection of the background with
its landscape of ruined buildings and wooden crosses, to be a
specific reference to the hope for national regeneration after the
devastation of the Franco-Prussian War. This kind of "real allegory"—an icon of faith for a faithless age—was Puvis's forte
and, as Picasso may have realized, was ideally suited to his own
post-war uses.

Yet, whether Picasso was consciously thinking of Puvis's

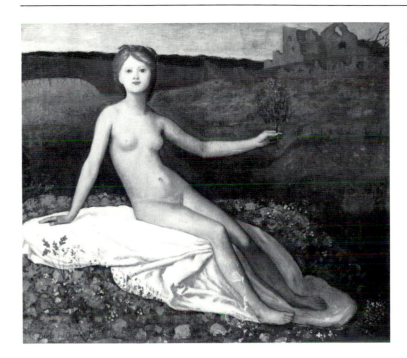

196. P. Puvis de Chavannes, *Hope*, 1871.

Hope or any of the other patriotic symbols, there is little question that his *Woman in White* of 1923 relies for its meaning
upon the significance of French allegorical figures. Self-pos-
sessed, looking backward (i.e. to the left) with an expression
that combines resolve, high-mindedness, and concern, she is
the incarnation of the word *classique*, an idealized expression of
France's national identity. She is bleached white, like the ruins
of Antiquity; all the color that remains is the brown of her hair,
the pink tones of her flesh, and the ghostly green of a chair that
has been scumbled over behind her. Indeed, it is the scumbled
surface of the painting that most effectively creates the sense of
reverie; we seem to be observing this classic image through the
veil of centuries. We are able almost, literally, to read through
and into the image as if we were reading into time: we can see
the first charcoal sketch for the figure (particularly apparent in
the drapery of her lap); the first painted essay that included the
chair; then the scumbling that washes over the entire canvas,
obliterating the figure's means of support (and thus making her
autonomous and self-supporting, as if balanced by her own
magical powers of equilibrium); and finally, in order to give her
noble head an intense, living presence, Picasso adds touches of
brown to her tresses on top of the scumbling, outlines the brow,

chin, and neck, and works up the flesh tones and highlights on the face.

In fact, we can do more than merely posit the war as an essential background for the *Woman in White*, and we can be even more certain of the telescoping of history that seems to be embedded in the scumbled surface of the picture, because there exists a torn section of the front page of the newspaper *L'Excelsior* (fig. 197) for Monday, 23 July 1923—a fragment that Picasso kept till he died and that is now in the collection of the Musée Picasso—that reveals the image's genesis. In the center of the page is a photograph of that summer's Tour de France champion, Henri Pelissier, with his wife—after some question as to the results, the cyclist emerged "vainqueur de la grande

197. P. Picasso, Drawing on fragment of *L'Excelsior* (23 July 1923), c. 1923.

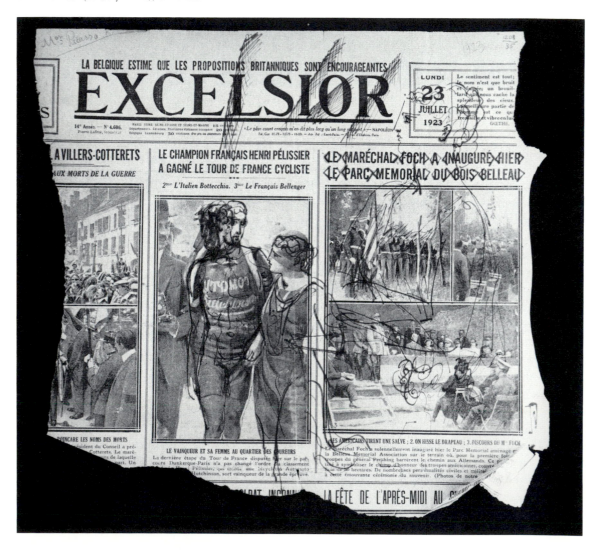

épreuve." Obviously, though, it is difficult to make out the specific features of the couple because, by means of a few strokes of the pen, Picasso has turned the Pelissiers into a pair of classical figures: he has traced the classically beautiful torso of the Greek athlete over the victor's "Automoto Hutchinson" jersey, and has turned the head from left to right; Mme. Pelissier has been metamorphosed from a typical woman of the 1920s in dress and hat, into an Antique goddess, with classical coiffure and drapery (perhaps Picasso means her to be a Victory). We have here a rare opportunity to watch the artist in the very process of transforming the mundane present into an idealized past. But even more important is what we see at the right: over an illustrated piece that bears the title "Le Maréchal Foch a inauguré le parc mémorial du Bois Belleau" Picasso has made a sketch for, or a recollection of, the *Woman in White*—her head and profile have been superimposed on the date at the upper right and her body, crossed arms and all, delineated over the photographs of the ceremony. The caption below informs us: "Yesterday Marshal Foch inaugurated the Memorial Park created by the Belleau Memorial Association, on the place where, for the first time, General Pershing's troops blocked the German advance. . . . Numerous civilian and military personalities took part in this moving ceremony of remembrance." Whether Picasso was consciously aware that his beautiful sitter was being given form, literally, on top of the tragic memory of war, we will probably never know; that his own visual associations bound the picture and the war together is apparent. Dense, mature, *évolué* in both the pictorial and the poetic sense, the *Woman in White* is Picasso's greatest post-war meditation on the endurance of culture.

Although much narrower in focus and less thoroughgoing, Braque's post-war neo-classicism was in some ways quite similar to Picasso's. His large series of *Canéphores* (ceremonial basket carriers), which he inaugurated in 1922–23 with two tall panels (figs. 198 and 199), are clearly derived from Picasso's contemporaneous image of monumentalized humanity (although their big-boned frames, small breasts, and well-developed stomach muscles, as well as their poses, also remind us of Michelangelo's Sibyls from the Sistine ceiling). Perhaps no one else in the Parisian avant-garde could have dared to come as close to Picasso's painting as Braque does here; he may well have felt that he had earned the privilege of "borrowing" from Picasso as a result of the reciprocity of their borrowings in the pre-war Cubist years. There may even be in the *Canéphores* a desire on Braque's part to reaffirm that now long-dissolved part-

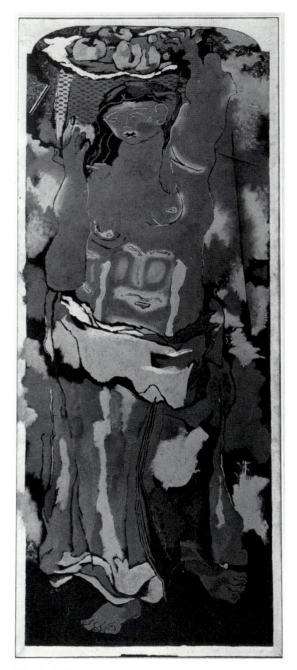 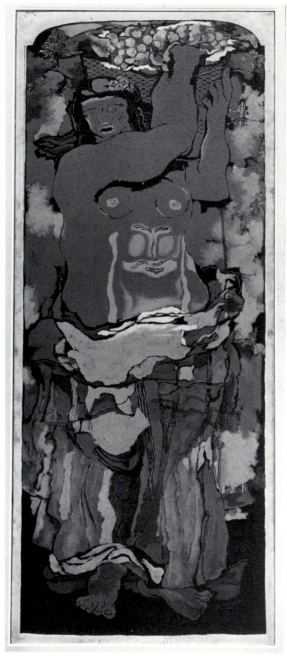

198. (*left*) G. Braque, *Canéphore*, 1922–23.

199. (*right*) G. Braque, *Canéphore*, 1922–23.

nership. At any rate, there is an almost palpable sadness in these paired images—not only are the facial expressions melancholy, but the poses, variations of the caryatid type, convey a sense of the tragic destiny of eternal burden.

Yet, at the same time, there is something in the pictorial fabric that is less than assured and even contradicts the monumentality of the women's proportions and their apparent allegorical significance as symbols of abundance. Unlike Picasso, who in his post-war classical vein seems as attentive to form, modeling, weight, and density as he had been uninterested in these qualities in his pre-war Cubism (at least after 1909), Braque plays a kind of hide-and-seek game with the physical presence of his canephoroe. While the linear description of their forms is as ample as it could be, they have been flattened up against the picture plane and made to conform to the very limited space of their tall vertical "niches." To be sure, this was intentional on Braque's part, since his points of reference are sculptural. There exists a study for a canephoros in which the figure is drawn as a piece of sculpture in a shallow niche,[117] and Braque may have also been thinking of Jean Goujon's sixteenth-century reliefs from the Fountain of the Innocents (Braque went so far as to add sand to the pigment to give the surfaces a stony quality). But there is too, I think, another and more surprising source for these two images—Antoine Bourdelle. Perhaps made newly aware of the sculptor after the recent installation of his twenty-foot *Virgin of the Offering* (1922) on a hillside in the reclaimed province of Alsace, Braque may have decided to give Bourdelle a closer look, specifically his well-known pre-war *Noble Burdens* (fig. 200), in which the "burden" of fecundity is allegorized as a peasant in caryatid pose, who bears aloft a basket of fruit, on her head, and holds an infant to her bosom. Whether intentionally or not—and, again, this may be more a matter of the general post-war atmosphere of "burden sustained" than a clearly considered iconography—Braque's theme in his *Canéphores* of 1922–23 seems quite close to that of Picasso's *Three Women at the Spring* of a year earlier.

Braque may himself have felt somewhat burdened at this point. Not only did he share with all members of the Parisian avant-garde the sense of a lost past, of being "advanced" artists in a distinctly conservative cultural moment; not only was his partnership with Picasso now merely a memory of youthful complicity; but he was at one of life's symbolic turning points: he reached the age of forty in 1922. Certainly, the devotion to Braque of an entire gallery at that year's Salon d'Automne must have been gratifying for the artist, not to mention the fact that all eighteen works exhibited were soon sold. Indeed, Braque's art was fetching high enough prices that two years later he was to move into a house that had been designed for him by Auguste Perret near the Parc Montsouris. But the recognition and the material comforts must also have reminded the artist that the old times were over forever. The critic Paul Husson, reviewing

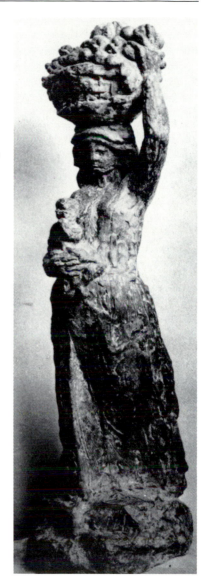

200. A. Bourdelle, *Noble Burdens*, 1910–11.

the Braque exhibit at the Salon d'Automne in 1922, said it first and most accurately:

> Braque, of the grayed harmonies; certainly all that is very fine, of great quality, very distinguished; but I feel that this sobriety is only the product of poverty, and under the exquisite sense of proportion, the elegance, and the precious refinement I sense depression and powerlessness.[118]

After Braque, Roger de la Fresnaye is probably the artist who most closely modeled his neo-classicism on Picasso's in the early 1920s. We have already seen examples of his vast output in the Ingres mode, and La Fresnaye continued to do a great deal of drawing in the post-war years, becoming increasingly classical in his style. His most forthright evocations of the An-

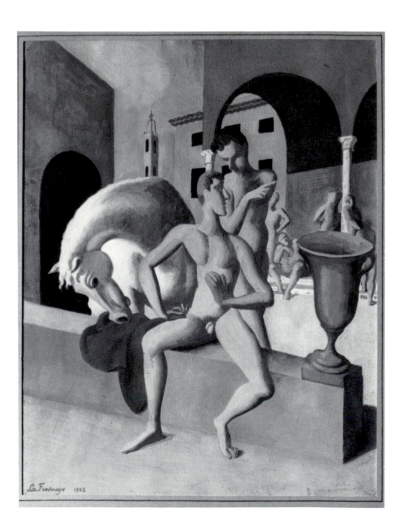

201. R. de la Fresnaye, *Les Palefreniers*, 1922.

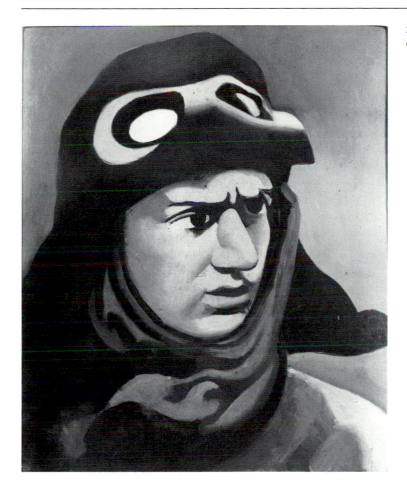

202. R. de la Fresnaye, *Portrait of Guynemer*, 1922.

tique past, though, are paintings, his series of *Palefreniers* (grooms or horse trainers of ancient Rome), typified by a picture of 1922 (fig. 201) in which Antique architecture of a distinctly Renaissance cast is juxtaposed with nude male figures and an accompanying horse.[119] The classical past is presented here in in all its supposed Arcadian innocence: we note both the unashamed nudity and athleticism of the men and their relaxed, easy relationship to the graceful horse. La Fresnaye's full-blown evocation of Antiquity notwithstanding, there is neither metaphorical power here nor, it must be said, technical proficiency: the figures are rubbery instead of noble and look more like denatured modern beach-goers than exemplars of classical beauty. Nor is there any evidence of what had been the artist's greatest strength as a pre-war painter: his ability to compose monumental pictures that were nonetheless dynamic and lighter than air. La Fresnaye looks very ill at ease as a neo-classicist.

He was slightly more successful when his post-war atavism took on less overtly remote themes and styles, and we even sense some real pictorial energy in his 1922 *Portrait of Guynemer* (fig. 202), which La Fresnaye based on a photograph of the legendary flying ace who had died a hero's death in 1917.

But if La Fresnaye seems to have been mostly confounded by the new traditionalism, it nevertheless provided him with what art had provided for so long, up until the invention of the photograph: a kind of immortality. In a series of pictures that he created after the war, La Fresnaye recorded his own illness and gradual decline first in imagined portraits and, toward the end, in self-portraits.[120] Beginning with a neo-classical line drawing of 1921 of a *Young Man Coughing*, which indirectly suggested the artist's own lung problems, La Fresnaye the next year made a pencil drawing of *The Sick Man in Bed* (fig. 203), with the invalid sighing in a theatrical gesture. For the next several years he made numerous studies of *les malades*; finally in 1925, the year of his death, he concentrated on his own anguished visage, in remarkably moving self-portraits that include a frighteningly close pen-and-ink study (fig. 204). It is not surprising to find La Fresnaye portraying his fatal illness in traditional-looking images. For an artist whose Cubism had been a

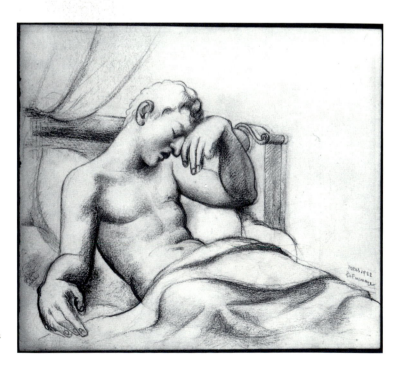

203. R. de la Fresnaye, *The Sick Man in Bed*, 1922.

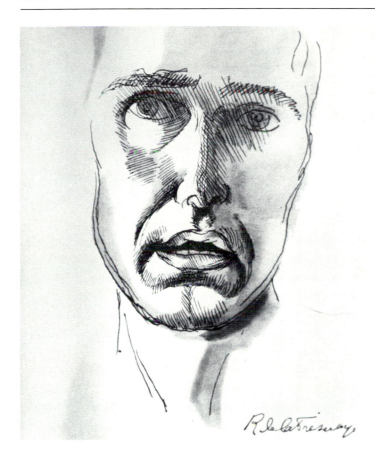

204. R. de la Fresnaye, *Self-Portrait*, 1925.

celebration of modernity, national pride, and industrial progress the modernist conceit did not really encompass anything as
disturbing as illness and death. For a subject that touched so
close and was so timeless, only the more trustworthy vehicle of
mimesis would do.

In a sense, though, death was a fitting subject for the various
pictorial modes of the post-war return to tradition within the
Parisian avant-garde. No matter how optimistic the image of
classical humanity was made—despite the intended confidence
of Braque's pictures of abundance or Picasso's *maternités* and
the elegant well-being of all the portraits in the Ingres style—
there was no avoiding the most basic fact that the iconography
of classicism had been the language of national defense in the
face of imminent extinction. Despite claims to the contrary,
there can have been no artist in the Parisian avant-garde who
did not know in his innermost heart that the new classicism was
a lament rather than a celebration. It was a style of loss, a

shadow play of mythic images that spoke more articulately of disillusionment than of tradition, stability, civilization, or hope. Perhaps the pantomime of classicism was the most appropriate fiction for a nation overwhelmed by grief. Picasso seems to have thought so. In 1923, the same year in which he painted his *Woman in White*, he said:

> From the painters of the origins, the primitives, whose work is obviously different from nature, down to those who, like David, Ingres, and even Bouguereau, believed in painting nature as it is, art has always been art and not nature. And from the point of view of art there are no concrete or abstract forms, but only forms that are more or less convincing lies. That those lies are necessary to our mental selves is beyond any doubt. . . .[121]

From Analysis to Synthesis

Sᴛʀᴀɴɢᴇ as it may seem, Cubism not only survived the war but, to a certain extent, flourished in post-war Paris.[1] After four long years of anti-modernist polemic—the outlines of which we know so well—the majority of pre-war Cubist painters nonetheless continued to make Cubist art in the 1920s, and a number of younger painters joined their ranks. Several factors conspired to bring about this formidable irony of Cubism's acceptance despite its wartime travails, including the passage of time, which shed the glow of legitimacy on the otherwise wayward aesthetic. By 1919, after all, Cubism was hardly new—it was now a familiar aspect of the Parisian arts and, as the French themselves had said often during the war, venerability provides its own *raison d'être*. In large part owing to the anti-modernist campaign, it retained more liveliness and topicality than it might have had if Cubism had simply been ignored during the war. It is a cardinal rule of modern society that, with a few rare exceptions, there is no such thing as bad publicity. Moreover, although any real sense of kinship among the pre-war modernists had been vitiated by the war, the nationalist imperative that the individual artist shed his "sacrosanct personality," as André Michel put it, and assume his place in the collective endeavor had been enormously effective. For the most part this meant no more than joining, or at least moving, toward the artistic mainstream (a tendency we have already witnessed in numerous cases). But it also meant, for some, a literal engagement in group activities, especially designing for the theatre.

The obvious precedent for theatrical collaboration was Picasso's work on *Parade*, the repercussions of which served as a warning for the painters who designed for the theatre in the post-war years. Picasso's own work for Diaghilev in the 1920s was thoroughly tasteful: he forsook all but the mildest forms of Cubism in favor of "Latin" and classical motifs. For the 1919 ballet *Le Tricorne* (set to the music of Manuel de Falla's famous

Three-Cornered Hat) Picasso created a curtain, set (fig. 205), and costumes *à l'espagnole*; and he made another ensemble in the style of the *commedia dell'arte* for Stravinsky's *Pulcinella* of 1920. The next year he did the sets and costumes for another Falla ballet, *Cuardo Flamenco*; in 1922 he collaborated with Jean Cocteau on the scenery for the latter's *Antigone*, which had music by Arthur Honegger and costumes by Chanel. And in 1924 he did the sets and costumes for two productions, Erik Satie's *Mercure* and Cocteau's *Le Train bleu*.[2]

Georges Braque and Juan Gris also worked for Diaghilev in the 1920s, making sets and costumes that, like Picasso's Ballets Russes designs, tended to be traditional rather than modernist. In 1924 Braque created the sets and costumes for Molière's *Les Fâcheux* (adapted by Boris Kochno to music by Georges Auric), with a curtain featuring "Venus on the half-shell" (fig. 206); and in 1925 he designed the Ballets Russes production of *Zéphyr et Flore* (which also had a story by Kochno, set to the music of Vladimir Dukelsky with choreography by Léonide Massine). In 1924, for Etienne de Beau-

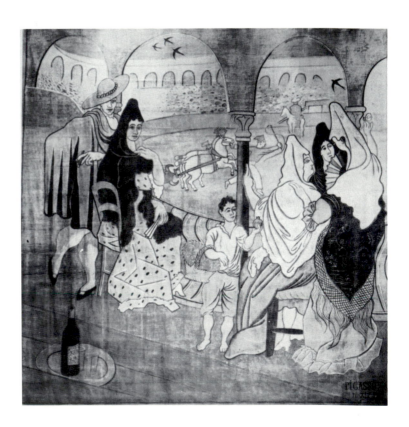

205. P. Picasso, Curtain for *Le Tricorne*, 1919.

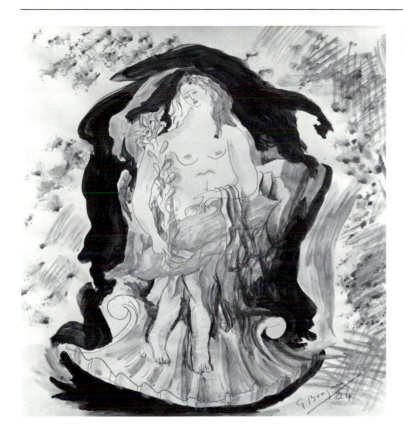

206. G. Braque, Curtain for *Les Fâcheux*, 1924.

mont's "Soirées de Paris," Braque also designed *Salade*, a *commedia dell'arte* adaptation with music by Darius Milhaud and choreography by Massine. That same year Gris designed his productions for Diaghilev: *La Colombe*, *Les Tentations de la bergère* (fig. 207), and *L'Education manquée*, as well as designing a Red Cross benefit staged by Diaghilev at the Printemps department store. In 1923 he had designed *La Fête merveilleuse*, another high-society benefit gala, also staged by Diaghilev, in the Hall of Mirrors at Versailles. Many other Parisian artists designed for the Ballets Russes as well: Delaunay, as we know, designed *Cléopâtre* in 1918; Matisse did the sets and costumes for Stravinsky's *Le Chant du Rossignol* in 1920; in the previous year Derain designed *La Boutique fantasque*, and Marie Laurencin did the same for *Les Biches* in 1924.

After Picasso, the painter who did the most work for, and gave the greatest commitment to, the theatre in the post-war period was Léger.[3] It is perhaps significant that he worked not for Diaghilev but for Rolf de Maré's Ballets Suédois,[4] an organization which, although (as is obvious from its name) it was

207. J. Gris, Costume design for *Les Tentations de la bergère*, 1924.

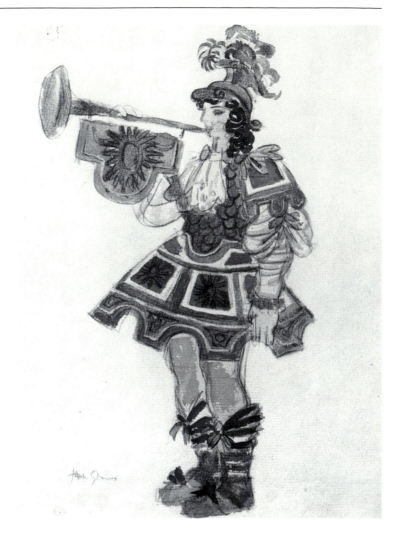

modeled after the Russian company, was nonetheless younger and more adventurous. Léger's two productions for the Ballets Suédois, Riccioto Canudo's *Skating Rink* (music by Arthur Honegger) of 1922 and Blaise Cendrars's *La Création du monde* (music by Milhaud) (fig. 208), can be distinguished both thematically and visually from the productions that his friends designed for the Russian Ballet: instead of the folkloric/Latin, classical/*grand siècle* range of subjects that Picasso, Braque, and Gris helped Diaghilev to realize, Léger's themes were contemporary working-class amusement in *Skating Rink* and African ritual in *La Création du monde*. Even more important, Léger's designs were innovative extensions of the Synthetic Cubist art (which we will discuss shortly) that he was making at the

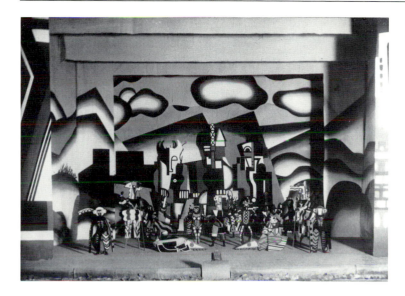

208. F. Léger, Set design for *La Création du Monde*, 1923.

same time. Instead of backing away from his pictorial innovations when making public art, Léger found in the ballet the perfect forum for his newest ideas. In fact, he considered the theatre to be the ideal medium for a collective aesthetic, and his ideas as expressed in an article in 1924 are a kind of updated version of the Wagnerian *Gesamtkunstwerk*. For Léger, *le spectacle* could bring about the defeat of the individualistic reign of the *vedette*—the star—so that the scenic conception as a whole could take on a life of its own, sharing the leading role with the actors (an idea that he may have derived from Picasso's "Managers" in *Parade*). Whereas in traditional theatre, Léger wrote, "a man or a woman, with or without talent, imposes himself and orders the spectacle in terms of scenic value"—that is, the ensemble is a function of the relative importance of the human presence—in the new theatre, in which the objects of the environment, formerly secondary, take an important place, "the prejudice of the individual-king disappears, the means of attraction come out of the shadows and are infinite. Lights, cinematographic projections join the ensemble."[5] Léger obviously retained a strong attachment to the values of the pre-war avant-garde, wherein the dismantling of the traditional hierarchy of figure and ground was perhaps the central tenet of the painterly revolution of Cubism.[6]

But it was not only time's inexorable progress and the avant-garde's concerted effort to meet the public at least halfway that account for the acculturation of the Cubists in post-war Paris.

Equally important was the appearance in France of the Swiss-born and German-affiliated Dada. Of course the Parisians already knew about Dada, if at a distance. The controversy after the première of Apollinaire's *Les Mamelles de Tirésias* in 1917 had probably been in part a reaction to real or imagined Dadaist aspects of the play. Apollinaire himself had been wary of forming too close an affiliation with the new movement from abroad: in a letter of February 1918 he explained to Tristan Tzara that he was sorry that he could not contribute to his new magazine *Dada*, but that unfortunately he found the journal's stance on Germany to be unclear; as a naturalized Frenchman, he explained to the Rumanian poet, he had to be circumspect and "I would be foolish to act otherwise" in the midst of war.[7] After the Armistice, though, the situation was very different indeed—the post-war euphoria meant that Dada could now even find a temporary home in Paris.

Francis Picabia and Georges Ribemont-Dessaignes[8] provided one of Dada's first post-war Parisian manifestations at the Salon d'Automne of 1919. Both showed paintings in the ironic, mock-scientific, mechanomorphic style that Picabia had inaugurated in 1915: among the works exhibited was Picabia's *L'Enfant carburateur*, a painting based on an actual diagram of an automobile carburetor, to which are affixed phrases like "méthode crocodile," "sphère de la migraine," and "détruire le futur." Ribemont-Dessaignes showed a rather similar-looking canvas, his *Jeune Femme*, now in the Société Anonyme Collection at Yale. Needless to say, the hanging committee of the Salon was loath to exhibit such obviously provocative if indecipherably sardonic works; but as both artists were associates of the Salon there was little that could be done aside from hanging the works in the least conspicuous and most inauspicious place at the Grand Palais—underneath the staircase. This, in turn, resulted both in a letter of protest written by Picabia to the *Journal du Peuple*, published on 2 November (aimed at Frantz Jourdain, president of the Salon),[9] and in Ribemont-Dessaignes's review of the Salon in a new issue of the Dada magazine *391*. This article managed to combine Dada politics and aesthetics in a furious attack on French cultural chauvinism. Referring to the galleries of the Salon, he said that "The skeleton of Marshal Foch prowls in the dark when the doors of the [Grand Palais] are closed and calls the muster. The teeth of the artists, which are almost as filthy as the nails of the sculptors, chatter with fright.—Am I enough of a corpse? Do I smell bad enough? Marshal! Marshal! I assure you, I have at least been to the censor!"[10] As far as one French artist was concerned, then, French art was now nothing more than the wartime regime perpetuated. Ribemont-Dessaignes's attack, in the same piece, on Maurice Denis and Henri Matisse led to his being summoned before the Salon committee, to more insults back and forth, and eventually to Louis Vauxcelles's demand for a duel with the artist.[11]

Soon the antics of Dada were receiving attention from a far larger public than only the members of the Salon directly concerned. Perhaps the most notorious attack in print appeared in the ultra-Right conservative daily *Le Gaulois* about six months later. This hysterical reaction to Dada's appearance in Paris, penned by Marcel Boulenger, helped to make Dada a household word of the moment. Featured in the first two columns of the paper's front page, the article (titled "Herr Dada") began, "It is rather curious today to see in our society—and sometimes in the best society—the smiles lavished on and encouragement given to revolutionaries, unforgivable enemies of civilization, of our nation, and of capitalism as well." And then, in case the reader had any question about where the writer stood on the issues, Boulenger continued:

> Let there be no doubt about it, it's all one and the same thing. Extremists, revolutionaries, bolsheviks, dadaists— same grain, same origin, same poison. . . . They have de- clared that . . . nothing which we consider reasonable, delicate, or beautiful interests them; that Greco-Latin cul- ture and the French culture—*parbleu!*—that derives from it are finished. . . . Do you sense what is lurking behind these strange goings-on? Do you see what this deliberate craziness is directed at? Yes! Against everything that has hitherto established the French intellectual empire and that still does so today, thanks to the inquiring spirit, the clarity, the chain of ideas, logic, moderation, and taste. And it is the disgraceful love of chaos and anarchy that hides behind these clown masks. As in Petrograd, as in Moscow, as in Berlin, so in the scum of society.[12]

In other words, by calling into question the most basic tenets of nationalist culture, Dada was providing a critique that no one could have dared to offer in wartime. Typical was Picabia's drawing, published in *391* on 10 July 1921—two days before the unveiling of Magrou's *Monument to the Genius of the Latin People* (fig. 180) in the Palais Royal—*Monument to Latin Stu- pidity (Monument à la Bêtise Latine)* (fig. 209), in which "er- ror," "truth," "Jew," and "Christianity" form part of an indeci-

209. F. Picabia, *Monument to Latin Stupidity* (*Monument à la Bêtise Latine*), 1921. Reproduced in *391* no. 16 (10 July 1921).

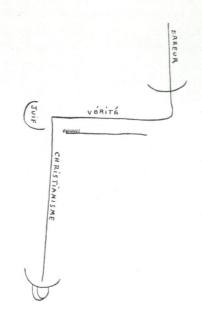

MONUMENT A LA BÊTISE LATINE

pherable, schematized circuit that is intended as a parody of the endless French theorizing on the greatness of Latinity.

It is certainly true that one of the essential thrusts of Dada activity in Paris was aimed at the conservative establishment in arts and letters—especially those of its members with strong political ties. It was not by chance that Maurice Barrès, one-time Symbolist and famous convert to nationalism (and to a very insidious form of racism), was chosen by the Parisian Dadas on 13 May 1921 to "stand trial" for "endangering the safety of the spirit." Although the writer himself did not of course appear at this kangaroo court, André Breton, Louis Aragon, and Philippe Soupault, among others, brought charges against Barrès. Not only were his books declared "literally unreadable," but his famous statement "I chose nationalism as a determinism" was called "1. obscure 2. absurd." His career was labeled one vast compromise from beginning to end.[13]

That is not to say that Dada's influence on Parisian art and culture was limited to political critique, or that the relationship between Dada and established Parisian culture was marked only by hostility. One of the points that Boulenger made in his article of 1920 was the extent to which the Parisian *beau monde* was willing to encourage Dada and take delight in its outrages;

and he specifically named Jean Cocteau, whom he otherwise found "charming," as one of those Parisians who had been swept up by the new movement. Not surprisingly Cocteau, who prided himself on his ability to reconcile the "Left" and "Right" in Parisian culture, and who had himself seen *Parade* as his first great attempt to forge the new wartime compromise of bohemia and High Society, saw his own relationship to Dada in the same way. In the first issue of *Le Coq*, the short-lived little magazine that Cocteau published during 1920, the poet wrote:

> The articles that group me with the Dadaists amuse me greatly because I am the very model of an anti-Dadaist. The Dadaists know this very well, and if they sometimes ask me to collaborate with them it is to prove that their system is to have no system. If they stand at the extreme Left, I am at the extreme Right. I invented the *extreme* Right. . . . Extremes touch. I feel myself so far from the Left and from the Right, so close to the *extreme* Left, with which I close the circle, that people confuse one of us with the other. I constantly have to keep specifying in a loud voice whether I am Right or Left, and this is tiring— whereas, just over the wall, without raising my voice, I can talk with Tzara and Picabia, my neighbors from the other end of the world. . . .[14]

One of the reasons that Cocteau was being grouped with the Dada artists and poets was, aside from his associations with people like Tzara and Picabia, that his highly visible theatrical productions of 1920–21 were frivolous, ironic, and lacking in anything that might have passed for seriousness or high artistic intention. This, of course, was deliberate on Cocteau's part, for he was finally having the opportunity to create the kind of simple and, by all appearances, charming spectacles that he had been imagining since at least the time of *Parade*, in 1917. Drawn from popular culture and mythology, Cocteau's two productions *Le Boeuf sur le toit* of 1920 and *Les Mariés de la Tour Eiffel* of 1921 were, in a sense, celebrations of peace regained and especially of the Franco-American effort that had brought about victory—the first production was set in an American bar, the "Nothing-Happens Bar," and the second at Paris's most famous monument (in fact, Tzara and a number of Dadaists disrupted the première of *Les Mariés* by shouting "Long live Dada" from seats in the orchestra).[15] Both were also in the spirit of *Grand Guignol* and looked like *images d'Epinal* brought to life—the former had set and costumes by Guy-Pierre Fauconnet

210. J. Hugo, Costume design for *Les Mariés de la Tour Eiffel*, 1921.

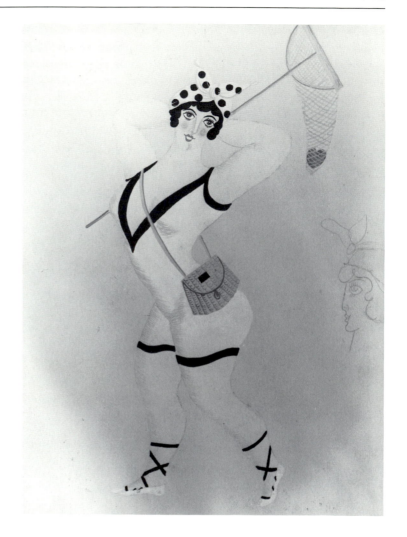

and Raoul Dufy, and the latter had sets by Irène Lagut and costumes (fig. 210) by Jean Hugo.

But if Cocteau's theatrical offerings of 1920–21 still seem at a great distance from anything we might call Dada—they were too sweet and nostalgic as well as too accessible, and they offered no political message or social criticism—they do seem to have shared in a mood of gaiety that also greeted Dada in Paris. Indeed, the French were almost too well suited for Dada: if the middle class and certain portions of the opinion-making Right were scandalized as they were intended to be, the same could not be said of the Parisian aristocracy and its intellectual entourage. This group was ever on the alert for a delightful event, for an excuse to throw a party, for a chance to put on fancy dress

or costume. The Count Etienne de Beaumont financed Cocteau's theatrical inventions at the same time that he gave a series of splendid theme-parties at his elegant *hôtel particulier* in
the rue Masseran.[16] Not only did his guest list consist of the
Parisian *beau monde* and the important artists (including Picasso, Satie, and Cocteau, of course), but his themes could
sometimes be found in the no man's land between the good life
and the Dada life—the big party for 1922 was the *Bal des Jeux*,
for which the guests were expected to arrive as their favorite
game or amusement; Picasso made sketches of the various costumes (fig. 211) as the guests arrived. In 1925 the Count and
Countess de Noailles threw a *Bal des Matières* for which the
guests were to come costumed only in synthetic materials—cel-
luloid, vulcanized rubber, etc.; Eugenia Errazuriz, Picasso's
patron, and Etienne de Beaumont wore coordinated plastic out-

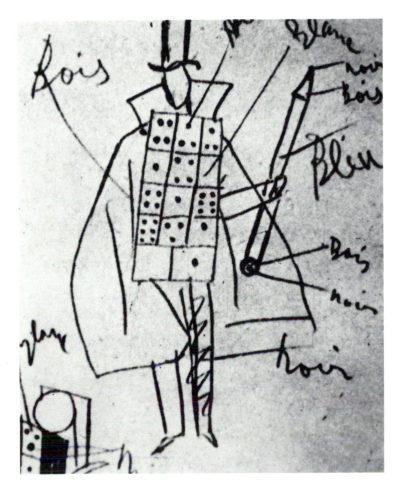

211. P. Picasso, Drawing of costume
worn at the Beaumont *Bal des Jeux*,
1922.

fits. "Just over the wall," as Cocteau would have it, were Oskar Schlemmer's theme-parties at the Bauhaus in Dessau, as for instance the "Dotted, Checkered, and Striped" event of March 1926.[17]

Most important for us, though, is the impact that Dada exerted on Cubism, as well as on the attitudes of those other Parisian artists who in one way or another considered themselves members of the avant-garde. At the beginning of December 1919, Juan Gris wrote to Kahnweiler: "I am alarmed about what happens next in painting. I see our serious efforts being swallowed up in waves of Dadaism and Expressionism. Raynal has been showing me copies of *Der Sturm*—it makes me sick."[18] Gris must have been aware that his feeling was reciprocated by the Parisian Dadas. In March 1919 Picabia wrote to Tzara, who was still in Zurich: "In Paris, nothing but idiotic gossip; all the geniuses pass the time by fighting with each other, then making up"; and this was followed by a reference to Picasso's popularity in all camps and to his arrivism.[19] In fact, as early as 1917—while residing in Barcelona—Picabia, in the inaugural issue of *391*, had begun to ridicule Picasso (and the other Parisian Cubists) for their accommodation to the wartime regime. Claiming that Picasso had given up "Germanic" Cubism in order to "return to the Ecole des Beaux-Arts (studio of Luc Olivier Merson)," Picabia (under the pseudonym "Pharamousse") noted that

> *L'Elan* has published his first studies from life. Picasso is henceforth the leader of a new school in which our collaborator Francis Picabia waits not a moment to enroll. The "Kodak" published above is the solemn sign of it.[20]

The "Kodak" referred to (fig. 212) was Picabia's parody of Picasso's portrait of Max Jacob (fig. 39), which, as we know and as Picabia tells the reader, was reproduced in *L'Elan* (in the final issue, of December 1916). Instead of depicting Jacob, Picabia makes a portrait of the poet and critic "Max Goth" (pseudonym for Maximilien Gauthier), drawn in simple linear style but with a photograph for the head (apparently a picture of Picabia himself), intended as a parody of the contrast between the schematized body and highly finished head in Picasso's portrait of Jacob. And in June 1919 Picabia again wrote to Tzara: "If you only knew what a sordid life [here] among all these Artists who dream only of academic glory. . . ."[21]

It was not long until Tzara had a chance to observe the comings and goings of the Parisian art world for himself; he moved to the French capital the next winter. But no sooner did he ar-

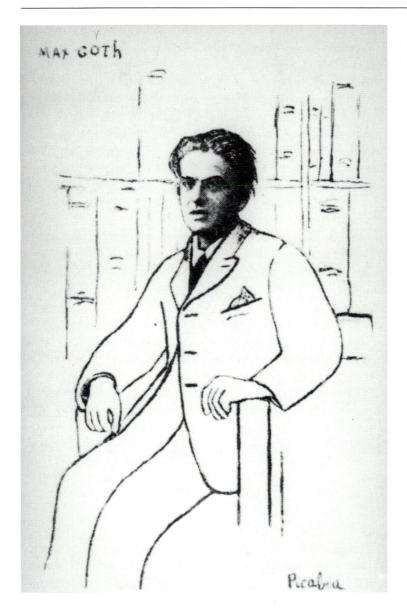

212. F. Picabia, *Portrait of Max Goth*, 1917. Reproduced in *391* no. 1 (1 February 1917).

rive than difficulties began to arise between the Cubists and the new insurgents, and once again it took the form of a political indictment of the now old avant-garde. On 23 January 1920 the magazine *Littérature*, edited by Louis Aragon, Breton, and Soupault, and allied to the Dada painters and poets, staged a *matinée* of the arts at the *Palais des Fêtes*. Among the various events were a talk by André Salmon, poetry readings by Max Jacob, Paul Eluard, Aragon, Breton, and Cocteau, and an exhibition of recent works by Giorgio di Chirico, Gris, and Jacques Lipchitz. All appears to have gone smoothly until

Tzara, who was making his eagerly awaited debut in Paris, began his portion of the program, which consisted of a "reading" (drawn from the newspaper) of Léon Daudet's latest speech in the Chamber of Deputies (the august legislative body to which the Royalist had recently been elected). Those who expected Tzara to read a poem, as had been announced, were merely disappointed. But others, specifically Gris and Salmon, were made furious not only by the Dadaist's lack of respect for the artistic event in which he was a participant, but also by his obvious ridicule of French nationalism (there was undoubtedly a fear of repercussions, as well). The critic Florent Fels shouted at Tzara: "Go back to Zurich! Go to Hell!"[22]

Albert Gleizes quickly found that he, too, was embroiled in the growing animosities between the Parisian Cubists and the Dadas, in part as a result of this attempt to revive the pre-war association of Cubist artists, the "Section d'Or" (their exhibition of 1912, largely arranged by the Villon brothers, had had a quasi-theoretical bias toward the "classical French" component of modern art). Almost immediately the situation became quite complicated: Picabia, who had provided the financial backing for the 1912 "Section d'Or" show, was soon invited into the new organization by Paul Dermée, poet and editor of the now-defunct *Nord-Sud*, and although it looked for a moment as if the Cubists and Dadas might present themselves to the public as allies, it was not to be. On 25 February, at a meeting of the organization at the Closerie de Lilas on the boulevard Montparnasse, the Dada artists (including Max Ernst, who was specifically named) were voted out of participation in the new "Section d'Or," and a rift between the Cubist artists and the Dadas was thus created that could not be repaired.[23]

To make matters worse, and most probably as a consequence of behind-the-scenes disputes, on 3 April Gleizes published a scathing attack entitled "L'Affaire Dada." Writing from a left-wing perspective, Gleizes referred to the Dada leaders as "products of the wealthy upper bourgeoisie," atop a hierarchy that he considered "already dead; what we see now is the decomposition of its corpse." Furthermore, he portrayed them as desperate men: "They cannot live alone. They seek the crowd, in which they believe. They are flat on their bellies before it," and he also made an oblique but clear reference to Cocteau and Parisian high society's fascination with Dada:

> The upper bourgeoisie is quite flattered to discover among its own a man sufficiently intelligent to keep his mind occupied for a while. Between Edmond Rostand and the

Dadaists, there is no insurmountable barrier. . . . The same devotees who swooned over Rostand already have their big toe on the step of the Dada car.

But even this, as damning as it was meant to be, was not the worst, for Gleizes seems to have developed an almost pathological hatred for the Dada artists. "Their minds are forever haunted by a sexual delirium and a scatological frenzy," he wrote; "They are obsessed with the organs of reproduction to such a degree that those of their works which may possibly reveal genius are inevitably of a genital character." Was he thinking of Duchamp, Picabia, and Ribemont-Dessaignes? Probably, for we can point to works by any of these three that might have justified such a description; but it is difficult to say what he was thinking of when he wrote the following:

> They have discovered the anus and the by-products of intestinal activity. . . . They make marbles with fecal matter, they gallop over it, they run probing fingers through it. This is a phenomenon well known to psychiatrists. They confuse excrement with the products of the mind. They use the same word to designate two different things.[24]

In May, Picabia replied to Gleizes in the pages of *Cannibale* (no. 2) attacking not only his wartime sojourn in Spain (Picabia claimed that Gleizes wanted to be naturalized a German) but also his politics ("a bread crumb socialist"); his marriage to a daughter of the "Grand Bourgeoisie Dada, with whom he is not even capable of making children!"; and—of course—his genitals: "His sexual apparatus, as he so elegantly names it, of what can it serve him? No doubt to construct aquatic cubism."[25] But this was not all. Waiting till the following autumn and the appearance of Gleizes's rather pedantic book *Du Cubisme et des moyens de le comprendre* (Cubism and How to Understand It), Picabia published a scandalous interview between Tzara and Jean Metzinger in *391*. "What do you think of Gleizes's book . . . ?" Tzara asked Metzinger; "Absolutely idiotic," the painter replied. Why did he write the book, then? "To explain Cubism to himself because he still has not understood it!" Finally the obvious question was asked of Metzinger: If all this is true, why did you collaborate on a book with Gleizes (*Du Cubisme*, of 1912)? "Because I am very lazy and I needed a secretary."[26]

In effect, by providing a new yardstick of artistic extremism, Dada helped to push Cubism much further toward the center of Parisian culture—not an altogether unhappy consequence as far as some of the Cubists were concerned. We know that Gris was worried that Dada might "swallow up" his serious efforts. But, as he also wrote to Kahnweiler, "The exaggerations of the Dada movement and of others like Picabia make us look classical, though I can't say I mind about that."[27] In fact, as again Gris told Kahnweiler, in January 1920, "The Salon des Indépendants has opened with something of a success for the Cubists, who are taken seriously by the whole—or almost—of the press. Even Vauxcelles admits he has wronged us," although he added, by way of qualification, "No one says much about me because I am a foreigner."[28] In part, the wartime argument in defense of Cubism and avant-garde art in general—that it was not German, but first a French and even a Latin artistic manifestation—had worked; also in its favor was the obvious fact that many of the practicing artists were loyal Frenchmen and courageous veterans. Although this meant that foreign artists (with the exception of Picasso) were likely to get short shrift, as Gris told Kahnweiler, it nonetheless assured the survival of what André Lhote called "French cubism."

But because Cubism after 1918 differed so greatly, in both form and content, from the way it had been practiced and understood before 1914, it may be accurate to call Cubism one of the casualties of the Great War. We have already observed the gradual introduction of specifically French and Latin subjects into Cubist art during the war, as for example in Picasso's *L'Italienne* of 1917 (fig. 100) and Gris's Cubist version of Corot of the same year (fig. 116). From a pre-war aesthetic of modernity, the avant-garde had worked its way back to tradition by means of implicitly patriotic themes, a trend that continued after the Armistice. Surely the greatest Cubist painting that takes the *commedia dell'arte* for its subject is Picasso's *Three Musicians* (fig. 213) of 1921. As Theodore Reff has convincingly argued, *Three Musicians* is a portrait of three friends: in the guise of the clarinet-playing Pierrot is the recently deceased Guillaume Apollinaire; Max Jacob is presented as the singing monk at the right (a reference to the Jewish poet's conversion to Catholicism and his subsequent residence, in the spring of 1921, at a Benedictine monastery); and Picasso paints himself as the guitar-strumming Harlequin. Reff calls the painting an elegy for Picasso's "lost bohemian youth, for freedom of the Bateau-Lavoir days and the gaiety of Apollinaire and Jacob . . ."[29] The dog that sits beneath Pierrot's chair is, then, both a symbol of friendship (*fido*) and of death (Cerberus). Furthermore, Picasso had many reasons—after the war—to paint this ode to things past: not only had he experienced two terrible losses

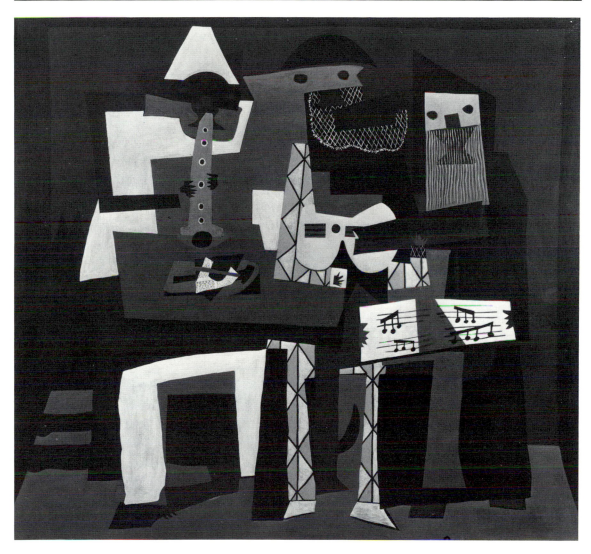

213. P. Picasso, *Three Musicians*,
1921.

since that fateful August 1914—the deaths of Eva and then of
Apollinaire—but his life had been transformed completely by
1921, the year he turned forty. He was now a married man, a
father, and a Parisian bourgeois living in one of the city's most
fashionable *quartiers*. It must have seemed that his youth was
really over, and in the juxtaposition of the bright carnival colors
of the figures and the deep tones of the ground we find the visual
sign for happy memories mixed with a sense of loss.

However, it is not just the choice of *commedia dell'arte* as the
vehicle for Picasso's memories that makes the *Three Musicians*
a distinctly post-war work. The large Cubist picture is obviously

the modernist counterpart to another picture of 1921, Picasso's *Three Women at the Spring* (fig. 184). The highly traditional three-figure grouping, the picture's large size, and the monumental proportion of figures to ground—all of these qualities attest to the contemporaneous creation of the two works. Nor is it only historical perspective that causes us to find correspondences between Picasso's neo-classicism and his Cubism in the post-war years. As he had demonstrated with the juxtaposition of the *Parade* curtain and set—and of Ingres and Cubism—so with his two great paintings of 1921 Picasso intended to establish an equivalence between his traditional and his modernist tendencies. This is made strikingly clear in a painting of the previous year (fig. 214), in which the artist combined, in a single work, classicizing and Cubist quotations from his own oeuvre: a dancing couple, a neo-classical head, and two fat classical hands are placed alongside six miniature Cubist still-life images.[30] The interplay of stylistic polarities in a single work—or, as in the case of *Three Women at the Spring* and *Three Musicians*, in two obviously related works—testified to the artist's ability to transform himself like Proteus, and thereby to rise above the banal categories that ensnared less powerful artists. At the same time, this joining of the modern and the ancient was a brilliant way of bringing Cubism into the fold of tradition while, conversely, diminishing the conservative sting of neo-classicism. The self-aggrandizement and the stylistic redefinition are in fact intimately linked. In making us concentrate on his artistic prowess, on his unique ability to be both the most traditional artist and the most gifted creator of new forms, Picasso removes himself from the group aspects of both Cubist and neo-classical aesthetics. He says with his two great paintings of 1921 not only that Cubism is more traditional than it had appeared to be before the war (and that traditional styles may be less retrograde than we had imagined) but, also, that his modernism and his atavism are personal choices. Where Picasso and Braque had attempted to create a group style of revolutionary impact by making almost identical paintings c. 1910–12 and agreeing not to sign their works, in the post-war years Picasso diametrically shifted the terms of his critical reception. Instead of presenting himself as one half of a revolutionary, pioneering team, he now appears as a lone artist with multiple personae. This is the Renaissance conception of a solitary, protean, overwhelming genius; Picasso in the 1920s becomes a modern Michelangelo.[31]

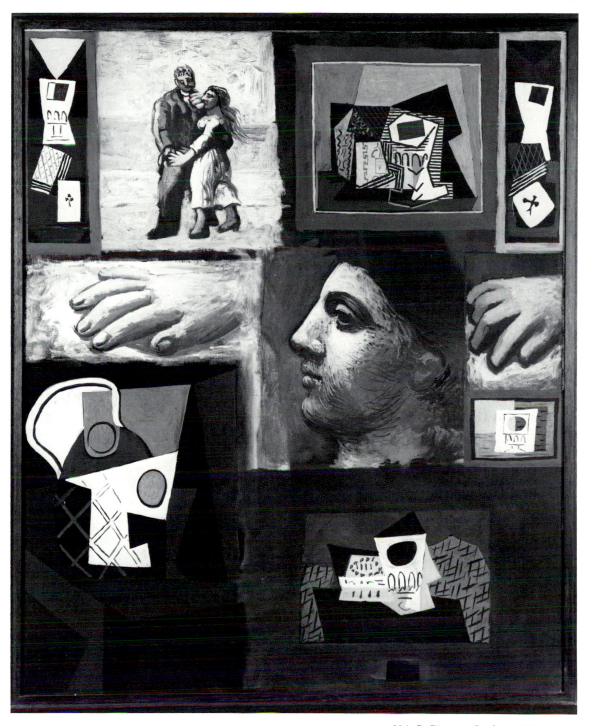

214. P. Picasso, *Studies*, 1920.

In the light of what we know about the status of individualism during the war, we might imagine that Picasso's new emphasis on his own artistic persona was a violation of the collective spirit as it was understood to be after August 1914. But we must keep several things in mind: first, that neither of his post-war artistic directions—classical or Cubist—was especially provocative at this point; second, that we must not confuse the French Right's conception of the state, of the collective unit of French people and their accumulated culture, with a Left notion of collectivism. From a conservative perspective, to invoke the collective unit as the highest national value was in no way to denigrate the concept of genius. To the contrary, as we have shown previously, the Right had never been averse to the notion of genius, which was—and remains to this day—one of the keystones in the construction of hierarchy. What the conservative meant by "dangerous" individualism was not superiority or talent, but dissent, anarchy, new ideas, social progressivism, and any kind of genius that did not reaffirm the *status quo*. Even Wagner was not derided for being a genius; he was despised for being an enemy genius. As long as it was put at the service of the established social order, as long as it served the state (as in the cases of Ingres and Puvis de Chavannes), genius was considered not an example of "individualism" but rather a sublime demonstration of the hierarchical principle. So too with Picasso. His genius came increasingly to be seen by the cultural establishment as a confirmation of the eternal rules of greatness, especially now that it was no longer at the head of a battalion of artistic dissidents and revolutionaries. Moreover, genius, as always, was bankable — Picasso's prices kept escalating,[32] along with those of other artists who were thought to possess "genius." And Picasso had now an added worth, to the extent to which he could lead the former revolutionaries *back* to the path of order, tradition, and French values. Needless to say, artists like Delaunay deeply resented Picasso in the role of leading neo-classicist, resented the fact that a foreigner could become the living exemplar of the French tradition. But there was little that Delaunay or anyone else could do about it. Picasso was both the best modernist and the best "retardataire" painter, and everyone knew it.

The *Three Musicians*—even apart from its Latin subject matter, its scale, and its three-figure grouping and obvious relationship to *Three Women at the Spring*—reveals in other formal respects a new conception of the Cubist aesthetic as monumental, static, classical. There is, for instance (as has been noted by William Rubin), a clear formal hierarchy in the painting: shapes are smaller and more intricately overlapped toward the center of the picture than at the edges; the brightest colors too are at the center—the yellow and orange of Harlequin's costume; the yellow guitar—with tones becoming more somber as we move outward.[33] Compared to a pre-war Cubist picture like *Ma Jolie* (fig. 101) of 1912, a painting that we previously compared to Picasso's 1917 *L'Italienne* (fig. 100), how well-mannered and traditional appears the large work of 1921. In place of the monochromatic pre-war palette, which served to mix up and generally confound our reading of space, the colors are either high-keyed or dark, but always distinct; instead of the infinity of nuanced brush-strokes that constitute the planes (such as they are) in *Ma Jolie*, the paint application is now smooth, with almost no evidence whatever of the artist's hand. The different handling of paint, from stippled to smooth, represents a shift in Picasso's conception of light between 1912 and 1921. For all its inconsistencies, the light that illuminates *Ma Jolie* is a Naturalist's light, composed of a multitude of readings, a kind of Impressionist light gone mad. In *Three Musicians*, on the other hand, the light is that of the studio; the figures are posed not only indoors, but in a closed compartment into which only an artificial illumination can penetrate—there is no changing daylight here at all, but rather the fixed intensity of dramatically disposed lights and darks.

The artificial illumination of the *Three Musicians* is a corollary of the illusionistic pictorial space. While it is very nearly impossible to speak of "figure" and "ground" in discussing *Ma Jolie*, so interwoven are they, figure and ground are reasserted in 1921. Not only are the three figures, although intricately entwined in jigsaw-puzzle fashion, distinguishable from each other, but the figures as a group are clearly distinguishable from the dark background against which they are placed, because a true spatial container has been devised for them. A back wall marks the recession in depth (which is not the least denied by the fact that the depth is so obviously askew at the left and the right); two side walls are indicated with receding orthogonals; and even a secure, if too drastically tipped, floor is provided. What Picasso has done is to insert his Cubist, jerry-built system of representation within a more or less conventional perspectival space—he has placed modernism, as it were, within a traditional frame of reference. Indeed, the entire picture resonates with art history, as becomes obvious when the musical theme here portrayed is compared yet again to *Ma Jolie*: in 1912 Pi-

casso proposed a conflation of themes allied to the multiple
meanings of his title—"Ma Jolie" as the title of a popular song,
as the title of his picture inscribed beneath this Cubist "portrait," as Picasso's very personal conception of the beautiful—
all in the context of a picture that is intended to be as weightless
as air, as insubstantial, evanescent, and contemporary as a popular tune. The *Three Musicians*, on the other hand, is a portrait
of three seventeenth-century stock characters put to the service
of a seventeenth-century theme, that of music-making or the
"Merry Company," which appears over and over again in Baroque art—in Le Nain, Honthorst, van Baburen, and many
others in the North; in Manfredi, Strozzi, and Caravaggio in the
South. But we should have probably realized from the start that
the *Three Musicians* is Caravaggesque (fig. 215)—the bright,
festive color of the clothes set off against the various browns of
the murky ground; the shallow space; the overly intense lighting
of the figures: in sum, those extraordinary pictorial equivalents
for Christian revelation that Caravaggio invented and that Picasso here uses in a picture about art, friendship, and death.
In effect, the old visual hierarchies and formulae that Picasso
had seemed to jettison before the war have returned, transforming Cubism from an art whose major theme had been change
itself (no matter what its ostensible subject) into an art whose

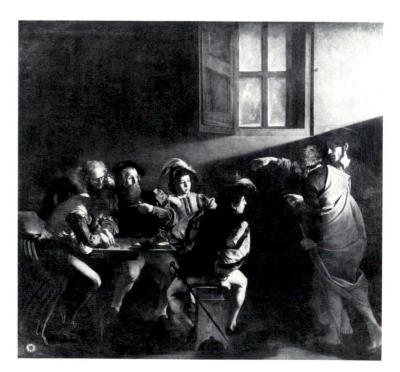

215. Caravaggio, *The Calling of
Matthew*, 1599–1600. Contarelli
Chapel, S. Luigi dei Francesi, Rome.

major theme, at least in these immediate post-war years, is the tragic realization of inevitability.

As one might expect, these remarkable changes in Cubism were not taking place in a critical vacuum. One of the first and most important articles to take up the subject of Cubism's post-war status was Blaise Cendrars's "Why is the 'Cube' Disintegrating?" of 1919, which began by first relegating Cubism to the past (as Ozenfant and Jeanneret had done in *Après le Cubisme*) and then invoking that by now familiar term "construction":

> . . . One can already foresee the day, near at hand now, when the term "Cubism" will have ceased to have more than a nominative value, indicating in the history of contemporary painting the researches of certain painters between 1907 and 1917. To refuse to recognize the importance of the Cubist movement would be fatuous, just as to laugh at it was idiotic. But it is quite as idiotic and fatuous to try to stop at a doctrine which today is dated, and to refuse to recognize that Cubism no longer offers enough novelty and surprise to provide nourishment for a new generation. . . . The "home from the Front" generation has its mind aroused by other problems, and its researches point in a new direction. First of all, it feels very much its own master. It wants to construct.[34]

Again, so many familiar notions: that the account has been closed on the pre-war period; that there is a new generation, distinct from its pre-war counterpart, with a new sense of mastery (a term we heard as early as 1916); that this masterful new generation "wants to construct." Although he does not say that pre-Armistice Cubism was destructive, Cendrars does imply that it was decadent (though he seems to find this exciting) and he says so in terms that are also familiar to us:

> At this point we touch on sorcery, and I am sure that, examined from the point of view of occultism, Cubism will yield some alarming and terrible secrets. Some Cubist paintings remind one of black magic rites; they exhale a strange, unhealthy, disturbing charm; they almost literally cast a spell. They are magic mirrors, sorcerer's tables.[35]

Germanic primitivism and Oriental mysticism; Métivet's green "Kubist" and delirious Marianne—all that seems rather remote in comparison to Cendrars's conviction that it is the Cubist pictures themselves that are as potent as savage fetishes. Nonetheless, he goes on to say, the artists "home from the front" cannot be encumbered with this pre-1917 Cubism:

> [The] younger generation, being healthy, muscular and full of life, is turning away from Cubism. In spite of its more sinister aspects, in spite of the purity of the means employed, Cubism does not succeed in troubling the young. They lay their emphasis on precisely the point which was left out of the Cubist experiment: the study of depth. The young have a sense of reality. They abhor a vacuum; they abhor destruction. They do not rationalize vertigo. They stand on their feet. They are alive. They want to construct; and one can only construct in depth.[36]

We need not posit a relationship between Cendrars's discussion of constructing in depth (as an antidote to the destructive, vertiginous Cubist experiment) and the new perspectival depth in Picasso's post-war pictures, for example. Yet there is some sense in these post-war years that the amorphous, ambiguous space of pre-war Cubism was in the process of being replaced by a surer, more traditional notion of illusionistic pictorial space. Perhaps the visual metaphor of depth was an inevitable result of the fact that architecture and solid construction were now the paradigmatic artistic processes.

Léonce Rosenberg, whose art gallery L'Effort Moderne and the accompanying *Bulletin* were important for post-war Cubist activity, also invoked the constructive metaphor in his *Cubisme et tradition* of 1920. His title was obviously meant to forge the new alliance between the avant-garde and the old guard. He explained in his book that "at the birth of an artistic movement, hostile but unequal forces are always pitted against each other," and that at this early stage "he who defends tradition . . . blindfolds himself," but that at the same time "he who exaggerates and protests against tradition is a demolisher." Still, the "demolisher" is essential to all artistic movements because "his work has prepared the coming of him whose return the present moment celebrates: the *constructeur*."[37] In this teleogical view of things, while destruction or demolition may have been appropriate and even essential to pre-war Cubism, their time has passed and the saviors of art are now "constructors." Just as Saroléa had asked Bergson when he would "put the coping stone" to his theory of flux, since change and mutability could only be a preparation, a beginning and not an end, so Rosenberg admits the necessity of Cubism's pre-war destructive phase so long as it prepares for the coming of the constructor.

Rosenberg also shared the preference for Platonic stasis over Bergsonian dynamics. In another article of the same year, after citing Braque's statement that "I love the rule which corrects emotion," Rosenberg went on to cite Marshal Foch's comparison of the principles of war to the principles of architecture, which the critic evidently found applicable to painting. "So, at certain epochs," Foch wrote, "the art of construction launches into a particular style, with greater spans and finer work which new materials permit, without . . . having modified the static principles that rule architecture in every era."[38] And Rosenberg's conclusion that "Forms evolve, the guiding principles remain"[39] was another way of saying that the post-war Cubist "constructor" had found his way back to tradition.

So all-pervasive were the constructive and architectural metaphors in the 1920s that Paul Valéry, in his 1921 tract *Eupalinos ou l'Architecte*, actually brought the reader back to the Elysian Fields, where Socrates himself and his enthusiastic and somewhat naive disciple Phaedrus are discussing architecture. The impetus for their dialogue is Phaedrus' recollection of having observed Eupalinos, architect of the temple of Artemis, at work on the construction site. He remembers the superb relationship that existed between Eupalinos and his workmen:

His instructions and their acts were so perfectly aligned that one would have said that these men were his limbs. Socrates, you would not believe what a joy it was for me to know something so well ordered. I no longer separate the idea of a temple from its construction [*édification*]. In seeing [a temple] I see an admirable action, more glorious than [military] victory and more contrary to miserable nature. To destroy and to build are of equal importance, and the soul is necessary for the one and for the other, but to build is the more cherished of the two. O, very happy Eupalinos![40]

Slightly later the following exchange ensues:

Phaedrus (to Socrates): You seem yourself to be seized with a love of architecture! See how you cannot speak without borrowing the images and the firm ideal of the highest art [*l'art majeur*].
Socrates: . . . There was an architect in me that circumstances did not succeed in forming.[41]

Like Socrates, the Parisian artists and critics of the 1920s could not "speak without borrowing the images and the firm ideal" of the art of architecture. We know that French society at large was preoccupied with the problems of reconstruction. Typical was the illustration on a 1920 calendar (fig. 216) above which was the slogan *So that France will Prosper*. Here we see modern industrial techniques applied to stone quarrying (presumably the granite blocks will be used to build a modern temple of some sort). A mechanical crane, operated by a single workman, lifts the blocks of stone from a waiting flatcar as another single worker measures the blocks at the right. A vignette at the upper right, for contrast, shows outmoded methods: there, with none of the efficiency of modern ways, no fewer than

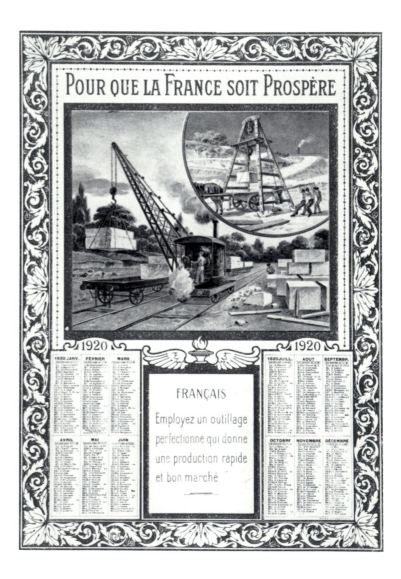

216. Anonymous, Calendar: "Pour que la France soit prospère," 1920.

four men toil with pulley and lever to load blocks into (or lift them from) a horse-drawn cart! The statement that appears beneath the two images makes the point: "Frenchmen: Use a perfected tool which makes for rapid and inexpensive production." This exhortation to efficiency would have pleased the authors of *Après le Cubisme*, especially Le Corbusier, a fervent supporter of Taylorism, the American system of labor discipline and plant organization based upon ostensibly scientific investigations of labor efficiency and incentive systems. We have already seen Henri Lebasque's Peace Loan poster (fig. 191) in which postwar industrial production was equated with human reproduction (e.g. *natalités*). But on the most basic level, reconstruction meant the rebuilding of the destroyed territories in the northeast: for instance, the new city of Lens-Méricourt arose on the site of the totally destroyed city of Lens, and within six months after government authorization, in May 1919, 800 houses were built by the railway company, Nord.[42]

The French obsession with architecture and "firm ideals" in the 1920s led to a re-examination of the modern movement's origins in the late nineteenth century specifically in terms of the concept of "construction." More than that of any other artist, the reputation of Paul Cézanne underwent a minor but important shift in critical opinion after the war. If there was a single artistic figure of the late nineteenth century who had dominated the thinking and the art of the pre-war avant-garde, it was unquestionably Cézanne. Albert Gleizes and Jean Metzinger wrote in *Du Cubisme*, in 1912:

> To understand Cézanne is to foresee Cubism. Henceforth we are justified in saying that between this school and previous manifestations there is only a difference of intensity, and that in order to assure ourselves of this we have only to study the methods of this realism, which, departing from the superficial reality of Courbet, plunges with Cézanne into profound reality, growing luminous as it forces the unknowable to retreat.[43]

This stunning passage conveys the poetry of visionaries, of *chercheurs* like Louis Pasteur stalking microbes or the Curies in search of their radioactive particles. They are carried aloft by a sense of historical inevitability, and it is Cézanne who plays the role of the mentor. But the passage has more complex nuances as well. On the one hand, Gleizes and Metzinger make clear that both Cubism and the art of Cézanne are realist in intention; but, on the other hand, they distinguish between the "profound" realism of their mentor and the "superficial" realism of Courbet. (Elsewhere in the essay, they explain that the Impressionists, with the exception of Cézanne, partake of this same superficial realism.) Gleizes and Metzinger read this distinction as a matter of "intensity"; they do not disdain or repudiate the realism of Courbet and the Impressionists, they only find it to be insufficient. The reason for this was quite simple: according to the Cubists, the realism of Courbet and the Impressionists was based on a total reliance on the senses, while Cézanne's realism, so they felt, combined the empiricism of the senses with the conceptualizations of the mind—that is, Cézanne was a profound, a thinking man's realist. Fernand Léger made the same point in an article of 1913. Speaking of the art of the late nineteenth century, he wrote:

> I shall insist particularly on that period of French painting, for I think it is at that moment that the two great concepts of painting—*visual realism* and *realism of conception*— meet, the first completing its curve, which includes all the old painting down to the Impressionists, and the second— realism of conception—beginning with them. Visual realism, as I have said, necessarily involves an object, a subject, and perspective devices that are now considered negative and anti-realist. Realism of conception, neglecting all this cumbersome baggage, has been achieved in many contemporary paintings. Among the Impressionists, one painter, Cézanne, fully understood what was incomplete about Impressionism. He felt the necessity of renewing *form* and *design* to match the new *color* of the Impressionists. His life and his work were devoted to the quest for this new synthesis . . .[44]

When during the war, in 1916, Daniel-Henry Kahnweiler wrote *Der Weg zum Kubismus* (The Road to Cubism) from his Swiss exile, it still seemed reasonable to proclaim that Cézanne's art was "the point of departure for all contemporary painting."[45] By 1920, however, Cézanne's reputation was under attack from certain quarters, and what specifically was being challenged was this pre-war idea of the master as a classicist and as a conceptual, "constructive" painter. Moreover, the attack on Cézanne was being launched not by an obscure critic or a disinterested party but by Cézanne's leading advocate and protégé, Emile Bernard, who, with his misquotations and distortions of the master's views, had been most responsible for

Cézanne's pre-war reputation as a classicist. Bernard, at the beginning of his article "La Méthode de Paul Cézanne" (which appeared in the *Mercure de France* on 1 March 1920), was quick to point out that he had been one of Cézanne's earliest champions: "I can say without deceiving myself that I was one of those, and surely among the first, who loved, knew, explained, and appreciated Cézanne. My loyalty to him is above suspicion."[46] It apparently had not occurred to Bernard that the kind of mischief in which he was about to engage had a quite specific name—betrayal—or that the killing-off of a father-figure is a fairly banal procedure, especially common when the father-surrogate is indisputably more powerful than the son.

Bernard's rhetorical stance toward Cézanne was much like one that Apollinaire had assumed in an article entitled "Baudelaire dans la domaine publique," which he published in *Nord-Sud* in May 1917. There the poet made a careful distinction between Baudelaire unto himself, as it were—the Romantic, Symbolist Baudelaire—and the public artist, who could serve as an example and an inspiration for his literary descendants (concluding, in fact, that Baudelaire was not appropriate for this second role). Thus Bernard says of Cézanne, whose art he had championed at the beginning of the century:

> The point of view changes; now it is necessary to examine what his system was, if it was true or false, if he followed the essential path or abandoned it, if his influence is good or bad—in a word, if he should be a guide (since he has been chosen as one), and a guide who will lead us back in the direction of the great works that are the glory of a nation and of a race.[47]

In other words, asks Bernard, no matter what conclusions we had drawn before the war, can we still say that Cézanne was a classicist, and that he can teach the post-war Frenchman to make truly French paintings? The answer, of course, is no, and the reason he offers, reversing his earlier opinions, is that Cézanne really was a Naturalist after all! "Cézanne's method has its origin in Naturalism. Before becoming what he was, Cézanne studied Courbet and Manet," he writes, in defiance of his own opinions at the turn of the century, when he had emphasized Cézanne's relationship to Poussin. Instead of pulling Cézanne out of the Impressionist circle, Bernard places him right back in the midst of a movement which was at the low point of its critical reception:

> One can recognize no difference between the aesthetic of
> the Impressionists and that of Cézanne: both tend toward
> the expression of things that we see, despising invention,
> by a style subordinate to nature. It's Naturalism.[48]

This was as severe a criticism of Cézanne as was possible in the
1920s without actually damning him outright.

But Bernard's most stinging criticism, for which the accusation of being a Naturalist was only a part and a prelude, was
really psychological. He repeatedly uses words like "impo-
tence" and "imperfection" to describe Cézanne, and even goes
as far as to say that in the master's devotion to observing nature
"There is a servility that touches on moral decline in this will
to restrict oneself to the thing seen, that is to say, in the con-
formity of the copy."[49] Cézanne as a mere copier? No matter;
Bernard was out to get Cézanne and nothing was too distorted
to include in his diatribe. "There was in his system a cause for
suicide,"[50] the critic writes, despite the fact that the master died
an old man and of natural causes. However, Bernard did indeed
mean something quite specific when he referred to the unhealthy nature of Cézanne's system; for where Cézanne's effort
to wrest a permanent art from the Impressionist aesthetic had
been the very substance of his glory before the war, Bernard
now, in 1920, saw Cézanne's "method" as a sign of his neurotic
ambivalence:

> Therefore, it was at once an attempt at objective truth and
> at mental logic . . . the dualism that he had created from
> the beginning between his exterior vision and the fulfill-
> ment of his system plunged him into error and kept him
> from going beyond sketches. It is in that that the Cézan-
> nean drama resides, and that the weak point of his poten-
> tial is proven. How to accommodate the optical—which is
> relative—with theory—which is absolute? How to resolve
> the contradiction of sensation, often mistaken, always var-
> iable, with the rigorous application of accepted principle?
> Finally, how can this lead to an accord between the senses
> and reason? It seems insoluble. . . . It is this difficulty,
> met at every brushstroke, that killed Cézanne.[51]

This critique is familiar by now: the denigration of sensations
and feelings, which are variable and unreliable, in favor of theory, which is "absolute"; the invocation of "drama," with its
implication of conflict, and its association with a tortured, anarchic Romanticism. Moreover, Bernard was not content just to

rewrite his own former opinions of Cézanne; he also now offered
another nineteenth-century master as an appropriate model for
contemporary art, and as an antidote to Cézanne's aesthetic:

> Puvis de Chavannes, who derives from the spirit, had been
> an affirmer, in the nineteenth century, of the synthesis of
> the essential laws of art. By the retinal sensualism that
> directs him, Cézanne shows us the contrary. While one
> simplifies, the other complicates. While one does not have
> enough wall space to display his vast compositions, the
> other reduces his format, renounces all conception, con-
> fines himself to the representation of the most vulgar ob-
> jects. For one, everything is grand; for the other, every-
> thing is complex, small, difficult.[52]

It was hardly by accident that this was the same antidote that
André Michel had offered in his prescription for post-war
French art. Deriding "landscape, plein-airism, Impressionism,
division[ism], optical mixing," which he considered "in defen-
sible eccentricities and even aberrations," Michel asked rhetor-
ically: "At the moment when, on so many fronts, mediocrity
seemed about to triumph, didn't a Puvis de Chavannes appear,
in the nick of time, to restore all her dignity to French art?"[53]
Puvis, the sanctioned master who gave the French capital the
story of her patron saint, Geneviève, on the walls of the Pan-
théon, exemplified the grand and enduring myth of France,
whereas Cézanne looked neurotic and idiosyncratic.

As far as the Parisian avant-garde was concerned, Bernard's
attack on Cézanne was probably less important than the contemporaneous attack on Cézanne by Gino Severini. In *Du Cubisme au Classicisme*, the 1921 textbook of avant-garde reaction, Severini said precisely the same things about Cézanne that
Bernard had, except in language that was more direct and up-
to-date:

> I believed, like everyone else, in the "classical tendency"
> of Cézanne; but now that I see clearly the sensory origin of
> his "intentions," I can no longer believe in a man who
> wants to "redo Poussin according to nature," who wants "to
> become classical again by nature, that is to say, by sen-
> sation."[54]

And he goes on:

> In recent years we believed that, finally, we had found a
> point of departure in the work of Cézanne. Many paint-

ers—one can almost say all of them—still have this conviction; for my part, while putting Cézanne's talent aside
for the moment, I believe that this point of departure is
false and that anything that one would want to build on
him will crumble, having as a basis all that is most ephemeral, most unstable, most variable on earth: our own sensations. . . . I think that I can affirm today that the path
to follow is precisely the opposite of that followed by Cézanne. One does not become classical by sensation, but by
the mind; the work of art must not commence by an analysis of *effect* but by an analysis of *cause*; and one does not
construct without method, by basing oneself uniquely on
the eyes and good taste, or on vague general notions.[55]

According to Severini, then, Cézanne was neither of the things
that a post-war French painter had to be, a classicist or a constructor, and his brushstroke as well as his unfinished canvases
proved this:

. . . Cézanne was too much a painter of "temperament" to
make use of the compass and of number; he based his
work only on his eyes—more intelligently than Claude Monet, with his vision governed by a strong enough will—but
his point of departure remained visual and sensual. That
is why he was never satisfied, why he ceaselessly started
the same painting over again and made the brushstroke
larger and more modulated, but this stroke, becoming a
surface, could never be constructive.[56]

On these criteria Severini concludes that, "while having a gift
of the first order, he is not a master."[57]

It must be understood that this critical condemnation of Cézanne—of his art, working methods, and life—coming as it did
from Bernard and Severini, was an important issue for the Parisian avant-garde. If Cézanne was neither a classicist nor a
constructor, and therefore was no longer an appropriate "point
of departure" for new painting, then Cubist pictures would inevitably have to look very different than they had before the
war. If the individual, subtly nuanced brushstroke could never
be "constructive"; if Cézanne's refined palette represented
moral decline rather than careful observation; if the attempt to
reconcile what the eye sees with what the mind knows was regarded as a preliminary to suicide; and if "temperament," visual dynamism, ambiguity, lack of finish, the depiction of the
"vulgar objects" of daily life were all signs of weakness and

failure, then there was not a great deal left of Cubism that could
be rescued from the pre-war years.

Robert Delaunay, like almost every other Cubist in pre-war
Paris, had seen Cézanne as the origin of the modern movement.
We have only to look at one of his Eiffel Towers, as for instance
a version done in 1911 (fig. 217), to see what a devoted, though
innovative, follower of Cézanne he had been. The broken
planes, the modulated brushstrokes, and the attempt to resolve
surface and depth in a single visual "skin"—here represented
by the effort to align the tower with the apartment buildings and

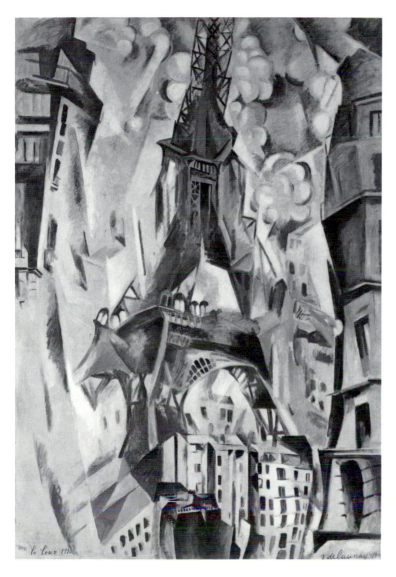

217. R. Delaunay, *Eiffel Tower*,
1911.

the ambient space—are all derived from ideas in Cézanne. The theme, too, is related to Cézanne: as Mont Sainte-Victoire had been a looming, beckoning presence for Cézanne in Aix, so the Eiffel Tower rises above the buildings, commanding the skyline in Delaunay's Paris of 1911. Moreover, the two monuments occupy similar places in each artist's consciousness—as a fixed point of reference and as an embodiment of aspiration. With the obsessiveness of Cézanne, Delaunay kept returning to the tower, depicting it in painting after painting and drawing after drawing. Can it be doubted that Cézanne's tenacity was as crucial to the Cubist enterprise as his imagery and picture structure?

We have already seen tendencies of two basic kinds in Delaunay's art after 1914: on the one hand, in marginally Cubist works like *Le Gitan* (fig. 109), the use of new, rather traditional notions of figure, ground, and volume; and on the other hand, in his "Ingres-style" portraits, a shift toward illusionism. It is clear that by 1915 his art had already begun to lose the direction and single-mindedness of his pre-war work. After six years of exile, Robert Delaunay was extremely disoriented upon his return to Paris in 1920. As we know, his military status during the war had come under attack; apparently, there were difficulties over Sonia's associations with the Maison Martine and Paul Poiret; the word "calumny" appears repeatedly in his correspondence.[58] He saw little of the pre-war Cubists (aside from Gleizes, who continued as a friend). He was close to a number of the Dada poets, but at the same time he wrote of "pure painting" and of a desire to move toward construction; he declared that "rule and order are the basis of audacity";[59] and he also made fun of Germans: ". . . the *pedantry and false science* from Germany. Herr critic who sees nothing through his binoculars—puritan, academic purism (False interpretation of genius)."[60] His post-war writings are so confused that they do no more than demonstrate his bewilderment, but it is clear that Delaunay, although he had been producing scores of academic drawings, was furious over the new classicism: "Who cares about the word *classical* with all the Cubist labels, neo-Greek and neo-Platonist. . . . Unable to bring about a new construction, the opportunists, in a rush to produce, ask Antiquity to give them a backbone; but even the marbles are broken!!!"[61] Consistent with this opinion, Delaunay made no neo-classical pictures or paintings with Antique references in the 1920s.

But he did not paint Cubist pictures either, and the pictures he did paint lacked the energy of his pre-war years. A series of

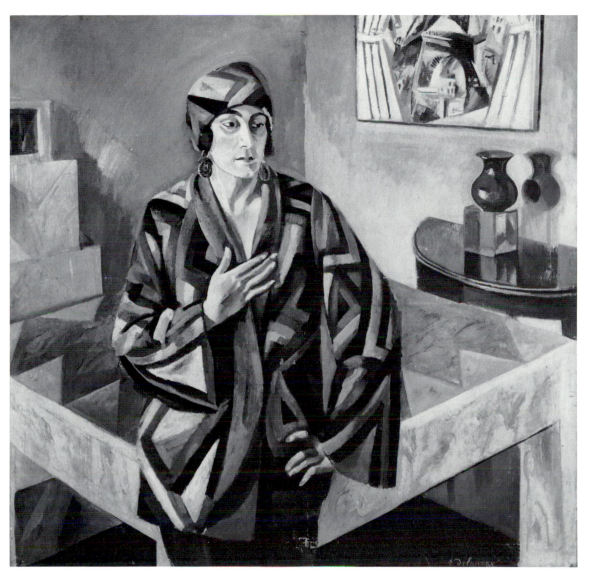

218. R. Delaunay, *Portrait of Mme. Mandel*, 1923.

portraits, including one of Mme. Mandel (fig. 218) done in 1923, demonstrates Delaunay's aesthetic disillusionment. The engagement with the art of Cézanne and even with his own pre-war art is now tangential at best: the fragmented vision of the Eiffel Tower is now pushed to the rear. Otherwise, the only visible remnants of modernism are the abstract geometry of the Sonia Delaunay hat and jacket that the sitter wears and a somewhat abstract decoration on the tabletop. The pictorial space is now completely conventional, and the creation of volume has nothing Cubist whatever to it. Cubism has literally become embellishment.

Perhaps the best way of comparing Robert Delaunay's pre-war and post-war Cubism is to look at one of his Eiffel Tower paintings from the later period, an example from 1926 (fig. 219). Here we see what Cubism became without "Cézannisme" or Bergsonian dynamics—without amibguity, movement, or change. Despite Delaunay's protest against the "neo-Platonists," he has nonetheless himself now produced a Cubism, or an Orphism—if those terms still apply—of stasis; or perhaps we should just say that we have a modernist version of the old notion of impressive monumentality. Now the tower is viewed from the ground, so that it rises to the top of the image without interruption, and its identity as a monumental construction is kept intact and even reinforced. Where the *Tower* of 1911 was an exercise in fragmentation and a symbol of urban dynamism, now we have, at best, a rather colorful tourist's-eye-view. To be sure, there is a degree of abstraction here in the artist's use of color, but it is really no more than an intense-hued infilling of the spaces in the iron fretwork.

When Delaunay did try to create a more dynamic image, as in a decorative panel titled *The City of Paris: The Woman and the Tower* (fig. 220) that he created for the *Ambassade Française* pavilion at the 1925 Exposition Internationale des Arts Décoratifs et Industriels Modernes,[62] the structure of the tower itself remained intact. The tower's image is complexly interwoven with Cubistic treatments of a nude at the lower left (presumably "la ville" herself), the Palais Bourbon at the lower right (just behind the obelisk from Luxor and the Pont de la Concorde), an abstracted version of the Arc de Triomphe and the Etoile above, as well as a view of the Seine at the upper left with various bridges crossing it, topped off by several "disks" of color and a small bi-plane. Nonetheless the central image is a perfectly conventional one, surrounded by freely disposed vignettes.

Even when Delaunay had been at his most traditionally allegorical before the war, as in the 1912 *City of Paris* (fig. 110), he was still deeply concerned with weaving all his elements into a consistent pictorial fabric, with finding a pictorial equivalent (by using *passage* and the adjustment of planes) for a space of the mind. By 1925, that psychic/physical ambiguity and concomitant attempt at resolution are of no concern, because pre-war ideas of truth to the surface of the painting (which had been bequeathed by Cézanne) have fallen out of favor. Now, as in the Renaissance formulation, the picture plane is transparent and

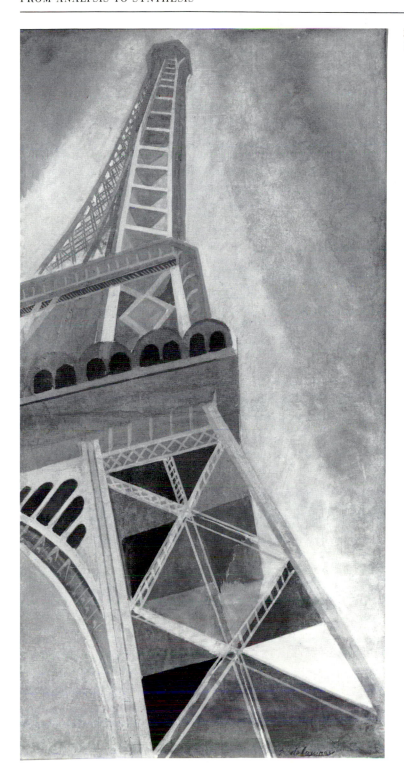

219. R. Delaunay, *Eiffel Tower*, 1926.

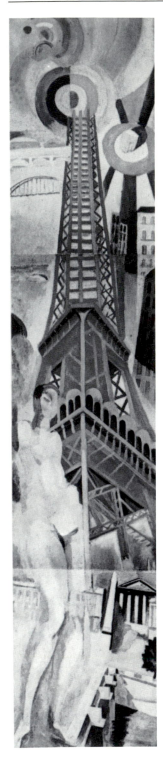

220. R. Delaunay, *The City of Paris: The Woman and the Tower*, 1925.

the world of the painting is entirely a fiction (even when it parades as an imitation of the world). To investigate the mechanics of illusion, as the pre-war Cubists had done, has become a heresy, just as any serious attempt to analyze the ideology of French culture became after August 1914 a sign of the most blatant treason. Fictions and myths, whether social or pictorial, were not to be scrutinized, because the value of mythic structures was a given. Cubism and its visual complexities—inspired by Cézanne's "torment," indecision, and irreconcilable dualisms—were now considered to be part of a pre-war mentality that the French wanted to forget. Too intense a self-scrutiny and too intense a pictorial examination were considered unhealthy, destructive, and dangerous.

Yet a new interpretation of history requires not only that former gods and mentors be revealed as less formidable than previously thought, but that new "old masters," new sources, be found to replace the former influences. If, as we have seen, Cézanne's reputation was at a discount after the war, so in turn the reputation of Georges Seurat achieved new esteem. In fact, there is a kind of see-saw phenomenon in the shifting reputations of Cézanne and Seurat in the 1920s: the degree to which Cézanne was devalued was the degree to which Seurat gained new prestige; the qualities that were now thought lacking in Cézanne were the same qualities that Seurat now seemed to possess in abundance. According to André Salmon in 1920, Seurat, in contrast to Cézanne, had been a *constructeur*:

> Seurat was the first to construct and compose. . . . In truth, Cézanne would not have sufficed to preside at the great task which engages the strongest and most spontaneous energies of today. There is a certain sylvan vulgarity in the candor of Cézanne. From Seurat comes the aristocratic feeling and the austerity without sterility of modern creations.[63]

Where Cézanne was "vulgar," Seurat was dignified; where Cézanne was vulnerable (i.e. candid), Seurat was strong and constructive. Moreover, Seurat's pictures were stable and finished, while the work of the Impressionists was too vague: "Georges Seurat was the first of the great reconstructors," Salmon wrote, "while the Impressionists . . . never finished their work of enslaving art to the armorphous." Besides, Seurat loved tradition: "He opened the way to the true tradition and prepared the work of the constructors. If he was truly classical in his habit of premeditation, it was because he had control of his natural riches."[64]

To a certain extent, this post-war view of Seurat was not in-correct, for he had seen himself as a classicist and a respectful reconstructor of Impressionist aesthetics. In 1921 Lucie Cou-sturier found the classical spirit to be so deep in him that "Seu-rat does not need to introduce figures and Greek temples into his landscapes to give them gravity and style. It is his entire oeuvre that suggests a temple with thousands of pillars or col-umns, with repeated verticals on clear horizontals."[65] Amédée Ozenfant took a more humorous approach when he said, "don't reproach Seurat for being on the Athens line rather than that from Flanders; the train from Greece is a good train, are you going to reproach it for not taking you to Amsterdam?" and, with complete seriousness, "We love in Seurat the dryness of the great French tradition of all times. . . ."[66] Moreover, André Lhote's point that "Seurat's theories, in fact, are a large part of his oeuvre"[67] was further proof, if any were needed, that Seurat was the antithesis of an empirical artist.

In many ways, Seurat seemed the perfect French artist for deification in the 1920s, and his popularity could be measured in facts and figures: although in the preceding decade not a single exhibition was devoted exclusively to his work, no mon-ograph on the artist appeared, and only four articles appeared in print which were specifically concerned with his oeuvre, dur-ing the 1920s Seurat's work was exposed, propounded upon, and explained in no fewer than five one-man shows (three in Paris, one each in London and Berlin), eight monographs, and thirty-four articles.

Seurat's art seemed in the 1920s to be at once ideal and prac-tical, classical and efficacious. Gustave Coquiot, in his mono-graph on Seurat, described one of Seurat's landscapes this way:

> Seurat gives us a solemn image of a naked landscape, which has come into the world with no gnashing of teeth, with no devastation, with no barrel-organ obbligato. Every-thing there is well established for living: very straight white walls, a very rigid chimney; and, above all, the wasteland only waits—"indifferent"—for an industralist to build a vast shed for work and production. . . . This, then, is a graphic definition of style![68]

It was no coincidence that Coquiot was writing in this way about Seurat in the midst of France's post-war reconstruction. Seurat's pictures offered the French an image of the world that they found reassuringly ordered, geometric, and much like the world that they themselves hoped to reconstruct on their own devas-tated territories. The critic's definition of "style" and the industrialist's choice of an ideal building site are, extraordinarily, one and the same. Not surprisingly, when in the autumn of 1920 Ozenfant and Jeanneret launched their new post-war, post-Cubist magazine of art, architecture, design and culture in general, *L'Esprit Nouveau* (which we shall discuss in detail shortly), their first issue was devoted to the art of Seurat, and only in the second issue did they pay tribute to Cézanne: the magazine's first page featured a full-color reproduction of Seurat's *La Poudreuse*, and facing the page of the artist's transfixed, powder-puffing mistress Madeleine Knoblock were the words "*L'esprit nouveau*. There is a new spirit. It is a spirit of construction and of synthesis guided by a clear conception."[69] While this particular iconographic puzzle may forever remain shrouded in mystery, there was nothing secret about the editors' taste: the same issue contained, as well, an article on Seurat by Bissière, accompanied by eight other reproductions of the artist's work.

Indeed, all the new attention being paid to Seurat was a source of amusement to Coquiot, especially the great frequency with which the term "constructor" was linked with the artist's name. He chided his colleagues,

> . . . it would perhaps be appropriate here—without waiting any longer—to use the word *constructor*. . . . Constructor of what, in what way? It doesn't matter! This word means everything. . . . Therefore, if you like, Seurat is a constructor. . . . But alas . . . he painted obstinately, simply, without knowing that he was Seurat-the-Constructor! Oh, if only he had known it! Seurat-Constructor! Construc-tor! Cons-truc-tor! Oh, how this word pleases me![70]

Of course, Coquiot knew that the constant use of this word in connection with Seurat by the post-war artists and critics was a measure of the high esteem in which they held him; but he was more than a little cynical about the new interest in "construction," despite the fact that he himself was contributing to the new "constructive" spirit. He concluded his book by saying:

> At this moment, it is above all "the constructors" who ally themselves to Seurat. Now, what are the names of these constructors? I don't know; there are too many of them! The young painter-constructors today are swarming. They all want to be constructors! That means, I think, that they paint *solidly*, these chaps. Oh! but! . . . the old days, Impressionists, Symbolists, Naturalists! . . . Now, you have to be serious, to trace verticals, horizontals, diago-

nals, angles, triangles, polyhedrons, dodecahedrons, who knows what? You have to *construct*, since we're constructors! . . . Oh! it was well worth it, O Seurat, to have sought "cleanliness" [only] to engender such nincompoops who ally themselves with you, O Prince of light and style![71]

Coquiot's irony does not alter the reality of Seurat's influence on French art of the 1920s. One of the most telling examples is that of Léger: although Cézanne would remain for him the indisputable generating force for the entire modern movement, there was nonetheless a subtle shift in his tastes. Before the war he had said that "Seurat was one of the great victims of this [i.e. neo-Impressionist] mediocre formula . . . he wasted a great deal of time and talent . . . ," but that "Cézanne, I repeat, was the only one of the impressionists to lay his finger on the deeper meaning of plastic life";[72] but by 1922 he was sounding quite a different note on the two artists: "My artistic sources: color, Impressionist; influence — Renoir, Seurat; form—Ingres, David," and in the same piece, "Ingres, the brothers Lenain, and Cézanne invented sometimes, Poussin often, Clouet and Fouquet almost always . . . ."[73] Even more strikingly, in Léger's art a subtle but definite shift is apparent from Cézanne to Seurat (with the myriad pictorial and cultural ideas that this shift represented), as a comparison between *La Ville* (fig. 221) of 1919, and *Le Grand Dejéuner* (fig. 222) will demonstrate.

As Christopher Green has said, "the impetus behind Léger's *La Ville*—its subject—was above all his simultaneist experience of the most dissonant and most modern part of Paris,"[74] and in this commitment to a modern, dissonant theme Léger has remained true to his pre-war interests. To be sure, the picture painted the year after the Armistice is markedly different from his earlier paintings: now there is almost none of the Impressionist-derived atmosphere, the clouds, smoke, etc., that could be found in his art before the war; the paint handling is smooth and the colors are more varied; the planes are now flatter and more expansive. In more general terms, though, in theme and style, *La Ville* is a continuation of the artist's pre-war artistic efforts. Modern urban life is rendered in a fragmented, multifaceted way; figures and ground are in an irrational relationship; the collapsed and ambiguous space is a space of the mind, in which all attempts to measure depth would be confounded, and in which abstract bits of lettering testify both to the conceptual nature of the image and to the modern commercial environment. This is a moving, pulsating, dynamic vision of the city, a pic-

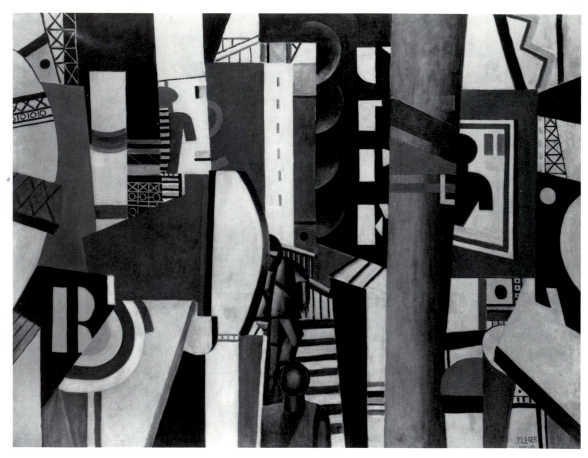

221. F. Léger, *La Ville (The City)*,
1919.

ture that is optimistic about the malaise we call anomie, cheerful in the face of the visual and aural cacophony that constitutes the urban experience.

Le Grand Déjeuner, although closely related to *La Ville*, nevertheless represents a drastic change in Léger's notion of modernity. The subject has now shifted from the cityscape, with heroic men who venture forth into the urban machine, to a domestic interior, where three large, classically cool women lounge on a day-bed, eating their breakfast. The scale of the figures has obviously changed: these women are monumental and dominate their setting, whereas the human presence is almost insignificantly small in the earlier painting. The relationship of *Le Grand Déjeuner* to *Three Women at the Spring* and *Three Musicians*, Picasso's two large paintings of 1921, is striking: all three show a triad of monumental figures depicted in a new, rationally constructed space. *Le Grand Déjeuner* occupies a middle position between Picasso's two paintings: the figures

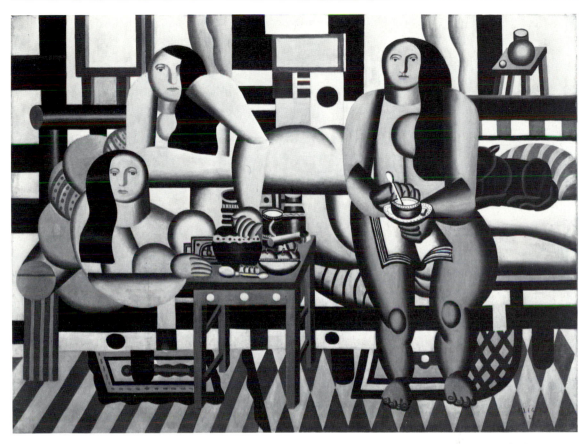

222. F. Léger, *Le Grand Déjeuner*,
1921.

are classically modeled as in *Three Women at the Spring*, and
the setting is articulated in the late-Cubist style of *Three Musicians*. Although the picture is activated by multiple patterns,
shapes, colors, and motifs, the composition is now calmer, more
static, and more classical than *La Ville*. One of the major reasons for the new pictorial stability in *Le Grand Déjeuner* is
Léger's use of the horizontal. In the painting of 1919 we notice
that there is no continuous horizontal in the entire picture and
even few horizontal lines at all. Indeed, the use of the repeated
vertical elements causes the image to "jump." In the painting
of 1921, though, the horizontal formed by the couch and the
two odalisques imparts a sense of calm and monumentality.

Obviously, Léger has looked to the art of Seurat for his new
sense of architectonic classicism—to paintings like *La Grande
Jatte* with its monumental catalogue of modern types (perhaps
Léger's title is meant as a humorous allusion to Seurat's) and to
La Parade, with its strict yet subtle grid, its juxtaposition of the

organic human form and the perfect geometry of its setting (in fact, both of these Seurat paintings were reproduced in that first issue of *L'Esprit Nouveau* in October 1920). Léger was too good an artist, and too deeply committed to the visual power of contrasts, to make a picture that was merely calm and horizontal—he adds the strong vertical element created by the upright nude (painted a darker color), who is in much the same position and serves the same activating function as the large red pillar to the right in *La Ville*. This big picture (it measures six by eight feet) of modern domestic well-being also aspires, much as Seurat's does, to be both thoroughly up-to-date and timeless.

Indeed, *Le Grand Déjeuner* is a very self-consciously "artistic" picture—from the Venus-Odalisque-harem iconography to the posed attitudes and prettily decorated surfaces. Robert Herbert argues convincingly that these three women are not, in fact, "real women, in the fiction of the picture, but *works of art*. Léger's evocation of past art constitutes a kind of visual quotation. His three nudes are art works within a work of art. Two of them are colored like marble statues and the third a terra-cotta sculpture"[75]—this last aspect perhaps an adaptation of the male/female color distinctions in ancient art. One wonders whether Léger's picture is not partly dependent on a well-known Greek vase painting of a feast of the gods (fig. 223). Although we can only speculate here that the loungers may be artistic ideas rather than real people, in a variation on the picture of the same year, *Women in an Interior* (fig. 224), Léger makes the distinction between real and ideal manifest—he juxtaposes a "real" post-war mother-and-child (1921 was the year of the Mother-and-Childhood exhibition in Paris) with the artistic idea

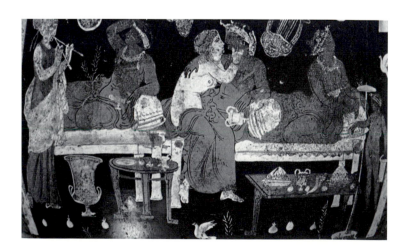

223. Greek vase (South Italian), fourth century B.C.

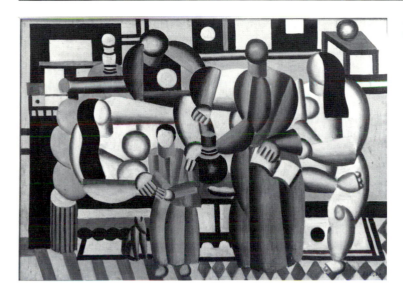

224. F. Léger, *Women in an Interior*, 1921.

of woman, his three modern Graces. In an article of 1924, Léger wrote that "we are coming close to tomorrow's realities," which he saw as a kind of Golden Age and which, like his painting, would be "society without frenzy, knowing how to live naturally within the Beautiful without exclamation or romanticism."[76]

Even if, with its bright colors and lively profusion of pattern, *Le Grand Déjeuner* looks "Romantic" in comparison to a picture like Picasso's *Three Women at the Spring*, the artist was nevertheless attempting to make a classical picture. Many years later, Léger explained to Alfred H. Barr, Jr. (writing in the artist's own idiosyncratic English):

"It is a painting more classical, I think, than *La Ville*, a little romantic by the sentiment of evocation of a modern city. *Les 3 femmes* [i.e. *Le Grand Déjeuner*] evokes nothing it is that: classicism," and then went on to explain:

All my life, I have been in conflict between the mural idea and the easel painting idea. When I realized La Ville (mural) I felt the imperious need for an easel painting: "Le grand déjeuner," like a contrary strength. So more or less consciously, after one realization of some elements taken out of modern life, to try on subjects or objects which have been treated during all the times by painters of other times. One background of classicism dominate in myself, I believe, some romantic pranks as: La Ville 1919 . . . but some women's bodies, one table, a dog, every time's sub-

ject without any expression of evocation. It is the classical
line, at my opinion . . . Le grand déjeuner is one [where]
my classical fighting won.[77]

Still, it should be said that Léger did not embrace the new classicism as unreservedly as many other members of the Parisian
avant-garde: he never made "Ingres-style" portraits; he always
avoided, as he said, "any expression of evocation" (that is,
there is no direct classical allusion in his classicized Cubism
and no allusion to the *commedia dell'arte*); and at another point
he even referred to *Le Grand Déjeuner* as "connected to the Romance period,"[78] for he recognized that his modern odalisques
were the cousins of Delacroix's exotic figures.

Of all the artists of the pre-war Parisian avant-garde, Léger
must have been aware that to give oneself up wholly to the post-
war traditionalism was tantamount to declaring Right-wing political allegiance, which, with his own Left sympathies, was out
of the question. However, he had come (as we know) to see his
own pre-war affiliations with the avant-garde as too narrow and
elitist: "I left Paris completely immersed in an abstract method
. . . Without any transition I found myself on a level with the
whole of the French people . . . I discovered the French nation." Léger had lost neither his idealism nor his desire for social change, but he had, by the post-war period, come to see
the possibilities and even the desirability of compromise and
moderation. Although he was ostensibly discussing his art he
was obviously also enunciating his politics when he wrote in
1923:

> To arrive at a fixed state, an enduring state that is not too
> far to the right, not too far to the left, but in the middle, is
> extremely difficult. There must be perfect balance between
> the artist's instinct and his control. The romantic pushes
> toward the left—an excess of subjectivity (a warm state).
> His opposite pushes toward the right—an excess of objec-
> tivity (a cold state).[79]

This might well be taken as a description of the visual program
of *Le Grand Déjeuner*: romanticism and classicism, subjective
and objective, warm and cool, vertical and horizontal joined in
a unified "society without frenzy."

By the time Léger painted *Le Grand Déjeuner*, a pair of terms
seemingly more neutral than "romantic" and "classical" had
come to prevail within the artistic discussions of the Parisian
avant-garde: "analytic" and "synthetic." Cousturier, for in-

stance, in her discussion of Seurat in 1921, felt the need to distinguish carefully between the two ideas. "Seurat was misunderstood," she wrote,

> insofar as he was thought to have stopped at analysis, at the representation of the immediate, the fortuitous play of light, he, the synthesizer—better, the implacable logician—who made use of this light only to preserve for objects the appearance that characterizes them once and for all time.[80]

As a result of the re-evaluations of both Cézanne and Seurat, we understand what all of this means: contrary to general opinion, Seurat is a deeply classical, traditional artist who paints "for all time," not, as his pointillist technique might lead one to suppose, an empiricist who had no sense of enduring values (as Léger would have put it at this moment, he was a classic not a romantic). This is expressed, in supposedly formal terms, by Cousturier's words "analysis" and "synthesizer": i.e., Seurat used analysis as only the first step in a process, as a means to an end, of which synthesis was the destination. In part because these words seemed culturally neutral and historically non-partisan (again, in comparison to words like "classical" and "romantic," or "destructive" and "constructive") and because they also had the ring of science, philosophy, and rhetoric, the terms "analytic" and "synthetic" became, in time, the most popular descriptions of Cubism's history. Nowadays it is common to invoke the terms "Analytic" and "Synthetic" whenever Cubism is discussed; the distinction between the supposed two phases—analytic and synthetic—is considered basic to any understanding of Cubism, and this is because the terms are considered to be merely descriptive. As originally used, though, to describe Cubism's history, they were qualitative terms, culturally freighted with specific social meanings.

We find, for instance, the analytic/synthetic dichotomy being used in reference to Cubism in the midst of war by one of the movement's detractors, the redoubtable Mme. Aurel. "Suddenly and without transition," she wrote in about 1915,

> . . . Cubism, Derain, Picasso, and Braque consummated the divorce between themselves and the wider public, arriving at a divisionism of form, turning us back to fragmented analysis, when art has always worked so hard to raise itself to synthesis. At that point, happily, no one could any longer follow them. French good sense does not

go backward. . . . The Cubists and Futurists announce
that they put their subject within the universal movement
but their confusion impedes all movement. They say that
they are analysts and synthesizers. But one cannot be
both. And synthesis cannot be expected of beginners. It is
the laurel wreath won by those who finish. It is the recompense of masters.[81]

Aurel here uses "analysis" to characterize the social and pictorial fragmentation of the pre-war period: "Cubis[ts], Derain
[sic], Picasso, and Braque" are guilty both of making fragmented, divisionist paintings and of fragmenting society, of di-
vorcing themselves from the public. In other words, their elitism is an aspect of their analytic stance. Moreover, according
to her, analysis is contrary to the eternal goal of art, which is to
arrive at its opposite, at synthesis. The critic is well aware, as
she herself says, that the terminology is not of her invention,
that the Cubists and Futurists had, if arbitrarily, used the terms
"analysis" and "synthesis" before the war. Severini, for example, wrote in 1913, "Synthesis will never be reached by the
path of analysis. While the cinematograph is an analysis of
movement, our art is, on the other hand, a synthesis";[82] Léger,
we may remember, referred to Cézanne's art and life as a quest
for "a new synthesis" (in which form and color would be
united); and in an essay in 1912, Maurice Raynal said that the
Cubists "have called to their aid that law of synthesis which—
though they have been so much reproached on its account—
today governs all conscientious speculation," and in the same
piece wrote: "Before all else, they separate out—according to
their own analytical methods and the characteristics of the object—the principal elements of the bodies they propose to
translate."[83] Not surprisingly, Aurel can accept the Cubists and
Futurists referring to their art as "analytic," filled as the term
was with destructive associations, but "synthetic" is a term that
she wants reserved exclusively for art that meets with her approval. Synthesis, for the critic, is a kind of *revanche* of tradition over the avant-garde; it is "the laurel wreath won by those
who finish. . . . the recompense of masters."

As the war progressed, the distinction between analysis and
synthesis—between a breaking-down and a putting-together—
became more and more popular within the Parisian avant-
garde, no doubt encouraged by the topical invocations of construction and firm architecture. Albert-Birot, in a 1916 article
in *Sic*, said that the artist should move from "qualitative analy-

sis" toward "synthesis," that "with these known elements (selected by a process of analysis) the artist goes on to construct
his work as an architect builds a house out of stones, iron, and
wood beams."[84] We also now realize that when Braque observed
during the war that "the pre-classic style is a style of rupture;
the classic style is a style of development," he was formulating
an early version of this concept of Cubism's development from
analysis to synthesis.

By the post-war period, the analytic/synthetic formulation
was complete: "analytic" was used to describe pre-war painting
and "synthetic" was used for contemporary endeavors. Bissière
wrote that the artist now wanted "to replace analysis with synthesis and thereby return to tradition,"[85] signifying, as Aurel's
statement had, that synthesis was an attribute of a master; an
extension of this is his observation, in 1920, that Braque was
experiencing "an ever-increasing desire for synthesis."[86] In his
book *Picasso* (1922) Raynal, who before the war had freely applied both terms to Cubist painting, now made a definitive judgment on the "analytic" versus the "synthetic" processes. Referring to the pre-war period, he said:

> . . . the cold figure of induction was also evoked. Art crit-
> ics did not hesitate to claim that art went from the partic-
> ular to the general. What heresy! . . . Artistic induction
> signifies the complete negation of all aspiration on the part
> of the creative artist; it is no more than a method for vul-
> garization, for assembly-line work, and above all for the
> perfecting of artistic manufacture.[87]

Indeed, it was with these remarks in mind that Raynal's friend
Gris wrote:

> I work with the elements of the intellect, with the imagi-
> nation. I try to make concrete that which is abstract. I pro-
> ceed from the general to the particular, by which I mean
> that I start with an abstraction in order to arrive at a true
> fact. Mine is an art of synthesis, of deduction, as Raynal
> has said.

And he continued with a statement that became famous:

> Cézanne turns a bottle into a cylinder, but I begin with a
> cylinder and create an individual of a special type: I make
> a bottle—a particular bottle—out of a cylinder.[88]

Now we can understand the context in which Gris distinguishes
his own art from that of his father-figure, Cézanne: Gris's pref-

erence for deduction and synthesis—over the Impressionist's inductive and analytic method—means that he has moved from general laws of truth to the particulars of experience. Indeed, this had more or less become doctrine at the Galerie de l'Effort Moderne, where along with Léger, Metzinger, and Severini, Gris was exhibiting in 1921 when he wrote the foregoing passage. Léonce Rosenberg was apparently quite well aware that propounding this new "Synthetic" Cubism might make some of the practitioners of the old "Analytic" Cubism angry (which had already begun to happen, as we know, as early as 1916–17); thus he wrote, also in 1921: "Hardly has an epoch of synthesis succeeded an epoch of analysis than an irreconcilable discord arises between persons of different epochs." Analysis was old-fashioned; synthesis was modern.[89]

Even more precise in drawing the distinctions between earlier analytic artistic tendencies and current synthetic practices in the post-war years was the Italian Futurist F. T. Marinetti. As we are already aware, the Futurists had been found guilty during the war of the same aesthetic crimes as the Cubists— only even more so. But now, in 1921, in the introduction to a show of Futurist work in Paris, Marinetti wrote:

> We were led, naturally, by our experiments toward too trifling an analysis of forms, and to too fragmentary a decomposition of bodies, obsessed as we were with endowing them with all the formal developments. This long analysis, which permitted us to thoroughly understand forms in their pure plastic essences, is today completed. That is why we feel an imperative need to enter into a larger and more synthetic plastic vision. We are entering a period of firm and sure constructionism, because we want to make a synthesis out of analytic deformation, with the knowledge and the penetration that became second nature for us through all our analytic deformations. This is true for color as well as for form. We must systematically avoid the analysis that we imposed on ourselves for such a long time.[90]

For at least one critic, in 1925, Marinetti's period of synthesis was manifesting itself in all domains of life. In Rosenberg's *Bulletin de l'Effort Moderne*, Marcel Bauginet offered the following dicta:

> Above organized things, there are the laws of organization.
> Above the individual, there is the collectivity.
> Above analysis, there is synthesis.
> Above hate, there is love.

> Above the small love for self and friends, there is the great
> love for humanity.[91]

Obviously, the terms "analysis" and "synthesis" had become
thoroughly established in the rhetorical vocabulary of post-war
French culture to describe not just Cubism, but nearly all social
phenomena. In time, though, these terms were to lose their social coloration and become strictly formal terms, useful in the
characterization of Cubism's "progressive" evolution.

Although most Cubist artists and their supporters appear to
have been satisfied with the analytic/synthetic formulation, and
even to have endorsed and promulgated it within the avant-
garde—speaking of a progression from the analytic, fractured,
early style of their pre-war work to the synthetic, complete, mature style of their post-war art—Pablo Picasso objected strenuously to the application of this developmental model to his art.
Just as Gris's "deductive" description of his working method is
now better understood in the context of post-war aesthetic, so
Picasso's famous statement of 1923 should also be understood
as a quite specific reaction to this reading of Cubism's evolution
from analysis to synthesis:

> I also often hear the word evolution. Repeatedly I am
> asked to explain how my painting evolved. To me there is
> no past or future in art. If a work cannot live always in the
> present it must not be considered at all. The art of the
> Greeks, of the Egyptians, of the great painters who lived
> in other times, is not an art of the past; perhaps it is more
> alive today than it ever was. Art does not evolve by itself,
> the ideas of people change and with them their mode of
> expression. . . . Variation does not mean evolution. If an
> artist varies his mode of expression this only means that
> he has changed his manner of thinking, and in changing,
> it might be for the better or for the worse. The several man-
> ners I have used in my art must not be considered as an
> evolution, or as steps toward an unknown ideal of painting.
> All I have ever made was for the present. I have never
> taken into consideration the spirit of research. . . . Many
> think that Cubism is an art of transition, an experiment
> which is to bring ulterior results. Those who think that way
> have not understood it. Cubism is not either a seed or a
> fetus, but an art dealing primarily with forms, and when a
> form is realized it is there to live its own life. A mineral
> substance, having geometric formation, is not made so for
> transitory purposes; it is to remain what it is and will al-
> ways have its own form. But if we are to apply the law of

evolution and transformation to art, then we have to admit
that all art is transitory. On the contrary, art does not enter
into these philosophic absolutisms. If Cubism is an art of
transition I am sure that the only thing that will come out
of it is another form of Cubism.[92]

The issue here is not whether Picasso attempted to make a more
"synthetic" art after August 1914, or even earlier; he most certainly did, and in precisely the traditional, deductive, and architectonic terms that we have been elucidating. The question,
as Picasso correctly perceived, was whether Cubism had
evolved—as in the scientific (biological, geological) paradigm,
which is what the analytic/synthetic notion presumes. What Picasso makes perfectly clear is that there was no "evolution" in
his art because his art admits of no predetermined destination—maturity is a given at the outset, not a goal to be
achieved. Rather, like any artist, Picasso had changed his
mind, his ideas had changed, and hence so did his art. "Synthetic" Cubism, for Picasso as well as for the others, had been
a conscious choice of direction, not a developmental "stage." It
was a choice as firmly rooted in post-1914 French history as
Analytic Cubism had been of the pre-war period. Yes, Picasso
had changed his mind; but unlike so many other Parisian painters, he had no intention of denigrating his pre-war work (by
reducing it to a "seed" or a "fetus") for the sake of the post-war
rewriting of art history.

But it was the paintings that were, after all, the point of making a distinction between pre-war "analytic" and post-war "synthetic" Cubism. We have already remarked, in our discussions
of *Three Musicians* and *Le Grand Déjeuner*, as well as of many
other works after August 1914, on the formal qualities that
characterize the work: pictorial stability, hierarchical organization, smooth facture, an increased sense of illusionism (especially in the creation of pictorial space) juxtaposed with abstract
and unmodulated bright colors. We have noted, as well, distinctly Latinate themes (like the *commedia dell'arte*) and classical allusions—the traditional, mythic, and often fictional
quality of the subject matter of Cubist art after 1914, which is
in such sharp contrast to the predominantly "Realist" iconography of pre-war Cubism. Yet the power of the wartime and
post-war cultural consensus can be demonstrated not only in the
obviously traditional subjects that are so pervasive in Synthetic
Cubism, but also in more subtle iconographic inflections, as for
instance in still-life. A beautiful gouache by Picasso, the small
Still-Life in Front of a Window at St. Raphaël (fig. 225) painted

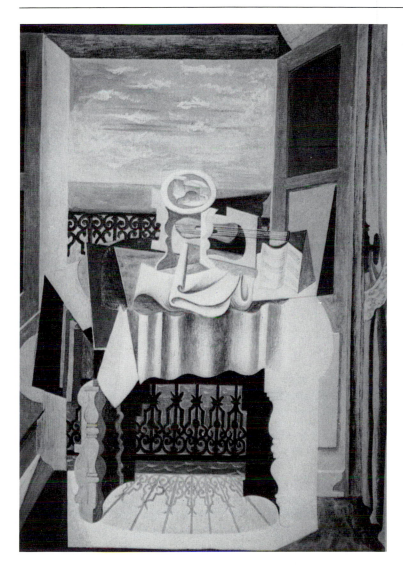

225. P. Picasso, *Still-Life in Front of a Window at St. Raphaël*, 1919.

in Paris in the fall of 1919, is a case in point. Apparently conceived as an autumnal recollection of the previous summer on the Riviera, the St. Raphaël still-life was inspired, at least in part, by the series of *guéridon* pictures that Braque showed at Rosenberg's L'Effort Moderne the previous March—for example, the so-called *Guitar and Compotier* (fig. 226). Picasso seems not only to have taken the image of the pedestal table from Braque (although such tables can be found earlier in the art of both men), but also to have elaborated on an equivocal passage in his friend's picture: above and behind the somber-colored and variously textured still-life, table, and woodwork,

226. G. Braque, *Guitar and Compotier*, 1919.

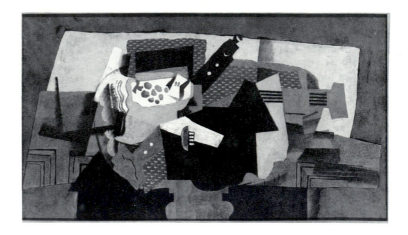

Braque has placed an ambiguous patch of blue that may or may not be intended as a blue sky seen through a window. In Picasso's picture, on the other hand, there is no ambiguity: as in *Three Musicians*, there is a clearly delineated spatial container, replete with walls and floor, and the open window reveals a panorama of sky and sea beyond. The only passages that can be called Cubist are the table and the still-life (we note a vase, a stringed instrument, and sheet music on a white drape); all the rest—windows, iron balustrade and shadow, and even the lace curtain pulled aside to the right—is naturalistically rendered. In other words, Cubism is presented here not as a world-view but as one mode of perception among other modes, not as an alternative vision intended to replace the rationalized pictorial space of Renaissance perspective but merely as a sub-category of illusionism. This "synthetic" image is all that the critics and artists have said it should be: idealized, generalized, firmly constructed, and attractive. The Cubist picture has been relieved of its pre-war hermeticism, when still-life was depicted (as it was almost always) in a neutral, unidentified place, or (when a location was indicated) in a place that was part of the tight-knit world of urban studio-café-street. Now a clear, bright, reassuring Mediterranean panorama provides the background for modernity. Surely there is a bit of irony here, in the amusing juxtaposition of modernist still-life with the super-realism of the setting, and also in the too-sweet pink, azure, and cream palette. But this only heightens the impression of Cubism's well-being: the shifting perspective and relativistic renderings of the still-life objects seem like so many ripples in the water beyond; Picasso's pictorial revolution of the pre-war years appears humbled by the immensity of sea and sky, made to appear insignif-

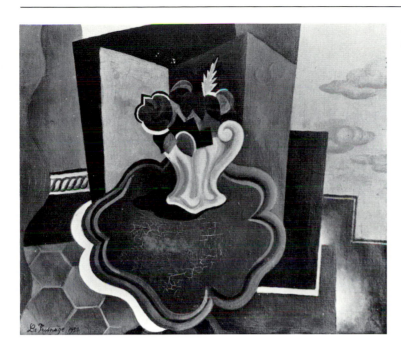

227. R. de la Fresnaye, *The Louis-Philippe Table*, 1922.

icant in the face of nature itself. Can we fail to sense the very traditional kind of elegance that, as we know, had become part of the artist's life? As Picasso was attempting to acclimate himself to the *grandes appartements* of the rue la Boétie and the lovely villas of the Emerald and Azure Coasts, so his Cubist forms were being domesticated as well.

In 1922 La Fresnaye, undoubtedly inspired by Picasso and Braque, painted a very similar image, *The Louis-Philippe Table* (fig. 227), which, perhaps not suprisingly, is also an amalgam of elements drawn from his life on the Riviera—in his case Grasse, where he rented the Villa Cresp (a house that had previously been occupied by Paul Poiret, who left it elegantly decorated with deep-rose-colored walls and white-lacquered Louis XV furniture upholstered in violet). In a rather ungainly fashion, La Fresnaye depicts an impossibly tilted tabletop on which a floral arrangement is placed, set in front of a purple *paravant*; the sinuous line of a red curtain can be glimpsed at the left, beside a bit of chair-rail; and at the lower left we see a section of hexagonal *provençale* terra-cotta flooring. The artist literally "cubifies" a part of the bouquet that functions in much the same way as the Cubist still-life in Picasso's gouache, and he places several completely abstract planes to the right of the table; these "modernist" elements are in turn juxtaposed, again, with "nature" in the form of a lurid sunset with floating clouds, glimpsed at the right. If rather more heavy-handedly, the message is nonetheless much the same as the *Still-Life in Front of a Window at St. Raphaël*: to wit, that Cubism had extricated itself from revolutionary entanglements in order to join the canon of sanctioned styles in a twilight of "modernism."

Gris, too, invoked this motif in no fewer than three remarkably similar pictures in 1921, *The Open Window* (pl. VII), *The View Across the Bay*, and *The Mountain "Le Canigou,"* all of which were painted on the Riviera, and all of which measure exactly 65 × 100 cm.[93] *The Open Window*, painted at Bandol, presents us with the theme at its most distilled: through the shutters of an open window in front of which are placed a guitar, glass, bottle, sheet music, and fruit-bowl with grapes, we observe an expanse of perfectly calm blue water, alongside a Vesuvius-like mountain (really a high hill) over which hang two clouds, one opaque (at left), the other translucent (at right). Of course, this theme was not new for Gris: he had, with enormous complexity, explored the subject of the open window in his great painting of 1915, *Still-Life Before an Open Window: Place Ravignan* (fig. 228). Yet how instructive is the comparison of the two pictures, a mere six years apart in time, and how different is the moral that the artist draws from his tale. In the earlier work, created during the first year of war, Gris had fashioned a scene at once cerebral and dramatic: the objects scattered on the table in the foreground, which include a newspaper (indicated by the words "Le Journal"), a bottle of Médoc, a compotier, a glass and carafe, and a book and/or package in the lower left, are intricately bound up with their immediate surroundings, including the wrought-iron balustrade and curtained window at left. Several passages are rendered as photographic negatives, and others are reduced to an eerie blue monochrome; black and blue predominate in this noctural scene, and it has been suggested, rightly I think, that this image makes reference to occult theories of the fourth dimension and to Roentgen's X-ray photography.[94]

Nothing could be further from this dark night of the Cubist soul than the *Open Window* of 1921. Now it is daytime, and we glimpse the Mediterranean vista from within the cool confines of a shuttered room; interior and exterior are distinct and separate realms, with only the slightest invasion of the lilting clouds into our interior space; the painting is calmly horizontal rather than vertical; the palette is muted and unaggressive, in striking

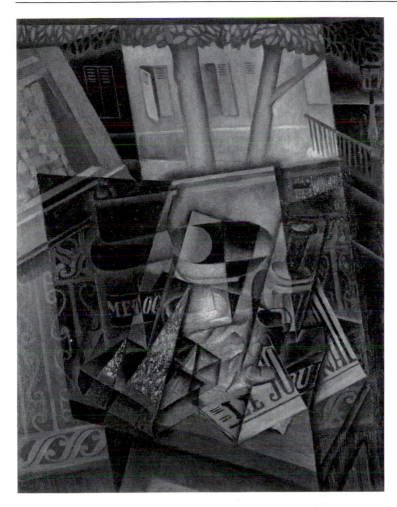

228. J. Gris, *Still-Life Before an Open Window: Place Ravignan*, 1915.

contrast to the blacks, deep blues, red, and greens of the 1915 picture. Perhaps most important, the post-war still-life is generalized—in place of the mundane specificities of the Parisian newspaper and the bottle of wine, we are shown two pristine pages of sheet music, whose empty staffs are made to rhyme with the repeated slats of the shutters and the radically simplified "Platonic absolutes" of guitar, glass, carafe, and fruit-bowl. "Though in my *system* I may depart greatly from any form of idealistic or naturalistic art," Gris was quoted as saying in *L'Esprit Nouveau* this same year, "in practice I do not want to break away from the Louvre. Mine is the method of all times, the method used by the old masters: there are technical *means* and they remain constant."[95]

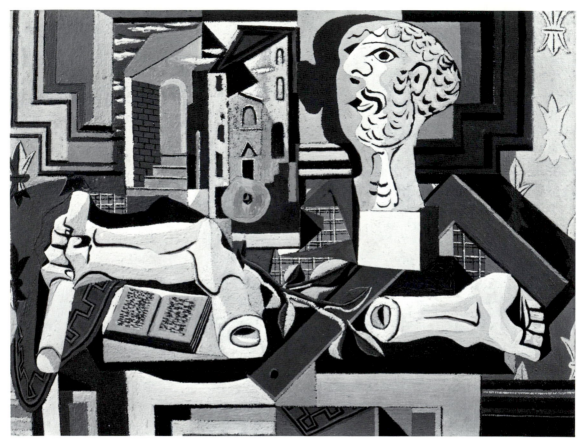

229. P. Picasso, *Studio with Plaster
Head*, 1925.

Indeed, in reference to Picasso's *Studio with Plaster Head*
(fig. 229), painted at Juan-les-Pins in the summer of 1925, Arthur Stevens has remarked upon the old-master iconography:
"The still life is no longer a collection of familiar and intimate
objects of life and sociability used as the basis of formal destruction and reconstruction, but traditional objects of culture—literature, art, drama and architecture. Reactionary elements rule *The Studio*: the return to the use of allegorical
objects; the clarity and readability of the subject matter; the
architectonic ordering of the composition."[96] In fact, it is not
altogether apparent that this is a painter's studio—the Roman
head and plaster anatomical parts are of course a standard part
of the Beaux-Arts education, but in and of themselves they
could as easily be owned by a sculptor; the right-angle square,
the text (or treatise), and the glimpse of a Mediterranean cityscape indicate that this could as easily be an architect's table.

Had Picasso heard statements like those of Adolphe Dervaux to
the effect that architecture was the "art of peace," and might
that account for the laurel branch in the center of the table?
Certainly Picasso knew of Paul Valéry's work, and perhaps he
knew what Phaedrus had said to Socrates in *Eupalinos ou l'architecte*: "See how you cannot speak without borrowing the images and the firm ideal of the *art majeur*," to which the philosopher replied, ". . . There was an architect in me that
circumstances did not succeed in forming." At any rate, this
Synthetic Cubist still-life is, like Gris's post-war still-lifes,
worlds away from Picasso's own past on the place Ravignan; the fleur-de-lis pattern of the wallpaper insures that the
picture's French affiliations are not too subtle to be read.

The previous year Léger had made a not dissimilar image,
his *Still-Life with Statue* (fig. 230). As in Picasso's painting, the
iconography is unequivocally male: the sculpted head is again
Roman (in Léger's picture it is a Caesar-type, whereas Picasso's
appears to be that of a bearded "philosopher"); the attributes
indicate, again, architecture or engineering. The male head,
seen in profile, looks fixedly across the canvas and seems to
dominate the scene like an ancient emperor or a modern *constructeur*. The composition reminds us of the *Le Grand Déjeuner*—the multiplication of horizontals countered by the strong
verticals, the compartmentalized spatial structure, the variation
of pattern. Now, though, there is none of the curvilinear sen-
suousness created by the women's bodies in the painting of
1921. However, when Gris took up the motif in 1926 (fig. 231),
in a picture that was almost certainly inspired by Picasso's 1925
Still-Life with Antique Head now in the Musée National d'Art
Moderne, it is not the creator (be he painter, sculptor, architect,
or philosopher) that is embodied in the Antique head, but the
muse. We are reminded of the statement that Kahnweiler tells
us the artist himself made to him in the post-war period, that
his work "may be bad great painting, but at any rate it is great
painting."[97] Mixing classical allusion with Synthetic Cubism,
the so-called *Musician's Table* (which is in fact an allegory of
the arts) does not seem a real synthesis of any kind. The guitar
floats in the middle of the image, upstaging the lyre behind; the
sheet music appears to be falling off the table rather than lyri-
cally unfurling toward the viewer, as it was meant to; the vase
is crudely twisted, and its shadow is fused with the edge of the
guitar in an ungainly fashion; the canvases stacked behind the
table at the right merge into an unspecified piece of what ap-

230. F. Léger, *Still-Life with Statue*,
1924.

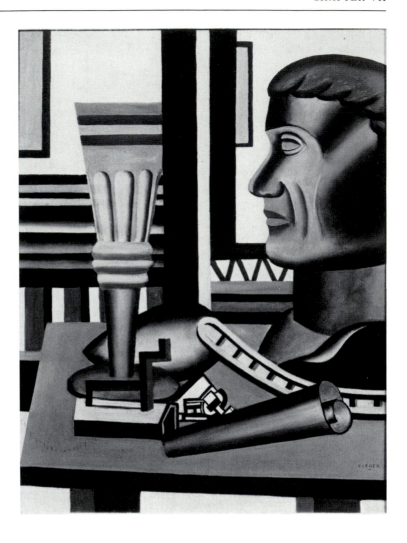

pears to be a granite tablet at the upper left; what we can only
imagine to be the back of a chair (or could this be a stretcher?)
juts awkwardly across the painting at the lower right. Mostly
uncomfortably, the junction of guitar, head, and vase—Gris has
made the statue's right eye "rhyme" with the mouth of the
empty vessel—has no real pictorial or thematic significance. In
picture after picture, between 1923 and 1927, Gris tried to
unite the disparate and disconnected pieces of his paintings by
means of an enclosing outline that runs around the furthest edge
of all the forms, literally pulling all the elements toward the
center of the picture. But the intended effect does not work.
Instead, the central image is merely detached from the ground,

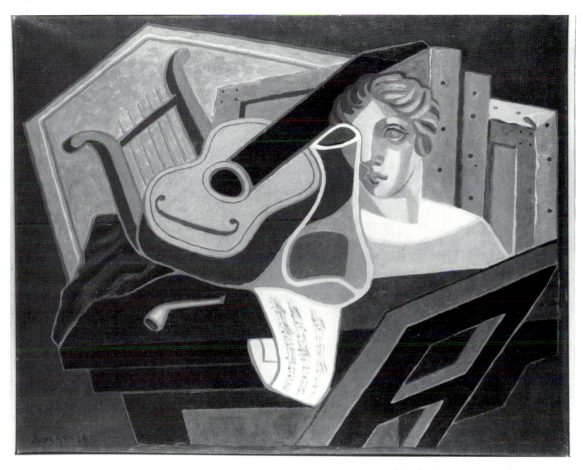

231. J. Gris, *The Musician's Table*,
1926.

undoing the process of weaving together figure and ground, surface and depth, that had been central to the modernist enterprise—and to which he himself was an important contributor—
since at least the time of Cézanne.[98]

Certainly Gris's biography cannot be disregarded in discussing these works of the early to mid 1920s. The artist had first
recognized in 1920 the symptoms of the renal disorder (tragically misdiagnosed as a respiratory ailment) that would plague
him and eventually lead to his death in 1927. Almost as much
as La Fresnaye, Gris had to fight against a diminishing vitality
in these years. Yet I think it is obvious that the "bad great
painting" which Gris produced in the 1920s cannot be attrib-
uted solely to the artist's personal difficulties, but rather form
part of a larger phenomenon in the post-war period. Severini
claimed that Gris had said to him sometime in the 1920s, "We

are all a generation of failures," and whether or not these words are in fact Gris's,[99] they go to the heart of what has often been a rather densely obfuscated history. Can it be denied that after the war not only Gris but Severini, Delaunay, La Fresnaye, and even Braque made much art that was lifeless, uninteresting, simply bad, to the same extent that these very artists had made much art that was exhilarating and beautiful before August 1914 and even for a while after that date? Youth came to a sudden end for all of these pre-war members of the Parisian avant-garde, even sooner and more inexorably for some than it might have if the Great War had not aged or debilitated them. Suddenly, and without warning, a new set of values replaced those of Parisian bohemia: instead of an art of Bergsonian simultaneity, they were now expected to make pictures that embodied Platonic absolutes; in place of internationalism, they were expected to recognize France, the Mediterranean, and *la grande tradition*; whereas to a greater or lesser degree all had made art based on a conception of innovation and novelty before the war, now all were attempting to forge a "synthetic" art of supposedly mature pictorial and thematic values. Having ridden a wave of extraordinary cultural self-confidence before the war, most of the avant-garde artists, faced with the "return to order," were at a loss (they could no longer even claim with pride to be *en avant*). They might talk and paint as if they believed in the new traditionalism and sense of construction. But, contrary to the intentions behind Delaunay's post-war Eiffel Towers and portraits, La Fresnaye's neo-classicism, Braque's *Canéphores*, Severini's Harlequins, or Gris's *Musician's Table*, the effect of their post-war art is of artificiality, an obvious lack of conviction. Without the capacity for adaptation of a Picasso—who, having lost if temporarily his iconoclastic fervor, retreated into a highly productive self-involvement—or the social utopianism of a Léger (or the Purists), most of the pre-war members of the Parisian avant-garde had little to fall back on. They came of age at a moment and in a milieu that idealized contemporaneity; the myths they had helped create were about the modern world, not the "Occident" or eternal values. As Mauclair had said, the war had dug a trench between "yesterday's ideas and those of today," and that—despite appearances—meant that the unqualified optimism of the pre-war years was an outmoded point of view. Henceforth a desperate effort to resuscitate a fading vision of a hegemonic "West" would compel attention in French cultural circles. Picasso

seemed to understand this instinctively: for him all forms were
more or less convincing lies that man could not do without. Unless the artist could be a convincing classicist or a credible *constructeur*, there was not much chance of crossing over the yawn-
ing abyss of the war. The bottom had fallen out of a system of
belief, and the world of the Parisian avant-garde was left with a
bankrupt social identity.

VIII Perchance to Dream

BETWEEN the months of April and October 1925, the Exposition Internationale des Arts Décoratifs et Industriels Modernes was installed in the heart of Paris (fig. 232): the ensemble of official French buildings and commercial pavilions, along with structures created by the twenty-one foreign countries that participated, stretched from the Grand Palais and the Cours la Reine, on the Right Bank, across the Seine on the Pont Alexandre III (which was lined with prestigious boutiques), and along the *quais* on both sides, and culminated in a great Roman-inspired closed court built on the Esplanade des Invalides on the Left Bank. There were a total of fourteen entrances to the Exposition scattered around the fair's perimeter, with the main point of entry—the Porte d'Honneur—situated between the Grand Palais and the Petit Palais. It was an impressive gateway (fig. 233) designed by the architects Favier and Ventre, with grillwork by Edgard Brandt and metal figural reliefs by Navarre; its polished granite columns were topped by capitals of neon and molded glass by René Lalique. The entire event was sponsored by the Minister of Commerce and was intended as a colossal advertisement for the French decorative and in-

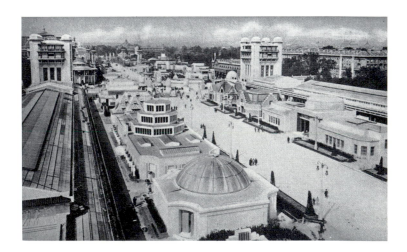

232. General view: Esplanade des Invalides, Exposition Internationale des Arts Décoratifs et Industriels Modernes, Paris, 1925.

dustrial arts. More generally, it was also a proclamation of France's successful and nearly complete post-war recovery.[1]

The Great War, now six years in the past, played a subdued but noticeable role at the Exposition, as, for instance, in the decision to exclude Germany from participation. "German Art Can Wait" was the title of an article published in *Le Figaro* in 1919, in which the critic Louis Vauxcelles—responding to the recent decision to hold the Exposition—said that the Germans should not be allowed to participate, having all too recently shown themselves to be the "the ferocious enemies, the pitiless destroyers, of all that was most venerable and precious in our art."[2] Although other critics, like Roger Allard, responded that to exclude the Germans would give the impression that the French were afraid to be compared with German designers and manufacturers,[3] it was to no avail; the former enemy would be allowed no place at this French post-war event. Instead, France seized the opportunity to congratulate itself on the victory over barbarism: Bourdelle's statue of *La France* stood on the steps of the Grand Palais, and the national tapestry works at Gobelins presented a *Salon de la Guerre* that featured a tapestry by Gustave Jaulmes, *The Embarkation of American Troops for France in 1917* (with profiles of Washington and Lafayette woven into the left and right borders), and a suite of furnishings with war emblems rendered in tapestry, designed by Robert Bonfils. The recovery and *revanche* were represented in less obvious ways as well. A *Village Français*, on a plan designed by Adolphe Dervaux, rendered in "provincial" style — with wooden beams, stucco, and much evidence of folk handicraft—was Parisian

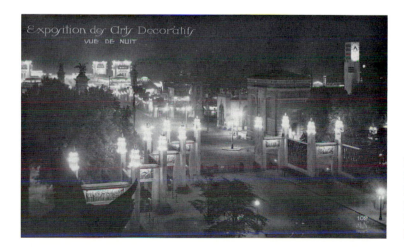

233. View of the *Porte d'Honneur* (by Favier, Ventre, Brandt, Navarre, and Lalique): Pont Alexandre III, Exposition Internationale des Arts Décoratifs et Industriels Modernes, Paris, 1925.

publicity for the very real post-war reconstruction that was taking place throughout the northeast.[4] Indeed, it took a good deal
of familiarity with names and places to recognize some of the
various tales of resurrection. For instance, a piece of garden
architecture, the *Pergola de la Douce France*, in which a number of sculptors who worked in the *taille-directe* technique participated, was constructed mostly from stone quarried in Verdun and, again, Lens. But the accomplishment of *revanche* was
generally apparent to everyone. There were not only a *Pavillon
de Nancy et l'Est* and a *Pavillon de Mulhouse*, but also a *Maison
d'Alsace*, a *Pavillon "L'Art en Alsace"* (sponsored by the magazine of that name), and even, all by itself in a wooded area
alongside the Grand Palais, an *Oratoire Alsacien*—designed in
vernacular style—where one went to thank the Lord, presumably, for liberation from the *boches*.

Although the reclaimed provinces of Alsace and Lorraine
were, naturally enough, well represented at the Exposition, many
of France's other regions also participated and came to show
their wares. Tony Garnier designed an imposing if somewhat
bland pavilion, composed of a ziggurat rotunda of stacked oc-
tagons on a large, flat single-storied base, for Lyons-St. Etienne
(with an equally imposing display of textiles inside); the region
of Berry-Nivernais presented a small modern farm; Bordeaux
had a tower with a restaurant serving—what else?—*vins de
pays*. Limoges, Roubaix-Tourcoing, and the Franche-Comté all
had pavilions, along with Provence, Brittany, and Normandy.

> To the international character that entailed the participa-
> tion of twenty-one foreign nations [said one writer after the
> fair] the Exposition added a regional character; in 1900
> Octave Mirbeau could write that the provinces around
> Paris formed "an immense wasteland." On the contrary,
> the France that is born of the post-war era is in certain
> respects a regional France. . . . Neo-regionalism creates
> appropriate forms for the needs of the modern world, in
> using local materials and processes . . . Provincial partic-
> ipation found its natural place in an Exposition of the mod-
> ern spirit. Alongside the wares of Paris appeared the wares
> of France.[5]

Of course, the economic revitalization of France depended on a
strong regionalist spirit—each province, region, and/or city had
to produce what it made best. Furthermore, it was not only regionalism narrowly defined that was essential to the post-war

economic recovery and to the decorative and industrial arts that made up the Exposition of 1925. The French colonies—that extended and wholly artificial form of regionalism, or regionalism in reverse—were also a part of the national picture: there was a *Pavillon de l'Asie Française*, designed by Delaval in part-French, part-Vietnamese style; a *Pavillon de l'Afrique Française*, in frenchified mock-African mud architecture by Olivier; and a *Pavillon de L'Afrique du Nord*, a whitewashed Moroccan-style house by Fournez. Each pavilion showed displays of the indigenous crafts and local commodities so valuable to the *patrie*.

Indeed, *La France d'Outre-mer* was a key image at the Exposition: the major official French presentation, contrived by the Société des Artistes Décorateurs (under the aegis of the Commissioner of Beaux-Arts) took the form of a model French embassy—*une Ambassade Française*—located in the great building of the Cours des Métiers, the central structure of the entire fair (and it is worth noting that the structure stood right in front of the Invalides, with its bas-relief of *Ludovicus Magnus* and Napoleon's tomb, and also in the midst of the embassy district just behind the Quai d'Orsay). The *Ambassade Française*, designed by Boileau and Carrière, consisted of twenty-five rooms, each created under the direction of a different designer or group of designers. Included here was a reception room by Selmersheim; an art gallery by Roux-Spitz; an office-library by Chareau; a smoking room by Dunand; a lady's bedroom by Groult; a small gymnasium by Jourdain; and a reception hall by Mallet-Stevens. The critic Waldemar George found the entire production of the make-believe *Ambassade Française* both socially irresponsible and politically objectionable. "In choosing as theme an Embassy rather than a *Maison du Peuple*," he wrote in *L'Amour de l'Art*, "the Société des Artistes Décorateurs has given us a good sense of the spirit in which our architects, furniture-makers, and ornamentalists work. These architects and designers are reactionary not only in their devotion to the "powers of money" but also in their failure to understand the needs that modern life imposes . . ."[6] Indeed, the greatest objection to the Exposition as a whole was that not only in the French pavilions but also in a number of foreign ones as well there was little evidence at all of social responsibility. The exhibition seemed dedicated to the good life of the upper bourgeoisie, ruthlessly so even by the standards of 1925. Typical of this attitude was Emile-Jacques Ruhlmann's *L'Hôtel du Collectionneur*, which the famous furniture-maker created with a group that included the designers Puiforçat, Brandt, Jallot and Legrain as well as the artists Pompon, Bernard, Bourdelle, and Janniot (the last of whom created a monumental group, *A la gloire de Jean Goujon*, that stood outside of Pierre Patout's half-modern, half-classicized townhouse). Filled with the luxury *bibelots* and *objets d'art* produced by this prestigious group, Ruhlmann's contribution was frankly and unabashedly elitist, a mid-1920s fantasy of a renovated *hôtel particulier* of the eighteenth century. And the tone was overwhelmingly one of *luxe* throughout the French portions of the exhibition: Lalique the luxury glassmaker and Brandt the master craftsman in wrought iron were well represented in numerous pavilions. There was also a Pavilion of Diamonds and a hall of French perfume; a joint pavilion of Baccarat crystal and Christofle silver; and a *Pavillon de l'Elégance* shared by Lanvin, Worth, Carlier, and Callot. The Gobelins tapestry pavilion has already been mentioned; and, prominently situated in the middle of the Esplanade des Invalides, the twin pavilions of the Manufacture Nationale de Sèvres, with eight monumental urns to catch the spectator's eye. Among the most important commercial structures at the Exposition were the four pavilions of the major department stores, each of which produced its own line of home furnishings: *Studium-Louvre* of the Grand Magasins du Louvre, designed by Laprade; the *Pavillon Pomone*, the display of Bon Marché, designed by Boileau; the *Pavillon de La Maîtrise* of Galeries Lafayette, designed by Hiriart, Tribout, and Beau; and, perhaps the most interesting of the four, the *Pavillon Primavéra* of the Printemps stores, designed by Sauvage and Wybo. If one gets the impression (at least in photographs) that none of the department-store pavilions, each with its house line of goods, was especially innovative or forward-looking, they were nonetheless presenting mass-produced goods available to a fairly large audience, rather than the custom-made objects that elsewhere prevailed. But the preponderance of *luxe* at the fair was, after all, a commercial decision—France was the world's foremost manufacturer of luxury goods and was intent upon remaining so. The conception of well-designed mass-produced objects was not one with which the French felt comfortable, as the Exposition International des Arts Décoratifs et Industriels Modernes made clear in spite of its title.

No one should have been surprised at the regressive character of the Exposition, especially as nearly fifteen years had elapsed since the idea for a decorative-arts fair in Paris had first been proposed. That was on 1 June 1911, when a commission appointed by the government, reporting to the Chamber of Deputies, drew up plans for an exposition to take place in 1915. It was no accident that the proposal was made less than eight months after the infamous exhibition of Munich decorators at the Salon d'Automne—the French decorative-arts industry was fighting for survival in the face of superior German design and manufacture. In order to rally French designers to the national cause and to focus international attention on French products, a fair seemed an excellent idea. "For centuries, since the Middle Ages," the report asserted, "with the exception of the Italian Renaissance, France has imposed her taste on the world. Today, we know only how to boast of the talent of our ancestors. Will we sink to being nothing but imitators and copyists? We must react courageously, we must get back on our feet. We owe it to ourselves to renew our relationship to our tradition and remain creators. It is a primary duty of the Republic to help in the realization of modern styles."[7] The Republic agreed and voted for the exhibition, although not until 1912, at which point it had become necessary to delay the event until 1916. Of course, that date was mooted as of 1 August 1914, but the proposal was by no means forgotten (indeed, as we know well, propagation of French taste seemed all the more imperative in the aftermath of the war). Perhaps in part as a result of the impressive showing that the French decorators made at the Fêtes de la Victoire, a Commissioner General of the long-postponed fair was appointed on 29 July 1919, and a new target date of 1922 was set for the Exposition. "Artists and industrialists ought to be aware," the editors of *Art et Décoration* cautioned in the autumn of 1919, "that the struggle will be intense, that much time has already been lost, and that we are talking about their winning for us a new Battle of the Marne."[8] In fact, still more time was to be lost before, as Léon Rosenthal said rather ominously, "architects, furniture-makers, glassmakers, or ceramicists will find the next Exposition the occasion to finally constitute a living fasces and to affirm the principles of reason, the solid basis on which all styles develop."[9]

When, after all the proposals and delays, the Exposition finally opened in the spring of 1925, Raymond Escholier perceived in the event a triumph of French taste over foreign encroachment, a glorious manifestation of the post-war sense of national identity. His argument is worth citing at length:

> Hasn't the war of 1914–18, which has had such a profound impact on our recent literature, also influenced artistic life

and the development of the modern city? . . . The *muni-chois* furniture of ten [sic] years ago has given way to sober and elegant furniture in the good and forthright French tradition. In other words, the era of cosmopolitanism has passed. Were not all people, constrained for nearly five years to live by their own resources, forced to adopt a sort of economic, financial, and political nationalism—in sum, a veritable literary and artistic protectionism?

On top of that there are purely emotional causes. Threatened at the very sources of life, France became aware of herself again. Since they feared they might lose her, her sons have felt a greater tenderness for her and—having returned to peacetime leisure—want to find nothing foreign in her dear maternal smile. Our museums, like our pilgrimage sites—of this we have certain proof—have experienced an increase in attendance: Frenchmen today put nothing above French spirit and taste.

We should not then be surprised if, after a long eclipse, the native virtues of the race—order, proportion, clarity, discipline—now prevail. That means an end to the anarchy of 1900 and to *munichois* hegemony. Just as our painters, abandoning Cubism and Futurism, have only one concern — to return to the school of Poussin — so our decorators and cabinet-makers, although retaining a feeling for modern life, no longer hesitate to ally themselves with the tradition of Louis XVI and the Directory.[10]

Here at the Exposition's opening, Escholier gives voice to what the French perceived as a decade and a half of cultural war with Germany (of which only four years were accompanied by military combat). The critic went on to mention, in passing and disparagingly, that "the influence of a Poiret on contemporary furniture is diminishing," and that, in place of the couturier's insouciance and fantasy, "an attentive study of pure, harmonious, simple line, of volumes and proportions"[11] was being reinstated. Ironically, not only was Poiret exhibiting at the fair, by means of three barges docked on the Seine—*Amours, Délices,* and *Orgues*—but so was his arch-nemesis, Henri Lapauze, whose magazine, *La Renaissance de l'Art Français et des Industries de Luxe* was represented by a small neo-classical pavilion nearby.

Perhaps the decorators who best exemplified the new postwar spirit of traditional "order, proportion, clarity, and discipline" as Escholier meant it were Louis Süe and André Mare, both of whom had long been involved with the French decorative arts—most recently, of course, as the creators of the Cenotaph for Bastille Day 1919. Further back, in partnership with Raymond Duchamp-Villon, Mare had designed the *Maison Cubiste* of 1912, one of the earliest French attempts to formulate an appropriate response to the Munich exhibition of 1910.[12] "Make something very French," Mare wrote to himself in his notebooks in preparation for the *Maison Cubiste*, "make things a bit severe of line, the coldness of which will be diminished by a decor that is pleasant, fresh-colored, and wholly within the French tradition."[13] Once the idea for a new French decorative-arts program had come to him, Mare held fast to his hopes for a more permanent association of designers. The opportunity to realize his plans appeared in 1917, in the midst of war, when the architect Louis Süe, who had also dreamt of challenging the Germans as *ensembliers* (and had in fact gone as far as to establish a small company to that end, the Atelier Français, also in 1912), agreed to join with Mare in forming a design collective. In great excitement Mare wrote to his friend the glassmaker Maurice Marinot: "Our intention is to realize what I have always tried to do at the Salon d'Automne with our comrades, that is to say, to work in common and to have representatives of all the arts."[14] There was even a chance for a trial run when Mare—who had been a member of the camouflage division of the army during the war—was asked, along with J. L. Boussingault, another *camoufleur*, to help create the decorations for the victory celebration, and they in turned asked Süe and Gustave Jaulmes to collaborate. As we know, despite the general success of the decorations the Cenotaph was labeled *munichois*. But that did not discourage Süe and Mare: that same year they founded the Compagnie des Arts Français, located at the intersection of the faubourg St. Honoré and the Avenue de Matignon, and financed largely by Robert de Rothschild, who warned Mare to avoid anything revolutionary in his designs.[15] He need not have worried: the partnership of Süe and Mare was intended not to revolutionize but to restore. In 1921 Mare wrote in his notebook, "France is in the process of again assuming the first place in the arts that she had occupied since the Renaissance,"[16] and the conception of a new French renaissance in the arts was the guiding principle—much as it was for Henri Lapauze—behind the deluxe album *Architectures* of 1921. It included architectural and interior design plans by Süe and Mare, as well as reproductions of works and original designs by artists like Jacques Villon, Roger de la Fresnaye, Marie Laurencin, André

Dunoyer de Segonzac, and Luc-Albert Moreau, along with Boussingault, Jaulmes, Paul Véra, and others. "*Architectures,* collection published under the direction of Louis Süe and André Mare," reads the title page (fig. 234), "including a Dialogue by Paul Valéry and the presentation of works of architecture, interior decoration, painting, sculpture, and engraving, contributing since 1914 to form the French style"—significantly, it is 1914, the "liberating date for French culture" according to the French Right, that is the *terminus post quem* for the formation of "French style," so that the pre-war years of cosmospolitanism are relegated to pre-history. And it was in Süe and Mare's *Architectures* that Paul Valéry's platonizing *Eupalinos, ou l'Architecte* first appeared.[17]

All of this helps us to understand how it was that Süe and Mare's Compagnie des Arts Français came to play such a large

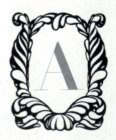

234. L. Süe and A. Mare, *Architectures* (Paris, 1921). Title page.

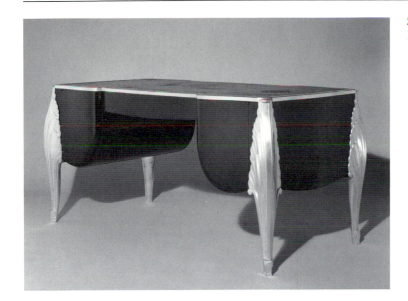

235. L. Süe and A. Mare, *Desk*, 1925.

role at the Exposition in 1925. Not only did the Compagnie display its wares in its own pavilion, the so-called *Musée Contemporain*, but Süe and Mare also designed the Fontaine company pavilion (a twin of their own pavilion, directly across the Esplanade des Invalides), as well as one of the most important public spaces at the fair, the Salle des Fêtes in the Grand Palais, which included a series of murals by Jaulmes depicting "les mois en fête." As was evident in many venues at the fair, the Süe and Mare style was luxurious and traditional, a streamlined version of the Louis-Philippe, with large, swinging curves rendered in rare materials, as in the desk (fig. 235) exhibited in their *Musée Contemporain*, made of Gabon ebony and bronze.

Although cultural chauvinism and reactionary taste were everywhere in evidence at the Exposition—of which the mausoleum-like appearance and fascist sponsorship of the Italian national pavilion, designed by Armando Brasini, represented the aesthetic and political nadir—the fair was not without a few redeeming values. For instance, many of the most important architects of the early twentieth century were represented at the fair in one way or another: Auguste Perret designed the official theatre building; Tony Garnier, the Lyon pavilion; Victor Horta, the Belgian pavilion (which was not, it must be admitted, an artistic triumph); Josef Hoffmann, the Austrian pavilion, which included a handsome greenhouse-tearoom by Peter Behrens (although he would have been denied participation at the fair as a German, he was at that point a professor at the Vienna Academy of Fine Arts); J. F. Staal, the Dutch pavilion; Henri Sauvage, the Primavéra (Printemps) building; Pierre Chareau, the *bureau-bibliothèque* in the *Ambassade Française*; and Robert Mallet-Stevens, two choice designs—the Pavilion of Tourism (in simplified, Cubist-derived planes, including a modernist campanile) and a reception hall in the *Ambassade* which caused, in fact, a mild contretemps. When Paul Léon, Director of Fine Arts and Adjunct Commissioner General of the Exposition, visited Mallet-Stevens's ensemble he demanded that two works commissioned by the architect for the space—an abstract panel by Léger and *The City of Paris: The Woman and the Tower* by Delaunay (fig. 220)—be removed, as he considered them wholly inappropriate to represent the French nation in an overseas embassy. The panels were removed but were put back in place shortly thereafter.[18] Aside from the architecture, among the best-known modernist contributions at the fair were the Cubist "trees," placed in a garden, by the Martel brothers

But far and away the most famous, and indeed the best, modern buildings at the fair were the Soviet pavilion, designed by Konstantin Melnikov, and the *Pavillon de l'Esprit Nouveau*, designed by Charles-Edouard Jeanneret, now calling himself Le Corbusier (fig. 236). Situated, in terms of the fair's typology, somewhere between the design-company pavilions (like Süe and Mare's or Ruhlmann's) and the magazine pavilions (like those of *Art et Décoration* or *La Renaissance*), the Purists' pavilion was given one of the poorest sites at the fair, right up against the side of the Grand Palais, in a grove of trees that could not be cut down or in any way altered. It was perhaps fitting that the pavilion, which ran into extraordinary obstacles at the hands of officialdom,[19] should have derived its name from Ozenfant and Jeanneret's magazine *L'Esprit Nouveau*, for the collaboration of painter and architect had ended when the magazine ceased publication in the preceding January.

That collaboration had been, at the time of their publication of *Après le Cubisme* in 1918, essentially reactive: although it was the first time the authors enunciated the term "Purism," the essay was more concerned with criticizing the parent-figure—Cubism—than with articulating the contours of a new aesthetic. By 1920, however, the Purists had left their own "analytic" phase behind and were ready to propose an artistic synthesis, which they did on 20 October in the first issue of their new magazine *L'Esprit Nouveau* (a title whose significance we already understand). In fact, in almost every way, Purism and *L'Esprit Nouveau* represented synthesis. First was the nature of

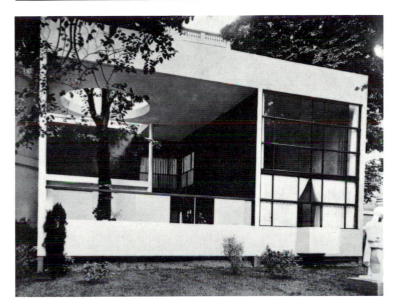

236. Le Corbusier, *Pavillon de l'Esprit Nouveau* (destroyed), Exposition Internationale des Arts Décoratifs et Industriels Modernes, Paris, 1925.

the collaboration: the partnership of Ozenfant, a painter (who was the son of a major French building contractor), and Jeanneret, an architect (who also painted)—a perfect pair of postwar "constructors." Their magazine, in turn, was the realization of its creators' interests, a pictorial and literary synthesis that was also a survey of diverse issues that included contemporary art and art history; architecture and city planning; politics and economics; theatre, music, and literature; as well as reports on the latest scientific developments and the newest industrial processes. This diversity could easily have made their magazine merely eclectic or fashionably dilletantish. Yet *L'Esprit Nouveau* is anything but motley or *mondain*. Not only are the magazine's editorial comment and pictorial layout robust and full of humor, but the authors have a rare ability to make a synthesis of the magazine's varied content. This is mostly owing to Ozenfant and Jeanneret's confident and optimistic outlook. On every page their belief that the world makes sense and can be explained—as well as intelligently managed—shines through.[20]

The partners' confidence and optimism as well as their non-French affiliations—Jeanneret was Swiss by birth, Ozenfant was married to a Russian—gave their magazine an internationalist cultural outlook that was rare among French publications in the immediate post-war years, and this was an integral part of its *esprit de synthèse*. Included in *L'Esprit Nouveau* were, for example, a manifesto of Futurist dance by Marinetti, and articles on Expressionism in Germany, on the work of the Russian painter Ivan Pougni (or Puni), on Walter Gropius and German architecture, and even on contemporary music in Soviet Russia—a list that certainly would not have pleased Daudet or Mauclair. Moreover, *L'Esprit Nouveau* had an irreverence, irony, and lightheartedness that set it apart from the humorless chauvinism of other art magazines such as *La Renaissance* and *L'Amour de l'Art*. For instance, in issue no. 3 appeared the *enquête* "Doit-on brûler le Louvre?" (Should We Burn the Louvre?), for which a space for reply was provided. In issue no. 6 a number of replies were duly published, including that of Léonce Rosenberg, "No, because it is a den of iniquity that only ruins the weak"; of Pierre Bohin, "Naturally, and the Galeries Lafayette too!!"; and the critic Jean Violier's earnest response, "*L'esprit nouveau* is a spirit of construction and not of destruction." Yet the open-minded progressivism of *L'Esprit Nouveau*, so unusual in the context of post-war Paris, was at the same time limited and shaped by the official cultural regime. Indeed (although the fact is not widely known), according to Ozenfant *L'Esprit Nouveau* enjoyed a subvention from the French government for all of its history; when that support was withdrawn in 1925, the magazine folded.[21] That is not to say that the authors were dictated to from above; only that at the very least they shared a commonality of attitude and interest with those in power. There is, for example, the importance of the war, a significance that had already been insisted upon by the partners in 1918, when they wrote that "the Great Test" had helped to make France a modern nation by forcing her to industrialize efficiently. This kind of theme is further elaborated in *L'Esprit Nouveau*. Le Corbusier, in his article "The Illusion of Plans," which appeared in the issue of February 1922, wrote:

> Now the plan is the generator, "the plan is the determination of everything; it is an austere abstraction, an algebrization, and cold of aspect." It is a plan of battle. The battle is composed of the impact of masses in space and the *morale* of the army is the cluster of pre-determined ideas and the driving purpose. Without a good plan nothing exists, all is frail and cannot endure; all is poor even under the cluster of the richest decoration.[22]

Here Le Corbusier makes use of war imagery as a metaphor for architecture, a plan of battle as the model for the plan of construction. But in another article, "Eyes Which Do Not See: Airplanes," published in the issue of June 1921, Le Corbusier tells us that it is specifically *la Grande Guerre* that has transformed society:

> The War was an insatiable "client," never satisfied, always demanding better. The orders were to succeed at all costs and death followed a mistake remorselessly. We may then affirm that the airplane mobilized invention, intelligence and daring: *imagination* and *cold reason*. It is the same spirit that built the Parthenon.[23]

Le Corbusier is expanding upon his metaphor of "the Great Test," but now the war has been transformed into a client, a ferocious industrialist, who galvanizes the forces of invention. But in whatever guise the Purists presented it, the war remained the pivotal event in the modern history of France. When, in a kind of rhetorical blitz, Le Corbusier associates the war and its fatalities with reason and Antiquity, he is invoking the same discursive chain that France had called upon in her darkest hour—that classical civilization provided a model and a precedent for the modern war against the barbarians. We recall that the authors of *Après le Cubisme* had said: "If the Greeks triumphed over the barbarians, if Europe, inheritor of Greek thought, dominates the world, . . . it is because . . . the Greeks loved intellectual beauty . . ."

It was not only in wartime that classical civilization could provide a model for contemporary endeavor. In the midst of post-war reconstruction, Le Corbusier also saw analogies to the Antique past. In an article entitled "La Leçon de Rome," published in *L'Esprit Nouveau* in February 1922, he wrote:

> The Romans did not have before them the problem of the devastated regions [i.e. the northeast of France], but that of equipping the conquered regions; it is all one and the same. So they invented methods of construction and with these they did impressive things—"Roman." The word has a meaning. Unity of operation, a clear aim in view, classification of the various parts.[24]

It was with this same Roman spirit that the Purists had embarked on their new post-war synthesis of the arts.

Classical Antiquity—not only in any neo-classical revivalist form, but in its pure ruined state—was the most important historical reference in *L'Esprit Nouveau*; ancient Mediterranean civilization functioned as the historical justification for the Purist revision of contemporaneity. Among the most striking examples of the way in which the Antique was used to validate—

124   TOWARDS A NEW ARCHITECTURE

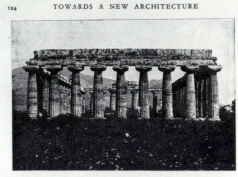

PAESTUM, 600–550 B.C.

When once a standard is established, competition comes at once and violently into play. It is a fight ; in order to win you must do better than your rival *in every minute point*, in

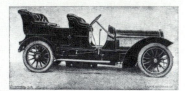

HUMBER, 1907

AUTOMOBILES   125

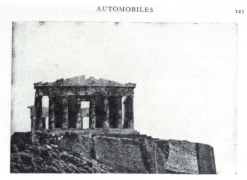

THE PARTHENON, 447–434 B.C.

the run of the whole thing and in all the details.   Thus we get the study of minute points pushed to its limits.   Progress. A standard is necessary for order in human effort.

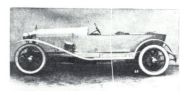

DELAGE, "GRAND-SPORT," 1921

237. Le Corbusier, "Eyes which do not see: Automobiles," from *Towards a New Architecture*, 1927 (originally published in *L'Esprit Nouveau*, July 1921).

indeed, to aggrandize—the present was a two-page spread in Le Corbusier's article "Eyes which do not see: Automobiles," published in the issue of July 1921 (fig. 237). Across the two pages, at the top, are an image of the "Basilica" at Paestum (at the left), captioned with the date 600–550 B.C., and an image of the Parthenon (at the right), similarly captioned 447–434 B.C. Below (also from left to right) are a Humber automobile of 1907 and a Delage "Grand-Sport" roadster of 1921. The text that accompanies these images reads:

> When once a standard is established, competition comes at once and violently into play. It is a fight; in order to win you must do better than your rival *in every minute point*, in the run of the whole thing and in all the details. Thus we get the study of minute points pushed to its limits. Progress. A standard is necessary for order in human effort.[25]

Obviously, the photographs are supposed to make the point that the laws of progress and competition are eternal: as the Doric style developed from Paestum to Athens, so the modern machine style develops from the older carriagework of the Humber to the streamlined silhouette of the Delage "Grand-Sport" (and this progress results, significantly, from Le Corbusier's notion of a violent competition between rivals). But something else too has been established—the classical past and the industrial present have been made into a pair of equivalences: just as the Humber of 1907 is equivalent to the archaic Doric style of Paestum and the Delage of 1921 embodies the full, mature High Classic style of the Parthenon, so, Le Corbusier implies, the pre-war automobile is the infant version of the fully realized post-war model. We have already seen a related equivalence made that same year (1921) by Picasso: the mock-Antique *Three Women at the Spring* and the modernist *Three Musicians*. The subtle difference between Picasso's and Le Corbusier's juxtapositions of old and new, however, points to an essential element of the Purist world-view, i.e. the developmental model and the notion of cultural progress, which we know Picasso repudiated. From Paestum to Athens; from childhood to maturity; from pre-war to post-war; from Analysis to Synthesis; from old buildings to new machines—with four illustrations, the Purists encapsulate a cultural discourse that had been long in the making.

It was not only their belief in the beneficial aspects of the war and their love of the classical past that linked the Purists with conservative post-war artistic attitudes. Their tastes in art history, for instance, were also biased in the direction of the well-established French repertory, especially as it had been refined since about 1917. In the January 1921 issue of *L'Esprit Nouveau* appeared Bissière's article on Ingres, and in the next issue his article on Fouquet; in April 1921 there was a piece on Poussin; in May an article titled "La Vie de Corot," followed in June by another article on Corot (again by Bissière); and in July an article on the Le Nain brothers—that is to say, the French tradition as it was being constantly invoked throughout the wartime and post-war period. And, as we already know, *L'Esprit Nouveau* played a significant role in the revival of interest in Seurat. Concomitantly, although Cézanne was not attacked—at least not by the editors themselves—he was relegated, literally, to second place: issue no. 2 of *L'Esprit Nouveau* included a color reproduction of a *Portrait d'Homme* by Cézanne, along with seventeen other reproductions of his work, accompanied by articles on Cézanne's life and his letters. Still, the Purists were to allow Gino Severini to assume the role of hired gun when, in issues nos. 11/12 and 13 (November and December

1921), he extended his attack on Cézanne (begun in his *Du Cubisme au Classicisme*) in a two-part article "Cézanne et le Cézannisme," an indictment not only of Cézanne's art but of his followers and of modern culture in general as it was exemplified in his painting. Moreover, the editors themselves managed to pay Cézanne a savage backhanded compliment in their most famous essay, "Le Purisme," published in issue no. 4 of January 1921. "As for Cézanne," they wrote,

> who practiced the obstinate, maniacal search for volume with all the confusion and trouble which animated his being, his work became monochrome; all his beautiful, vivid greens, all the precious vermilions, all the chrome yellows and azure blues of his palette were in the end broken to such a degree that his painting is one of the most monochromatic of any period . . . the paradoxical activity of an orchestra leader . . . who tries to make violin music with an English horn and bassoon sounds with a violin.[26]

Stubborn and obsessive; confused, troubled; committed to a futile and inefficient method—these were now the standard ways in which to describe Cézanne, mentor of the pre-war "Analytic" Cubists. He might be an important figure from the past, but Cézanne could not be a guide for the Purist painting of the future.

But this seminal essay demands closer attention. Although, unlike *Après le Cubisme*, it contains no mention whatever of *la Grande Epreuve*, or of the decadent pre-war society for which it was the radical cure, the social realities and myths of pre-war, wartime, and post-war France are nonetheless evoked throughout the essay. "Le Purisme" begins:

> Logic, born of human constants, and without which nothing is human, is an instrument of control, and, for him who is inventive, a guide toward discovery; it controls and corrects the sometimes capricious march of intuition and permits one to go ahead with certainty.[27]

If *Après le Cubisme* had been the movement's Armistice statement, then here was Purism's Treaty of Versailles, a document that would establish, in no uncertain terms, the Purist aesthetic parameters. We can hear much of France's own recent history in these opening lines: just as by means of logic, order, and self-discipline the French had controlled their own capriciousness and, in turn, stopped the "capricious march" of the invaders from beyond the Rhine, so the Purists now offered "logic," "human constants," and "control" as the antidote to aesthetic caprice. Logic as an antidote to caprice, or reality as an antidote to dreaming, had been one of the rewards of the war from the very first. The new sense of proportion and value that the war had bestowed on the French—the new sense of limit that would rouse France from its troubled sleep, and which was referred to so often early in the war—was a central image to the Purists:

> We affirm that the mind claims imperative rights in what is called the work of art . . . we have sought to push aside all factors of futility or disaggregation; we have sought to bring together the constructive means; we have kept to physical questions and have tried in that way to throw out bridges toward mathematical order.[28]

Can there be any doubt that "Le Purisme" was an essay written in the immediate post-war period, or that it was in the face of terrible devastation that the "constructive means" were brought together? That same year, in 1921, the political analysts Bornecque and Drouilly had said that a battle for "moral unity" was being waged against the "divisive and revolutionary forces that the demobilization had unleashed." The chaos of the war was the base line for Ozenfant's and Le Corbusier's "Purism"; terms like "formidable fatality" and "perilous agent" proliferate throughout the essay. Although such figures are always used to discuss the formal properties of painting and never as social terms, in fact there is little in the essay that does not speak clearly, if hermetically, of France in peril.

For instance, as an extension of their preference for logic over caprice and intuition, the Purists wrote:

> With regard to man, aesthetic sensations are not all of the same degree of intensity or quality; we might say that there is a hierarchy. The highest level of this hierarchy seems to us to be that special state of a mathematical sort to which we are raised, for example, by the clear perception of a great general law (the state of mathematical lyricism, one might say); it is superior to the brute pleasure of the senses; the senses are involved, however, because being in this state is as if in a state of beatitude. The goal of art is not simple pleasure; rather, it partakes of the *nature of happiness.* . . . There are obviously those arts whose only ambition is to please the senses; we call them "arts of pleasure." Purism offers an art that is perhaps severe, but

one that addresses itself to the elevated faculties of the mind.[29]

Almost everything here is familiar from French wartime discussion: the sanctioning of hierarchy; the preference for clarity and general laws over "brute pleasure"; and the argument, in purely aesthetic terms, that an art that speaks to the mind is better than an art that addresses the senses. As was evident in *Après le Cubisme* and is equally evident here, the Purists preferred the collective to the individual, in both social and artistic matters. "The highest delectation of the human mind," they wrote, "is the perception of order, and the great human satisfaction is the feeling of collaboration in that order"[30]—a statement with which one could surely argue, but one that Ozenfant and Le Corbusier clearly considered indisputable:

> It does not seem necessary to expatiate at length on this elementary truth that anything of universal value is worth more than anything of merely individual value. It is the condemnation of "individualistic" art to the benefit of "universal" art.[31]

As the Purists were well aware, this marked an about-face for French avant-garde aesthetics. In their joint essay of 1913, "Du Cubisme," Gleizes and Metzinger had spoken of "that negative truth, the mother of morals and everything insipid which, true for many, is false for the individual." And about the maker of paintings they had said:

> Let the forms which he discerns and the symbols in which he incorporates their qualities be sufficiently remote from the imagination of the crowd to prevent the truth which they convey from assuming a general character.[32]

This was written before the Great War, before the French felt so acutely the need for unity, before truths that assumed a general character became not only desirable but the means by which the war effort and Reconstruction came into being. As we know, after August 1914 a position such as Gleizes and Metzinger's would have seemed almost treasonous in the face of France's "call to order." But, for that matter, the entire tone of "Du Cubisme" would have seemed amorphous, elitist, and decadent. When Gleizes and Metzinger spoke of the Cubist painting as "a sensitive passage between two subjective spaces" and wrote that "the picture, which only surrenders itself slowly, seems always to wait until we interrogate it, as though it reserved an infinity of replies to an infinity of questions,"[33] they were speaking in a language that would become anathema to the French after war began. By 1921, Le Corbusier had reduced their infinity of questions to the simplest of postulates: "The primordial physical laws are simple and few in number. The moral laws are simple and few in number."[34] His statement was precisely the kind of static, unequivocal world-view that the post-war French could ratify.

Although Purism was intended as a cure for Cubist decadence, by 1920 Ozenfant and Jeanneret had actually moved closer than ever to the art of their predecessors, appropriating many of its formal motifs for their own pictures. If Le Corbusier's 1920 *Still-Life with Pile of Plates* (fig. 238) is compared with his earlier *Still-Life with Book, Glass, and Pipe* (fig. 152), it is clear that the Purist stance has shifted from a rejection of Cubism to a revision of the pre-war aesthetic. Where Le Corbusier's painting of 1918 had been almost anecdotal, now, in 1920, the image is mute and iconic; where his style had been more or less naturalistic, now, under the influence of Cubism, it is highly abstract; and where the previous image, for all its rectitude and even asceticism, had been personal, in 1920 the entire picture is governed by geometry and rendered in an immaculate chiaroscuro—decidedly more modern and "cold of aspect."

If we turn to the critique of Cubism that is found in "Le Purisme"—a far more moderate appraisal of the movement than that found in *Après le Cubisme*—we can see precisely how this revision of Cubism is undertaken:

> Of all the recent schools of painting, only Cubism foresaw the advantages of choosing selected objects, and of their inevitable associations. But, by a paradoxical error, instead of sifting out the general laws of those objects, Cubism showed their accidental aspects, to such an extent that on the basis of this erroneous idea it even re-created arbitrary and fantastic forms. Cubism made square pipes to associate with matchboxes, and triangular bottles to associate with conical glasses. From this critique and all the foregoing analyses, one comes logically to the necessity of a reform, the necessity of a logical choice of themes, and the necessity of their association not by deformation, but by *formation*.[35]

This is just the kind of misreading of pre-war Cubism that Picasso objected to in his statement of 1923; it is the evolutionary interpretation that treated art as if it were science instead of aesthetics. Contrary to the Purist interpretation, the Cubists

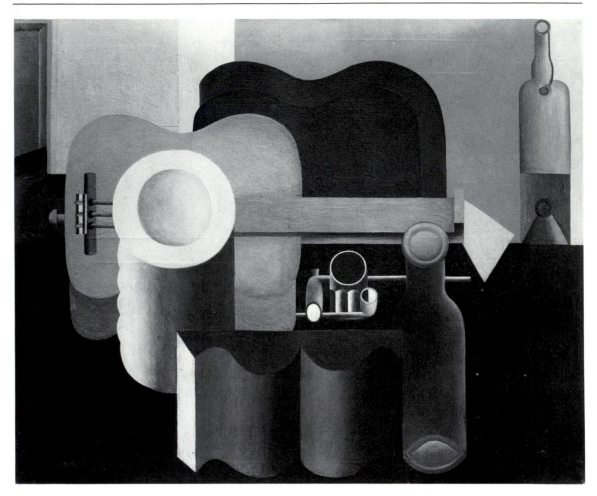

238. C.-E. Jeanneret (Le Corbusier),
Still-Life with Pile of Plates, 1920.

had never been interested in the supposed "advantages of choosing selected objects"; they had made no "paradoxical error" by showing objects in their "accidental aspects," because they had never *intended* to "sift out general laws." Indeed, Gleizes and Metzinger did not believe in the existence of general laws of objects. "There are as many images of an object," they wrote, "as there are eyes which look at it; there are as many essential images of it as there are minds to comprehend it"[36]—a statement made, of course, before the rise of a new Platonism in the 1920s. Yet it was by means of this intentional misreading of Cubist art—this teleological reading that rendered pre-war art as a failed, or less than perfect, effort—that the Purists could carry Cubism's "evolution" to its logical conclusion. In their proclamation that their critique led to "the necessity of a reform" the political rhetoric is unmistakable, and in their call for a "logical choice of themes, and the necessity of their association not by deformation, but by *formation*" they were describing both the shift from analysis to synthesis and the movement from pre-war divisiveness to post-war unity.

In pictorial terms, the reforms of Purism are obvious: in Le Corbusier's *Still-Life* and in Ozenfant's *Glasses and Bottles* (pl. VIII) we can see the themes of selection, of the reinstatement of general laws, and of formation as opposed to deformation. All objects have been reduced to their simplest geometric forms: a guitar becomes a kind of perfect, Platonic ideal of a guitar (smooth, regular, non-specific), and a particular bottle is transformed into an absolute; modeling has become regularized because the illumination is for the most part consistent; and in place of the pre-war Cubist idea of the visual "rhyming" of formally similar but essentially different shapes, we now see a kind of visual incantation—shapes are not so much rhymed as repeated (cylinders, circles, verticals, and horizontals). This is a still-life image that leaves nothing to chance, for there is nothing accidental here. Or, as the Purists say (with Cubism again serving, *sotto voce*, as both progenitor and antagonist),

> Purism would never permit a bottle of triangular shape, because a triangular bottle, which eventually [éventuellement] could be produced by a glassblower, is only an exceptional object, a fantasy, just like the idea that conceived it.[37]

We know, of course, how thoroughly "constructive means" had come to supersede "fantasy," with its anarchic, German, and Orientalist implications. Like the French wartime and post-war collectivity, a painting must exemplify a "sacred union":

> A painting is an association of purified, related, and architectured elements. A painting should not be a fragment, a painting is a whole. A viable organ is a whole, a viable organ should not be a fragment.[38]

We can probably go even a bit further, because although the extreme abstraction of Purist paintings—the compression of space, simplification of forms, implied transparencies—accounts for their "modern" look, a rather old-fashioned notion of hierarchies (specifically, Charles Blanc and André Michel's academic concept of architecture as the primary discipline from which the other arts descend) endows the paintings with their monumental sense of wholeness. Ozenfant's forms, particularly

the fluted bottles and glasses he painted so often, begin to re-
semble Roman arcades and Doric columns; the large simple objects have the monumentality of built structures and cast shadows that seem closer to those in De Chirico's *piazzi* at high noon
than anything in the history of still-life. Indeed, the very title
of a work like *Les Vases Doriques* of 1925 conflates still-life and
architecture, just as the images themselves represent this su-
perimposition. Jeanneret's paintings, if less literal in their architectural references, are perhaps even more architectonic in
their structure: especially in the early 1920s, the objects are
highly modeled and set in a clear, readable space. Slightly
later, as in the *Still-Life with Numerous Objects* (fig. 239) of
1923, where the arrangement of objects is more complex (and
the forms are more often transparent and flattened), the picture's morphology is not of still-life but of landscape, and spe-

239. C.-E. Jeanneret (Le Corbusier),
Still-Life with Numerous Objects,
1923.

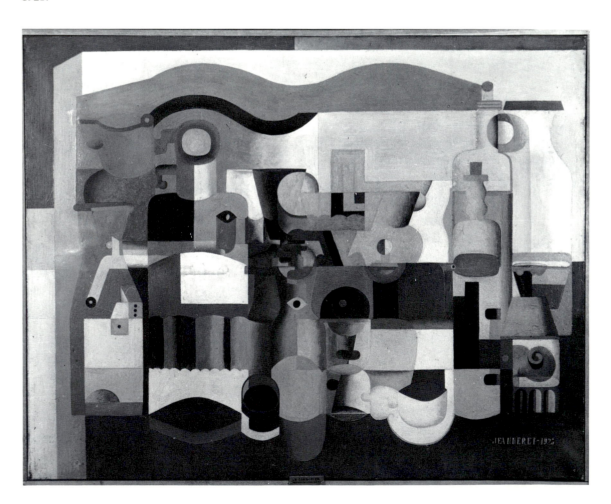

cifically cityscape. Might there even be in this work, where the profile of a violin at the top of the picture creates a mountain ridge underneath which the various bottles, glasses, cups, etc. appear nestled like so many buildings in a hill-town, a recollection of the Swiss landscape of his childhood in La Chaux-desfonds or of the Italian hill-towns he visited and admired in 1907 and 1911?

Of course, the earth-tones and soft pastels of the Purist palette encourage the sense that we are gazing at a kind of noble and timeless architecture. As we know from *Après le Cubisme*, Ozenfant and Jeanneret preferred form to color (an old academic prejudice), in part because they were wary of the emotional power of color. In "Le Purisme" they put it this way:

> When one says painting, inevitably one says color. But color has properties of shock (sensory order) that strike the eye before form (which is a creation already cerebral in part). . . . In the expression of volume, color is a perilous agent; often it destroys and disorganizes volume . . .[39]

As it had been for so many other wartime and post-war critics, color is here presented as the subversive element of art, ever poised to create havoc among the wholesome elements of form and volume; it is in a tone of pained resignation that they concede the equating of "painting" with "color." Consequently, the earthbound color schemes of Ozenfant—brown, red, ochre, black, and white, with touches of blue, rose, and green (the latter often rendered in nacreous tonalities)—and of Jeanneret—brown, terra-cotta, gray, ochre, tan, buff, black and white, again with touches of blue, red, and green—are calculated to soothe and reassure. Once more these early works are reminiscent of Picasso, for it was the same Mediterranean palette that he was just then employing for his pantheon of classical bathers.

But what of Purist iconography? Why an art devoted exclusively to still-life, especially since the range of allusions is so squarely and classically humanistic, leading one to expect an engagement with the human figure and with architectural imagery? Why not an art of classical quietude, depicting the radically simplified figure in an abstracted but classicized architectural setting, like the pictures that were being painted in Italy by Carlo Carrà and Mario Sironi?[40] Although Purism as a movement was highly moral, even moralistic, in its artistic stance, its subject matter could not be less moralizing, consisting as it did of glasses, bottles, pipes, books, plates, and musical instruments. To a certain extent, of course, this was logical for two artists who also saw themselves as propagandists for social utility. Manufacturing, modern industrial processes, and efficient production were all important elements in the synthetic program of *L'Esprit Nouveau*; beautifully rendered objects demonstrated the power of the machine to successfully replace hand-crafted artifacts. But it was only in part the modernity of manufacturing that attracted the Purists to these still-life objects. They were really more interested in the "eternal laws" of which these objects seemed to be the result. They applied Darwin's law of natural selection to objects:

> Mechanical selection began with the earliest times and from these times provided objects whose general laws have endured; only the means of making them has changed, while the laws have endured. . . . In all ages, for example, man has created containers: vases, glasses, bottles, plates, which were built to suit the needs of maximum strength, maximum economy of materials, maximum economy of effort.[41]

In other words, the objects which the Purists were painting had already been purified by time—just as the French nation itself had, according to Ozenfant and Jeanneret, been purified and refined by "the Great Test." Indeed, people and objects were not distinct and separate categories for the Purists:

> Man and organized beings are products of a natural selection. In every evolution on earth, the organs of beings are more and more adapted and purified, and the entire march forward of evolution is a function of purification . . . these artificial objects obey the same laws as the products of natural selection . . . consequently, there reigns a total harmony, bringing together the only two things that interest the human being: himself and what he makes.[42]

Without recourse to the *commedia dell'arte* or to classical figures, the post-war Frenchman was expected to see himself in the things of his manufacture, to locate his identity in the bottles and glasses of these Purist still-lifes. As if in "total harmony" between "himself and what he makes," he was to recognize his own heritage in the venerable tradition of Baccarat, Limoges, and Sèvres, to celebrate through these mute arrangements of time-honored vessels his victory and even his survival. Of course, it was imperative that the French not meditate too long on real buildings and real people, that they not see themselves as they really were after 1918: burnt-out, ravaged, and mutilated. *La Belle France* might regain her poise and dignity, in time showing herself again in her perfect, classical profile. But not, so it was believed, if she saw herself mirrored in her northeastern landscape, so shattered that many thought it could never be cultivated again; or in the devastated towns to which, after centuries of family history and tradition, many would never again return; or in her mutilated soldiers. Nothing less than an extraordinary, renewed sense of *élan*, the "new spirit," would suffice to see France through her recovery. When the Purists wrote that "a painting surface should make one forget its limits, it should be *indifferent*,"[43] they were also talking about Frenchmen in the wake of the Great War, who could afford to be neither too sensitive nor too vulnerable. Far better to contemplate a purified and enduring collection of French objects than to concentrate on the uncertain, ephemeral, and vulnerable products of nature. Man might be his own most compelling subject, but he was imperfect and likely to break down under pressure. The post-war Frenchman could feel more certain of his power to make and remake things than he could in his power to repair his countrymen or to enrich the land torn by shrapnel.

The formal revision of Cubism exemplified in Ozenfant's 1925 line drawing, *Fugue* (fig. 240), represents, then, much more than a mere change in taste—or perhaps there are no "mere" changes in taste, ever, anywhere. In the clean contours of *Fugue*, with its perfect profiles of bottle and vase, its equilibrated relationship between larger and smaller vessels, its hierarchies and its perfectly bounded limits, we find André Michel's "return to style, to composition, which makes itself heard even at the very base of contemporary anarchy." *Fugue* is a picture of organizational harmony, a blueprint, and a social contract for post-war France, in which order is maintained, deviation is controlled, and the nightmare through which the French had passed is banished. The recovery of "the sense of limits and of the relative, father of the arts," had been cited by Gabriel Boissy as one of the rewards of war, during that terrible year of 1916; "the war's violent necessities reestablish the sapped hierarchy. . . . Freed from their vanquished soul, the French will have, they have already, a soul of masters, a creative spirit . . . Henceforth they will flower with the impetuous ease of a people rejuvenated or, rather, purified by sacrifice."

But there was also in Purist painting and theory a very definite social and political attitude, one that was far more specific

240. A. Ozenfant, *Fugue*, 1925.

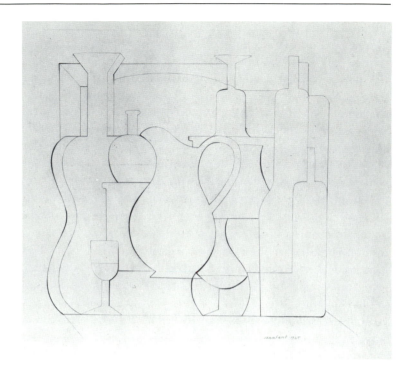

than the program of turning one's gaze away from unpleasant realities. For Purism was in the deepest sense a self-consciously anti-revolutionary theory and was, equally self-consciously, a movement that depended on the maintenance of the social order and believed in that social order. When Ozenfant and Jeanneret asserted in "Le Purisme" that "if Ingres paper and Whatman paper have a fixed format, and if canvases of 40 × 32, for example, have a format unchanged for so many years, it is because their proportions satisfy physiological needs,"[44] they were talking not just about formal issues but about society. Le Corbusier comments directly on the social aspects of this fatalistic doctrine in his article "Eyes which do not see: Automobiles":

> All men have the same organism, the same functions. All men have the same needs. The social contract that has evolved through the ages fixed standardized classes, functions, needs, producing standardized products.[45]

In other words, the static, Platonic world of eternal values (which nonetheless, according to the Purists, encompasses an ineluctable progress toward perfection) was predicated on a society of fixed classes (in which Ozenfant and Jeanneret naturally considered themselves members of the elite). In the article

"What we have done, what we will do," published in 1921, the editors claimed that "Intellectual progress has created vast human resources among the cultural and technological elite. The aim of *L'Esprit Nouveau* is to provide indispensable links among such groups and to offer a clear idea of the main currents of contemporary thought."[46] As Susan Ball has said of the social complexion of Purist theory, "What emerges . . . is a Platonic belief in the ability of a few people to change the course of the future with a clearly stated program, a fundamental belief in the power of the elite, the power of a Platonic oligarchy."[47]

Indeed, as Reyner Banham has noted, the final image of Le Corbusier's book of 1926, *L'Urbanisme*, is an engraving of Louis XIV supervising the construction of the Invalides. The caption beneath reads: "Homage to a great town-planner—This despot conceived great projects and realized them. Over all the country noble works still fill us with admiration. He was capable of saying 'We wish it,' or 'Such is our pleasure.' " Recognizing that he might be taken for a Royalist, the architect added: "This is not a declaration of the *Action Française*."[48] But if Le Corbusier was wary of being thought a member of the extreme Right, neither was he, nor did he want to appear to be, allied to the far Left. The Purists' elitism was real, and it was unsurprisingly (especially considering the cultural climate in France just after the war) anti-socialist: "We must see trade unionism and the experiments of bolshevism as unfortunate episodes," they wrote; "The *esprit nouveau* is the result of a faith in the possible organization of the forces of progress—the disturbed conditions around us are proof of the enormous job that awaits."[49] It is on a specifically anti-revolutionary note that both *Vers une architecture* of 1923 and *L'Urbanisme* conclude. The former concludes with these famous lines: "Society is filled with a violent desire for something which it may obtain or not. Everything lies in that: everything depends on the effort made and the attention paid to these alarming symptoms. Architecture or Revolution. Revolution can be avoided."[50] And the final lines of the latter are these: "Things are not revolutionized by making revolutions. The *real* Revolution lies in the solution of existing problems."[51]

It was this post-war climate that Le Corbusier counted on to give meaning and urgency to the *Pavillon de L'Esprit Nouveau* at the Exposition in 1925 (fig. 236): the Parisian public was given an architectural means of avoiding revolution in the form of a fully furnished two-storey module, extracted from Le Corbusier's projected *immeubles-villas* (apartment houses made up entirely of duplexes, a kind of stacked-up *cité-jardin*) plunked down beside the Grand Palais. Not that it was only by way of these supposedly affordable *petits palais* that social upheaval would be avoided; the real revolution, as Le Corbusier meant it, could be found next door to the villa, in the *Stand d'Urbanisme*, where his two city plans—the "Ville Contemporaine" and the "Plan Voisin" (a scheme for the remaking of central Paris)—were on display (fig. 241).[52]

Yet the *Pavillon de l'Esprit Nouveau* marked not only the climax but also the demise of Purism. Before the pavilion even opened in April, the magazine had ceased publication: the final issue is dated January 1925. From here on Jeanneret and Ozenfant would go their separate ways, undoubtedly sensing that Purism had served its purpose and was about to outlive its time. Indeed, while its anti-revolutionary stance had given voice to a very real fear abroad in post-war France, such a position seemed less and less interesting as the spectre of international Marxism became less forbidding (in fact, Melnikov's Soviet pavilion at the Exposition was awarded first prize for design by a specially established French commission). The Cartel des Gauches, a coalition of Radicals and Socialists, led by Edouard Herriot, former mayor of Lyon, was swept into power at the polls in 1924. Although Herriot would resign the next year, and the cabinet would slip back to the center under Painlevé, the Right's hold on the French imagination—so powerful since August 1914—had been broken. If the Purists' New Spirit can be said to have been born of the Armistice, then we might also say that the umbilical chord that connected the movement to the Great War had been stretched about as far as it would go. Purism was essentially an aesthetic of Reconstruction, and as the rebuilding of France drew toward completion, so the movement lost its *raison d'être*.

In fact, just a month before the final issue of *L'Esprit Nouveau*, there appeared on 1 December 1924 the first issue of André Breton's *La Révolution Surréaliste*. The thoughts of Louis Aragon, as published alongside a photograph of Pierre Patout's Place de la Concorde entryway to the Exposition (with the facetious caption "Report on the Exposition des Arts Décoratifs") in the 15 July 1925 issue of *La Révolution Surréaliste*, typify the magazine's editorial tone:

> . . . if you ask me what distinguishes this year [1925] with which the century sews together its first two quarters—this year that was supposedly celebrated in Paris by an Expo-

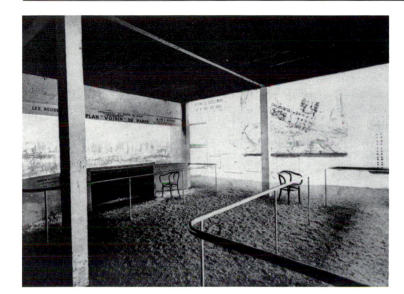

241. Le Corbusier, Urbanism display, *L'Esprit Nouveau* pavilion, Exposition Internationale des Arts Décoratifs et Industriels Modernes, Paris, 1925.

sition of Decorative Arts that is a huge joke—I will tell you that it is, in the very bosom of Surrealism and under its gaze, the advent of a new spirit of revolt, a spirit determined to attack in all directions.[53]

Indeed, this *nouvel esprit de révolte* was quite precisely aimed, as Picabia's Parisian Dada had been a few years earlier, at the nationalistic and classicizing *esprit nouveau* of wartime and post-war France. It is worth repeating Breton's definition of the new movement as he enunciated it in the autumn of 1924:

> SURREALISM. noun, masculine. Pure psychic automatism, by which one intends to express verbally, in writing or by any other method, the real functioning of the mind. Dictation by thought, in the absence of any control exercised by reason, and beyond any aesthetic or moral preoccupations. ENCYCL. Philos. Surrealism is based on the belief in the superior reality of certain forms of association heretofore neglected, in the omnipotence of dreams, in the undirected play of thought. . . .[54]

Contrary to the most basic tenets of the Sacred Union's newly awakened and orderly sense of alertness after August 1914, Breton calls for a re-engagement with the psyche, unimpeded by the "control exercised by reason"—in other words, for an abandonment of the very self-control and discipline that the French had been inculcating for a decade. To write of the "omnipotence of dreams" and to promulgate the "undirected play of thought" was a heresy, an anarchic point of departure on which Breton would base his entire Surrealist program. Aragon wrote that as early as 1922 "an epidemic of trances broke out among the surrealists . . . there were some seven or eight who now lived only for those moments of oblivion when, with the lights out, they spoke without consciousness, like drowned men in the open air. . . ."[55] *La Révolution Surréaliste* ran a regular column, called simply "Rêves," in which various Surrealists transcribed their dreams. Included in issue no. 3 of April 1925, for instance, were Paul Eluard and Antonin Artaud's nocturnal adventures. And, to what would have been the horror of every *bon bourgeois*, J. A. Boiffard, Eluard, and Roger Vitrac exclaimed, "Parents, tell your children your dreams!"[56]

The spokesmen for the nation, both official and not, had reminded the French almost daily since 1914 that theirs was the civilization of reason and clarity. But if reactionary values of hierarchy and cultural elitism were considered reasonable, then Reason itself was now considered repellent: "Ideas, logic, order, Truth (with a capital T)," said Artaud in 1925, "—we consign everything to nothingness of death. Watch out for your logics, Gentlemen, watch out, you don't know how far our hatred of logic can take us."[57] It took the Surrealists very far indeed, to the point of embracing everything that the Sacred Union (which now included a good part of the so-called avant-garde) disdained, including "the right to opium, the right to alcohol, the right to love, the right to abortion, the right of the individual to do with himself as he will . . . ,"[58] as Robert Desnos put it. Anything that smacked of officialdom was fair game: Breton and his friends wrote excoriating open letters, which they published in issue no. 3 of *La Révolution Surréaliste*, to the Rectors of European Universities, to the Doctors-in-Chief of Insane Asylums, and to the Pope; in issue no. 6 they reproduced all of the doodles that were found one day on the blotters of the Council of Ministers (the Surrealists obviously had friends in high places). Needless to say, the Surrealists disdained patriotism and were thoroughly irreverent when anyone mentioned the war or the heroic French dead. In the second issue appeared the "Extract of a letter from Fernand Fontaine, 1st Class, killed 20 June 1915: 'No, really, it's not nearly so amusing as I thought it would be,' " the soldier wrote from the trenches, " 'And if I die, let it be known that it will be in opposition to France.' "[59] That was fairly scandalous, but slightly less so than the Surrealists cheering *en groupe* at a banquet in 1925, "Long live Germany!"[60] Of course, Breton and many of his friends were also avowed Marxist revolutionaries of one complexion or another, and their radical politics was one of the surest signs of the alienation from established culture.

As a result, the Surrealists were able to scrutinize and comprehend the subtleties of regnant cultural positions as were few others of their contemporaries. One example is "Orientalism." In issue no. 8 Breton noted that there were currently circulating ". . . certain *rubber-stamp words* like 'Orient.' This word . . . has been uttered more and more in recent years . . . the reactionaries today . . . never pass up an opportunity to implicate the Orient," and he went on to name the chief offenders, who included Charles Maurras, Paul Valéry, and Henri Massis, the right-wing author whose *La Défense de L'Occident* of 1927 was perhaps the period's most celebrated attack on the Oriental vogue.[61] In revenge, the Surrealists exalted the Orient, which Desnos referred to as "the Citadel of every hope," calling the Asians "the archangels of Atilla."[62] In an article entitled "Address to the Dalai-Lama," he wrote: "We are your faithful servants, O great Lama, give us, send us your illumination, in a language which our contaminated European minds can understand . . .";[63] and in another article, "Letter to the School of Buddha," he called out to the Buddhists: "Logical Europe crushes the mind endlessly. . . . But now the strangulation is at its crisis, we have suffered in harness too long. . . . Like you, we reject progress: come, demolish our houses . . ."[64]— which was, during Reconstruction, about the worst thing that a Frenchman could wish on *la patrie*. Again, in direct challenge to the French Right, which during the Dreyfus Affair had cast the Jew as the central antagonist in their nationalist drama, Desnos—who considered Jews "Orientals"—proclaimed in relation to the issue of Zionism, "The Israelites must remain in exile as long as the cause of the West is still not lost, as long as this Latin, Greek, Anglo-Saxon, German spirit, which is the most terrible menace against the soul, is not yet crushed."[65] Of course, this kind of talk was not calculated to do France's Jews much good, but then the Surrealists were hardly do-gooders. What they wanted was complete disruption of the status quo. In issue no. 4 of July 1925 of *La Révolution Surréaliste*, Aragon laid it squarely on the line (even if it was all a fuzzy, adolescent fantasy of holocaust and personal triumph):

We shall triumph over everything. And first of all we'll destroy this civilization that is so dear to you, in which you are caught like fossils in shale. Western world, you are condemned to death. We are Europe's defeatists . . . Let the Orient, your terror, answer our voice at last! We shall waken everywhere the seeds of confusion and discomfort. We are the mind's agitators. All barricades are valid, all shackles to your happiness damned. Jews, leave your ghettos! Starve the people, so that they will at last know the taste of the bread of wrath! Rise, thousand-armed India, great legendary Brahma. It is your turn, Egypt! And let the drug-merchants fling themselves upon our terrified nations! . . . Rise, oh world! See how dry the earth is, and ready, like so much straw, for every conflagration. Laugh your fill. We are the ones who always hold out a hand to the enemy . . .[66]

In contrast, the gleeful part of the Surrealist insurrection was the attack on the sacred cows of the French cultural world, the indigenous intelligentsia. Our old friend Mme. Aurel, scourge of the Cubists and fervent nationalist, was the target of Surrealist abuse at yet another banquet, in February 1924. As Aurel rose and commenced to speak in her usual flowery prose, Breton and Desnos shouted "Assez"—and Desnos added, so that everyone in the room could hear, "For twenty-five years now she's bored the shit out of us, but no one's had the nerve to tell her!"[67] But Aurel was merely a popular commentator and not a major figure; the Surrealists had their sights set on bigger game, no matter at which end of the French socio-political spectrum. In 1924, Breton wrote this epitaph for three of the nation's most famous spokesmen, who had died that year:

> Loti, Barrès, Anatole France, any year deserves a gold star that lay these three sinister gentlemen to rest: the idiot, the traitor, and the policeman. . . . With Anatole France, a little bit of human servility leaves the world. Let the day be a holiday when we bury cunning, traditionalism, patriotism, opportunism, skepticism, and lack of heart. Let us remember that the lowest actors of this period have had Anatole France as their accomplice, and let us never forgive him for adorning the colors of the Revolution with his smiling inertia.[68]

State funerals and national mourning for *les grands hommes* augured well for the future, since what the Surrealists hoped for was the death of French culture in general.

What gave the Surrealist critique of contemporary culture its power was Breton's remarkable understanding of visual art and his ability to analyze what he saw (coupled with a disposition to embarrass and even publicly humiliate all those who disagreed with him); among his favorite targets were those members of the avant-garde who had, in his opinion, capitulated to the bourgeois regime. Although he exempted Picasso from censure—"Picasso, released from every obligation of simple morality on account of his genius . . . , remains the master of a situation that we would often think was desperate without him"—Breton went on to say that "it seems in fact that most of his friends from the early days are now embarked on a path that is the most contrary to ours and to his."[69] The poet had specific artists in mind, whose recent compromises and cultural conformism he described with the poignantly appropriate image of the lion-cage at the circus:

> Those who called themselves "the Fauves," with so exceptional a prophetic sense, do not more than execute, within time's prison, [their] ridiculous turns and their latest leaps, which are so little to be feared; the least important art dealer or lion-tamer protects himself with a chair. Matisse and Derain are just such elderly lions, discouraged and disconcerting. From the forest and the desert, for which they no longer retain any nostalgia, they have passed into this minuscule arena . . . A *Nude* by Derain, a new *Window* by Matisse; what more certain proof of the truth of the maxim that "all the water in the sea would not suffice to wash clean a stain of intellectual blood"?[70]

Obviously, Breton had been keeping a close eye on the art and the careers of the leading Parisian painters and knew, better than many cared to be reminded, just how far many had strayed from their youthful pre-war principles. His most famous indictment was of Giorgio de Chirico, an artist for whom Breton had felt a special reverence owing to the Italian's extraordinary pre-war proto-Surrealist cityscapes. Now, though, in June 1926, Breton spoke out against Chirico's obvious lack of conviction or principle: "Chirico, who in continuing to paint has for ten years done no more than abuse a supernatural power, is today astonished that no one wants to follow him in his lame conclusions, of which the kindest thing one can say is that the spirit is totally lacking and that nothing but shameless cynicism prevails." According to Breton, Chirico had fallen prey to one temptation and spurious involvement after another: "Italy, fascism—there is a

242. Editorial defacing of Giorgio de
Chirico, *Orestes and Electra*. *La
Révolution Surréaliste* (1 March 1926).

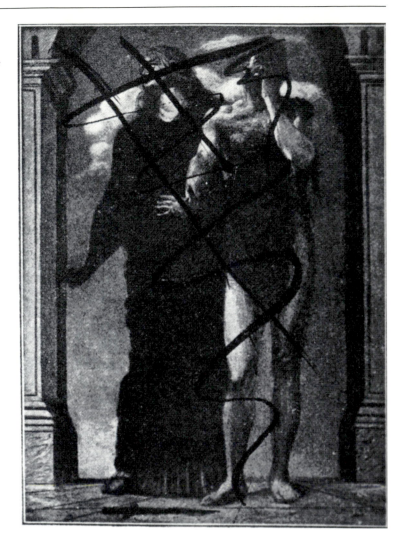

painting by him vile enough to be entitled *Roman Legionary
Surveying the Conquered Territories*—artistic ambition, and,
most mediocre of all, even avarice," the catalogue of crimes
culminating in a scene which Breton says he himself witnessed:
Chirico's sitting down to make copies of his own early paintings.[71] As the concluding image of the second part of his four-
part series "Le Surréalisme et la peinture," Breton reproduced,
in the issue of 1 March 1926, a neo-classical work by Chirico
of 1922–23, *Orestes and Electra*, which the magazine's editor
defaced with a scribble of ink (fig. 242).

The Surrealist program with its reclamation of the pre-war
values that had been relinquished after August 1914—internationalism and cosmopolitanism, with the concomitant interest in

the so-called primitive nations and non-Western cultures; revolutionary sentiment, both specifically in Marxist terms and more generally in a desire to disturb, upset, and overturn the status quo; the anti-hierarchical aesthetic attitudes that valued above all the disenfranchised, the common, and the ephemeral—challenged in the most direct and vocal way the widespread capitulation of the Parisian avant-garde to the forces of "order" and reaction. In terms of painting alone, by the middle of 1925 the work that was being made in and around Surrealist circles represented the first real alternatives seen in Paris to either late Cubism or neo-traditionalism; issue no. 4 of *La Révolution Surréaliste* of 15 July is powerful proof. It includes not only a Man Ray "Rayograph" (*Marine*) but also two major works by the newcomer Joan Miró, *Maternité* and *Le Chasseur*; two of Max Ernst's most important pictures, *2 Enfants sont Menacés par un Rossignol* and *La Révolution la Nuit*; and—perhaps of greatest moment—two major works by Picasso, *Les Demoiselles d'Avignon*, which appears with the date of 1908, and a brand-new work of 1925, *Jeunes Filles dansant devant une fenêtre*, usually referred to as *The Dance* (fig. 243).

Indeed, Picasso's *The Dance*, painted by an artist who had made so many artistic and social adjustments necessary to survive and even to thrive in the Sacred Union of wartime and postwar France, is perhaps the best evidence we have that the enforced consensus was waning by the middle of the decade. It is not merely as a gesture of nostalgia on Breton's part that the *Demoiselles d'Avignon* was reproduced in the same issue as *The Dance*, printed several pages earlier and intended to establish both a precedent for the later work and a direct link with the values of the pre-war Parisian avant-garde. Having passed through the entire repertory of sanctioned styles since 1914 (a canon that the artist in large part had helped to create)—classicism, *commedia dell'arte*, *belle-peinture*, "Synthetic" Cubism—Picasso was preparing to become once again an iconoclast, and to join, if from a distance, the ranks of the cultural insurrectionists. In almost every way, *The Dance* is a picture that violates the wartime and post-war artistic code. Primitive and ecstatic, Picasso's bacchic trio could not be further from either the monumental classicism of *Three Women at the Spring* or the well-tempered, nostalgic Cubism of *Three Musicians*. The figures are ruthlessly distorted, impossibly flat, and terrifyingly ugly; the colors are discordant, jarring, and subversive of normal expectations; the theme of death is neither subtly alluded to nor perspicaciously avoided, but heraldically proclaimed in

243. P. Picasso, *The Dance*, 1925.

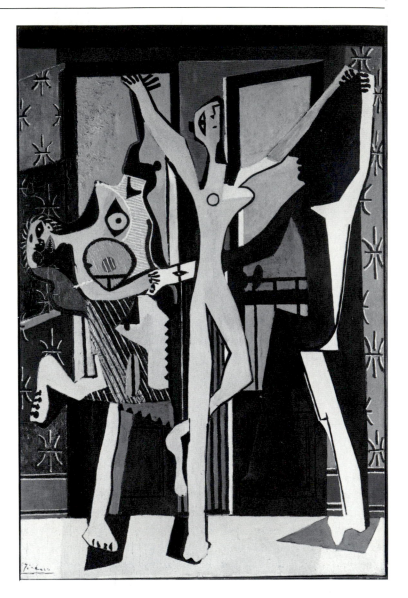

the cruciform central figure and in the dark male profile silhou-
etted against the french windows (is the abstracted fleur-de-lys
pattern on the wallpaper, which now looks like a Satanic tri-
dent, intended ironically?). Most important, the picture's image
of ritual loss-of-self represents the kind of pictorial intoxication
that had seemed to disappear from the art of the Parisian avant-
garde in August 1914, when self-control, self-abnegation, and
self-denial of so many kinds became a national *modus vivendi*.
Perhaps with the nightmare of the war beginning to fade into

the past, Parisian artists could again allow themselves the luxury of inventing a world less tragically circumscribed than the France of *la Grande Guerre*.

Notes

1. Picasso made the comment at a later date to his dealer Daniel-Henry Kahnweiler, who spoke of it to Francis Crémieux: "Picasso told me many years later, 'On 2 August 1914, I took Braque and Derain to the Gare d'Avignon. I never saw them again.' This was a metaphor, of course. He did see them again, but by this he meant that it was never the same." Kahnweiler, *My Galleries and Painters* (London, 1971; orig. Paris, 1961); as quoted in the original French in Pierre Cabanne, *Le Siècle de Picasso*, 2 vols. (Paris, 1975), I, p. 279.

2. "Il y a une grande mélancholie à feuilleter les publications et les revues de tout genre qui parurent au moment où la guerre éclatait. . . . Comme elles nous semblent heureuses, les époques où nous discutions sérieusement de l'avenir du cubisme ou des mérites respectifs du vers libre et du vers régulier. Il fut un moment, au mois d'août, où je crus fermement que tout cela était fini, à tout jamais, qu'il ne serait plus jamais question ni d'art, ni de poésie, ni de littérature, ni de science même . . ." Rémy de Gourmont, *Pendant l'orage* (Paris, 1915), pp. 57–58.

3. Juan Gris to D.-H. Kahnweiler, Collioure, 1 August 1914, *Letters of Juan Gris*, collected by D.-H. Kahnweiler, trans. and ed. Douglas Cooper (London, 1956), p. 6. (All passages from Gris's letters here quoted are Cooper's translations presented without alteration.)

4. Gris to D.-H. K., Collioure, 3 August 1914, in ibid., p. 7.

5. Gris to D.-H. K., Collioure, 16 August 1914, in ibid., pp. 8–9.

6. Although it lacks any scholarly apparatus, the best source for a general overview of life in France during the war is Gabriel Perreux's *La Vie quotidienne des civils en France pendant la Grande Guerre* (Paris, 1966). Of Picasso specifically, Pierre Cabanne has written: "Picasso traverse une période d'amère solitude. . . . [Pablo and Eva] traînent le soir de café en café, mais les hommes en uniforme, qui souvent reviennent du front, détaillent sans complaisance ce robuste 'embusqué' accompagné d'une jolie femme. Gêné, Pablo se terre chez lui durant des semaines et peint. 'Je vois peu de monde' écrit-il à un ami Italien." *Le Siècle de Picasso*, I, p. 284. Gris told Kahnweiler on 19 April 1915 that he would have liked to eat at the canteens, because it was inexpensive, except that he would have had to face unpleasant accusations there. *Letters*, ed. Cooper, p. 26. The basic source for Cocteau's activities during wartime is Francis Steegmuller's *Cocteau*,

I "In the nightmare through which we are passing"

A Biography (Boston, 1970), where Cocteau's attempt to enlist is discussed pp. 122–29 and appendix I (Portions of Cocteau's Military Dossier). Also essential for Cocteau is Frederick Brown, *An Impersonation of Angels—A Biography of Jean Cocteau* (New York, 1968), who writes, "Cocteau, though declared physically unfit, wore a blue officer's uniform far spiffier than ordinary military issue" and cites André Gide's remark that when he saw Cocteau in August 1914 "he was wearing something like a soldier's uniform" (p. 100). He also explains that "Cocteau had various reasons for contriving what resembled a pilot's uniform. He did so partly from sibling rivalry, for Paul, his older brother, had become a pilot as soon as war broke out" (p. 101), and he notes that "Cocteau's nurse's outfit had been designed by Paul Poiret" (p. 104). Cocteau's substitute wartime activities for soldiering are by now almost legendary: he founded an ambulance corps with his friend Misia Sert; took the role of a volunteer male nurse; eventually saw action at the front, where he performed bravely; and even began flying with the French ace Rolland Garros. All this is in Steegmuller and was also fictionalized by Cocteau in his novel of 1918, *Thomas l'Imposteur*.

7. Gris to D.-H. K., 19 April 1915, in *Letters*, ed. Cooper, p. 26.

8. ". . . des 'Huns' et des 'Vandales' qui ont, après les plus cruels massacres, incendié les plus beaux monuments, détruit tout ce que la science vénérait et tout ce dont l'art se glorifiait!" Baron H. Kervyn de Lettenhove, *La Guerre et les oeuvres d'art à Belgique* (Paris and Brussels, 1917), p. 178. This passage is dated 24 October 1916. Paul Fussell's *The Great War and Modern Memory* (New York and London, 1975), a study of the war's impact on English literature, has an interesting section on the symbolism of the destruction of the Cloth Hall at Ypres (pp. 40–41). The imagery of German barbarism was constantly invoked, as for example when René Viviani, President of the Council of Ministers and Minister of Foreign Affairs, declared in August 1914 that in her role of "emancipator" (a role bequeathed to the nation by Napoleon) France had an obligation to pursue the "barbarians." Quoted in A. Augustin Rey, *Les Grandes Pensées de la France à travers ses grandes hommes, 1914–1916* (Paris, 1916), I, p. 6.

9. Romain Rolland, *Au-dessus de la mêlée* (Paris, 1915); here in its English translation, *Above the Battle* (Chicago, 1916), pp. 24–25. Indeed, the bombing of Reims (publicized by French propaganda) was very damaging to the Germans in world opinion—so much so that the Germans felt they had to reply to the accusations of barbarism. Consequently, on 4 October there appeared in the German newspapers the "Aufruf an die Kulturwelt" (Call to the Civilized World), a proclamation of innocence signed by ninety-three leading German intellectuals. The document was probably aimed primarily at Italy and the United States, both of whom were still "neutral" nations in 1914 (although they would join the Allies in 1915 and 1917 respectively). It

appeared in France first in extracts in Charles Maurras's *Action Française* on 10 October, and three days later the full text was published
in French in *Le Temps* (followed on 16 October by a complete list of
the signatories, which included the architect Peter Behrens; the art
historian Wilhelm Bode; the painters Adolphe von Hildebrand, Max
Klinger, Max Liebermann, and Franz von Stuck; the composers En-
gelbert Humperdinck and Siegfried Wagner; the writer Frederik Nau-
mann; the theatrical director Max Reinhardt; and the physicist Max
Planck).

10. "Je veux vous parler de l'influence croissante et néfaste qu'avait
prise sur l'art français, pendant ces vingt dernières années, la corporation de marchands de tableaux.

"Je veux vous montrer par quels agissements ils étaient arrivés à
fausser le goût français; quelles influences ils ont mises en oeuvre
pour faire entrer dans nos grandes collections publiques des spéci-
mens d'un art dont ils avaient au préalable amplement garni leurs
offices, et comment ils ont imposés à l'admiration de nos snobs des
oeuvres empreintes de la culture allemande, pointillistes, cubistes,
futuristes, etc.

". . . Tout, musique, littérature, peinture, sculpture, architecture,
art décoratif, mode, tout subissait déjà l'influence délétère des gaz
asphyxiantes de nos ennemis." Tony Tollet, *De l'influence de la corporation judéo-allemande des marchands de tableaux de Paris sur l'art
français* (Lyon, 1915), pp. 6–7. (No publisher is named.) Tollet gave
another lecture, also published, on 28 March 1916 to the Académie
des Sciences, Belles-Lettres, et Arts de Lyon, entitled *Sur les origines
de notre art contemporain (Discours de Reception)*, which was also
anti-modernist and anti-Semitic (he blamed the entry of the Impressionists into the Louvre on the collection of the "*juif Camondo*"). He
was himself a champion of Baudry, Puvis de Chavannes, and Bouguereau among others.

11. For the confiscation of the Uhde and Kahnweiler stocks during the
war and the sale of the goods in the early 1920s, see Malcolm Gee,
*Dealers, Critics, and Collectors of Modern Painting: Aspects of the Pa-
risian Art Market Between 1910 and 1930* (New York, 1981), and the
same author's article "The Avant-Garde, Order and the Art Market,
1916–1923," *Art History* 2, no. 1 (March 1979), pp. 95–106.

12. The wartime attack on Cubism was a continuation of pre-war attacks that attempted to link modernism and the Germans, the only
difference being that before the war these attacks were relatively
harmless, whereas after August 1914 it was a serious charge indeed
to call Cubism an enemy style. For the anti-Cubist and anti-modernist
campaign before and during the war see Theda Shapiro, *Painters and
Politics: The European Avant-Garde and Society, 1900–1925* (New
York, 1976), and Elizabeth Kahn Baldewicz, "*Les Camoufleurs*: The
Mobilization of Art and the Artist in Wartime France, 1914–1918"

(Ph.D. dissertation, U.C.L.A., 1980), pp. 189–200. See also Ellen Oppler, "Fauvism Re-examined" (Ph.D. dissertation, Columbia University, 1969), for the pre-war political emplacement of the Parisian avant-garde, especially pp. 180–95, 215–22, 223–36, 249 and 250. Léka's series, like many other wartime images in this study, is in the collection of the Musée d'Histoire Contemporain (formerly the Museé des Deux-Guerres), Hôtel National des Invalides, in Paris. It was probably intended for publication, although whether it ever was published is open to conjecture. (Many of the images in this museum's collection were so intended, and when I am aware of their eventual publication I so indicate here.) Of the Kub affair, Gabriel Perreux writes: "Dès avant la déclaration de guerre, une foule en folie s'est ruée, pour les piller, sur les magasins ennemis ou réputés tels: les dépôts *Maggi*, accusés de vendre du lait empoisonné aux enfants, et leurs filiales, les *Bouillons Kub*, dont on dit que les panneaux-réclames servent de points de repère pour une avance éventuelle des troupes du Kaiser," *La Vie quotidienne*, p. 250. Although it is doubtful that the anti-Cubist commentators had ever looked long enough at the paintings to notice, it is nonetheless interesting that Picasso himself—as has long been realized—liked to pun on Kub-brand bouillon cubes and Cubism in his pre-war art, as for instance in a *Landscape with Posters* of 1912 (present location unknown), no. 501 in Pierre Daix and Joan Rosselet, *Picasso: The Cubist Years 1907–1916, A Catalogue Raisonné of the Paintings and Related Works* (Boston, 1979), p. 285.

13. ". . . cet art dont Glaize [sic], Metzinger, Apollinaire, Joccioni [sic] et hier Severini ont fixé les statuts avec la plus érudite malice, cet art pour être éclos chez nous, n'en est pas plus français." Aurel, *Le Commandement d'amour dans l'art après la guerre* (Geneva, c. 1917), p. 1 (the word *éclos* may be translated as simply "born" or, more figuratively, as "hatched"). Aurel mentions specifically "cubisme, futurisme, orphisme" as the modern artistic movements to which she is referring. She also makes use of another argument that in fact was a popular one, to wit, that even if the Germans didn't invent Cubism, the reason they imitated the French in their artistic waywardness was to encourage French cultural decline: "Quand je l'ai vu imité en Bochie, j'ai bien compris pourquoi. C'est qu'il nous contredit, c'est que l'Allemagne, en accentuant cet art nous aidait à tuer nos forces de droiture . . ." (p. 1).

14. "Le cubisme peut être considéré comme la dernière et indépassable conséquence de ce dévoiement total des directions naturelles du coloris et du dessin. Il n'est pas exact de dire que cette bizarre conception . . . soit d'origine d'allemande. Elle est espagnole et française, comme le futurisme est italien." Camille Mauclair, *L'Avenir de France* (Paris, 1918), pp. 519–20. Like so many others, Mauclair saw Cubism as only one part of a much larger picture of cultural deviation

that resulted from the defeat of 1870: "Nous avons durant un demi-siècle porté le poids d'une défaite. . . . C'est par là que nos curiosités passionnées du roman russe, de Wagner, de Nietzsche, d'Ibsen, ont été nuisibles après avoir été profitables" (p. 517).

15. For the history of the Franco-Prussian War and its aftermath see Jean Chaudordy, *La France à la suite de la guerre, 1870–71* (Paris, 1887); Jean Joughlin, *The Paris Commune in French Politics, 1871–80* (Baltimore, 1955); Roger Soltau, *French Parties and Politics, 1871–1921* (New York, 1965); David Thomson, *Democracy in France since 1870* (London and New York, 1964).

16. "C'est dans le plus beau pays du monde, . . . que naquit notre Marianne, un jour de grand orage. Fusils et canons faisaient rage, et, de l'Est, soufflait en tempête sur la capitale la rafale d'une injuste défaite. Or, tandis que hurlait le vent, l'enfant . . . eut la singulière fortune de devenir la souveraine d'un magnifique domaine . . ." Lucien Métivet, "Marianne et Germania, histoire d'un bonnet et d'un casque," with illustrations by Métivet, *La Baïonnette* 4, no. 146 (18 April 1918), p. 242 (the pagination is continuous for the year).

17. ". . . poèmes, problèmes, romans et pièces de théâtre, sévères, tendres ou folâtres, sciences, littérature: tout le répertoire des charmantes Soeurs." Ibid., p. 245.

18. For the Dreyfus Affair, see *Alfred Dreyfus, Five Years in My Life* (New York, 1901); Guy Chapman, *The Dreyfus Case: A Reassessment* (London, 1955); Georges Clemenceau, *La Honte* (Paris, 1903); Cecile Delhorbe, *L'Affaire Dreyfus et les écrivains français* (Neuchâtel, 1943); and Louis Snyder, *The Dreyfus Case: A Documentary History* (New Brunswick, 1973). For general French history of the period, political, cultural, and social, see Paul Gagnon, *France since 1789* (New York, 1964).

19. "Elle a reçu des amis,—des empereurs et des rois des pays chaud, des pays froid, venus de tout près ou des antipodes en habits, dorés, en bonnets pointus ou carrés, d'aucuns même coiffés de pagodes.

"Avec sa grâce coutumière, elle sait bien la manière de les distraire: défilés et cavalcades, et régalades, grandes eaux-ci et grands vins-là, dans les festins en tralala et, à l'Opéra, des galas—Faust—Roméo—Samson et Dalila! . . ." Métivet, "Marianne et Germania," p. 251.

20. Maurice Barrès, *The Undying Spirit of France* (New Haven, 1917), pp. 2–3.

21. "La France d'avant-guerre était bien près de penser d'elle-même ce qu'en pensait le monde. Elle se savait femme, femme de tête et de coeur, certes, mais femme tout de même, par son nervosisme, ses

abattements, ses colères brusques, ses périodes de faiblesses et l'injustice de ses verdicts." Henri Bornecque and Germain Drouilly, *La France et la Guerre: Formation de l'opinion publique pendant la guerre* (Paris, 1921), p. 13. Numerous other sources echoed this same opinion, as for instance: "Dans les années qui ont précédé 1914, nous avions, à l'étranger, une réputation de légèreté et d'immoralité. Cette réputation, c'étaient nos ennemies surtout qui travaillaient à la créer afin de discréditer la France dans le monde. Mais nous avions . . . une petite part de résponsabilité, nous complaisant un peu trop dans cette stupide habitude de chercher à nous dénigrer, à nous poser en esprits forts, amoureux de dillettantisme, d'éclectisme." Alexandre Gilbert-Rivière, *Les Forces matérielles et morales de la France* (Tours, 1922), p. 101. Also, "What was the opinion of France commonly held in 1914? That the race was wearied; the industries behind the times; the nation helplessly divided by political dissension." Information Bureau of the French High Commission, *What France Has Done in the War* (Washington, D.C., 1919), n.p.

22. "Germania la despotique reçoit aussi dans son palais, son palais gothique, ostrogothique, non des amis mais des valets. . . . Elle ne tend jamais la main,—le poing, toujours, dans un gant qui n'est pas de velours." Métivet, "Marianne et Germania," p. 251.

23. "Marianne jolie! prends garde!—ton bonnet à cocarde prend des façons de bonnet de folie! Voici qu'elle semble entraînée dans un vertigo fantastique: danses effrénées, robes inopinées, culottes d'odalisque, turbans de sultane—tête à l'envers et cheveux verts,—à croire qu'elle a perdu la tramontane." Ibid., p. 252.

24. "Avec sourires indulgents elle regarde se pâmer les gens devant les saugrenus travaux de cubistes, cucubistes, des ameublements 'art nouveau' dus à des ébénistes fumistes.

"Elle veut voir et voir encore danser de barbares ballets, dedans des tartouillades de décors coloriés à coup de balai, en carré, en losange, en rond, par des Sioux ou des Hurons." Ibid. Métivet was known for his parodies of Cubism before the war as well, in 1911–12; for this see Adam Gopnick, "High and Low: Caricature, Primitivism, and the Cubist Portrait," *Art Journal* 43, no. 4 (Winter 1983), p. 371.

25. The history of *Le Sacre du Printemps* has been told often, as for instance in Charles Spencer, *The World of Diaghilev* (Chicago, 1974), pp. 78–79. For the confusion between Left Bank Cubism and Right Bank Ballets Russes, see below, chapter III.

26. "Et elle ne rêve que musique d'une clique de pitres . . . d'amazones poussant des clameurs gutturales et hennissant comme cavales." Métivet, "Marianne et Germania," p. 252.

27. The German word *Kultur* (usually spelled "Kulture") was often invoked during the war, by the French, as a way of signifying the sectarian, "prussianized" culture of the Germans in comparison to

their own supposedly disinterested, universal *civilisation*. The French were apparently aware of the German term *Kulturkampf*, and they may have known that it was Bismarckian in origin. In fact, though, the term was narrower in meaning: when it was first used in the wake of the Franco-Prussian War to signify German anti-clericalism of the 1870s. See Erich Eyck, *Bismarck and the German Empire* (New York, 1964), pp. 202–10.

28. "Avec Wagner, il s'agit de tout autre chose: d'une glorification méthodique, systématique des annales légendaires germaniques. . . . Il fait, qu'on le veuille ou non, partie intégrante des intentions conquérantes et absorbantes de l'impérialisme allemand. . . ." (pp. 75–86); "Mais si je répète à mes compatriotes: 'adhésion à Wagner se paie cher,' c'est parce que, à mon sens, il dénationalise les Français à la façon d'un Kant, d'un Hégel ou d'un Schopenhauer" (p. 85); "Ces 'motifs' de Wagner sont des commandements militaires en langue allemande" (p. 91); ". . . mais il faut savoir aussi que les drames de Wagner sont une avant-garde et qui ne lache pas aisément ses positions une fois conquises" (p. 81). Léon Daudet, *Hors du joug allemand: Mesures d'après-guerre* (Paris, 1915).

29. "La France, avant la guerre, était envahie par les produits allemands; elle s'était mise à l'école de l'Allemagne. L'avenir de son industrie, les plus belles qualités de son génie national en étaient menacés, déjà compromis. . . ." (p. 1). "Nous nous sommes fait des 'âmes de vaincus,' nous avons abdiqué nos meilleures traditions nationales; nous avons considéré l'Allemagne comme la nation supérieure, comme la nation maîtresse. . . ." (p. 9). Edouard Driault, *Plus rien d'allemand* (Paris, 1918), p. 1.

30. Edith Wharton, *Fighting France: From Dunkerque to Belfort* (New York, 1915), p. 25.

31. "Elle sera héroïquement defendue par tous ses fils dont rien ne brisera devant l'ennemi l'union sacrée . . ." President Poincaré as cited in Anon., *La Journée du 4 Août* (from the series "Pages d'Histoire") (Paris, 1914), pp. 6–7.

32. "Socialistes, radicaux, progressistes, conservateurs, républicains, monarchistes, francs-maçons, cléricaux, blocards, nationalistes: voilà encore des 'mots diaboliques' qui ont été trop longtemps les uns contre les autres les fils de la même mère." G. Lacour-Gayet, "L'Union Sacrée," *L'Assistance Éducative* 10, no. 103 (June 1915), p. 111. David Thomson has said of Poincaré's *union sacrée*: "The Socialists agreed not to exploit the murder of Jaurès and the Right agreed not to conspire against the civil government of the Republic. It was an agreement 'not to shoot the pianist.' " *Democracy in France since 1870*, p. 1512. See also François Aubry de la Noë, *La France meilleure, l'Union Sacrée* (Dijon, 1916), and Julien de Nafron, *Que subsistera-t-il de l'Union Sacrée?* (Paris, 1916).

33. See Harvey Goldberg, *Jean Jaurès* (Madison, Wisconsin, 1968). Jaurès was killed by Raoul Villain, who may well have been provoked to action by an anti-war speech that Jaurès delivered on 25 July 1914. On 1 August Gris wrote to Kahnweiler: ". . . everyone is talking about the latest news—Jaurès's death and the attempt on [Joseph] Caillaux's life. Is there any truth in this? Is it really true that war is imminent? I just don't know what to do." *Letters*, ed. Cooper, p. 6.

34. Anatole France's letter read in full: "Monsieur le Ministre, Beaucoup de braves gens jugent que mon style ne vaut rien pendant la guerre. Comme ils peuvent avoir raison, je renonce à écrire et demande à changer ma plume contre un fusil. Je ne suis plus jeune, mais je me porte bien. Faites de moi un soldat." This letter is reproduced (in facsimile) in Jacques Suffel, *Anatole France: par lui-même* (Paris, 1954), p. 107.

35. The best book on Charles Maurras and *Action Française* is Eugen Weber, *Action Française: Royalism and Reaction in Twentieth-Century France* (Stanford, 1962), on which I have relied heavily. For a discussion of the paper's circulation figures, see p. 111; for a discussion of the "Kub" affair, in which Maurras played a role, see p. 94. More generally on the French Right see Weber's *The Nationalist Revival in France, 1905–1914* (Berkeley, 1959), as well as Jeffrey Bader, *The Nationalist Leagues in France after Dreyfus, 1896–1906* (New York, 1975); Maurice Barrès, *Scènes et doctrines du nationalisme* (Paris, 1925); Henry Contamine, *La Revanche, 1871–1914* (Paris, 1957); Charles S. Doty, *From Cultural Rebellion to Counterrevolution: The Politics of Maurice Barrès* (Athens, Ohio, 1976); David Shapiro, *The Right in France, 1890–1919* (London, 1962); Zeev Sternhell, *La Droite révolutionnarie 1885–1914: Les origines françaises du fascisme* (Paris, 1978); and René Rémond, *The Right Wing in France, from 1815 to De Gaulle* (Philadelphia, 1966).

36. "L'Allemagne a tout ignoré de l'âme française et elle subit, en ce jour, la châtiment de son erreur. Elle croyait trouver devant elle une nation dissociée et frivole." Rey, *Les Grandes Pensées*, I, p. 9.

37. "Depuis le commencement de la guerre, la France, par tous ses actes, dans les revers comme dans le succès, a donné démenti à ses ennemis. Elle a donné raison à ceux qui l'aimaient et qui croyaient en elle. Elle a déconcerté ses critiques et les a remplis d'étonnement. . . . C'est l'ancien héroïsme, l'ancienne vitalité qui s'affirment. Les journalistes étrangers bien informés, ceux dont tout l'horizon se borne aux cafés de boulevards, sont surpris par cette révélation soudaine d'ordre et de retenue, de dévouement et de sacrifice." Charles Saroléa, *Le Réveil de la France* (Paris, 1916), p. 71; also translated into English as *The French Renascence* (New York, 1916).

38. Barrès, *The Undying Spirit of France*, pp. 3–4.

39. "C'est fini. La France nouvelle aura conscience de sa force, non pour en abuser, mais pour n'être plus timide." André Beaunier, *Les Idées et les hommes* (Paris, 1915), II, p. 324. Beaunier's cultural stereotypes were very close to those of Barrès, especially as concerned France's supposed pre-war decadence: "La France, à la veille de la présente guerre, a bien de l'analogie avec cette aristocratie charmante qui, à la veille de la Révolution meurtrière, multiplia les gentillesses et fut exquise plus que jamais jusqu'au moment de mourir" (p. 323).

40. "Il était temps que la date guerrière et libératrice de 1914 mît une barrière à ce débordement. Un des plus beaux privilèges des armes est de restaurer les valeurs de tout genre, et principalement intellectuelles, antérieurement négligées ou reniées." Daudet, *Hors du joug allemand*, p. 16.

41. ". . . la guerre qui n'est pas que déstructrice, mais qui est aussi féconde . . ." Clément Janin, "Les Estampes et la Guerre," part 3, *Gazette des Beaux-Arts* 59 (1917), p. 508.

42. "Un champ immense, qu'encombrait la culture allemande, s'ouvre ainsi à notre activité intellectuelle, artistique et scientifique." Daudet, *Hors du joug allemand*, p. 128.

43. "La guerre a creusé au figuré mais puissamment, une tranchée entre nos idées et nos goûts d'hier et de demain. . . . Nous avons tous été jetés hors de nous-mêmes par une secousse inouie." Mauclair, *L'Avenir de France*, p. 512.

1. "Afin d'avoir quelques données au sujet de l'influence que la guerre pourra exercer sur l'art, *Sic* serait heureux que ses *lecteurs* mobilisés veuillent bien lui exposer leur idées sur cette question . . ." *Sic* no. 1 (January 1916), n.p.; "Pas besoin de cinq lignes, la guerre marquera le vrai départ d'une ère nouvelle. Victor R. . . . Corps d'A. Secteur . . ." Ibid. no. 3 (March 1916), n.p.; "La guerre, c'est comme une purge de cheval qui guérit quand elle ne tue pas. Louis B. . . . d'Infanterie . . . Cie . . ." Ibid.

2. "12 Mars 1916, Secteur 139, Gabriel Boissy: Bien sanglant de fatalité terrestre; cette guerre enracine nos sensations, nos sentiments, nos idées. Les unes et les autres reposeront sur des réalités, non plus sur des rêves, ni sur des souvenirs. Le sens de la limite et du relatif, père des arts, nous revient et nous écartons les chimères de l'absolu extra-humain, dont l'Allemagne meurt.

"Nous daterons de cette guerre, pivot d'histoire, au lieu de dater d'un passé trop lointain. *Elle mesure les hommes entre eux et d'elle surgit une nouvelle noblesse.* Ses nécessités violentes rétablissent la hiérarchie sapée. . . . Dépouillant leur âme de vaincus, les Français auront, ils ont déjà, une âme de maîtres, un esprit de créateurs; ils croient enfin en eux, sans attendre d'approbation rétrospective ou ex-

II   The Rewards of War

otique. Ils s'épanouiront désormais avec l'aisance impétueuse des peuples rajeunis ou plutôt épurés par le sacrifice." *Sic* no. 4 (April 1916), n.p.

3. "Le péril fait seul mesurer toute la beauté de ce qu'on possède." Camille Mauclair, *L'Avenir de France*, pp. 525–26.

4. Juan Gris to D.-H. Kahnweiler, 16 August 1914, in *Letters*, ed. Cooper, p. 26.

5. Ibid., p. 41.

6. "Mobilisé à Lisieux, Derain écrit à Vlaminck qu'il pense 'tout le temps' à 'cette bon dieu de peinture' mais, 'tout va être changé et on aura des idées plus simples.' " Derain to Vlaminck, in Cabanne, *Le Siècle de Picasso*, I, pp. 284–85.

7. Matisse to Hans Purrmann, dated 1 June 1916, in Alfred H. Barr, Jr., *Matisse: His Art and His Public* (New York, 1951), pp. 181–82. A variation of this is, as he wrote to Charles Camoin the next month (19 July 1916), "I may not be in the trenches, but I am in a front line of my own making." Cited in John Elderfield, *Matisse in the Collection of the Museum of Modern Art* (New York, 1978), p. 112.

8. " 'Derain, Braque, Camoin, Puy, sont au front, risquant leur peau. . . . Nous en avons assez de rester à l'arrière. . . . Comment pourrions-nous servir le pays?'

"Sembat n'eut qu'une réponse, très brève:

" 'En continuant, comme vous le faites, à bien peindre.' " Matisse to Marcel Sembat, quoted in Raymond Escholier, *Matisse ce vivant* (Paris, 1956), p. 112. Matisse's "nous" was an allusion to his friend, the painter Albert Marquet.

9. "Le Hun, le Hun stupide, à la peau sale et rance"; "Voyez-là cette étonnante nation, d'ordinaire si mobile, aujourd'hui si calme, dans sa sereine espérance. . . . La vie a recommencé partout. . . . tout le monde apporte une bonne volonté évidente, sous l'impulsion des pouvoirs publics, à établir en parallèle de notre force défensive la force morale, dont la source première est dans l'emploi normal de nos facultés. . . . Et voilà que les lettres et les arts, eux aussi, reprennent!" Clément Janin, introduction to catalogue *La Triennale, Exposition de l'art français* (Paris, 1916), p. 14.

10. "Ah! quelle revanche, si l'historien qui écrira sur la lutte gigantesque et la vaillance épique de notre peuple, trouvait, ici ou là, le chef-d'oeuvre éclos dans la tempête et acclamé de l'avenir!

"Quel triomphe, s'il pouvait s'écrier: 'Pendant que les barbares détruisaient les cathédrales de Reims, de Louvain, de Soissons, Les Halles d'Ypres, le Beffroi d'Arras, la France, sentant s'exalter son génie, réparait ses désastres. Elle rendait à l'Humanité ce que celle-ci avait perdu!'

"C'est pourquoi ce renouveau des préoccupations artistiques, quand la horde d'Atilla est à quatre-vingt-dix kilomètres de la Ville-Lumière, quand celle-ci est obligée de s'éteindre chaque soir, pour atténuer la gravité des attentats, a quelque chose de très noble. Il a aussi quelque chose de très touchant." Ibid., p. 17.

11. "Notre armée a dressé une si forte barrière devant l'ennemi en lui intimant: 'Tu n'iras pas plus loin' que le peintre, en confiance, a ressaisi ses pinceaux, le statuaire son ébauchoir, le graveur son burin, le céramiste son tour et son émail. Tous se sont mis à l'oeuvre, et, sans se désintéresser une seconde des tragédies qui se jouent communément dans les tranchées, vibrant d'accord avec des coeurs des héros, qui souvent sont leurs fils ou leurs frères, ils ont voulu participer selon leurs moyens, à la défense sacrée et à la Victoire." Ibid., p. 15.

12. "La reprise de notre vie intellectuelle en ce moment? Impossible! . . . Trop de sang, trop de râles. . . . Faisons la guerre! . . .

"Faire la guerre? . . . Comment? Chacun selon son métier.

"Je vous prie, depuis qu'il y a la guerre, est-ce que le médecin—non pas seulement celui qui soigne nos blessés, mais aussi le vieux médecin civil—cesse de guérir, le juge de juger, le maître d'enseigner, l'industriel et le commerçant de produire et de vendre? Pourquoi, seuls, l'écrivain et l'artiste seraient-ils contraints à faire grève? Par quel exclusif privilège leur serait-il interdit de travailler et de vivre quand, plus que tout autre, leur effort peut s'associer à la pensée patriotique, s'en inspirer et la propager, quand ils sont, eux aussi, des guérisseurs, des arbitres, des éveilleurs d'âmes, et de bons combattants, à leur façon?" Charles Morice, "Nécessité présente du travail intellectuel," *L'Homme Libre* (20 December 1917), p. 1.

13. "Dans la stupeur et désarroi des premières semaines de la grande guerre, les écrivains et les artistes ont d'abord ressenti douloureusement le sentiment de leur inutilité . . ." Mauclair, *L'Avenir de France*, p. 509.

14. "Là je travaille énormément toute la journée, et avec ardeur, je sais qu'il n'y a que ça, de bon et de sûr. Je ne puis faire de politique, comme hélas, presque tout le monde en fait, aussi pour compenser il faut des toiles fermes et sensibles. Métier de forçat que nous avons, sans les certitudes qui font dormir tranquille. Il faut chaque jour avoir peiné toute la journée pour d'accepter l'irresponsabilité qui met la conscience en repos. . . . Que dis-tu des évenements?" Matisse to Charles Camoin on 10 April 1918, in Danièle Giraudy, "Correspondance Henri Matisse—Charles Camoin," *Revue de l'Art* no. 12 (1971), p. 21.

15. The best discussion to date of *The Piano Lesson* is Theodore Reff, "Matisse: Meditations on a Statuette and a Goldfish," *Arts* 51, no. 3

(November 1976). See also the discussion in my M.A. thesis, "Classicism, Construction, and *La Grande Guerre*" (Yale University, 1975), pp. 47–48.

16. For the mutual influence of Gris and Matisse c. 1914–16, see Kenneth E. Silver, "Eminence Gris," *Art in America* 72, no. 5 (May 1984), pp. 152–61, as well as Silver, "Juan Gris y su arte en la gran guerra [1914–1918]," in Biblioteca Nacional (Salas Pablo Ruiz Picasso), *Juan Gris 1887–1927*, exhibition catalogue (Madrid 1985), pp. 45–52.

17. Cabanne, *Le Siècle de Picasso*, I, pp. 281 and 284.

18. The sketch was drawn on a letter dated 6 May 1915. Depicted is a *tricolore* waving in front of a sunset, over which is written "Vive la France." See the catalogue Grand Palais, *Picasso: Oeuvres reçues en paiement des droits de succession* (Paris, 1979–80), p. 66.

19. Most of the documents relating to Apollinaire's military service are reproduced in Pierre Cailler, ed., *Guillaume Apollinaire* (Geneva, 1965).

20. "Encore un autre effet de la guerre: la renaissance de l'image d'Epinal! . . . L'image vient donc de reparaître. Elle était 'dans l'air' depuis que M. Lucien Descaves avait prononcé son panégyrique en 1899." Clément Janin, "Les Estampes et la Guerre," part 3, pp. 483–84. See also Kenneth E. Silver, "Jean Cocteau and the *Image d'Epinal*: An Essay on Realism and Naiveté," in *Jean Cocteau and the French Scene*, ed. Arthur King Peters (New York, 1984), pp. 80–105.

21. See, for example, "Les Gardes du Corps du Roy" of 1774, in Jean Mistler et al., *Epinal et l'imagerie populaire* (Paris, 1961), p. 142.

22. Dufy to Simon Bussy, letter of 30 May 1916, describing his meeting with Michel Bréal of the propaganda office; the letter is cited in Pierre Schneider, *Matisse* (New York, 1984), p. 734. Amédée Ozenfant wrote: ". . . je travaillais à la Propagande, rue de Valois, où j'étais chargé de contribuer à éditer des publications illustrées comme . . . la série des Images de Guerre par Dufy . . ." *Mémoires 1886–1962* (Paris, 1968), p. 95. I am grateful to Susan Ball for this reference.

23. See Baldewicz, *"Les Camoufleurs."*

24. See, for example, La Fresnaye's program design (c. 1917) for his regiment's production of *Navarre sans peur! (Revue du 5ième Régiment d'Infanterie)*, reproduced in Germain Seligman, *Roger de la Fresnaye* (Greenwich, Ct., 1969), p. 104.

25. See Judith Zilczer, "In the Face of War: The Last Works of Raymond Duchamp-Villon," *Art Bulletin* 65, no. 1 (March 1983), pp. 138–44.

26. "La coiffure réalisée par Dunand, après de nombreux essais était, au contraire, d'acier au manganèse, emboutie d'une seule pièce. La loyauté de cette solution s'est, comme de juste, traduite dans le domaine de la forme: sobre, robuste et mâle, sous sa patine le casque de Dunand est un véritable oeuvre d'art. Quelques milliers d'exemplaires seulement avaient été fabriqués et mis en essai quand la signature de l'armistice vint rendre l'inventeur à des recherches plus pacifiques." Emile Sédeyn, "Jean Dunand," *Art et Décoration* 36 (1919), p. 126.

27. Gleizes received an honorable discharge in 1915 (whereupon he went to New York) thanks to a friendly government bureaucrat, Joseph Granié. See Daniel Robbins, "From Cubism to Abstract Art," *Baltimore Museum News* 25, no. 2 (1962), p. 15; and for Granié, Pierre Cabanne, *L'Epopée du Cubisme* (Paris, 1963), p. 88.

28. Like many other Cubists, Gris was eventually represented by Rosenberg, but out of loyalty to Kahnweiler he refused to deal with another dealer for several years. In a letter of 14 January 1915 he wrote to Kahnweiler, "M. Rosenberg came here with the idea of buying something. He was very discreet and did not insist when I told him that I considered myself bound to you by our agreements . . ." (*Letters*, ed. Cooper, p. 23). For the wartime perturbations in the Parisian art market, see Malcolm Gee, "The Avant-Garde, Order and the Art Market."

29. See Schneider, *Matisse*, p. 735, and Gino Severini, *La Vita di un pittore* (Milan, 1965), p. 206.

30. "Ah! Sauvegardons le trésor de la France. Qu'on n'abîme pas par hâte et par erreur toute une lente architecture; qu'on prenne garde de ne pas jeter le bon grain avec le mauvais grain. Déjà, des confusions se dessinent. On pousse dans le même sac la pacotille de Munich et des chefs-d'oeuvres de pure tradition française, et on reproche à des jeunes peintres l'influence berlinoise . . ." "Nous voudrions vous dire un mot," *Le Mot* no. 14 (13 March 1915), n.p.

31. "Wagner est indigeste MAIS génial. . . . "L'Art Munichois est atroce MAIS il ne faut pas le confondre avec un pur retour Français à la simplicité sublime. . . .

   "Je ne me laverai plus les dents avec l'Odol MAIS je ne me priverai ni de Schubert, ni de Bach, ni de Beethoven." "Soyons raisonables," *Le Mot* no. 15 (27 March 1915), n.p.

32. "La Grande Pitié des Victimes de France (à Maurice Barrès)," by Jean Cocteau, appeared in *Le Mot* no. 8 (30 January 1915). In part it read: "Péguy j'entends ta voix terreuse qui m'appelle!/. . . fantômes de Kant, de Beethoven, de Goethe,/Ne Leverez-vous pas une farouche émeute/Contre votre Empereur?" This in effect set Germany's great thinkers of the past *against* the contemporary "Boche."

33. "Avant la guerre, que de guerres! Que de tranchées! Que de mines! Que de malaises, de jeûnes, d'alliances, de provinces envahies, d'atrocités, de frontières qui bougent!" "Nous voudrions," n.p.

34. "Eclate la guerre; aussitôt un canon qui tonne et une cathédrale qui flambe révèlent à chacun son oreille et son oeil. Il entend! Il voit! Il est désabusé! Son amorphe se métamorphose en passion . . . l'évidence concrète du drame lui révélant l'intérêt relatif de vivre . . ." Ibid.

35. "Notre programme, c'est de faire un journal qui montre toujours le même visage, mais animé chaque semaine d'une différente expression . . ." "A notre Public," *Le Mot* no. 5 (9 January 1915), n.p.

36. "Entre le 'GOUT' et la 'VULGARITÉ,' l'un et l'autre fastidieux, il reste un élan et une mesure: LE Tact de COMPRENDRE JUSQU'OÙ ON PEUT ALLER TROP LOIN. Le *Mot* souhaite qu'on le suive sur ce chemin de France." Ibid.

37. "Le Mot demande à ses fidèles de le suivre, de le croire, d'avoir confiance en lui. Il souhaite devenir peu à peu l'organe de la bonne parole, de l'équilibre et de l'ordre intellectuel." "Nous voudrions," n.p.

38. "Espérons que l'après-guerre apportera la mort de l'isme. Cubisme fut commode pour un gros public . . . Cubisme fut commode et un peu simple, comme Impressionisme, à son âge . . . Prenons bien garde au GermanIsme." "Isme," *Le Mot* no. 18 (1 June 1915), n.p.

39. "Que suscitera-t-elle chez des musiciens comme Igor Stravinsky et Maurice Ravel, chez des peintres comme Albert Gleizes et Bonnard, chez des poètes comme la comtesse de Noailles et Paul Claudel, chez des conteurs comme Gide et Valéry-Larbaud?" "Pallas et les Muses," *Le Mot* no. 5 (9 January 1915), n.p.

40. "Métèques . . . un métèque ne peut aimer notre journal." *Le Mot* no. 7 (23 January 1915), n.p. In common parlance, "métèque" was a highly pejorative word for an alien, with a racial or ethnic slur implied.

41. "Le conflit actuel anarchise toutes les directions intellectuelles de l'avant-guerre, et les raisons en sont simples: les chefs sont aux armées, toute la génération de trente ans est éparse. . . . *Le Mot* veut, dès maintenant, vous préparer l'après-guerre. . . . *Le Mot* veille sur l'esprit de France, audacieusement créatif. Les Ecrivains et les Artistes, dont un jour tu revendiqueras l'honneur d'être de leur race, sont presque tous sur les lignes du feu. Néanmoins, rien n'aveugle leur conscience et leur amour. Le Passé est révolu. Il fut grand. Sachons ne pas le rendre odieux en abdiquant en lui. Nous lui resterons fidèles en allant avec courage le plus loin qu'il nous sera possible." Albert Gleizes, "C'est en allant se jeter à la mer que la fleuve reste fidèle à sa source," *Le Mot* no. 17 (1 May 1915), n.p.

42. "Charles Péguy, vous auriez vengé Reims! La Fresnaye, vous auriez, sur une seule de vos fraîches toiles, concentré l'héroisme inventif de notre jeunesse tricolore de la terre et du ciel." "Pallas et les Muses." The apology for this gaffe appeared in the next issue, no. 6, under the title "Une Bonne Nouvelle."

43. Seligman says of *Artillery* only that "it was painted at a time when Europe was already tense with political conflict and the Agadir incident had even brought open talk of war," and notes that the artist's brother was an artillery officer (Seligman, *La Fresnaye*, p. 32). Catherine Bock gave a lecture (which I did not have the opportunity to hear) specifically addressing the issues of La Fresnaye's pre-war militaristic paintings, "Cubism and Artistic Imperialism: De la Fresnaye's Military Themes, 1910–1913," at the College Art Association annual meeting in 1984, in Toronto.

44. Intended by Dufy as a patriotic demonstration of Allied fellow-feeling, it was misunderstood by some of *Le Mot*'s readers, who thought that it depicted the French and the English firing on each other. The editors set the record straight in issue no. 11 (20 February 1915) in the article "Un peu de détente, s'il vous plaît!"

45. "Voilà de l'excellente tradition d'Epinal tricolore . . ." Ibid.

46. See Ozenfant, *Mémoires*, pp. 31–36.

47. For the relationship of the word *élan* to the French military, see Barbara Tuchman, *The Guns of August* (New York, 1962), pp. 48–49 and 77. Also, see my discussion of Ozenfant's *L'Elan* in "Purism: Straightening Up After the Great War," *Artforum* 15, no. 7 (March 1977), pp. 56–63.

48. "*L'Elan* s'affirme ainsi la revue de l'avant-garde des recherches de l'Art et de l'Esprit—il accueille tout effort libre et témoigne que la guerre n'a pas ralenti en France l'élan de la pensée," *L'Elan* no. 8 (1 January 1916), p. 3.

49. "D'ailleurs, il nous semble que M. Léon Daudet avait fait cette remarque dans sa remarquable ouvrage *L'Avant-guerre*. N.D.L.R." "Une Enquête," *L'Elan* no. 5 (15 June 1915). The monkey's response to the question of what he thought of the war was to say that the new uniform of the French army, in which the *pantalon* was changed from the former bright red to the new "horizon blue," was something he had advocated for years. The parallel to Daudet is unmistakable—like the monkey he took credit for having advocated anti-modernist, xenophobic doctrines long before the outbreak of war, when they become popular.

50. Granié, "Aux camarades cubistes," *L'Elan* no. 8 (1 January 1916).

51. "Depuis Claude Lorrain, l'art français est souillé de germanisme." (Untitled), *L'Elan* no. 9 (February 1916).

52. "l'étranger croit peut-être qu'en France l'art appartient qu'à la Paix. Ceux qui se battent, nos amis, nous écrivent combien la guerre les a attachés d'avantage à leur art: ils aimeraient des pages où le réaliser.

"ce journal sera ces pages.

"l'étranger ne pourra qu'admirer cette élégante insouciance, cette fidélité à l'art.

"ce journal français, est aussi le journal de nos alliés et de nos amis. . . .

"il luttera contre l'Ennemi partout où il recontrera, fut-ce en France.

"entièrement désintéressé, il se rendra au prix coûtant, son seul but étant la propagande de l'art français, de l'indépendance française, en somme, du véritable esprit français." (Untitled), *L'Elan* no. 1 (15 April 1915), p. 2.

53. "C'est au cours de la guerre, pendant les loisirs de la tranchée, que Braque, Derain, de La Fresnaye, Léger, L.-A. Moreau, A.-D. de Segonzac, Allard, Apollinaire et tant d'autres s'obstinent—ô paradoxe!—à perpétrer ou prôner . . . LA PEINTURE BOCHE." "Aux camarades cubistes."

54. Although Ozenfant takes up an argument close to that offered by Janin in his introduction to the Triennale catalogue, Ozenfant's review of the exhibition, in *L'Elan* no. 9 (February 1916), p. 19, was as follows: "et maintenant parlons de la Triennale

La Triennale . . . .
La Triennale . . . .
La Triennale .Renoir . . . .
La Triennale . . . ."

55. "Le beau dessin . . . de notre collaborateur et ami A.-D. de Segonzac est une preuve ajouté à cette certitude que les Français, même hors de leur cadre et malgré la diversité constante d'une existence si nouvelle, peuvent conserver avec une insouciance vraiment PAISIBLE, la possession parfaite de tous leur moyens. . . . Devant la lucidité de ces lignes comment imaginer que l'auteur est lui-même un soldat, qu'il se bat et que la même main en des instants consécutifs, a commandé l'attaque et construit ce contour? . . . Admirons cette force qui est la force française." "A propos d'un dessin," *L'Elan* no. 8 (15 May 1915), p. 2 (with Segonzac's drawing of a *poilu* on the facing page 3).

56. For official censorship during the war, see Marcel Berger and Paul Allard, *Les Secrets de la Censure pendant la Guerre* (Paris, 1932).

57. "Pourquoi ces images sanglantes, ces cadavres, ces agonisants, sur chaque page des plus timides journaux? . . . Pauvres héroïques soldats, dure tâche de combattre! mais quand vous tombez, lamentables, ne serait-il pas décent qu'on se detournât? Agonie, le civilisé tire le rideau. On doit aimer la vie; oh, oui! admirons nos pauvres

frères soldats qui sacrificent la leur, mais voilons leurs cadavres et aussi ceux de nos ennemis." (Untitled), *L'Elan* no. 7 (15 December 1915), p. 1.

58. "Cézanne, autre géant, inaugura cette série d'efforts individuels . . . de technique rationnelle, dont le Cubisme qu'il pressentit, fut la plus ardente expression . . . "; ". . . malgré certain malaise de la surenchère, malaise produit par la hantise de la personnalité à tout prix et concluant parfois à la systématisation de techniques précaires et trop experimentales"; ". . . mais la suspension de ces luttes esthétiques, qui furent trop souvent des querelles d'atelier, incite aujourd'hui chaque conscience studieuse reposée des exagérations agressives d'hier, à une évaluation juste des procédés picturaux . . ."; "Profitons donc de ces tragiques vacances . . . pour tenter . . . une totalisation expressive des valeurs picturales. Avertis de l'insuffisance d'une méthode unique, ne nous cantonnons dans aucun parti-pris exclusif." André Lhote, "Totalisme," *L'Elan* no. 9 (February 1916), p. 3. See also Nathalie Reymond, "Le Rappel à l'ordre d'André Lhote," in Université de Saint-Etienne, *Le Retour à l'ordre dans les arts plastiques et l'architecture 1919–25* (Paris, 1975), pp. 209–24.

59. "L'Elan étant complètement indépendant, s'intéresse à toute recherche . . . Les opinions exprimées n'engagent que leur signataire. N.D.L.R." Editorial note at the end of Lhote, "Totalisme." Severini says that Ozenfant was already expressing anti-Cubist opinions in the midst of wartime (*Vita*, p. 205).

60. Aside from my dissertation of 1981, on which this book is based, Pierre Schneider is the first to discuss the Bohain series (*Matisse*, p. 735).

61. "Ce sont encore certaines oeuvres faites à l'occasion de la guerre, pour des oeuvres de guerre, mais ne représentant nullement des sujets de guerre. Elles sont incontestablement de notre domaine par leur inspiration, par leur destination, et par leur procédé. Telles les simples figures, dessinées d'un trait d'eau-forte, d'une pureté de contour qui fait tour à tour songer à des calques d'Ingres et à des dessins de M. Rodin, que M. Henri Matisse a tirées à quinze épreuves, au profit des prisonniers de Bohain-en-Vermandois. M. Henri Matisse dont il est souvent difficile d'accepter la formule d'abbréviation picturale, est, au contraire, dans ses eaux-fortes et dans ses croquis lithographiques, entièrement digne d'approbation, je dirai même d'admiration." Clément Janin, "Les Estampes et la Guerre," p. 382.

62. "Cette tendance arbitraire a été représentée de plus en plus, après le triomphe des grands impressionistes, par Cézanne et Gauguin et par les artistes issus d'eux, symbolistes, 'fauves,' et enfin cubistes et futuristes." Mauclair, *L'Avenir de France*, pp. 518–19.

63. For one commentator at least, portraiture was a concomitant of war. In the introduction to *Exposition des Cent Portraits* (L'Union In-

teralliée, Paris, 15 May–15 June 1922), André Dezarrois wrote: "Si suivant la légende antique, la main tremblante de la fille d'un pottier de Corinthe, voyant se détacher en ombre portée sur un mur le profil de son amant, le fixa de son mieux, créant ainsi le premier portrait, on pourrait remarquer qu'aux périodes des grandes guerres, les héros de tout genre qu'elle font naître, suscitent chaque fois une pléiade de portraitistes. L'on compte, paraît-il, plus de 2,000 portraits contemporains de Napoléon Ier. Combien, notre temps en laissera-t-il à la postérité?"

64. ". . . cet art non allemand comme on l'a dit, mais métèque et rasta par son côte sur-combiné. Il est tout le moins cosmopolite . . . l'art véritable est toujours terrien, même nationaliste, portant la trace de chaque terre, même les tics de chaque nation." Aurel, *Le Commandement d'amour*, p. 6.

65. ". . . nous avons appris depuis la guerre—pour ne le plus l'oublier—combien tout ce qui est la manifestation d'un art pour un pays est également le témoignage de sa force morale . . ." Francis Carco, preface to the exhibition catalogue *Arc-en-Ciel* (Galerie du Luxembourg, 5–29 December 1917).

66. "Il faut donc que l'art entre à son tour dans la bataille . . . attachions à voir en lui non le domaine des voluptés ou des tristesses éternelles, mais le programme d'une race et le résumé de ses instincts." Henri Focillon, *Technique et sentiment: Etudes sur l'art moderne* (Paris, 1919), p. 166.

67. "Revenons à nous-mêmes, à notre passé, à nos origines les plus lointaines, à tous les monuments de notre effort, à tout ce que nous avons donné d'intelligence et de vertu. L'histoire n'est pas un méditation aride, un recul dans le temps. C'est la mémoire des peuples. Elle ne détourne pas, elle exhorte, elle entraîne à l'action." Henri Focillon, *Les Evocations française: Les pierres de France* (Paris, 1919), p. ii of Introduction (dated "23 Mai 1918," and thus written in the midst of the last German offensive).

68. "Chaque pays . . . a son caractère propre. Il représente un ensemble distinct de qualités intellectuelles et morales, issues du sol, du climat, de la race, surtout de la culture et de l'histoire . . . la patrie, c'est, avec tout cela, une certine forme particulière de sentir, de penser, de vouloir, c'est une certaine manière de comprendre et d'exprimer le vrai . . ." Lucien Roure, *Patriotisme, impérialisme, militarisme* (Paris, 1915), p. 9. Roure was here paraphrasing Hippolyte Taine, who had written in his famous doctoral dissertation of 1853 ("Essai sur les fables de La Fontaine"): "A race is found which has received its character from the climate, the soil, the elements, and the great events which it underwent in its origin. . . . The more perfect the poet, the more national he is. The more he penetrates into his art, the more he has penetrated into the genius of his age and his

race." Quoted in S. J. Kahn, *Science and Aesthetic Judgement: A Study in Taine* (Weston, Ct., 1953).

69. Picasso's *The Painter and His Model* only came to light in the exhibition *Picasso: Oeuvres reçues en paiement des droits de succession* (Grand Palais, 11 October 1979–7 January 1980). I know of no reference to the work whatsoever before that point.

70. The drawing is reproduced in Denys Sutton and Paolo Lecaldano, *The Complete Paintings of Picasso Blue and Rose Periods* (New York, 1968), cat. no. 89A, according to which the present location of the study is unknown.

71. For other works in the series see Zervos II, part 2, 507, 858; VI, 1189–1191, 1194–1201, 1204–1216, 1218, 1223, 1227–1229, 1232, 1233, 1243. There is also a small oil on panel "Head of a Young Man," in the Cézanne mode, from 1915. In Daix and Rosselet, *Picasso: The Cubist Years*, cat. no. 813.

72. Albert Gleizes and Jean Metzinger, *Du Cubisme* (1912), trans. in Robert L. Herbert, ed., *Modern Artists on Art* (Englewood Cliffs, N.J., 1964), pp. 2–3.

73. Daix and Rosselet write of "The unfinished state, with some parts already painted . . . there is good reason to believe that it was the war which interrupted this impetus, this return to natural forms which Picasso was to resume only when he began working on *Parade*." *Picasso: The Cubist Years*, cat. no. 763. The authors do not give their reasons for believing that the war interrupted work on the picture, rather than provoking it. Yet their (and the traditional) reason for assuming that Picasso's return to naturalism pre-dated the mobilization is based on a statement that Kahnweiler made to Francis Crémieux: "in the spring of 1914, Picasso showed me two drawings that were not Cubist, but classicist, two drawings of a seated man. . . . This proves that this idea must already have been germinating in him then, but it had not reached the stage of painting" (Kahnweiler, *My Galleries and Painters*, p. 54). This does not mean, of course, that *The Painter and His Model*, or even the idea for the painting, pre-dates the mobilization, but only that—if the statement is accurate—the idea for the seated man (the "painter") pre-dates the start of war, and even perhaps that a general return to naturalistic appearances, by way first of Cézanne, may be an idea that pre-dates the war.

74. Robert Rosenblum suggested to me, in March 1986, that if (as is assumed) it is a portrait of Marcelle Humbert, who was to die of tuberculosis in the following years, Picasso may have preserved it as a *memento mori*.

75. ". . . et enfin à celui que nous choyons plus que tous les autres et qui, heureusement, ne court point de risques, s'élargit chaque jour, tout en se précisant, et vient, par des crayons qui font penser à Ingres,

de le dépasser en se jouant." *Correspondance de Guillaume Apolli-naire*, I: *Guillaume Apollinaire—André Level* (Paris, 1976), p. 10.

76. "Après la secousse formidable d'une guerre quasi-universelle, il est certain qu'il naîtra, d'efforts nouveaux et d'épreuves passées, des formes, des idées et des aspirations inédites.

"Ainsi le veut la marche de l'avenir. Sans comparer aussi rigou-reusement que le font certains retardataires le passé au présent, on peut rappeler qu'après 1870 ce fut un ensemble de tendances nou-velles qui succéda aux traditions trop figées du second Empire.

"Mais où l'on risquerait de se tromper, c'est de conclure à un mouvement rigoureusement calqué sur celui-là, et de considérer que l'art ira encore 'plus loin,' si l'on peut parler ainsi, sur les routes où, avant la guerre, il croyait s'avancer.

"En réalité, si les choses procédaient de façon absolue par actions et réactions, flux et reflux . . . après ces sortes de grandes secousses on voyait . . . ce qui se produirait après la guerre de 1914 serait diamétralement différent de ce qui s'est passé après celle de 1870.

"Ce serait une réaction ou une renaissance, comme on voudra, de tendances classiques contres celles de liberté à outrance. On se re-mettrait à chercher la forme, la ligne, aussi passionnément qu'on cherchait la déformation entre 1900 et 1913, et on ferait aussi peu de cas de l'arabesques et des rapprochements exaspérés de tons plats qu'on faisait consister dans ces recherches un peu simplificatrices, pour ne pas dire un peu simplistes, la fin du fin." Jacques Vernay, "La Triennale, exposition d'art français," *Les Arts* no. 154 (April 1916), pp. 25–26. It is interesting that Vernay's idea of pre-war artis-tic extremism is based not on his views of Cubism, but rather on an art that seems, with its "arabesques" and "*rapprochements* of flat tones," to be akin to that of Matisse.

III *Comme il faut*

1. "La Tradition Française: c'est briser les entraves
"La Tradition Française: c'est tout voir et tout comprendre
"La Tradition Française: c'est chercher, découvrir, créer . . . Donc, la tradition française C'EST NIER LA TRADITION. Suivons la tradition." "Tradition/Mort, France/Vie," *Sic* no. 4 (April 1916), n.p.

2. Christopher Green, *Léger and the Avant-Garde* (New Haven and London, 1976), pp. 120–21.

3. Gleizes's *Le Retour* was probably inspired by Jacques Villon's *Sol-diers on the March*, 1913 (Galerie Louis Carré, Paris).

4. This is a quotation from Elizabeth Kahn Baldewicz's lecture "Mak-ing Art at the Front," delivered at the symposium "Art in Time of Crisis," Department of Art History, U.C.L.A., May 1978. Generally, see Baldewicz, "*Les Camoufleurs*," chapter IV.

5. Raymond Duchamp-Villon to John Quinn, from a translation of a

lost letter, from the New York Public Library, published in Knoedler & Co., *Raymond Duchamp-Villon 1876–1918*, ed. George Heard Hamilton and William C. Agee (New York, 1967), p. 119.

6. Baldewicz, "*Les Camoufleurs*," chapter v.

7. Severini, *Vita*, p. 193. The full title of the exhibition was "Gino Severini: Ire Exposition Futuriste d'Art plastique de la Guerre et d'autres oeuvres antérieures."

8. Severini, *Vita*, pp. 213, 216.

9. ". . . e poi cominciava una serie di critiche e di reserve di alcuni di essi, ch'egli diceva 'portati ad adottare un'attitudine astrusa, e sdegnosa del pubblico, e a giudicarlo imbecille.' In conclusione, pur risparmiando Picasso e Braque, lanciava anatemi a destra e a sinistra senza precisare, contro quei cubisti che, quei cubisti come, ecc. ecc. . . ." Ibid., p. 207.

10. "Più conoscevo Matisse, e più ne apprezzavo il valore come pittore e come uomo. Era allora all'inizio dei suoi grandi successi, già in piena maturità artistica e maturità di pensiero." Ibid., p. 206.

11. Ibid., pp. 216–17. In the end, the French government would not allow the paintings to leave the country. But things started to get a bit better for Severini at this point: Diaghilev came to visit his studio and bought four works for Massine; Picasso brought his Chilean patron, Eugenia Errazuriz, who bought work from Severini too.

12. Severini showed a drawing titled *Portrait de ma femme et de ma fille* (no. 23) in his Boutet de Monvel exhibition. See Joan M. Lukach, "Severini's 1917 Exhibition at Stieglitz's *291*," *Burlington* 93, no. 817 (April 1971), pp. 196–207.

13. See Susan L. Ball, *Ozenfant and Purism: The Evolution of a Style 1915–1930* (Ann Arbor, Michigan, 1981), pp. 22–24.

14. Severini, *Vita*, p. 199: "I cubisti, soprattutto Metzinger, ne furono irritatissimi; altri invece, fra gli artisti e critici, ne furono interessati . . ."

15. "Mais la vie de la littérature continue et un instinct très sûr la guide dans son évolution! A une période d'exubérance et de force doit succéder une période d'organisation, de classement, de science, c'est-à-dire un âge classique." Paul Dermée, "Quand le Symbolisme fut mort," *Nord-Sud* 1, no. 1 (15 March 1917), p. 3.

16. "—Je ne savais pas, Gretchen, que nos troupes avaient passé par Rome . . .
    "—Mais, Fritz, elles n'y ont pas passé . . .
    "—Alors, qui a commencé leur ouvrage?" "Devant les Ruines du Colisée," illustration by Quesnel, cover of *Le Pêle-Mêle* 21, no. 46 (14 November 1915).

17. "Nous ne prétendons pas suffire à nous-mêmes. Nous sommes les disciples de l'antiquité, d'où vient notre langue directement. Le meilleur de 'l'humanité' ancienne a passé en nous." Ernest Lavisse, *France = Humanité* (Paris, n.d. [after July 1917]), p. 20. See also Pierre Nora's article "Lavisse, instituteur national," in *Les Lieux de mémoire*, I: *La République*, ed., P. Nora (Paris, 1984), pp. 247–89.

18. ". . . cette langue française si sublime par se clarté, sa limpidité, sa loyauté, proclamant la foi invincible de la race dans ses destinées." Rey, *Les Grandes Pensées*, II, p. 3. "Sa pensée imagée, nerveuse, incisive, la beauté classique de l'expression, s'unissent étroitement à une adaptation merveilleuse des exigences de l'heure présente." Ibid.

19. "On a défini la Renaissance: 'd'un nouveau qui n'est pas neuf'; elle resuscitait un passé magnifique, l'antiquité. La nouveauté qu'annoncent ces deux mots d'une 'France Nouvelle' n'est pas neuve non plus. . . . Une tradition très ancienne se renoue. . . . nous remet sur la belle et bonne voie, large et bien éclairée par le soleil de France." André Beaunier, *Les Idées et les hommes*, II, p. 317.

20. "J'essaie de définir ce que je vois: du fond des siècles je vois une perpétuelle marche des populations d'Outre-Rhin pardessus le fleuve vers des régions plus douces. . . . Nous devons nous protéger par des bastions à l'est de France. Ces bastions, ce sont des fortifications, et plus encore, s'il est possible, des peuples organisés pour filtrer à travers leurs sympathies françaises et latines les éléments germaniques." Maurice Barrès interviewed by Frédéric Lefèvre, "Une Heure avec M. Maurice Barrès," *Les Nouvelles Littéraires* 2, no. 26 (14 April 1923), p. 2.

21. Gabriele d'Annunzio, "Ode to the Latin Resurrection," quoted in Philippe Jullian, *D'Annunzio* (New York, 1973), pp. 252–53.

22. "Saluons avec tendresse un peuple qui pouvait dormir sur les palmes et sous les oliviers du Latium et qui, une touffe des plumes de notre coq sur l'oreille, nous épouse, . . . —Saluons, au seuil d'un enfer sacré, la rencontre du Dante et de Marianne." [Jean Cocteau and Paul Iribe], "Saluons l'Italie," *Le Mot* no. 19 (15 June 1915), n.p.

23. "Si la pensée française procède de la tradition dite classique, elle est également héritière de la tradition chrétienne. Celle-ci ne contredit nullement la tradition classique" (p. 9); "L'idée française de la liberté n'est pas une invention moderne, c'est le fruit de la double tradition gréco-romaine et chrétienne" (p. 7). Emile Boutroux, *L'Idée de Liberté en France et en Allemagne* (Paris, n.d. [c. 1915–18]). (On Boutroux, see also chapter IV, n. 48, below.)

24. All cited in Jean Vic, *La Littérature de guerre*, 5 vols. (Paris, 1918–23), the most extensive bibliography—although far from complete—of wartime literature (most remarkably, it was compiled while the war was still going on).

25. "L'Amphitrite britannique, qui se moque du Kaiser, de ses mines et ses zeppelins, prend le pauvre pêcheur sous sa protection."

26. The legend reads: "Ça, la victoire! Ben, mon colon, qu'est-ce que l'autre a dû prendre pour son rhume?" A slightly different version of this cartoon appeared in *Le Pêle-Mêle* on 14 November 1915, p. 11. Here two Germans, one a civilian and one a soldier, peruse a statue and make the following comments: "—Hoch!. . . hoch!. . . kolossal! . . . superbe!. . . ." "—Tiens! Vous êtes donc connaisseur? . . ."

"—Ya! Connaisseur! . . . C'est du vrai bronze! . . . Envoyer à la fonte! . . ."

If the form is like Reb's cartoon, the meaning is identical with that of Quesnel's image of Fritz and Gretchen before the Colosseum.

27. ". . . l'art français si pur, si sobre, si classique, se laissait envahir par le mauvais goût allemand . . ." Driault, *Plus rien d'allemand*, p. 10. "Nous avons enfin compris que l'Allemagne menait la guerre contre toute la civilisation latine . . ." Ibid., pp. 16–17.

28. "Toute notre activité artistique devra être un retour de passion pour notre mère. Nous redeviendrons par cet amour que l'angoisse exaspéra, des classiques, des fervents de la cathédrale, du village, du site, du ciel, les chérissant d'avantage pour les avoir défendus, en ayant mesuré tout le prix, ne les confondant avec rien d'autre, ne rêvant que les mieux vénérer. Les époques où refleurit une tradition classique ne sont pas faites d'autre chose que de ce sentiment simple et sain." Mauclair, *L'Avenir de France*, p. 525.

29. "Voilà ce que je pense:—Nous ferons bien d'abandonner toutes les chimères provenant d'un cerveau malade et de retourner à la véritable tradition ancienne, vieille de tant de siècles, au lieu de faire des choses sans valeur.

"Depuis quelque temps les villes de l'Europe sont abîmées par cette barbarie.

"Nous n'avons pas besoin de l'influence allemande, mais de celle de nos belles traditions classiques." Auguste Rodin, as quoted in "De l'art français et des influences qu'il ne doit pas subir," *La Renaissance* 5, no. 19 (15 September 1917), pp. 17–18 (pp. 2955–56 in series).

30. "De quel ton parler des magnificences ou des beautés dont le génie a pu doter des ennemis? A travers ces images même, une Allemagne obsédante apparaît. La pensée gréco-romaine, la pensée française classique s'adressent à la raison universelle, à l'homme de partout et de toujours. . . . L'art de l'Allemagne moderne repose sur l'homme allemand, sur la raison allemande, sur la nature allemande"; "Jamais l'on n'a été plus éloigné de l'esprit de la Renaissance, des formes classiques de la pensée, de la méthode gréco-latine—inventée, non pour la tribu, mais pour l'humanité tout entière." Focillon, *Technique et sentiment*, pp. 167, 175.

31. "Le devoir des Français a une supériorité sur tous les autres patriotismes: c'est que la France à toutes les époques de son histoire ne s'est jamais désintéressée des destins de l'humanité. Si bien que le devoir des Français se confond avec la grande tradition humaine." Guillaume Apollinaire, "La Guerre et nous autres," *Nord-Sud* 1, no. 9 (October 1917), p. 10.

32. "Sans doute, il est utile de percer à jour l'erreur des néoclassiques qui veulent un appauvrissement de notre lyrisme et de notre langue en nous donnant comme modèle notre XVIIᵉ siècle!" Dermée, "Quand le Symbolisme fut mort," p. 3.

33. "Ils prétendent que le vers classique est nécessaire au classicisme. Certains croient même que le classicisme est un idéal auquel nous n'atteindrons pas si nous ne possédons un roi . . ." Ibid., p. 3.

34. Again, I have relied on Eugen Weber's *Action Française* for basic information on Maurras.

35. ". . . les jeunes Français devront devenir aux humanités, à cette formation latine notamment, que rien ne remplace . . ." Daudet, *Hors du joug allemand*, p. 121. The classical revival in French literature of the pre-war years is discussed in Henri Peyre, *Le Classicisme français* (New York, 1942), pp. 211–20. On the pre-war cultural conservatism of French youth, see also Robert Wohl, *The Generation of 1914* (Cambridge, Mass., 1979), chapter 1.

36. "L'étalon fougueux de les passions est solidement bridé. On le tient de court. . . . La maîtrise de soi-même est l'idéal moral et esthétique des époques classiques." Paul Dermée, "Un Prochain Age classique," *Nord-Sud* 2, no. 11 (January 1918), p. 3.

37. "En art le progrès ne consiste pas dans l'extension mais dans la connaissance de ses limites." "J'aime le règle qui corrige l'émotion." Georges Braque, "Pensées et réflexions sur la peinture," *Nord-Sud* 2, no. 10 (December 1917), pp. 3, 5.

"Les sens déforment, l'esprit forme. Travailler pour perfectionner l'esprit. Il n'y a de certitude que dans ce que l'esprit conçoit." Ibid., p. 4.

38. Georges Braque, "Personal Statement," *Architectural Record* (May 1910), p. 405, quoted in Edward F. Fry, ed., *Cubism* (London and New York, 1966), p. 53.

39. "Le style pré-classique est un style de rupture; le style classique est un style de développement," cited (without source or date) by Phoebe Pool, "Picasso's Neo-Classicism: Second Period, 1917–1925," *Apollo* 85, no. 61 (March 1967), p. 198. It is included in the Braque "notebook" (no. 28), although no date for the specific citation is given: see *Cahier de Georges Braque, 1914–1947*, published jointly by Curt Valentin and Galerie Maeght (New York, 1948).

40. A French non-combatant certainly would be even worse off than a non-combatant foreigner. It may be for this reason that we find so many wartime excursions overseas by French civilians in the Parisian avant-garde: Marcel Duchamp to New York in 1915; Albert Gleizes, after being honorably discharged from the army, to New York the same year; and Robert Delaunay to the Iberian peninsula for the duration.

41. Quoted in Steegmuller, *Cocteau*, p. 149, based on a recording of his recollections made much later (date unspecified).

42. "Dès la mobilisation, nous avons assisté à un splendide sursaut national. Instantanément, les partis oubliaient leur querelle. Plus de politique; au lieu de politicaillerie, cette volonté unanime: sauver la France." Beaunier, *Les Idées et les hommes*, II, p. 328.

43. *Thomas l'Imposteur*, written in 1918, was published in 1923.

44. Quoted in Steegmuller, *Cocteau*, p. 147.

45. See my discussion in "Jean Cocteau and the *Image d'Epinal*."

46. For *Parade*, see: Richard Axsom, *"Parade": Cubism as Theater* (New York, 1979); Douglas Cooper, *Picasso Theater* (New York, 1968); Marianne Martin, "The Ballet *Parade*: A Dialogue between Cubism and Futurism," *Art Quarterly*, n.s., 1, no. 2 (Spring 1978).

47. This is the scenario as provided by Cocteau on the original piano score by Satie:

"Parade. Ballet réaliste.
"Le décor représente les maisons à Paris un Dimanche.
"Théâtre forain. Trois numéros de Music-Hall servent de Parade.
    Prestidigitateur chinois.
    Acrobates.
    Petite fille américaine.
"Trois managers organisent la réclame. Ils se communiquent dans leur langage terrible que la foule prend la parade pour le spectacle intérieur et cherchent grossièrement à le lui faire comprendre.
    "Personne n'entre.
"Après le dernier numéro de la parade, les managers exténués s'écroulent les uns sur les autres.
    "Le chinois, les acrobates et la petite fille sortent du théâtre vide. Voyant l'effort suprême et la chute des managers, ils essayent d'expliquer à leur tour que le spectacle se donne à l'intérieur."

48. ". . . reserver ces arts révolutionnaires à la Russie Rouge, si toutefois elle s'en accommode." Quoted in Cabanne, *Le Siècle de Picasso*, I, p. 309.

49. Martin, unconvincingly I think, suggests that the company depicted on the overture curtain consists of specific portrayals: ". . . Massine, the harlequin with his back to the audience, Cocteau as

Pierrot and a sleepy Columbine, perhaps the dancer Marie Shebelska
. . . The lovely auburn-haired girl wearing a large straw hat has some
features of Olga Koklova, Picasso's future wife . . ." "The Ballet *Parade*," p. 103.

50. I first mentioned this source in "Jean Cocteau and the *Image d'E-
pinal*," p. 89.

51. Axsom discusses the color scheme but not its significance, as
noted by Linda Nochlin in her article "Picasso's Color: Schemes and
Gambits," *Art in America* 68, no. 10 (December 1980), p. 115.

52. See my discussion in "Jean Cocteau and the *Image d'Epinal*."

53. ". . . qui ne manquera pas de séduire l'élite, et se promet de
modifier de fond en comble les arts et les moeurs dans l'allégresse
universelle." Quoted in Cabanne, *Le Siècle de Picasso*, I, p. 308.

54. *Nord-Sud* nos. 4/5 (June–July 1917), p. 9.

55. "Il faut bien que ceux qui sont de votre avis vous aident. . . .
Vous pouvez toujours correspondre avec moi par la voie du journal
sous le vocable *trépané*," quoted in Weber, *Action Française*, p. 111,
note 8.

56. This is mentioned by Gilbert Guilleminault, *La France de la Madelon* (Paris, 1965), p. 214.

57. "L'Esprit nouveau qui s'annonce prétend avant tout hériter des
classiques un solide bon sens, un esprit critique assuré, des vues
d'ensemble sur l'univers et dans l'âme humaine, et le sens du devoir
qui dépouille les sentiments et en limite ou plutôt en contient les manifestations." "L'Esprit nouveau et les poètes" (1917), *Oeuvres com-
plètes de Guillaume Apollinaire*, ed. Michel Décaudin (Paris, 1966),
III, p. 900.

58. Ibid.

59. "[Ils] parlent aujourd'hui d'un 'esprit nouveau,' d'une dramatique
transformation du caractère français. . . . Mais cette explication est
. . . superficielle. . . . Ce que nous observons aujourd'hui en France
n'est pas nouveau, mais c'est une chose très ancienne et très fami-
lière." Charles Saroléa, *Le Réveil de la France*, p. 71. In fact, the
term *l'esprit nouveau* has an interesting and significant history in the
late nineteenth century. According to Debora L. Silverman, "Eugene
Spuller, Gambetta's close collaborator through the early 1880s, formulated the theory of the "*esprit nouveau*" in 1894, as Minister of
Public Instruction and Beaux-Arts under Prime Minister Casimir-Pe-
rier;" and this was the "practical extension" of the *ralliement*, the new
center-and-right coalition to combat the rise of socialism. See Silverman, "Nature, Nobility, and Neurology: The Ideological Origins of Art

Nouveau in France, 1889–1900" (Ph.D. dissertation, Princeton, 1983).

60. Published in *L'Excelsior* the same day as *Parade*'s première (18 May 1917), and quoted in Steegmuller, *Cocteau*, p. 183.

61. "Tout le mérite de cette 'création'—si mérite il y a—revient sans que cela puisse être contesté à Pablo Picasso et Georges Braque. Ce sont les véritables 'créateurs' d'une école qui pourrait être qualifiée par conséquent de franco-espagnole ou plus simplement de latine.

"Il est vrai que depuis la guerre elle s'est étendue au point qu'il s'en faudrait de peu qu'on put l'appéler cosmopolite si sa latinité ne s'était encore une fois affirmée par l'absorption importante qu'elle a faite du futurisme italien. Il est juste par conséquent qu'on appelle latine une école dont les principaux adeptes sont français, espagnols et italiens. De toute façon, elle est née sur le sol français et les artistes qui la composent travaillent à Paris, ce qui fait le qualificatif de 'parisienne' ne lui irait pas mal." Guillaume Apollinaire, letter to the *Mercure de France*, 22 September 1917 (published in the magazine on 16 October).

62. See the "*Cahier roman*" in Axsom, "*Parade*" pp. 340 and 363. Axsom rightly points out (ibid., pp. 36–37) that Cocteau's street theatre is specifically of the Parisian—not the provincial—type.

63. There is, for example, a *Loterie Alphabetique des Cris de Paris*, no. 178, in the collection of the Musée Carnavalet, Paris, where under the letter "Y" one again finds a Chinese porcelain vendor looking much like Picasso's Chinese Magician, wearing a red and yellow tunic and with a long pigtail down the back of the head. Reproduced in Massin, *Les Cris de la Ville* (Paris, 1978), p. 154.

64. Quoted in Steegmuller, *Cocteau*, p. 138.

65. Cocteau discusses the post-history of *Parade* in "Scandales," *New Criterion* 4, no. 1 (January 1926), pp. 131–32.

66. Quoted in William Rubin, *Picasso in the Collection of the Museum of Modern Art* (New York, 1972), p. 98. After 1905, Picasso ceased to depict the *commedia dell'arte* themes that had hitherto been so prominent in his art. Aside from four depictions of Harlequin in 1909, this is the first time he returned to the theme.

67. Rubin has offered this interpretation, Ibid.

68. Willette's Pierrot sings: "Ohé! là-haut! Les zeppelins de K.K. . . . Oh! . . . Ça, ça t'mange à Berlin, n'empestez plus les anges, par le grand Merlin! Sachez qu'on ne craint pas les croquignolles aux Batignolles!"

69. It is interesting to note that Cocteau was not at this point a fan of

Harlequin. On p. 7 of *Le Coq et l'Arlequin* he writes: "Vive le Coq! à bas l'Arlequin," for he considered the Coq virile and pure, and Harlequin "eclectic," i.e. impure, in part because of his motley costume.

70. "Le Tact dans l'audace, c'est de savoir jusqu'où on peut aller trop loin." Ibid., p. 11.

71. "Il faut s'entendre sur le malentendu de 'l'influence allemande.' La France, insouciante, avait ses poches remplies de graines et en laissait tomber autour d'elle; l'allemand ramassait les graines, les emportait en Allemagne, les plantait dans un terrain chimique d'où poussait un monstre fleur sans odeur." Ibid., p. 24.

72. "Debussy a devié, parce que de l'embûche allemande, il est tombé dans le piège russe. . . . Quand je dis 'le piège russe,' 'l'influence russe,' je ne veux pas dire par là que je dédaigne la musique russe. La musique russe est admirable parce qu'elle est la musique russe. La musique française russe ou la musique française allemande est forcément bâtarde, même si elle s'inspire d'un Moussorgsky, d'un Stravinsky, d'un Wagner, d'un Schoenberg." Ibid., p. 69.

73. "Je demande une musique française de France" (Ibid., p. 29); "L'impressionisme est un contre-coup de Wagner, les derniers recoulements de l'orage. L'école impressioniste substitue le soleil à la lumière et la sonorité au rythme" (p. 52); "Notre musique doit être construite à mesure d'homme" (p. 32); "On ne peut pas se perdre dans la brouillard Debussy comme dans la brume Wagner, mais on y attrape du mal" (p. 53); "Le jeu latin se joue sans mettre les pédales; le romantisme enfonce les pédales. Pédale Wagner; Debussy pédale" (p. 53).

74. "Travailler avec trois couleurs, trop de couleurs font de l'impressionisme." Quoted in Axsom, *"Parade,"* p. 333, where Cocteau's notebook from Rome is reproduced in its entirety.

75. A similar image was found and reproduced by Giovanni Carandente in the exhibition catalogue Centro di Cultura di Palazzo Grassi, *Picasso: Opere dal 1895 al 1971 dalla Collezione Marina Picasso* (Venice, 1981), p. 49.

76. The sexual connotation of slimy fish was of long standing in Picasso's oeuvre. See for example *The Mackerel*, c. 1902 (Museo Picasso, Barcelona).

77. "Voici donc un Espagnol, pourvu des plus vieilles recettes françaises (Chardin, Poussin, Lenain, Corot) . . ." (p. 11); "Je n'insiste pas sur l'Espagne, Picasso est de chez nous. Il a mis toutes les forces, toutes les ruses de sa race à l'école et au service de la France" (p. 11, footnote). Jean Cocteau, *Picasso* (Paris, 1923).

78. See the catalogue of Picasso drawings, Galerie Berggruen, *Pablo Picasso: Pour Eugenia* (Paris, 1976), with preface and commentary by Douglas Cooper.

79. "C'était un temps béni nous étions sur les plages / Va-t-en de bon matin pieds nus et sans chapeau / Et vite comme va la langue d'un crapaud / L'amour blessait au coeur les fous comme les sages." Guillaume Apollinaire, "Les Saisons" (1917), translated by Anne Hyde Greet, *Calligrammes: Poems of Peace and War (1913–1916)* (Berkeley, Los Angeles, and London, 1980), p. 195.

80. The letter, dated 4 September 1918, is translated and quoted in full in *A Picasso Anthology: Documents, Criticism, Reminiscences*, ed. Marilyn McCully (Princeton, 1982), pp. 130 and 132.

81. "Debussy transpose Claude Monet à la russe," Cocteau, *Le Coq et l'Arlequin*, p. 28; "Satie reste intact . . . Satie parle d'Ingres," Ibid.

82. Pool, "Picasso's Neo-Classicism: Second Period," p. 201.

83. Gris in a letter to Kahnweiler dated 3 September 1919 (*Letters*, ed. Cooper, p. 67); the references to Max Jacob and Georges Braque in Cabanne, *Le Siècle de Picasso*, I, p. 331.

84. Ibid., p. 318.

85. "Chez Paul Rosenberg, Pablo Picasso descendit en courant le grand escalier, m'étreignit longuement avec émotion et me conduisit dans le salle du haut où étaient des tableaux de lui.

"Je me trouvai en présence d'un grand portrait dans ce qu'on appelle le 'style Ingres'; le convenu de l'attitude, une sobriété voulue, semblaient y réprimer un pathétique secret; . . . Que signifiaient donc ces tableaux? Etait-ce un termède, un jeu, beau, mais sans portée. . . . Ou bien, en un temps où la haine régissait les hommes, où la circonspection romane, consciente d'elle-même, se dressait avec hostilité contre la nuageuse métaphysique allemande, se sentait-il montre du doigt par d'innombrables gens qui reprochaient à ses sentiments profonds des affinités germaniques et l'accusaient d'être secrètement de connivence avec 'l'ennemi'? Souffrait-il d'isolément moral en pays 'étranger'? Cherchait-il à se ranger du côté spécifiquement 'français,' et ces tableaux attestent-ils les tourments de son âme?

"Il est difficile de trouver la réponse à ces questions. Quant à l'obtenir de lui-même, il n'y fallait point songer." Wilhelm Uhde, *Picasso et la tradition française* (Paris, 1928), pp. 55–56.

86. Pierre Daix, "Le Retour de Picasso au portrait (1914–1921), une problématique de généralisation du cubisme," in Université de Saint-Etienne, *Le Retour à l'ordre*, p. 84.

IV Internecine Warfare

1. "Tout d'abord, je m'excuse d'employer ce mot 'cubiste.' Il qualifie une école qui a peut-être été nécessaire à son heure, mais dont l'utilité a cessé de se faire sentir et dont la disparition semble un fait à peu près accompli." Bissière, "Le Réveil des cubistes," *L'Opinion* (15 April 1916), p. 382.

2. "Rappelez-vous—avant la guerre—la divergence de vues, d'opinions, de tendances, de directions, de théories, dans l'art pictural

français. Le spectacle des extravagances les plus grossières y était devenu quotidien et nous devions lutter dans ce désordre—pour déclarer que le Cubisme n'était qu'une erreur et la recherche pour la recherche qu'une oisive préoccupation." Francis Carco, introduction to exhibition catalogue, *L'Arc-en-ciel*, Galerie de Luxembourg, Paris (December 1915), n.p.

3. ". . . des vieux . . . se sont servis ou laissé faire ces villaines manoeuvres, ont même, tel ou tel, declaré déserteur, insoumis, etc. etc. . . . des tas de calomnies infecte. . . . Il y a aussi des jeunes . . . qui ont eu un rôle dégouttant . . . jusqu'à dire que la peinture moderne était Allemande . . . ont attaqués [unclear] dans le dos . . ." Robert Delaunay, letter to Albert Gleizes, undated but with an address in Portugal c. 1915–17. The Delaunay letters are all from the Delaunay archive now on deposit in the Manuscripts Division of the Bibliothèque Nationale, Paris. The original orthography is preserved wherever I have quoted from these, but I have tried where possible to make use of only those sentences or phrases that are clear and unequivocal (hence the ellipses). Most of these letters are unpublished, but a few have appeared in Pierre Francastel (ed.), *Robert Delaunay: Du Cubisme à l'art abstrait* (Paris, 1957): I indicate these with page numbers from Francastel. See also Bibliothèque Nationale, *Sonia et Robert Delaunay* (Paris, 1977).

4. "Je partage tout à fait vos idées ou projets des grandes manifestations de cet art le plus nouveau (en réaction ou plutôt en opposition à toutes les tendences peintures ou art dit cubiste-futuriste) . . . il y a parmi les jeunes une grande réaction contre cet art amorphe et ces profiteurs ne sont plus à la mode—c'est fini. . . . Je suis très cont.[ent] de ce que vous dites que . . . ne réagit plus sur cette peinture stupide qui étaient faites par certains mystificateurs la plupart des étrangers à la France mais qui ont faire marché le monde en disant *made in Paris* [written by Delaunay in English] . . . je suis heureux de voir qu'il y a des hommes . . . qui ne se sont pas laissés envahir par toute cette pourriture: [qui] comme je le dit n'est pas française mais dont nous nous chargerons maintenant de nettoyer Paris— le grand Paris qui se renouvelle toujours." Delaunay to Weichsel, 12 December 1916 (Delaunay letters, BN).

5. In an undated wartime letter to Albert Gleizes: "le balai commence pour cette époque" (Delaunay letters, BN).

6. "Il y a un groupe de jeunes français qui ont commencé ce nettoyage." Delaunay to Felin Elias, 13 September 1917 (Delaunay letters, BN).

7. "Epoque de la peinture pauvre, hystérique, convulsive, déstructive, . . . ces fumisteries, futuristes, cubistes . . . ni de la peinture ni de l'Art." Delaunay, letter to *Vell I Nou* published 15 December 1917 (Francastel, p. 131).

8. "Les étrangers et les vieux ont trop profité du manque de cohésion existant." Delaunay to Gleizes, undated (but to the latter in New York, therefore c. 1915–1916) (Delaunay letters, BN); "[unclear] a dessein de faire passer les peintres français comme suiveurs du fameux génie . . ." Ibid.

9. "Je vous ai dit pour *Parade*. C'est tout à fait une histoire de fou— aucun succès ici, même de curiosité devant cette chose hystérique, c'est le seul mot adéquat . . . hystérie—peinture d'esprits malade— torturé . . ." Delaunay to Gleizes, undated, but after the premiere of *Parade* in Barcelona (10 November 1917) (Delaunay letters, BN); "Ce que vous dites à propos de Picasso . . . avec sa maintenant, ayant quitté l'incompréhensibilité cubiste . . . il s'y prêt à merveille avec sa soi-disant période classique de ces dessins qui n'ont ni père ni mère . . ." Ibid.

10. ". . . comme Picasso, qui fait du Bouguereau ne pouvant obtenir la pureté d'un Ingres (Ingres étant déjà du néo, il n'y a pas de suite de développement sérieux et possible) . . ." Delaunay notes, dated 1919–20 by Francastel (p. 100).

11. I have not seen Severini's *Appearance of the Angel to Pulcinella* except in reproduction, but Joan Lukach, who has seen it, mentioned to me in 1980 that she does not believe it was painted in 1917. As it appears in black-and-white reproduction, I find the picture quite convincing as a work of 1917 (which is the date ascribed to it by Lionello Venturi, *Gino Severini* (Rome, 1961), although it may well have been retouched afterwards.

12. Severini, preface to exhibition catalogue for show at *291*—Stieglitz Gallery, New York, March 1917, as quoted in Joan Lukach, "Severini's Writings and Paintings 1916–17 and His Exhibition in New York City," *Critica d'Arte* 20, no. 138 (November–December 1974), pp. 61–62.

13. Umberto Boccioni, Carlo Carrà, Luigi Russolo, Giacomo Balla, Gino Severini, "Manifesto of the Futurist Painters," 11 April 1910, as translated and quoted in Umbro Apollonio, *Futurist Manifestos* (New York, 1973), pp. 24–31.

14. Typical of his wartime feelings, Gris wrote to Raynal, on 22 February 1916: "Here it's always the same, work and boredom." *Letters*, ed. Cooper, p. 35.

15. Gris to Kahnweiler (7 September 1915), in ibid., p. 31.

16. ". . . la Comédie Italienne renaît toujours . . . les Fratellini, Grock, . . . les ballets russes, . . . Molière, . . . Marivaux, Verlaine, Debureau, . . . Callot, . . . Gillot, Watteau, Lancret, Jean-Baptiste Tiepolo, . . . Guérin, Picasso, Severini, Gris, Lombard, Brunelleschi, Claude-Lévy, et tant d'autres . . . petits et grands se font signe de la main à travers les siècles; ils sont tous un peu membres de

l'illustre, joyeuse et toujours reverdissante famille qui pourrait porter sur son bannière comme devise: 'Tous les genres, hors les genres ennuyeux.' " Pierre Duchartre, *La Comédie italienne* (Paris, 1925), p. 7.

"Pas d'Othello, pas d'Hamlet, pas de Phèdre ni de Chimère, pas de gens qui se barattent la cervelle avec des sentiments exceptionnels. . . . La Commedia dell'Arte est un monde complet où chacun peut trouver sa pâture." Ibid., p. 332.

"Les poètes, les musiciens, les écrivains, les peintres du talent ou de génie les plus opposés se sont rencontrés dans un commun amour de la Commedia dell'Arte." Ibid.

17. For the issue of Gris's relationship to Cézanne and, in comparison to this, Emile Bernard's relationship, see Kenneth E. Silver, "Eminence Gris."

18. Braque wrote in the same article: "9. One must not imitate what one wishes to create." "Pensées et réflexions sur la peinture," as quoted in Fry, *Cubism*, p. 147.

19. Gris to Kahnweiler (c. 1919), as quoted in D.-H. Kahnweiler, *Juan Gris: His Life and Work* (London, 1947), p. 93.

20. Gris to Raynal, 17 October 1916, *Letters*, ed. Cooper, p. 42.

21. For the Poueigh-Satie affair see Brown, *An Impersonation of Angels*, pp. 151–53. For the exact figures and sentences involved see the *Gazette des Tribunaux* (Paris), for Monday, 16 July 1917, on file at the Hôtel de Ville. The records of the Poueigh-Satie trial are still closed to the public, owing to the statute of limitations.

22. Gris to Raynal, 10 January 1917, *Letters*, ed. Cooper, p. 44.

23. Gris to Raynal, 24 March 1917, ibid., p. 45.

24. Max Jacob, letter to Jacques Doucet, 22 March 1917, quoted in Ramon Favela, *Diego Rivera: The Cubist Years*, Phoenix Art Museum (Phoenix, Ariz., 1984), p. 144.

25. Ibid., p. 145.

26. Anonymous author, "La querelle cubiste . . . ou le cubisme expliqué," in an unidentified publication found in the Fonds Vauxcelles of the Bibliothèque Jacques Doucet at the Institut d'Art et Archéologie, Paris.

27. "Peintres et sculpteurs cubistes, nous protestons contre la fâcheuse liaison que l'on tend à établir entre nos oeuvres et certaines fantaisies littéraires et théâtrales qu'il ne nous appartient pas de juger. Ceux d'entre nous qui ont assisté aux manifestations 'd'Art et Liberté' et de 'Sic' déclarent formellement qu'elles n'ont rien de commun avec leurs recherches plastiques." Originally published in *Le Pays* (date

unknown), and reproduced in the anonymous article cited in note 26, above. Gee discusses the letter, in different terms, in "The Avant-Garde, Order and the Art Market."

28. Apollinaire's angry letter to Reverdy is reproduced in full in *Pierre Reverdy 1889–1960* (various authors) (Paris, 1962), pp. 9–10. It is dated 28 June 1917, which means that the letter in *Le Pays* must have appeared between 25 June and 28 June. In a letter of the next day, 29 June 1917 (ibid., pp. 10–11), Apollinaire tells Reverdy that he now knows the identity of the instigator of the letter, which he will reveal at a later unspecified date.

29. "Nous avons tous crié très haut contre les modes boches, munichoises, et berlinoises, qui étaient imposées aux Français. Les Allemands se chargent dans leurs journaux de nous confirmer dans nos indignations d'avant-guerre, comme dit M. Léon Daudet.

"Un dessin du *Simplicissimus*, montre un cavalier allemand qui console sa femme:

"—Na, lui dit-il, ne pleure pas, Else, je te commanderai moi-même ta nouvelle robe chez Poiret!

"Chez Poiret, vous avez bien lu! Qu'en pense M. Poiret? Faut-il que, malgré lui sans doute, il ait eu le goût boche pour que des Allemands le reconnaissent, à ce point, pour l'un des leurs?

"Après la guerre, M. Poiret se fera pardonner par les Françaises: il en a, certes, grand besoin." Anonymous [Henri Lapauze?], "Juste Sévérité," *La Renaissance (politique, . . .)* 3, no. 14 (7 August 1915), pp. 15–16. Carlton Hayes, in *France, a Nation of Patriots* (New York, 1930), describes the magazine as "moderate Left" (p. 426).

30. "Elle ne se laissera plus influencer par certain goût munichois; tout le monde nous l'affirme et même M. Poiret ne cesse pas de déclarer la nécessité de revenir aux traditions nationales. Pourquoi ne pas croire la bonne volonté de M. Poiret lui-même? Il en a entendu de si cruelles qu'il lui faudrait être inconscient pour persister. Et M. Poiret n'est pas inconscient: c'est un homme intelligent et averti. Si averti qu'il poussait à l'excès, bien certain qu'il serait suivi par le snobisme des étrangères et aussi par les énervées que la vie surchauffée d'avant-guerre nous avait faites." Anonymous [Lapauze?], "La Mode changera," *La Renaissance (politique, . . .)* 3, no. 19 (16 October 1915), p. 13.

31. "Pour la mode, donc, je crois bien que nous sommes tous d'accord ou à peu près.

"Mais . . . pour l'ameublement? . . . Est-ce que nous consentirons encore à être tributaires du goût immonditieux de Mlle Martine, de l'école Martine, de la maison Martine? Est-ce que nous tolérons encore les noirs, les verts, les rouges, les jaunes b. . .ochonneries qu'on nous a imposa sur nos tables, nos consoles, nos sièges, etc.? Est-ce que nous ne mettrons pas le feu à toutes ces ordures allemandes, influencées de Munich, de Dresde, et de Stuttgart, et que prônaient nos revues d'art, toutes ou à peu près toutes nos revues d'art?

"Au feu, dis-je, au feu tout cela,—et qu'on n'en entende plus jamais parler." Ibid.

32. See Palmer White, *Poiret* (New York, 1973), esp. pp. 83–88, 137.

33. "L'assignation de M. Poiret réjouit *La Renaissance*. Jamais occasion plus propice ne nous fut offerte de nous expliquer sur ce que nous entendons par l'art boche ou, si l'on préfère, par l'influence allemande dans l'art décoratif français et dans la mode française.

"Il était temps que certaines choses fussent dites: *La Renaissance* les dira. Elle apportera devant les magistrats français de la neuvième chambre des faits precis, et des textes. La voix éloquente et particulièrement autorisée de M. Léon Bérard traduira, ce jour-là, le sentiment de tous. Et, puisqu'il a plu à M. Poiret qu'il en fut ainsi, il aura bien vite fait de s'apercevoir que, pour juger une cause nationale entre toutes, il y a des juges à Paris." Anonymous [Lapauze?], "Le Procès de l'influence allemande dans l'art décoratif français et dans la mode française," *La Renaissance (politique, . . .)* 3, no. 22 (27 November 1915), p. 17.

34. Paul Poiret, *En habillant l'époque* (Paris, 1930), pp. 142–49, 194–99.

35. On the decorative arts in France before the war, see especially Nancy Troy, "Towards a Redefinition of Tradition in French Design, 1895–1914," *Design Issues* 1, no. 2 (Fall 1984), pp. 53–69.

36. Louis Vauxcelles, "Les décorateurs munichois à Paris," 1910 (exact date and place of publication unknown; from Fonds Vauxcelles, Bibliothèque Jacques Doucet, Paris). See also Vauxcelles's lengthy survey of the exhibition in *L'Art Décoratif*, "Le Salon d'Automne de 1910" (October 1910), pp. 113–76.

37. The committee members of the Salon d'Automne are listed in the preface to the exhibition catalogue for the 1910 show.

38. "Rappelez-vous la section germanique à l'Exposition bruxellois de 1910, ou bien les ensembles du Salon d'Automne, quand on y convia les décorateurs bavarois? Que ces pavillons et ces 'chambres de musique' étaient donc mornes et funéraires! . . . le vestibule orange et vert clair de herr Karl Jaeger, avec mosaïques néopompéiennes; le boudoir colossal de herr Theodor Veil; la bibliothèque du Professeur Paul-Ludwig Troost (l'ennui y suintait des murailles); la chambre à coucher violette de herr Adalbert Neimeyer, où le lit était de plomb et l'armoire de granit; et cette morose caserne, la salle de 'restauration' faite pour qu'on s'y empiffre de saucisses protestantes en écoutant une compact symphonie de Mahler,—toute cette affreuse archi-

tecture tudesque où trima l'innombrable armée des 'professoren' à lu-
nettes d'or, nous fit apprécier par contraste le goût exquis et nuancé
de nos meubliers de France, petits neveux des Crescent et des Rie-
sener. Le sens de la mesure, l'harmonie, le tact ailé sont choses de
chez nous. On crèverait de malle mort en un intérieur boche." Louis
Vauxcelles, "L'Art social chez eux et chez nous," 1915 (exact date
and source unknown; from Fonds Vauxcelles, Bibliothèque Jacques
Doucet, Paris).

39. ". . . un style où tout est violent, heurté, bruyant, où les tons
pétaradent les uns à côté des autres, les plus crus et les plus vifs
qu'on puisse imaginer. C'est là le style munichois. Et on y voit des
verts dont l'acidité crispe l'estomac, les barres de filets lilas qu'on
accompagne une ligne de rouge sang; et quels jaunes! et quels roses!
Le but poursuivi—et atteint—est de vous faire voir trente-six chan-
delles, de frapper sur la rétine un coup d'une brutalité toute germanique: le coup boche!" Frédéric Masson, "Nos Leaders: l'art munichois et ses apôtres," *L'Excelsior* (30 March 1915), p. 31.

40. It is worth pointing out in this regard that Auguste Perret was
attacked for Germanic taste in the designs for his Théâtre des
Champs-Elysées, of 1911. See Paul Jamot, *A.-G. Perret et l'architecture du béton armé* (Paris, 1927), pp. 76–77. I am grateful to Mary
McLeod for this reference.

41. "Le problème, plus haut et plus grave, d'ordre économique, social, national, est de savoir si le goût français, la mode francaise,
l'architecture et l'ameublement français baisseront pavillon devant les
produits berlinois et munichois. Et cela seul importe." Vauxcelles,
"L'Art social," n.p.

42. In an article in 1923, Léon Rosenthal wrote: "Dès 1851, à l'Exposition universelle à Londres . . . Léon de Laborde découvrait, chez
nos clients traditionnels, des efforts d'émancipation, les germes d'une
concurrence, et, dans un rapport justement célèbre, il jetait un premier cri d'alarme. . . . Au lendemain de l'Exposition universelle de
1900, il apparut singulièrement redoutable." He also said that in the
decorative-arts market in 1913, based on a figure of 3 billion francs'
worth of business in all of Europe, Germany accounted for 2 billion of
that figure and France, along with the rest of the European nations,
accounted for the other billion. "L'Art et la cité: L'Exposition internationale des arts appliqués," *Les Nouvelles Littéraires* 2, no. 46 (8
September 1923), p. 1.

43. "Après la guerre à coups de canon, une autre guerre, sur le terrain des industries d'art, devra reprendre avec âpreté. Et là encore il
faut que nous vainquions." Vauxcelles, "L'Art social," n.p.

44. "Tournons-nous vers cette tradition française! la seule susceptible
de satisfaire aux conditions de notre tempérament, par la mise en

oeuvre intelligente de nos ressources matérielles, sous notre climat.

"Oublions tous efforts étrangers s'ils opposent à ces conditions.

"Ne suivons ni 'l'art' munichois dont, à juste titre, on ne veut pas, ni aucun art désuet ou éxotique." Adolphe Dervaux, "Le Beau, le vrai, l'utile, et la réorganisation de la cité," *La Grande Revue* 90, no. 584 (April 1916), p. 33.

45. In fact, by 1917, so thoroughly had the ideas *"munichois"* and "Oriental" become conflated in the minds of French artists that the decorative artist Maurice Marinot could say: "Le Maroc est beau malgré les orientalistes, beau en lui-même, beau pour les Marocains, beau pour la décoration marocaine. Je sais bien des gens qui trouveraient les intérieurs d'ici munichois, au sens que vous savez." Marinot in a letter to André Mare, inscribed "Casablanca, 30 September 1917" (Françoise Mare-Vène Collection, Paris).

46. Apollinaire thought (incorrectly, it appears) that Gerda-Wegener was German, and gave the illustrator some difficulty during the war. See Michel Sanouillet, *Dada à Paris* (Paris, 1965), note 1.

47. "Cette architecture, cette peinture, cette gravure, ce mobilier, . . . envahi la scène parisienne. Après l'hellénisme allemand, nous eûmes l'orientalisme allemand, ce modernisme criard de l'esthétique, dont les malheureux étaient si fiers, . . . On distinguait néanmoins, dans ces monstres bariolés, les aspirations de l'impérialisme allemand, ses pointes vers Bagdad et ailleurs. L'estampille qu'il mettait sur ses turqueries théâtrales conservait une signification politique." Daudet, *Hors du joug allemand*, p. 129.

48. ". . . l'Orient, qui soumettait l'homme et le monde à l'empire absolu de pouvoirs transcendants et de fatalités inéluctables." Emile Boutroux, *L'Idée de Liberté*, p. 7. Boutroux was one of France's best known academic philosophers. A student at both the Ecole Normale and the University of Heidelberg (hence his expertise on German philosophy), he later was a professor at the Ecole Normale and was elected to the French Academy in 1912. He died in 1921.

49. ". . . la civilisation gréco-orientale est, sans nulle contestation possible, de qualité inférieure." Abbé Delfour, *La Culture latine* (Paris, 1916), pp. 13–14. He goes on to explain that "Macedonian" Hellenism of Alexander was a bastardization of that pure Hellenism of which the French are the inheritors.

50. ". . . fantaisies vestimentaires, faisandées, batignolle-persanes de certains tailleurs pour dames." Vauxcelles, "L'Art social," n.p.

51. "Il eût été difficile, l'année qui précéda la guerre, d'entreprendre une critique sérieuse de la mode, parce que l'absence de principe présidant aux créations des couturiers condamnait d'avance toute analyse. L'anarchie la plus radicale régnait alors; c'était en tout la fan-

taisie individuelle et momentanée, fantaisie guidée par le souci de réaliser des modèles originaux et surprenants, et encouragée par l'abdication de la volonté des femmes entre les mains du couturier." Jeanne Ramon Fernandez, "L'Esprit de la mode," *Gazette des Beaux-Arts* 8, no. 4 (1917), p. 121.

52. The precise wording is as follows: "Ce procès menaçait donc de déchainer les uns contre les autres des artistes également convaincus et appartenant à des écoles différentes. M. Poiret a pensé que le moment n'était pas opportun d'ouvrir cette lutte.

"Pour l'éviter—et mettant ce souci au-dessus de des intérêts personnels—il déchire aujourd'hui son assignation. De notre côté nous associant à ce geste, nous déchirons la page qui l'avait motivée: nous y avions traduit avec vivacité des préoccupations inspirées par les événements tragiques au milieu desquels nous vivons mais il ne s'y était mêlé de notre part aucune intention malveillante à l'égard de M. Poiret.

"Aujourd'hui, d'accord avec lui, nous publions toutes les lettres qui étaient destinées aux dossiers de nos avocats." Henri Lapauze, introductory remarks to "De l'art français et des influences qu'il ne doit pas subir," *La Renaissance (politique, . . .)* 5, no. 19 (15 September 1917), p. 11.

53. "Le style *Martine* venait en droite ligne de Munich, pour la raideur des formes, et de Polynésie, pour la violence barbare des couleurs." Maurice de Waleffe in ibid., p. 19.

54. "L'influence allemande . . . hélas! cher ami, elle fut indéniable, détestable . . ." Eugène Delard in ibid., p. 15.

55. "L'influence allemande sur l'architecture et surtout sur l'art décoratif fut incontestable dans les dix dernières années qui précédèrent les hostilités." M. R. Falcou in ibid., p. 15.

56. "Ma réponse est simple et pourrait se résumer en quatre mots: 'Vous avez absolument raison.' " Georges Cain in ibid., p. 13.

57. ". . . cette alliance de la *simplicité*, de la *clarté* et du *sens de la mesure*"; "Vous comprenez à quel point les Allemands et leurs agents ou leurs dupes avaient intérêt à ruiner tout cela . . ."; "Le mal a été profond." Arsène Alexandre in ibid., p. 12.

58. "Je ne puis que m'associer à la campagne de ceux qui s'efforcent de combattre tout ce qui persiste de l'influence d'outre-Rhin dans nos arts, et particulièrement dans nos arts décoratifs. Il est à souhaiter que nos artistes se retrouvent tous après cette grande crise et sachent se rattacher en toute liberté à nos vieilles traditions de goût, c'est-à-dire de mesure et de tact." Léonce Bénédite in ibid., p. 12.

59. "Je savais qu'on vous avait quelque peu maltraité ces temps-ci, et quoique en principe je pense que l'on doit supporter ces choses

avec une complète indifférence, je conviens qu'il est amer en ce moment d'être insulté de telle façon." André Derain in ibid., p. 21.

60. "J'entends dire que vous êtes accusé de défendre l'art boche! . . . Vous, dont le caractère est si français, si parisien, a justement fait le succès en France et dans le monde entier, être l'objet de l'accusation de M. Lapauze! C'est stupéfiant!" Raoul Dufy in ibid., p. 22.

61. "J'ai été, mon cher ami, plus indigné que surpris des attaques dont vous êtes l'objet depuis la guerre et avant elle. Peu surpris parce que les hommes de votre valeur ont toujours été des victimes, mais indigne parce que l'injustice est par trop criante." Max Jacob in ibid., p. 23.

62. "On peut être très bon patriote et ne rien connaître à la chimie. Tout le monde est d'accord là-dessus. Mais quelques bons patriotes s'appuieront sur leurs sentiments pour déclarer, par ignorance, que le cubisme est allemand. Cela s'est déjà produit. La vérité est qu'ils ne connaissent rien à la peinture. Le cubisme a été fondé, si on peut le dire, par Picasso et Braque; l'un est Espagnol et l'autre Français. C'est en France qu'il s'est développé et c'est un produit latin. . . ." G. Fauconnet in ibid., p. 22.

63. "Puisqu'il est question, ici, de *modes* et puisque le nom de M. Poiret est prononcé, il reste à dire que M. Poiret me semble avoir eu sur les *modes* une influence considérable et des plus heureuses, par sa hardiesse, et le goût oriental de ses productions. Je n'y puis voir rien *d'allemand*; mais, je le répète, l'influence allemande en art me paraît tout simplement *nulle*. L'ameublement, les bibelots, les jouets dits munichois datent des ballets russes. La seule authentique nouveauté, dans les combinaisons de lignes et de couleurs décoratives, c'est le génie russe qui nous l'apporta. Le nom de Léon-Bakst, le plus populaire en Amérique comme en Europe, est lisible, si l'on s'en donne la peine, sur beaucoup d'étiquettes d'où l'on a voulu effacer." Jacques E. Blanche in ibid., p. 13.

64. "C'est donc ça 'l'Union Sacrée.' C'est la revanche de la 'critique' et des 'Fonctionnaires d'art' contre tous ceux qui ont eu le courage de s'affirmer en créant quelque chose. . . . Te traiter de Boche, c'est vraiment si bête! Toi, qui a toute l'indépendance d'esprit, la fantaisie et la franchise de l'enfant de Paris que tu es. . . . Si on n'ose pas faire d'hypothèse sur la mentalité française après la guerre, on peut du moins formuler des voeux. Tous ceux qui aiment le pays et comprennent son véritable intérêt souhaiteront lui voir abandonner son esprit de routine qui déconcertait les forces vives et paralysa tant d'initiatives. A bien des points de vues, la France révolutionnaire était devenue plus conservatrice que l'Allemagne moyenageuse. Les exemples sont malheureusement trop nombreux." André Dunoyer de Segonzac in ibid., p. 22.

65. For "Art et Liberté" see Gee, *Dealers, Critics, and Collectors*, pp. 218–21. Its manifesto was first published in *L'Opinion* no. 48 (25 November 1916), and among its founders were the writer Sébastien Voirol and Joseph Granié, the magistrate and friend of the Parisian avant-garde.

66. ". . . les soussignés tiennent à protester publiquement contre la désunion, qu'en pleine guerre, certains tentent de créer à l'encontre d'artistes de valeur, parfaitement français et participant au rayonnement essentiel de la patrie.

"Ils constatent que, lorsque ces critiques, insinuations et attaques ne se bornent pas à une impudente accusation d'immoralité, elles se manifestent sous un forme actuellement injurieuse entre toutes, celle de stigmatiser tout effort neuf comme 'oeuvre de boche.' " *La Renaissance* (15 September 1917), p. 24 (p. 2962).

67. "Je signe cela pour tout art renouvelé, sauf pour les cubes, n'aimant pas la géométrie, et j'interdis qu'on prenne ma signature sans la faire précéder de cette mention." Mme. Aurel in ibid.

68. Ibid., p. 25.

69. "Même dans cette déclaration il conviendrait d'établir des nuances qui m'empêchent de signer en bloc." Jean Cocteau in ibid.

70. ". . . c'est de réalisations que nous avons besoin maintenant. L'école française a, durant ces dix dernières années, amassé toutes sortes de matériaux, tenté des expériences de toute nature et souvent hasardeuses. Il serait temps de mettre de l'ordre dans tout ce chaos et de bâtir. On déplore de ne point rencontrer parmi tous ces chercheurs audacieux, et souvent admirablement doués, les constructeurs que notre génération apelle de tous ses désirs et qui, ne se contenter point de grouper de belles pierres, sauront les agencer ensemble pour élever une vaste et solide maison." Bissière, "Le Réveil des cubistes," p. 382.

1. These figures, provided by the French Minister of the Liberated Regions, are found in William MacDonald, *Reconstruction in France* (New York, 1922). See also the excellent article by Mary McLeod, " 'Architecture or Revolution': Taylorism, Technocracy, and Social Change," *Art Journal* 43, no. 2 (Summer 1983), pp. 132–47.

V *Fluctuat nec mergitur*

2. MacDonald, *Reconstruction*, p. 40.

3. "La guerre, avec toutes les mutilations et déformations qu'elle a causées, a favorisé le développement de ce qu'on pourrait appeler la chirurgie esthétique . . . rien n'est devenue plus commun comme un oeil de verre habilement placé ou . . . des cicatrices hideuses savamment masquées." Anonymous, "L'Art de restaurer les visages," *La Renaissance (politique, . . .)* 5, no. 6 (17 March 1917), pp. 15–16.

4. "Il y a la guerre! Tous les efforts, toutes les pensées, sont tendus

par le souci terrible du moment: LA GUERRE! Cependant et à cause de la catastrophe, il est de toute urgence de s'occuper de l'architecture—en même temps que des canons, des munitions, de la reprise des affaires. La question se pose, depuis août 1914, de savoir comment seront rétablis villes et villages détruits ou endommagés par les obus et les incendies." Dervaux, "Le Beau, le vrai," p. 33. For post-war reconstruction in France, see also McLeod, " 'Architecture or Revolution.' "

5. "Or, créer ou reconstruire une ville, c'est assurément de l'économie nationale, mais c'est aussi de l'architecture!

"Assainir une région étroitement peuplée, relier les rives d'un fleuve par un pont, c'est de l'architecture.

"Aménager convenablement un local, étudier les coutumes sociales et les exigences des habitants pour la commodité de leur labeur, de leur éducation ou de leur repos, c'est faire de la psychologie professionnelle, individuelle ou collective; c'est toujours de l'architecture." Dervaux, "Le Beau, le vrai," p. 324.

6. "L'âme française refaite et la France reconstituée: ces deux phénomènes se réunissent en une seule épiphanie." Beaunier, *Les Idées et les hommes*, II, p. 341.

7. "Des appréciateurs malveillants ont pu dire que la France oscillait entre le despotisme et l'anarchie. Et il est de mode, notamment outre-Rhin, de soutenir que les Français sont voués à un individualisme ingouvernable. L'individu, selon cette opinion, se considérerait, en France, comme littéralement souverain. Il placerait dans la satisfaction de ses volontés propres, de ses désirs, de ses caprices, la loi unique de sa conduite" (p. 13); "Si la présente guerre a particulièrement rappelé les Français au devoir de soumettre leur volonté individuelle à une loi supérieure, elle les a, par cet appel, simplement excités à développer harmonieusement toutes leurs tendances" (p. 15); "Il est conforme à leur nature la plus intime de concilier la valeur individuelle avec la soumission à la règle et au devoir" (p. 35). Boutroux, *L'Idée de Liberté*.

8. "Sans aspirer à voir les races latines se transformer en automates disciplines comme c'est un peu le cas de nos voisins d'Outre-Rhin . . ." L. Hauser, *Les Trois Léviers du monde nouveau* (Paris, 1918), pp. 104–105.

9. On the question of the French birthrate see Michel Huber, *La Population de la France pendant la guerre* (Paris and New Haven, 1931).

10. Barrès, *The Undying Spirit of France*, p. 3.

11. "Tous se donnent à l'oeuvre commune, chacun selon la place qu'il occupe ou qu'il est assignée . . . il est indispensable que les Français se persuadent profondément du rôle . . . de l'organisation dans l'accomplissement des tâches humaines" (pp. 13–14); "Tenir son rang

dans le monde, c'est pratiquer, le plus largement possible, les méthodes d'organisation les plus perfectionnées." Boutroux, *L'Idée de Liberté*, pp. 34–35.

12. Information on French economies and rationing during the war is from Perreux, *La Vie quotidienne*, pp. 98–110.

13. "Sans doute, Kant n'a pas pointé les canons qu'ont ruiné la Cathédrale de Reims, pas plus que Jean-Jacques Rousseau n'a actionné le déclic de la guillotine; mais ils ont formé les cervaux des bombardeurs et des sans-culottes." Sar Péladan, "Revisions des valeurs philosophiques allemands," *Mercure de France* 111, no. 416 (1 August 1915), p. 695.

14. "Non que l'individu se suffise et ait le droit de se regarder comme supérieur à toute loi. La pensée française ne ratifie pas l'assertion exagérée de Rousseau, attribuant à l'individu 'une existence absolue et naturellement indépendante.' " Boutroux, *L'Idée de Liberté*, p. 11.

15. "Jean-Jacques [Rousseau] lui-même est une dérivation très directe de Martin Luther et . . . son introspection passionnée est une fille indéniable du libre examen . . ." (p. 17); "On sait où mène et mènera, ce chemin: à *l'individualisme*" (p. 18). Daudet, *Hors du joug allemand*.

16. "Derain, Picasso et Braque consommaient le divorce entre eux et le publique extérieur . . ." Aurel, *Le Commandement d'amour*, p. 7.

17. "L'individualisme . . . n'a pu se suffire: le besoin d'une doctrine d'Ecole française est général . . ." Mauclair, *L'Avenir de France*, p. 522.

18. "Qu'attendons-nous pour qu'une nouvelle grande époque soit possible en France? Oh! d'abord, la victoire! Et puis, le retour au bon sens. Les préjugés révolutionnaires, les excès de l'individualisme, le goût du paradoxe, le fétichisme de l'inédit de l'original, toutes les tares de notre art sont aussi les tares de la société française." Maurice Denis, preface to M. Storez, *L'Architecture et l'art décoratif en France après la guerre (comment préparer leur renaissance)* (Paris, 1918), n.p.

19. Weber, *Action Française*, p. 74.

20. "Je m'expose d'un coeur léger au mépris de ces grands hommes en rappelant comme une vérité d'évidence qu'aux plus grandes époques créatrices l'artiste fut à la fois le serviteur et le porte-parole de la communauté; il avait charge d'exprimer, non pas sa sacro-sainte personnalité, son intangible indépendance, son ésotérique originalité—(ah! l'originalité, que de sottises, de notre temps, ont été commises en son nom!)—mais les croyances communes sur lesquelles était fondée la cité et autour desquelles elle organisait sa vie. Et il s'est trouvé qu'au lieu de pâtir de cette dépendance, la force plastique de l'artiste, si je puis parler ainsi, y trouvait comme un appui, un

renfort et une inspiration plus sûres et plus efficaces." André Michel, "L'Art français après la Guerre," *La Revue Hebdomadaire* 26, no. 11 (17 March 1917), p. 321.

"On peut aller plus loin, et les excès de l'individualisme et l'abus de la raison raisonnante s'en mêlant, on peut ébaucher si l'on veut une théorie du cubisme. Oui, il n'est rien de tout à fait absurde, comme disait l'indulgent Renan; mais nous sommes arrivés à une heure où il faut bien s'apercevoir que tous les sophismes ne sont pas également inoffensifs. Et c'est ici que pour la santé, pour l'avenir, pour le rayonnement de notre art français, je me permettrai de faire appel au bon sens, à la raison et à la conscience de tous ceux qui en sont responsables devant la France et devant le monde. . . . Le besoin, on peut dire fervent, d'un retour au style, à la composition, qui s'est fait entendre du fond même de l'anarchie contemporaine, n'est pas une mystification nouvelle, j'en ai le grand espoir; c'est une de nos plus fermes raisons de compter sur demain. C'est par là, c'est dans ce besoin que les artistes, même les plus individualistes, au sens dangereux du mot, comprendront la nécessité des lois, le bienfait de la subordination où des individualités vraiment fortes se retrempent et triomphent." Ibid., pp. 328–29.

21. ". . . le groupe de la rue Penthièvre semblant considérer la singularité comme une fin et non comme un moyen, s'attarde aux recherches avec un plaisir un peu maladif et une excessive complaisance. Chacun . . . se complait dans la contemplation de sa trouvaille." Bissière, "Le Réveil des cubistes," p. 382.

22. Fernand Léger, 1920, as quoted in Jean Cassou and Jean Leymarie, *Fernand Léger: Drawings and Watercolors* (Greenwich, Ct., 1973), p. 33.

23. Ibid.

24. "Cette exposition organisée dans un espace fatalement très restreint exige de chaque artiste, quel qu'il soit, un petit sacrifice de sa personnalité. Quel qu'il soit, il n'aura droit qu'à une oeuvre." Anonymous, Introduction to exhibition catalogue, Petit Palais, "Exposition au Profit des Oeuvres de Guerre" (Paris, May–June 1918), n.p.

25. Schneider, *Matisse*, pp. 330–39.

26. The Parisian critics were quick to note all defections from the avant-garde. Reviewing the Salon d'Automne in 1919, Emile Sédeyn remarked that, in comparison to his *Music* and *Dance* of 1910, Matisse's current Salon entries were, happily, on their way to becoming "paintings, in the proper sense of the word." "Le Salon d'Automne, II: La Peinture et la sculpture," *Art et Décoration* 36 (Fall 1919), p. 164.

27. "Le goût de l'architecture . . . on le retrouve chez Poussin, Claude Lorrain, David et Ingres qui trouvent souvent des équilibres

parfaits." André Lhote, "De la composition classique," *Gazette d'Hollande* (1917), quoted by Reymond, "Le Rappel à l'ordre d'André Lhote," p. 251.

28. "On peut blâmer la couleur des chambres, peu importe si la maison est solidement construite, sans rien qui manque du haut en bas." Cocteau, *Le Coq et l'Arlequin*, p. 52.

29. "Qu'en en mot, l'art du statuaire, et celui de peintre, s'ils sont dans leur émancipation, plus animés, plus vivant et plus libres, ne sont jamais plus grands et plus fiers que dans leur austère obéissance aux lois de l'architecture." Charles Blanc, *Grammaire des arts de dessin* (Paris, 1870), p. 71. Blanc himself was a strong Republican, and if architecture was symbolic for him, it was undoubtedly as a strong republic facing its enemies.

30. "Jusqu'ici, l'Architecture indiqua le degré de civilisation de chaque epoque . . . L'historien futur . . . jugera après la Grande Guerre, notre intellectualité à l'étiage de celui des arts que l'on nomme art de la Paix: l'Architecture." Dervaux, "Le Beau, le vrai," p. 346.

31. "A toutes les grandes époques créatrices, c'est elle qui fut l'art central et comme la matrice de tous les autres arts subordonnés à ses directions et bénéficiant de ses inspirations." Michel, "L'Art français après la Guerre," p. 320.

32. "Il serait beaucoup trop long de rappeler ici comment la sculpture et la peinture ne furent longtemps que ses collaboratrices, et quelle grandeur, quelle force elles puisaient, dans les contraintes apparentes qu'elle leur imposait. En même temps qu'une vertu plastique plus haute, qu'une allure plus fière, plus monumentale, elles y gagnaient de prendre plus pleinement conscience de leur destination sociale. Nous en sommes aujourd'hui, c'est entendu, à l'indépendance, à la souveraineté, je dirais même: bientôt à la tyrannie de la fantaisie de l'artiste, qui méprise d'abord le philistin incapable de pénétrer la sublimité de son génie ou de ses intentions." Ibid., pp. 320–21.

33. "Ce qu'on peut dire de moins fort à cet égard c'est que, si notre France tient ensemble, c'est que les morceaux en ont été réunis par les architectes classiques. On reconnait les traces de leur main énergique et fine; je les appelle, entr'autres, l'Eglise catholique et l'Administration romaine, antique conseillère des Rois de France. Enfin notre langue littéraire est gréco-latine." Charles Maurras, "Prologue d'un essai sur la critique" (1896), *Oeuvres capitales*, III (Paris, 1954), p. 30.

34. Léon Daudet, *Le Stupide XIXième siècle (exposé des insanités meurtrières qui se sont abattues sur la France depuis cent trente ans, 1789–1919)* (Paris, 1922).

35. Weber, *Action Française*, p. 9.

36. Ibid., p. 77.

37. "Rousseau, l'adoration de la nature, l'effréné du lyrisme, l'insurrection des esclaves, les droits des peuples, le 'vivre sa vie,' Bernstein, Bergson enfin et sa métaphysique de l'élan vital, ne sont qu'une seule et même attitude devant le monde: le Romantisme. Les arts classiques n'existent que par le règne de l'intelligence." Paul Dermée, "Un Prochain Age classique," p. 3.

38. "Depuis Giotto, dont il a la grandeur, David fut le plus considérable des maîtres dont l'enseignement clair et logique galvanisa une génération. Le vague ROMANTIQUE dont l'Impressionnisme fut l'aboutissement, renouvelant les déliquescences mal refrénées du XVIIe siècle provoqua la défaveur de tout enseignement précis . . . et aboutit à un empirisme pictural basé sur la seule sensibilité." André Lhote, "Totalisme," p. 3.

39. ". . . religion de l'instinct, du don pur . . . négation de tous principes, innovation totale, anarchie." André Lhote, "Tradition et troisième dimension," *Nouvelle Revue Française* no. 85 (October 1920), quoted in Reymond, *Le Rappel à l'ordre*, p. 211.

40. "L'étude minutieuse des caprices de la lumière et la notation de la vie moderne ont conduit l'impressionnisme à négliger le style et la composition, à nier tout influence de tradition et d'école après en avoir discrédité . . ." Mauclair, *L'Avenir de France*, p. 518.

41. Quoted in Katherine Kuh, *Léger* (Urbana, Ill., 1953), p. 24.

42. See Cocteau's "Roman notebooks" reproduced in Axsom, *"Parade,"* p. 333.

43. "Il est évident dans ce tableau, l'effort de concilier l'esprit des recherches futuristes (continuation de l'impressionnisme) avec l'esprit des recherches cubistes (réaction à l'Impressionisme). Et en ce moment tous les peintres sont là . . ." Quoted in Lukach, "Severini's Writings," p. 79.

44. "Ne vous y trompez point. Le Cubisme a été un classicisme après le romantisme des Fauves." Quoted (without original source indicated) in Pool, "Picasso's Neo-Classicism: Second Period," pp. 200–202.

45. Cocteau to Gleizes, January 1918, in Steegmuller, *Cocteau*, p. 201.

46. "Le peintre impressionniste regardait la nature entre ses cils clignés au soleil; aujourd'hui le cubisme retrouve la discipline austère des grandes époques, renonce à des jeux charmants, et l'univers lui devient le prétexte d'une nouvelle architecture de la sensibilité . . ." Jean Cocteau, *Dans le ciel de la patrie* (Paris, 1918), n.p.

47. Saroléa, *The French Renascence* (translation of *Le Réveil de la France*), p. 36.

48. "Paris, personnifiant la France dont en ces heures haletantes se précipite et se joue le destin, Paris absorbe depuis quinze jours les pensées du monde entier. . . . Alors Paris . . . reprend à ce moment sa figure de blason, son effigie traditionnelle et sacrée. Sur l'océan de sa vieille histoire, soulevé depuis quatre ans, on revoit bondir, descendre et remonter la Nef. Sur ses couleurs ruisselantes de larmes, de sang, se ravive en lettres d'or l'inébranlable devise: *Fluctuat nec mergitur.*" Henri Lavedan, "Fluctuat," *L'Illustration* no. 3928 (15 June 1918), p. 568.

49. See Silverman, "Nature, Nobility, and Neurology," pp. 62–63.

50. See Charles Maurras, *Les Amants de Venise* (Paris, 1902).

51. "Les peintres modernes n'ont pas eu le sens de la construction, ils ont fait les palais roses, des reflets dans l'eau et des gondoles, mais ils n'ont pas compris que l'eau mouvente n'était que l'antithèse d'une architecture rigide et sévère toute en ligne en ombres et en plans où la couleur n'est pas un revêtement et jamais un but." André Mare, notebook no. 9 (1916), Collection Françoise Mare-Vène, Paris.

52. ". . . je pense que l'esthétique collective et anti-individualiste à laquelle je viens de faire allusion se prépare une époque d'art réalisant enfin l'universalité et le style." Gino Severini, "La Peinture d'avant-garde," *Mercure de France* 445, no. 121 (1 June 1917), p. 468.

53. Excerpts from Plato's *Philebus* were published in *L'Elan* no. 9 (February 1916), pp. 12–13.

54. "Ce dessin d'un trait précis et strict, où la tricherie ne trouverait point place, cette lumière juste et tempérée sans zone de clair-obscur propice à cacher les défaillances et qui jamais ne se décompose en papillôtements impressionnistes, ce subtil et savant équilibre de la partition gravée sur ces feuillets, c'est un peu comme si M. Ingres, à la demande de Victor Cousin, eût illustré ces passages des *Dialogues* de Platon." René Chalupt, Introduction to Satie's *Socrate* (Paris, 1919), n.p.

55. Saroléa, *The French Renascence*, pp. 282–83.

56. "L'évolution d'un véritable artiste connait successivement les trois phases suivantes:
    "L'imitation—L'interprétation—La création.
    "Première phase: Il reproduit *directement* l'apparence de la Nature. Il rend une image.
    "Deuxième phase: Il exprime l'aspect de la Nature à travers son *humanité*; il extériorise une *impression*.
    "Troisième phase: Ne conservant de la Nature que le constant et l'absolu, libre du choix des éléments nécessaires à la *construction* de son oeuvre, il réalise *l'Esprit*. Son oeuvre devient *la Réalité*." Léonce Rosenberg, "Pourquoi choyez-vous," *Nord-Sud* no. 16 (October 1918), p. 21.

VI   Blue Horizons

1. After noting that the peasants carried *images d'Epinal*, Mare wrote in his notebook: "Je ne croyais jamais avant ce voyage un sentiment français bien vivace chez les Alsaciens; je suis [forcé] de convenir non seulement qu'il existe mais qu'il a dépassé les prévisions les plus optimistes et qu'il étonne les Alsaciens eux-mêmes." André Mare, notebook no. 10 (1918), Collection Françoise Mare-Vène, Paris.

2. For the Victory celebration, see Rosemonde Sanson, *Les 14 Juillet: Fête et conscience nationale, 1789–1975* (Paris, 1976), pp. 105–14.

3. "Puis dans la grande porte au travers de laquelle brillait le plus beau soleil d'Austerlitz, des silhouettes surgirent. Les poilus s'engageaient sous l'Arc de Triomphe . . ." Maurice Barrès, "Les Poilus sous l'Arc de triomphe," *L'Echo de Paris* (15 July 1919) as quoted in Sanson, *Les 14 Juillet*, p. 112.

4. Pictures of the cenotaph, descriptions of it, and articles referring to it are all from the Collection Françoise Mare-Vène, Paris.

5. "Sous l'Arc de Triomphe le monument aux morts est en voie d'achèvement. Il bouche fâcheusement la porte triomphale; il y semble écrasé et lourd et de style un peu munichois malgré son haut mérite d'art et d'émotion grave." Anonymous, "Le Monument aux morts," *L'Eclair* (13 July 1919).

6. "Il est beaucoup plus regrettable que M. Jean Cocteau, qui se donne carte blanche dans *Paris-Midi*, ait écrit que le cénotaphe 'aurait pu venir tout droit de Munich, rempli de camelote boche.' " Roger Allard, "A propos du Cénotaphe," *Le Nouveau Spectateur* 1, no. 6 (10 August 1919), p. 140.

7. "M. Clemenceau a vu le cénotaphe et il a dit: 'C'est grandiose.' . . . M. Clemenceau a revu le cénotaphe le jour du 14 juillet et il a dit: 'C'est ignoble,' avec son laconisme hautain ennemi des circonlocutions. Puis il a pris la peine bien inutilement d'étayer sa nouvelle opinion. Et il a parlé 'd'art boche,' 'd'inspiration munichoise.' Enfin— puisqu'en France, présentement, tout finit par des démolitions—il a donné l'ordre de tout démolir." André Chevalier, "M. Clemenceau, Critique d'Art," *Le Pays* (23 July 1919).

8. Allard, "A propos du Cénotaphe," p. 140.

9. "C'est déjà à l'histoire un peu ancienne. Mais les gaffeurs et les ignorants méritent toujours d'être relevés. Nul n'a oublié la noblesse rigide, la simplicité grave du cénotaphe dû à Louis Süe, André Mare et Gustave Jaulmes. Malgré les conditions précaires de temps et d'argent où fut exécuté ce monument funéraire, tous les artistes s'accordèrent à en admirer les lignes pures et simples. Une ou deux voix discordantes s'élevèrent. Et naturellement, l'accusation 'd'art boche'—injure aujourd'hui classique, fut décochée à nos amis—qui sont parmi les rénovateurs des arts appliqués français, les plus ardents, tenants de la lutte contre Munich—et qui ont fait la guerre

. . ." Anonymous, "Gaffe et incompétence," *Carnet de la Semaine* (10 August 1919).

10. The *poilu*'s helmet was an especially popular motif for post-war wallpaper; see for example Boigegrain's "toile de Rambouillet" composed of the helmet surrounded by festoons and cornucopias (*Art et Décoration* 36, May–June 1919, p. 36) and Guy Arnoux's more child-like paper, made for the house of "Patria," that depicts the helmet surrounded by what appear to be laurel leaves and cockades (*La Renaissance de l'art français*, etc., January 1918, p. 17).

11. Barr reproduces *Fleurs, 14 Juillet* on p. 431 of *Matisse: His Art and His Public* (dated July 1919), as in the Gaston Bernheim de Villers Collection, Monte Carlo.

12. Mentioned in Steegmuller, *Cocteau*, p. 190.

13. "Le combat pour l'unité morale du pays fut poursuivi contre les éléments de division et de révolution que la démobilisation déchaînait. . . . Il y eut des défiances et des heurts, des conflits et des grèves, des tentatives de révolution même; mais les semences jetées avaient lentement germé et, quand les ennemis intérieurs de la France, métèques, mercantis et fauteurs de troubles réunis pensèrent que l'heure était venue d'achever le pays blessé, ils le trouvèrent levé tout entier contre eux et n'eurent plus qu'à rentrer dan l'ombre." Bornecque and Drouilly, *La France et la Guerre*, pp. 24–25.

14. Herbert Tint, *The Decline of French Patriotism, 1870–1940* (London, 1964), p. 162.

15. "On prêcha les sacrifices nécessaires aux riches et aux patrons, la production intense et l'économie la plus stricte à tous, la réconciliation des classes sur l'autel du travail le retour à la terre nourricière de tous les déracinés, l'hygiène élémentaire indispensable à l'amélioration de tant de santés, l'amour de la famille seule force sociale puissante, procréatrice d'une génération nouvelle." Bornecque and Drouilly, *La France et la Guerre*, p. 24.

16. "Une belle Minerve est l'enfant de ma tête" ("Tristesse d'une Etoile"), cited in Pool, "Picasso's Neo-Classcism, Second Period," p. 199.

17. "L'Art avant la Grande Epreuve n'était pas assez vivant pour tonifier les oisifs, ni pour intéresser les actifs; cette société là s'ennuyait parce que la directive de la vie était trop incertaine, parce qu'aucun grand courant collectif n'entraînait au travail ceux qui devaient travailler, ni tentait au travail ceux qui pouvaient ne pas travailler. Epoque de grèves, de revendications et de protestations où l'art lui-même n'était qu'un art de protestation. Ils sont passés ces temps lourds et trop légers." Amédéc Ozenfant and Charles-Edouard Jeanneret, *Après le Cubisme* (Paris, 1918), p. 11.

18. "La Grande Concurrence a tout éprouvé, elle a achevé les méthodes séniles et imposé à leur place celles que la lutte a prouvé les meilleures." Ibid.

19. "Le dernière venue des écoles d'art fut le Cubisme. Il fut bien de son époque, cet art trouble d'une époque trouble." Ibid., p. 12.

20. "L'Art d'aujourd'hui, qui fut art d'avant-garde, n'est plus qu'un art d'arrière-garde, d'avant-guerre, celui d'une société jouisseuse." Ibid., p. 11.

21. "Les Fauves nient; leurs tableaux sont, en effet, d'une technique faible, leur conception ne laisse pas de l'être aussi; la mode en est déjà passée." Ibid., p. 28.

22. "Jusqu'au Romantisme, les artistes vivaient avec leur temps; les Romantiques rompaient le contact en se considérant comme des êtres à part, hors l'époque. Peut-etre motivée en cette période de régression, une telle attitude ne se justifieraient plus aujourd'hui." Ibid.

23. "Assez de jeux. Nous aspirons à une rigeur grave." Ibid., p. 34.

24. Gris to Kahnweiler, 16 February 1921, *Letters*, ed. Cooper, p. 95.

25. "La science et le grand Art ont l'idéal commun de généraliser, ce qui est la plus haute fin de l'esprit . . . l'Art doit généraliser pour atteindre la beauté." Ozenfant and Jeanneret, *Après le Cubisme*, pp. 39–40.

26. "L'idée de forme précède celle de couleur." Ibid., p. 55.

27. "Si . . . les Grecs ont triomphé des barbares, si l'Europe, héritière de la pensée des Grecs, domine le monde, c'est parce que les sauvages aimaient les couleurs criardes et les sons bruyants du tambour qui n'occupent que leurs sens, tandis que les Grecs aimaient la beauté intellectuelle qui se cache sous la beauté sensible." Ibid., p. 48.

28. "La Guerre finie, tout s'organise, tout se clarifie et s'épure; les usines s'élèvent, rien n'est déjà plus ce qu'il était avant la guerre." Ibid., p. 11.

29. "Voici que l'ordre, la pureté, éclairent et orientent la vie; cette orientation fera de la vie de demain une vie profondément différente de celle d'hier. Autant celle-là était troublée, incertaine de sa voie, autant celle qui commence la discerne lucide et nette." Ibid., p. 12.

30. ". . . tout est changé. Le ciel se dégage; il se purifie et s'allège. . . . Nous étions malades; et nous recouvrons la santé. Dans nos âmes, dans nos esprits et dans nos coeurs, il se fait de l'ordre." Beaunier, *Les Idées et les hommes*, II, p. 324.

31. "Le Purisme craint le bizarre et 'l'original.' Il recherche l'élément pur pour en reconstruire des tableaux organisés qui semblent être faits par la nature-même." Ibid., p. 60.

32. "Le Purisme . . . estime que le Cubisme est demeuré, qui qu'on en dise, un art décoratif, ornémanisme romantique." Ibid., p. 59.

33. "L'ère des virtuoses est close." André Salmon, *L'Art vivant* (Paris, 1920), p. 9. Originally published in *Montjoie* (March 1914).

34. "Soldes avant inventaire. Demain, on va recommencer sur nouveaux frais. Le Salon d'Automne de 1919 ressemble trop à celui de 1913 pour n'être pas un Salon de liquidation des stocks. Nous n'espérions pas un miracle, un feu d'artifice d'éblouissantes révélations et nous envisageons 'les bienfaits de la guerre' avec le scepticisme qui convient. Mais à défaut de bienfait, il y a un fait. . . . qu'aux valeurs nouvelles, les moyens ne correspondent plus. *Tout augmente de prix*: la nouveaute, la vraie richesse, le précieux métal du talent n'ont plus de prix. Ce qui suffisait naguère à conférer une manière d'originalité et permettait à un réalisateur adroit de faire figure dans un salon de peinture excite aujourd'hui par son air d'indigence ou par son opulence usurpée une commisération mêlée d'agacement.

"De certains mots ont recouvré une signification pleine. Ce sont des gongs sonores qu'on n'ose plus frapper sans motif. On ne dira plus, si généreusement, qu'une oeuvre est 'audacieuse'; on ne feindra plus de croire que le clown qui fait chaque soir la même cabriole est 'audacieux.' " Roger Allard, "Le Salon d'Automne: La peinture," *Le Nouveau Spectateur* 1, nos. 11/12 (25 October/10 November 1919), p. 5.

35. "Mais la guerre . . . nous laissant de dures leçons, qui ne serait pas perdues. . . . Il s'agit d'émonder les branches mortes . . . pas de la nouveauté à tout prix, de la maison à l'envers et de la chaise à cinq pieds . . ." Jean Laran, untitled article, *Art et Décoration* 36 (May–June 1919), p. 180.

36. "L'innovation à tout prix n'est plus à la mode. On se calme et on s'organise." Jean-Louis Vaudoyer, "Le Salon d'Automne, II: L'art décoratif," *Art et Décoration* 36 (December 1919), p. 180.

37. "Nous remarquerons que le passé n'est plus l'ennemi qu'il faut abattre ou dédaigner, mais, au contraire, un auxiliaire, un allié, une inspiration discrète, aux vertus vivantes et éprouvées." Ibid.

38. "L'histoire n'est pas une méditation aride, un recul dans le temps. C'est la mémoire des peuples. Elle ne détourne pas, elle exhorte, elle entraine à l'action." Henri Focillon, *Les Evocations françaises: Les Pierres de France*, p. II.

39. For Monet's Orangerie commission see Charles F. Stuckey and Robert Gordon, "Blossoms and Blunders: Monet and the State" in two parts, *Art in America* 67, no. 1 (January–February 1979), pp. 102–17, and no. 5 (September 1979), pp. 109–25.

40. See Christopher Green's discussion in Tate Gallery, *Léger and Purist Paris* (London, 1971), p. 64.

41. ". . . après une longue période de fermeture le Louvre nous est réapparu, beaucoup d'entre les peintres d'aujourd'hui l'ont abordé d'un coeur nouveau . . . avec le désir de rencontrer là quelques grandes oeuvres et l'espoir secret de trouver en elles un enseignement et une justification." Bissière, "Jean Fouquet," *L'Esprit Nouveau* 5 (February 1921), p. 516.

42. "Ils ont préféré aux splendeurs italiennes, les petites salles perdues où dort l'art des hommes de leur race, témoignage du clair et lucide esprit français, esprit des réalités terrestres. . . . Ils se sont trouvés en présence de leur véritables origines et ont compris qu'il ne fallait pas chercher ailleurs des guides et des soutiens." Ibid.

43. Reymond, "Le Rappel à l'ordre," p. 222.

44. ". . . notre plus haute référence nationale." André Lhote, "L'Enseignement de Cézanne," *N.R.F.* no. 86 (November 1920), quoted in ibid.

45. "Jean Fouquet, Le Nain, Ingres avec ses dessins prodigieux d'acuité et de style . . ." André Lhote, "Première Visite au Louvre," *N.R.F.* no. 72 (September 1919), quoted in ibid.

46. "Trois pommes sur un plat peuvent suffire à donner l'idée d'un peintre excellemment doué, mais un paysage de Claude Lorrain ou *Les Bergers d'Arcadie* donnent une idée plus fière de l'art et de l'humanité." Roger Allard, untitled article, *Le Nouveau Spectateur* 1, no. 1 (10 May 1919), p. 9.

47. Kahnweiler, *Juan Gris*, p. 94.

48. Gris to Kahnweiler, 25 August 1919, *Letters*, ed. Cooper, p. 65.

49. "Il me suffit de reconnaître en cet artiste l'essentiel des dons de notre race; cette mesure et cette grace sévère qui ne naissent qu'en France, comme aussi ce dédain des aspects éphémères, et ce besoin de profondeur." Bissière, *Georges Braque* (Paris, 1920), n.p.

50. All of these works are reproduced, and most of their sources indicated, in Seligman, *La Fresnaye*, pp. 233–37.

51. Ibid., p. 79.

52. "Je voudrais te voir faire de grands tableaux comme Le Poussin, quelque chose de lyrique comme ta copie de Le Nain." Grand Palais, *Picasso: Oeuvres reçues*, pp. 95–96. The entire letter, with a slightly different English translation, is reproduced in McCully, *Picasso Anthology*, p. 130.

53. Robert Rosenblum cites Ingres's *Turkish Bath* as a source for the picture: it is certainly that in general terms, but not, I think the specific reference here intended by Picasso. Rosenblum, "Ten Images," in Walker Art Center, *Picasso from the Musée Picasso, Paris* (Minneapolis, 1980), p. 49.

54. "Est-ce qu'à l'heure où la médiocrité semblait, sur tant de points, triomphante, un Puvis de Chavannes n'a pas paru, comme à point nommé, pour rendre à l'art français toute sa dignité?" Michel, "L'Art français après la Guerre," p. 328. For the influence of Puvis's art on Picasso before the war, see Art Gallery of Ontario, *Puvis de Chavannes and the Modern Tradition*, ed. Richard Wattenmaker (Toronto, 1975), pp. 168–77.

55. The photograph on which Picasso based his drawing was taken by Léon Marotte in 1913. It is reproduced in Georges Rivière, *Renoir et ses amis* (Paris, 1921).

56. Certainly more than just Degas is evoked by Picasso's ballet pictures, because the ballet was generally a popular subject, especially for printmakers and sculptors, in the nineteenth century.

57. For an example of the Puvis-type drawings, see Zervos, IV, no. 6, dated 1920.

58. ". . . tout, y compris Léonard, Durer, Le Nain, Ingres, Van Gogh, Cézanne, oui, tout . . . excepté Picasso." Roger Allard, "Expositions diverses," *Le Nouveau Spectateur* 1, nos. 11/12 (25 October–10 November 1919), p. 28.

59. "L'exposition qui vient d'avoir lieu rue de la Ville-l'Evêque arrivait, semble-t-il, à son heure. . . . Tandis que Delacroix est un peu relégué dans l'ombre, Ingres, depuis des années, sollicite l'attention des artistes et du public." Léonce Bénédite, "Une Exposition d'Ingres," *Gazette des Beaux-Arts* 63, no. 3 (1921), pp. 326–27.

60. ". . . M. Picasso, comme mes jeunes compatriotes André Lhote et Bissière, si compréhensifs de la sensibilité ingriste—dont ils sont pourtant plus éloignés qu'ils ne se l'imaginent—seront suivis à leur tour par des cadets ardents, comme ils ont suivi leurs anciens. Car c'est la loi désormais: chacun entend, à son heure, pouvoir se réclamer de M. Ingres." Henri Lapauze, "Une Nouvelle Leçon de Ingres," *La Renaissance de l'Art Français et des Industries de Luxe*, special Ingres issue (April 1921), p. 191.

61. "Les cubistes d'aujourd'hui ont été devancés dans leur admiration pour Ingres par des révolutionnaires qui se sont assagis." Ibid.

62. ". . . cette exposition, au profit des blessés de la face, vaillants qui se sont sacrifiés à la Patrie, arrivait à son heure. Nos jeunes artistes vont, hélas! à la dérive, ne sachant au juste quel entendre. Je vois bien qu'ils cherchent leur voie avec une entière bonne foi, mais personne n'est là pour la leur indiquer. On parle volontiers de reconstruction, d'ordre, de disciplinne. Et on croit entendre M. Ingres lui-même." Ibid.

63. ". . . la France est, avant toute autre parenté, la plus hellénique des nations glorieuses"; "Il ne s'agit pas, bien entendu, de la Grèce

actuelle. . . . Mais de cette Grèce d'Euripide, de Socrate, de Platon, de Praxitèle, de Phidias . . .”; “. . . les tendances d'une race . . . il y a entre l'oeuvre de Ingres . . . et nos propres penchants, d'assez frappantes analogies”; “. . . cette vertu d'hellénisme suprême chez Ingres . . .”; “telle oeuvre procurera toujours aux hommes de race et de culture Gréco-Latine une légère et calme ivresse, capable d'aider à supporter les doutes et le poids de la vie.” “Cet enseignement capital ne saurait trop être souligné du moment présent, où nous nous réveillons à peine de l'emprise germanique qui s'était abattu sur nos esprits sous formes de systèmes asphyxiants beaucoup plus nuisibles que les gaz empoisonnés . . .” Arsène Alexandre, “Comprendre Ingres, c'est comprendre la Grèce et la France,” in ibid., pp. 194–205.

64. “La consécration du temps fait de telles rivalités une harmonie . . . on se réjouit que la France ait ainsi, par un merveilleux équilibre qui n'appartient qu'à elle, pu donner naissance, au même moment, au même pays, à deux génies aussi représentatifs des tendances opposées.” Ibid., p. 194.

65. “Un siècle de recul opère bien des rapprochements et des métamorphoses, égalisant les sommets les plus abrupts, ainsi que le fait pour nos yeux un observatoire élevé, il transforme un révolutionnaire en classique et un classique en révolutionnaire, ce qui est une manière de les mettre d'accord.” Ibid., pp. 194–95.

66. See Kahnweiler, *My Galleries and Painters*, pp. 67–71, and Gee, *Dealers, Critics, and Collectors*, pp. 19–85.

67. Although Gris's series (Kahnweiler, *Gris*, p. 323) must be understood in the light of the Ingres “revival,” it may well have in fact a German source: these prints are strikingly close to works like Peter von Cornelius's pencil drawing of Konrad Eberhard, now in the Staatliche Graphische Sammlung, Munich.

68. Gris to Kahnweiler, 27 November 1921, *Letters*, ed. Cooper, p. 128.

69. “. . . le superficiel de l'autre [i.e. Picasso] et son snobisme habituel”; “cette continuité dans le pillage que les individualistes osent appeler ‘la tradition.’ ” Robert Delaunay, “Fragments, Notes,” c. 1923–24, in Delaunay, *Du Cubisme*, p. 101. Delaunay was using the term “individualists” in a negative sense—this passage begins with a phrase from Léonce Rosenberg: “l'individualisme exagéré conduit au pillage.”

70. “P avec ses périodes. Steinlen, Lautrec, Van Gogh, Daumier, Corot, Nègres, Braque, Derain, Cézanne, Renoir, Ingres, etc., etc., etc. . . . Puvis de Chavannes, néo-italiens. Ces influences prouvent le peu de sérieux au point de vue de la construction et de la sûreté.” Ibid.

71. La Fresnaye's homosexuality has been unacknowledged in the literature until recently; the silence was broken by Eric Hild, curator at the Musée de l'Annonciade in Saint-Tropez, in the catalogue (by that museum and the Musée d'Art Moderne, Troyes) *Roger de la Fresnaye* (1983), n.p.

72. "Il m'avait dit en le peignant 'je veux faire ça comme M. Ingres.' " André Mare in his notebook, c. 1921–22 (Collection Françoise Mare-Vène, Paris).

73. I know of at least one other Gleizes drawing in a wholly traditional mode during this period, a pencil portrait of Mme. Walter Fleischer, dated 1918, in the collection of the Musée National d'Art Moderne, Centre Georges Pompidou, Paris.

74. I lectured on this subject at the 1985 annual meeting of the College Art Association, at Los Angeles: "From Cosmopolitan to Colonial: Henri Matisse's Esthetic of the Orient." My own thinking on the subject also owes much to my former student Yona Zeldis, who wrote an M.A. qualifying paper on the subject for Columbia University (1981): "Remembrance of Things Past: Matisse's Odalisques of the Twenties."

75. "Oh! Renoir était une merveille! . . . J'ai toujours pensé qu'aucune époque n'offre d'histoire plus noble, plus héroïque, d'accomplissement plus magnifique que celui de Renoir." Matisse to Ragnar Hoppe (June 1919) in Dominique Fourcade, "Autres propos de Henri Matisse," *Macula* 1 (1976), p. 97.

76. "Reste M. Matisse qui demeure trop en dehors de la peinture, quoi qu'il se serve de couleurs, pour qu'il soit parlé de lui ici." Vernay, "La Triennale," p. 29.

77. *La Mise en valeur des colonies françaises*, quoted in Christopher M. Andrew and A. S. Kanya-Foster, *France Overseas: The Great War and the Climax of French Imperial Expansion* (London, 1981), p. 212.

78. Ibid.

79. For the cultural dimension of "Orientalism" and colonialism, see Edward Said, *Orientalism* (New York, 1978), and Linda Nochlin, "The Imaginary Orient," *Art in America* 71, no. 5 (May 1983), pp. 118–31, 187–91. See also Jean-Claude Lebensztejn, "Les Textes du peintre," *Critique* (May 1979), pp. 400–433.

80. Romy Golan will expand upon the colonialist issue in the 1920s and 1930s in her forthcoming Ph.D. dissertation (Courtauld Institute of Art, University of London).

81. ". . . les artistes d'Europe, sans s'*africaniser*, s'*asiatiser*, ou s'*océaniser*, peuvent cependant toujours tenter pour se rafraîchir l'imagination et s'aiguiser la vue" (emphasis in the original). Arsène Al-

exandre, "Les Richesses Artistiques de la France Coloniale," *La Renaissance de l'Art Français* (April 1922), p. 154.

82. L. Bénédite, "Une Exposition d'Ingres," p. 327 (with the caption: "*L'Odalisque à l'Esclave*, Par Ingres (1842), Appartient à Sir Phillip Sassoon)."

83. Matisse wrote to Bénédite on 7 March 1922 that he was "greatly honored by the offer that you have made me concerning the odalisque currently on exhibit at Bernheim-Jeune," and that he was sure there would be no problem since it was a question of a museum purchase. The picture was painted in Nice the previous year. See Isabelle Monod-Fontaine, *Matisse: Oeuvres de Henri Matisse (1869–1954)*, *Collections du Musée National d'Art Moderne, Paris* (Paris, 1979).

84. ". . . un anarchiste, dès qu'il en est venu à admettre un jour l'existence d'une autorité, menace, par la suite, de devenir plus autoritaire, et plus *purement* autoritaire que personne au monde." Jean Paulhan, "Du Cubisme à propos de *L'Elan*," *Les Annales* (January 1916), p. 63.

85. "Au commencement du XXe siècle, l'anarchie artistique est à son comble malgré les très louables efforts de quelques-uns. Cela tient à des causes d'ordre moral et social, sans doute, mais ce n'est pas mon intention d'examiner cet aspect du problème. Peut-être de temps en temps serai-je forcé d'y faire allusion, mais si je me décide à publier ces notes, c'est avant tout pour montrer et souligner aux artistes de ma génération les causes esthétiques et techniques de ce désordre, et leur indiquer le chemin pour en sortir." Gino Severini, *Du Cubisme au Classicisme: Esthétique du compas et du nombre* (Paris, 1921), p. 13.

86. "On a cherché âprement *l'originalité*, mais n'ayant que la fantaisie et le caprice comme base, on n'a atteint en général que la *singularité*" (p. 14); "Après Ingres, dont l'influence heureuse nous a beaucoup soutenus, des essais de plus en plus hardis, souvent divergents et contradictoires . . ." Ibid., p. 18.

87. ". . . évidemment, non pas une vieille Ecole replâtrée et repeinte aux fraîches couleurs impressionnistes, comme l'Ecole des Beaux-Arts, mais un *Edifice*, un Monument tout neuf, depuis la base jusqu'au toit, tout en ayant comme génératrices les éternelles lois de la construction, que nous retrouvons à la base de l'art de tous les temps . . ." Ibid., p. 15.

88. "Les meilleurs peintres, les plus doués, ont cru sincèrement et beaucoup le croient encore, pouvoir ramener la peinture à la construction et au style par la *déformation*. . . . Les plus intelligents parmi les artistes commencent cependant à se rendre compte qu'il n'est pas possible d'édifier quelque chose de solide sur le caprice, la fantaisie

ou le bon goût, et qu'en somme, rien de bon n'est possible sans l'Ecole." Ibid., pp. 14–15.

89. "Ces causes peuvent se résumer en quelques mots: Les artistes de notre époque ne savent pas se servir du compas, du rapporteur et des nombres.

"Depuis la Renaissance Italienne, les lois constructives sont graduellement rentrées dans l'oubli." Ibid., pp. 13–14.

90. "Au lieu d'exalter Homère, Virgile, Cicéron, etc., il aurait mieux valu suivre de près Orphée, Pythagore, Aristote, Platon . . ." Ibid., p. 121.

91. "Nous nous retrouvons aujourd'hui, à plusieurs siècles d'interval, devant une situation identique.

"Aujourd'hui on parle beaucoup de la grande civilisation grecque, on se réclame d'elle, et on se déclare hellénistes, mais il est sousentendu que c'est de l'hellénisme Ionien, du paganisme et de l'Epicurisme qu'on entend parler en général . . .

"Aurons-nous un nouveau Pythagore capable de réunir et ordonner toutes les bonnes forces que nous sentons autour de nous et qui tendent vraiment vers une nouvelle renaissance?" Ibid., pp. 121–22.

92. "Dans l'immense destruction où nous vivons, faute d'un homme poète, soldat, législateur capable de regrouper tout ce qui est valable en France et de donner un âme à la nation indifférente . . ." André Mare, in his notebook, c. 1921–22 (Collection Françoise Mare-Vène, Paris).

93. For example, A. Augustin Rey, "Napoléon: Ingénieur et Architecte," a lecture delivered at the Association des Hygiénistes et Techniciens Municipaux on 5 May 1921, and a glut of books: Elie Faure, *Napoléon*; G. Montorgueil, *Napoléon*; A. Dayot, *Napoléon*; C. N. Rados, *Napoléon I et la Grèce* (all published Paris, 1921). Marshal Foch also delivered a speech in commemoration on 5 May (the actual day of the centennial).

94. Quoted in F. L. Carsten, *The Rise of Fascism* (Berkeley, 1967), p. 79.

95. The revival of the Olympics in modern times had been in large measure a French initiative, led by Pierre, Baron de Coubertin. See his account of the revival of the games in *Entre deux batailles* (Paris, 1922). The first winter Olympic games were held in 1924 at Chamonix.

96. "Aller de l'anarchie à l'Action Française n'est pas se contredire, mais construire. . . . Son oeuvre est une suite de constructions destinée à créer ou à maintenir une harmonie. Il prise par dessus tout et fait admirer l'ordre, parce que tout ordre représente de la beauté et

de la force." André Malraux, 1923, as quoted in Weber, *Action Fran-*
çaise, pp. 518–19.

97. See Martin Caiger-Smith, "Gino Severini: The Montegufoni Frescoes" (M.A. thesis, Courtauld Institute of Art, University of London,
1983).

98. This information was conveyed to me by a member of the staff of
the Bureau des Bâtiments in December 1976. The statue is inscribed:
"Hoc monumentum ad ingenii latini gloriam a latinis gentibus anno
MCMXXI erectum est. (Ce monument à la gloire du Génie latin a été
érige en l'année 1921 par les peuples latins.)" File from the Bureaux
des Bâtiments Civils et des Palais Nationaux, at the Palais Royal,
Paris. It is interesting to note that the Commission du Vieux Paris
objected strenuously to the placing of the statute in the garden of the
Palais Royal (according to a notation on the above file).

99. "Nous pensons apercevoir une direction où l'instinct créateur de
notre race, aussi neuf et aussi hardi que jamais, est en train de s'en-
gager . . . nous dirons tout ce qui semble nous faire prévoir une renaissance classique." Jacques Rivière, "Introduction," *N.R.F.* 69
(June 1919), as quoted in Reymond, "Le Rappel à l'ordre d'André
Lhote," pp. 209–10.

100. "Je m'occupe de la *Vie de Socrate* . . . que je voudrais blanche
et pure comme l'antique." Erik Satie to Valentine Hugo, 6 January
1917, as quoted in Valentine Hugo, "Le Socrate que j'ai connu," *La
Revue Musicale* no. 214 (June 1952), p. 140.

101. Reproduced in Green, *Léger and the Avant-Garde*, p. 234.

102. Hans Baron, *The Crisis of the Early Italian Renaissance* (Princeton, 1966), p. 3.

103. "Nous [sommes] voici . . . aux premiers jours d'une indiscutable
renaissance" (p. 12); "Il semble que le XXe siècle commence à l'armistice et qu'il y ait eu, depuis l'exposition universelle, vingt ans
d'entre-siècles" (p. 206); "Certes, l'Ordre classique nous saisfait . . .
Il fallait une alliance étroite, désinteressée, généreuse, tant d'amour,
c'est à dire capable de création authentique pour atteindre à cela. Le
bénéfice d'une telle rencontre est inéstimable. . . . C'est une si rare
et si complète alliance qui peut vraiment et seule favoriser l'Ordre
classique" (p. 10); ". . . tout ce que conditionne l'impressionnisme
appartient désormais à un cycle fermé. Le premier Salon libre
d'après-guerre, Le Salon d'Automne de 1919, 'ce mortel triomphe des
valeurs classés,' selon l'expression du plus raisonnable des peintres
sachant écrire, nous en fournit la certitude" (p. 34). Salmon, *L'Art
vivant*. I do not know the identity of this "most reasonable of painters."

104. "Cette conception, qui tend de toutes ses jeunes forces vers une

libération du passage et de l'exceptionnel, en un mot, de tout individualisme, implique nécessairement une universalité du nombre et de
durée. . . . Cette technique que nous définissons "classique" est op-
posée à la technique directe." E. Viollier, "A l'ordre classique—technique classique," *Bulletin de l'Effort Moderne* no. 10 (January 1924),
p. 15.

105. Zervos, IV, no. 243.

106. See Rubin, *Picasso in the Collection of the Museum of Modern
Art*, pp. 116, 220. Elaine Johnson, author of the entry for the museum's drawing *La Source*, has reproduced the painting *Nymph of
Fontainebleau* from the chateau; it is the work on which Picasso based
his drawings and painting of 1921. The attribution of the work in the
chateau reads: "Cartoon by Couder, painted by Alaux, based on an
engraving of the original composition (c. 1532–41) by Rosso" (Rubin,
p. 220).

107. We now know that the *Three Women at the Spring* has a san-
guine-and-oil study, also of 1921, in the collection of the Musée Picasso.

108. Picasso may have been influenced by the various funerary monuments, cenotaphs, etc. that were being produced by students at the
Ecole, as for instance Jeanniot's *Le Retour du Héros* that was the Prix
de Rome winner in sculpture for 1919. See "Chronique," *Art et Décoration* 36 (November 1919), p. 3.

109. See Pool, "Picasso's Neo-Classicism: Second Period," p. 206,
and also Anthony Blunt, "Picasso's Classical Period (1917–25)," *Burlington* 110, no. 781 (April 1968), p. 188.

110. Robert Judson Clark and Marian Burleigh-Motley, "New Sources
for Picasso's *Pipes of Pan*," *Arts* 55, no. 2 (October 1980), pp. 92–
93.

111. See Theodore Reff, "Picasso's *Three Musicians*: Maskers, Artists, and Friends," *Art in America* 68, no. 10 (December 1980), pp.
126–42.

112. In a seminar on Cubism conducted at Yale University in the fall
of 1973, Anne Hanson pointed out the reference in Apollinaire's wartime satire *Les Mamelles de Tirésias* (1917): "Smoke the shepherd's
pipe . . ."

113. "Au lendemain d'une guerre où, malgré son infériorité numé-
rique, la France de la Marne et de Verdun triompha, par son héroïsme
et son génie, de la sauvage ruée d'un empire de 60 millions d'habitants, il devenait indispensable de condenser, dans une puissante
synthèse visuelle, les désastreux effets de la Dénatalité, et les
remèdes qu'on doit, à tout prix, mettre en oeuvre pour l'enrayer.

"L'avenir même de la race est en jeu et rien ne serait d'une ironie plus cruelle que de voir s'éteindre le flambeau quand il rayonne de son plus vif éclat. Si la France est la lumière du monde, il importe, non seulement à notre pays mais encore à l'espèce humaine, que ce phare ne cesse jamais de projeter, sur la route incertaine, son faisceau lumineux. Que fait-il pour cela? Que les délicieux porteurs de torches que sont nos enfants viennent au monde en assez grand nombre! Pour toute lampe qui s'éteint, il faut au moins qu'une lamp s'allume." Q. Albertini, "La Genèse et les buts de L'Exposition Nationale de la Maternité et de l'Enfance," in catalogue of *L'Exposition Nationale de la Maternité et de l'Enfance* (Paris, 1921), p. 9.

114. Alfred H. Barr, Jr., *Picasso: Fifty Years of His Art* (New York, 1946), p. 128.

115. Linda Nochlin, "Picasso's Color," p. 117. By way of substantiating Nochlin's interpretation, it should be pointed out that the couple dancing on Bastille Day was a popular subject of late-nineteenth-century sculpture—for example, Carabin's (undated) and Bourdelle's of 1906, both reproduced in Maurice Rheims's *La Sculpture au XIXe siècle* (Paris, 1972).

116. Robert Goldwater, "Puvis de Chavannes: Some Reasons for a Reputation," *Art Bulletin* 28, no. 1 (March 1946), pp. 42–43.

117. See Nadine Pouillon and Isabelle Monod-Fontaine, *Braque: Oeuvres de Georges Braque (1892-1963), Collections du Musée National d'Art Moderne, Paris* (Paris, 1982), p. 76.

118. "Braque, de grises harmonies; certainement tout cela est très fin, très qualitif, tres distingué; mais je devine que cette sobriété n'est que le produit de l'indigence, et sous la mesure esquise, l'élégance et la précieux raffinement, je sense la dépression et l'impuissance." Paul Husson, "Le Salon d'Automne—la peinture," *Montparnasse* no. 17 (November 1922), p. 2.

119. See Eric Hild's discussion of the picture in Musée de l'Annonciade, *Roger de la Fresnaye*, n.p.

120. Ethlyne J. Seligman and Germain Seligman, "Of the Proximity of Death and Its Stylistic Activations—Roger de la Fresnaye and Juan Gris," *Art Quarterly* (Spring 1949), pp. 146–55.

121. Picasso, in an interview with Marius de Zayas (1923), in Barr, *Picasso: Fifty Years*, p. 270.

VII From Analysis to Synthesis   1. The post-war history of Cubism will be considered by Christopher Green in *Cubism and Its Enemies* (New Haven and London, 1987).

2. Picasso's work for the theatre is the subject of Deborah Menaker's forthcoming doctoral dissertation (Institute of Fine Arts, New York University).

3. Léger's work for the theatre is the subject of Judy Freeman's forth-coming Ph.D. dissertation (Yale University). See also Elisabeth Blondel, "Fernand Léger et les arts du spectacle" (unpublished thesis, Bibliothèque Jacques Doucet, Institut d'Art et d'Archéologie, Paris, 1969).

4. For the Ballets Suédois, see the exhibition catalogue Musée d'Art Moderne de la Ville de Paris, *Cinquantenaire des Ballets Suédois, 1920–1925: Collections du Musée de la Danse, Stockholm* (Paris, 1971).

5. Fernand Léger, "Le Ballet Spectacle: L'Objet-Spectacle," *Bulletin de l'Effort Moderne* 12 (1925), here as translated in Léger, *Functions of Painting*, ed. Edward F. Fry (New York, 1973), pp. 71–73.

6. It is important to remember that Léger's interest in creating new theatrical effects also led to his work in film. See, for instance, G. Sadoul, "Fernand Léger et le ciné-plastique," *Cinéma* 59, no. 35 (1959).

7. "Mais pour ce qui me concerne, je suis, quoique soldat et blessé, quoique volontaire, un naturalisé, tenu, par conséquent, à une très grande circonspection. Je crois qu'il pourrait être compromettant pour moi, surtout au point où nous en sommes de cette guerre multiforme, de collaborer à une revue, si bon que puisse être son esprit, qui a pour collaborateurs des Allemands, si Ententophiles qu'ils soient. Je dois cela à mes opinions et à ma conduite même, mais je serais imprudent si j'agissais autrement." Letter dated 6 February 1918, in Sanouillet, *Dada à Paris*, p. 98.

8. The following account of Dada activity has been drawn mainly from three sources: Sanouillet, *Dada à Paris*; William Camfield, *Francis Picabia: His Art, Life and Times* (Princeton, 1979); and John Russell, *Max Ernst: Life and Work* (New York, 1967).

9. Camfield, *Picabia*, p. 129, n. 20.

10. Ibid., p. 129 (*391*, no. 9, November 1919).

11. Ibid., p. 130. For contemporary accounts of Vauxcelles's challenge and Ribement-Dessaignes's refusal, see *391* no. 10 (December 1919), and *Carnet de la Semaine* (28 December 1919).

12. "Il est assez curieux de voir aujourd'hui dans notre société, et parfois dans la meilleure, prodiguer les sourires et les encouragements aux révolutionnaires, ennemis inexpiables de notre civilisation, de notre patrie, et du capital aussi. . . . Or, c'est la même chose, qu'on ne s'y trompe pas. Extrémistes, révolutionnaires, bolchévistes, dadaistes,—même farine, même origine, même poison. . . . Ils ont déclaré que . . . rien de ce que nous estimons raisonnable, délicat, ou beau ne les intéressait; que la culture gréco-latine, et la fran-çaise—parbleu!—qui en découle, avait fait leur temps. . . . Sentez-

vous bien ce que cela cache, ces étrangetés? Voyez-vous contre quoi ce délire très conscient est principalement dirigé? Eh! contre tout ce qui a jadis établi l'empire intellectuel français, et maintenant aujourd'hui encore notre incontestable supériorité, quant à l'esprit à savoir, la clarté, l'enchaînement des idées, la logique, la mesure et le goût. Et c'est l'indigne volupté du bouleversement et de l'anarchie qui se dissimule sous ces masques bariolés de fous. Comme à Petrograde, comme à Moscou. *As in Berlin*, dans les bas-fonds." Marcel Boulenger, "Herr Dada," *Le Gaulois* (26 April 1920), p. 1.

13. For the Barrès trial, see "L'Affaire Barrès," *Littérature* 3, no. 20 (August 1921), pp. 1–24, and Frederick Busi, "Dada and the 'Trial' of Maurice Barrès," *Boston University Journal* 23, no. 2 (1975), pp. 63–71.

14. Originally published in *Le Coq* no. 1 (May [?] 1920), quoted Steegmuller, *Cocteau*, pp. 257–58.

15. See Brown, *An Impersonation of Angels*, pp. 208–209.

16. See the exhibition catalogue Galerie Artcurial, *Au temps du "Boeuf sur le Toit"* (Paris, 1980), text by Georges Bernier.

17. See Hans Wingler, *The Bauhaus* (Cambridge, Mass., 1969), p. 483.

18. Gris to D.-H. Kahnweiler, 2 December 1919, in *Letters*, ed. Cooper, p. 70.

19. "A Paris il ne se passe rien potins idiots, tous les génies passent leur temps à se fâcher puis à se raccommoder . . . Picasso est de plus en plus admiré par tous, étant de plus en plus arrivé, où, je ne sais mais ceux qui l'admirent le savent . . ." Picabia to Tristan Tzara, 28 March 1919, in Sanouillet, *Dada à Paris*, p. 485.

20. "—Pablo Picasso, à qui le mage Max Jacob vient de révéler les origines germaniques du cubisme, a décidé de retourner à l'Ecole des Beaux-Arts (atelier Luc-Olivier Merson). *L'Elan* a publié ses premières études 'd'après modèle.' Picasso est désormais le chef d'une nouvelle école à laquelle notre collaborateur Francis Picabia n'hésitant pas une minute, tient à donner son adhésion. Le kodak publié ci-dessus en est le signe solennel." "Pharamousse," "Odeurs de Partout," *391* no. 1 (25 January 1917).

21. "Si vous saviez quelle vie maussade parmi tous ces Artistes qui ne rêvent que glorie académique." Picabia to Tzara, 4 June 1919, in Sanouillet, *Dada à Paris*, p. 487.

22. See Sanouillet, *Dada à Paris*, pp. 146–47.

23. Ibid., pp. 160–62, and also Paul Dermée, "Premier et Dernier Rapport du secrétaire de la Section d'Or: Excommuniés," *391* no. 12 (March 1920), p. 6.

24. "The Dada Case," by Gleizes, 1920, is both translated into English and reproduced in full in *The Dada Painters and Poets: An Anthology*, ed. Robert Motherwell (New York, 1951), pp. 298–303.

25. In Camfield, *Picabia*, p. 147. Mme. Gleizes, born Juliette Roche, was apparently the daughter of an important national figure from the Ardèche.

26. Ibid., p. 127, and Tristan Tzara, "Interview de Jean Metzinger sur le cubisme," *391* no. 14 (November 1920), p. 8:
"Tz.— —que pensez-vous du livre de Gleizes *Du cubisme et des moyens de le comprendre?*
"M.— —absolument idiot.
"Tz.— —quel but a-t-il poursuivi en écrivant ce livre?
"— —s'expliquer le cubisme à lui-même, parce qu'il ne l'a pas encore compris!
"Tz.— —pourquoi avez-vous écrit un livre en collaboration avec Gleizes?
"M.— —parce que je suis très paresseux et qu'il me fallait un secretaire."
It is unclear whether the interview is real or imagined, although included is the following editorial statement (presumably written by Picabia): "Voici la conversation qui s'échangea entre Metzinger et Tzara à propos d'Albert—ajoutons que l'authenticité de cette conversation nous est garantie par Metzinger lui-même et que celui-ci nous a autorisé à la reproduire dans *391*."

27. Gris to D.-H. Kahnweiler, 25 August 1919, *Letters*, ed. Cooper, p. 65.

28. Gris to Kahnweiler, 31 January 1920, in ibid., p. 75.

29. Reff, "Picasso's *Three Musicians*."

30. See my discussion of *Etudes* in "Hockney, Center Stage," *Art in America* 73, no. 11 (November 1985), pp. 148–49.

31. For a consideration of Picasso's critical fortunes in the 1920s, see Eunice Lipton, *Picasso Criticism, 1901–39: The Making of an Artist-Hero* (New York, 1976), pp. 140–213.

32. For Picasso's prices, as well as those of the rest of the Parisian avant-garde, see Gee, "Dealers, Critics, and Collectors."

33. Rubin, *Picasso in the Collection of the Museum of Modern Art*, pp. 112–13.

34. Blaise Cendrars, "Why is the 'Cube' Disintegrating?" (English translation of "Pourquoi le 'Cube' s'effrite?" *La Rose Rouge*, 15 May 1919), in Fry, *Cubism*, p. 154.

35. Ibid., p. 155.

36. Ibid.

37. "A la naissance de tout mouvement artistique, des forces enne-mies mais non égales, se sont toujours aussitôt dressées les unes contre les autres . . ."; "L'homme qui croit défendre la tradition . . . en se couvrant les yeux . . ."; ". . . celui qui, s'insurge contre un système établi . . . fait oeuvre de démolisseur"; "Son travail cepen-dant a préparé la venue de celui dont les temps présents fêtent le retour: du *constructeur*." Léonce Rosenberg, *Cubisme et tradition* (Paris, 1920), pp. 2–3.

38. "Tel, à de certaines époques, l'art de la construction s'élance par-fois dans un style particulier, à portées plus grandes, que lui permet-tent de réaliser des matériaux nouveaux, sans que . . . se trouvent modifiées, pour cela, les principes de statique qui régissent l'archi-tecture de tous les temps." Marshal Foch, as quoted in Léonce Rosen-berg, "Parlons peinture . . . ," *L'Esprit Nouveau* no. 5 (February 1921), pp. 580–81.

39. "Les formes évoluent, les principes directeurs subsistent." Léonce Rosenberg in ibid., p. 581.

40. "Ses discours et leurs actes s'ajustaient si heureusement qu'on eût dit que ces hommes n'étaient que ses membres. Tu ne saurais croire, Socrate, quelle joie c'était pour mon âme de connaître une chose si bien réglée. Je ne sépare plus l'idée d'un temple de celle de son édi-fication. En voyant un, je vois une action admirable, plus glorieuse encore qu'une victoire et plus contraire à la misérable nature. Le dé-truire et le construire sont égaux en importance, et il faut des âmes pour l'un et pour l'autre, mais le construire est le plus cher à mon esprit. O, très heureux Eupalinos!" Paul Valéry, *Eupalinos ou l'Ar-chitecte*, as it appeared in Louis Süe and André Mare, *Architectures* (Paris, 1921), p. 11.

41. "PHÈDRE: Tu semble conquis toi-même à l'adoration de l'archi-tecture! Voici que tu ne peux parler sans emprunter de l'art majeur, ses images et son ferme idéal.

"SOCRATE: . . . Il y avait en moi un architecte que les circon-stances n'ont pas achevé de former." Valéry, in ibid., pp. 34–35.

42. See McLeod, " 'Architecture or Revolution.' "

43. Gleizes and Metzinger, *Cubism* (English translation of *Du Cu-bisme*), in Fry, *Cubism*, p. 105.

44. Fernand Léger, "The Origins of Painting and Its Representational Value" (English translation of "Les Origines de la peinture et sa va-leur représentative," *Montjoie!* no. 8 [29 May 1913]), and no. 9/10 [14/29 June 1913]), in Fry, *Cubism*, p. 123.

45. "Elle [i.e. Cézanne's art] constitue le point de départ de toute peinture actuelle." D.-H. Kahnweiler, *Confessions esthétiques* (Paris, 1963), p. 15; this is the French version of an excerpt from Kahnwei-ler's *Der Weg zum Kubismus* (Munich, 1920).

46. "Je puis dire, sans m'abuser, que j'ai été de ceux, et des premiers sans doute, qui ont aimé, fait connaître, expliqué et apprécié Cézanne. Je ne suis donc pas suspect à son égard." Emile Bernard, "La Méthode de Paul Cézanne," *Mercure de France* 138, no. 521 (1 March 1920), p. 289.

47. "Le point de vue change; il s'agit maintenant d'examiner ce qu'est son système, s'il est juste ou faux, s'il a suivi la voie essentielle ou l'a abandonnée, si son influence est bonne ou mauvaise, en un mot s'il peut être un guide (puisqu'on l'a choisi comme tel) et un guide favorable à un retour vers les grandes productions qui font la gloire d'une nation et d'une race." Ibid.

48. "La méthode de Cézanne tire son origine du naturalisme. Avant que d'être ce qu'il fut, Cézanne étudia Courbet et Manet"; "Quant à l'esthétique des impressionnistes et celle de Cézanne, on ne peut y reconnaître aucune différence: elles tendent toutes deux à l'expression des choses que nous voyons, au mépris de l'invention, par un style soumis à la nature. C'est le naturalisme." Ibid., pp. 290–91.

49. "Il y a une servilité qui touche à la déchéance morale en cette volonté de se renfermer dans la chose vue, c'est-à-dire dans la conformité de la copie." Ibid., p. 308.

50. "Il y avait dans son système une cause de suicide." Ibid., p. 301.

51. "C'était à la fois une tentative de vérité objective et de logique mentale . . . le dualisme qu'il avait créé dès le début entre sa vision extérieure et l'accomplissement de son système le jeta dans l'erreur et l'arrêta sur des ébauches. C'est en cela que réside tout le drame Cézannien, et par lui se prouve le point faible de sa possibilité. Comment accorder l'optique—qui est relative—avec la théorie—qui est absolue? Comment résoudre la contradiction de la sensation, souvent trompeuse, toujours variable, avec l'application rigoureuse d'un principe accepté? Enfin, comment aboutir à l'accord des sens et de la raison? Cela semble insoluble" (p. 293); ". . . C'est cette difficulté, rencontrée à chaque coup de pinceau qui a tué Cézanne" (p. 301). Ibid.

52. "Puvis de Chavannes, qui partait de l'esprit, a été au XIXe siècle, un affirmateur de la synthèse des lois essentielles de l'art. Cézanne nous offre le spectacle contraire par le sensualisme rétinien qui le dirige. Alors que l'un simplifie, l'autre complique. Alors que l'un n'a pas assez de murailles pour étaler ses vastes compositions, l'autre réduit son format, renonce à toute conception, se confine dans la représentation des objets les plus vulgaires. Pour l'un tout est grand, pour l'autre tout est complexe, petit, difficile." Ibid., pp. 300–301.

53. "Prédominance et triomphe du paysage d'abord, pleinairisme, impressionisme, division du ton, mélange optique . . ."; "l'apparition des excentricités et même des aberrations les moins défendables."

"Est-ce qu'à l'heure où la médiocrité semblait sur tant de points, triomphante, un Puvis de Chavannes n'a pas paru, comme à point nommé, pour rendre à l'art français toute sa dignité?" Michel, "L'Art français après la Guerre," pp. 327–28.

54. "J'ai cru comme tout le monde à la 'tendance classique' de Cézanne; mais maintenant que je vois clair dans l'origine sensorielle de ses 'intentions,' je ne puis plus croire à un homme qui veut faire 'du Poussin sur nature,' qui veut 'redevenir classique par la nature, c'est-à-dire par la sensation.' " Severini, *Du cubisme au classicisme*, p. 20.

55. "Ces dernières années, enfin, nous avons cru trouver un point de départ dans l'oeuvre de Cézanne. Beaucoup de peintres, et on peut dire la presque totalité, ont encore cette conviction; pour ma part, tout en mettant hors de discussion le talent de Cézanne, je crois que ce point de départ est faux et que tout ce qu'on voudra bâtir sur lui s'écroulera, ayant comme base ce qu'il y a de plus éphémère, de plus instable, de plus variable sur cette terre: nos propres sensations . . . je crois pouvoir affirmer aujourd'hui que le chemin à suivre est précisement l'opposé de celui suivi par Cézanne.

"On ne devient pas classique par la sensation mais par l'esprit; l'oeuvre d'art ne doit pas comencer par une analyse de *l'effet*, mais par une analyse de la *cause*, et on ne *construit* pas sans méthode et en se basant uniquement sur les yeux et le bon goût, ou sur de vagues notions générales." Ibid., pp. 19–20.

56. "Mais Cézanne était trop peintre de 'tempérament' pour faire un usage utile du compas et du nombre; il ne se basait que sur ses yeux, plus intelligemment que Claude Monet, avec une volonté bien établie de régler la vision, mais son point de départ restait quand même visuel et sensuel. C'est pourquoi il ne sera jamais satisfait, il recommencera sans cesse le même tableau, et il fera de la tache de pinceau une tache plus grande et modulée, mais cette tache, devenue une surface, ne sera jamais constructive." Gino Severini, "Cézanne et le Cézannisme," *L'Esprit Nouveau* nos. 11/12 (November 1921), p. 1260.

57. ". . . tout en ayant une qualité de premier ordre, il n'est pas un maître." Ibid., p. 1261.

58. There is a letter from Delaunay to an unknown correspondent ("Mon cher ami"), dated 20 August 1920, that says, "Je vous envoie copie de la lettre surprenante que vient de recevoir Sonia en réponse d'une lettre écrite par son associé, le comte de Maubon, à la maison Poiret. . . . Notre première et dernière impression a été que nous sommes enchantés d'une telle bétise de la part de cet homme et pour la première fois je me trouve en possession d'une preuve écrite de la calomnie qui court . . . vous voyez la lettre est sur entête [unclear] . . . papier de la Maison Martine et signée Poiret. . . . Par la tournure de cette lettre il est clair et évident que l'idée de cet homme est de

nuire par une arme radicale, moralement et matériellement. . . . Une telle calomnie ne peut peser plus longtemps . . ." (Sonia Delaunay archive, Paris). It is impossible to know precisely what calumny Delaunay is talking about; it may even be that the dispute was with Poiret, but what kind of calumnies would have resulted from this I do not know.

59. ". . . règle et ordre sont à la base de l'audace . . ." Robert Delaunay, "Fragments, Notes," c. 1923–24 in *Du Cubisme*, p. 103.

60. "—le *pédantisme et fausse science* venue d'Allemagne. Herr critique qui ne voit rien à travers ses binocles—puritain, purisme academique (Fausse interprétation du génie)." Ibid.

61. "Qu'importe le mot *classique* où vont les étiquettes des cubistes, néo-grec ou néo-platoniciens. . . . Ne pouvant pas tenir par une nouvelle construction, les opportunistes pressés de réaliser redemandent à l'antique une épine dorsale; mais même les marbres sont brisés!!!" Ibid., p. 105.

62. For Delaunay's collaboration with Robert Mallet-Stevens in 1925, see Michel Hoog, *Robert Delaunay* (New York, 1976), pp. 87, 89. See also chapter VIII below.

63. André Salmon, "Georges Seurat," *Burlington* 37, no. 210 (September 1920), pp. 120–21.

64. Ibid., p. 122.

65. "Seurat n'a pas besoin d'introduire des figures et des temples grecs dans ses paysages pour leur donner de la gravité, du style. C'est son oeuvre entière qui nous suggère un temple aux mille piliers ou colonnes, avec ses verticales répétées sur des horizontales nettes . . ." Lucie Cousturier, *Seurat* (Paris, 1921), p. 18.

66. "Nous aimons dans Seurat le sec de la grande tradition française depuis toujours . . . ne reproche pas à Seurat d'être de la lignée d'Athènes et non de celle des Flandres; le train de Grèce est un bon train, allez vous lui reprocher de ne pas conduire à Amsterdam?" Amédée Ozenfant, "Seurat," *Cahiers d'Art* (September 1926), p. 172.

67. "[Seurat's] theories, en effet, font tellement partie de son oeuvre." André Lhote, "Parlons peinture" (1922), in Lhote, *Ecrits sur la peinture* (Paris, 1946), p. 88.

68. "Seurat nous donne une image grave d'un paysage nu, venu au monde sans grincement de dents, sans désolation, sans accompagnement obligé d'un orgue de Barbarie. Tout y est bien établi pour vivre: les murs blancs très droits, la cheminée très rigide; et le terrain vague, au premier plan, n'attend—'indifférent'—que la venue d'un industriel qui saura édifier là un vaste hangar de travail et de production. . . . Cela, c'est une définition graphique du style!" Gustave Coquiot, *Seurat* (Paris, 1923), pp. 195–96.

69. "L'Esprit nouveau. Il y a un esprit nouveau: c'est un esprit de construction et de synthèse guidé par une conception claire." *L'Esprit Nouveau* no. 1 (October 1920), p. 3.

70. ". . . il conviendrait peut-être d'employer ici—et sans tarder plus!—ce mot *Constructeur*, . . . Constructeur de quoi, en quoi? n'importe! ce mot veut tout dire. . . . Donc, si vous y tenez, Seurat est un constructeur . . . Mais, hélas! moins heureux que ces deux considérables romanciers, il a peint, lui, avec obstination, simplement, sans se douter qu'il était Seurat-le-Constructeur! Ah! s'il avait pu se douter de cela! Seurat-constructeur! cons-truc-teur! cons-truc-teur! Ah! que ce mot me plaît!" Ibid., pp. 201–202.

71. "En ce moment, ce sont surtout 'les constructeurs' qui se recommandent de Seurat.

"Or, quels sont les noms, de ces constructeurs? Je ne sais pas; ils sont trop! Les jeunes peintres-constructeurs aujourd'hui pullulent. Ils veulent tous être des constructeurs! Cela veut dire, je pense, qu'ils peignent *solidement*, les bougres. Ah! mais! . . . Aux vieilles lunes, les Impressionnistes, les Symbolistes, les Naturalistes! . . . Maintenant, il s'agit d'être serieux, de tracer des verticales, des horizontales, des diagonales, des angles, des triangles, des polyèdres et des dodecaèdres, que sais-je? il faut *construire*, puisqu'on est des constructeurs! . . .

"Ah! c'était bien la peine, ô Seurat, d'avoir tant recherché la 'netteté' pour engendrer de tels nigauds qui se recommandent de toi, ô Prince de la lumière et du style!" Ibid., pp. 241–42.

72. Fernand Léger, "Contemporary Achievements in Painting," originally in *Soirées de Paris* (Paris, 1914), translated in Léger, *Functions of Painting*, p. 17.

73. Fernand Léger, "A Letter," originally published in the *Bulletin de L'Effort Moderne* no. 4 (April 1924, there dated 1922), translated by Charlotte Green in Tate Gallery, *Léger and Purist Paris*, p. 85.

74. Green, *Léger and the Avant-Garde*, p. 182.

75. Robert L. Herbert, in Minneapolis Institute of Arts, *Léger's "Le Grand Déjeuner,"* exhibition catalogue (Minneapolis, 1980), pp. 25–26.

76. Léger, "Le Spectacle: Lumière, couleur, image mobile, objet-spectacle," here as translated in Léger, *Functions of Painting*, p. 47.

77. Léger to Barr, 20 November 1943, from Museum of Modern Art Archives, published in Minneapolis, *Léger's "Le Grand Déjeuner,"* p. 72 (orthography as here).

78. Léger to Barr, 13 November 1942, in ibid., p. 70.

79. Fernand Léger, "Notes on the Mechanical Element" (unpublished, 1923), in Léger, *Functions of Painting*, p. 30.

80. "On a méconnu Seurat jusqu'à le croire attardé à l'analyse, à la représentation de l'immédiat, les jeux fortuits de la lumière, lui, le synthétiste, mieux, le logicien implacable qui ne s'est servi de cette lumière que pour conserver aux objets les apparences qui les caractérisent une fois pour toutes." Cousturier, *Seurat*, pp. 18–19.

81. "Tout à coup et sans transition, . . . le cubisme, Derain, Picasso et Braque consommaient le divorce entre eux et le public extérieur, arrivant au divisionnisme de la forme, nous reculant à l'analyse fragmentée, quand l'art eut toujours tant de peine à s'élever à la synthèse. Là, nul esprit heureusement, ne pouvait plus les suivre. Le bon sens français ne recule pas. . . .

"Ils annoncent bien, les cubistes, les futuristes qu'ils mettent leur sujet dans le mouvement universel mais leur tohu bohu gène tout mouvement. Ils disent bien qu'ils sont analyse et synthèse. Mais l'on n'est pas l'un et l'autre. Et la synthèse ne peut être exigée par les partants. Elle est le palme cueillie par les arrivants. C'est la récompense des maîtres." Aurel, *Le Commandement d'amour*, p. 7.

82. Gino Severini, in the preface to the Marlborough Gallery (London) catalogue of his exhibition there in 1913. I am grateful to Joan Lukach for pointing this out to me.

83. Maurice Raynal, preface to exhibition catalogue, "Salon de Juin: Troisième exposition de la Société Normande de Peinture Moderne," Rouen, June 1912, translated into English and quoted in Fry, *Cubism*, p. 92.

84. Albert-Birot, "Dialogues Numiques," *Sic* no. 11 (November 1916), n.p., translated into English and quoted in Green, *Léger and the Avant-Garde*, p. 126.

85. "Nous sommes à une époque où semble s'opérer une révision des valeurs . . . remplacer l'analyse par la synthèse et par là retourner à la tradition." Bissière [c. 1920?] as quoted (without indication of source) in Cabanne, *Le Siècle de Picasso*, I, p. 351.

86. ". . . un désir toujours grandissant de synthèse . . ." Bissière, from the Introduction to *Georges Braque*, n.p.

87. ". . . l'on a également évoqué la froide figure de l'induction. Des écrivains d'art n'ont pas hésité à soutenir que l'art allait du particulier au général. Quelle hérésie! . . . L'induction artistique signifie la négation complète de toute tentative de l'artiste créateur; elle n'est qu'une méthode pour la vulgarisation, pour l'application en série et surtout le perfectionnement de l'usinage artistique." Maurice Raynal, *Picasso* (Paris, 1922), p. 19.

88. Juan Gris, "Personal Statement" (English translation of untitled article from *L'Esprit Nouveau* no. 5, February 1921), in Fry, *Cubism*, p. 162.

89. "A peine une époque de synthèse succède-t-elle à une époque d'analyse, qu'un désaccord irréductible s'établit aussitôt entre personnes d'époques différentes." Léonce Rosenberg, *Cubisme et empirisme* (Paris, 1921), p. 10.

90. "Nous fûmes amenés naturellement, par ces recherches, à une analyse trop menue de formes, et à une décomposition trop fragmentaire des corps, obsédés que nous étions d'en donner tous les développements formels.

"Cette longue analyse, qui nous a permis de comprendre intégralement les formes dans leurs pures essences plastiques, est aujourd'hui achevée. C'est pourquoi nous sentons un besoin impérieux d'entrer dans une plus large et plus synthétique vision plastique.

"Nous entrons dans une période de constructionisme ferme et sûr, car nous voulons faire la synthèse de la déformation analytique, avec la connaissance et la pénétration qui nous sont devenues faciles à travers toutes nos déformations analytiques. Ceci pour la couleur aussi bien que pour la forme. Il faut éviter systématiquement l'analyse que nous nous sommes imposée depuis longtemps." F. T. Marinetti, 1921, quoted in Victor Servranckx, "Les Voies nouvelles de l'art plastique," *Bulletin de l'Effort Moderne* no. 18 (October 1925), p. 10.

91. "Au-dessus des choses organisées, il y a les lois organisatrices.
"Au-dessus de l'individu, il y a la collectivité.
"Au-dessus de l'analyse, il y a la synthèse.
"Au-dessus de la haine, il y a l'amour.
"Au-dessus du petit amour de soi et ses amis, il y a le grand amour de l'humanité." Marcel Bauginet, "Vers une synthèse esthétique et sociale." *Bulletin de l'Effort Moderne* no. 14 (April 1925), p. 11. Nor is it surprising to hear Bauginet state, in the same article, "Il y a un art primaire et dominant; c'est l'architecture."

92. Pablo Picasso, "Picasso Speaks" (1923), in Barr, *Picasso: Fifty Years*, pp. 270–71.

93. See my article "Eminence Gris" for a fuller discussion of these themes.

94. This was suggested by Tom Gibbons in "Cubism and the 'Fourth Dimension' in the Context of the Late Nineteenth-Century and Early Twentieth-Century Revival of Occult Idealism," *Journal of the Warburg and Courtauld Institutes*, vol. 44 (1981), pp. 130–47.

95. Juan Gris, quoted in Vaucrécy (pseud. of Amédée Ozenfant), "Juan Gris," *L'Esprit Nouveau* no. 5, here as translated in Kahnweiler, *Juan Gris*, p. 193.

96. Arthur Dene Stevens, "The Counter-Modern Movement in French and German Painting after World War I" (unpublished Ph.D. dissertation, Indiana University, 1971), p. 145.

97. Gris to D.-H. Kahnweiler (c. 1919), quoted in Kahnweiler, *Juan Gris*, p. 93.

98. Gris to Kahnweiler (December, 1923), quoted by Mark Rosenthal in the exhibition catalogue University Art Museum (Berkeley) et al., *Juan Gris* (New York, 1983), p. 165.

99. Severini, as quoted in Kahnweiler, *Juan Gris*, p. 15.

1. The principal document for the study of the 1925 Exposition is the twelve-volume catalogue of the fair: Imprimerie Nationale, *Encyclopédie des arts décoratifs et industriels modernes au XXième siècle* (Paris, 1925; reprint, New York and London, 1977). See also the catalogue *Cinquantenaire de l'Exposition de 1925* (Musée des Arts Décoratifs, Paris, 1976–77) and the accompanying text volume, Yvonne Brunhammer, *1925*, 2 vols. (Paris, 1976).

VIII   Perchance to Dream

2. ". . . ceux qui se sont montrés les ennemis féroces, les impitoyables déstructeurs, de tout ce que notre art avait de plus vénérable et plus précieux . . ." Louis Vauxcelles, "L'Art allemand peut attendre" (undated clipping from *Le Figaro* in Vauxcelles archive), p. 1.

3. Roger Allard, "A propos de l'exposition internationale des arts décoratifs," *Le Nouveau Spectateur* 1, no. 10 (10 October 1919), p. 210.

4. See p. 311 above; and see McLeod, " 'Architecture or Revolution.' "

5. "A ce caractère international que consacra la participation de vingt et une nations étrangerès, l'Exposition devait joindre une caractère régional; en 1900 Octave Mirbeau pouvait écrire que la province formait autour de Paris 'un immense terrain vague.' Au contraire, La France née de l'après-guerre est, à certains égards, une France régionale. . . . Le néo-régionalisme crée des formes appropriées aux besoins du monde moderne, en usant des matériaux & des procédés locaux. . . . La participation provinciale trouvait sa place naturelle dans une Exposition d'esprit moderne. Près de l'article de Paris, figuraient les articles de France." Anonymous, "Programme de l'Exposition," in *Encyclopédie des arts décoratifs*, i, p. 95.

6. "En choisissant comme thème une Ambassade plutôt qu'une Maison du Peuple, la Société des Artistes Décorateurs a donné la mesure de l'esprit dans lequel travaillent nos architectes, nos meubliers, nos ornemanistes. Mais ces architectes et ces meubliers ne sont pas seulement réactionnaires par leur dévotion aux 'puissances d'argent,' mais aussi par leur incompréhension des exigences qu'impose la vie moderne . . ." Waldemar George, "L'Exposition des Arts Décoratifs et Industriels de 1925: Les tendances générales," *L'Amour de l'Art* no. 8 (August 1925), pp. 285–86, cited in Brunhammer, *1925*, p. 60.

7. ". . . Pendant des siècles, depuis le moyen-âge, la Renaissance Italienne excepté, la France a imposé son goût au monde. Aujourd'hui, nous ne savons plus que nous faire gloire du talent qu'ont eu nos ancêtres. Tomberons-nous à n'être plus qu'un peuple de mouleurs et de copistes? Il faut réagir courageusement, nous relever. Nous nous devons de renouer avec notre tradition et de rester des créateurs. Il est d'un devoir premier pour la République d'aider à la réalisation des styles modernes." *Rapport sur une exposition internationale des arts décoratifs modernes, Paris 1915* (dated 1 June 1911, Paris), reprinted in Brunhammer, *1925*, p. 16.

8. "Artistes et industriels doivent savoir que le combat sera dur, qu'il y a eu déjà beaucoup de temps perdu et qu'il ne s'agit de rien moins pour eux que de nous gagner une nouvelle bataille de la Marne." Anonymous, "Chronique," *Art et Décoration* 36 (September–October 1919, p. 2.

9. "Architectes, constructeurs de meubles, verriers ou céramistes troueront, dans l'Exposition prochaine, l'occasion de constituer enfin un faisceau vivant et d'affirmer les principes de raison, base solide des styles qui s'élaborent." Léon Rosenthal, "L'Art et la cité," p. 1.

10. "La guerre de 1914–1918 qui impressionna si profondément notre jeune littérature, n'a-t-elle pas eu d'influence sur la vie artistique, sur la développement de la cité nouvelle? . . . Le mobilier munichois d'il y a dix ans a fait place à des meubles sobres et élégants, de bonne et franche tradition française. C'est que les temps du cosmopolitisme sont révolus. Contraints, durant près de cinq années, de vivre sur leur propre fonds, les peuples, tous les peuples n'ont-ils pas dû adopter une sorte de nationalisme économique, financier, politique et, pour tout dire, un véritable protectionnisme littéraire et artistique?

"Joignez à cela d'autres causes purement sentimentales. Menacée dans les sources mêmes de sa vie, la France a repris conscience de soi. D'avoir craint de la perdre, ses fils ont ressenti pour elle une plus vive tendresse et, rendus aux loisirs de la paix, ils sont souhaité que rien ne leur fut étranger du cher visage maternel. Nos musées, comme nos sites, nous en avons des preuves certaines, ont reçu des visites plus nombreuses: les Français d'aujourd'hui ne placent rien au-dessus de l'esprit et du goût français.

"Ne soyons donc pas surpris si, après une longue éclipse, les vertus natives de la race—ordre, mesure, clarté, discipline—l'emportent décidément. C'en est fini de l'anarchie de 1900 et de l'hégémonie munichoise. Tandis que nos peintres, délaissant cubisme et futurisme, n'ont plus qu'un souci: se remettre à l'école de Poussin, nos décorateurs, nos ébénistes, tout en gardant le sentiment de la vie moderne, n'hésitent plus à renouer avec la tradition de Louis XVI et du Directoire." Raymond Escholier, "Le Meuble," special supplement to *L'Illustration* 83, no. 4286 (25 April 1925), n.p.

11. "L'influence d'un Poiret sur l'ameublement actuel s'atténue . . . l'étude attentive de la ligne pure, simple, harmonieuse, des volumes et des proportions." Ibid.

12. See Marie-Noël Pradel, "La Maison Cubiste en 1912," *Art de France* I (1961), pp. 177–86, and Nancy Troy, "Towards a Redefinition of Tradition."

13. "Faire quelque chose de TRÈS FRANÇAIS. . . . faire des choses un peu sévères de lignes dont la froideur sera corrigée par un décor aimable, coloré franchement et le tout dans une tradition bien française." Mare notebook (pre-war), in Collection Françoise Mare-Vène, Paris (original orthography).

14. "Notre intention est de réaliser ce que j'ai toujours essayé de faire au Salon d'Automne avec les camarades, c.à.d. de travailler en commun et d'avoir des représentants de tout les arts." Mare to Maurice Marinot, 11 September 1917, in Collection Françoise Mare-Vène, Paris.

15. See Baldewicz, *"Les Camoufleurs,"* p. 322, as well as the exhibition catalogue L'Ancienne Douane, *André Mare et la Compagnie des Arts Français (Mare et Süe)*, ed. Victor Beyer (Strasbourg, April–June, 1971).

16. "La France est en voie de reprendre à la tête du mouvement artistique la première place qu'elle avait occupée depuis la Renaissance." Mare, Notebook no. 14 (1921), n.p. Collection Françoise Mare-Vène, Paris.

17. "1921/ARCHITECTURES/Receuil publié sous la direction de Louis Süe et André Mare comprenant un Dialogue de Paul Valéry et la présentation d'ouvrages d'architecture, décoration intérieure, peinture, sculpture, et gravure contribuant depuis Mil Neuf Cent Quatorze à former le Style Français." Süe and Mare, *Architectures*, title page. For a brief and interesting discussion of the album, see Gérard Monnier, "Un retour à l'ordre: Architecture, géometrie, société," in Université de Saint-Etienne, *Le Retour à l'ordre*, pp. 45–54. For Valéry as an architectural critic, see Claude Bouret, "Paul Valéry et l'architecture: Un amateur compétent," *Gazette des Beaux-Arts* 76, no. 1220 (September 1970), pp. 185–208.

18. George, "L'Exposition . . . Les tendances générales," p. 289.

19. See, for example, Le Corbusier's own account in Le Corbusier and Pierre Jeanneret, *Oeuvre Complète*, vol. I, 1910–1929 (Geneva, 1967), pp. 98–100.

20. See Françoise Will-Levaillant, "Norme et forme à travers *l'Esprit Nouveau*," in Université de Saint-Etienne, *Le Retour à l'ordre*, pp. 241–76.

21. Amédée Ozenfant mentioned this himself in "Le Cubisme, crime national—Le Cubisme et le Parlement," *La Revue Nouvelle* (December 1929–January 1930), p. 16. I am grateful to Romy Golan for this information.

22. Le Corbusier, "L'Illusion des plans," *L'Esprit Nouveau* no. 15 (February 1922), translated (by Frederick Etchells) in Le Corbusier, *Towards a New Architecture* (New York, 1946; original edition London, 1927), p. 166.

23. Le Corbusier, "Des yeux qui ne voient pas: Les Avions," *L'Esprit Nouveau* no. 9 (June 1921), translated in Le Corbusier, *Towards a New Architecture*, p. 101.

24. Le Corbusier, "La Leçon de Rome," *L'Esprit Nouveau* no. 14 (January 1922), translated in ibid., p. 146.

25. Le Corbusier, "Des yeux qui ne voient pas: Les Automobiles," *L'Esprit Nouveau* no. 10 (July 1921), translated in ibid., pp. 124–25.

26. Amédée Ozenfant and Charles-Edouard Jeanneret (Le Corbusier), "Le Purisme," *L'Esprit Nouveau* no. 4 (January 1921), translated in Herbert, *Modern Artists on Art*, p. 71. This article is hereafter cited as "Purism," with page numbers referring to *Modern Artists on Art*.

27. Ibid., pp. 59–60.

28. Ibid., pp. 72–73.

29. Ibid., pp. 60, 66.

30. Ibid., p. 73.

31. Ibid., p. 62.

32. Gleizes and Metzinger, *Du Cubisme*, translated in Herbert, *Modern Artists on Art*, p. 6. This essay is hereafter cited as *Cubism*, with page numbers referring to *Modern Artists on Art*.

33. Ibid., p. 14.

34. Le Corbusier, "Les Tracés Régulateurs," *L'Esprit Nouveau* no. 5 (May 1921), translated in Le Corbusier, *Towards a New Architecture*, p. 70.

35. Ozenfant and Jeanneret, "Purism," p. 65.

36. Gleizes and Metzinger, *Cubism*, p. 13.

37. Ozenfant and Jeanneret, "Purism," p. 66.

38. Ibid., p. 67.

39. Ibid., p. 70.

40. See Pia Vivarelli's article "Classicisme et arts plastiques en Italie entre les deux guerres," in the exhibition catalogue Centre Georges Pompidou, *Les Réalismes, 1919–1939* (Paris, 1980–81).

41. Ozenfant and Jeanneret, "Purism," pp. 63–64.

42. Ibid.

43. Ibid., p. 68.

44. Ibid., p. 67.

45. In Le Corbusier, *Towards a New Architecture*, p. 126.

46. Ozenfant and Jeanneret, "La Direction ce que nous avons fait, ce que nous ferons," *L'Esprit Nouveau* no. 11–12 (1921), cited as "What we have done, what we will do" in Ball, *Ozenfant and Purism*, p. 123.

47. Ibid., p. 124.

48. Le Corbusier, *L'Urbanisme* (Paris, 1926), cited in Reyner Banham, *Theory and Design in the First Machine Age* (New York, 1960), p. 256.

49. Ozenfant and Jeanneret, "What we have done," in Ball, *Ozenfant and Purism*, p. 123.

50. Le Corbusier, *Towards a New Architecture*, p. 269.

51. Le Corbusier, *L'Urbanisme*, cited in Banham, *Theory and Design*, p. 256.

52. Le Corbusier's post-war city plans are the subject of Francesco Passanti's forthcoming Ph.D. dissertation (Columbia University).

53. ". . . si vous me demandez ce qui marque cette année par laquelle le siècle coud l'un à l'autre ces deux premiers quarts, cette année qu'on a cru célébrer à Paris par une exposition des arts décoratifs qui est une vaste rigolade, je vous dirai que c'est au sein même du surréalisme, et sous son aspect, l'avènement d'un nouvel esprit de révolte, un esprit décidé à s'attaquer à tout." Louis Aragon, "Fragments d'une Conférence," *La Révolution Surréaliste* no. 4 (15 July 1925), p. 25.

54. André Breton, "Manifesto du Surréalisme" (Paris, 1924), translated in William Rubin, *Dada, Surrealism, and Their Heritage* (New York, 1968), p. 64.

55. Louis Aragon, "Une Vague des rêves," *Commerce* (Paris, Autumn 1924), in Maurice Nadeau, *The History of Surrealism* (New York, 1967 ed.), p. 83.

56. J. A. Boiffard, Paul Eluard, and Roger Vitrac, undated leaflet (1924?), as quoted in ibid., p. 93.

57. Antonin Artaud, "Diner est servi," *La Révolution Surréaliste* no. 3 (15 April 1925), in ibid., p. 105.

58. Robert Desnos, in ibid., p. 106.

59. "Extrait d'une lettre de Fernand Fontaine, classe 1916, tué le 20

juin 1915: 'Non vraiment, ce n'est pas si amusant que je le croyais
. . . Et si je meurs crois bien que ce sera contre la France.' " *La
Révolution Surréaliste* no. 2 (15 January 1925), p. 15.

60. See Nadeau, *History of Surrealism*, p. 113.

61. ". . . à certains *mots-tampons* tels que le mot 'Orient.' Ce mot
. . . est prononcé de plus en plus depuis quelques années. . . . les
réactionnaires d'aujourd'hui . . . ne perdent aucune occasion de
mettre l'Orient en cause." André Breton, "Légitime Défense," *La Révolution Surréaliste* no. 8 (1 December 1926), p. 35.

62. Desnos, "Description d'une révolte prochaine," as quoted in Nadeau, *History of Surrealism*, p. 106.

63. Desnos, "Adresse au Dalai-Lama," *La Révolution Surréaliste* no.
3 (15 April 1925), as quoted in ibid., p. 106.

64. Desnos, "Lettre aux écoles du Bouddha," *La Révolution Surréaliste* no. 3 (15 April 1925), in ibid.

65. "Il faut que les Israélites restent en exil tant que la cause occi-
dentale ne sera pas perdue, tant que ne sera pas écrasé cet esprit
latin, grec, anglo-saxon, allemand, qui est le plus terrible menace
contre l'esprit." Desnos, "Pamphlet contre Jérusalem," *La Révolution
Surréaliste* no. 3 (15 April 1925) p. 9.

66. Aragon, "Fragments," as quoted in Nadeau, *History of Surrealism*,
p. 111.

67. Desnos, February 1924 (original source not indicated), in ibid.,
p. 95.

68. André Breton, "Refusal to Inter," *Un Cadavre* [1924], in ibid., p.
96.

69. "Alors que Picasso, délié par son génie de toute obligation morale
simple . . . reste maître d'une situation que sans lui nous eussions
tenue bien souvent pour désespérée; il semble en effect que la plupart
de ses compagnons de la première heure soient dès maintenant en-
gagés dans la voie la plus contraire à la nôtre et à la sienne." Breton,
"Le Surréalisme et la peinture," part 2, *La Révolution Surréaliste* no.
6 (1 March 1926), p. 31.

70. "Ceux qui s'appelèrent 'les Fauves,' avec un sens prophétique si
particulier, ne font plus qu'exécuter derrière les barreaux du temps
des tours dérisoires et de leurs derniers bonds, si peu à craindre, le
moindre marchand ou dompteur se garde avec une chaise. Matisse et
Derain sont de ces vieux lions décourageants et découragés. De la
forêt et du désert dont ils ne gardent pas même la nostalgie, ils sont
passés à cette arène minuscule . . ." Ibid. ". . . Un *Nu* de Derain,
une nouvelle *Fenêtre* de Matisse, quels plus sûrs témoignages à l'appui de cette vérité que 'toute l'eau de la mer ne suffirait pas à laver
une tache de sang intellectuelle.' " Ibid.

71. "Chirico, qui, en continuant à peindre, n'a fait depuis dix ans que mésuser d'un pouvoir surnaturel, s'étonne aujourd'hui que l'on ne veuille le suivre en ses piètres conclusions, dont le moins qu'on puisse dire est que l'esprit en est totalement absent et qu'y préside un cynisme éhonté . . . (L'Italie, le fascisme—on connait de lui un tableau assez infame pour être intitulé: *Légionnaire romain regardant les pays conquis*—l'ambition artistique qui est la plus médiocre de toutes, la cupidité, même) a eu tôt fait de dissiper les enchantements." Breton, "Le Surréalisme et la peinture," part 3, *La Révolution Surréaliste*, no. 7 (15 June 1926), p. 4.

Bibliography

Accademia di Francia a Roma (Villa Medici). *Picasso e il Mediterraneo*. Exh. cat. Marie-Laure Besnard-Bernadac, ed. Rome, 1982.

Albertini, Q., ed. *L'Exposition Nationale de la Maternité et de l'Enfance*. Paris, 1921.

Allard, Roger. "A propos du Cénotaphe," *Le Nouveau Spectateur* 1, no. 6 (10 August 1919).

Andrew, Christopher M., and A. S. Kanya-Forstner. *France Overseas: The Great War and the Climax of French Imperial Expansion*. London, 1981.

Anonymous. "Le Monument au génie latin," *L'Illustration* no. 4087 (16 July 1921), p. 46.

Association Générale des Hygiénistes et Techniciens Municipaux. *L'Exposition de la cité reconstituée*. Paris, 1916.

Aurel. *Le Commandement d'amour dans l'art après la guerre*. Geneva, c. 1917.

Axsom, Richard H. *"Parade": Cubism as Theater*. New York, 1979.

Bachollet, Raymond, Daniel Bordet, and Anne-Claude Lelieur. *Paul Iribe*. Paris, 1984.

Badisches Landesmuseum. *Picasso und die Antike*. Karlsruhe, 1974.

Baldewicz, Elizabeth Kahn. *"Les Camoufleurs*: The Mobilization of Art and the Artist in Wartime France, 1914–1918." Ph.D. dissertation, U.C.L.A., 1980.

Ball, Susan L. *Ozenfant and Purism: The Evolution of a Style 1915–30*. Ann Arbor, Michigan, 1981.

Banham, Reyner. *Theory and Design in the First Machine Age*. New York, 1960.

Barbara Mathes Gallery. *Purism and the Spirit of Synthesis*. Exh. cat. Essay by Kenneth E. Silver. New York, 1986.

Barr, Alfred H., Jr. *Matisse: His Art and His Public*. New York, 1951.

Barr, Alfred H., Jr. *Picasso: Fifty Years of His Art*. New York, 1946.

Barrès, Maurice. *The Undying Spirit of France*. New Haven, 1917.

Bauginet, Marcel. "Vers une synthèse esthétique et sociale," *Bulletin de l'Effort Moderne* no. 14 (April 1925), pp. 11–14.

Beaunier, André. *Les Idées et les hommes*. 2 vols. Paris, 1915.

Bénédite, Léonce. "Une Exposition d'Ingres," *Gazette des Beaux-Arts* 63, no. 3 (1921), pp. 325–37.

Bérard, Léon. "L'Art français et la guerre," *Revue Politique et Littéraire* 55, no. 11 (26 May/29 June 1917), pp. 321–25.

Bernard, Emile. "La Méthode de Paul Cézanne," *Mercure de France* 138, no. 521 (1 March 1920), pp. 289–318.

Biblioteca Nacional (Salas Pablo Ruiz Picasso), *Juan Gris 1887–1927*. Exh. cat. Madrid, 1985.

Bibliothèque Nationale. *Diaghilev: Les Ballets Russes*. Exh. cat. Paris, 1979.

Bibliothèque Nationale. *Sonia et Robert Delaunay*. Exh. cat. Paris, 1977.

Bissière, [Roger]. *Georges Braque*. Paris, 1920.

Bissière, [Roger]. "Le Réveil des cubistes," *L'Opinion* (15 April 1916), p. 382.

Bissière, [Roger]. "Notes sur Ingres," *L'Esprit Nouveau* no. 4 (January 1921), pp. 387–409.

Blunt, Anthony. "Picasso's Classical Period (1917–25)," *Burlington* 110, no. 781 (April 1968), pp. 187–91.

Bonnefous, Edouard. *Histoire politique de la Troisième République*. Vols. I–IV (1906–1929). Paris, 1968.

Bornecque, Henri, and J. Germain Drouilly. *La France et la Guerre: Formation de l'opinion publique pendant la guerre*. Paris, 1921.

Boudar, Gilbert, and Michel Décaudin. *Correspondance de Guillaume Apollinaire*, no. 1: *Guillaume Apollinaire–André Level*. Paris, 1976.

Bouret, Claude. "Paul Valéry et l'architecture: un amateur compétent," *Gazette des Beaux-Arts* 76, no. 1220 (September 1970), pp. 185–208.

Boutroux, Emile. *L'Idée de Liberté en France et en Allemagne*. Paris, n.d. [c. 1915–18].

Braque, Georges. "Pensées et réflexions sur la peinture," *Nord-Sud* 2, no. 10 (December 1917), pp. 3–5.

Brendel, Otto. "The Classical Style in Modern Art," in Whitney Oates, ed., *From Sophocles to Picasso*. Bloomington, Indiana, 1962.

Brion-Guérry, L. ed. *L'Année 1913: Formes esthétiques de l'oeuvre d'art à la veille de la première guerre mondiale*. Paris, 1971.

Brown, Frederick. *An Impersonation of Angels—A Biography of Jean Cocteau*. New York, 1968.

Brunhammer, Yvonne. *1925*. 2 vols. Exh. cat. Musée des Arts Décoratifs, Paris, 1976.

Buchloh, Benjamin H. D. "Figures of Authority, Ciphers of Regression: Notes on the Return of Representation in European Painting," *October* 16 (Spring 1981), pp. 39–68.

Bury, J.P.T. *France: The Insecure Peace*. New York, 1962.

Busi, Frederick. "Dada and the 'Trial' of Maurice Barrès," *Boston University Journal* 23, no. 2 (1975), pp. 63–71.

Cabanne, Pierre. *L'Epopée du Cubisme*. Paris, 1963.

Cabanne, Pierre. *Le Siècle de Picasso*. 2 vols. Paris, 1975.

Caiger-Smith, Martin. "Gino Severini: The Montegufoni Frescoes." M.A. thesis, Courtauld Institute of Art, University of London, 1983.

Cailler, Pierre, ed. *Guillaume Apollinaire*. Geneva, 1965.

Camfield, William. *Francis Picabia: His Art, Life and Times.* Princeton, 1979.

Carsten, F. L. *The Rise of Fascism.* Berkeley, 1967.

Cendrars, Blaise. "Pourquoi le 'Cube' s'effrite?" *La Rose Rouge* (15 May 1919), pp. 33–35. Trans. as "Why is the 'Cube' Disintegrating," in Fry, ed., *Cubism*, pp. 154–56.

Centre Georges Pompidou. *Les Réalismes, 1919–1939: Entre révolution et réaction.* Exh. cat. Paris, 1981.

Centro di Cultura di Palazzo Grassi. *Picasso: Opere dal 1895–1971 dalla Collezione Marina Picasso.* Exh. cat. Giovanni Carandente, ed. Venice and Florence, 1981.

Christie's East. *Jean Cocteau: The Collection of Louis Shorenstein.* Sales cat. New York, 1984.

Clark, Robert Judson, and Marian Burleigh-Motley. "New Sources for Picasso's *Pipes of Pan*," *Arts* (October 1980), pp. 92–93.

Cobb, Richard. *French and Germans, Germans and French: A Personal Interpretation of France under Two Occupations 1914–1918/1940–1944.* Hanover, New Hampshire, and London, 1983.

Cocteau, Jean. "Autour de La Fresnaye," *L'Esprit Nouveau* no. 3 (December 1920), n.p.

Cocteau, Jean. *Dans le ciel de la patrie.* Paris, 1918.

Cocteau, Jean. *Le Coq et l'Arlequin (notes autour de la musique).* Paris, 1918.

Cocteau, Jean. *Le Retour à l'ordre.* Paris, 1917.

Cocteau, Jean. *L'Ode à Picasso.* Paris, 1917.

Cocteau, Jean. *Picasso.* Paris, 1923.

Cocteau, Jean. *Thomas l'Imposteur.* Paris, 1923.

Codding, George A., Jr., and W. Safron. *Ideology and Politics: The Socialist Party of France.* Boulder, Colorado, 1979.

Cogniat, Raymond, and Waldemar George. *Oeuvre complète de Roger de la Fresnaye.* 2 vols. Paris, 1950.

Comité de Propaganda Socialiste pour la Défense Nationale. *Les Socialistes dans la nation et pour la nation.* Paris, 1916.

Cooper, Douglas. *Picasso Theater.* New York, 1968.

Cooper, Douglas, and Meg Potter. *Juan Gris: catalogue raisonné de l'oeuvre peint.* Paris, 1977.

Cousturier, Lucie. *Seurat.* Paris, 1921.

Crespelle, Jean-Paul. *La Folle Epoque.* Paris, 1968.

Daix, Pierre, and Jean Rosselet. *Picasso: The Cubist Years, 1907–1916.* Boston, 1979.

Daudé-Bancel, A. "La Reconstruction des cités détruites," *La Grande Revue* 91, no. 597 (May 1917), pp. 1–32.

Daudet, Léon. *Hors du joug allemand: Mesures d'après-guerre.* Paris, 1915.

Daudet, Léon. *L'Avant-guerre: Etudes et documents sur l'espionnage juif-allemand en France depuis l'affaire Dreyfus.* Paris, 1913.

Daudet, Léon. *Le Stupide XIXe Siècle (exposé des insanités meurtrières qui se sont abattues sur la France depuis cent trente ans, 1789–1919)*. Paris, 1922.

Delaunay, Robert. *Du Cubisme à l'art abstrait*. Pierre Francastel, ed. Paris, 1957.

Delfour, Abbé. *La Culture latine*. Paris, 1916.

Dermée. Paul. "Quand le Symbolisme fut mort," *Nord-Sud* 1, no. 1 (15 March 1917), pp. 2–4.

Dermée, Paul. "Un Prochain Age classique," *Nord-Sud* 2, no. 11 (January 1918), p. 3.

Dervaux, Adolphe. "Le Beau, le vrai, l'utile, et la réorganisation de la cité," *La Grande Revue* 90, no. 584 (April 1916), pp. 33–58.

Dimier, Louis. *L'Appel des intellectuels allemands*. Paris, 1915.

Dimnet, Ernest. *France Herself Again*. New York, 1914.

Doesburg, Theo van. "Vers un style collectif," *Bulletin de l'Effort Moderne* no. 4 (April 1924), pp. 14–16.

Domenach, Jean-Marie, ed. *Barrès par lui-même*. Paris, 1954.

Driault, Edouard. *Plus rien d'allemand*. Paris, 1918.

Ducasse, André, Jacques Meyer, and Gabriel Perreux. *Vie et mort des Français 1914–1918 (Simple histoire de la Grande Guerre)*. Paris, 1959.

Duchartre, Pierre. *La Comédie italienne*. Paris, 1925.

Duchène, André. *Pour la reconstruction des cités industrielles*. Paris, 1919.

Ehrenberg, Alain. *Le Corps militaire: Politique et pédagogie en démocratie*. Paris, 1983.

Elderfield, John. *Matisse in the Collection of the Museum of Modern Art*. New York, 1978.

Espatallier, Lt. Col. G. *Pour rebâtir nos maisons détruites*. Paris, 1917.

Faure, Elie. *Les Constructeurs*. Paris, 1914.

Faure, Elie. *The Dance Over Fire and Water*. New York, 1926.

Fels, Florent. "Propos d'artistes: Fernand Léger," *Les Nouvelles Littéraires* 2, no. 37 (30 June 1923), p. 4.

Fels, Florent. "Propos d'artistes: Picasso," *Les Nouvelles Littéraires* 2, no. 41 (28 July 1923), p. 2.

Fernandez, Jeanne Ramon. "L'Esprit de la mode," *Gazette des Beaux-Arts* (1917), pp. 121–25.

Fierens, Paul. *Gino Severini*. Milan, 1936.

Focillon, Henri. *Les Evocations françaises: Les pierres de France*. Paris, 1919.

Focillon, Henri. *Technique et sentiment: Etudes sur l'art moderne*. Paris, 1919.

Fondation Nationale des Arts Graphiques et Plastiques. *Albert Gleizes 1881–1953: Legs de Madame Juliette Roche Gleizes*. Exh. cat. Paris, 1982.

Fourcade, Dominique. "Autres propos de Henri Matisse," *Macula* 1 (1976), pp. 92–115.

Fraternité des Artistes. *Album nationale de la guerre.* Paris, 1915.

Fromage, Georges. *Pendant et après la guerre.* Rouen, 1917.

Fry, Edward F., ed. *Cubism.* London and New York, 1966.

Fundaçao Calouste Gulbenkian. *Sonia e Robert Delaunay em Portugal 1915–1917.* Exh. cat. Lisbon, 1972.

Fussell, Paul. *The Great War and Modern Memory.* New York and London, 1975.

Gagnon, Paul. *France since 1789.* New York, 1964.

Galerie Artcurial. *Au temps du "Boeuf sur le toit."* Exh. cat. Georges Bernier, ed. Paris, 1981.

Galerie Berggruen. *Pablo Picasso: Pour Eugenia, une suite de 24 dessins exécutés en 1918.* Exh. cat. Douglas Cooper, ed. Paris, 1976.

Galerie Boutet de Montvel. *Gino Severini: ler Exposition Futuriste d'art plastique de la Guerre et d'autres oeuvres antérieures.* Exh. cat. Paris, 1916.

Galerie Louise Leiris. *Juan Gris: Dessins et gouaches 1910–27.* Paris, 1965.

Galerie Paul Guillaume. *Catalogue des oeuvres de Matisse et de Picasso.* Exh. cat. Essays by Guillaume Apollinaire. Paris, 1918.

Galerie Paul Rosenberg. *Exposition de dessins et aquarelles par Picasso.* Exh. cat. Paris, 1919.

Galerie Paul Rosenberg. *Exposition Picasso.* Exh. cat. Paris, 1921.

Gallatin, Albert Eugene. *Art and the Great War.* New York, 1919.

Garcin, Paul. *Les Socialistes et la Guerre.* Lyon, 1916.

Gee, Malcolm. *Dealers, Critics, and Collectors of Modern Painting: Aspects of the Parisian Art Market between 1910 and 1930.* New York, 1981.

Gee, Malcolm. "The Avant-Garde, Order and the Art Market, 1916–1923," *Art History* 2, no. 1 (March 1979), pp. 95–106.

Geldzahler, Henry. "World War I and the First Crisis in Vanguard Art," *Art News* 61, no. 8 (December 1962), pp. 48–51ff.

George, Waldemar. *Pablo Picasso.* Paris, 1924.

George, Waldemar. "Roger de la Fresnaye," *L'Amour de l'Art* no. 8 (1926), pp. 317–23.

Gilbert-Rivière, Alexandre. *Les Forces matérielles et morales de la France.* Tours, 1922.

Giraudy, Danièle. "Correspondance Henri Matisse–Charles Camoin," *Revue de l'Art* no. 12 (1971), pp. 7–34.

Gleizes, Albert. "C'est en allant se jeter à la mer que la fleuve reste fidèle à sa source," *Le Mot* no. 17 (1 May 1915), n.p.

Gleizes, Albert. *Du Cubisme et des moyens de le comprendre.* Paris, 1920.

Gleizes, Albert. "Vers une époque des bâtisseurs," *Clarté* 1 (1920), 5 parts: no. 13 (20 March); no. 14 (3 April); no. 15 (17 April); no. 22 (26 June); no. 32 (11 September).

Gleizes, Albert, and Jean Metzinger. *Du cubisme.* Paris, 1912.

Goldberg, Harvey. *Jean Jaurès.* Madison, Wisconsin, 1968.

Golding, John. "Picasso and Surrealism," in *Picasso in Retrospect*, Roland Penrose and John Golding, eds. London, 1973.

Golding, John. *Cubism: A History and an Analysis.* London and New York, 1959.

Goulinat, J. C. "Vers un classicisme nouveau: L'inquiétude chez les peintres d'aujourd'hui," *Les Nouvelles Littéraires* 2, no. 48 (15 September 1923), p. 1.

Gourmont, Rémy de. *Pendant l'orage.* Paris, 1915.

Grand Palais. *Exposition des arts décoratifs de Munich.* Paris, 1910.

Grand Palais. *Picasso: Oeuvres reçues en paiement des droits de succession.* Exh. cat. Paris, 1979.

Green, Christopher. "Juan Gris, el cubismo y la idea de tradicion," in Biblioteca Nacional, *Juan Gris 1887–1927*, pp. 93–104.

Green, Christopher. *Léger and the Avant-Garde.* New Haven and London, 1976.

Green, Christopher. "Purity, Poetry, and the Painting of Juan Gris," *Art History* 5, no. 2 (June 1982), pp. 180–204.

Green, Christopher. "Synthesis and the 'Synthetic Process' in the Painting of Juan Gris," *Art History* 5, no. 1 (March 1982), pp. 87–105.

Gris, Juan. *Letters of Juan Gris (1913–27).* Collected by D.-H. Kahnweiler, Douglas Cooper, ed. London, 1956.

Gromaire, Georges. *L'Occupation allemande en France 1914–18.* Paris, 1925.

Grunwald Center for the Graphic Arts, U.C.L.A. *Images of the Great War 1914–1918.* Exh. cat. Los Angeles, 1983.

Guilleminault, Gilbert. *La France de la Madelon.* Paris, 1965.

Hauser, L. *Les Trois Léviers du monde nouveau.* Paris, 1918.

Hayes, Carlton J. H. *France, a Nation of Patriots.* New York, 1930.

Herbert, Robert, L., ed. *Modern Artists on Art.* Englewood Cliffs, N.J., 1964.

Hoog, Michel. *Robert Delaunay.* New York, 1976.

Hope, Henry R. *Georges Braque.* New York, 1949.

Hôtel de la Monnaie. *Images de Jeanne d'Arc.* Exh. cat. Paris, 1979.

Hourticq, Louis. "Au salon des artistes décorateurs," *Art et Décoration* (May–June 1919), pp. 35–38.

Huber, Michel. *La Population de la France pendant la guerre.* Paris and New Haven, 1931.

Hughes, Judith M. *To the Maginot Line: The Politics of French Military Preparation in the 1920s.* Cambridge, Mass., 1971.

Huinck and Scherjon Gallery. *Gino Severini: Exposition rétrospective.* Exh. cat. Amsterdam, 1931.

Imprimerie Nationale. *Encyclopédie des arts décoratifs et industriels modernes au XXième siècle.* 12 vols. Paris, c. 1926. Reprint: New York and London, 1977.

Janin, Clément. "Les Estampes et la Guerre," *Gazette des Beaux-Arts* 59 (1917), 3 parts: pp. 75–94, 361–83, 482–508.

Jessner, Sabine. *Edouard Herriot: Patriarch of the Republic.* New York, 1974.

Jones, Barbara, and Bill Howell. *Popular Arts of the First World War.* London, 1972.

Judkins, Winthrop. *Fluctuant Representation in Synthetic Cubism: Picasso, Braque, Gris 1910–20.* New York, 1976.

Jullian, Philippe. *D'Annunzio.* New York, 1973.

Kahn, Elizabeth Louise. "Art from the Front: Death Imagined and the Neglected Majority," *Art History* 8, no. 2 (June 1985), pp. 192–208.

Kahnweiler, Daniel-Henry. *Juan Gris: His Life and Work.* London, 1947.

Kahnweiler, Daniel-Henry. *My Galleries and Painters.* London, 1971 (orig. Paris, 1961).

Kern, Stephen. *The Culture of Time and Space 1880–1918.* Cambridge, Mass., 1983.

Kervyn de Lettenhove, Baron H. *La Guerre et les oeuvres d'art en Belgique.* Paris and Brussels, 1917.

Knoedler and Co. *Raymond Duchamp-Villon 1876–1918.* Exh. cat. George Heard Hamilton and William C. Agee, eds. New York, 1967.

Koechlin, Raymond. "L'Art français moderne n'est pas *Munichois*," *L'Art Français Moderne* no. 1 (January 1916), pp. 1–37.

Krauss, Rosalind. "Re-Presenting Picasso," *Art in America* 68, no. 10 (December 1980), pp. 90–96.

L'Ancienne Douane. *André Mare et la Compagnie des Arts Français (Mare et Süe).* Exh. cat. Victory Beyer, ed. Strasbourg, 1971.

Lapauze, Henri. "De l'art français et des influences qu'il ne doit pas subir," *La Renaissance (politique, économique, littéraire, artistique)* 5, no. 19 (15 September 1917), pp. 11–25.

Lapauze, Henri, ed. "Ingres," special issue, *La Renaissance de l'Art Français et des Industries de Luxe* (April 1921).

Larson, Philip. "Matisse and the Exotic," *Arts* 49, no. 9 (March 1975), pp. 72–73.

La Sizeranne, Robert de. *L'Art pendant la guerre 1914–1918.* Paris, 1919.

Lavedan, Henri. "Fluctuat," *L'Illustration* no. 3928 (15 June 1918), p. 568.

Lavisse, Ernest. *France = Humanité.* Paris, n.d. [after July 1917].

Le Corbusier. *Towards a New Architecture.* New York, 1946 (orig. London, 1927).

Lefebvre, Raymond. "Chronique de la vie intellectuelle en France," *Clarté* no. 4 (29 November 1919), p. 2.

Lefèvre, Frédéric. "Une Heure avec M. Maurice Barrès," *Les Nouvelles Littéraires* 2, no. 26 (14 April 1923), p. 2.

Léger, Fernand. *Functions of Painting.* Edward F. Fry, ed. New York, 1973.

Léger, Fernand. "L'Esthétique de la machine," *Bulletin de l'Effort Moderne* no. 1 (January 1924), pp. 5–7.

Leighten, Patricia. "Picasso's Collages and the Threat of War, 1912–13." *The Art Bulletin* 67, no. 4 (December 1985), pp. 653–72.

Lepage, Jacques. "Picasso à Rome," *Vie des Arts* no. 51 (Summer 1968), pp. 42–49.

Lhote, André. *Ecrits sur la peinture*. Paris, 1946.

Lhote, André. "Totalisme," *L'Elan* no. 9 (February 1916), pp. 3–4.

Ligue Navale Français. *Les Peintres de la mer*. Exh. cat. Louis Vauxcelles, ed. Paris, 1917.

Lipton, Eunice. *Picasso Criticism, 1910–1939: The Making of an Artist-Hero*. New York, 1976.

Lukach, Joan. "Severini's 1917 Exhibition at Stieglitz's *291*," *Burlington* 93, no. 817 (April 1971), pp. 196–207.

Lukach, Joan. "Severini's Writings and Paintings 1916–17 and His Exhibition in New York City," *Critica d'Arte* 20, no. 138 (November–December 1974), pp. 59–80.

Lyons, Lisa. "Matisse: Work, 1914–1917," *Arts* 49, no. 9 (March 1975), pp. 74–75.

McCully, Marilyn, ed. *A Picasso Anthology: Documents, Criticism, Reminiscences*. Princeton, 1982.

MacDonald, William. *Reconstruction in France*. New York, 1922.

McLeod, Mary. " 'Architecture or Revolution': Taylorism, Technocracy, and Social Change," *Art Journal* 43, no. 2 (Summer 1983), pp. 132–47.

Mahar, William John. "Neo-Classicism in the Twentieth Century." Ph.D. dissertation, Syracuse University, 1972.

Maier, Charles S. "Between Taylorism and Technocracy: European Ideologies and the Vision of Industrial Productivity in the 1920s," *Journal of Contemporary History* 5, no. 2 (1970), pp. 27–61.

Maier, Charles S. *Recasting Bourgeois Europe: Stabilization in France, Germany, and Italy in the Decade after World War I*. Princeton, 1975.

Mallory, Keith, and Arvid Ottar. *The Architecture of War*. New York, 1973.

Martin, Marianne. "The Ballet *Parade*: A Dialogue Between Cubism and Futurism," *Art Quarterly*, n.s., 1 no. 2 (Spring 1978), pp. 85–111.

Martin du Gard, Maurice. "Charles Maurras," *Les Nouvelles Littéraires* 2, no. 23 (24 March 1923), p. 1.

Massis, Henri. "Defence of the West," *New Criterion* 4, no. 2 (April 1926), pp. 224–43.

Massis, Henri. *La Défense de l'Occident*. Paris, 1927.

Mauclair, Camille. *L'Avenir de France*. Paris, 1918.

Mauclair, Camille. *Le Vertige allemand*. Marseille, 1916.

Maurras, Charles. *Oeuvres capitales*. 4 vols. Paris, 1954.

Mayer, Arno J. *The Persistence of the Old Regime, Europe to the Great War*. New York, 1981.

Meyer, Jacques. *La Vie quotidienne des soldats pendant la Grande Guerre*. Paris, 1966.

Meyer, Susan. "Ancient Mediterranean Sources in the Works of Picasso." Ph.D. dissertation, Institute of Fine Arts, N.Y.U., 1980.

Michel, André. "L'Art français après la Guerre," *La Revue Hebdomadaire* 26, no. 11 (17 March 1917), pp. 307–30.

Minneapolis Institute of Arts. *Léger's "Le Grand Dejeuner."* Exh. cat. Robert L. Herbert, ed. Minneapolis, 1980.

Mistler, Jean, François Blaudez, and André Jacquemin. *Epinal et l'imagerie populaire*. Paris, 1961.

Morice, Charles. "Nécessité présente du travail intellectuel," *L'Homme Libre* (20 December 1917), p. 1.

Motherwell, Robert. *The Dada Painters and Poets: An Anthology.* New York, 1951.

Mullins, Edwin. *The Art of Georges Braque*. New York, 1968.

Musée d'Art Moderne de la Ville de Paris. *Cinquantenaire des Ballets Suédois, 1920–1925: Collections du Musée de la Danse, Stockholm.* Exh. cat. Paris, 1971.

Musée d'Art Moderne de la Ville de Paris. *Léger et l'esprit moderne.* Exh. cat. Paris, 1982.

Musée d'Art Moderne de la Ville de Paris. *Robert et Sonia Delaunay.* Exh. cat. Paris, 1985.

Musée de la Guerre. *1914–1918: Témoignages d'artistes et documents.* Exh. cat. Paris, 1964.

Musée de la Mode et du Costume, Palais Galliéra. *Paul Poiret et Nicole Groult: Maîtres de la mode art déco.* Exh. cat. Paris, 1986.

Musée de l'Annonciade (Saint-Tropez) and Musée d'Art Moderne (Troyes). *Roger de la Fresnaye.* Exh. cat. Eric Hild, ed. Saint-Tropez and Troyes, 1983.

Musée de l'Orangerie. *Catalogue de la collection Jean Walter et Paul Guillaume.* Michel Hoog, ed. Paris, 1984.

Musée des Augustins. *Picasso et le théâtre.* Exh. cat. Denis Milhaud, ed. Toulouse, 1965.

Musée des Deux Guerres Mondiales. *André Fraye: Oeuvres de guerre, 1914–1918.* Exh. cat. Paris, 1979.

Musée des Deux Guerres Mondiales. *Armistice et Paix (1918–1919).* Exh. cat. Paris, 1968.

Musée National d'Art Moderne, Centre Georges Pompidou. *Braque: Oeuvres de Georges Braque (1892–1963), Collections du Musée National d'Art Moderne, Paris.* Collection cat. Nadine Pouillon and Isabelle Monod-Fontaine, eds. Paris, 1982.

Musée National d'Art Moderne, Centre Georges Pompidou. *Matisse: Oeuvres de Henri Matisse (1869–1954), Collections du Musée National d'Art Moderne, Paris.* Collection cat. Isabelle Monod-Fontaine, ed. Paris, 1979.

Musée Picasso. *Catalogue sommaire des collections.* Paris, 1985.

Museo Correr. *Le Corbusier: Pittore e scultore.* Exh. cat. Milan, 1986.

Museum of Modern Art. *Art of the Twenties.* Exh. cat. William S. Lieberman, ed. New York, 1979.

Museum of Modern Art. *Pablo Picasso: A Retrospective.* William Rubin, ed. New York, 1980.

Nadeau, Maurice. *The History of Surrealism.* New York, 1967 ed.

Neue Nationalgalerie, et al. *Tendenzen der Zwanziger Jahre.* Exh. cat. Berlin, 1977.

Nochlin, Linda. "Picasso's Color: Schemes and Gambits," *Art in America* 68, no. 10 (December 1980), pp. 105–23.

Nochlin, Linda. "The Imaginary Orient," *Art in America* 71, no. 5 (May 1983), pp. 118–31, 187–91.

Nora, Pierre, ed. *Les Lieux de mémoire,* I: *La République.* Paris, 1984.

Orangerie des Tuileries. *Georges Braque.* Exh. cat. Michèle Richet and Nadine Pouillon, eds. Paris, 1973.

Orangerie des Tuileries. *Juan Gris.* Exh. cat. Paris, 1974.

Ozenfant, Amédée. *Foundations of Modern Art.* New York, 1931.

Ozenfant, Amédée. *Mémoires 1886–1962.* Paris, 1968.

Ozenfant, Amédée, and Charles-Edouard Jeanneret. *Après le cubisme.* Paris, 1918.

Ozenfant, Amédée, and Charles-Edouard Jeanneret. *La Peinture moderne.* Paris, 1927.

Ozenfant, Amédée, and Charles-Edouard Jeanneret, "Le Purisme," *L'Esprit Nouveau* no. 4 (January 1921), pp. 369–86.

Pacini, Piero. *Gino Severini.* Florence, 1966.

Pacini, Piero. *La "Sala Gino Severini" nel museo dell'accademia di Cortona.* Cortona, 1972.

Palazzi Casali. *Gino Severini: Prima e dope l'opera.* Exh. cat. Maurizio Fagiolo dell'Arco. Cortona, 1984.

Penrose, Roland. *Picasso: His Life and Work.* New York, 1962.

Perreux, Gabriel. *La Vie quotidienne des civils en France pendant la Grande Guerre.* Paris, 1966.

Peyre, Henri. *Le Classicisme français.* New York, 1942.

Picasso, Pablo. *Picasso on Art.* Dore Ashton, ed. New York, 1972.

Poiret, Paul. *En habillant l'époque.* Paris, 1930.

Ponge, Francis. *Braque, le réconciliator.* Geneva, 1947.

Pool, Phoebe. "Picasso's Neo-Classicism: Second Period, 1917–1925," *Apollo* 85, no. 61 (March 1967), pp. 198–207.

Raynal, Maurice. *Georges Braque.* Rome, 1921.

Raynal, Maurice. *Juan Gris.* Paris, 1920.

Raynal, Maurice. *Picasso.* Paris, 1922.

Read, James Morgan. *Atrocity Propaganda 1914–1919.* New York, 1941.

Reff, Theodore. "Matisse: Meditations on a Statuette and a Goldfish," *Arts* 51, no. 3 (November 1976).

Reff, Theodore. "Picasso's *Three Musicians*: Maskers, Artists and

Friends," *Art in America* 68, no. 10 (December 1980), pp. 124–42.

Rémond, René. *The Right Wing in France, from 1815 to De Gaulle.* Philadelphia, 1966.

Reverdy, Pierre. *Pablo Picasso.* Paris, 1924.

Rey, A. Augustin. *Les Grandes Pensées de la France à travers ses grands hommes, 1914–1916.* 2 vols. Paris, 1916.

Rey, Robert. *La Renaissance du sentiment classique dans la peinture française du XIXième siècle.* Paris, 1931.

Reymond, Nathalie. "Le Rappel à l'ordre d'André Lhote," in Université de Saint-Etienne, *Le Retour à l'ordre,* pp. 209–24.

Rickards, Maurice. *Posters of the First World War.* New York, 1968.

Robert, Stephen. *The History of French Colonial Policy 1870–1925.* London, 1963.

Rolland, Romain. *Au-dessus de la mêlée.* Paris, 1915.

Rosenberg, Léonce. *Cubisme et empirisme.* Paris, 1921.

Rosenberg, Léonce. *Cubisme et tradition.* Paris, 1920.

Rosenberg, Léonce. "Parlons peinture . . . ," *L'Esprit Nouveau* no. 5 (February 1921), pp. 578–84.

Rosenblum, Robert. *Cubism and Twentieth-Century Art.* New York and London, 1960.

Rosenthal, Léon. "L'Art et la cité: L'Exposition internationale des arts appliqués," *Les Nouvelles Littéraires* 2, no. 46 (8 September 1923), p. 1.

Roskill, Mark. *The Interpretation of Cubism.* Philadephia, 1985.

Roure, Lucien. *Patriotisme, impérialisme, militarisme.* Paris, 1915.

Rubin, William. *Picasso in the Collection of the Museum of Modern Art.* New York, 1972.

Russell, John, *Georges Braque.* London, 1959.

Said, Edward. *Orientalism.* New York, 1978.

Salmon, André. *L'Art vivant.* Paris, 1920.

Sanouillet, Michel. *Dada à Paris.* Paris, 1965.

Sanson, Rosemonde. *Les 14 Juillet: Fête et conscience nationale 1789–1975.* Paris, 1976.

Saroléa, Charles. *Le Réveil de la France.* Paris, 1916.

Schneider, Pierre. *Matisse.* New York, 1984.

Seligman, Ethlyne J., and Germain Seligman. "Of the Proximity of Death and Its Stylistic Activations—Roger de la Fresnaye and Juan Gris," *Art Quarterly* (Spring 1949), pp. 146–55.

Seligman, Germain. *Roger de la Fresnaye.* Greenwich, Ct., 1969.

Servranckx, Victor. "Les Voies nouvelles de l'art plastique," *Bulletin de l'Effort Moderne* no. 17 (July 1925), pp. 1–10.

Severini, Gino. "Cézanne et le Cézannisme," *L'Esprit Nouveau* nos. 11/12 (November 1921), pp. 1257–66.

Severini, Gino. *Du cubisme au classicisme: Esthétique du compas et du nombre.* Paris, 1921.

Severini, Gino. "La Peinture d'avant-garde," *Mercure de France* 455, no. 121 (1 June 1917), pp. 451–68.

Severini, Gino. *La Vita di un pittore*. Milan, 1965.

Shapiro, Theda. *Painters and Politics: The European Avant-Garde and Society 1900–1925*. New York, 1976.

Silver, Kenneth E. "Eminence Gris," *Art in America* 72, no. 5 (May 1984), pp. 152–61.

Silver, Kenneth E. "*Esprit de Corps*: The Great War and French Art, 1914–1925." Ph.D. dissertation, Yale University, 1981.

Silver, Kenneth E. "Fernand Léger: Logic and Liberalism," *Art Journal* 42, no. 2 (Summer 1982), pp. 151–54.

Silver, Kenneth E. "Jean Cocteau and the *Image d'Epinal*: An Essay on Realism and Naiveté," in Arthur King Peters, ed. *Jean Cocteau and the French Scene*. New York, 1984.

Silver, Kenneth E. "Juan Gris y su arte en la gran guerra [1914–1918]," in Biblioteca Nacional, *Juan Gris 1887–1927*, pp. 45–52.

Silver, Kenneth E. "Purism: Straightening Up After the Great War," *Artforum* 15, no. 7 (March 1977), pp. 56–63.

Silver, Kenneth E. Review of Christopher Green, *Léger and the Avant-Garde* (New Haven, 1976), in *Journal of the Society of Architectural Historians* 38, no. 1 (March 1979), pp. 48–49.

Silver, Kenneth E. Review of Pierre Daix and Jean Rosselet, *Picasso: The Cubist Years 1907–1916* (Boston, 1979), in *Art in America* 68, no. 10 (December 1980), pp. 35–37.

Silverman, Debora L. "Nature, Nobility, and Neurology: The Ideological Origins of Art Nouveau in France, 1889–1900." Ph.D. dissertation, Princeton University, 1983.

Singer, Barnett. *Modern France: Mind, Politics, Society*. Seattle and London, 1980.

Société des Artistes Français. *Exposition du profit des oeuvres de guerre*. Exh. cat. Paris, 1918.

Solomon R. Guggenheim Museum. *Albert Gleizes*. Daniel Robbins, ed. New York, 1964.

Sotheby's. *Modern Pictures from the Paul Rosenberg Family Collection*. Sales cat. New York, 1979.

Steegmuller, Francis. *Apollinaire: Poet among the Painters*. New York, 1963.

Steegmuller, Francis. *Cocteau: A Biography*. Boston, 1970.

Sternhell, Zeev. *La Droite révolutionnaire 1885–1914: Les origines françaises du fascisme*. Paris, 1978.

Stevens, Arthur Dene. "The Counter-Modern Movement in French and German Painting After World War I." Ph.D. dissertation, Indiana University, 1971.

Storez, M., and Maurice Denis. *L'Architecture et l'art décoratif en France après la guerre (comment préparer leur renaissance)*. Paris, 1915.

Süe, Louis, and André Mare. *Architectures*. Paris, 1921.

Tate Gallery. *Léger and Purist Paris*. John Golding and Christopher Green, eds. London, 1971.

Tate Gallery. *The Essential Cubism: Braque, Picasso, and Their Friends, 1907–1920*. Exh. cat. Douglas Cooper and Gary Tinterow, eds. London, 1983.

Taylor, A.J.P. *A History of the First World War*. New York, 1966.

Thomson, David. *Democracy in France since 1870*. Oxford, 1969.

Tint, Herbert. *The Decline of French Patriotism, 1870–1940*. London, 1964.

Tollet, Tony. *De l'influence de la corporation judéo-allemande des marchands de tableaux de Paris sur l'art français*. Lyon, 1915.

Tollet, Tony. *Sur les origines de notre art contemporain (Discours de Reception)*. Lyon, 1916.

Troy, Nancy. "Towards a Redefinition of Tradition in French Design, 1895–1914," *Design Issues* 1, no. 2 (Fall 1984), pp. 53–69.

Tuchman, Barbara. *The Guns of August*. New York, 1962.

Turner, Paul. "The Education of Le Corbusier," Ph.D. dissertation, Harvard University, 1971.

Uhde, Wilhelm. *Picasso et la tradition française*. Paris, 1928.

Université de Saint-Etienne. *Le Retour à l'ordre dans les arts plastiques et l'architecture 1919–25*. Paris, 1975.

University Art Museum (Berkeley), Solomon R. Guggenheim Museum, and National Gallery of Art. *Juan Gris*. Exh. cat. Mark Rosenthal, ed. New York, 1983.

University of Iowa Museum of Art. *Jean Metzinger in Retrospect*. Exh. cat. Joann Moser, ed. Iowa City, 1985.

Vaillat, Léandre. *La Cité renaissante*. Paris, 1918.

Vaudoyer, Jean-Louis. "Le Salon d'Automne ii: L'art décoratif," *Art et Décoration* (December 1919), pp. 179–83.

Venturi, Lionello. *Gino Severini*. Rome, 1961.

Vernay, Jacques. "La Triennale, exposition d'art français," *Les Arts* no. 154 (April 1916), pp. 25–29.

Vic, Jean. *La Littérature de guerre: Manuel méthodique et critique des publications de langue française*. 5 vols. Paris, 1918–23.

Ville-Chabrolle, M. de. "Les Mutilés et réformés de la guerre 1914–1918 en France," *Bulletin de la Statistique Générale de la France* 21 (July 1922), pp. 387–422.

Vriesen, Gustave, and Max Imdahl. *Robert Delaunay: Light and Color*. New York, 1967.

Walker Art Center. *Picasso: from the Musée Picasso, Paris*. Exh. cat. Minneapolis, 1980.

Weber, Eugen. *Action Française: Royalism and Reaction in Twentieth-Century France*. Stanford, 1962.

Weber, Eugen. *The Nationalist Revival in France, 1905–1914*. Berkeley, 1959.

Wharton, Edith. *Fighting France: From Dunkerque to Belfort*. New York, 1915.

White, Palmer. *Poiret le magnifique: le destin d'un grand couturier*. Paris, 1986.

Will-Levaillant, Françoise. "La *Danse* de Picasso et le surréalisme en 1925," *L'Information d'Histoire de l'Art* 11, no. 5 (1966), pp. 210–14.

Willett, John. *Art and Politics in the Weimar Period: The New Sobriety, 1917–33.* New York, 1978.

Wohl, Robert. *French Communism in the Making 1914–1924.* Stanford, 1966.

Wohl, Robert. *The Generation of 1914.* Cambridge, Mass., 1979.

Zeldis, Yona. "Remembrance of Things Past: Matisse's Odalisques of the Twenties." M.A. thesis, Columbia University, 1981.

Zervos, Christian. "Confrontations de Picasso des oeuvres d'art d'autrefois," *Cahiers d'Art* 33–35 (1960), pp. 9–119.

Zervos, Christian. "Le Classicisme de Braque," *Cahiers d'Art* 6 (1931), pp. 35–40.

Zervos, Christian. *Pablo Picasso.* 33 vols. Paris, 1932–78.

Index